BOBBY FISCHER *and* HIS WORLD

Other book by John Donaldson include:

Alekhine in the Americas
Alekhine in Europe and Asia
A Legend on the Road: Bobby Fischer's 1964 Simultaneous Tour
The Life & Games of Akiva Rubinstein: Volume 1: Uncrowned King
The Life & Games of Akiva Rubinstein: Volume 2: The Later Years
The Unknown Bobby Fischer
Elmars Zemgalis: Grandmaster Without the Title
The Life and Games of Frank Ross Anderson

BOBBY FISCHER *and* HIS WORLD

International Master
John Donaldson

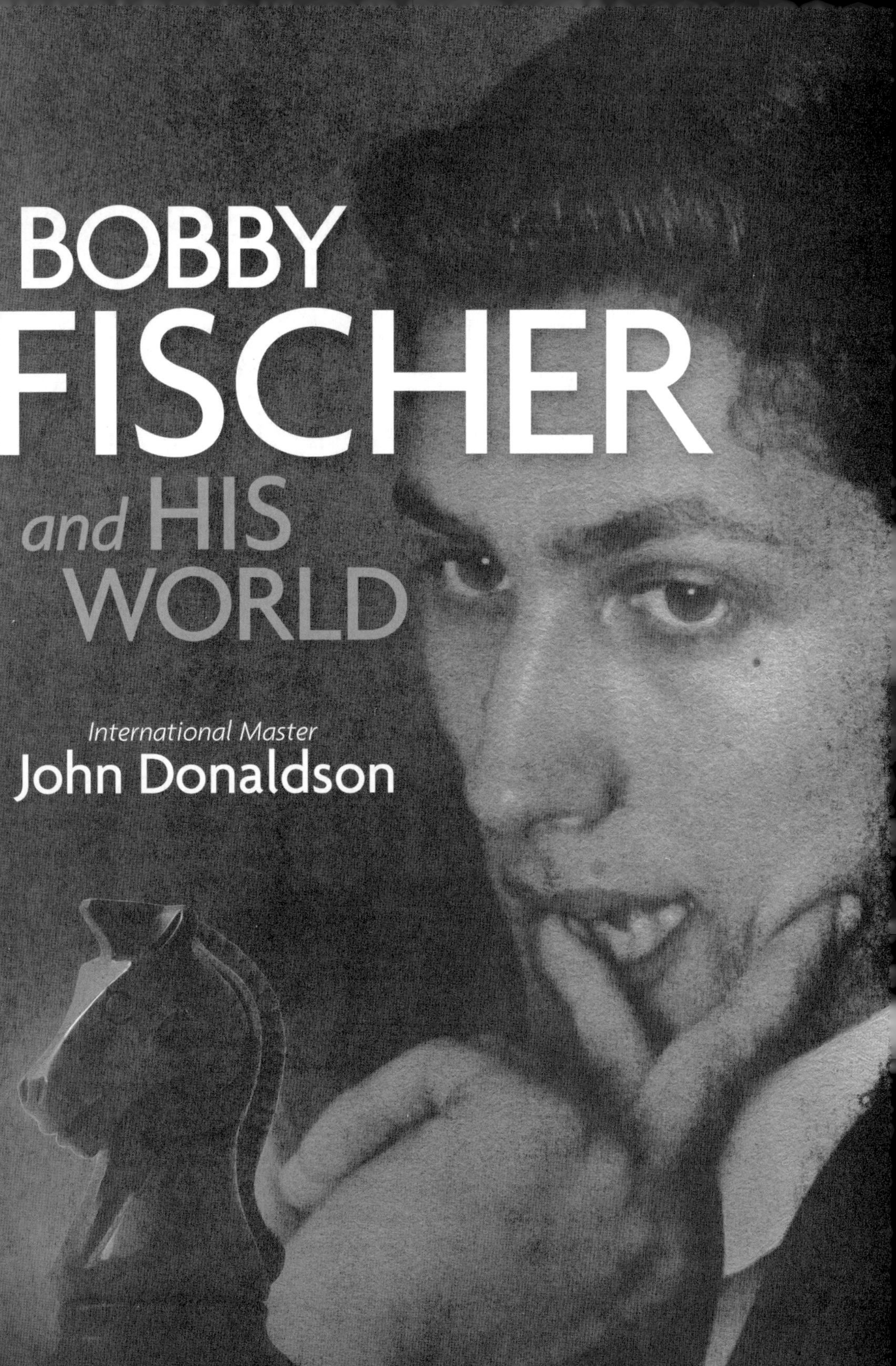

SILES PRESS LOS ANGELES

First Edition
10 9 8 7 6 5 4 3 2

Library of Congress Cataloging-in-Publication Data
Names: Donaldson, John (William John), 1958- author.
Title: Bobby Fischer and his world / by John Donaldson.
Description: First Edition. | Los Angeles : Siles Press, 2020.
Includes index.
Identifiers: LCCN 2020031501
ISBN 9781890085193 (Trade Paperback)
ISBN 9781890085544 (eBook)
Subjects: LCSH: Fischer, Bobby, 1943-2008. | Chess players--United States--Biography. | Chess players--Anecdotes. | Chess--Collections of games. | Chess--Middle games. | Chess--Anecdotes. | Chess--History.
Classification: LCC GV1439.F5 D66 2020 | DDC 794.1092 [B]--dc23

Cover Design and Artwork by Wade Lageose

SILES PRESS
a division of Silman-James Press, Inc.
www.silmanjamespress.com
info@silmanjamespress.com

To Holly whose help and support made this book possible.

CONTENTS

LIST OF GAMES

Part Eight – Comeback

Part Nine

ACKNOWLEDGMENTS

The idea for *Bobby Fischer and His World* originated ten years ago and I'm grateful to International Master Eric Tangborn for his help and encouragement from inception to completion. Eric and I have been fascinated with Bobby since our early days at the Tacoma Chess Club in the fall of 1972.

I want to give a special thanks to: David and Alessandra DeLucia for their generosity in sharing their collection of Bobby Fischer letters and other ephemera, a wealth of original source material; Gary Forman for unselfishly sharing several never-before-published Fischer games, a strong believer that chess information should be made available to all, Gary practices what he preaches; Lou Hays, one of the key people that got Bobby to play again, for his permission to reprint the story of Fischer's comeback, a story only he could write; Anchorage attorney Robert Stoller, long fascinated with Bobby's legal battles, for his analysis; Tom Crispin for detailing his experience with Fischer and chess computers; Richard Fireman, for his warm account of the "Good Bobby" before tragic life events and the demons got to him; Dan Scoones for his translations of Russian language chess articles and insights into the Soviet chess scene of the 1950s; Bruce Pandolfini for kindly sharing his experiences of Bobby and books from the mid-1960s; Bernard Zuckerman, who probably spent more time studying and talking about chess with Bobby than anyone else; and Edward Winter, whose *Chess Notes* were an invaluable resource in the preparation of this volume (no one has done more to make chess history a serious field of inquiry).

I would like to extend my thanks and give a tip of the hat to the many people who generously shared their memories of Fischer, as well as those who assisted with research: Paul Albert, Leighton Allen, Andy Ansel, Mike Archer, Alexander Baburin, Dan Bailey, Todd Bardwick, Eduardo Bauzá Mercére, Jonathan Berry, Peter Biyiasas, Frank Brady, Nikolai Brunni, Curtis Carlson, Charles Crittenden, David Daniels, Art Drucker, Alex Dunne, Larry Finley, Bill Goichberg, Carl Gorka, Sanford Greene, Mig Greengard, Ron Gross, Bruce Harper, John Hartmann, Paul Heaton, Pedro Hegoburu, Peter Holmgren, Robert Hungaski, Dr. Albert Jenkins, Eric Johnson, Allyn Kahn, Brian Karin, Jeff Kastner, Allen Kaufman, Larry Kaufman, Lubos Kavalek, Keven Korsmo, Jesse Kraai, Kerry Lawless, Ron Lohrman, Shelby Lohrman, J. Ken MacDonald, Rusty Miller, Stella Monday, Michael Negele, Bill "Tommy"

Nigro, John O'Donnell, Helgi Ólafsson, René Olthof, Erik Osbun, Joseph G. Ponterotto, Orest Popovych, David Presser, Viktors Pupols, Jason Radley, Theron Raines, Gil Ramirez, Dr. Richard Reich, Donald Reithel, Larry Remlinger, Tony Rich, John Rinaldo, Aben Rudy, Hanon Russell, Andy Sachs, Dr. Anthony Saidy, Dr. Franklin Saksena, Miguel A. Sánchez, Yasser Seirawan, Peter Sepulveda, Swami Shankarananda, James Sherwin, Richard Shorman, David Siudzinski, Sam Sloan, Sarah Sneider, Andy Soltis, Steve Stepak, Jesús Suárez, Duncan Suttles, Jeffrey Tannenbaum, James Tarjan, Frank Thornally, Joe Tracy, John Upper, Bill Wall, Tibor Weinberger, Paul Whitehead, Mark Wieder, Fred Wilson, Elliott Winslow, Judy Winters, and the many other chess players who contributed.

In memoriam, I am grateful to Mike Franett, best remembered as the editor of *Inside Chess*, for his fine portrait of Ron Gross; Nancy Roos, one of the greatest chess photographers of all time; Jack Spence an unsung hero of American chess, for without his tireless efforts (and the many tournament bulletins he produced) many Fischer games would be lost; Beth Cassidy for the photographs she took of Fischer and his contemporaries throughout the mid-to-late-1960s; and Frank Berry who tracked down Ms. Cassidy and scanned her slides and photographs saving them from oblivion; Alan Benson, John Blackstone, Stephen Brandwein, Walter Browne, William Haines, Jerry Hanken, Ruth Haring, Eliot Hearst, William Lombardy, Dr. Nikolay Minev, Jack O'Keefe, Mike Schemm, and Walter Shipman.

Many thanks to U.S. Chess, *Chess Life*, and *Chess Review*, no other publications covered Bobby's formative years as well. All serious chess players in the United States are members of U.S. Chess, and I'm proud to have first joined almost fifty years ago.

Thank you to the staff of the John G. White Collection at the Cleveland Public Library, the Lilly Library at Indiana University, the Mechanics' Institute Library of San Francisco, and the World Chess Hall of Fame in St. Louis where Chief Curator Shannon Bailey, Curator Emily Allred, and Registrar Nicole Tessmer were especially helpful.

The WCHOF, through the support of Rex and Jeanne Sinquefield, has by far the largest publicly held collection of Fischer memorabilia and is continually adding to and exhibiting the materials. Hopefully one day all the treasures in Fischer's Pasadena storage locker will be reunited in St. Louis.

I'm indebted to John Watson, who not only proofread the entire book but offered constructive criticism throughout that markedly improved it.

Last, but certainly not least, I would like to thank Jeremy Silman for his continuous support and enthusiasm for this book, and especially Gwen Feldman who is everything one could hope for in an editor and more.

INTRODUCTION

In the spring of 2013 I was invited by officers of the Marshall Chess Club to view a collection of material donated to the club by Bobby Fischer's brother-in-law. Much of the donated material consisted of family documents. However, a small portion of the collection dealt directly with Bobby's chess career, and within this mix were score sheets from some of his games, many of which had not previously surfaced. These games are what piqued my interest as they are the essence of Fischer's creative genius.

I first joined the U.S. Chess Federation in the fall of 1972, inspired by the Fischer–Spassky match in Reykjavík. Media interest in chess in those golden times was at a level never witnessed before or since, with daily coverage in newspaper and broadcast media around the world. It was in the Tacoma News Tribune that September I found an announcement for the local chess club, which started my nearly fifty-year involvement with the game.

My experience was hardly unique. Many giants of American chess of my generation, inspired by Fischer's World Championship run, began their careers around this time including: Yasser Seirawan, Joel Benjamin, Larry Christiansen, Nick de Firmian, and John Fedorowicz. Like myself, most of these players never encountered Fischer, as our "Chess Godfather" stopped playing after winning the World Championship.

Despite his early retirement Bobby stayed in the public eye until the beginning of the 1980s, with reports of a possible comeback periodically surfacing. Fischer's rematch with Spassky in 1992 led to hopes he would again play regularly but although that was not to be, his domination of the 1970-72 World Championship cycle and one-man crusade against the Soviet chess empire insured he would never be forgotten.

In the early '90s I spent a considerable amount of time tracking down Fischer's simul games for my book *Legend on the Road: Bobby Fischer's 1964 Simul Tour*. This book was followed in 1999 with *The Unknown Bobby Fischer*, written with International Master Eric Tangborn. My aforementioned visit to the Marshall confirmed there was still plenty of Fischer gold to be found and a more substantial work was needed.

I was interested in answering a number of nagging questions about the eleventh World Champion: Who was Fischer's chess teacher? How did Bobby make his incredible jump in strength from early June of 1955 to late August of 1958? Why did he have such a hatred of the United States government? Why, with his mother a doctor and his sister a nurse, did he possess such an aversion to Western medicine? Why did Fischer play Spassky a rematch after so many earlier planned matches had fallen through? What happened to his belongings, particularly those lost after his storage locker was auctioned off?

Despite his incredible talent and tremendous work ethic, Bobby did not become World Champion by himself. As I thought about this and dug deeper into my research it became apparent that the answers to my questions weren't absolute. I realized the first-hand observations, documentations, and opinions (some contradictory of others) that I had gathered from players, friends, supporters, and other people in Fischer's orbit wove a story. And that story is what developed into this book, a portrait of Fischer's world.

With so much already written about Fischer's life and career, I was selective as to the material presented. Accordingly, I only touch briefly on many aspects of Bobby's life. For example, I didn't include well-known Fischer games unless I could offer new analysis. For the most part, the games I've chosen are ones that shed light on lesser known moments in Fischer's career.

There are a few exceptions to these choices. A case in point is Bobby's game with Edmar Mednis from the first round of the 1963/64 U.S. Championship. This tournament, well known for Fischer's 11-0 sweep, is also remembered for Fischer's brilliancies against Robert Byrne, Pal Benko, and the good knight versus bad bishop last round endgame squeeze versus Anthony Saidy. Edmar Mednis points out that he should have won their first round encounter and stopped Bobby's sweep before it even started.

Tigran Petrosian and Fischer appeared to have little in common in the way they approached chess, but they shared an interest in playing the Maróczy Bind, the only World Champions to do so on a regular basis. Playing 1...c5 followed by a kingside fianchetto was Bobby's habitual answer to 1.Nf3 and 1.c4 in the late 1960s and early 1970s and he scored heavily with it. Allowing the Maróczy was the price of admission, and due to Bobby's success fighting the "Bind" these games are examined in depth.

Fischer's love of the "old ones" could be seen in his resurrecting many of Steinitz's opening ideas: 9.Nh3 in the Two Knights and 5.d3 in the Ruy Lopez are but two examples. He didn't confine his borrowing to just the beginning of the game. My chapter on the Hedgehog shows just how far ahead of his time Fischer was. While this middlegame structure wouldn't become popular until after his retirement, Bobby had already played it as early as 1966 (vs. García Soruco).

There are other examples of Fischer as a pioneer. His famous win in the King's Indian Attack against Myagmarsuren from the Sousse Interzonal (the heretical 13.a3 violated the classical rule of not opening lines on the side of the board where one is weaker) is well-remembered. Not so its predecessor Bisguier–Fischer (20...a6) from the 1963 Western Open, an earlier, less known example, albeit with colors reversed.

It's been almost fifty years since Fischer won the World Championship, but information about his life and games continues to come forward. In 2019 forty games he played against masters and experts in simuls in Solingen and Münster resurfaced. This year Florido–Fischer, Havana 1956, was made public for the first time and I was thrilled to have made contact with Tommy Nigro, son of Carmine Nigro, who was Bobby's first teacher.

In 1982 I played in the British Columbia Open held at the University of British Columbia. After round four, for relaxation, I watched the film *Body Heat* in the theater of the UBC Film Society. It was not until many years later that I realized this theater, previously called the Student Union Auditorium, was the site of the Fischer–Taimanov Candidates match, and that some of the stage lights were those specifically requested by Fischer. I was on hallowed ground!

Researching Bobby Fischer is a job that could go on forever. There are so many nooks and crannies in Fischer's life that it would be easy for me to go down the rabbit hole and never resurface. I did draw the line, but my quest goes on and I welcome readers' comments, additions, and corrections.

I hope you enjoy reading this book as much as I did writing it.

John Donaldson
Berkeley, California
imwjd@aol.com
October 2020

A NOTE TO THE READER

The spelling of names has been standardized as far as possible using Jeremy Gaige's *Chess Personalia: A Biobibliography* and the FIDE rating list. There are a few exceptions where a source has been quoted that used an alternative spelling— for example Fischer refers to Tchigorin instead of Chigorin.

Foreign players names are given as they appear in the Latin alphabet, including accents and diacritical marks. However, these marks are not used on the names of players who immigrated to North America. One exception: for clarity, I used the Americanized spelling of Polgar, (instead of Polgár) as Susan resides in the United States while sisters Judit and Sofia live in Hungary and Israel.

Place names follow standard American usage.

PART ONE

Beginner *to* U.S. Junior Champion

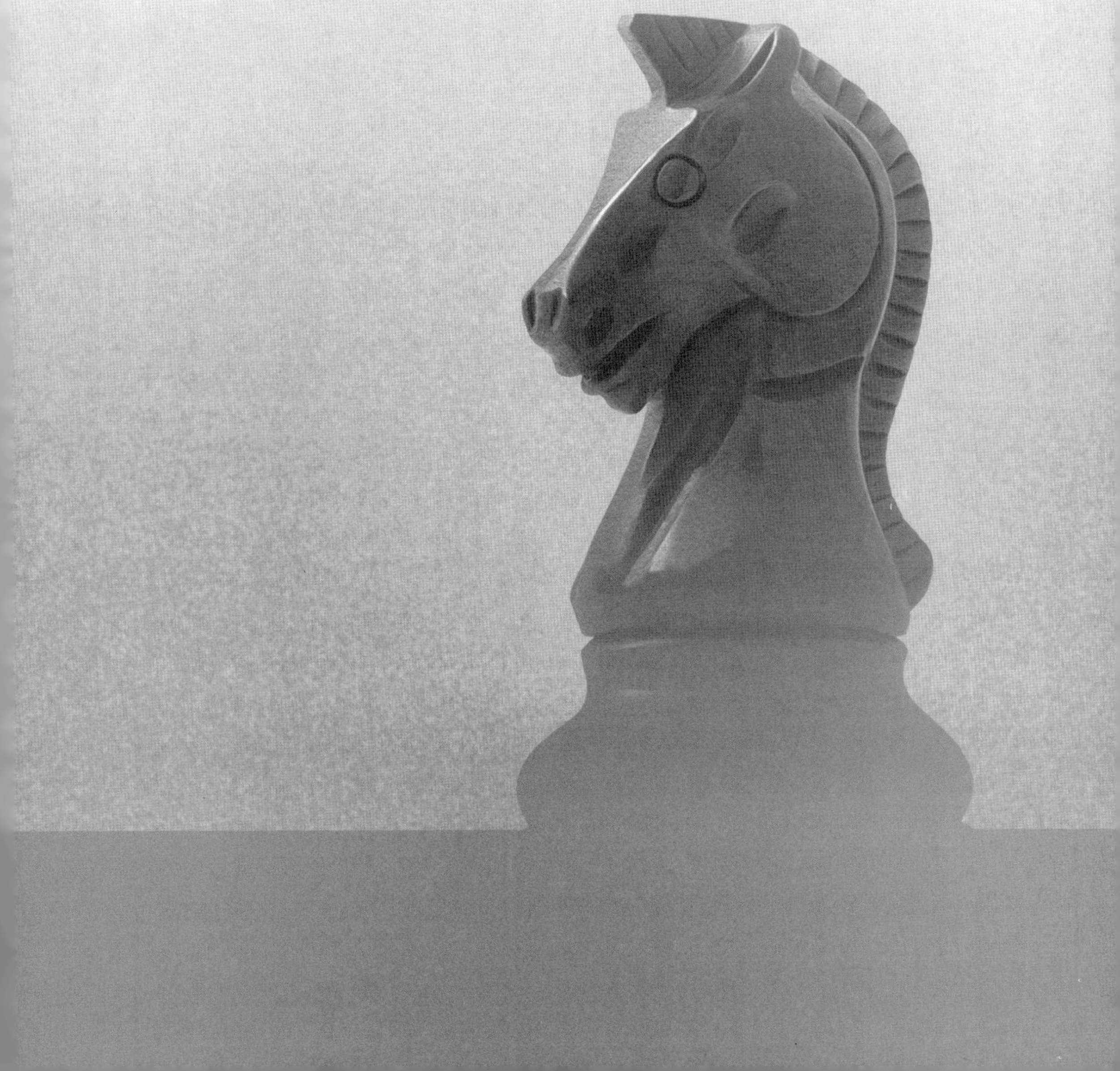

The many faces of young Bobby Fischer in a game at the Manhattan Chess Club, 1956 (Photos: Courtesy of the Cleveland Public Library, John G. White Collection). Another photo of this game, that includes opponent Karl Forster, can be found on page 80.

1

GROWING UP IN BROOKLYN

> I was born in Chicago, Illinois, on March 9, 1943, and learned the chess moves early in 1949 from my sister Joan, who was eleven. She often bought different games at a local candy store and one day happened to buy a chess set. We figured out the moves from the directions that came with the set. For the next year or so I played chess occasionally with the boys I taught or by myself.

Thus wrote fifteen-year-old Bobby Fischer in the introduction to his first published book *Bobby Fischer's Games of Chess.*[1]

> On November 14, 1950, my mother sent a postcard to the chess column of the old *Brooklyn Eagle* (we were now living in Brooklyn) asking if they knew any boys my age I could play chess with. A reply came from Mr. Hermann Helms, dean of American chess. He suggested I go to a chess exhibition at the Grand Army Plaza Library on January 17, 1951. There I played against Senior Master Max Pavey and managed to last about fifteen minutes. Watching in the crowd was Mr. Carmine Nigro, president of the Brooklyn Chess Club. After the game he came up and invited me to join his club.
>
> Mr. Nigro was possibly not the best player in the world, but he was a very good teacher.[2] I went to the Brooklyn Chess Club practically every Friday night. Later I started playing chess at Mr. Nigro's home on weekends and often went with him to play chess at Washington Square Park.

As an adult, Fischer rarely talked about his early years. He made a rare exception and offered a glimpse in one of his *Boys' Life* columns:[3]

> After I was playing a year or so, my mother took me to the Brooklyn Chess Club where I took lessons a couple of times a week from Carmine Nigro, one of the best players in the club. The lessons cost me a dollar an hour. I'm sure he wasn't interested in the dollar, but this was his way of making sure I took the lessons seriously.
>
> One of the biggest thrills of my life was when I won first prize at the YMCA children's championship. (One critical game, incidentally, was against

[1] Bobby Fischer, *Bobby Fischer's Games of Chess*. New York: Simon & Schuster, 1959, (p. xi).

[2] Carmine Nigro was rated 2028 on the May 5, 1957, USCF rating list.

[3] *Boys' Life*, December 1966, (p. 87).

> my teacher's son. I was nervous in that game, but the training I got from my early games was important to me and gave me confidence.) I still have that medal at home.

Does a genius appear from nowhere? Are they simply born, or do they require nurturing to emerge? In Bobby's case, we know he came from an intelligent and well-educated family. We also know, with his family's move to Brooklyn in 1949, he was transported to the best place in the United States to develop as a chess player—New York City. If Bobby had stayed in Mobile, Arizona (thirty-five miles southwest of Phoenix near the Sierra Estrella Mountains) where his family lived for a year (his mother taught school there), it's almost inconceivable that he would have developed into a World Champion. Today, with the Internet, databases, computer programs, and tons of chess literature, a player from an isolated area can go far. This was not the case when Bobby was growing up. It was pretty much New York City, or forget it.

Bobby Fischer's name first appeared in print in Hermann Helms' *Brooklyn Daily Eagle* chess column. Helms (1870–1963) was instrumental in promoting American chess for over seventy years. In 1893, he began a chess column in the *Brooklyn Daily Eagle* that ran until the paper's 1955 demise. He founded the *American Chess Bulletin*, and served as editor for the magazine's entire run, 1904 to 1963. Over his career, Helms wrote for *The New York Times* as well as the other major New York newspapers. In his January 18, 1951 column, Helms recounted the Max Pavey simul: Played on thirteen boards, Pavey scored +11, =2. The two draws were with Sylvan Katske and Edmar Mednis (1937–2002). The future Grandmaster Mednis was only thirteen and already showing promise (he would take second behind Boris Spassky in the World Junior four years later). Bobby was only mentioned because of his age, which was mistakenly given as eight—actually, he was seven.

Sadly, few games are preserved from the beginning of Bobby's career. He started playing tournament chess in 1953, but the earliest recorded games in standard Fischer game anthologies[1] date from the summer of 1955 and the U.S. Junior Open in Lincoln, Nebraska.

Three casual games played at the Brooklyn Chess Club take us back a little further in time. Game (1) is against Dan Mayers, a former English Senior Champion who played tournament chess into his nineties. Games (2) and (3), appear to be from the end of 1954 or the beginning of 1955.

[1] Robert G. Wade and Kevin J. O'Connell, *The Games of Robert J. Fischer*. Garden City: Doubleday, 1972. Lou Hays, *Bobby Fischer: Complete Games of the American World Chess Champion*. Dallas: Hays Publishing, 1995.

(1) King's Gambit
Dan Mayers – Fischer
Brooklyn (blitz) 1953

1. e4 e5 2.f4 exf4 3.Bc4

This is the Bishop's Gambit, a line Bobby made his own later in his career. He played it twice in tournament games (beating Grandmasters Evans and Minić) and countless times during his 1964 simul tour. His interest in 3.Bc4 didn't wane with the years. When he faced the Greenblatt computer in 1977 he trotted out the Bishop's Gambit to win a miniature.

Bobby wrote his famous article "A Bust to the King's Gambit,"[1] advocating 3.Nf3 d6! a year after his loss to Boris Spassky (Mar del Plata 1960) in the 3.Nf3 g5 line.

Interestingly enough, while Fischer consistently played 3.Bc4 throughout his career, he varied at least once with 3.Nf3 and his opponent chose Bobby's Bust! Fischer–K. Mott-Smith, Chicago (simul) 1964, saw 1.e4 e5 2.f4 exf4 3.Nf3 d6 4.d4 h6 5.Bc4 g5 6.0-0 Bg7 7.c3 Ne7 8.g3 (all according to Bobby's analysis), but now Black varied from 8...d5! (Fischer), with 8...Ng6 9.Qb3 0-0 10.gxf4 gxf4 11.Kh1 Nc6 12.Qc2 Nce7 13.Nd2 Be6 14.Rg1 Bxc4 15.Nxc4 d5 and unclear play.

3...Nf6

Evans tried 3...Qh4+ and Minić 3...Ne7. Fischer faced 3...d5 on several occasions in simuls and against the Greenblatt computer.

4.Nc3 c6 5.d4 Bb4 6.e5 Ne4 7.Qh5 0-0 8.Nge2 d5 9.Bb3 g6 10.Qh6 Bg4 11.Bd2 Nxd2 12.Kxd2

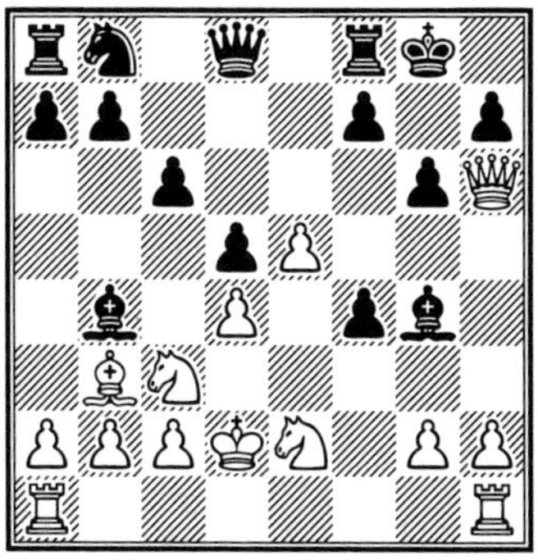

12...g5 13.h4 gxh4 14.Rxh4 Bf5 15.Rah1 Be7 16.Rg4+ Bg6 17.Qxh7, 1–0.

[1] *American Chess Quarterly*, Bobby Fischer, "A Bust to the King's Gambit," Vol.1 No.1, Summer 1961, (pp. 3–9).

(Seated from left to right) Unknown, Herman Steiner, Reuben Fine, George Sturgis, I. Walter Stephens, Weaver Adams, Boris Blumin and Hermann Helms. (Standing) sixth from the left is Erich Marchand, and on the far right are Joseph Rauch and Bruno Schmidt (Photo: Piatigorsky Collection, courtesy of the World Chess Hall of Fame).

Jacob Altusky (1931–2017) does not appear to have ever had a USCF over-the-board rating (he did have a USCF postal rating of 1869 in 1998). However, he was not unknown in New York chess circles having lost to Arnold Denker (1945) and drawn with Hans Kmoch (1947) in simuls. Games (2) and (3) clearly do not show him at his best.

(2) King's Indian
Fischer – Jacob Altusky
Brooklyn (offhand) December 1954 or January 1955

1.d4

No 1.e4! Several years were to pass before Bobby started to consistently open with 1.e4. Six months after this game, at the U.S. Junior in Lincoln, Nebraska, Fischer was opening with 1.e4, but hadn't yet progressed to his later standard Ruy Lopez.

1...g6 2.c4 Nf6 3.Nc3 Bg7 4.e4 0-0 5.Bg5 d6 6.Nf3 Nbd7

Here 6...c5 and 6...h6 are seen more often.

7.e5 dxe5 8.dxe5 Ng4 9.Nd5 Ngxe5?? 10.Nxe7+ Kh8 11.Nxg6+ hxg6 12.Bxd8, 1–0.

(3) Ruy Lopez
Jacob Altusky – Fischer
Brooklyn (offhand) December 1954 or January 1955

1.e4 e5 2.Nf3 Nc6 3.Bb5 a6 4.Ba4 d6 5.d4 b5 6.Bb3 Bg4?!

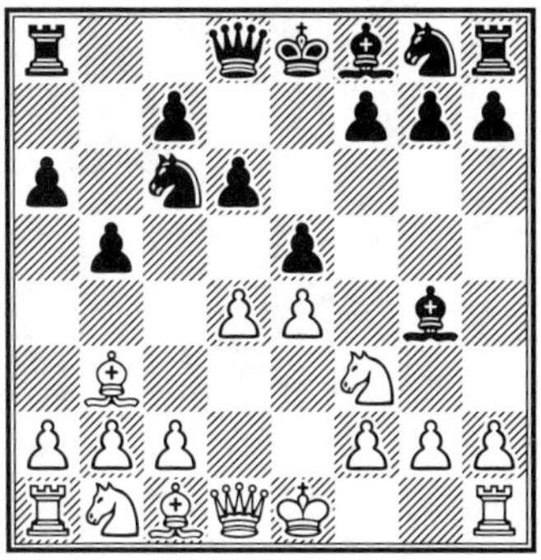

7.Bxf7+??

White overlooks Black's eighth move. The correct way to take advantage of 6...Bg4?, is by 7.dxe5 Nxe5 (7...dxe5 8.Qd5! Qxd5 9.Bxd5 Nge7 10.Nxe5 Nxd5 11.Nxc6 Nb4 12.Nxb4 Bxb4+ 13.Bd2 Bd6 14.f3 and Black's two bishops don't offer sufficient compensation for the pawn; 7...Bxf3 8.Bxf7+ Kxf7 9.Qd5+ Ke7 10.Bg5+ Nf6 11.exf6+ gxf6 12.Qxc6 fxg5 13.gxf3 with the better position and an extra pawn.) 8.Nxe5! Bxd1 9. Bxf7+ Ke7 10.Nc6+ Kxf7 11.Nxd8+ Rxd8 12.Kxd1 and White is a clear pawn up.

7...Kxf7 8.Ng5+ Qxg5, 0–1.

Many remember Fischer played in his first simul against Senior Master Max Pavey (1918–1957), but few today know Pavey was one of America's top players in the 1950s and held a plus score against Bobby in tournament games. A real gentleman, noted for his good sportsmanship, Pavey and his wife Violet were very active in working on behalf of the U.S. Chess Federation.

Pavey's chess career is profiled in an obituary written by *Chess Life* editor Montgomery Major:[1]

> Death claimed Max Pavey on September 4, 1957 at the age of thirty-nine after a long confinement in the Mt. Sinai Hospital. Leukemia and coronary complications "with a suspicion of radium intoxication" were the causes ascribed for his untimely passing.
>
> Ranked as a Senior U.S. Master, Pavey had a very distinguished career in chess. While a student in Edinburgh in 1939 he won the championship of Scotland. In 1947 he won the U.S. Lightning Chess Championship in New

1 *Chess Life*. September 20, 1957, (p. 4).

[above] Paul Keres against Max Pavey from their 3rd game in round four of the 1954 USSR–USA match. The position on the board has Black to move after 34.Kh2. Keres had a winning position after 34...Bg4, but blundered horribly in time pressure and eventually lost.

[above] Bobby at bat in 1955.

[left] The four-story apartment building at 560 Lincoln Place in Brooklyn. Bobby Fischer lived in apartment Q on the top floor with his mother Regina, and sister Joan (Photo: John Donaldson).

York and in 1949 the New York State Championship. He finished second to Donald Byrne in the 1953 U.S. Open at Milwaukee, and was a member of the U.S. team that traveled to Moscow in 1955. He was also a ranking tournament bridge player.

Max Pavey was a chemist by profession and for several years had been manager of the Canadian Radium and Uranium Corp. Laboratory in Mt. Kisco, New York. It is suggested that he might have been the victim of radioactivity, according to a statement from the State Labor Department of New York, which has brought court action against the Canadian Radium and Uranium Corp., alleging laxity in reprocessing and salvaging radium.

Chess players in the USA owe a great debt of gratitude to Max Pavey, not only for his distinguished career which reflected glory on American chess but for his faithful and efficient labors as the chairman of the USCF International Affairs Committee. His zeal for chess was such that he continued to conduct important international chess negotiations from his hospital bed at Mt. Sinai;

> the participation of an American team in the first International Women's Team Tournament at Emmen, Holland was his final successful negotiation on behalf of American Chess.
>
> Invariably soft-spoken and affable in his relationship with others, Max Pavey will be long remembered and his premature passing deeply regretted by all who cherish the best in American chess. Our sympathy goes to his widow, parents and sister.

Pavey was the first strong player Bobby was exposed to. In addition to facing him in the simul, Bobby witnessed him play in the USA–USSR match in 1954 that was held at the Hotel Roosevelt (Madison and 45th). This event, one of the best attended in U.S. chess history, attracted over 1000 spectators per round (only the last two rounds of the Second Piatigorsky Cup are in the same ballpark) and saw Pavey score a very creditable one out of three against Paul Keres on board three. Bobby might not have been able to watch an entire round as the games were played from 8PM to 1AM. Admission was $3 ($28 in 2020 dollars) making the attendance figures all the more remarkable.

Growing up in Brooklyn, just a short distance from Ebbets Field, naturally Bobby was a Dodgers fan. He also loved to play the game himself. His lifelong friend Jim Buff (1944–2010) was a semi-pro baseball player, who is said to have introduced Bobby to the finer points of stickball. Buff, who as an adult was even bigger than Bobby, was a good hitter but an even better pitcher. San Francisco Master Joe Tracy remembers that Buff's fastball was clocked at ninety-two miles per hour, and he had a decent curve ball in his youth. Buff never had a good enough slider or changeup to reach the majors, although he did pitch briefly in the minors. He and Bobby played catch in Golden Gate Park on more than one occasion when Fischer stayed with him at 521 3rd Avenue in San Francisco in 1981.

Buff was the grandson of Harry Zirn, a well-known Brooklyn chess organizer in the 1920s and 1930s. He was an enthusiastic attacking player who played Bobby many times growing up as related in the following newspaper article.

San Francisco Examiner columnist Dick Nolan wrote of Buff:[1]

> I got to thinking and chuckling (insanely, insanely) about the 'hand that shook the hand' when I received proper humiliation the other night in a casual coffee house chess match. My defeat was at the skilled professional hands of Jim Buff. And Jim Buff is the boyhood (and lifelong) friend of World Chess Champion Bobby Fischer. Jim, as a matter of fact and record, has played more chess games with Fischer than anybody has, and on occasion has handled the champ roughly; not often, but once in a while.

---

1 *San Francisco Examiner*, March 6, 1975.

2
FIRST TOURNAMENTS

U.S. AMATEUR CHAMPIONSHIP (1955)

Prior to 1955, all of Bobby's chess was played at the Brooklyn Chess Club or in informal settings such as Washington Square Park—this changed in May of that year, which marked the beginning of his participation in weekend tournaments.

How good was Fischer at the time? He may have been 1700 strength by the beginning of 1955, but was not yet rated by the U.S. Chess Federation.

> My first tournament out of New York City was the United States Amateur, held May 1955 at Lake Mohegan in upstate New York. Mr. Nigro (Carmine Nigro, president of the Brooklyn Chess Club) had to persuade me to play in this tournament as just before the beginning of it I lost my nerve and only wanted to watch. I played, got a minus score, but found it interesting.[1]

These words are the only first-hand account we have from Bobby from what appears to have been his first U.S. Chess Federation rated tournament. Curiously, in Fischer's tournament and match record that is given in *My 60 Memorable Games,*[2] Lake Mohegan is mistakenly given as being in New Jersey, possibly confusing the venue with Lake Hopatcong, home of important tournaments in 1923 and 1926, which is in the Garden State.

The 1955 U.S. Amateur Championship was held May 20–22 at the Mohegan Country Club on Lake Mohegan, roughly fifty miles north of New York City in northern Westchester County. Open to anyone except masters (masters then being defined by the USCF as anyone rated 2300 and over), it attracted seventy-five players and was won by Clinton L. Parmalee of New Jersey. The event was covered in both *Chess Life*[3] and *Chess Review,*[4] but neither published a crosstable. *The American Chess Bulletin*[5] published the names and scores of the first thirty-two finishers (those scoring 3½ points or more), but Bobby was not among them.

---

1 Bobby Fischer, *Bobby Fischer's Games of Chess*. New York: Simon & Schuster, 1959, (p. xi).

2 Bobby Fischer, *My 60 Memorable Games*. New York: Simon & Schuster, 1969, (pp. 381–382).

3 *Chess Life*, June 5, 1955, (p. 1).

4 *Chess Review*, June 1955, (p. 164).

5 *The American Chess Bulletin*, May–June 1955, (p. 48).

His score in the tournament was two wins, one draw and three losses and his post-tournament provisional USCF rating was 1826. It's clear from this result and others around the same time that Bobby at age twelve was a promising young player, but far from being a prodigy

To put things into perspective, Sergey Karjakin, who currently holds the world record for being the youngest grandmaster, made his final norm at the age of twelve years and seven months, almost three years earlier than Bobby who was awarded the title at fifteen years and six months. Since Bobby's accomplishment, over twenty players have become grandmasters before reaching their fifteenth birthday.

Boris Spassky (who at age sixteen finished equal fourth at Bucharest 1953 with a victory over world number two Smyslov) and Garry Kasparov (who at age sixteen took first at Banja Luka 1979, a point and a half over the grandmaster norm as a FIDE unrated) were probably close to Fischer in strength in their mid-teens but were already strong masters at the age of twelve. Neither experienced the "quantum leap" that Bobby did.

It is very unlikely, almost impossible, that we will ever see another player undergo such a massive jump in playing strength.

For many years, Bobby's earliest surviving USCF rated games were from the 1955 U.S. Junior Championship played in July. New York City book dealer Fred Wilson, an accomplished chess historian and teacher (who still plays master level chess at the age of seventy-four), pushed the clock back by two months with his discovery of Game (4), played in May at the 1955 U.S. Amateur Championship. Wilson picked up this game score by accident when he found it hidden in the pages of a book he acquired at an auction in the mid-1990s.

Bobby's opponent in Game (4), Albert B. Humphrey (1911–1997), was an amateur player from Great Barrington, Massachusetts. A college chess champion while attending law school at the University of Virginia, Humphrey was stricken with polio at the age of four. He drove a specially built car with hand levers, and with Lake Mohegan only ninety miles from his home, he decided to play in the 1955 U.S. Amateur. There in the sixth round, the forty-four-year-old Humphrey met the twelve-year-old Robert James Fischer. Humphrey earned a rating of 1791 from this event.

(4) King's Indian
Albert Humphrey – Fischer
Lake Mohegan (6) 1955

1.d4 Nf6 2.c4 g6 3.Nc3 Bg7 4.Nf3 0-0 5.e4 d6 6.h3 Nbd7 7.Be3 e5 8.d5 a5 9.Be2 b6 10.0-0 Ne8 11.Qc2 Nc5 12.Nh2 f5 13.f3 f4 14.Bf2 Qg5 15.Kh1 Bd7 16.Rg1 Nf6 17.g4 fxg3 18.Rxg3 Qh6 19.Nd1 Nh5 20.Rg1 Bxh3 21.Be3 Nf4 22.Nf2 Bf6 23.Rg3 Bd7 24.Ng4 Bxg4 25.Rxg4 Qg7 26.Rag1 Be7 27.Qd2 Rf7 28.R1g3 Raf8 29.Bxf4 Rxf4 30.Rh3 Qf7 31.R4g3 Bh4 32.Rg4 Bf2 33.Bd1, Draw.

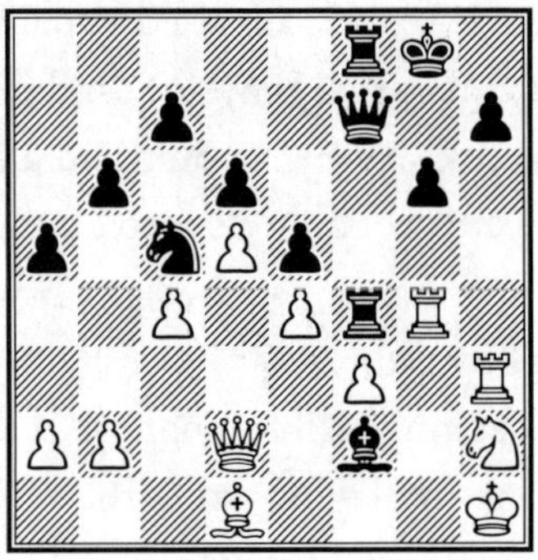

The final position is more than a bit puzzling. Bobby is a pawn up with a big positional advantage. Yes, there still is some work to be done, but White has no counterplay. So why did the young Bobby accept the draw offer? Maybe he was in time pressure or just not feeling confident. The latter theory is supported by what he wrote in *Bobby Fischer's Games of Chess*. Three years later this same player qualified for the Candidates tournament at Portorož, scoring 12–8 for equal 5th versus the world's best.

Partial information for another game Bobby played at Lake Mohegan was provided by Sanford (Sandy) Greene, who fifty years later recalled their draw at the 1955 U.S. Amateur:

> Yes, I did play Bobby a tournament game, in Westchester County, I think at the U.S. Amateur Championship. I drew on the black side of a Yugoslav Dragon, which I still play today. It was an uneventful draw in the old ...Nxd4...Be6 and ...Qa5 line.
>
> Bobby and I were very good friends for a long time. We played hundreds of five-minute games, generally my giving him five-to-two. He would occasionally get annoyed. I think I was the last person to give him odds!

Greene was six years older than Bobby and higher rated in 1955. Going into the U.S. Amateur he had a 1950 USCF rating. Greene would later become a master and was still rated in the top fifty correspondence players in the United States at age eighty.

(5) Sicilian
Fischer – Sanford Greene
Lake Mohegan 1955

1.e4 c5 2.Nf3 d6 3.d4 cxd4 4.Nxd4 Nf6 5.Nc3 g6 6.Be3 Bg7 7.f3 0-0 8.Qd2 Nc6 9.Bc4 Nxd4 10.Bxd4 Be6 11.Bb3 Qa5 (remaining moves unavailable), Draw.

Unfortunately, without the missing moves it's impossible to see how twelve-year-old Fischer handled the Yugoslav Attack. To attain the type of mastery exhibited by his crushing win over Larsen at the 1958 Interzonal, Game (29), Bobby first had to absorb some painful losses. Game (5a) is one, played in a blitz tournament at the Manhattan Chess Club first published in Hermann Helms' column in the *New York World Telegram and Sun* on August 31, 1957.

(5a) Sicilian
Fischer – Donald Byrne
New York 1957

1.e4 c5 2.Nf3 Nc6 3.d4 cxd4 4.Nxd4 g6 5.Nc3 Bg7 6.Be3 Nf6 7.f3?!

7. Bc4 0-0 8.Bb3 d6 9.f3 transposes to the Yugoslav Attack. 8.f3?! Qb6! was Fischer–Panno, Portoroz (izt) 1958 and Black was already equal.

7...0-0 8.Qd2 d5!

Byrne is a full tempo ahead of the Dragon having played ...d5 in one move.

9.Nxc6 bxc6 10.0-0-0 Bb7 11.e5 Nd7 12.Bh6?

Bobby goes for the throat but 12.f4 was necessary.

12...Bxh6!

Accurately judged. Byrne realizes White's attack can easily be repelled.

13.Qxh6 Nxe5 14.h4 f6! 15.h5 Nf7 16.Qf4 Qd6 17.Qg4 Kg7 18.hxg6 hxg6 19.Bd3 Ne5 20.Qd4 Rh8 21.Ne2 c5 22.Qf2 c4 23.f4 Ng4 24.Qg3 f5 25.Nd4 cxd3 26.cxd3 Qc5+ 27.Nc2 Rac8, 0–1.

U.S. JUNIOR OPEN (1955)

The 1955 U.S. Junior in Lincoln, Nebraska, was Fischer's first tournament outside of New York State. The young Bobby took the train from New York to Philadelphia where he hooked up with Charles Kalme. The two then made an over twenty-four-hour journey to Lincoln where they were met by organizer Alexander Liepnieks.

Today young players in the United States have many big events to choose from—the World, Chicago, and North American Opens to mention but three—but go back sixty years and the situation was markedly different. American players in the 1950s didn't have the luxury of being able to choose which tournaments to play in—they played in what was available.

These days the U.S. Junior Open is not an especially significant event, having been superseded by the U.S. Junior Closed, which brings together the best young players in the country. Things were different when Bobby travelled to Lincoln. The Junior really meant something then and the best players traveled considerable distances to participate at a time when plane travel was not the norm.

Lincoln, Nebraska, might seem an unlikely venue for a chess tournament. The hometown of the acclaimed University of Nebraska Cornhusker football team could have passed for a typical Midwestern steak and potatoes kind of place but for one unusual ingredient: Latvians.

Many of the citizens of this small Baltic nation, which was savaged during the Second World War, immigrated to the United States in the late 1940s and early 1950s. A small colony of them settled in Lincoln and brought with them a love for chess. Their numbers included the master-strength player and organizer Alex Liepnieks, who was to bring the U.S. Open to Lincoln in 1969. Liepnieks was the driving force behind the 1955 U.S. Junior, taking command of every detail.

One of his first duties was to schedule the event for July 15–24, to enable twenty-year-old Viktors Pupols, with a July 31 birthday, to meet the age requirement. Pupols was one of several Latvian-born players (Kalme, Staklis, Briska were others) competing in the event, and had ties to Lincoln, having moved there with his family in the early 1950s, before relocating to the Pacific Northwest.

In 1992, shortly after the second Fischer–Spassky match, the Seattle Chess Club held a special Bobby Fischer night with Grandmaster Yasser Seirawan, International Master Nikolay Minev, and Master Viktors Pupols as guest speakers. The event, which was videotaped and later shown on local cable television, was a great hit. Pupols, whose skills as a raconteur were documented in *Viktors Pupols, American Master,* entertained the audience with his impressions of the young Bobby.

The first thing Pupols stressed in his talk was that Bobby was very much an unknown player in 1955. He was only twelve and hadn't yet begun the growth spurt that would later enable him to reach 6'2". This was his first trip away from home and it's doubtful that Bobby would have been allowed to make it if his mother hadn't had the assurances he would be spending the next two weeks in a domestic environment with the Liepnieks family.

Bobby is often portrayed in the media as a loner who formed few close personal relationships, but conversations with Bobby's friends and an examination of written records show no basis for this judgment. Fischer may initially have been on his guard, but once he understood you respected chess he was very friendly.

The friendship with Liepnieks and his wife, their two daughters (Ruth and Sylvia) and son (Andy), which began with Bobby's first stay, lasted for decades. Fischer, subject to some teasing as the youngest player in the event, got a little homesick, but greatly enjoyed his stay.

Alexander Liepnieks was a member of the Fischer camp at the 1972 World Championship match against Spassky in Reykjavík, where his skills as a Russian translator proved invaluable for Fred Cramer and other high-ranking members of the American delegation. When Liepnieks died in 1973 the Latvian-American publication *ChessWorld/Sacha Pasaule* ran a letter of condolence from Bobby:

> **AN INSPIRING EXAMPLE TO ME**
>
> Thank you for your note informing me of your father's death. I was very sorry to hear this because I considered him to be a good friend. His enthusiasm, good will, dedication and love of chess was an inspiring example to me. And I am sure to many others.
>
> I have certainly enjoyed *Chess World* very much over the years and especially the section on the Latvian Gambit, which was highly entertaining and instructive. It is my sincere hope that someone will follow in your father's footsteps and continue the monthly publication of this fine magazine.
>
> Again please accept my condolences.
>
> Sincerely,
> Bobby Fischer

The 1955 U.S. Junior was easily won by top-rated (2186) Charles Kalme, who defeated two of his chief rivals, Larry Remlinger and Ron Gross, in the first four rounds. His sole loss, en route to a 9–1 score, which garnered him the title and a seventy-five dollar suit, was to Robert Cross.

Charles Kalme (1939–2002), a talent with great potential, was only fifteen at the time of his victory in Lincoln, setting a record as the youngest U.S. Junior winner. Bobby would break this record the very next year.

California Master Charles Henin covered Kalme's career up to the early 1960s in a *Chess Life* article. Shortly thereafter Kalme retired from chess to concentrate on a career in academia:[1]

> There is no doubt that the rise of the United States to the No.2 spot in world chess has been due mainly to the emergence in recent years of some very talented young players. Along with the spectacular rises of Fischer and

[1] *Chess Life*, March 1961, "Young American Grandmasters," (p. 86).

Lombardy have been those, less spectacular but no less important, of several other young masters.

One among these is Charles Kalme of Philadelphia. That city's leading player for several years, Kalme is a former U.S. Junior and U.S. Intercollegiate titleholder, having won the former title in 1955 and the latter in 1957. He tied for first place in the strong North Central Open in 1957, in which he defeated Fischer, a feat that has not since been duplicated in an American chess tourney. Charley has competed twice on the U.S. student team, and his most outstanding success was in the recent student team tournament in Moscow, where his dazzling score of 12½–1½ on board two helped in no small way to bring the United States its first international team title in over twenty-five years.[1] In the recent U.S. Championship event Kalme scored a respectable 5–6, good for seventh prize in a powerful field. Only a loss in a rather wild last round game with Lombardy prevented a really fine result, for if Kalme had won that game he would have tied for third place, so close was the finish.

Kalme was born in Riga, Latvia, home of many fine chess players including the present World Champion [Mikhail Tal]. Just after the war his family fled to Germany, where they lived for several years in Displaced Persons Camps in the Allied zone. It was here that Charley learned chess, though he didn't play seriously until his high school days in Philadelphia, where he and his family came to settle in 1951. His rapid development to master strength he attributes mainly to his association with Master Attilio Di Camillo.

Tall, thin, and blond, Kalme presents a physical picture of ease and relaxation. He is in fact known for his nonchalance, and I am told that in a recent tourney, half an hour after the first round was scheduled to have begun, into the playing room leisurely strolled Kalme and asked "Where do I register?"

When it comes to chess though, Charley becomes very serious. He has a complex style which often leads him into difficult and complicated positions in which he fights intensely. With regard to his part in the student team victory he says, "For many reasons, some best understood only by me and my native country Latvia, this was the greatest thrill of my life. I do not think there has been anything in my life that I wanted more than for our team to win the title, and it was definitely the most determined effort ever put into chess by me. That is not to say that the quality of my play was so high but that the effort was great. Generally I seldom find the effort to sit through forty or so moves and try to make every one of them to the best of my ability. In the Student's Team Tournament however I did so in thirteen of the fourteen games played. The one exception was in the fifth round against Yugoslavia. With the U.S. leading by some 4 or 5 points over the field (including Russia) I left a piece in take in an even position, after having played rather carelessly throughout. We lost the match by ½–3½ and this enabled Russia later to

[1] The U.S. won the 1937 Olympiad so it was a twenty-three-year drought.

> catch up with us and even move ahead. After this disaster I walked around sulking till 5AM next morning, only then feeling convinced that there was no reason for us still not to win the championship!

Kalme always did well playing for the United States, scoring close to 80% in three Student Olympiads. He took home team gold in 1960, silver in 1961, and would almost certainly have added a bronze medal to his collection at Krakow 1964 if the U.S. team, which finished fourth, had more than four players to use. Raymond Weinstein's performance was so poor he had to be benched half way through—this was one of the last events he played in before being committed to a home for the criminally insane. Second reserve Mitchell Zweig was much weaker than the other players and only played one game.

In 1955, soon-to-be International Master James Sherwin wrote about Kalme's style and personality in a *Chess Life* article "Masters of the Future."[1]

> He has a solid positional style and prefers not to take too many chances (which accounts for his very few losses and many draws—he was undefeated in three recent tournaments). He is remarkably modest for a strong chess player and is always announcing that the best he can do is draw—only when a rook ahead does he admit there are some winning chances. And unfortunately, he is a good poker player. This deprives him of needed sleep during most tournaments in return for pocket money. It's hard to see what is more necessary. As soon as he begins to take his games more seriously he should become a master.

Kalme stayed away from the tournament play for thirty years during which time he earned his Ph.D. in Mathematics and taught at the University of California at Berkeley. Returning to play in the mid-1990s, his performance at the 1994 World Open was impressive (2450 USCF) considering the long layoff. This might not seem that remarkable for a player of such great talent, but as Philadelphia International Master Richard Costigan points out:

> He was getting absolutely nothing from the opening, even against experts. His strength was a strongly developed positional sense.

Kalme, who had escorted Bobby to Lincoln in 1955, returned there twenty years later to speak on his behalf at the U.S. Open regarding regulations for the World Championship and Fischer's demand for a ten-win match. Kalme did an exhaustive analysis of Fischer's proposal in *Chess Life & Review*[2] and came to the conclusion that with draws not counting, normally one of the two players would reach ten victories before game thirty. He believed that the ten-game win format would lead to a shorter match than one with a fewer number of victories required, but a set number of games.

---

1 *Chess Life*, "Masters of the Future," July 5, 1955, (p. 3).

2 *Chess Life & Review*, November 1975, (pp. 717–729).

Subsequent to this article, two matches tested Kalme's hypothesizes with mixed results. The first, Karpov–Kasparov (1984–85), ended inconclusively after game forty-eight, with the score 5–3 in favor of Karpov but with Kasparov having won the last two games. Karpov was up 4–0 after nine games, and it looked like he would quickly get to the required six wins, but things were not so simple. Kasparov went into survival mode and Karpov played cautiously. The result was Karpov only notched up win number five after game twenty-seven and failed to add to that in the next twenty-one games.

The second test was the 1992 Fischer–Spassky match. Here things went pretty much as Kalme predicted: it lasted thirty games with Bobby winning ten wins to five losses, with fifteen draws.

Latvian authorities reported that Charles Kalme died on March 20, 2002:

> [Kalme] died a mysterious death in Latvia at the age of sixty-two, which some reliable sources say may have been the result of a brutal mugging he suffered on the streets of Riga.[1]

Bobby scored 5–5 in Lincoln, good for shared eleventh to twenty-first place, with two wins, two losses, and six draws. His play gave no indication he would become a world class grandmaster in just three years.

Fischer wasn't the top young talent to play in the 1955 U.S. Junior—that distinction belonged to thirteen-year-old Larry Remlinger of Long Beach, California. Remlinger was considered a brilliant prospect at the time and was strongly supported by his parents. A regular at the Long Beach Chess Club, then a full-time facility, he was clearly stronger than Bobby in 1955 and would almost certainly have become a strong grandmaster if he'd been born in the Soviet Union or had lived in New York City.

Larry Remlinger is a good example of a promising young player who came up at the same time as Fischer but did not have the same opportunities. A year-and-a-half older than Bobby, Remlinger was rated 2114 to Bobby's 1830 when the two competed in the U.S. Junior in Lincoln, Nebraska in the summer of 1955. Larry finished second (for the second year in a row) with 7½, while Bobby ended up with an even score. Remlinger would soon take a break from the game that lasted for fifteen years (he did temporarily come back to share first with Raymond Weinstein at the 1958 U.S. Junior but lost the title on tiebreak).

Remlinger grew up in Long Beach and during the summers was a constant presence at the Lincoln Park Chess Club, one of the most important in the Los Angeles area. Larry had a key to the club and would open it at eight in the morning, often not coming home until after dark. He didn't have a coach or formal study program, learning and improving through constant play.

---

[1] *Chess Life*, November 2010, (p. 31).

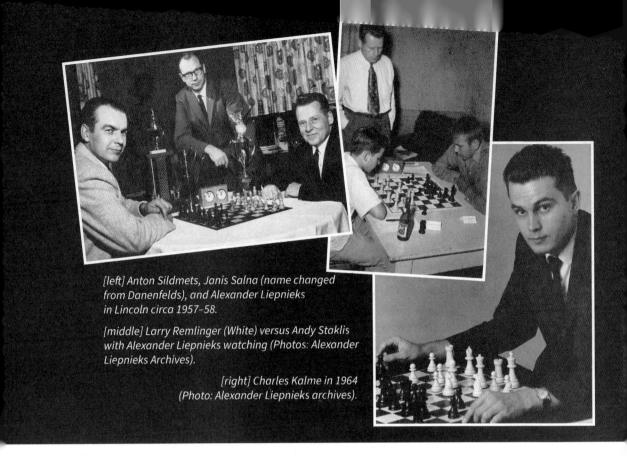

[left] Anton Sildmets, Janis Salna (name changed from Danenfelds), and Alexander Liepnieks in Lincoln circa 1957–58.

[middle] Larry Remlinger (White) versus Andy Staklis with Alexander Liepnieks watching (Photos: Alexander Liepnieks Archives).

[right] Charles Kalme in 1964 (Photo: Alexander Liepnieks archives).

However, unlike New York, which had almost all the top players in the country, Long Beach had few masters. Once Larry reached 2200–2300 strength there were few opportunities to consistently face stronger opposition. On top of that, when he hit a plateau there was no coach that could explain this was a natural occurrence and what he could do to work his way through it. Like Kalme, Remlinger "retired" from tournament play well before realizing his full potential, preferring to concentrate on college. He played in the occasional event off and on until the 1990s when he rededicated himself to chess, quickly earning the International Master title in his early fifties.

One person in California who might have helped Remlinger was International Master Herman Steiner. A one-time U.S. Champion and member of the American Olympiad team, Steiner was a great promoter of the game who died much too young—in 1955 at only fifty years of age. *Chess Life* published photos of him with Larry and Jim Cross, a slightly older junior star from southern California, but neither were actually coached by Steiner.

Sherwin described Remlinger in his article "Masters of the Future:"[1]

> Most New York players provincially determine the strength of 'out of towners' by examining their records against the New York masters. That was how Larry Remlinger's play came to be respected in New York. Karl Burger

[1] *Chess Life*, "Masters of the Future," July 5, 1955, (p. 3).

[left] Mitzi Mayfair, Herman Steiner, Hector Rossetto, and Carmen Miranda, at the Pan American Chess Championship held in Pasadena during the summer of 1945 (Photo: Nancy Roos);

[right] Larry Remlinger at the Mechanics Institute, in a California State Championship, 1950s.

attended the Kansas City Junior two years ago and returned to report that an eleven-year-old named Remlinger was going to be U.S. Champion in six years and that Karl was lucky to have drawn with him.

Larry learned to play chess from an uncle when he was ten and a year later joined the Lincoln Park Chess and Checker Club. Fortunately Mr. John L. Looney, the club secretary, and Lionel Joyner [one of Canada's top players in the 1950s and early 1960s] recognized Larry's talent and helped him study the theory of the openings and endings—midgame theory must be learned more by experience. The members of the club and local merchants contributed to send Larry and his parents to the Kansas City tournament where he was coached by Herman Steiner.

Last year in Long Beach, Larry finished second in the U.S. Junior ahead of Kalme, Harrow, Gross, Shelby Lyman and Bob Cross, to mention only a few.

Bobby, Kalme, and Remlinger were not the only players in Lincoln destined to become well-known names. Robert Cross, who finished third, would develop into a strong correspondence player. Max Burkett became a noted chess bookseller and produced the Lone Pine tournament bulletins for many years.

John Rinaldo (1938–) finished sixth in the 1955 U.S. Junior Open—he was not paired against Bobby in that tournament. In a 2000 interview he recalled his friendship with Fischer:

It was during this period that I became friends with Bobby. He was playing a line that had recently (1955) been analyzed in Euwe's *Chess Archives*. I was from Long Beach, California and had ridden with Larry Remlinger and his

Larry Remlinger, Steve Brandwein, Jeremy Silman (standing), and Yasser Seirawan (sitting) watch Larry Christiansen and Walter Browne (back to camera) go over a game. San Francisco 1977.

mother and father to Lincoln. As I watched Bobby play I called over Ron Gross, also from Long Beach, to see Bobby's game, telling him I couldn't believe this kid knew this line. After the game Bobby and I analyzed the post mortem and developed a friendship that we continued over to the next year where we played together in the U.S. Open in Oklahoma City.

During this Open we spent most of our time together, playing, studying, and going to the movies. I accompanied him to a couple of TV interviews. (Already he was standing out as a young prodigy.) During these interviews the topics spanned not only chess but also such diverse topics as baseball where Bobby predicted the Dodgers would win the pennant! (And indeed they did but lost in the World Series to the Yankees).

After the Open we kept in contact and as the summer of '57 rolled around we agreed we would spend the summer together. Bobby won the Junior and joined me in Long Beach where we studied and played together, swimming and playing the chess hustlers at West Lake Park! During that period Bobby stayed with me and for the most part he and I ate and slept chess. We would wake up at about 9AM, have breakfast, play and study various lines, including the famous Petroff line where Walter Browne played Bh6! Sorry Shawn but Bobby found it first!

Viktors Pupols was Bobby's opponent in round seven. The Northwest Master is one of the top senior players in the United States and still maintains a rating over 2200 in his mid-eighties. He provided the background for Game (6) in the pages of *Chess World/Sacha Pasaule.*[1]

[1] *Chess World/Sacha Pasaule*, April 1972.

[left] Viktors Pupols at the U.S Junior Open 1955 (Photo: Alexander Liepnieks Archive) and at the Mechanics' Institute Chess Club with a forty year gap—1974 [middle] and 2014 [right].

U.S. JUNIOR CHAMPIONSHIP LINCOLN, NEBRASKA JULY 1955

1	Charles Kalme	Philadelphia, PA	15	2186	+23	+6	+2	+4	-3	+11	+5	+8	+9	+12	**9.0**
2	Larry Remlinger	Long Beach, CA	13	2114	+17	+15	-1	=5	+14	+6	=4	+3	+11	=8	**7.5**
3	Robert Cross	Santa Monica, CA	20	2068	=7	+16	=14	+12	+ 1	=4	=11	-2	+5	+6	**7.0**
4	Ronald Gross	Compton, CA	19	2123	+22	+10	+11	-1	+6	=3	=2	-5	=8	=9	**6.0**
5	Andris Staklis	Lincoln, NE	16	1823	+21	=12	+15	=2	-11	+13	-1	+4	-3	+18	**6.0**
6	John Rinaldo	Long Beach, CA	16	1847	+25	-1	+17	+7	-4	-2	+12	+11	=13	-3	**5.5**
7	Robert Lorber	Reseda, CA	16	1600	=3	=8	+9	-6	-12	+24	+14	=13	=15	=10	**5.5**
8	Sanford Greene	Mt. Vernon, NY	18	1950	=16	=7	+23	=14	=13	=12	+18	-1	=4	=2	**5.5**
9	Victor Pupols	Tacoma, WA	20	2027	+24	-11	-7	-13	+25	+16	+20	+17	-1	=4	**5.5**
10	Barton Lewis	Lincoln, NE	20	1785	+18	-4	-16	=17	-19	=22	bye	+24	+23	=7	**5.5**
11	Elliott Fromes	Palo Verdes, CA	19	unr	+13	+9	-4	+16	+5	-1	=3	-6	-2	=14	**5.0**
12	Kenneth Warner	Bakersfield, CA	17	1550	+20	=5	=13	-3	+7	=8	-6	+15	=14	-1	**5.0**
13	Ben Schaeffer	San Bernardino, CA	19	1700	-11	+24	=12	+9	=8	-5	=15	=7	=6	=16	**5.0**
14	William Whisler	Concord, CA	17	unr	bye	=20	=3	=8	-2	=18	-7	+19	=12	=11	**5.0**
15	Dale Ruth	Midwest City, OK	18	1785	+19	-2	-5	+23	=18	=17	=13	-12	=7	+22	**5.0**
16	Kenneth Stone	Los Angeles, CA	19	1600	=8	-3	+10	-11	=20	-9	=21	bye	+25	=13	**5.0**
17	Max Burkett	Carlsbad, CA	16	1600	-2	+22	-6	=10	+21	=15	+19	-9	-18	+23	**5.0**
18	David Ames	Quincy MA	18	unr	-10	bye	+19	=20	=15	=14	-8	=21	+17	-5	**5.0**
19	John Briska	Albany, NY	17	unr	-15	=21	-18	+25	+10	=20	-17	-14	bye	+24	**5.0**
20	Robert Fischer	Brooklyn, NY	12	1830	-12	=14	+21	=18	=16	=19	-9	=23	=22	+25	**5.0**
21	James Thomason	Ft. Worth, TX	14	1600	-5	=19	-20	+22	-17	+25	=16	=18	=24	bye	**5.0**
22	John Winkelman	Lincoln, NE	14	1650	-4	-17	+24	-21	bye	=10	-23	+25	=20	-15	**4.0**
23	Robert Blair	Midwest City, OK	18	1650	-1	+25	-8	-15	-24	bye	+22	=20	-10	-17	**3.5**
24	Jim Dick	Lincoln, NE	15	1600	-9	-13	-22	bye	+23	-7	+25	-10	=21	-19	**3.5**
25	Franklin Saksena	Ft. Worth, TX	17	1600	-6	-23	bye	-19	-9	-21	-24	-22	-16	-20	**1.0**

We had known all day what the pairings and the colors would be (Alex Liepnieks directed the tournament), and I tried to impress Bobby Fischer (he was only twelve years old) with the glories of the Latvian Gambit. Fischer refused to believe that this opening would indeed be played and analyzed other open games.

There was a continuing poker game at Alex Liepnieks' home, and throughout the day Charles Kalme, the eventual tournament winner, and I kept playing skittles games using the Latvian Gambit against Fischer, whenever we folded at poker, but at the end of the day Fischer was still analyzing the Ruy Lopez and Giuoco Piano. Bobby took his loss very hard. I did, of course, announce in advance my intention of playing the Latvian Gambit.

(6) Latvian Gambit
Fischer – Viktors Pupols
Lincoln (7) 1955

1.e4 e5 2.Nf3

Bobby was greatly interested in double King-pawn openings. He not only played the standard Ruy Lopez, but also the King's Gambit with 3.Bc4 in tournament practice. During 1964 his repertoire was even greater with a good mix of Vienna Games. Dr. Leroy Dubeck, whose term as USCF president (1969–1972) coincided with Bobby's World Championship run, had much unpublished Weaver Adams analysis on the Vienna which he and Fischer looked at a couple of times in the early 1960s.

2...f5

Bobby would probably have played 3.Bc4 against 2...Nc6.

3. Nxe5 Qf6 4.d4 d6 5.Nc4 fxe4 6.Nc3

The opening sequence of this game is sometimes given as 6.Ne3 and 7. Nc3, but as Pupols points out Black might be able to avoid having to play ...Qg6 by answering 6.Ne3 with 6...Nc6.

6...Qg6 7.Ne3

This blockading move is often attributed to the "Great Blockader" Aron Nimzowitsch, who was born in Riga, Latvia.

7...Nf6 8.Bc4 c6 9.d5

This stops ...d6-d5 but yields the e5 square. The more Nimzowitschian strategy was to allow Black to play ...d5 and then attack the pawn chain with c2-c4.

9...Be7

Here 9...c5 yields the b5 square.

10.a4 Nbd7 11.a5?

The plan of a2-a4-a5 loses valuable time.

11...Ne5 12.Be2

12.Ba2 c5 and White doesn't control b5.

12...0-0 13.0-0 Bd7 14.Kh1 Kh8 15.Nc4 Nfg4 16.Qe1

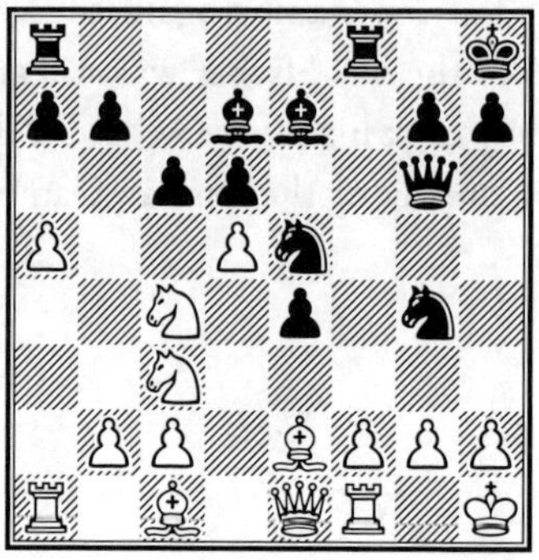

16...Rf7

Missing a win with 16...Nf3! 17.gxf3 exf3 when the threat of 18...Qh5 forces White to return the piece with no satisfactory way to protect his king.

17.h3 Nf6?!

Black could have again played the very interesting piece sacrifice 17...Nf3!. The position after 18.Qd1 Raf8 looks very promising for him.

18.Nxe5 dxe5 19.Bc4 Rff8 20.Be3 Nh5 21.Kh2 Bd6 22.Bb3 Nf4

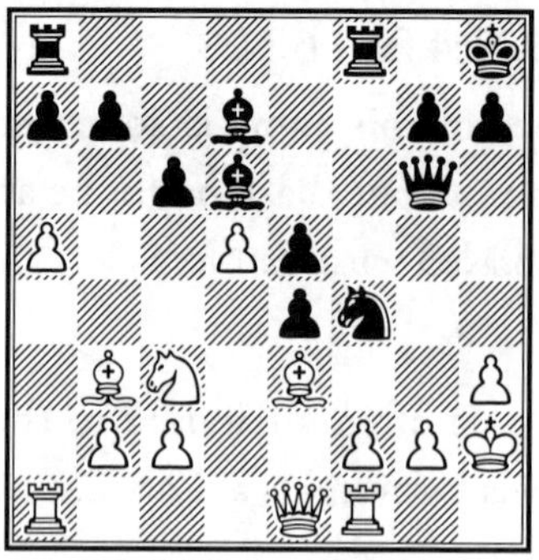

23.Bxf4?

This exchange brings Black's dark-squared bishop to life and gives him strong mobile pawns on e4 and f4. A better try is 23.Rg1 meeting 23...Qh5 with 24.Qf1.

23...exf4 24.Qxe4?

This should lose immediately. 24.f3 had to be played, but Black would of course have a large advantage after 24…Rae8.

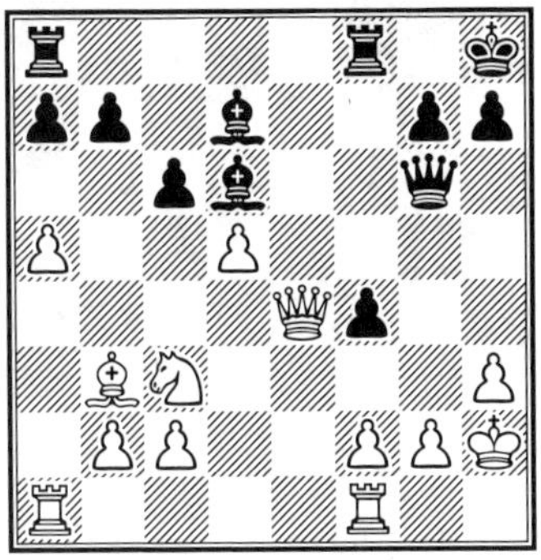

24...f3+ 25.g3 Bf5?

Here 25...Qh6! or 25...Qh5! would have won immediately, as 26.h4 is met by 26... Rf4! with the threat of 27...Rxh4+ mating.

26.Qh4 Rae8 27.Rae1 Be5

Avoiding exchanges.

28.Qb4?

28.dxc6 bxc6 29.Re3 Bd7 would have left White much worse but still fighting. The text should lose immediately.

28...Qh6 29.h4

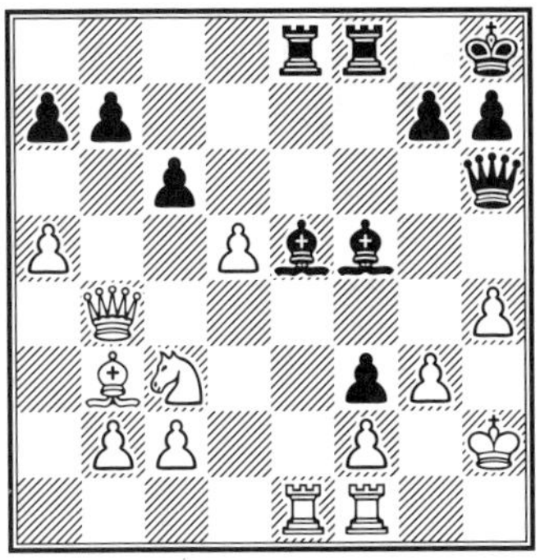

29…g5?

Black had a forced win with 29...Bxg3+: 30.fxg3 Qd2+, 30.Kh1 Bf4 and 30.Kxg3 Qg6+ all lead to mate.

30.Rh1?

Bobby could have tired to complicate matters with 30.Rxe5!, hoping for 30…Rxe5 31.Qd4 with some fighting chances, but the intermezzo 30…gxh4!, settles matters on the spot.

30...gxh4 31.Kg1

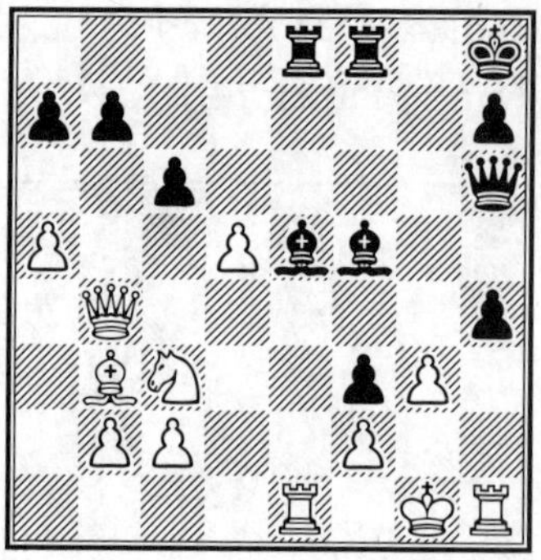

31...h3?

This mistake, which closes lines for the attack, overlooks two forced wins. Black had much better in 31...Bxg3! 32.Qd4+ Be5 33.Rxe5 Qg7+ or if 33.Qxh4 Bh2+! (Pupols). Also winning is 31...Qg7! 32.Rxe5 hxg3 33.Ne4 gxf2+ 34.Kxf2 Qxe5 35.dxc6 Bxe4.

32.dxc6?

Better is 32.Ne4, although Black still has a large advantage after 32...Bxb2 33.Kh2 Be5.

32...bxc6?

Pupols overlooks 32...Bxg3!. Black wins after 33.Qd4+ Be5 34.Rxe5 Qg7+ 35.Kf1 Rxe5.

33.Qc5?

This wastes valuable time with the queen. White should have brought his knight to the defense with 33.Ne4.

33...Qg7?

The contestants continue to have a blind spot for ...Bxg3. Here 33...Bxg3! is again crushing. For example: 34.Qd4+ Be5 35.Rxe5 Qg7+ 36.Kf1 Rxe5 37.Ne4 c5.

34.Kh2

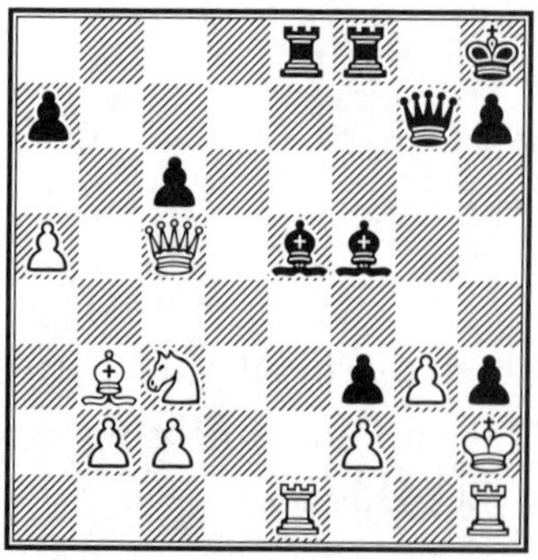

34...Qf6?

34...Bd4! 35.Qd6 Rd8 wins.

35.Qxa7 Bd4? 36.Qc7 Bf2

Here 36...Be5 allows 36.Rxe5. Pupols no longer has the advantage.

37.Rxe8 Rxe8 38.Rf1 Bd4

The time control was forty-five moves in two hours. For the following phase White had only two minutes on his clock; Black but one.

39.Rxf3?

Bobby had to play 39.Qf4. After the text Black has a powerful shot.

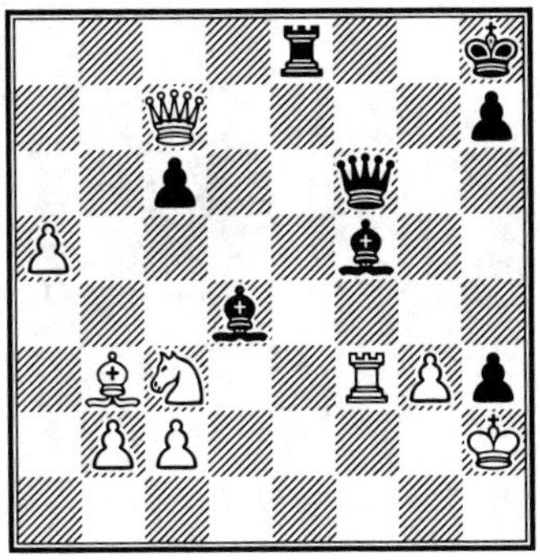

39...Bxc3?

Pupols misses a chance to conclude the game in brilliant fashion. Black has a forced win with 39...Bg1+!! White loses whether he captures the bishop or not: 40.Kh1 Be4 41.Qf4 Bxf3+ 42.Kxg1 Re1+ 43.Kf2 Qxf4 44.gxf4 h2 45.Kxe1 h1=Q+ or 40.Kxg1 Qd4+ 41.Kf1 h2 42.Kg2 h1=Q+ 43.Kxh1 Re1+ mating.

40.bxc3 Re2+ 41.Kh1 Be4 42.Qc8+ Kg7 43.Qg4+?

White could have drawn with 43.Qd7+ Kh6 44.Qxh3+ Kg7 45.Qd7+ Kh6 46.Qh3+ with a draw by perpetual check. After the text Black has a significant advantage.

43...Qg6 44.Qd7+?

Bobby misses the last chance to continue to fight. White had to play 44. Qf4 when Black has two choices, though neither one leads to a forced win. On 44...Bxf3+ White has 45.Qxf3 Rg2 46.Qe3 when 46...Qd6 keeps a small edge. The alternative is 44...h5 45.a6 Bxf3 46.Qxf3 Re1+ 47.Kh2 h4 48.Kxh3 Qxg3+ 49.Qxg3+ hxg3 50.Kxg3 and White should hold.

44...Kh6, 0–1 time.

Black is winning after 45.Qxh3+ Qh5.

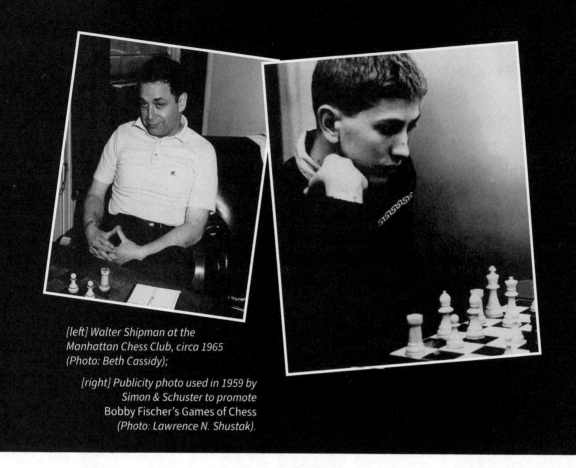

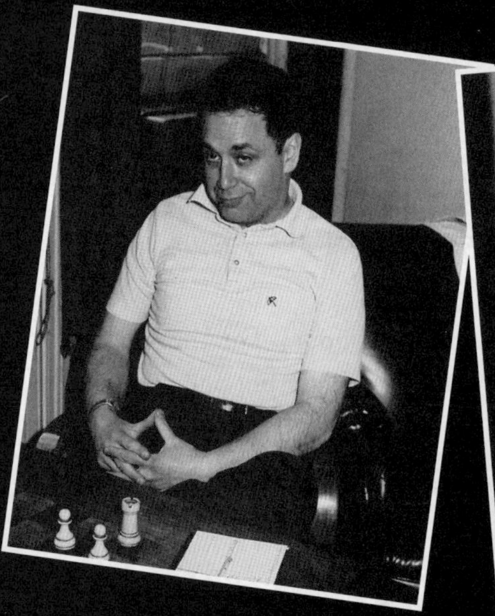

[left] Walter Shipman at the Manhattan Chess Club, circa 1965 (Photo: Beth Cassidy);

[right] Publicity photo used in 1959 by Simon & Schuster to promote Bobby Fischer's Games of Chess *(Photo: Lawrence N. Shustak).*

Game (6), a 1956 loss to Reshevsky from the Rosenwald, and a defeat against Sherwin from a 1957 Log Cabin game (unpublished) are the only occasions Fischer lost on time in his career.

The Lincoln event is one of the rare U.S. Juniors that has a bulletin—thanks to the efforts of chess enthusiast Jack Spence (1926–1978). Omaha born and raised, Spence did an incredible amount to preserve American chess history. Thousands of games would be lost if not for the dozens of bulletins he produced of U.S. Opens and other important American tournaments. Besides these bulletins, Spence found the time to serve as the editor of the *Nebraska Bulletin and Midwest Chess News* (from 1947–1959), and the *Ohman Memorial Club Newsletter* (1969–1978). He served as a tournament director and officer (at both the local and state level) for much of his life.

The bulletin for Lincoln doesn't have all the games of the event but offers a good selection. Bobby, who was not one of the top finishers, had his first four games selected for publication (Warner, Whisler, Thomason, and Ames). This tallies with Wade and O'Connell's *The Games of Robert Fischer*—the first systematic attempt to locate all of Bobby's games—which undoubtedly used Spence's bulletin as primary source material.

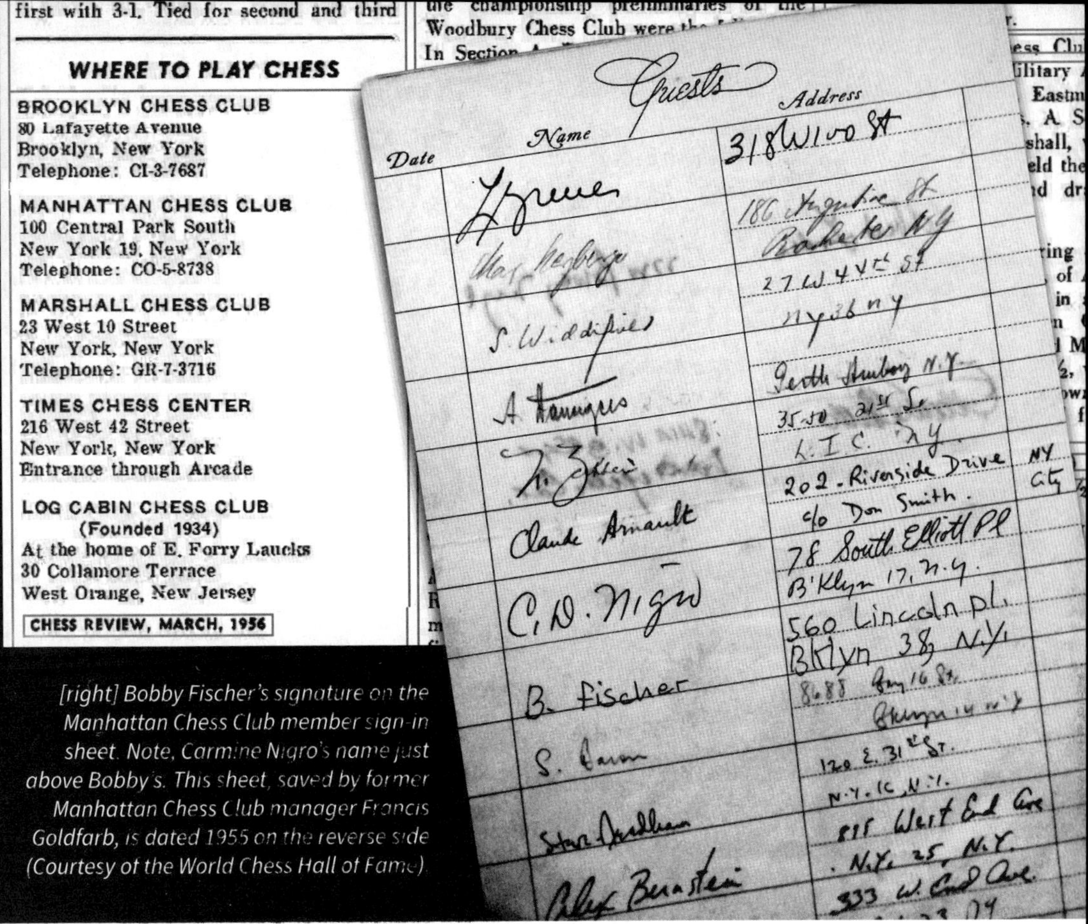

[right] Bobby Fischer's signature on the Manhattan Chess Club member sign-in sheet. Note, Carmine Nigro's name just above Bobby's. This sheet, saved by former Manhattan Chess Club manager Francis Goldfarb, is dated 1955 on the reverse side (Courtesy of the World Chess Hall of Fame)

Years later Pupols and Franklin Saksena made their games with Bobby public—Game (6) and (8). This brings the tally of known games to six plus the following Game (7) that was played against either Briska or Winkelman.

In his notes to 3.Bc4 in a Two Knights Defense game with Bisguier,[1] Bobby wrote, "The last time I played this move in a tournament was when I was twelve, at the 1955 Championship." This appears to be that game.

---

(7) Two Knights
Fischer – Briska!? or Winkelman!?
Lincoln 1955

1.e4 e5 2.Nf3 Nc6 3.Bc4 Nf6 4.Ng5

Here 4.Nc3, as Bobby played against Ames at this tournament, has the widely held reputation of being a beginner's mistake. The fork trick after 4...Nxe4 is supposed to easily equalize for Black, if not lead to a better game, but rarely are things 100% clear in chess.

[1] Bobby Fischer, *My 60 Memorable Games*, New York: Simon & Schuster, 1969, Game 45, (pp. 280–285).

Check out Morovic–Sagalchik, North Bay 1996, (*Chess Informant*, 67/406) where the GM duel saw White emerge with an advantage after 5.Nxe4 d5 6.Bd3 f5 (6…dxe4 7.Bxe4 Bd6 Ivanchuk–Karjakin, Moscow (blitz) 2009) 7.Nc3 e4 (7...d4 8.Qe2!) 8.Bb5 exf3 9.Qxf3 Be6 10.0-0 Qd7 11.Ne2! Bd6 12.d4! 0-0 13.Bf4 Bxf4 14.Qxf4 Rae8 15.Qd2 a6 16.Bxc6 Qxc6 17.Nf4 Bd7 18.f3 Qb6 19.b3 Qh6 20.Rf2! c6 21.Nd3 f4 22.Re1 g5 23.Rxe8 Rxe8 24.Re2 Rxe2 25.Qxe2 Qe6 26.Ne5. White's superior minor piece gives him a long-term advantage.

4...Bc5

Fischer, annotating his game with Bisguier from the 1963 New York State Open for *Chess Life*[1] remarks after 4...d5:

"On that last occasion in Nebraska, referred to above, my opponent played 4...Bc5, alias the Wilkes-Barre line of the Two-Knights. At that time I was unfamiliar with this variation and nearly laughed out loud at the thought of my opponent making such a blunder in a tournament of this importance. I was just about to let him have it, when I noticed that he had brought along a friend who was watching the game very intently. This aroused my suspicion —maybe this was a trap, straight from Horowitz's *Traps and Pitfalls*. But a rook is a rook—so I continued with...."

5.Nxf7 Bxf2+ 6.Kxf2 Nxe4+ 7.Ke3? Qh4

"And somehow I got out of this mess. Afterwards I showed him a forced win that he had missed. The game was actually drawn on my request. I had no chance for first place and my trophy for the best scoring player under thirteen was assured already, since I was the only one under thirteen!"

This note was included in an early draft of what was to become *My 60 Memorable Games*, but didn't make the final cut.

Game (8) surfaced when Dr. Franklin Saksena responded to Alex Dunne's request for information for his book on the U.S. Junior Championship.[2]

Saksena was seventeen and living in Fort Worth, Texas, when this game was played in the last round of the 1955 U.S. Junior Open. He finished last in Lincoln, but improved enough over the course of the next twelve months to make an even score in the 1956 U.S. Junior Open in Philadelphia. He went on to become a well-respected cardiologist.

---

1 *Chess Life*, December 1963, (pp. 302–303).

2 Alex Dunne, *The United States Junior Open Chess Championship, 1946–2016*. Jefferson, NC: McFarland, 2016. This game was first presented in *Chess Life* August 2017, (pp. 46–47).

(8) Giuoco Piano
Fischer – Franklin Saksena
Lincoln (10) July 24, 1955

1.e4 e5 2.Nf3 Nc6 3.Bc4 Bc5 4.c3 f5?

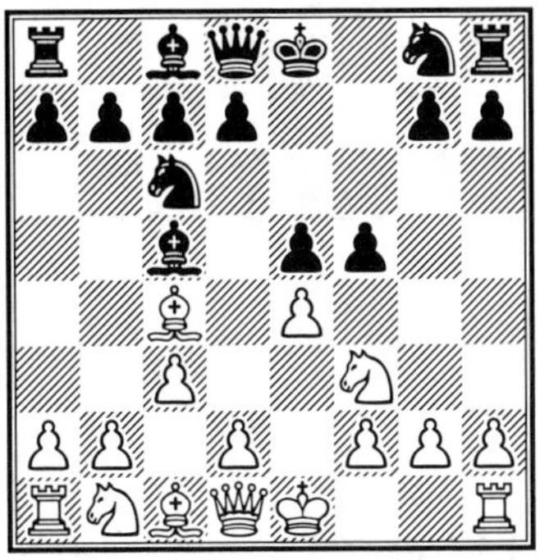

With White's bishop on b5 (1.e4 e5 2.Nf3 Nc6 3.Bb5 Bc5 4.c3 f5) the f-pawn advance makes much more sense and has been played by Grandmasters Ivan Sokolov, Ian Rogers, and Jonny Hector. Here it is just bad as the bishop on c4 is perfectly placed to exploit the weakened a2–g8 diagonal.

5.d4 exd4

As 5...fxe4 6.Nxe5 Nxe5 7.dxe5 e3 8.Bxe3 Bxe3 is met by 9.Qf3! with a winning position.

6.Nxd4

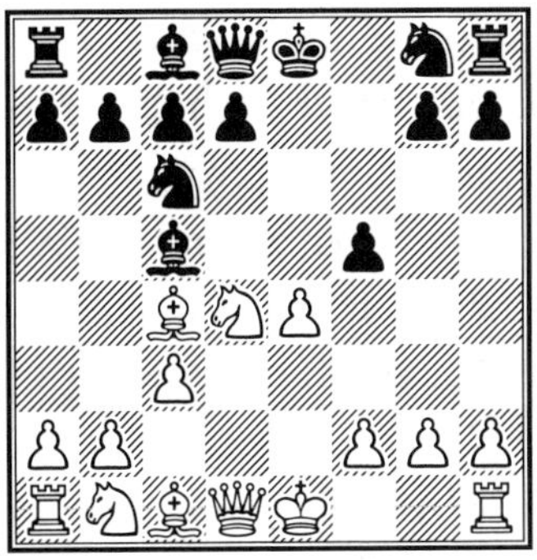

6.Ng5 was more challenging.

6...Bxd4?

6...Nf6 had to be played, meeting 7.Nxf5 with 7...d5. White is better after 8.Nxg7+ Kf7 9.exd5 Kxg7 10.dxc6 Qxd1+ 11.Kxd1, but Black is not without counterplay after 11...Ng4.

7.cxd4 Nf6 8.e5

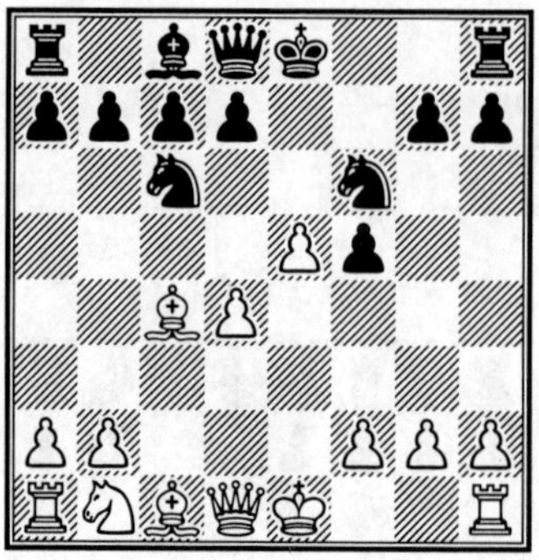

8...Ne4?

8...d5 put up more resistance though 9.exf6 and 9.Bb5 both leave White with a big advantage.

9.Nc3 Nxc3 10.bxc3 d5 11.exd6 Qxd6 12.0-0 Na5 13.Qa4+ Nc6 14.d5 0-0 15.dxc6+ Kh8 16.Ba3 Qf6 17.Bxf8 Qxf8 18.Qb4 Qxb4 19.cxb4 bxc6 20.Rfe1 Bb7 21.Re7 Rc8 22.Rae1, 1–0.

Bobby won the Dittmann trophy for the top scoring player under thirteen. Herman A. Dittmann (1890–1954) of Salt Lake City was internationally known for his artistic creations in wood: beautiful chess trophies, chess sets, and inlaid boards. Some of his sets sold for over $500 in the 1950s! Among his masterpieces was a trophy for the World Championship, which Botvinnik possessed. A tireless promoter and a key figure at the Salt Lake City Chess Club, his collection of over 200 chess magazines and books was donated to the Salt Lake City Public Library.

August 1955 was a milestone for Bobby—he became a member of the Manhattan Chess Club. Unlike the Marshall, the Manhattan was considered off-limits to younger players, rarely giving membership to anyone under eighteen. International Master Walter Shipman (1929–2017) was instrumental in persuading the powers that be at the Manhattan that Bobby was something special. Frank Brady and Walter Shipman agreed that Bobby's first visit to the Manhattan club definitely was in August, although they didn't remember what the circumstances were.[1] Possibly, it was for a league match between the Manhattan and Brooklyn Chess Clubs.

[1] Frank Brady, *Endgame: Bobby Fischer's Remarkable Rise and Fall from America's Brightest Prodigy to the Edge of Madness*. New York: Crown Trade, 2010, (p. 38).

3

RON GROSS, THE MAN WHO KNEW BOBBY FISCHER

Another important figure who played in the 1955 U.S. Junior, and would soon become a close friend of both Bobby and Larry Evans, was Ron Gross.

Mike Franett (1941–2004), best remembered as the editor of *Inside Chess* for its entire run (1988 thru 2000), was also a fine player (three-time Washington State Champion). For the article that follows, he interviewed National Master Ron Gross of Los Angeles and Las Vegas, who witnessed first-hand how Fischer went from a shy twelve-year-old 1700 rated player in 1955 to U.S. Champion at the end of 1957.

> National Master Ron Gross of Las Vegas has been playing chess in the United States for close to fifty years. Most of us who have been involved in chess for a long time have gotten in and out over the years but Ron has remained steadily active from 1952 to this day. As a result, he knows just about everybody who has been seriously involved in American chess for the last five decades.
>
> He started to play in Long Beach, California in 1952. An early teacher was a strong master named Lionel Joyner who later became Canadian Champion. In 1954, at the age of nineteen, Ron played in the New Orleans U.S. Open and scored a very respectable 8–4. He was hooked.
>
> In 1955 he met an intense twelve-year old named Bobby Fischer at the U.S. Junior Championship in Lincoln, Nebraska. The tournament was won by Charles Kalme and Ron finished tied for fourth. Fischer lost to Viktors Pupols but still had a respectable score. But the real up-and-comer was thought to be the slightly older Larry Remlinger of California who was generally regarded as a bigger talent than Fischer.
>
> Ron recalls Fischer at the time wearing a large military-style dog tag around his neck which his mom had attached to him with all his vital information on it: name, address, phone number etc. Bobby would twist the dog tag nervously when he was losing. Fischer was skinny and fidgety but pleasant in a distracted way. Ron played a lot of five-minute chess with Bobby and won the majority of the games. At the time, Ron was rated over 2100 and Fischer's rating was in the 1700s.

[left] National Master Mike Franett in the early 1980s (Photo: Archive of John Braley);

[below] Hans Kmoch in the mid-1960s (Photo: Beth Cassidy).

[right] William Addison playing black against Guðmundur Sigurjónsson at Caracas 1970;

[below] Ron Gross takes in the action at Lone Pine 1976. Jack Peters is closest to him playing Ken Rogoff (not pictured). Next to Peters is Győző Forintos facing Kim Commons. Behind Peters is Vassily Smyslov and John Grefe. The man in the flowered shirt adjusting the chair is assistant tournament director Myron Lieberman (Photo: Alan Benson).

Gross and Fischer also both played in the U.S. Junior Rapid Transit Championship in Lincoln which was at ten seconds a move with a warning buzzer at eight seconds and then a bell. This method of rapid play preceded five-minute chess in general usage and was quite popular in those days. Fischer was familiar with it from the New York clubs and Ron had played a lot of rapid transit in California.

As it turned out, Ron played Bobby in the last round of their preliminary section and had to win in order to get into the final. Gross got into a losing position, complicated things, and managed to win the game. He says now, "Fischer wasn't a bad loser. He would just get real quiet, twist that dog tag even more and immediately set up the pieces to play again. He was a real fighter, always." Ron got hot in the final, beat Kalme and Remlinger, and won his first national championship as Bobby looked on.

Ron didn't see Fischer again until the spring of 1957. Gross had become a master and moved to New York to play chess. He spent a lot of time at the Marshall and Manhattan clubs and so did Bobby who had begun to skip school to play chess all day. Ron was stronger than he had been the previous year and he expected to still be able to handle Fischer. "I was stronger but Bobby was a LOT stronger than he had been." They played skittles chess daily for small stakes. "Even though Bobby was still rated lower than me (Gross was 2198), he won four or five games to my one."

Just before Ron got to New York, Fischer had beaten Donald Byrne in spectacular style in the Rosenwald tournament and people were starting to think he might be something special. *Chess Life* columnist and opening theoretician Hans Kmoch had even started to collect Fischer score sheets and spoke of him as a budding genius.

[Hans Kmoch (1894–1973) moved to the United States after World War II, and it was in his new home that he wrote the groundbreaking work *Pawn Power in Chess*. Kmoch served as manager of the Manhattan Chess Club from 1951 until his death and was the games editor for *Chess Review* for much of this period. It was in that publication that he dubbed D. Byrne–Fischer from the 1956 Rosenwald tournament, the "Game of the Century." Kmoch directed several of Bobby's early tournaments.]

"Bobby and I became friends and would tramp around the city together. Go down to the Marshall and play in the rapid transit tournament there. Things like that. One day we were on our way downtown at a time we were both playing in a little Ruy Lopez thematic tournament that Kmoch had arranged. All of sudden Bobby said, 'You know, I can beat all those guys.' I thought he meant the people in the thematic tournament and thought that was a funny thing to say because it wasn't that strong. We both had perfect scores in fact. But he didn't mean that. He meant he could beat anyone in the U.S. And by the end of the year he did it."

Another side of Fischer started to emerge: "One day we were playing skittles for something like twenty cents a game and Bobby had accumulated a stack of dimes and had another good position against me. It so happened that Hans Kmoch had made an appointment that day with Gregor Piatigorsky [renowned cellist and chess philanthropist] for Bobby to show him his win against Donald Byrne. Just about the time that Piatigorsky showed up to see the game, Bobby made a slip and I sacked the exchange for a pawn and good positional compensation. Fischer started to take more and more time and Kmoch started to get nervous as the game dragged on." Despite his best efforts, Fischer lost and angrily flipped two dimes back to Ron's side of the table as Kmoch rushed up. "Please Bobby. It's been forty minutes! Mr. Piatigorsky is waiting!"

Bobby blew up. "I don't care! I don't have to show anybody my games just because they're a big shot!" And with that, he stormed out of the club. That was the first time that Ron had ever seen that side of Fischer and he was shocked. "The amazing thing to me was that it didn't bother Kmoch and Piatigorsky very much. The Piatigorskys' later sponsored his match against Reshevsky and all. I guess a certain amount of temperament is expected of geniuses."

Ron remembers, "Fischer was a good kid but very unsophisticated about anything but chess. It was all chess for him, every waking moment. We'd go down to the Four Continents bookstore and he'd buy any Russian chess material he could get his hands on. He'd learned enough Russian to get the gist of prose and he just absorbed the chess part." Bobby was just a little kid but with a big talent. "He was in the perfect atmosphere to learn chess. There weren't so many good books then but guys like Arthur Bisguier, Bill Lombardy, Kmoch, and Walter Shipman would help him all they could. Anything he wanted to know, they would try to help him with."

He was also spoiled and easily frustrated. One day, Ron and a friend, Arthur Feuerstein, picked up a letter for Fischer that was an invitation from the Hastings organizers to play in the annual event. Max Euwe, who had played two exhibition games with Bobby the year before, had recommended him. Before giving the letter to him they teased him, both pretending that the other had the letter. "We were just kidding around a little but Bobby started crying and clawing at us, jumping up and down like a little kid. Of course we gave it to him and then he ran out the room in tears, with the letter clutched in his hand. In the end, he turned the invitation down anyway. Not enough money." [Fischer actually declined the Hastings invitation to play in the 1957/58 U.S. Championship which was a Zonal.]

Later in 1957, Fischer and Gross along with Larry Evans played in the Western Open in Milwaukee and Fischer lost a game to a little-known player named Milton Otteson [who later changed his name to Alex London]. It was to be the next to last game he lost in the U.S. for quite a while. The rocket was about to take off.

After the Western Open, they all headed west to Long Beach in southern California and Fischer waited a couple of weeks for the U.S. Junior in San

Francisco. Fischer spent his time playing Remlinger and then went up to San Francisco and took the title by winning all his games, save one draw. He returned to Long Beach[1] and got a ride to the Cleveland U.S. Open, along with junior players Gil Ramirez and John Rinaldo, from Bill Addison. A lowlight of the trip was a fight Fischer got into with the older Ramirez in the back seat that left Gil with bite marks on his arm that can be seen to this day [see pages 121 and 264 for other versions of this story]. Bobby proceeded to win that tournament on tiebreak points ahead of Arthur Bisguier, which qualified him for the U.S. Championship, which in turn was a zonal qualifier for the World Championship cycle.

When Addison and Fischer left for Cleveland, Ron Gross stayed behind in California because he had decided to go to college. He found that he liked school quite well, eventually becoming a high school teacher in Compton, California. He had spent much of 1957 with Fischer and then his pal from New York won the U.S. Championship to close out the year. The next year, at fifteen, Fischer shocked the chess world by qualifying for the Bled Candidates tournament at the 1958 Portorož Interzonal and the next year he became the youngest grandmaster in history.

Ron later spent more time with Bobby when Fischer came out to California in 1961 to play his ill-fated match with Sammy Reshevsky. When asked what Fischer was like to hang out with then Ron says, "Well, he was pretty intense all right but when something struck him as being funny, he had a great laugh. It's like he tried to hold it in and then this big, booming laugh kind of escaped. We always got along well. He could be fun but the subject was almost always chess. And, by the way, there was no trace of antisemitism in him back then. That came later, after his religious phase in the early '70s. When he got involved with The Church of God he blamed the Jews for killing Christ and then, when he became an atheist, he blamed them for everything."

Ron saw a lot of Fischer again when Bobby came out to Los Angeles before the great Piatigorsky Cup tournament in 1966. They played table tennis, took walks and drives and scoped out pretty girls from the terrace of the Miramar Hotel. "Bobby liked to look at pretty girls all right. He had a good eye. He was way too shy to ever go up and talk to them though." Mainly, they would look at chess, chess and more chess. "I like to analyze as well as most but Bobby would just go on and on. I had to get out of there sometimes and take a break."

At the tournament, Ron helped Mrs. Piatigorsky run the event and Fischer got off to a bad start. After his games, Bobby's usual goal was to get through the crowd as fast as possible, get to his room and analyze his game. Ron would often look at the games with him. But after his loss to Spassky, Fischer lingered at the board and made a move possible for him in an earlier position. Spassky reached out and immediately made a move in reply. Fischer flushed

[1] Gross has the details right, just not the chronology. Actually, Bobby went immediately from Milwaukee to San Francisco, and then Long Beach before returning to San Francisco for the ride to Cleveland.

and rushed away, giving Ron the high sign to come with him. In his room, Bobby kicked the wastepaper basket in anger. Ron asked, "What's wrong? I thought that was a really good game." Fischer replied, "Yeah, it was. That's not what's bothering me. I usually never stay at the board after a game. Especially against Spassky. I made a dumb suggestion and he refuted it instantly! I know I'm going to have to play him some day and it was really stupid to look like such a jerk in front of him." Then he calmed down and very thoroughly went over his loss and of course he later made a stunning comeback in the second half of the double round-robin event.

After the tournament, Bobby decided he wanted to spend some time in California and stayed on at the exclusive Miramar at the Piatigorskys' expense. Finally, Lina Grumette, on behalf of Mrs. Piatigorsky asked Ron to speak to Bobby. "Ron, everybody else has left. He's running up a huge bill. Room service, phone calls all over the place. Please talk to him."

"So I said, 'Bobby, if you're going to stay out here, you should get an apartment.'"

"Yeah, you're right. That's a good idea."

Fischer saw some apartments he liked but the problem was that he couldn't make up his mind which one to take so he stayed on the hotel for ten more days. Finally, Ron just came out with it. "Bobby, you've been at the hotel a long time. Everybody else is gone. The Piatigorskys are paying for everything."

"Oh. I didn't know. Yeah, I guess I should move."

Ron says, "He knew what was going on. He just waited until someone broached the subject. He had learned that people were often hesitant to say anything to him he might not want to hear and he used that to his advantage."

Ronnie Gross saw Fischer again when Bobby returned to California early in 1970 to prepare for the World vs. USSR match. This time Bobby found his own lodgings without any trouble and saw Ron, Larry Evans and other friends in the area who showed him around.

Ron remembers that Fischer's apartment had chess books stacked everywhere, usually open and marked to whatever he was studying. He was preparing to play Spassky on first board in the upcoming match. One surprise he was working on was that he was preparing 1.d4 for Spassky and had good lines against all of Boris' favorite defenses. As it turned out, he played second board against Petrosian whom he handled fairly easily, 3–1, though the chess world was surprised that Fischer acceded so readily to Bent Larsen's demand that he play first board against Spassky.

Ron explains, "It was simple. Bobby hadn't played in a long time. He knew Spassky was a much more dangerous opponent for him than Petrosian and he got to save all his preparation for another day." Ron saw a lot of the ideas that Fischer showed him pop up in the Reykjavík World Championship match two years later. [One bit of Fischer preparation from 1970 that surfaced in the 1972 match was 13.Qa3 and 14.Bb5 in game six. Bobby found 14.Bb5 prior to the game Furman–Geller, Moscow 1970.]

During this 1970 stay in California, Fischer would often visit Ron and his wife Marilyn at their home in Compton. During these visits, Bobby met a friend of Marilyn's named Cindy who would sometimes give him a ride back to his Los Angeles apartment at the end of an evening of chess and Chinese food. When Ron asked him if he was interested in going out with her, Fischer said no.

"Why not? She's really cute."

"Yeah. But she knows I'm Bobby Fischer."

Bobby wouldn't go out with women who knew who he was but he was too shy to ask out the ones who didn't.

Throughout the 1970's Gross continued to see Fischer whenever Bobby came to southern California. Ron was teaching in Compton and Bobby would come over and they would play 10-second chess just like in the old days. Fischer loved it when Ron would play offbeat openings and he would try to refute them over-the-board. He was particularly struck when Ronnie, as black, played a weird gambit against the Tarrasch French: 1.e4 e6 2.d4 d5 3.Nd2 e5!? Bobby asked where Ron had found that one and Gross explained that a correspondence player friend of his had showed it to him. Further, the originator of the gambit was Steinitz! Bobby, of course, was a big admirer of Steinitz and had included him on his personal list of the ten best players of all time. Fischer sat back, shook his head, and repeated admiringly, "that guy, that guy!"

Fischer was also very good about looking at other people's games. He was genuinely interested and obviously could be pretty helpful. Here's a game of Ron's that Bobby particularly liked.

(9) Dutch
Ron Gross – Anthony Saidy
Seattle 1966

1.d4 f5 2.Bg5 Nf6 3.Bxf6 exf6 4.e3 d5 5.Bd3 Be6 6.Qf3 Qd7 7.Ne2 g6 8.Nbc3 c6 9.Nf4 Rg8 10.Nce2 a5 11.h4 h5 12.Nxe6 Qxe6 13.Nf4 Qf7 14.Rc1 b5 15.a4! b4 [15...bxa4 16.c4!] **16.c4 bxc3 17.bxc3 Na6 18.0-0 Bd6 19.c4 Nb4 20.cxd5 Bxf4 21.exf4 cxd5 22.Rc5 Kf8 23.Rfc1 Ra7 24.Qg3 Nxd3 25.Qxd3 Kg7 26.Qb5 Rd8 27.Qb6 Rdd7 28.Rxa5 Rab7 29.Qa6 Rb4 30.Qc8! Rxd4 31.Ra8 Kh6 32.Qh8+ Qh7 33.Qxf6,** 1–0.

In 1980–81 Fischer lived in Mexicali for several months. Ron went to see him and they went down to Tijuana. Fischer wanted to buy two things: a battery for his Casio watch and an illustrated anti-Semitic book in Spanish. He looked all over for it and was really happy when they finally found it.

Sometime before this, Ron's daughter Ember had started to take a picture at his home of Bobby and Ron playing 10-second chess. Bobby said, "Oh.

You're not going to take my picture are you?" and the idea was dropped. He seemed to remember that incident in Tijuana and offered to have his picture taken with Ron by a street vendor who took gag photos of people sitting on a donkey painted to look like a zebra. Ron was in a hurry to get down to Ensenada so he passed on the idea. "I've since regretted that. It was a chance to get my picture taken with Bobby Fischer sitting on a zebra-painted donkey. I think the caption was something like, 'On my ass in Mexico.' Now, that would have been a collector's item!"

In Ensenada, they fished, drank beer and generally had a good time. "No one knew who Bobby was, which was one of the reasons he liked Mexico so much. One day he was hungry and told me he didn't have any money so I gave him some and he went off to get something to eat by himself. Later that day I told him that Mexico was a great place to get inexpensive shoe repairs and so we went and found a shoe shop."

Ron got his shoes re-soled on the spot and when Fischer heard how cheap it was he wanted to get his done too. And he badly needed the work done because his shoes were falling apart. When Ron mentioned their dilapidated condition, Bobby said, "These are the shoes I got in Buenos Aires when I beat Petrosian." That had been almost ten years before. Ron thought, "Gee, I wonder if he expects me pay for this too." Bobby didn't. "He pulled out a wad of cash, several hundred dollars at least. He had a LOT more money on him than I did." Fischer seemed unaware that there was anything odd about the fact that he had asked for food money a couple of hours before and paid for the shoe repairs for both of them.

They stayed in Ensenada for four or five days and one morning went out on a fishing boat at dawn. "It was a calm day but Fischer was seasick before the boat left the harbor. Despite everyone's best efforts, Bobby had refused to take Dramamine the night before and now everybody else on the boat was having a great time. There were flying fish and dolphins following us, whales in the distance and to top it all off we got into a big school of fish and everyone was landing them like crazy." Except Bobby. "By the time he got over his seasickness the fish were gone but we still had a good time. We were talking and I mentioned that Mexico was also a good place to get inexpensive dentistry done because it looked like he needed it badly. He had all these open cavities in his teeth."

"Bobby said, 'No way.' He said he knew a guy in New York who had a metal plate in his head and it picked up radio signals." Bobby was afraid the Russians would be able to beam all sorts of things into his head through his fillings. "I said, 'Do you mean you're going to let your teeth rot out?' Bobby said, 'Yes, I'll gum my food if I have to!'"

In fact, Fischer still has his teeth and Ron thinks that Bobby's sister Joan finally talked Bobby into taking care of them.

The money issue was one of Bobby's growing eccentricities. Fischer's friend from the old junior chess days, John Rinaldo, had become a successful banker.

One day he got a call from the woman who handled Bobby's business affairs. She said that Bobby needed a computer and wanted to know if Rinaldo would buy it for him. It turned out that was a pattern. Whenever Fischer heard that someone from the old days had done well, his surrogate would hit them up for money. In Bobby's defense, Ron says, "Bobby was sentimental about the old days too. For instance, whenever he heard that someone he had known and liked from the past had died, he would often send a note of condolence to the family."

"Bobby was still fun sometimes in the early '80s. He would joke around a little but more and more he always came back to the so-called Jewish conspiracy. And he would send you tracts, 'The Myth of the Six Million,' that sort of thing. Even worse, he would call at all hours and want to talk about the stuff he had sent and you had to pretend that you had read it. Once he even had me go into a bookstore and buy a couple of anti-Semitic books for him. He had had a falling out with the owner but he still wanted his junk. He even told me, 'Be sure to ask for the 10% discount!' There was some secret phrase, I forget what it was. Probably something like 'Holocaust? What Holocaust?'"

Fischer's behavior was getting more bizarre. One night he called Ron and asked him to pick him up in front of the Los Angeles Library. "I got there. No Fischer in sight. I drove around the block several times and all of a sudden he came flying out of the bushes and jumped into the car like demons were after him. It's a bit unsettling to be around that sort of thing."

Fischer kept up with chess but he told Ron that he would never play in another tournament though he would still play matches. He often carried the latest *Chess Informant* around with him and analyzed on his beloved chess wallet.

Around this time, in 1981, a man named Kevin Burnett was writing a newspaper piece on Fischer. He knew Ron was a friend of Bobby's and asked him to check the piece for accuracy. Ron did and told Burnett that Fischer still considered himself World Champion because of the way FIDE had deprived him of his title. Ron defended Fischer's views and he also mentioned that Bobby was doing just fine and that he had recently been fishing with him in Mexico. That was all. Ron knew Fischer probably wouldn't like it if he found out about it but by that time his attitude was, "so be it."

A short version of the story appeared in a local southern California paper and it wouldn't have been seen by very many people, but, because it was about Fischer, it was picked up by a wire service and it ran in a San Francisco paper. A friend of Fischer's there saw it, called Bobby and told him, "Gross has been talking to the press."

Shortly thereafter, on a hot summer night in 1982, Ron got a call from Fischer that sounded like it was from a phone booth next to a carwash. Bobby was very mad and wanted to know if it was true that he had been "talking." Gross asked him if had seen the article in question.

"No."

"Well, why don't you read it. It's just a short article . . ."

"No. You broke our friendship."

"I defended your title claims and just mentioned that we went fishing."

"I don't care. It turns out you're just a dirty Jew after all."

Ron sadly replied, "You just had to get that in didn't you, Bobby?"

Bobby Fischer hung up and Ron has never heard from him again though they still have friends in common.

Ron Gross looks at Fischer's games sometimes and remembers the old days. The games are still wonderful.

4
CORRESPONDENCE PLAYER

Bobby's career as a correspondence player is a bit of a mystery. His mentor, John "Jack" W. Collins, who was a strong postal master and correspondence columnist for *Chess Review*, wrote:[1]

> Bobby never played correspondence chess. Probably the pace was too slow and the dramatic personal confrontation, which is such a large part of the excitement of the game, was lacking. Consulting books while the game was in progress would not be his idea of legitimate chess either. In fact, very few grandmasters, and potential grandmasters, with the exception of Paul Keres in his formative years, have cottoned to correspondence chess. This is in contrast to the popularity with experts and lower-rated players who delight in it. Possibly the difference of appeal is due to the reasons just mentioned, the preference for public or private competition, or to causes which are psychological in nature.

Actually, Bobby did play in at least one correspondence tournament. Collins probably wasn't aware of it because by the time he first met Bobby on Memorial Day Weekend in 1956, Bobby's short-lived postal career appears to have either finished or was winding down.

The first indication that Bobby played correspondence chess is attested to by Donald P. Reithel, (Reithel also played Bobby during his 1964 simul tour[2]):

> In 1955 I played Bobby in postal chess—a prize tourney in *Chess Review*. I remember him as a typical American kid: Brooklyn Dodger fan, somewhat opinionated about school and somewhat desirous to exchange ideas and thoughts. He printed his name in lower case letters, 'bobby fischer.' He didn't finish the event because he was starting to play over-the-board tournaments.

In a later communication, Reithel added:

> A.W. Conger was one of my opponents in [a] *Chess Review* Prize Tourney... [a player named Fisher played in 54-P 38-100] ...That is the event Bobby

[1] John W. Collins, *My Seven Chess Prodigies*. New York: Simon & Schuster, 1975, (p. 55)

[2] John Donaldson, *A Legend on the Road: Bobby Fischer's 1964 Simultaneous Exhibition Tour.* Seattle: I.C.E., 1994, (p. 12).

> Fischer competed in …For myself, I discarded many of my early tournament results and no longer have my scorepads covering that period of time.
>
> I did have several of Bobby's cards, but they too were tossed out in spring cleanups. What was interesting about them was that Bobby had notes on all of them covering various subjects.
>
> Our individual game was a King's Indian Defense [I was White] and the game lasted twelve to fifteen moves when he wrote me that he was withdrawing from the tourney to pursue a lengthy cross-country trip and series of over-the-board tournaments, which, he said, was his entry toward capturing the world chess title—build skills, gain exposure, make results and earn a reputation. A year or two later he won the U.S. Championship for the first time and he was true to his word. [The cross-country trip might have been to the 1955 U.S. Junior Open in Lincoln, Nebraska.]
>
> I did not find his comments to be egotistic, but rather showing youthful optimism and self-confidence as to his talent and ability.
>
> We shared considerable note exchanges, as I was only a teen myself and I think he related to that, as we had similar interests outside of just chess. I recall responding to his direct statement that he intended to win the World Championship and return it to the USA, advising him to complete his education, which he would need to handle his affairs during his adulthood. His response was that I sounded just like his sister and teachers. His follow-up card listed only the moves. But then he responded in a more friendly way to my comments about his note…
>
> In all, I found him to be a rather lonesome kid who was trying to find himself and purpose. He no doubt caught the chessbug early and it was a burning fire inside him. Who exactly contributed to his maturity, I cannot say. He told me that he studied the bible and I wrote that he might find Rev. Rice and Herbert W. Armstrong and Garner Ted Armstrong's religious broadcasts informative, which he apparently checked out, as he later became interested in the latter's Worldwide Church of God.
>
> …I found him to be a nice, normal kid with a lot of dedication to chess, but also having interests that all kids seem to share. He was a Dodger fan and a Yankee fan. Maybe that is why we hit it off. Anyway, I followed his career and was most pleased that his youthful dream was fulfilled."

Al Horowitz's *Chess Review* was one of the major organizers of correspondence tournaments in the 1950s. The record is spotty, but it appears Bobby played in a Prize Tourney section during 1955 and 1956. The May 1955 issue of *Chess Review*,[1] lists an R. Fischer under new postalites, assigning him a 1200 correspondence rating. The piece mentions that newcomers to postal chess are rated on their estimated ability with class A running from 1300 on up, and class B was from 1000 to 1298. Note, that at the time, postal ratings were about 500 to 600 points lower than over-the-board USCF.

[1] *Chess Review*, May 1955, (p. 159).

Postal ratings appeared in *Chess Review* approximately twice a year. The August 1955[1] issue lists a B. Fischer at 1198. Later he drops to 1082 in March 1956. The August 1956 issue again lists him at 1082, which suggests that he was no longer active.

Game (10) is the only correspondence effort of Bobby's that has surfaced. A.W. Conger of Pennsylvania was rated 1274 in the August 1955 issue of *Chess Review*. It first appeared in *Zugzwang*,[2] the newsletter of the King of Prussia Chess Club (located in King of Prussia, Pennsylvania, twenty miles northwest of Philadelphia).

POSTAL GAMES
from CHESS REVIEW tourneys
Our Postal players are invited to submit their BEST games for this department. The moves of each game must be written on a standard score sheet, or typed on a single sheet of paper, and marked "for publication"——
annotated by JOHN W. COLLINS
Notice in Chess Review *April 1957.*

(10) King's Indian
Anthony Wayne Conger – Fischer
Correspondence Game 1955

1.d4 Nf6 2.c4 g6 3.Nc3 Bg7 4.e4 d6 5.Bg5

This line, sort of a hybrid between the Averbakh (5.Be2 and 6.Bg5) and the Four Pawns Attack (5.f4), was a long-time favorite of American Grandmaster Arthur Bisguier. White aims for an aggressive formation combining Bg5, f4 and Bd3.

5...h6 6.Bh4 0-0

Spassky–Fischer, Belgrade (m-16) 1992, saw 6...c5 7.d5 g5 8.Bg3 Qa5! and both 9.Bd3 Nxe4 and 9.Qd2 Nh5 are fine for Black.

This game is deeply annotated in *No Regrets*,[3] the classic book on the 1992 Revenge match.

7.f4 c5 8.d5 Qa5 9.Qd2 Qc7?!

This is an incomprehensible move. Black not only loses time with his queen, but puts it on an unfortunate square to boot. Correct is 9...e6.

10.Bd3 e6 11.Nb5?

---

1 *Chess Review*, August 1955, (p.252).

2 *Zugzwang*, Spring 1976.

3 Yasser Seirawan and George Stefanović, *No Regrets: Fischer–Spassky*. Seattle: International Chess Enterprises, 1992, (pp. 155–159).

11.Nf3! is much better.

11...Qb6 12.Nxd6, 1–0.

Correct is 12...Qxd6 then 13.e5 Qd8 is very nice for Black.

[Note: *Zugzwang* gives the date of the game as June 27, 1955, but it's unclear if this is the starting or ending date. Bobby was rated around 1800 over-the-board at that time, which might suggest the game started earlier. His play vs. Conger suggests a less-experienced player conducting the Black pieces.]

5
CACHE OF GEMS (THE TARG DONATION)

[**Note:** In the spring of 2013 author John Donaldson was invited to the Marshall Chess Club to view the Targ donation. This chapter is a first-hand account.]

In 1960 Bobby's mother Regina left the long-time family home in Brooklyn to join the San Francisco to Moscow Walk for Peace [see pages 215–217]. With no clear plan of when she might return to New York, if ever, Regina judged it prudent to give the family records and papers (which included many of Bobby's score sheets) to her daughter Joan (then newly married to Russell Targ), for safekeeping. She no doubt figured entrusting them to the teenage Bobby (whom she was leaving by himself in the Brooklyn apartment) was not the right thing to do.

All indications are that these records were in storage for over fifty years, first in New York and later in Palo Alto where the Targ family relocated. In 2008, a few months after Bobby's death, Russell Targ (Bobby's brother-in-law) donated the entire collection of Fischer family records and papers to the Marshall Chess Club.

A number of years ago, Max Wilkerson (1925–2009), who served as the director of the Mechanics' Chess Club in San Francisco from 1980–1996, mentioned to me that he had played Fischer a series of games in 1955. According to Max, who was living in New York City exploring a career as an artist, the games were played at the Manhattan Chess Club. Years later, during Fischer's 1964 tour, the two would split a pair of exhibition games. The 1964 games are a matter of public record, but those earlier efforts appeared to be lost forever with the odds of them surfacing a million to one. However, sometimes miracles do occur.

In the spring of 2013 I was invited to the Marshall Chess Club to view the Targ Collection. Much of the donated material was family related (not dealing directly with Bobby's chess career) and provided great background material: Frank Brady had access to it when he wrote *Endgame.*[1] Joseph Ponterotto relied heavily on it as a primary source for *A Psychobiography of Bobby Fischer.*[2] However, the real gold was hidden under the family papers—Bobby's score sheets from his youth.

I would guess there might be anywhere from seventy-five to one hundred score sheets (some signed and some not) dating from 1955 to around 1960. Approximately half are carbons (not originals) from major tournaments that Bobby played in from 1958 to 1959—these games are well-known and contribute nothing new.

To my delight the collection included a number of games thought to be lost forever. Recording the games was not permitted, so I made the following list from memory a few hours after viewing the score sheets.

Previously unknown games

- Five non-tournament games played with Max Wilkerson in 1955.
- The game versus Florido at Havana 1956 (Log Cabin Chess Club vs. Capablanca Chess Club match). [Note: This game has since been made public.]
- Two of the three missing games from Montreal 1956 (Canadian Open). Round one vs. G. Lepine; and round five vs. V. Judzentavicius. I don't recall seeing round three vs. J. Boyer.
- Sklaroff—round four U.S. Amateur 1956 at Asbury Park—a picture of this game in progress is on the cover of *Chess Life*, July 20, 1956
- There were a bunch of games circa 1956 from the Manhattan Chess Club reserves—two against Aben Rudy (one being a very short draw) There may also be a game where Bobby is Black in a Sämisch KID against Karl Forster—a picture of which appeared in a NYC newspaper around this time.
- Four games (Seropian, Gore, Feuerstein, and Tamargo) from a Ruy Lopez Thematic tournament held at the Manhattan Chess Club in the spring/summer of 1957.
- A long hard-fought draw with Szedlacsek from the last round of the North Central Open held in Milwaukee over Thanksgiving weekend in 1957. This game is missing from the Spence book on the event.
- All five games from the match with Daniel Beninson played in the fall of 1957.

---

[1] Frank Brady, *Endgame: Bobby Fischer's Remarkable Rise and Fall from America's Brightest Prodigy to the Edge of Madness*. New York: Crown Trade, 2010.

[2] Joseph G. Ponterotto, *Psychobiography of Bobby Fischer: Understanding the Genius, Mystery, and Psychological Decline of a World Chess Champion*. Springfield: Charles C. Thomas, 2012.

- A training game with Anthony Saidy from the summer of 1958, Game (26). [Note: This game has since been made public.]
- Fischer's two wins from the match with Milan Matulović played before the 1958 Interzonal.
- A training game between Fischer and Collins from the spring of 1957, Game (28). [Note: This game is in the Collins Collection at Indiana University.]
- The score of the second game between Euwe and Fischer from their 1957 match. I'd seen this game before as The Marshall Chess Club had allowed it to be published in *Chess Life*.
- There is a game with Lombardy from around 1957.
- There were several Feuerstein games but close study is needed to see if they are already known. One exception is the Ruy Lopez Thematic game that is definitely unpublished. It is possible two of the games were played in round one of the 1956 U.S. Junior in Philadelphia and the 1956 Greater New York Open respectively.

Games still Missing (I do not recall seeing them):

- The draw with Tautvaisas from the last round of the Western Open held over the July 4th weekend in Milwaukee in 1957.
- The drawn game from the Fischer–Matulović match (Belgrade 1958).
- The missing moves from Fischer– Radojčić, New York State Open (Poughkeepsie) 1963.

Whether the other games will ever be made public is difficult to say. Unpublished Fischer game scores can have a high monetary value and the Marshall Chess Club is not a wealthy club with only membership dues and rental income to keep it afloat. One need look no further than the demise of the Manhattan Chess Club to realize that operating in New York City is an expensive proposition. The Governors of the Marshall Chess Club are required to act in the club's best financial interest regardless of their own personal feelings, particularly as the Targ donation has been appraised at $300,000. While some might feel that optimistic, the fact remains that this is a rare and large windfall for the Marshall. One can hope that "lost" Fischer games will one day be made available to the public.

One interesting aside to the Targ donation are the appeals Bobby made in his *Chess Life* column "Bobby Fischer Talks Chess" for readers to send in missing games from early in his career. All too often players are not good record keepers, and this seems to have been the case with Bobby. The September 1963 issue of *Chess Life*[1] carried a boxed item:

> WANT TO GET PUBLISHED?
>
> Bobby Fischer is compiling his early games, 1955, 56 & 57, for publication. He is missing quite a few—and he was on the losing side of many of these. If you have any of the scores, send them to *Chess Life*, c/o J.F. Reinhardt, 80 E. 11th Street, New York 3, N.Y.

Had Bobby forgotten about the game scores his mother had entrusted to Joan and her husband for safekeeping?

1 *Chess Life*, September 1963, (p. 224).

6

"THE YEAR 1956 TURNED OUT TO BE A BIG ONE FOR ME IN CHESS."

Today we know *Chess Life*, the U.S. Chess Federation's publication, as a monthly glossy, but in the 1950s it appeared twice a month as a broadsheet. One of the first issues of 1956 had a mention of Bobby and from then on news of Bobby appeared regularly within it's pages:

> USCF master William Lombardy of the Bronx won the first Greater New York Open with a score of 6–1, nosing out Dr. Ariel Mengarini, also 6–1, by one-half a median point. Arthur Feuerstein of the Bronx and Edgar McCormick of East Orange, New Jersey, scored 5½–1½ each, but third prize went to the former on tiebreaking points. The Class A trophy was captured by McCormick, while the Class B trophy went to twelve-year-old Bobby Fischer of Brooklyn. Fischer tied for fourth at 5–2 with Anthony Saidy and E.S. Jackson in the event held January 21–26 at the Churchill Chess Club in Manhattan [see crosstable on next page].

During the 2016 World Championship, Heritage Auctions of New York (located only a few miles from the match) offered fifteen of Fischer's score sheets dating from 1956 to 1960 up for sale—fourteen carbon and one in Bobby's hand. Ten of the carbons were from the 1959/60 U.S. Championship—they were well-known games of little historic importance. However, the five games from 1956 were previously unknown. How did they surface after sixty years?

The answer only became apparent after they initially failed to sell and appeared again in a subsequent auction, paired with a letter Bobby wrote to his mother in 1965. The letter suggests the materials came from Russell Targ, perhaps items he discovered after he made the large donation to the Marshall Chess Club.

The first two of these games were played on February 16, 1956, and recorded on Manhattan Chess Club score sheets. It's possible that they were skittles games, as they don't fit into any tournaments that Fischer played at the time.

Bobby's opponent in Game (11), Dr. Isaac Spector, was a strong amateur player and a regular at the Manhattan Chess Club in the 1950s and 1960s. He was rated 1877 on the May 20, 1956 USCF rating list.

1956 GREATER NEW YORK CITY OPEN

W = WIN, w L = LOSS, FL = FORFEIT LOSS, WD = WITHDREW, BYE = UNPLAYED GAME

Rank	Participants	Rs.`	Rd. 2	Rd.3	Rd. 4	Rd. 5	Rd. 6	Rd. 7	Total
1	Lombardy, William	W23	W46	W18	W2	L3	W5	W13	6
2	Dr. Mengarini, Ariel	W38	W37	W11	L1	W12	W15	W3	6
3	Feuerstein, Arthur	W7	W8	D5	W6	W1	W10	L2	5.5
4	McCormick, Edgar	W44	W28	D6	W13	L3	W11	W14	5.5
5	Saidy, Anthony	W51	W31	D3	W9	W4	L1	D6	5
6	Jackson, Edward	W16	W30	D4	L3	W25	W8	D5	5
7	**Fischer, Robert J.**	**L3**	**W50**	**W28**	**L10**	**W31**	**W32**	**W18**	**5**
8	Pflumm, Eugene	W24	L3	W37	W33	D14	L6	W26	4.5
9	Linn, Stanley	D29	W17	W35	L5	D20	W37	D12	4.5
10	Steinberger, Eugene	D17	W29	D15	W7	W32	L3	D21	4.5
11	Krauhs, Gustave	W43	W12	L2	D40	W27	L4	W23	4.5
12	Baczynski, Chester	W48	L11	W38	W22	L2	W20	D9	4.5
13	Kalme, Charles	W50	W32	W14	L4	D15	W21	L1	4.5
14	Bakos, Nicholas	W49	W20	L13	W25	D8	W17	L4	4.5
15	Green, Matthew	D25	W40	D10	W23	D13	L2	W22	4.5
16	Bass, Robert	L6	W39	L32	W41	W43	L18	W37	4
17	Hauck, Siegfried	D10	L9	D19	W47	W29	L14	W30	4
18	Hays, Rhys	W36	W47	L1	L32	W28	W16	L7	4
19	Greene, Sanford	D45	L25	D17	L37	W42	W34	W32	4
20	Plock, Richard	W26	L14	D27	W30	D9	L12	W33	4
21	Dr. Spector, Isaac	L31	W42	D44	W38	W40	L13	D10	4
22	Condon, F.E.	L37	W36	W47	L12	D35	W27	L15	3.5
23	Goldsmith, Julius	L1	W24	W48	L15	D37	W35	L11	3.5
24	Dr. Greenberg, I.	L8	L23	W49	L28	W41	W29	D25	3.5
25	Holodny, Edward	D15	W19	W33	L14	L6	D30	D24	3.5
26	Kleeger, Harry	L20	L33	W34	D36	W44	W31	L8	3.5
27	Kramer, Manfred	L40	W51	D20	W44	L11	L22	W36	3.5
28	Beach, Winthrop	W39	L4	L7	W24	L18	D36	D35	3
29	Brady, Frank	D9	L10	W45	D49	L17	L24	W43	3
30	Daniels, Stewart	W41	L6	D31	L20	W38	D25	L17	3
31	Martinez, M.	W21	L5	D30	D35	L7	L26	W41	3
32	Salome, Eugene	W42	L13	W16	W18	L10	L7	L19	3
33	Schiller, Sid	D33	W26	L25	L8	D36	W43	L20	3
34	Mrs. Selensky, Mary	L46	L44	L26	W39	W47	L19	W42	3
35	Westing, Edward	D33	W45	L9	D31	D22	L23	D28	3
36	Curtis, Clinton	L18	L22	W42	D26	D33	D28	L27	2.5
37	Dorn, Fred	W22	L2	L8	W19	D23	L9	L16	2.5
38	Laucks, E. Forry	L2	W41	L12	L21	L30	D39	BYE	2.5
39	Roberts, Bertrand	L28	L16	L41	L34	BYE	D38	W45	2.5
40	Tilles, Michael	W27	L15	W43	D11	L21	WD	WD	2.5
41	Dr. Altman, Vladimir	L30	L38	W39	L16	L24	W45	L31	2
42	Fisch, M.	L32	L21	L36	W45	L19	BYE	L34	2
43	Offenberg, Robert	L11	BYE	L40	W48	L16	L33	L29	2
44	Hersch, Paul	L4	W34	D21	L27	L26	WD	WD	1.5
45	Kawas, George	D19	L35	L29	L42	W49	L41	L39	1.5
46	Cohler, Alfred	W34	L1	WD	WD	WD	WD	WD	1
47	Jones, Leo	W52	L18	L22	L17	L34	WD	WD	1
48	Sklaroff, Samuel	L12	W49	L23	L43	WD	WD	WD	1
49	Cossino, P.	L14	L48	L24	D29	L45	WD	WD	0.5
50	Hans, Julius	L13	L7	WD	WD	WD	WD	WD	0
51	Higler, William	L5	L27	WD	WD	WD	WD	WD	0
52	Dr. Ponstein, M.	FL47	WD	WD	WD	WD	WD	WD	0

1956 Greater New York City Open was held January 20 to 22. The crosstable surfaced in 2010 when long-time Fischer researcher Nikolai published it in an article on Arthur Feuerstein in the *Atlantic Chess News*. This was the event where Frank Brady (who later wrote two definitive Fischer biographies) first met Bobby.

(11) Sicilian
Fischer – Isaac Spector
New York, February 16, 1956

1.e4 c5 2.Nf3 d6 3.d4 cxd4 4.Nxd4 Nf6 5.Nc3 a6 6.Bg5 e6 7.Qf3

The twelve–year-old Bobby, who was already recognized as a rising talent from his success in the weekly Friday night rapids at the Manhattan, varies from the main line starting with 7.f4. The queen move was a popular way of combating the Najdorf in the 1950s.

7...Be7 8.0-0-0 Qc7 9.Qg3 Nbd7

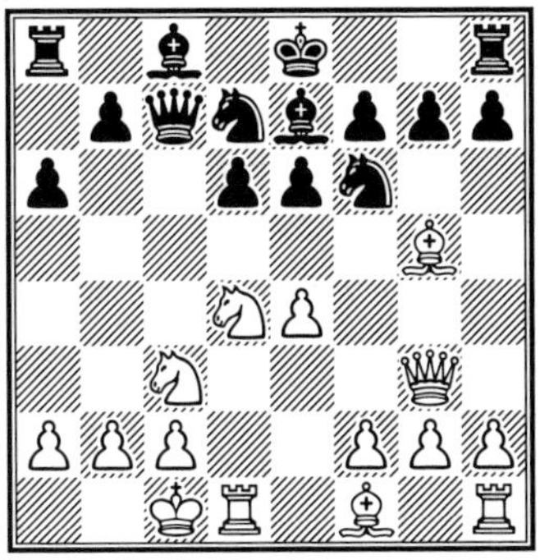

10.Nb3?!

10.f4, 10.Be2, 10.h4 and 10.Kb1 all look more logical than the text, which takes the knight from the center. Fischer's idea, as we shall see, is to clear the d-file in preparation for meeting ...b5 with Bxb5, Nxb5 and Nxd6+.

10...b5 11.a3 Bb7 12.f3 0-0-0

12...0-0 was also quite playable and in fact maybe better, with the point that 13.Bh6 Nh5 14.Qh3 can be met by 14...Ndf6 15.Be3 d5! 16.exd5 Nf4! with good play for Black. After the text White is able to justify his previous play.

13.Bxb5

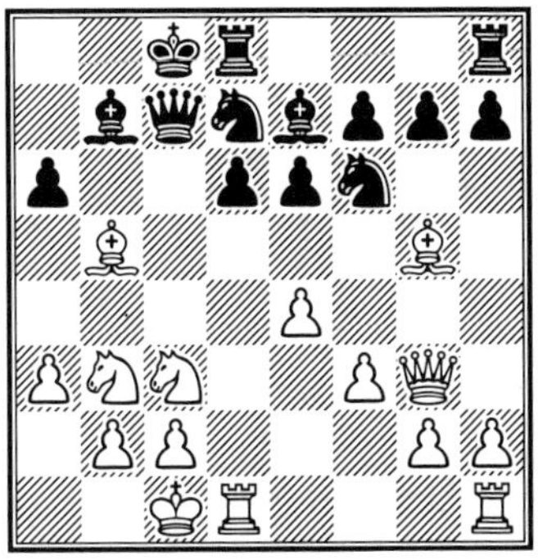

13...Ne5?

This loses a pawn for nothing. 13...axb5 14.Nxb5 Qb6 15.Nxd6+ Bxd6 16.Qxd6 Qxd6 17.Rxd6 Ne5 leads to an unbalanced ending with mutual chances. After the text Fischer wins in convincing fashion.

14.Be2 h5 15.h4 Nc4 16.Rd4 Na5 17.Nxa5 Qxa5 18.Ra4 Qb6 19.Rb4 Qa5 20.Be3 Nd7 21.Ra4 Qe5 22.Bf4 Qf6 23.Bxd6 Nb6 24.Bxe7 Qxe7 25.Rb4 Qc5 26.Kb1 Rd2 27.Bd3 Qc7 28.Qg5 Rxd3 29.cxd3 f6 30.Qe3 Nd7 31.Rc4 Bc6 32.Rc1 Kd8 33.Ne2 Ne5 34.Nd4 Nxc4 35.Rxc4, 1–0.

(12) Four Knights
Pat(?) Smith – Fischer
New York, February 16, 1956

Bobby's score sheet leaves it unclear as to who his opponent was—no first name was written. Walter Shipman, who was an important member of the Manhattan Chess Club for several decades, remembers that a Pat Smith, who attended Yale and was a good friend of Robert Byrne, was a regular at the Manhattan Chess Club in the 1950s.

1.e4 e5 2.Nf3 Nc6 3.Nc3 Nf6 4.Bb5 Nd4

Although he was not the first to play it, this move is associated with Akiva Rubinstein. He analyzed it extensively and played it with success for over twenty years, except for his 1920 match with Bogoljubow where he lost three games with 4...Nd4.

5.Nxd4

Seemingly every legal move has been tried here including 5.Ba4, 5.Bc4, 5.Nxe5, 5.0-0, 5.Bd3, 5.Be2 and 5.d3.

5...exd4 6.e5 dxc3 7.exf6 Qxf6 8.bxc3?!

8.dxc3 (rapid development overwrites the rule of capturing towards the center) 8...Qe5+ has led to many draws.

8...c6

8...Qe5+ was still quite playable if dull.

9.Be2 d5

Black is already better.

10.Rb1

10.0-0 Bd6 11.d4 0-0 12.Bd3 looks more normal although after 12...Qh4 Black is for choice.

10...Bd6 11.d4 0-0 12.Be3 b5

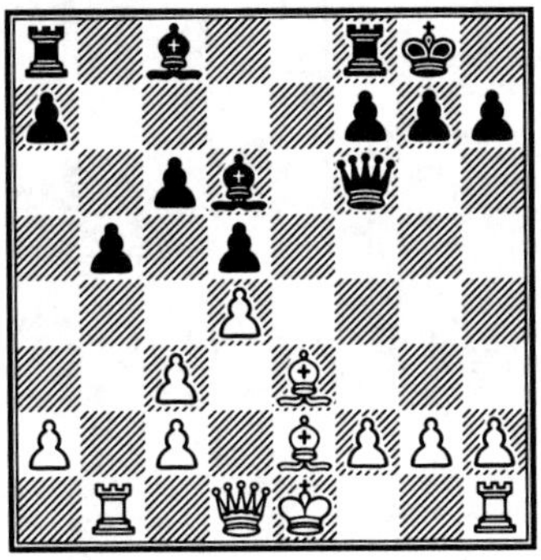

Young Bobby takes time out to insure White will never undouble his pawns with c4.

13.Qd2 Qg6 14.Kf1?

14.0-0 Bh3 15.Bf3 Bf5 16.Rb2 a5 intending ...a4-a3 is awkward to meet, but the text is even worse.

14...Bf5 15.h4 Be4!

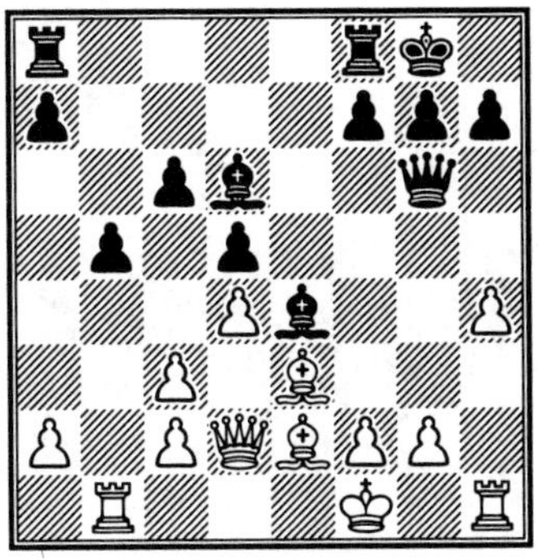

This classy intermezzo, forcing a weakness before picking up the pawn, is a sign that Bobby had improved a great deal from the previous year.

16.f3 Bxc2 17.Rc1 Rae8 18.h5 Qe6 19.Kf2 Ba4

Black is a pawn up with much the better position and not surprisingly, the game ends quickly.

20.Rh3 f5 21.Bg5 h6 22.Re1 hxg5 23.Qxg5 Qh6, 0–1.

This group photo was taken at the St. Petersburg Chess Divan (still in operation over sixty years later as the St. Petersburg Chess Club) in late February 1956.

Those identified in the picture are: (front row) Nestor Hernandez, unknown, E. M. Weeks, Bobby, unknown, Norman Whitaker, E. Forry Laucks (last seated on right); (standing) First six unknown, Glenn Hartleb (tallest), Regina, Ralph Houghton (wearing a bow tie), Raymond Glover, William Walbrecht (?) and Ted Miller (standing on the far right).

7
"LET'S SCHUSSE!"

Much has been written about Fischer's participation in the Capablanca Memorial tournaments—1965 from New York via teletype and 1966 in person in Havana [see pages 317–330]. However, what is rarely mentioned is his first trip to Cuba a decade earlier—in February 1956 he visited the Caribbean island as a member of the colorful Log Cabin Chess Club. The twelve-year-old Fischer was accompanied by his mother who doubled as a photographer for *Chess Review*. Bobby needed a chaperone, as the Log Cabin crew included several larger than life characters including convicted felon International Master Norman Whitaker and Log Cabin founder E. Forry Laucks.

The Marshall and Manhattan Chess Clubs reigned supreme as the New York area's top clubs for much of the last century, but for a while the Log Cabin Chess Club gave them a run for their money. The name Log Cabin might suggest the club was formed back in the 1800s in a rural town, but in fact, it was started in 1934. Located in West Orange, New Jersey, a stone's throw from New York City, the Log Cabin Chess Club was a true original.

E. Forry Laucks (1897–1965) was an unorthodox and enthusiastic promoter. Besides running strong events at the club, which was located in his large basement, he also took to the road. The Log Cabin irregulars made trips to all corners of the United States, even Alaska! This was more of an accomplishment than it might seem, as Laucks, who typically did much of the driving, had the disconcerting habit of taking his eye off the road and talking face to face with riders in the backseat—for minutes at a time!

Palo Alto Master Art Wang, who played in a U.S. Junior organized by the Log Cabin, stayed as a guest at Laucks' home for a few weeks with fellow Northern California juniors. Wang remembered Laucks as a good-natured eccentric and a dedicated patron of the game. Laucks often took the California juniors out to dinner, but when they dined at home, he had certain specific rules that had to be obeyed. For example, bananas were to be eaten only at breakfast with cereal which was to be consumed only with a soup spoon. Failure to comply with the rules wasn't tolerated.

Laucks' father, a successful safe maker, passed on much of his wealth to his son, enabling E. Forry's wild streak. Wang recalled E. Forry's penchant for excessive speeding, which he witnessed first hand. Laucks loved to race his cars and would often try to outrace pursuing police cars—a practice that kept his lawyer busy. During major cross-country trips it was not uncommon for Laucks to abandon a troubled car on the highway and buy a new vehicle in the next town.

T.A. Dunst gave tribute to the quirky club:[1]

FIRST HERE, FIRST THERE, FIRST EVERYWHERE

The year is 1980. The first American space-liner has just landed on Mars. Who are those passengers briskly climbing out ahead of all the other people in the ship? There can only be one answer: the space-traveling chapter of the Log Cabin Chess Club of West Orange, New Jersey, led by that intrepid pioneer, E. Forry Laucks. They are seeking Martian chess players for the purpose of engaging in the first interplanetary chess match, the greatest and grandest "first" in the interminable history of "firsts" piled up by the Cabineers.

Do you think, tough-minded reader that we are jesting? Nothing of the kind. This is as sure a prophecy as that the Irish will celebrate next St. Patrick's Day. In order to extrapolate, we merely need to take a look at some of the actual "firsts" on the log of these ubiquitous wanderers: They were first in the Western Hemisphere to travel by yacht and plane to other clubs, first to be televised while en route to Fairbanks and first to play matches in forty states. Whimsically, they were first to play a tournament by gas light in modern times and first in the Western Hemisphere to hold a blindfold tournament. As for their heavy guns, they have won the championship of the country's strongest chess league (beating out the powerful Marshall Chess Club in New York City to do so) and have had on their membership list all classifications of U.S. Champions, including the national, open, amateur, women's, correspondence and junior. Even the bright face of danger has been stared down by the Cabineers, as on the occasion when they went on a hazardous trip of exploration to snow-capped mountains near Mexico City, almost losing one of their two motor cars during the journey.

Who is this almost legendary figure, Log Cabin chieftain E. Forry Laucks, the man with the vast enthusiasms, untrammeled imagination and passionate devotion to the cause of chess? Born back in 1898, he looks like a man in his forties, darkish, intense, and ready at a moment's notice to laugh at himself and at any of life's ludicrous situations. Neatly balancing his social and business interests is his gift for art, as evidenced by the paintings which hang upon the walls of his home and which have been exhibited at the Montclair Art Museum, the Trenton Academy of Art, and the Art Center of the Oranges.

[1] T.A. Dunst, *Chess Review*, "First Here, First There, First Everywhere," January 1958, (pp. 14–15).

He was reared in York, Pennsylvania, as the son of a prominent industrialist and attended Dummer Academy, Mercersburg Academy and Philips Exeter. He first took notice of chess when he was about nine years old and at eleven visited the Manhattan and Marshall Chess Clubs in New York City. During his boyhood, however, the game did not mean much to him, so that it was not until many years later that he began his checkered career (harmless pun intended) as player and impresario.

In 1933, four years after his marriage to Josephine Frances Lehmann, Laucks joined the West Orange YMCA Chess Club. As far as he was personally concerned, he immediately discovered a fatal flaw in the set-up—the relatively early closing time. To a born "night person" such as Forry, who is at his best at three or four in the morning, midnight is the signal for coming awake, not going to bed. Surely, reasoned Forry, there must be nocturnal chess players like himself.

Inspiration: Why not establish a haven for these kindred souls, irked as they are by regulations which absurdly put the need for slumber above the lure of Caissa? With Laucks, to get an idea is to act; so he went to work at once to create the world's liveliest chess club.

In a way, the Log Cabin's "club personality," if one may use this term, was just a happy mushroom growth; in another sense, it was the natural result of effort, planning and devotion. When the idea for a chess club first took root in Laucks' mind, the spacious basement of his residence at 30 Collamore Terrace in West Orange, New Jersey (he has another home at Old Lyme, Connecticut, where he lives with his wife and two children) seemed just the thing for his purpose. He wanted a comfortable, relaxing, "different" atmosphere; the answer was to transform his basement into a "log cabin" with furnishings to match. Here, in his own words, is what he sought to accomplish:

"[The clubhouse was to be] a log cabin that would be neither too palatial, as some wealthy clubmen's are, nor so poor and roughshod that it would lack comfort or a certain degree of refinement...

"I realized that everything, even to the wall decorations, furniture and utensils, had to be in keeping with the surroundings, or else just one piece out of place could spoil the effect of the whole...Therefore I made and designed all furniture just as if I were in the backwoods where there can be no machined, finished pieces."

When this labor of love was done, Laucks' chess-playing friends descended with a cry of joy upon the new chess club. Where else, indeed, could they find rooms whose main house rule came close to avoiding all rules and whose perfect playing conditions were not marred by orders of "lights out" and other intolerable interruptions of chess genius in the throes of creation? The first session, held on January 31, 1934, did not break up until 4 AM. Subsequent meetings lasted till 5 AM or dawn or such time as Morpheus claimed his own.

Formal organization of the Log Cabin Chess Club took place on July 28, 1934 and resulted in the election of E. Forry Laucks as president. No constitution was drawn up at that time and none is in existence now; the club simply does not need this kind of machinery.

It did not take the Log Cabin long to become a rendezvous of champions, deep in tournaments and league matches. The greatest victory of all, duly celebrated at the Waldorf-Astoria Hotel in New York City, occurred when the Cabineers won the championship of the Metropolitan Chess League of New York ahead of the famous Marshall Chess Club. Although the perennial champions of the Manhattan Chess Club were not competing that year (1948), many of the nations' strongest players took part in these matches, and the triumph of the Cabineers therefore took on epic proportions.

Not to be outdone in any sphere of operations, the Log Cabin claims to publish, and to be the subject of, more reading matter than any other chess club. In addition to a stream of letters, circulars, advertisements, and so forth, literature includes *Log Cabin Chess Divertives*, issued irregularly as a news bulletin, the book of the Log Cabin Chess club Championship tournament of 1951, edited by A. N. Towsen, and Selected Games from the Log Cabin chess Club Spring Tournaments, 1957, edited by Jack Spence. Titleholder of 1951 was Weaver W. Adams, while joint winners of the 1957 Log Cabin Independent Open were A. Feuerstein, G. Fuster, M. Green, A. E. Santasiere, and S. Wanetick. Among titles of the future books will be Log Cabin Firsts and Tournament Games and Barnstorming Trips of the Log Cabin. Spence is also preparing a book of Log Cabin games which will include scores taken from its first 1957 Morphy Centennial Tournament (played in Alabama!), on the occasion of which the Log Cabin donated a monument and plaque in honor of Morphy.

It is safe to predict that any little thing that Laucks and his merry men have not yet attended to will be taken care of in due time. Laucks himself, the center of all this ferment, is determinedly unobtrusive and unassuming, as player, as host and as promoter. Thus, although strong enough to have defeated E. S. Jackson, Jr., in a New Jersey championship tournament, he grades himself as Class B and shrinks from having any of his winning scores included in Log Cabin publications "so people won't think this fellow Laucks is such hot stuff as a player." His hospitality has been likened to that of the Great Gatsby in Scott Fitzgerald's novel of the 1920's, except that Laucks entertains on a more modest scale and without benefit of a staff of servants. Chess players, after all, cannot be bothered with folderol when they are intent upon the serious business of stalking the opponent's King.

The membership card of the Log Cabin Chess club, as might be expected, is a unique item. On the front are listed no less than three telephone numbers—standard, loud-speaker and mobile car. Underneath the name, "Log Cabin Chess Club," we read, "The most diversified, animated chess club in the Western Hemisphere." On the other side of the card is printed the club's motto:

> "We are the pioneers for the most animation. First here, first there, first most everywhere, We are ready, up and forward! Let's schusse! Log Cabineers!!!"
>
> "Let's schusse," an expression of the Pennsylvania Dutch, is roughly translated as "Let's be up and doing." That just about sums up the club spirit. To return to our opening theme: if there is ever an interplanetary chess match, we know who will be first to face the extraterrestrials over the chessboard."

An ad for the club in a 1960 issue of *Chess Review* contained a capsule description of the Log Cabin's activities.

> Champions of the New York "Met" League 1948. Organized and founded the North Jersey Chess League and Inter-chess League. First to help in large inter-scale matches. First to fly by air to Deep River Chess Club. First to promote largest international matches of eighteen and nineteen boards. First to make transcontinental and international barnstorming tours. Played interclub matches in five Mexican states, five Canadian provinces and all forty-nine United States but five, to 1958. Visited eleven countries and flew by plane to three—all in 1958.

One of the Log Cabin club's longest trips was a February/March 1956, 3500-mile journey that saw it play matches in Miami, St. Petersburg (twice), Hollywood/Fort Lauderdale, Tampa, Havana, and Clinton, North Carolina. Representing the Log Cabin club, besides Laucks and Fischer were: the infamous Norman T. Whitaker then director of the Washington Chess Divan; team captain Ted Miller of the Fool's Mate Chess Club in Newark; William Walbrecht the secretary of the New Jersey Chess Federation; Ralph Houghton of the Public Service Chess Club in Newark; and E.R. Glover, president of the Franklin Mercantile Chess Club in Philadelphia. The players besides Whitaker and Fischer were not strong, but well respected in their local chess communities. Glover was particularly important at the Franklin Mercantile and for many years an annual memorial tournament was held in his honor.

It was difficult to reconstruct the date of each match—information wasn't provided in *Chess Life* or *Chess Review* and newspaper accounts contradict each other. The most accurate record seems to be the one provided in the *Tampa Daily News:*[1]

> The seven on circuit played in Miami, St. Petersburg, Hollywood, and Havana, Cuba, before returning to St. Petersburg yesterday and Tampa last night.

The proximity of St. Petersburg and Tampa suggests two matches were played on the same day with one in the afternoon and the other in the evening.

1 *Tampa Daily News,* March 2, 1956, (p. 2).

The information available translates into the following schedule:

February 18	Leave Philadelphia
February 20	Miami
February 21	St. Petersburg
February 23	Hollywood/Ft. Lauderdale (Broward County)
February 25	Key West to Havana
February 25–26	Havana
February 27	Havana to Key West
March 1	St. Petersburg and Tampa
March 2	Clinton, North Carolina

R. E. Burry, who played on the Broward County team, reported on the tournament for the *Fort Lauderdale Sunday News*.[1]

Log Cabin		Miami	
Fred Borges	1	Aron Goldman	0
Norm Whitaker	½	Marvin Sills	½
Bob Fischer	1	Chas. Shaw	0
Wm. Walbrecht	1	John Fulop	0
E.R. Glover	0	Murray Cohen	1
Forry Laucks	1	Arne Pedersen	0
R. Houghton	1	Norman Church	0
Tedd Miller	0	José Simonet	1
	5½		2½

[Why is Fred Borges, USCF rated 2000 playing above Whitaker and Fischer? Burry explains he played for the Log Cabin in the past when he lived up North and was still a member in good standing despite now living in Miami. Laucks put him on board one for old times' sake].

Log Cabin		St. Petersburg	
Norm Whitaker	0	R. G. Carlyle	1
Bob Fischer	1	Col. F. Lynch	0
E.R. Glover	½	C. Spicehandler	½
R. Houghton	0	C.L. Clarks	1
Forry Laucks	0	Sam Tilles	1
Wm. Walbrecht	0	Dan Bryant	1
Ted Miller	0	E.M. Weeks	1
	1½		5½

[This match demonstrated the lack of depth on the Log Cabin team. There was a big drop in strength after Whitaker and Fischer with Glover, rated 1976 on the May 20, 1956, USCF rating list. Then came Walbrecht at 1736, Laucks 1726, and Houghton at 1524. Miller didn't even have a rating.]

[1] *Fort Lauderdale Sunday News*, March 4, 1956, (p. 72).

On Thursday [February 23rd] we were pleased to have a visit from the Log Cabin Chess Club of New Jersey. Here is the result of a match we played with this well-known and much traveled team (Burry).

Log Cabin		Broward County	
Bob Fischer	1	Frank Rose	0
Norm Whitaker	1	Jim Hundley	0
E.R. Glover	1	John Roman	0
R. Houghton	0	John Harvey	1
Wm. Walbrecht	0	P. DeNoel	1
Forry Laucks	½	R.E. Burry	½
Ted Miller	1	Rudy Brunner	0
	4½		2½

[The match was played in Hollywood, Florida which is located next door to Fort Lauderdale in Broward County—hence the name of the team the Log Cabineers faced. This tour seems to be the only time Fischer was referred to as Bob. Same goes for Whitaker who was always listed as Norman. The next stop on the tour was Havana where Bobby gave a simul, but first, played in a match against the members of the Capablanca Chess Club on February 25.]

Log Cabin		Capablanca	
Whitaker	1	Gonzales	0
Fischer	1	Florido	0
Glover	0	Calero	1
Walbrecht	0	Cobo	1
Miller	0	Ortega	1
Houghton	0	Aleman	1
Laucks	0	Romero	1
	2		5

Long thought lost, both players' score sheets to Game (13) were found in the Targ Collection. Marshall Chess Club Governor Gary Forman wrote:

> Both score sheets are from Club de Ajedrez "CAPABLANCA de La Habana", and are dated February 25, 1956.
>
> Señor Florido's score sheet is signed, and it appears that Fischer printed his name on both sheets. Mr. Fischer's sheet is more accurate and shows Florido as White, Fischer as Black, in a Giuoco Piano opening, with Florido resigning on the twenty-eighth move. Señor Florido's sheet is less accurate as it is missing a few moves at the end, and does not show a clear resignation point.

José Florido of Cuba was rated 2210 on the May 20, 1953, USCF list and his results in the 1951–1953 U.S. Opens (8½–3½, 7½–4½, and 8½–4½) confirm he was a strong player and Bobby's most difficult opponent on the tour. Florido dominated Fischer most of the game before inexplicably blundering at the end.

Game (13) was played on board two.

(13) Guioco Piano
José Florido – Fischer
Havana February 25, 1956

1.e4 e5 2.Nf3 Nc6 3.Bc4 Bc5 4.d3 d6 5.Nc3 Nf6 6.Bg5

This move dates back to the 1850s and possibly earlier, but is most closely associated with the Peruvian Grandmaster Esteban Canal who scored 3 out of 4 with it at Carlsbad 1929.

6...Na5

6...h6 7.Bxf6 Qxf6 8.Nd5 Qd8 9.c3 with d3–d4 to follow is the Canal Attack proper.

The text is Black's fourth most commonly played move here after 6...h6, 6...Be6 and 6....Bg4, but still enjoys an excellent theoretical reputation. Fischer's playing it points to the soon-to-be thirteen–year-old having acquired some opening erudition.

7.Bb5+?

7.Bb3 is best here. After 7.Nd5, Black answers with 7...Nxc4 8.dxc4 c6 9.Nxf6+ gxf6 10.Bh4 Rg8 11.0-0 Bh3 with an unbalanced position where the second player is not worse. The text just loses time.

7...c6 8.Ba4 b5 9.Bb3 Nxb3 10.axb3 h6 11.Be3 Qb6 12.Bxc5 Qxc5 13.0-0 Bg4

13...0-0 was more flexible.

14.Ra5?!

Florido commences active operations in a position that does not warrant it. More prudent was 14.d4 exd4 15.Qxd4 with equal chances.

14...g5?

Bobby wants to attack, but his position doesn't justify it.

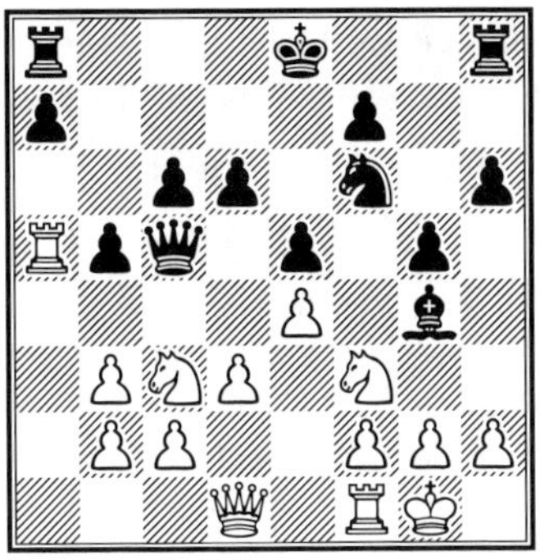

14...Qb6 15.Ra1 0-0 offered equal chances, but with White still having to deal with the annoying pin on his knight.

15.Qe2

The classic central counter 15.d4! was the correct response: 15...Qb6 (15...exd4 16.Qxd4 Qxd4 17.Nxd4 Bd7 18.b4, and 14.Ra5 turns out to be a brilliant move as White will soon double on the a-file. Note 15...Bxf3? 16.Qxf3 wins a piece.) 16.b4 and it is not clear how Black should proceed. White will break the pin with Qd3 and follow up with Nc3–e2–g3 and/or Rfa1.

15...Qb6 16.b4 Nh5

Bobby is nothing if not consistent and prepares to transfer his knight to the powerful f4 square.

17.Qe3!

Well played by Florido who breaks the pin advantageously.

17...Qb7

Trading queens prevents the knight from coming to f4.

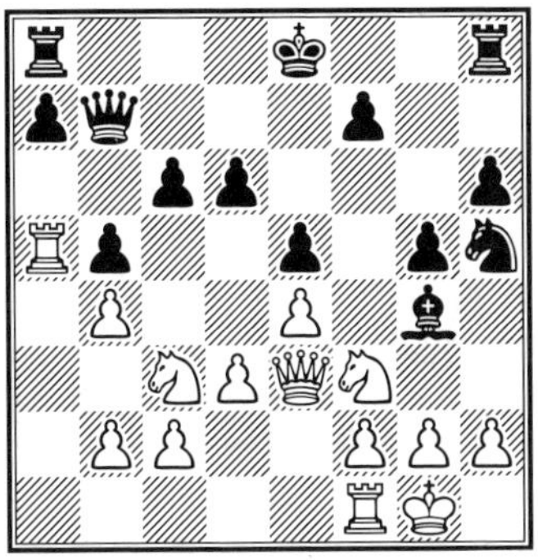

18.Rfa1 a6 19.d4 f6 20.d5

White has two equally attractive plans here, and which he chooses is largely a question of choice.

The text weakens Black's control of b5 but also to be considered was:

20.dxe5 dxe5 (20...fxe5 followed by ...Ke7 was safer although the d6 pawn can be a target and White has the idea of bringing a knight to f5.) 21.Nd2 Nf4 22.Nb3 (eyeing the c5 square) 22... Ne6 23.Qg3 Bh5 24.Qh3 Nf4 25.Qf5 0-0 26.Nc5 Qg7 27.Rxa6 winning a pawn while preserving a positional advantage.

20...Bd7 21.g3 f5?!

In for a penny in for a pound. Fischer is nothing if not consistent, but 21...0-0 was definitely safer.

22.exf5 cxd5

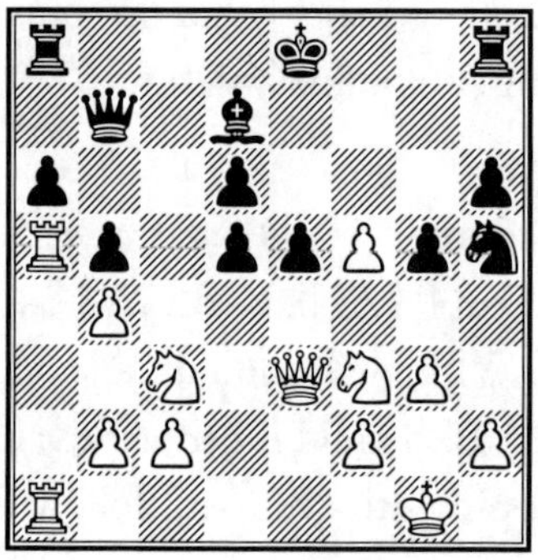

23.Nxe5!?

White had a stronger and much simpler alternative in 23.Qe2. After the forced sequence 23...Nf6 24.Nxb5 Bxb5 25.Qxb5+ Qxb5 26.Rxb5 Kd7 27.Rba5 (27.Rb7+ Kc6 28.Rg7 d4 29.Rg6 is a promising alternative.) 27...d4 28.c4 dxc3 29.bxc3 Rhc8 30.b5 White has excellent winning chances as 30...Rxc3 is met by 31.Rxa6 with Nxe5+ in the offing.

23...dxe5 24.Qxe5+ Kf7 25.Nxb5??

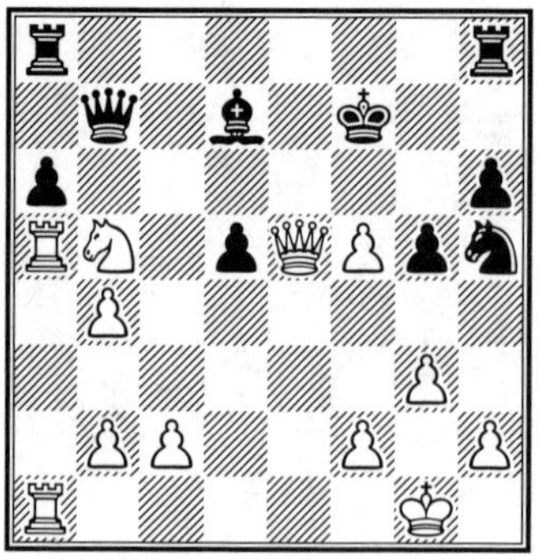

Florido blunders when he could have still kept the better of it with 25.Nxd5. The point is that 25...Rhe8 can be met by 26.Qd6 Bxf5 27.Qc7+ Qxc7 28.Nxc7 Bxc2 29.Nxa8 Rxa8 30.Rxa6 Rxa6 31.Rxa6 Nf6 32.f3 and White is a little better but a draw is the most likely result. It's hard to know what Florido was thinking when he played 25.Nxb5??.

25...axb5 26.Rd1 Nf6, 0–1.

The day after his win over Florido, Bobby gave a simul at the Capablanca Chess Club, and then, on the morning of February 27, the Log Cabin team headed north to Key West on the S.S. City of Havana.[1]

Bobby drew an unnamed opponent in the second match against St. Petersburg the afternoon of March 1st (no information about this match exists) and lost his only game of the tour that evening to unrated Nestor Hernandez of the Tampa Chess Club (regrettably this game has not been preserved).

The tiny town of Clinton, North Carolina, (1950 census population was 4,414) was the Log Cabineers' last stop on its tour. There they faced and lost to the best players from the "Tar Heel" chess clubs playing as one team. Master Charles "Kit" Crittenden, one of the top players in the South in the 1950s, fondly recalled the match:

> I was the highest rated player [in North Carolina at the time] having won the state chess championship several times by then. So I was number one on the North Carolina team. My opponent was not Bobby Fischer, number two on the Log Cabin team, but Norman Whitaker! So I missed out on a chance to play Bobby Fischer because he was not ranked highly enough! I'd known of Bobby from my friends in New York City—I'd played in various U.S. Opens, and a U.S. Junior in Fort Worth in 1949, and even been to New York and played chess there. I remember Bobby at the time—a gangly twelve-year-old kid, in sneakers and (I think) a long-sleeved shirt of some kind. I asked him if he wanted to play some five-minute chess, and he said OK, but somehow it never happened. Another lost opportunity!
>
> Bobby played Al Jenkins, our number two, and won. Al has told me that he has many times looked for the score of their game, but has not been able to locate it. He's in his seventies now, going strong, and lives in Raleigh still.
>
> Sometimes it happens that there are circumstances where I tell people that I won the North Carolina Championship when I was fourteen (in 1948). That sounds impressive. But then I tell them that Bobby Fischer won the U.S. Championship when he was fourteen!! That puts matters in perspective.
>
> Remlinger told me that when they were both up and coming juniors, he played BF a lot of five-minute chess, and they came out about even.

Dr. Albert Jenkins–Fischer Game (14) was recently rediscovered. Fischer's score sheet was among those auctioned off in the November 2016 Heritage Auction in New York City. Contacted in 2014, Al Jenkins recalled:

> Early in 1956 I was scheduled to participate in a match between teams from Raleigh, Chapel Hill, and Wilmington, which was to be held in Clinton, North Carolina—easy traveling distance for all involved. I believe it was in March. Dr. Norman Hornstein was bringing the Wilmington team.

[1] Fischer's first visit to Havana is covered in *Fischer in Cuba, Vol. 1*, by Miguel A. Sánchez and Jesús Suárez. Miami, 2019.

Sometime the day of the match he received a call from Norman Whitaker who represented the Log Cabin Chess Club (LCCC) and he told him they had been in Havana and were coming through North Carolina. Dr Hornstein told Whitaker to go to the meeting place in Clinton where the scheduled match was to be held.

When the three North Carolina teams reached Clinton they were informed of the availability of players from the LCCC and a new plan was made up to instead have a match between the LCCC and players on the North Carolina teams. Kit Crittenden was to play first board, Dr. Albert Jenkins was second board. I do not recall the other pairings, but in all there were maybe six or eight boards. Norman Whitaker was to play first board for the LCCC, with young Bobby Fischer to play second board.

Bobby was traveling with his mother and I was introduced to them. Bobby was quite young and didn't say much before the games began. We started around 7:30PM and I was playing White. I opened P-K4 and Bobby answered with the Sicilian. After a few moves things seemed fine for both players. Somehow, in the early middle game Black started to attack and White was quickly put on the defensive and began to play badly. Not long after Black obtained a strong material advantage and things went from bad to worse for White. I resigned the game and Bobby went out with his mother while the games on other boards continued.

I watched the game between Kit and Whitaker and it was a hard-fought battle which was eventually won by Whitaker. Players on the other boards continued and when the final game was finished, North Carolina had won the match!

Everyone was surprised at how easily Bobby had beaten me since I had won the NC Chess Championship in 1955 and was thirty-one years of age, more than two times older than Bobby. Kit's loss with Whitaker was not too unexpected, because his rating was so much lower than Whitaker's. The rest of the North Carolina players were surprised that they had won the match. It seems like other strong players from the LCCC had not been able to make the trip. Mr. E. F. Laucks, the leader of the LCCC, was a player in the match.

(14) Sicilian
Dr. Albert Jenkins – Fischer
North Carolina vs. Log Cabin Chess Club, March 2, 1956

Dr. Jenkins, was rated 1962 on the May 20, 1956, USCF rating list.

1.e4 c5 2.b3 Nc6 3.Bb2 e5 4.Nf3

The main line with 4.f4 or 4.Bc4 (Kramnik), intending to play f4 after Ne2 and 0-0, both seem more logical than the move played. White needs to attack Black's pawn triangle.

4...d6 5.Nc3 f5

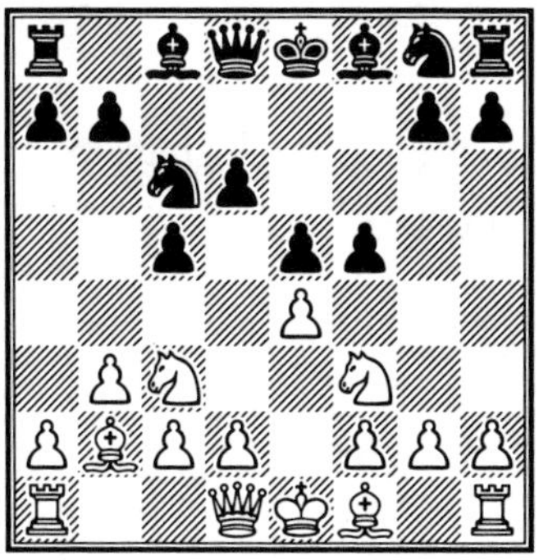

Ambitious play by Bobby. 5...Nf6 was more solid.

6.d3?!

Too passive. White had to play more actively. One possibility was 6.Bb5.

Another is 6.Bc4, which can lead to wild play. For example: 6...fxe4 7.Nxe4 d5 8.Nxe5 Nxe5 9.Bxe5 dxe4 10.Qh5+ g6 11.Bb5+ Kf7 (11...Bd7 12.Bxd7+ Qxd7 13.Qh3 favors White.) 12.Bc4+ with a draw by repetition.

Another option is 6.exf5 Bxf5 7.Bc4 Nf6 8.0-0 when 8...d5? walks into 9.Nxd5 Nxd5 10.Nxe5 Be7 11.Re1 with a winning position.

6...f4 7.h4?!

7.Be2 was more circumspect.

7...Bg4 8.Be2 Nf6 9.Nd5 Be7 10.Nxe7 Qxe7 11.Nd4?

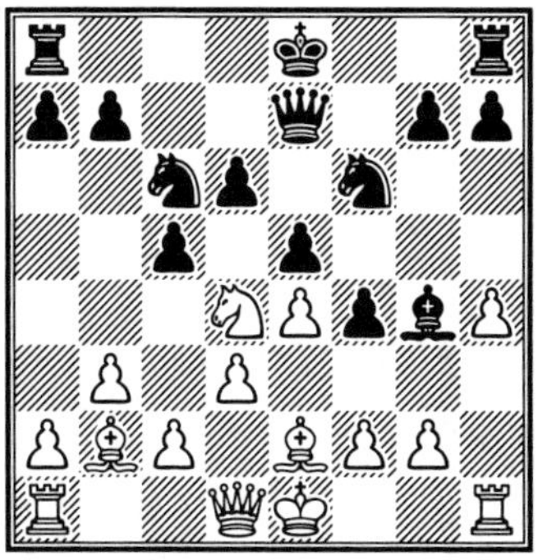

This fancy play only leads to the loss of material. 11.c3 was a better choice, although Black is already better.

11...Nxd4 12.Bxg4 Nxc2+ 13.Kf1?

13.Qxc2 was relatively best for White.

13...Nxa1 14.Bxa1 Nxg4 15.Qxg4 0-0 16.Bc3 b5 17.Qe2 a5 18.f3 b4, 0–1.

So far the moves from both sides have been plausible but here the score goes south with the remaining moves given as 19. P-R5 Q-B2 20. PxP PxP 21.Q-K3 K-K2 22.R-R8.

Carl Gorka suggests the finish might have been 19. Be1 a4 20.Qb2 axb3 21.axb3 Qe6 22.Ke2 Ra3 0-1.

The *Carolina Gambit*[1] reported on the match:

Clinton Chess Gala!
North Carolina 4 – Log Cabin 3
Wilmington B 2 – Chapel Hill 2
Raleigh Vass Barden 3 – Clinton 1

On March 2, 1956, the attractive city of Clinton became the scene of a mighty sextagonal chess battle. Thirty-two players and six teams competed. The North Carolina Chess Association team met and defeated the celebrated Log Cabin Chess Club of New Jersey. The score was 4–3. 1952 Carolinas Champion and veteran chess master, Norman T. Whitaker, defeated Kit Crittenden in the Exchange Variation of the Ruy Lopez. The twelve-year-old boy genius, Bobby Fischer, who was described by Whitaker as the equal to Reshevsky at the same age, defeated Dr. Albert Jenkins, state champion when the latter played an unusual variation of the Sicilian. Young Bobby showed that he is already a full-fledged chess master in spite of his tender years.

North Carolina		Log Cabin
1. Kit Crittenden	0-1	Norman Whitaker
2. Dr. Albert Jenkins	0-1	Bobby Fischer
3. Dr. Norman Houghton	1-0	William Walbrecht
4. Reverend M.J. McChesney	1-0	Ralph Houghton
5. Pete Henderson	1-0	Forry Laucks
6. Jack Godfrey	1-0	Ted Miller
7. Herman Vander Schalie	0-1	Raymond E. Glover

The brief *New York Times* recap of the tour mentions Whitaker and Bobby both finished with identical scores of 5½–1½. Fischer beat Rose (USCF 2030), Shaw (1858), Lynch (1922), Jenkins (1962), and Florido (a Cuban Master), lost to the unrated Hernandez and drew with an unknown opponent from the St. Petersburg Chess Club. This performance makes clear just how underrated Bobby was at the time. With ratings only calculated once a year, his USCF rating of 1726 from the previous May was over 300 points out of date by early 1956.

The Log Cabin produced booklets covering several of their tours including a 1955 trek from California to Alaska, but they didn't publish one for the February and March 1956 tour.

---

1 *Carolina Gambit*, May 7, 1956.

8

"BOBBY FISCHER RANG MY DOORBELL."

> Bobby Fischer rang my doorbell one afternoon in June 1956. I opened the door and a slender, blond typical thirteen-old American boy dressed in a plaid woolen shirt, corduroy trousers, and black-and-white sneakers, said simply: "I'm Bobby Fischer."[1]

Few individuals have contributed more to American chess than John Williams Collins (1912–2001). The man who wore many hats—including player, teacher, writer, administrator, and organizer—was born in Newburgh, New York. Collins' mother suffered a breach birth and he was born of small stature with spastic paralysis. Collins was able to walk until he was ten, but after that he had to rely on a small specially built tricycle for mobility. Growing up in Ontario, Canada, Collins rode to his elementary school each day in a sled pulled by the family dog, a huge collie named Tim. Raised in a loving and supportive environment, Collins would grow up to be a role model for the disabled at a time when few resources were available for the physically challenged.

In the early 1920s, Collins family returned to New York and settled in Brooklyn. It was there, at the age of sixteen, Collins was taught to play chess by his eighty-year-old upstairs neighbor. Despite his physical handicaps, which undoubtedly affected his stamina, by the early 1940s Collins had defeated Edward Lasker, Ulvestad, Morton, and Helms while drawing Marshall, Horowitz, Reinfeld, Santasiere, Hanauer, Seidman, Shainswit, and Polland. When the U.S. Chess Federation instituted ratings in the early 1950s, Collins was ranked among the top twenty-five players in the country.

Active in chess organization from an early age, Collins founded the Hawthorne Chess Club in 1931. Originally comprised of Hawthorne Street residents, within time the club would host some of Brooklyn's strongest players. Also, in the 1930s, Collins, with L. Walter Stephens, helped to organize the "latter day" Brooklyn Chess Club—this is the same club where Bobby got his start in the early 1950s.

---

[1] John W. Collins, *My Seven Chess Prodigies* (opening to the chapter on Fischer). New York: Simon & Schuster, 1975.

[above left] Harry Eckstrom, Ethel Collins, Jack Straley Battell, and Jack Collins circa 1950s on a trip to upstate New York;

[above right] Jack Collins (Photos: Courtesy of the Lilly Library, University of Indiana).

On November 26, 1955, Fischer, at the age of twelve, gave his first simultaneous exhibition. He played a dozen members of the Youth Group of the Yorktown Chess Club at the Manhattan Chess Club.

[left] The great chess journalist Hermann Helms and Jack Collins (Photo: Courtesy of the Lilly Library, University of Indiana);

[below] Louis J. Wolff and Jack Collins playing skittles at Collins' apartment at Stuyvesant Town in the mid-1960s (Photo: Beth Cassidy).

Besides the "Seven Prodigies" discussed in his 1975 memoir—Fischer, Lombardy, the Byrne brothers, R. Weinstein, Matera, and Cohen—Collins's other students included famous artists such as Marcel Duchamp and John Cage, as well as many players who would later become well known in the chess world. In 1991 Collins listed Max Dlugy, John Litvinchuk, Nawrose Nur, Greta Fuchs, Lisa Lane, and Shernaz Kennedy as some of those he had tutored.

Shortly after the 1956 Amateur at Asbury Park Bobby began frequenting the Hawthorne Chess Club. "There I have played thousands of skittles and rapid-transit games with Collins, Kaufman,[1] and other Collins regulars." The membership of the club read as a Who's Who of American chess of the 1950s: Jack Battell, Donald Byrne, Robert Byrne, Irving Chernev, Harry Eckstrom, Hermann Helms, William Lombardy, Aben Rudy, and Raymond Weinstein.

The standard accounting of the Fischer–Collins relationship, as given in numerous books as well as in the documentary *Bobby Fischer Against the World*, portrays Collins as Fischer's teacher and mentor.

Grandmaster William Lombardy, another claimant to the title of Bobby's teacher, begs to differ with this idea of Collins. In his 2011 memoir Lombardy repeatedly states that this wasn't the case:[2]

> I cannot imagine even today that anyone could consider that Collins had the strength or knowledge to coach the champion that Bobby already was by the time he reached the Collins apartment! Somehow the myth of Collins' professorial skill persists.
>
> By the way, Jack Collins was not in any way capable of teaching me, the Byrne Brothers, Raymond Weinstein, let alone Bobby Fischer. All had entered his home in friendship and were already superior masters, far past the ability of Collins to impart anything but trivial knowledge. I said this less vehemently in [Collins's] *My Seven Chess Prodigies*[3] where I practically wrote my corresponding chapter.

It's interesting to note Lombardy's dedication to Collins in his book *Chess For Children Step By Step:*[4]

> To John (Jack) W. Collins, the teacher of Grandmasters and World Champions, who made chess a truly happy experience for me and many others.

---

[1] Fischer refers here to Master Allen Kaufman who served for many years as executive director of the American Chess Foundation and later as the Secretary of the Frank P. Samford, Jr. Chess Fellowship.

[2] William Lombardy, *Understanding Chess: My System, My Games, My Life*. In association with Russell Enterprises, 2011, (p. 28 and p. 219)

[3] John W. Collins, *My Seven Chess Prodigies*. New York: Simon & Schuster, 1975.

[4] William Lombardy and Bette Marshall, *Chess For Children Step By Step*. New York: Little Brown, 1977.

Lombardy made the claim he was Fischer's teacher from the time Bobby was eleven-and-a-half years old (roughly, August 1954). If this was true, it would be curious as to where they would have met. Lombardy lived in the Bronx (961 Faile St.) and Fischer in Brooklyn, roughly an hour and a half away from each other by subway. Bobby didn't play in tournaments outside the Brooklyn Chess Club until 1955. He didn't go to the Manhattan Chess Club until the summer of 1955, nor to the Hawthorne Chess Club (Collins' club) until June of 1956.

On top of that, why did Lombardy wait so long to make the claim he was Fischer's teacher—over fifty years after the fact? Those of a suspicious mind will note Lombardy *never* made this claim while Fischer was alive. To Joseph Shipman (son of Walter Shipman), close friend and attorney in Lombardy's later years, the answer is clear: Lombardy, as an ordained Roman Catholic priest, was a keeper of secrets, and he believed he owed it to Bobby not to publicly air their early relationship until after Fischer's death.

Joseph Shipman believes the mentor/student relationship between Lombardy and Fischer can be seen in their stylistic similarities. To those who have only seen Lombardy's games after he left the priesthood this might be hard to see. The long layoff from full-time study caused him to adopt a cautious approach, particularly in the openings where he had fallen out of touch with theory. However, if you go through his games in the mid-to-late 1950s, he definitely had a more dynamic style; but Lombardy was hardly the only New York player besides Bobby to champion the Najdorf and the King's Indian as Black at the time. Ultimately, while Lombardy had a strong influence on the young Bobby as a player, he was not his teacher in any formal sense of the word.

The truth is that Collins never claimed to be Bobby's "teacher." Collins addressed this issue himself in his memoir:[1]

> "He taught Bobby Fischer to play chess" is the way I am sometimes publicly and privately introduced. Or "You taught Bobby Fischer, didn't you?" is the somewhat more tentative question often put to me. And usually there is no time for an answer, or the place is not right for a proper response. For one thing the response is not so simple. What is meant by "taught"? Obviously, I did not teach Bobby in the sense that I instructed him in the rules of the game or showed him how the knight moves two squares in one direction and one square in another direction, an L-shaped move. In his first book, *Bobby Fischer's Games of Chess,* he writes that one day his sister, Joan, "happened to buy a chess set" and that "we figured out the moves from the directions that came with the set." And two paragraphs later he writes, "Mr. Nigro was possibly not the best player in the world, but he was a very good teacher." And the book is dedicated: "To my chess teacher, Carmine Nigro."

[1] John W. Collins, *My Seven Chess Prodigies.* New York: Simon & Schuster, 1975, (pp. 47–49).

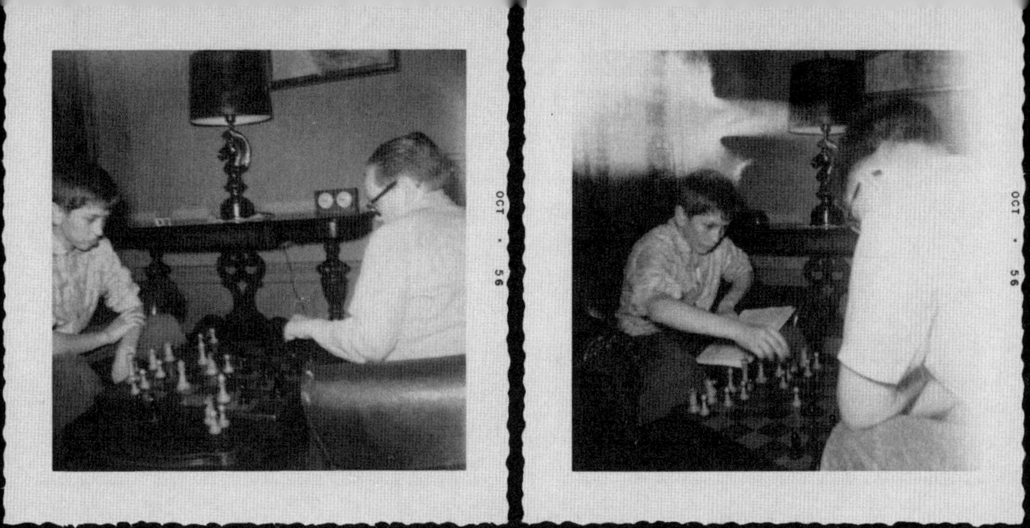

Bobby studying at Collins' apartment (October 1956).

Bobby once told me that Nigro[1] taught him the basic principles very well. Then why the bald assertion that I "taught Bobby Fischer to play chess"? Partly because it is an easy, popular one, and partly because definitions are not always precise and comprehensive. Consulting the American College Dictionary we find "taught" (tot), v. pt. and pp. of teach." And turning to teach we find:

Teach (tech), v. taught, teaching. – v.t. to impart knowledge of or skill in; give instruction in: he teaches mathematics. 2. To impart knowledge or skill to, give instruction to: he teaches a large class. – v.i.3 to impart knowledge or skill; give instruction.

In that sense I suppose I "taught" Bobby. At least something. After all I was a master and he had finished only twenty-first, in the U.S. Amateur Championship at Asbury Park two weeks before he first visited me. And we played thousands of fast games, a few simulated tournament games, we analyzed openings, we played over current and old games, we analyzed adjourned positions of our own games, and we talked endlessly about chess players, chess theory and chess history. All of which is a way "to impart knowledge." In "The Making of a Legend," a contribution in *Bobby Fischer's Chess Games*, by Robert G. Wade and Kevin J. O'Connell, Grandmaster Arthur Bisguier, former U.S. Champion, mentions that I was a friend, guide to Bobby during his early formative years. In this sense too, then, I could

[1] Carmine Domenico Nigro (1910-2001) definitely had an impact on Bobby. According to Carmine's son Tommy, almost every weekend from 1951 to the spring of 1955, Bobby would come to their home at 78 S. Elliott Place in Brooklyn and spend hours and hours being taught the fundamentals by his father. What started out to be a group chess class for the kids in the neighborhood invariably ended up with Carmine and Bobby studying chess for hours and hours while everybody else played stickball. Carmine, a latecomer to the game, only started to play seriously in his late 30s. He earned a rating of over 2000, and taught using the leading books of the day, chiefly treatises by Reuben Fine (including *Practical Chess Openings*, *The Middle Game in Chess*, and *Basic Chess Endings*).

> say "I taught Bobby Fischer." But in a larger sense neither Joan, nor Nigro, nor I, nor anybody else taught Bobby. Geniuses like Beethoven, Leonardo da Vinci, Shakespeare, and Fischer come out of the head of Zeus, seem to be genetically programed, know before instructed. So, I might have said of Bobby what Wenzel Ruzicka, a noted music teacher, said of Franz Schubert: "This one has learned from God!"

Certainly, Collins wasn't a teacher/trainer/coach in the way it's thought of today, where grandmasters take promising young players under their wing, systematically working with them on all aspects of their game, often for extended periods of time.

When Fischer was developing in the 1950s, that level of instruction was found only in the Soviet Union. This sort of professionalism in working with teenage talents only came to the United States in the 1990s with the arrival of former Soviet chess players. Before that Americans improved primarily by playing strong players in tournaments and working on their games by themselves. There were some exceptions, but that's pretty much the way it was. There is a world of difference between the current American chess scene and the past.

Collins definitely played a critical role in Fischer's meteoric rise from 1956 to 1958, not only by mentoring him, but even more importantly by providing a full-time chess center. That this club was only a short walk from Bobby's home and school, enabling him to spend roughly six hours each day there, was an added bonus. While Collins was not Fischer's "teacher" in a strict interpretation of the term, it's clear that without him and the Hawthorne Chess Club Bobby would not have developed as quickly as he did.

Lombardy's claim, that he was a stronger player than Collins when they first met and sat down to play a training game in July 1953, rings true. Less than a month later he would tie for thirteenth in the U.S. Open in Milwaukee. Over the next few years Lombardy would develop into one of the greatest talents in the history of American chess. Everyone remembers his winning the 1957 World Junior (11–0!) and playing first board (12–1!) for the gold-medal-winning U.S. entry in the 1960 World Student Team Championship. Equally impressive are his results in the 1958 and 1960 Olympiads and victory in the 1959 U.S. Invitational—a de facto national championship.

Possibly the greatest indication of Lombardy's talent can be found in his loss to Reshevsky in a training match held in 1956. This was organized to get Sammy ready for David Bronstein, but the match between the two giants never materialized. Lombardy, ably seconded by his friend Aben Rudy, lost by the barest of margins 3½–2½, dropping only the last game. He might have entered game six with a lead if he had more time on his clock to find the following trick.

(15) Ruy Lopez
William Lombardy – Sammy Reshevsky
New York m (3) 1956

1.e4 e5 2.Nf3 Nc6 3.Bb5 a6 4.Ba4 Nf6 5.d4 exd4 6.0-0 Be7 7.e5 Ne4 8.Nxd4 Nxd4 9.Qxd4 Nc5 10.Nc3 0-0 11.Rd1 d6 12.Be3 Nxa4 13.Qxa4 Bd7 14.Qd4 Be6 15.Bf4 dxe5 16.Qxe5 Bd6 17.Qe4 Qe7 18.Bxd6 cxd6 19.Nd5 Qd8 20.Ne3 Qd7 21.Rd4 Rac8 22.Rad1 Rc6 23.Qd3 Rd8 24.c4 Qc7 25.f4 f6 26.b3 Bf7 27.h3 Re8 28.Re4 Rxe4 29.Qxe4 Qd7 30.Qd4 Be6 31.a4 f5 32.b4 Qc7 33.Kh2 h6 34.b5 Rc5 35.Qxd6 Qxd6 36.Rxd6 Bxc4

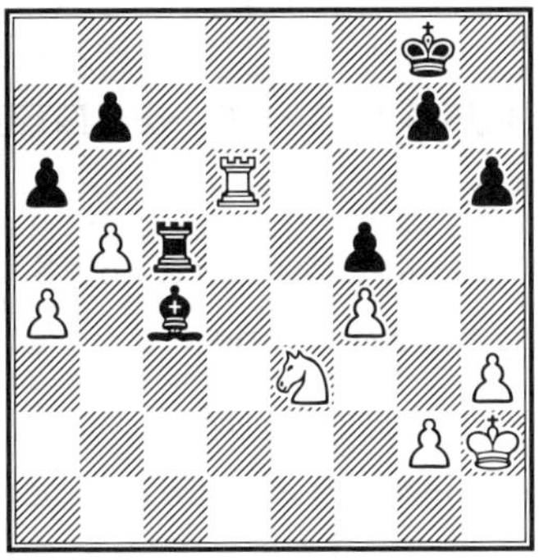

37.Nxc4

37.Rc6!! would have won.

37...Rxc4 38.bxa6 bxa6 39.Rxa6 Rxf4 40.a5, ½–½.

Lombardy was only eighteen when he played Reshevsky, one of the toughest match players of all time. Remember, Sammy didn't lose a match until he was in his fifties—to Lajos Portisch in 1964.

While he knew his own development better than anyone else, we believe Lombardy's claim that "all had entered his home in friendship and were already superior masters, far past the ability of Collins to impart anything but trivial knowledge," to be debatable.

Donald Byrne was twelve and his brother Robert was fourteen at their first meeting, while Raymond Weinstein and Bobby Fischer were both thirteen. None of them were rated masters, nor did their results at the time suggest superiority to Collins who was rated around 2350 for most of the 1950s.

Although Bobby was not rated master when he first met Collins, he was developing rapidly, and by 1958 Collins had imparted all the knowledge he had to offer Bobby. However, during the period 1956–57 he did much to set Bobby on the right track in many different ways beyond offering a second home. While Collins might have been more a mentor than a teacher to Bobby, his influence was unmistakable. Would 9.Nh3 in the Two Knight's Defense have ever been resurrected if Collins had not exposed Fischer to the games and writings of Steinitz through Bachmann's four volume collection of his games and the first official World Champion's *International Chess Magazine?*

Collins' Game (16) win over the great Edward Lasker emphasizes what a dangerous opponent he was in his prime. The circumstances surrounding this game are unknown, but it was likely played at the Marshall Chess Club as Collins recorded the game using one of the MCC's score sheets.

(16) Queen's Gambit
John Collins – Edward Lasker
New York February 12, 1960

1.d4 Nf6 2.c4 e6 3.Nc3 d5 4.Nf3 c5 5.cxd5 Nxd5 6.e3 Nc6 7.Bc4 cxd4 8.exd4 Nxc3

8...Be7 is the most common move here, and 8...Bb4 has also been played many times, but the text is not unknown.

9.bxc3 Bd6

9...Be7 to deny White's pieces g5 is more logical. The text is associated with the ...e5 advance, but as we shall see this can be difficult to implement safely.

10.0-0 0-0 11.Re1 Qa5

Grandmaster Thomas Luther's 11...Qc7 looks to be a safer way to prepare ...e5.

12.Bd2 e5 13.dxe5 Nxe5 14.Nxe5 Bxe5 15.Qh5 Bf5?

The hard to find 15...Qc5! was the only way to keep White's advantage to a minimum.

16.g4! g6 17.Qg5 h6 18.Qxh6

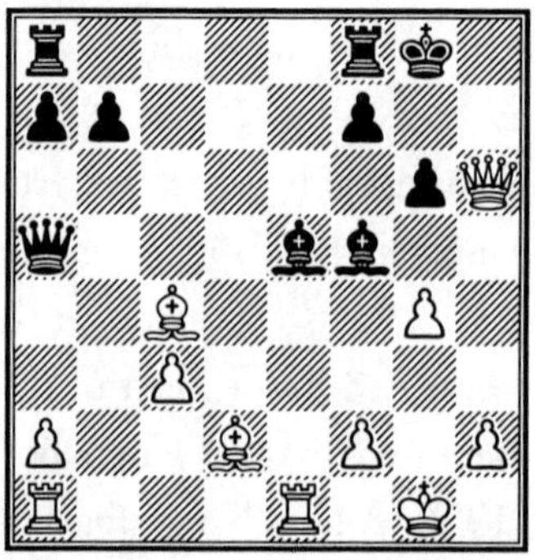

18...Bg7?

18...Bc2 had to be played. After the forcing sequence 19.Rac1 Rac8 20.Be6 Bg7 21.Qe3 Rfe8 22.Bxf7+ Kxf7 23.Qf3+ Bf5 24.gxf5 Qxf5

25.Qxb7+ Kg8 White is two pawns up, but Black has practical chances due to the exposed enemy king.

19.Qg5

19.Qf4! (more precise as it guards the bishop on c4) 19...Bd7 20.Re7 wins on the spot.

19...Qc7

19...Qa4! 20.Bxf7+ Rxf7 21.gxf5 gxf5 had to be played, although after 22.Re5 White is still on top.

20.Bb3 Bd3 21.Re3

The direct 21.Re7! was stronger.

21...Rad8 22.Rh3 Rfe8 23.Qh4

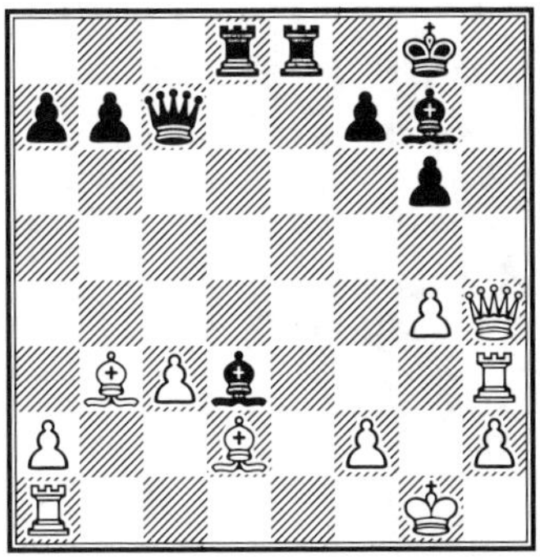

23...Re2?

Black had to play 23...Re4!, the point being that 24.Qh7+ Kf8 25.Bh6 Qxc3 26.Bxg7+ Qxg7 27.Qh8+ Qxh8 28.Rxh8+ Kg7 29.Rxd8 now loses to 29...Rxg4+ 30.Kh1 Be4+.

24.Qh7+ Kf8 25.Bh6

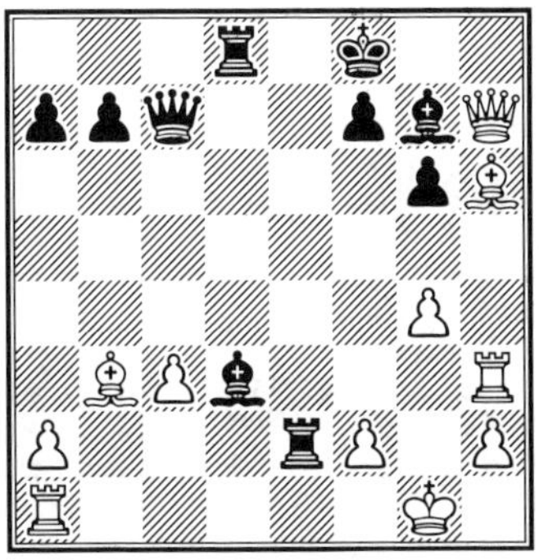

25...Bxh6

If 25...Qxc3 26.Bxg7+ Qxg7 27.Qh8+ Qxh8 28.Rxh8+ Ke7 29.Rxd8 Kxd8 30.Rd1 and White wins a piece.

26.Qxh6+ Ke8 27.Qg5 Qe7 28.Rh8+ Kd7 29.Rxd8+ Kxd8 30.Qd5+, 1–0.

Chess Life

America's Chess Newspaper

Copyright 1956 by United States Chess Federation

Vol. X, No. 22 | Friday, July 20, 1956 | 15 Cents

What's The Best Move?

Conducted by
RUSSELL CHAUVENET

SEND solutions to Position No. 188 to reach Russell Chauvenet, 721 Gist Ave., Silver Springs, Md., by August 20, 1956. With your solution, please send analysis or reasons supporting your choice of "Best Move" or moves.

Solution to Position No. 188 will appear in the September 5, 1956 issue.

Position No. 188
Contributed by
PAUL H. SMITH

IT'S FISCHER! IN JUNIOR

Bobby Fischer Youngest Titleholder, Henin Second, Feuerstein Third In Event

By WILLIAM ROJAM
Staff Writer

Setting a new record in the U.S. Junior Championship by winning the title at the age of 13 on his second try (Bobby placed 20th with 5-5 score at Lincoln in 1955), Fischer becomes the youngest player to hold the U.S. Junior title. He has outdistanced two other players who also began their Junior tournament careers at the age of 11—Ross Siemms and Larry Remlinger. Siemms began his career in the Junior at Cleveland in 1947, placing 5th, placed second on S-B at Milwaukee in 1950 (losing the title to James Cross) and did not win the U.S. Junior title until Long Beach in 1954 after six attempts. Larry Remlinger placed 8th (winning the Dittmann Trophy for contestants under 15) in his first appearance in Kansas City in 1953. He placed second in 1954 at Long Beach and second at Lincoln in 1955 but has yet to win the coveted title; he was not a contender this year.

The Eleventh Annual U.S. Junior Championship began auspiciously at Philadelphia with 28 participants, representing Canada, Texas, New York, Pennsylvania, California, Rhode Island, Michigan, Georgia, Maryland, Wisconsin, Illinois, New Jersey, and Massachusetts. It was held at the Franklin Mercantile Chess Club with Bill Ruth as tournament director, assisted by D. A. Gianguilio.

Early Dark Horse

Bobby Fischer of Brooklyn, a member of the Manhattan Chess Club, proved a menace to the favorites from the beginning. He drew Arthur Feuerstein, one of his most dangerous rivals, in the first round and proceeded to dispose of Carl Grossguth and William Whisler. By the fourth round, when Charles Henin of Chicago drew against Sanford Greene (he had already drawn with Feuerstein), Bobby was challenging the field, tied with George Baylor for first place with 3½-½. In the fifth round Bobby disposed of Baylor and took undisputed first place with 4½-½. Henin was second with 4-1, tied with Sydney Geller, and fighting for fourth with 3½-1½ were George Baylor, Thomas Levine, and Kenneth Blake.

Sixth Round Upset

A dramatic sixth round saw Fischer lose to his other principal rival, Henin, while Feuerstein, Geller, and Baylor also tallied wins. The lead quickly shifted with Henin ahead with 5-1, tied with Sydney Geller of Philadelphia. Fischer and Baylor followed with 4½-1½, trailed by Feuerstein with 4-2. Already the field seemed narrowed to these five contender.

U.S. JUNIOR
Final Standings—Leaders

1. B. Fischer	8½-1½	4. S. Geller	7 -3
2. G. Henin	8 -2	5. G. Baylor	6 -4
3. Feuerstein	8 -2	6. T. Levine	6 -4

Round seven saw Geller and Baylor drop points, while Fischer, Henin, and Feuerstein won. Henin holds undisputed lead with 6-1; on his heels is Fischer with 5½-1½, while pressing doggedly behind with 5-2 each are Feuerstein and Geller. Baylor has 4½-2½, tied with a new contender, Kenneth Blake. Pressing forward with 4-3 each are Thomas Levine, David Kerman, and Frank Jobin.

Henin Falters

Round eight, and Henin drops half-a-point in a game with Baylor. Feuerstein, Fischer, and Levine win; Geller and Baylor draw. Again the lead shifts with Fischer and Henin tied at 6½-1½, Feuerstein with 6-2, Geller with 5½-2½, followed by Baylor, Levine, Blake, and Jobin at 5-3. Forging ahead are Kerman and Joseph Tamargo with 4½-3½ each.

Round nine, and again Henin falters, drawing with Frank Jobin, while Fischer, Feuerstein, and Gel-

(Please turn to page 3, col. 1)

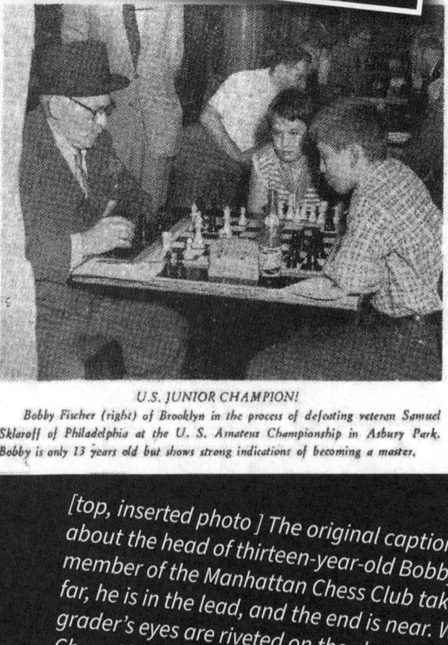

U.S. JUNIOR CHAMPION!

Bobby Fischer (right) of Brooklyn in the process of defeating veteran Samuel Sklaroff of Philadelphia at the U. S. Amateur Championship in Asbury Park. Bobby is only 13 years old but shows strong indications of becoming a master.

[top, inserted photo] The original caption of this photo was: "Restless hands play about the head of thirteen-year-old Bobby Fischer of Brooklyn, as the youngest member of the Manhattan Chess Club takes part in a current tournament there. So far, he is in the lead, and the end is near. While his hands may be fidgety, the eighth grader's eyes are riveted on the chessboard before him. His goal is the U.S. National Chess Championship—and he's made an excellent start toward it." Bobby's opponent is Karl Forster. See Game (19a) page 85. Other photos from this game are on page 2.

[bottom] This is the photo Judy (Hauck) Winters remembers of herself watching Bobby play Samuel Sklaroff at the U.S. Amateur Championship. The photo was originally published on the front page of Chess Life, July 20, 1956.

9
1956 TOURNAMENTS

U.S. AMATEUR CHAMPIONSHIP 1956

Asbury Park, New Jersey, was the site of the 1956 U.S. Amateur Championship held May 25–27, just before Bobby started to make his great leap forward.

Icelandic Grandmaster Helgi Ólafsson was intrigued by a curious story posted by Judy Winters of Port Charlotte, Florida online shortly after Bobby's death:[1]

> Bobby Fischer was my first boyfriend. Starting about 1955, I would go to the Manhattan Chess Club with my father. My father would play and I would drink soda. I saw Bobby a few times there and we would talk a little. (We were both the same age and very shy) I fell in love with him at a tournament at Asbury Park, in New Jersey. We went to the boardwalk together, went on rides and played games of chance. His mother was real mad at him when we got back because he was almost late for his game.
>
> I think it was Memorial Day or Labor Day, maybe 1955 or 1958. The Asbury Park newspaper had a picture of me watching one of his games. I wish I could get a copy of that picture. We wrote back and forth for a while, and then I got too cool for chess and he got famous. One time, a Jewish friend of mine said I couldn't marry him because he was Jewish and I wasn't. I wish I could have seen her when he converted.
>
> I love remembering him in such an innocent time. He was just a person, like you and me, with a wonderful gift (and he was very cute). If anyone can get that picture from the Asbury Park newspaper, please let me know. I think it was on the front page, because we were only about thirteen or fifteen, and he won.

Contacted in 2012, Judy Winters elaborated:

> My father was Sig Hauck. I forget [his rating], it was so long ago, but my father was in A class for a while but fell to B class. I think one year he was top in the B class. He would have loved to have done more with his chess but he was an accountant with a family! He was also a writer. In those days he took me all over for tournaments.

---

[1] Helgi Ólafsson, *Bobby Fischer Comes Home*. Alkmaar, The Netherlands: New In Chess, 2012, (p. 119).

> Some were in a big mansion in the northern part of New Jersey. I wish I could remember the names and places better. I loved going with him because the people would fuss over me because I was so young. They were very nice times. The chess world was its own community and naïve to the political world around it. You can tell by our picture it was a different world.

The big mansion Winters refers to was almost certainly E. Forry Laucks' home at 30 Collamore Terrrace in West Orange, New Jersey.

Bobby scored 4–2 in the U.S. Amateur. For many years only Bobby's game with Edmund Nash (born Adam Edmund Nasierawski) was available, but recently two more have surfaced. A fourth game, with Sklaroff, is in the Targ collection, so hopefully, soon, only rounds one and three will be missing.

---

(17) Catalan
Fischer – J.F. Bacardi
Asbury Park, New Jersey (2) May 25, 1956

Bacardi had a provisional rating of 1770 on the May 5, 1957, USCF list.

1.Nf3 Nf6 2.g3 Nc6 3.d4 d5 4.Bg2 e6

4...Bf5 and 4...Bg4 are more active and superior choices for Black. After the move played he will have a hard time activating his queen bishop.

5.0-0 Be7 6.c4 dxc4 7.Qa4 0-0

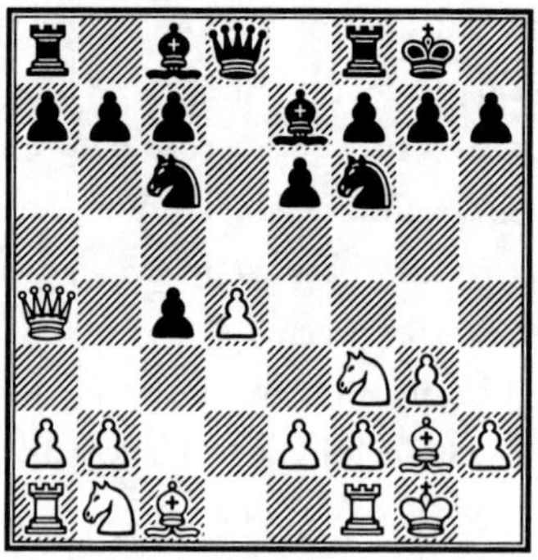

7...Bd7 8.Qxc4 Na5 9.Qc2 Rc8 10.Nc3 c5 11.dxc5 Bxc5 12.e4 Nc6 13.e5 Nb4 14.Qd2! (14.Qe2 allows 14...Nfd5 and Black is hanging on.) 14...Nfd5 15.a3 Nxc3 16.axb4 Bxb4 17.bxc3 Bxc3 18.Qa2 Bxa1 19.Qxa1 0-0 20.Qxa7 and White went on to convert his advantage in Fischer–Di Camillo, U.S. Ch. (11) 1957/58.

8.Qxc4 Bd7

8...Qd5 is a better try though after 9.Qd3 White has a clear advantage typical of the Catalan—he has more space (d4 vs. e6) and Black's light-squared bishop lacks mobility.

9.Rd1 a6

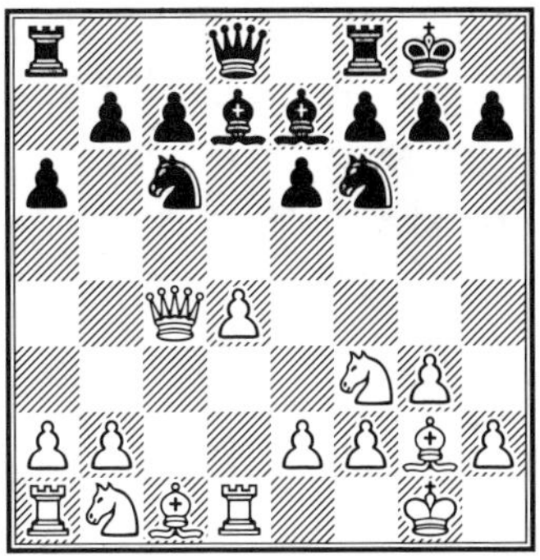

9...Na5 10.Qc2 (10.Qc3!? c5?! 11.dxc5 Rc8 12.Qe1! refutes Black's attempt to liberate his position. 12.b4 Nd5 13.Rxd5 exd5 14.bxa5 is also better for White) 10...Rc8 intending ...c5 does not solve Black's problems:

11.Nc3 c5 12.dxc5 Bxc5 13.Ne5 Qe7 14.Bg5 Bc6 15.Nxc6 Nxc6 16.Ne4 Bd4 17.Rac1 h6 (17...Rfd8 18.e3 Be5 19.f4) 18.Nxf6+ Bxf6 19.Bxf6 Qxf6 20.Rd7. The simplification has not eased Black's pain as the rook on d7 and powerful bishop ensures White's advantage.

9...b5!? had to be tried though after 10.Qxb5 Nxd4 11.Qd3 Nxf3+ 12.Bxf3 Rb8 13.Nc3 White still retains some advantage. The text is too passive.

10.Ne5

10.Nc3 preparing Ne5 was possibly even stronger.

10...Na5?

10...Nxe5 11.dxe5 Nd5 12.Nc3 c6 13.Ne4 Qb8 14.Bf4 leaves White with a clear positional advantage.

11.Qc3! c6??

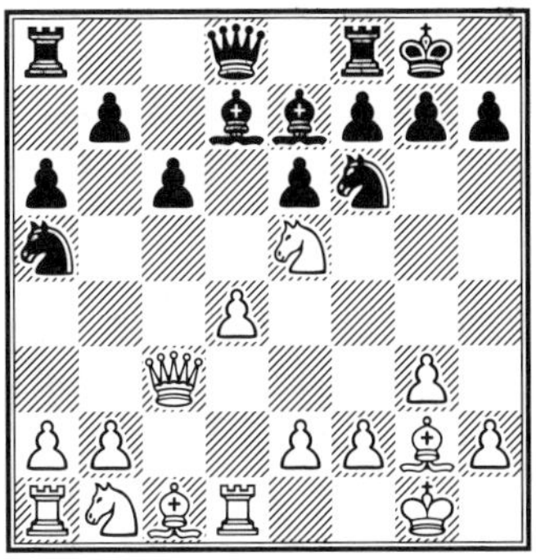

11...Nc6 was forced.

12.b4! Nd5 13.Bxd5 cxd5 14.Nxd7 Rc8 15.Qd3 Qxd7 16.bxa5 Bb4 17.Bd2 Bd6 18.Nc3 Bb4 19.Nxd5 Qxd5 20.Bxb4 Rfe8 21.e4 Qg5 22.d5 exd5 23.exd5 Rcd8 24.d6 Rd7 25.Re1 Rxe1+ 26.Rxe1 f5 27.Qd5+ Kf8 28.Re8+, 1–0.

(18) Sicilian
Richard Riegler – Fischer
Asbury Park, New Jersey (6) May 27, 1956

Dr. Richard Riegler was rated 1844 on the May 5, 1957 USCF rating list.

1.e4 c5 2.Bc4?

This move makes sense after 1.e4 c5 2.Nf3 d6, but here the text is weak as Black is able to play ...d7-d5 in one go.

2...Nc6 3.Ne2 e6 4.Nbc3 Nge7

4...Nf6 intending ...d5 was also good and more straightforward.

5.Ng3 d5 6.exd5 exd5 7.Bb3 c4 8.Ba4 g6

8...d4 and 8...a6 forcing the trade on c6 were equally strong alternatives.

9.0-0 Bg7 10.Bxc6+?!

10.d3 trying to complete development was more logical. White ends up spending four moves with his bishop only to trade it off.

10...bxc6 11.Nce2?

Why? Again 11.d3 was best preparing to develop the bishop on c1.

11...h5!?

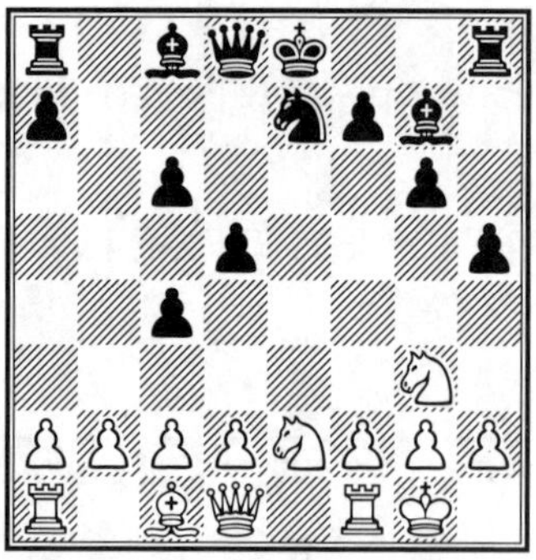

11...0-0 was the routine move, but Bobby plays more ambitiously trying to exploit the awkward position of the knight on g3.

12.Rb1?

This is asking for trouble. White had to play 12.Re1 to create a home for the knight on f1. It will have few prospects on h1.

12...h4 13.Nh1 h3!

This pawn will prove to be a bone in White's throat.

14.g3 Bg4 15.f3

This loses material but good moves are not to be found. On 15.d3 Black has 15...Bf3 with an unbreakable pin, which Black will soon exploit. For example: 16.dxc4 Nf5 17.c3 0-0 18.Re1 Re8 with ...Qe7 to follow. White's pieces are really sadly placed—look at the knight on h1!

15...Qb6+ 16.Nf2 Bxf3 17.c3 Nf5

Threatening to capture on g3!

18.Re1 0-0-0 19.Qc2

19.b3 Nxg3! 20.hxg3 h2+ 21.Kf1 h1Q+ 22.Nxh1 Rxh1+ 23.Ng1 Rxg1 mate

19...Rde8 20.d4 cxd3 21.Qxd3 Be4

White could resign here but struggles on.

22.Be3 Nxe3 23.Nxe4 dxe4 24.Qd4 Bxd4 25.Nxd4 Nc2 26.Red1 Nxd4 27.Rxd4 e3 28.Rb4 e2+ 29.Rxb6 e1Q+ 30.Rxe1 Rxe1+ 31.Kf2 axb6 32.Kxe1 Re8+ 33.Kf2 Rd8 34.Ke3 Rd1, 0–1.

Norman Hurttlen of Union City, New Jersey, played Bobby at least three times. His draw from the 1956 Eastern States Open and loss in an event held at the Log Cabin Chess Club in February 1957 are known, but their earlier draw from round three of the 1956 U.S. Amateur is missing. Hurttlen, rated 1985 on the May 20, 1956, USCF rating list, would go on to become a master as would his older brother Ralph.

Aben Rudy and Allen Kaufman both recognize Bobby's opponent in Game (19a) as Karl Forster, a Manhattan Chess Club habitué. Rudy remembers him as a master strength player who preferred blitz to tournament play, while Kaufman recalled that Forster was a heavy smoker with an equally heavy German accent. Fragment (19a) is a reconstruction of the opening position in the photo of Forster playing Bobby on page 80.

---

(19) Three Fragments, New York (1956)

(19a) **Karl Forster – Fischer**

1.d4 Nf6 2.c4 g6 3.Nc3 Bg7 4.e4 d6 5.f3 0-0

The game could also have gone 5...e5, a move order Fischer used on several occasions in 1959.

6.Be3 e5 7.d5 Nh5 8.Qd2 f5 9.exf5

9.0-0-0 f4 was Avram–Fischer, West Orange 1957

9.Nge2 a6 10.0-0-0 b5 was Ivkov–Fischer, Mar del Plata 1959

9.Bd3 Nbd7 10.Nge2 was Najdorf–Fischer, Bled 1961

9...gxf5 10.Bd3 (remaining moves unavailable)

[left] Karl Forster analyzing at the Manhattan Chess Club circa 1965 when it was located on 59th and Central Park South; [right] Norman Hurttlen circa 1965 (Photos: Beth Cassidy).

(19b) Aben Rudy – Fischer

Game notes and comments are by Aben Rudy.

I still remember the opening moves of my two draws with Fischer, but I have no idea why except that I seem to remember the openings of many of my games. In the first game, in which I was White, the opening went

1.e4 e5 2.Nf3 Nc6 3.Bb5 a6 4.Ba4 Nf6 5.0-0 Be7 6.Bxc6 dc 7.Qe1 0-0? 8.Nxe5

Despite Bobby's blunder and my win of a pawn, the game ended as a draw not many moves later. He had never seen 7.Qe1 before and simply assumed he could continue as usual.

(19c) Fischer – Aben Rudy

The second game, in which I was Black, began

1.e4 e6 2.d4 d5 3.Nc3 Nf6 4.Bg5 Be7 5.e5 Nfd7 6.Bxe7 Qxe7 7.f4 0-0

And the game was drawn about the fortieth move.

The event was indeed a six-man double round robin. I've racked my brains as best I can, but I can't come up with the name of anyone else in the tournament.

Although these two were the only tournament games we played, I contested scores of offhand blitz games with Fischer, both at the Manhattan and at the home of Jack Collins. Bobby, in those early days, also enjoyed playing in the Friday night rapid tournaments at the Manhattan. These tournaments were always played at ten-seconds a move, a speed greatly to my liking. In one of the very few newspaper clippings I still have, I am shown, with a score of 8½–1½, to have "outranked" Arthur Feuerstein and Bobby Fischer, both prize-winners in the recent tournament for the Lessing J. Rosenwald trophy. Feuerstein was second with a score of 7½–2½, and Fischer third with 6½–3½.

U.S. JUNIOR (1956)

The 1956 U.S. Junior, held July 1–7 in Philadelphia, was Fischer's first big breakthrough. He won his last round game versus David Kerman by adjudication, which took two hours of analysis by a panel of three referees. Bobby placed second behind Arthur Feuerstein, in the final of the U.S. Junior Blitz Championship (William Lombardy finished third).

Master David Kerman, who continued to play actively into his seventies, wasn't able to find the game score, but remembered he was Black in a Winawer French and that the game was very close until the last few moves of the time control.

Sanford (Sandy) Greene wrote of the event:

> In 1956 four of us roomed together during the U.S. Junior in Philadelphia at the YMCA—Arthur Feuerstein, Joe Tamargo, Bobby, and me. Fischer won the event with a score of 8½–1½, losing to Chuck (Charles) Henin in one of the middle rounds. Bobby kept us up all night, carrying on about what he was going to do to Henin. If he succeeded in half of what he wanted to do, Henin would have been in pieces! In one of the early rounds, the three aforementioned (not I) engaged in a pillow fight. One of them whacked Bobby with a pillow and he teetered against an open window (we were many floors up) and I put myself against his knees to keep him from possibly falling out the window.

Chess Life, which at that time appeared in newspaper format with the banner "America's Chess Newspaper," ran the headline:[1]

> **IT'S FISCHER! IN JUNIOR**
>
> Setting a new record in the U.S. Junior Championship by winning the title at the age of thirteen on his second try (Bobby placed twentieth with a 5–5 score at Lincoln in 1955), Fischer becomes the youngest player to hold the U.S. Junior title. He has outdistanced two other players who also began their junior tournament careers at the age of eleven—Ross Siemms and Larry Remlinger. Siemms began his career in the junior at Cleveland in 1947, placing fifth, placed second on S-B at Milwaukee in 1950 (losing the title to James Cross) and did not win the U.S. Junior title until Long Beach in 1954 after six attempts. Larry Remlinger placed eighth (winning the Dittmann Trophy for contestants under fifteen) in his first appearance in Kansas City in 1953. He placed second in 1954 at Long Beach and second again at Lincoln in 1955 but has yet to win the coveted title; he was not a contender this year.
>
> The Eleventh Annual U.S. Junior Championship began auspiciously at Philadelphia with twenty-eight participants, representing Canada, Texas, New York, Pennsylvania, California, Rhode Island, Michigan, Wisconsin,

---

[1] *Chess Life*, July 20, 1956, (p. 1).

[left] Stephan Popel drew with Bobby in round eleven of the 1956 U.S. Open; [middle] Arthur Bisguier, winner of the 1956 U.S. Open (on tiebreak over James Sherwin), in the opening stage of a game played in the mid-1960s in New York (Photo: Beth Cassidy); [right] Allen Kaufman playing in the 1988 U.S. Open in Boston (Photo: Steve Stepak).

Illinois, New Jersey, and Massachusetts. It was held at the Franklin Mercantile Chess Club with Bill Ruth as tournament director, assisted by D.A. Gianguilio.

Pennsylvania Master William Allen Ruth (1886–1975) was an early proponent of 1.d4 Nf6 2.Bg5. He played it extensively in the 1930s, the same time as Octávio Trompowsky who is commonly credited as its inventor. Dawid Janowsky played 2.Bg5 four times at Semmering 1926 but with no particular success.

Robert James Fischer	8½–1½
Charles C. Henin	8–2
Arthur William Feuerstein	8–2
Sydney Geller	7–3
George Baylor	6–4
Thomas S. Levine	6–4

U.S OPEN (1956)

Recorded in the U.S. Open tournament bulletin, July 16–28, Oklahoma City:

> Bobby Fischer, thirteen, who recently won the U.S. Junior Championship at Philadelphia, continues as the center of attraction for the spectators and newspaper men. The brilliant Brooklyn youngster has been on two television programs and his portrait was featured by the local press. Bobby chews gum continuously, is a Dodgers fan, likes Elvis Presley, and seems completely unaffected by all the publicity he is getting. Unlike most chess prodigies, his manners are excellent. He has been playing chess for about seven years.
>
> Mainly for publicity reasons, Bobby Fischer was paired in the first round with A.M. Swank of Oklahoma City, who is seventy-eight years old

Sammy Reshevsky (White) and Donald Byrne in the mid-1960s (Photo: Beth Cassidy).

> and boasts a long, flowing beard. Mr. Swank was no match for the Junior Champion who is playing with the strength of a master and has not lost a single game in nine rounds. His score of 6 points includes a win over Dr. Lapiken, California master, and draws with New York masters Santasiere and Owen. In the first eight rounds, all of Bobby's opponents, except Swank and Wilmer Stevens, were rated masters or experts. In the ninth round, Bobby was paired with Dale Ruth of Midwest City, Oklahoma, the most promising of the young local players. Ruth set a trap for Bobby but it boomeranged and cost the Oklahoma player the game.

The twelve-round Swiss, held in the Civic Room of the famous Biltmore Hotel, was won by Arthur Bisguier with a score of 9½. James Sherwin, who had the same score, lost out on tiebreaks. Bobby and Anthony Saidy, who tied for fourth-seventh at 8½, stayed at the home of Dr. Ernest Gill, a former Oklahoma state champion. The nineteen-year-old Saidy was acting as thirteen-year-old Bobby's legal guardian for the tournament!

Fischer befriended his round eight opponent Wilmer Stevens (a 1900 player) of Laramie, Wyoming, who along with 1957 Wyoming champion Robert McGregor regaled the young Bobby with tales of life in the Wild West—plans were discussed for Bobby to visit but they never materialized.

The Ukrainian Master Stephan Popel (1907–1987) was one of many Eastern Europeans who enriched American chess after the Second World War. While most of them settled on the East or West Coast, Popel landed first in Michigan where he won the state championship from 1956–59. He later became a professor of French language and literature at North Dakota State University in Fargo and was an institution in North Dakota chess, winning the state title eleven times between 1965 and 1980.

Bobby next traveled to Montreal, Quebec, where he played in the first Canadian Open. The eighty-eight-player, ten-round Swiss, held August 30–

September 2, was won on tiebreaks by Larry Evans over William Lombardy, both of whom scored 8-2. Bobby ended up tied for eighth to twelfth place. He gave a simultaneous in Montreal on September 5, scoring +18 =1–0.

THIRD LESSING J. ROSENWALD TROPHY TOURNAMENT

Allen Kaufman's *Chess Review* article written toward the end of 1956 confirms how much Bobby had progressed in the previous nine months.[1]

> Having returned from Washington, D.C. with equal second prize in his pocket, Bobby Fischer resumed his rapid transit play at the Manhattan Chess Club with a victory in the weekly event. In Washington he tied with Rossolimo, Lombardy, Feuerstein, etc..., behind Berliner. In New York he won the rapids ahead of local masters. Bobby has definitely arrived.
>
> His style of play is difficult to describe. His moves are confident and aggressive. In the Rosenwald tournament he displayed tactical brilliance (vs. Byrne) as well as the ability to "kvetch" out a positional game (vs. Seidman).
>
> His manner of kibitzing is clearer. All his opponent's moves are blunders, "Bobby keel!" he shouts. "Look at that move," he exclaims. "Boy is he weak!" But don't believe that Bobby is anything but a nice kid; his kibitzes are all in fun.
>
> Away from the board, Bobby (known to his chess friends as "Baby Fuscher") is quite like other thirteen-year olds. He is a Rock 'n' Roll fan ("I like music with the Big Beat") and loves comic books and cookies. Witches scare him more than a powerful kingside attack.
>
> Rumor says he may play at Hastings in the Christmas tourney. He is a master player, and afraid of no one. Watch his results!

Bobby's impressive performance in the Third Lessing J. Rosenwald Trophy Tournament (New York, October–November 1956) showed the thirteen-year-old could hold his own with the best players in the country. His high point was unquestionably the "Game of the Century" against Donald Byrne.

Bobby wasn't the only surprise. Arthur Feuerstein, who had drawn with Bobby in the U.S. Junior in Philadelphia during the summer was outstanding, scoring plus two. The report in the December 5, 1956, issue of *Chess Life* concluded he would have finished second if he had not weakened in a favorable game against Edmar Mednis.

Also scoring well was Abe Turner who was heading toward a high prize until his fiascoes against Bisguier and Reshevsky in the last two rounds. One of the few players with a lifetime plus record against Fischer (two wins and a draw in 1956–58), Turner was a good friend of Bobby's until his life was senselessly

[1] *Chess Review*, December 20, 1956.

ended in 1962, at the age of thirty-eight, stabbed to death by fellow *Chess Review* employee Theodore Smith. *Chess Review*[1] carried an account of the tragedy:

> On October 25 [1962], Abe Turner, an employee of a few weeks, and Theodore W. Smith, employed six months, left Chess Review at 2:50 PM. At 3:30, the building superintendent, following a trail of blood, found a body in a large safe in the basement. It was Turner's. Apprehended late that night when he returned home, Smith led police to a hunting knife buried in Central Park. Asked why he killed Turner, he replied: "The Secret Service told me to do it." He is now under observation in Bellevue Hospital. More than two hundred attended the funeral for Abe Turner.

Aben Rudy:

> I worked for Al Horowitz for two summers, when school was out. His second office, on West 72nd street (his first was on West 57th), was where Abe Turner was killed (actually in the basement of the building). Abe was a wonderful person, and it was a terrible shock to hear of his murder on the radio. An oddity that may not be well known is when he was rushed to the emergency room, the doctor in charge was Marlys Hearst, Eliot Hearst's sister.

Grandmaster Larry Evans, a good friend of Turner's, wrote a heartfelt appreciation for *Chess Life*.[2]

> **TOP CHESS PLAYER STABBED TO DEATH**
> **CHESS EXPERT KNIFED, BODY LEFT IN BASEMENT SAFE**
> **A CHESS PROBLEM WITH NO SOLUTION**
>
> So trumpeted the headlines. It never turns out to be someone you know, but in this case, it was. Someone I knew very well.
>
> Abe had been brutally and senselessly stabbed nine times by a demented employee at *Chess Review* stuffed in an eight by ten safe. His assailant, Theodore Smith, shortly confessed that "the Secret Service ordered me to do it . . . He was a Communist spy." (No doubt part of the cold war hysteria that induces us eventually to turn on ourselves and devour our own.) He was dispatched to Bellevue Hospital for the inevitable psychiatric examination after telling the judge he had been discharged from the army for mental reasons and was recently released from an asylum in 1959.
>
> Abe was a true coffee house chess pro. He referred to the chess den on 42nd Street, where he could be found every afternoon, as "my office." Weekends he scrupulously retired to his home in Mt. Vernon in order to write plays patterned after the style of Ionesco. We had collaborated earlier on a three-act unproduced play called "Do Horses Eat Meat?" based on Abe's whacky comedy of what happens when a twelve-year-old boy prodigy inherits a crime

---

1 *Chess Review*, December 1962, (p. 356).

2 *Chess Life*, December 1962, (p. 281).

Bobby is on the white side of a Ruy Lopez playing against Eliot Hearst in the 1956 Rosenwald tournament (Photo: Courtesy of the John G. White Collection at the Cleveland Public Library).

syndicate. We holed up a week in my apartment in order to finish. Although I had stuffed the refrigerator with food, it was never quite sufficient to satisfy his prodigious appetite.

Always colorful and in good spirits, his corpulence framed the role of the buffoon which he chose to play in life. "Fatso" may have been unhappy, but he was never bitter. People called him a chess bum. He was a strong player who could hold his own with nearly anyone. He seemed content to demonstrate his equality over the chessboard. He was always happy to draw with a strong player, but he came into his own when they over extended themselves trying to win. In tournaments he had a plus score against Fischer and Bisguier, it was only recently that I evened our personal score.

Turner was a late comer to the game, picking it up only in 1943 while recuperating in a naval hospital from shrapnel wounds inflicted during the war. He was a quick learner.

I met him in 1945 and we spent many hours on opening analysis. I was a knight-odds player in those days, and it was from Abe that I grasped the essence of positional play. He had enormous "sitzfleisch"—patience—the ability to sit on a position until his opponent got an idea (meaning "blundered"). Today playing "Turner style" means chopping pieces at every opportunity, particularly when a queen ahead, thus prolonging an easy win beyond human endurance.

Never really in financial difficulty because of his numerous friends and chess students—"clients" as he called them—Abe did not need the income or respectability of a job. One can only wish that he had remained jobless, even to endure the taunts of "chess bum." It is ironic, but had he not taken that fatal job he would be alive right now.

It's sad that Turner is best remembered for how he died rather than for how he lived. We can think of few players who reached Turner's level of play (rated over 2400) after such a late start—he didn't learn to play until his early twenties.

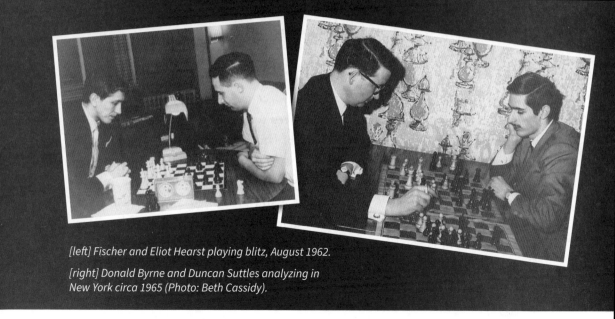

[left] Fischer and Eliot Hearst playing blitz, August 1962.

[right] Donald Byrne and Duncan Suttles analyzing in New York circa 1965 (Photo: Beth Cassidy).

An announcement that appeared in *American Chess Quarterly*[1] indicates Bobby's respect for Turner:

> Our editorial consultant, Bobby Fischer, who happened to come across the unpublished notes of the late Abe Turner covering the 1961 Fischer v. Reshevsky match for our magazine, suggested that Abe's notes merited being published, not only as a tribute to Abe's memory, but because they were good annotations.

International Master Lawrence Day spoke of the effect Turner's death had on Fischer:[2]

> According to Duncan and Dobrila Suttles (who only talked about it after Fischer's death) young Bobby considered Abe Turner as his major mentor and father figure. Turner's mysterious death was influential in Bobby's switch from atheistic Nietzscheism to Herbert Armstrong's popular radio cult Worldwide Church of God.
>
> Trusting that they wouldn't blab to the "creepy" media, Fischer opened up about some mysteries in his life. One was the split with his mother at age sixteen. According to Fischer this was when he was introduced to conspiracy theory. The Communist plot to take over the world was elaborated to him, and that he had a role to play in combating it. The problem: his mother, Regina, was herself a Communist. That motivated the family break, which lasted until the 1980s. Of his mentors, Fischer considered Abe Turner was his main influence as "father figure." It spooked Bobby greatly in 1962 when Turner was stabbed to death by ex-mental patient Theodore Smith. The murderer claimed the Secret Service had ordered it because Turner was a Communist spy. That mysterious death was the catalyst in Fischer switching his religious views from atheistic Nietzscheism to Herbert Armstrong's radio ministry.

---

[1] *American Chess Quarterly*, Spring 1964, (p. 295).

[2] Lawrence Day's chess column in the *Toronto Star*, May 3, 2008.

Grandmaster Duncan Suttles is correctly thought of as a Canadian player although he was born in San Francisco (December 21, 1945). His parents, Americans Wayne and Shirley Suttles, moved to Vancouver in 1951 where the young Duncan spent the next dozen years until his father received a position in the Anthropology department at the University of Nevada at Reno. While starting his university studies there, Suttles frequently played in U.S. tournaments, particularly in California. A series of successful events led him to qualify for the 1965/66 U.S. Championship where he played Bobby. We believe they may have first met in April 1964 during Fischer's clock simul at the University of California at Davis.

According to Day, Suttles knew Fischer in the '60s, but they didn't become friends until later. Bobby and Suttles competed in the Interzonal in Palma de Mallorca in 1970 and their paths would cross again in 1971 when Bobby played Taimanov in the first round of the Candidates matches in Vancouver.

In 1994, Suttles spent a week with Fischer in Budapest:

> We stayed at the same hotel he was living in. I spent a lot of time talking to Bobby at that time and we regularly ate dinner together.

Suttles' assessment of Turner's relationship to Bobby is plausible—Suttles has a reputation as someone with a good memory, trustworthy, and not prone to exaggeration. Of course, there are alternative explanations for the parting of Bobby and Regina—certainly, they were not the first mother and teenage son who had their differences.

Turner is not the only candidate that has been put forth as an important male figure in Bobby's formative years. Another name that has been mentioned is Harry Eckstrom. John Collins stated that Eckstrom was a regular at the apartment of Collins and his sister Ethel:[1]

> [Eckstrom and Bobby] hit it off to a T from the very beginning. Bobby could do no wrong in his eyes. And Bobby got a great kick out of playing, talking to him, and listening to his stories and jokes. I have the feeling of all those who visited us Bobby liked him best. As far as I know, Bobby is like me in that he seldom attends funerals, yet he was at Harry's and was as deeply grieved as the rest of us.

According to the Rosenwald Trophy Tournament report, Eliot Hearst (1932–2018) was under the psychological handicap of having just finished his master's thesis and of preparing for the Armed Forces. Hearst, who went on to earn a PhD and eventually became a Professor of Psychology at Indiana University, has a 50% lifetime score against Bobby, but is the first to admit that his timing

---

[1] John W. Collins, *My Seven Chess Prodigies*. New York: Simon & Schuster, 1975, (p. 40).

THIRD LESSING J. ROSENWALD TROPHY TOURNAMENT

Rank	Name	1	2	3	4	5	6	7	8	9	10	11	12	Total
1	Sammy Reshevsky	X	1	0.5	1	1	0	1	1	0.5	1	1	1	9
2	Arthur Bisguier	0	X	0.5	0.5	0	0.5	1	1	1	0.5	1	1	7
3	Arthur Feuerstein	0.5	0.5	X	0	1	0	0	0.5	1	1	1	1	6.5
4	Edmar Mednis	0	0.5	1	X	1	1	1	0.5	0.5	0*	0.5	0	6
5	Sidney Bernstein	0	1	0	0	X	1	0	0.5	1	0.5	1	0.5	5.5
6	Donald Byrne	1	0.5	1	0	0	X	1	0	0	1	0	1	5.5
7	Abe Turner	0	0	1	0	1	0	X	1	0	1	1	0.5	5.5
8	Robert Fischer	0	0	0.5	0.5	0.5	1	0	X	1	0	0.5	0.5	4.5
9	Hebert Seidman	0.5	0	0	0.5	0	1	1	0	X	0	0.5	1	4.5
10	Eliot Hearst	0	0.5	0	0*	0.5	0	0	1	1	X	0	1	4
11	Max Pavey	0	0	0	0.5	0	1	0	0.5	0.5	1	X	0.5	4
12	George Shainswit	0	0	0	1	0.5	0	0.5	0.5	0	0	0.5	X	3

* The double loss for Mednis and Hearst is not a mistake. It was a double forfeit. Hearst overstepped at move 40 and Mednis had quit keeping score. According to the rules of the time, both players got a zero!

was good. Hearst wrote about his game against Bobby at the Third Lessing J. Rosenwald Trophy Tournament, Game (20):[1]

> Of course I played him hundreds of games, starting with my giving him queen or rook odds and ending up in the 1960s with our playing blitz with me having 4½ minutes and him 1½ minutes. We were about even.
>
> I had been playing Bobby for two or three years before the following game took place. This was our first tournament game, as our prior games at the Marshall Chess Club and Columbia University Chess Club were all contested at very fast speeds. I believe I was able to give him rook odds in our initial games, but it soon became apparent that he was a chess genius and that someday in the near future I would no longer be able to hold my own against him. It is not well known that he used to appear occasionally at the Columbia Club after his high school classes were over for the day (or he might have failed to attend school that day at all!); Columbia's was the only club in New York where some strong players were usually available to play on weekday afternoons. At any rate, at the Rosenwald Tourney Bobby had beaten Donald Byrne a few days before in what became known as the "Game of the Century," and I was not at all sure that I should be considered the favorite in this game against a thirteen-year-old (I was twenty-four at the

[1] From a 2017 correspondence with chess historian Nikolai Brunni.

time, had been playing in tournaments since I was thirteen, and had gained a master's rating). Bobby had already established himself as someone who would virtually always open with the Ruy Lopez if his opponent permitted it. I decided beforehand to permit [it], but not to meet the opening with one of the most common defenses against it.

(20) Ruy Lopez
Bobby Fischer – Eliot Hearst
New York 1956

Annotations by Eliot Hearst.

1.e4 e5 2.Nf3 Nc6 3.Bb5 Bc5

The relatively unusual Classical or Cordel Defense to the Ruy Lopez.

4.0-0

Most common here is 4.c3, aiming for an early d4.

4...Nd4 5.Nxd4 Bxd4 6.c3 Bb6 7.d4 c6 8.Ba4 d6 9.Na3 Nf6 10.Re1 Qe7 11.Bg5 h6

Up to here the play has more or less followed some previously played grandmaster games.

12.Bh4

This is a mistake, in my opinion. Since Black can still castle queenside, he does not fear initiating a pawn storm on the kingside; he has no intention of castling on that side of the board.

12...g5 13.Bg3 h5 14.f3 h4 15.Bf2 g4 16.Nc4 g3!

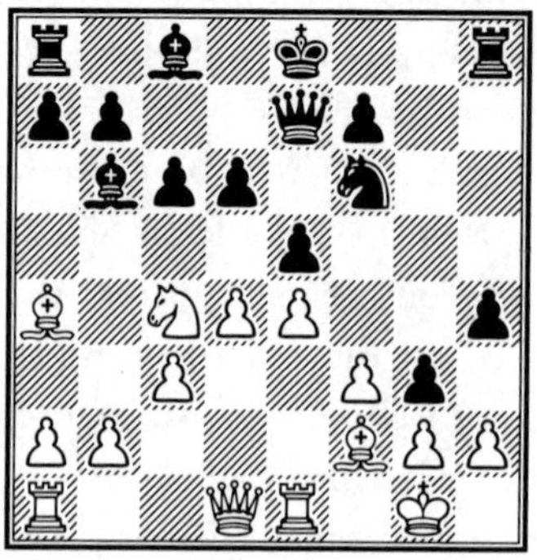

The opening of lines to White's king seemed to justify this pawn sacrifice.

17.hxg3 hxg3 18.Bxg3 Nh5 19.Bh2 Bc7

With the minor threat of ...b5, but the major purpose of saving this bishop for later use against White's king.

20.Ne3 Qh4 21.Qd2 Bd7 22.Bb3 Rh7 23.Qf2 Qg5 24.Rad1 Nf4

Of course threatening a disastrous fork with ...Nh3+.

25.Bxf4

The move 25.Qg3 gives Black much more trouble. (I was in a bookstore looking at Karsten Müller's book *Bobby Fischer: The Career and Complete Games of the American World Chess Champion*, and saw Müller's note: "25. Qg3 leads to a more or less forced draw: 25...Qh5 26. dxe5 dxe5 27. Qg8+ Ke7 28. Qxa8 Qxh2+ 29. Kf2 Qh4+." [In fact, 29...Rg7! Gives Black a winning position here.]

25...exf4 26.Nf5?

Appears aggressive but leaves the knight out on a limb. 26.Nc4 was much better [then 26...0-0-0 gives Black a winning game]. Now Black gains a definite advantage.

26...0-0-0

Black is fully mobilized for his attack against White's king. Recalling the game about thirty years later, Bobby told me "you gotta terrific compensation in that game!"

27.Kf1 Rh2 28.Bxf7

Losing a piece eventually but it is hard to suggest a better defense.

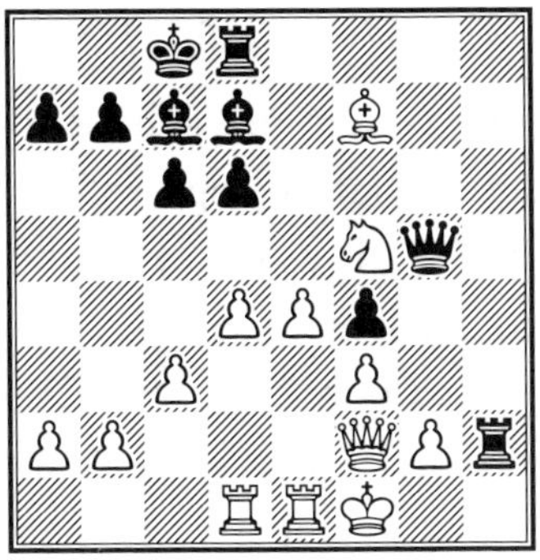

28...d5!

Trapping the bishop or at least giving White major defensive problems.

29.Rd2 Rf8 30.Qg1

If instead 30.Bg6 (hoping for 30...Qxg6 31.Ne7+) then Black simply replies 30...Kb8 and the bishop still has nowhere to go.

30...Rh7 31.exd5 Rhxf7 32.dxc6 Bxc6

Now White's knight is trapped, too. Against a grandmaster opponent Bobby would probably have resigned here. But we were both in tremendous time pressure to reach the fortieth move.

33.d5 Bb5+ 34.Ree2 Rxf5 35.Qxa7 Rxd5 36.c4 Bxc4 37.Qa8+ Bb8 38.Rc2 Rc5⁈

I was merely trying to play safe moves so that I could avoid a loss on time. Were I looking for an immediate tactical win I might have seen 38...Rd1+ 39.Kf2 Qg3 mate. As soon as the game was over everyone in the crowd surrounding our game (allowed in those days) pointed out this checkmate to me. I was abashed but so happy to win that I was able to laugh at my blunder.

39.Ke1 Bxe2 40.Qa5

In a totally lost position and extreme time pressure Bobby found this tricky move. Somehow I am impressed by this last-gasp try, even though it can be refuted in numerous ways.

40...Qg3, 0–1.

Now that I have reached the time control without overstepping the time limit, my recollection is that Bobby resigned right now. However, some collections of Bobby's games continue with the following moves, which I do not believe occurred: 41.Kd2 Rd8+ 42.Qxd8+ Kxd8 43.Rxc5 Qxg2. I consider this game one of the five best games I ever played, regardless of whether it was played against a future World Champion. My only regret about it was missing the forced mate on move thirty-eight.

Despite having turned in a very respectable performance in the Rosenwald Trophy (an even score against all but the top two finishers and a brilliant victory against Donald Byrne—the so-called "Game of the Century") a few months before, Bobby was unable to qualify for the top section of the Manhattan Chess Club Championship. He scored only 50% (2½–2½) in the semi-final held in late 1956 and early 1957, losing to Max Pavey and Abe Turner. The accepted ending of his win over Joe Tamargo might be wrong, or maybe not.

---

(21) Sicilian
Joe Tamargo – Fischer
New York 1956–57

1.e4 c5 2.d4 cxd4 3.c3 Nf6 4.e5 Nd5 5.cxd4 Nc6 6.Nc3 Nxc3 7.bxc3 d5 8.Bd3 e6 9.Ne2 Be7 10.0-0 Bd7 11.f4 g6 12.g4 Qc7 13.f5 gxf5 14.gxf5 exf5 15.Ng3 0-0-0 16.Nxf5 Be6 17.Kh1 h5 18.Qf3 Rdg8 19.Nh6 Rf8 20.Bf5 Qd7 21.Bd2 f6 22.Bxe6 Qxe6 23.Qf5 Qxf5 24.Nxf5 fxe5 25.Nxe7+ Nxe7 26.dxe5 Kd7 27.Bg5 Ke6 28.Bf6 Rhg8 29.Rab1 b6 30.Rfd1 Rc8 31.Bxe7 Kxe7 32.Rxd5 Rxc3 33.a4 Ke6 34.Rdb5 Ra3

35.a5 bxa5 36.R1b3 Rxb3 37.Rxb3 Rg5 38.Rb7 Kxe5 39.Rxa7 Kd4 40.h4

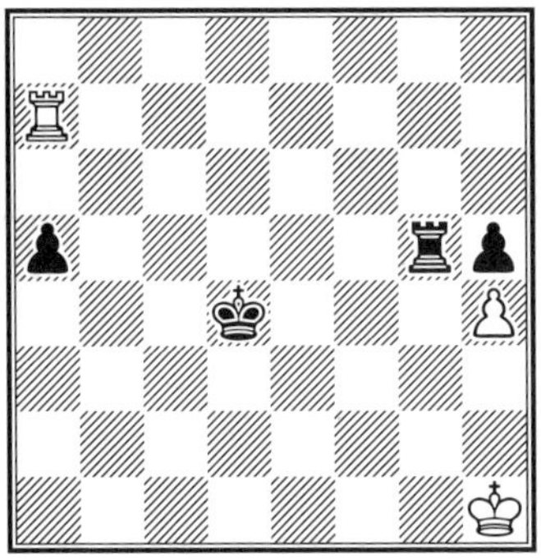

Here the end of the game has historically been given as....

40...Rg4, 0–1.

The original source for the game score was the booklet on this event done by Jack Spence. Spence had a tough job as many of the score sheets he worked from were not very legible. This led him to have to make educated guesses from time to time, with the occasional mistake slipping through.

That does not seem to be the case for this game. Spence used English description notation for his publications as was standard practice in the 1950s and 1960s. His game score reads: 40...R-N4, which makes one immediately wonder if Fischer's fortieth move wasn't 40...Rb5 (easily winning) instead of 40...Rg4 which allows 41.Rxa5 drawing. Indeed Robert Hübner and Karsten Müller have both given the game ending 40...Rb5, unable to believe Bobby would have committed such a blunder as 40...Rg4??.

This would seem to be the end of the story except that Tamargo had written that Bobby actually played 40...Rg4 with the game continuing a few moves longer.

Joe Tamargo (1938–2013) was a strong master who won the 1976 Marshall Chess Club Championship. He was also an accomplished Go player. Tamargo posted three times at chessgames.com in 2003 about this game:

> Oct-18-03: The explanation is that I put my rook en prise a move later. I was upset because I had offered a draw and little Bobby piped up "Are you crazy?" Note the spelling of my name. It's Tamargo, not "Tomargo." I'm a well-known New York master. They've been misspelling it for nearly fifty years, ever since Jack Spence (who was a nice man but maybe not the brightest guy in the world) got it wrong in the tournament book.

> Oct-19-03: I don't remember which move I made to hang the rook. It was a move or two later. Disgusted with myself I didn't bother to write it down,

just resigned. Of course I didn't think anybody would ever care. Bobby had all the talent anyway. Eventually I saw the light and made money betting on him.

Oct-20-03: No, we all found out in 1957 that he was the real article. My f5 was the kind of impetuous move a young player makes; probably should have built first. Also managed to trade off my good bishop. Enough of this. Bye.

PART TWO

Breakthrough!

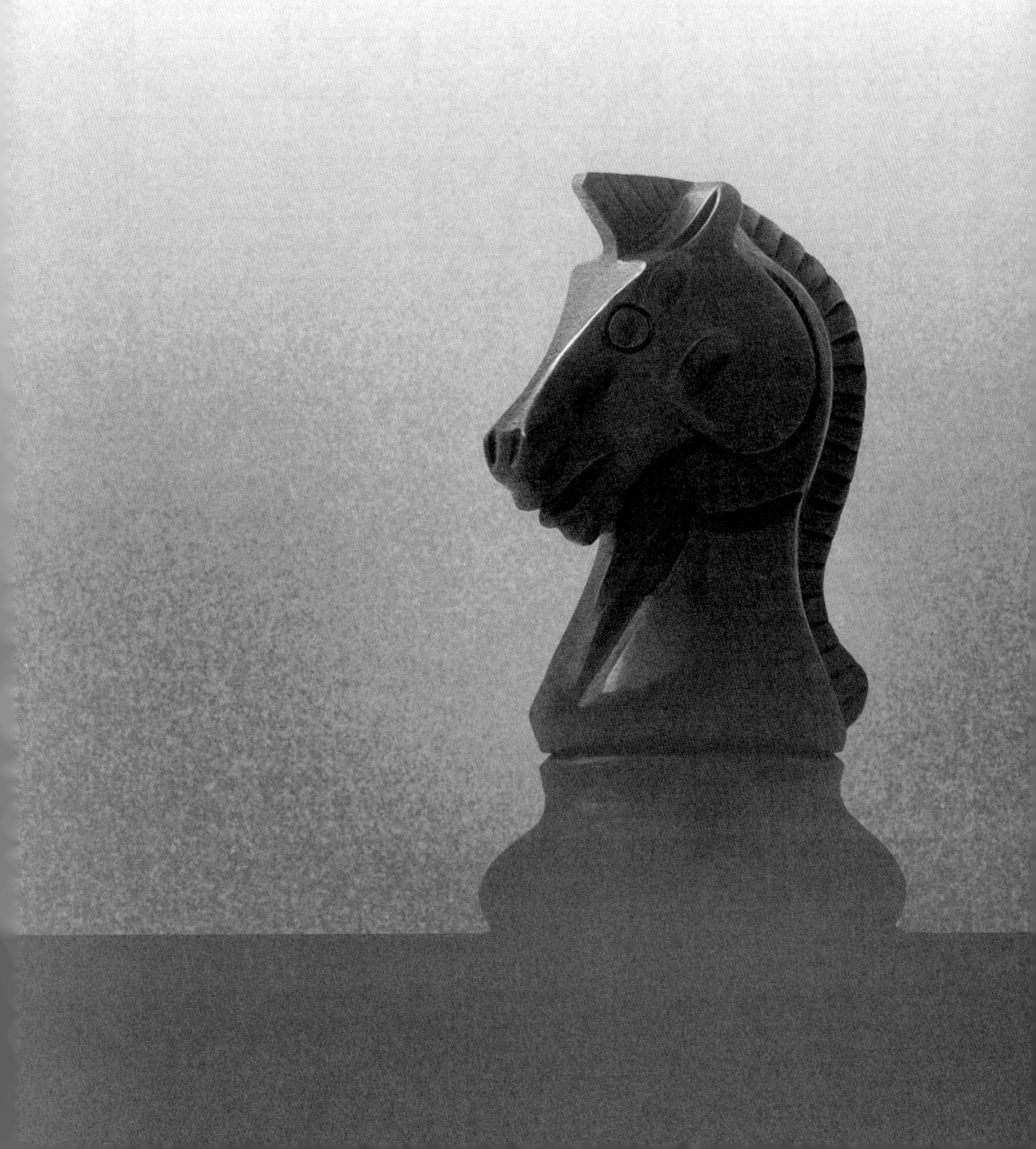

GAME No. 2

MANHATTAN CHESS CLUB

SINCE 1877

America's Oldest - Ever Progressive

Event E x H Round 2 Date March 10-57

White: Mr. Robert J. Fischer Black: Mr. Dr Max Euwe

WHITE		BLACK	WHITE		BLACK	WHITE		BLACK
P-K4	1	P-K4	B-Q4	31	P-KR4		61	
N-KB3	2	N-QB3	R-KB1	32	B-Q6		62	
B-N5	3	P-QR3	R-K1	33	R-B3		63	
B-R4	4	N-KB3	R-K3	34	B-K5		64	
O-O	5	NxP	Q-K2	35	Q-B4		65	
P-Q4	6	P-QN4	K-B2	36	P-R5		66	
B-N3	7	P-Q4	K-K1	37	PxP		67	
PxP	8	B-K3	PxP	38	B-R3		68	
P-B3	9	B-K2	K-Q2	39	B-N8		69	
QN-Q2	10	O-O	R-B3	40	B-R8		70	
Q-K2	11	N-B4	R-B1	41	Draw		71	
N-Q4	12	NxB		42			72	
QNxN	13	Q-Q2		43			73	
NxN	14	QxN		44			74	
B-K3	15	B-B5						
Q-Q2	16	P-QB4						
N-R5	17	Q-R5						
N-B6	18	KR-K1						
P-KN3	19	Q-R4						
NxB+	20	RxN						
BxP	21	R-B2						
B-Q4	22	B-N5						
P-KB4	23	R-B3						
P-QR4	24	PxP						
RxP	25	R-R3						
Q-B2	26	B-B4						
KR-R1	27	QR-B1						
R-N4	28	R-N3						
R-N6	29	RxR						
BxR	30	Q-N5						

[above] Bobby's score sheet from the second game of his match with Max Euwe;

[right] Cover of Chess Review *depicting Fischer–Euwe.*

1
A MATCH WITH EUWE

1957 started off slowly. Bobby played very little in the first half of the year and attended school on a regular basis. He tied for 6th–14th at 4–2 in the 61-player Log Cabin Independent Open, held February 22–24, with losses to Herbert Avram and Anthony Santasiere. However, by summer, Bobby had metamorphized from promising master to one of the country's best. In autumn, he made the next logical jump to national champion!

Anthony Santasiere (1904–1977) was one of the top American players from the mid-1920s to the 1950s. A frequent contributor to the *American Chess Bulletin,* Santasiere was noted for his love of romantic chess although his own play tended to be more practical.

The first World Champion Bobby faced was Max Euwe. Even though the fifty-five-year-old Dutchmen was no longer at his peak, he was still a formidable opponent when they met in a two-game match in the spring of 1957.

The two-game match was held at the Manhattan Chess Club and likely organized by the club manager Hans Kmoch who was always supportive of Bobby. The first game was held on Fischer's fourteenth birthday and he met Euwe's 1.d4 with his favorite Ragozin Defense. Unfortunately for Bobby he blundered in an equal position on move thirteen and had to resign before move twenty-one. The next day Bobby came back for the second game and gave a much better account of himself.

Until recently only the first fifteen moves of Game (22) were available—this changed in 2011 with the publication of the entire score.[1]

Brady provides some background:

> I found Bobby's personal score sheets of his match with Euwe stuffed at the bottom of a box[2] that Regina Fischer had kept for years, and that eventually went to Bobby's sister Joan. Now, more than a half-century later, this game—a true Fischer relic—can be seen. That a fourteen-year-old could draw with a

[1] The game, with annotations by Grandmaster Lev Alburt, appears alongside an interview with Frank Brady. *Chess Life*, February 2011, (pp. 22-23).

[2] The box of score sheets that Brady is referring to is part of the donation Russell Targ made to the Marshall Chess Club.

[top] Sonja Graf and Max Euwe;

[middle] Herman Steiner, the tournament director, young Arturo Pomar, and Max Euwe in London 1946;

[bottom] Max Euwe and George Koltanowski at the Paul Masson Chess Festival, Saratoga, California, 1976 (Photo: Richard Shorman).

former World Champion is testament to Bobby's growing talent at that time. The first score sheet (Bobby's loss to Euwe) was severely creased and damaged, but the score sheet of his draw was in fairly good condition, as indicated in the accompanying illustration.

(22) Ruy Lopez
Fischer – Max Euwe
New York (2) March 10, 1957

1.e4 e5 2.Nf3 Nc6 3.Bb5 a6 4.Ba4 Nf6 5.0-0 Nxe4

Certain opening lines were known to give Fischer problems at different points in his career, the Winawer variation of the French and the Two Knights line against the Caro Kann being early trouble spots. This said, arguably the most troublesome line Fischer faced throughout his career was the Open variation of the Ruy Lopez. Bobby was renowned for his skill in playing the Ruy, but in fact this was true of only the Closed variation (5...Be7) and not the Open (5....Nxe4). His career record against the latter was a modest two wins, one loss and four draws.

6.d4 b5 7.Bb3 d5 8.dxe5

Bobby tried the uncommon 8.Nxe5 against Addison at the 1966 U.S. Championship, but achieved nothing after 8...Nxe5 9.dxe5 c6 10.Be3 Be7 11.Nd2 Nxd2 12.Qxd2 0-0 13.Qc3 Bb7 14.f4 a5 15.a3 b4, the game ending in an uneventful draw at move thirty-one. White often wants to advance his f-pawn in the Open Ruy, so from that point 8.Nxe5 makes sense. However Black also wants to activate his pawn majority and trading knights makes ...c7-c5 easy to realize.

8...Be6 9.c3

The last time Bobby faced the Open Ruy, he tried 9.Qe2 and quickly won a pawn when his opponent blundered after 9...Be7 10.Rd1 0-0 11.c4 bxc4 12.Bxc4 Qd7!? 13.Nc3 Nxc3 14.bxc3 f6 15.exf6 Bxf6 16.Bg5 with 16...Na5? instead of 16...Kh8. After 17.Qxe6+ Qxe6 18.Bxd5 Qxd5 19.Rxd5 Bxc3 20.Rc1 Bb4 21.Rxc7 White soon won in Fischer–Ree, Netanya 1968.

9...Be7

9...Bc5 10.Nbd2 0-0 11.Bc2

Bobby faced the Dilworth Attack early in his career against Wilmer Stevens at the 1956 U.S. Open in Oklahoma City: 11...Nxf2 12.Rxf2 Bxf2+ 13.Kxf2 f6 14.exf6 Qxf6 15.Kg1 Rae8 16.Nf1 Ne5 17.Ne3? (17.Be3 Nxf3+ 18.Qxf3 Qxf3 19.gxf3 Rxf3 20.Bf2 Bh3 is the main line and has been tested many times.) 17...Nxf3+ 18.Qxf3 Qxf3 19.gxf3 Rxf3 20.Bd1 Rf7 (20...Rf6 is an improvement when Black is better) draw.

11...Bf5 12.Nb3 Bg4 13.Nxc5 Nxc5 14.Re1 Re8 with equal chances was Fischer–Larsen, Piatigorsky Cup 1966. Larsen went on to win this game after Fischer blundered in an equal position looking for a non-existent mating attack. This was the start of three consecutive losses that landed Bobby in the cellar before he launched one of the most celebrated comebacks in the history of chess.

Larsen had great results with the Open Ruy in 1966, using it to make a couple of draws with Geller in their Candidates match playoff. However, a year later a book by him appeared in German with the title loosely translated: *What should the club player play against the Ruy Lopez? The Open variation!* This was a signal the Dane had retired this line from his opening repertoire, which proved to be the case.

While Larsen may have personally discarded the line its adoption still makes a lot of sense for amateur players. Like the Tarrasch Defense against the Queen's Gambit, the Open Ruy offers activity for all of Black's pieces, albeit at some cost in the pawn structure.

10.Nbd2

Bobby later varied with 10.Bc2 0-0 (10...Bg4 11.h3 Bh5 12.g4 Bg6 13.Bb3 Na5 [13...Nc5! with the point that 14.Qxd5 0-0 15.Qxc6?? is met by 15...Be4] 14.Bxd5 c6 15.Bxe4 Bxe4 16.Qxd8+ Rxd8 17.Nbd2 and White is a pawn up although Black probably has enough compensation, Fischer–Ólafsson, Havana (ol) 1966.)

11.Nbd2 f5 12.Nb3 Qd7 13.Nbd4 Nxd4 14.Nxd4 c5 15.Ne2 (15.Nxe6 is much more common) 15...Rad8 16.Nf4 Qc6 (16...c4 Lékó–Kamsky, Zug 2013.) 17.a4 with a very small advantage for White, Fischer–Unzicker, Piatigorsky Cup 1966. This game, which was eventually drawn, was all that stopped Bobby from winning six games in a row against world class grandmasters in rounds eleven through sixteen.

10...0-0 11.Qe2 Nc5 12.Nd4 Nxb3 13.N2xb3

The zwischenzug 13.Nxc6 would be countered by the intermezzo 13...Nxc1.

13...Qd7 14.Nxc6 Qxc6 15.Be3

Euwe was familiar with this position, having played 15...Bf5 twenty-three years earlier against Botvinnik (Leningrad 1934) and 15...f6 versus Broadbent (England–Netherlands 1948).

15...Qc4

This is where the standard sources (i.e. *Bobby Fischer's Chess Games* by Wade and O'Connell and more recently Karsten Müller's *Bobby Fischer: The Career and Complete Games of the American World Champion)* have the game ending.

16.Qd2 c5?

This stops the threat of Nd4 and b3 winning material, but at a serious cost. Better is 16...Qg4 (Anand–Lékó, Amber Blindfold Rapid 2006) although after 17.Bc5 White has a small but persistent advantage.

17.Na5

Also quite attractive is throwing in 17.f4 first. For example 17.f4 Bf5 18.Na5 Qe4 (or 18...Qd3 19.Qxd3 Bxd3 20.Nc6 Bh4 21.Rfd1 Be4 22.Bxc5 Rfc8 23.Ne7+ Bxe7 24.Bxe7) 19.Nc6 Bh4 20.Bxc5 Rfc8 21.Ne7+ Bxe7 22.Bxe7. Whether the queens are left on or exchanged, Black is struggling.

17...Qh4 18.Nc6 Rfe8 19.g3

The point of Bobby's play—the queen is driven away from the bishop which protects the c-pawn. The direct 19.f4 is also good

19...Qh5 20.Nxe7+ Rxe7 21.Bxc5 Rc7 22.Bd4

Natural, but 22.Bd6, 22.Qe3, and 22.Qd4, intending b4 and a4, were all more accurate. The latter two are particularly attractive as they offer White good play in the center and the queenside.

22...Bg4 23.f4 Rc6 24.a4

[Lev Alburt in his annotations to the game for *Chess Life* online.]:
"Fischer creates counterplay, and a diversion, on the queenside. Note how the character of play somewhat resembles the Marshall Gambit—except that in the Marshall many endings are drawish, while here they would clearly favor White"

24...bxa4 25.Rxa4 Rh6

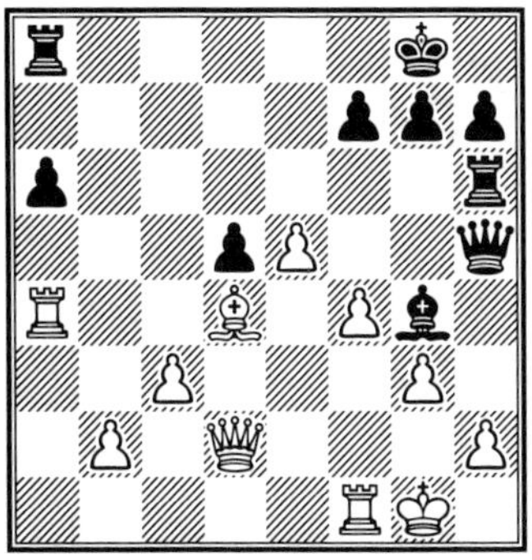

26.Qf2

Alburt points to 26.Be3 as very strong and indeed Stockfish seconds his assessment of the position. After 26...Bf5 27.Rd4 Be4 28.c4! Rc6 (28...Rc8 29.Rxd5 is very strong) 29. Rxd5! Rcc8 30.f5 is crushing.

26...Bf5 27.Rfa1 Rc8 28.Rb4

28.Rxa6?? Rxa6 29.Rxa6 Qd1+ 30.Qf1 (30.Kg2 Be4+ 31.Kh3 Qh5 mate) 30...Qxf1+ 31.Kxf1 Bd3+.

28...Rg6 29.Rb6

This exchanges off one aggressive piece, but Black's remaining forces are still very active.

29...Rxb6 30.Bxb6 Qg4 31.Bd4

White can win the enemy a-pawn, but after 31.Qf1 Be4 32.Rxa6 h5 Black has excellent counterplay against the White king.

31...h5

A typical move for these type of positions. Black prepares to attack the enemy king while gaining breathing space for his own monarch.

32.Rf1 Bd3

32...Be4 33.Re1 h4 was simple enough.

33.Re1 Rc6 34.Re3 Be4 35.Qe2

[Alburt]: "White misses a chance to better place his kingside pawns, thus securing his king's safety, and an edge: 35.Qf1 followed by 36.h3, and then 37.Kh2."

White can certainly initiate this plan with 35.Qf1 but after 35...Qf5 (35...Rc4?? 36.Rxe4) 36.h3 Rc4 37.Kh2 Ra4 it's not clear how to make progress and care must be taken—i.e. 38.Qe2?? Ra1.

35...Qf5 36.Kf2

Trailing in the match, having lost the first game, Bobby decides to transfer his king to the queenside so he can freely advance his kingside pawns. The flaw in this plan is that he makes his king a target for the Black pieces.

36...h4 37.Ke1 hxg3 38.hxg3?

Returning the pawn by 38.Rxg3 Qxf4 39.Qe3 was essential.

38...Rh6 39.Kd2 Bb1!

The threat of ...Qc2+ is deadly.

40.Rf3 Rh1

40...Qc2+ 41.Ke3 Qe4+ 42.Kd2 Rh2 43.Rf2 (43.Qxh2 Qc2+) 43...Qc2+ 44.Ke3 Qc1+ 45.Qd2 Qg1 46.Qe2 Bf5 and White is completely tied up and unable to defend against the threat of...Bg4. (46...Qxg3+ 47.Kd2 Rh1

48.Rf1 lets White escape)) 47.Bc5 Bg4 followed by taking on g3 ends all resistance.

40...Rh2 41.Rf2 Qc2+ 42.Ke3 Qc1+ 43.Qd2 Qg1 transposes. Euwe's move also wins.

41.Rf1, ½–½.

Grandmaster Alburt is correct when he writes: "Perhaps Euwe was happy with the draw (after all, he won the match) and also felt that Bobby, who played very well and indeed was better through most of the game, deserved this one draw."

However his assertion that White can hold in the final position is mistaken: 41...Rh2 42.Rf2 Qc2+ 43.Ke3 Qc1+ 44.Qd2 Qg1 45.Qe2 Bf5 and again there is no defense against ...Bg4.

On June 13, 1957, Fischer was among four players that beat Sammy Reshevsky (the top player in the U.S.) during a blindfold exhibition he gave at the Manhattan Chess Club in celebration of the club's victory in the Met League. Reshevsky was challenged by ten players, one after another, at ten seconds a move and won six of the games (two of the strong players who went down in defeat were Gresser and Shipman).

Bobby was improving at a fast pace—less than six months later he was national champion!

In this classic photo (photographer unknown) of Bobby at the Manhattan Chess Club, June 1957, he is pictured on the black side of the Queen's Indian—an opening never associated with Fischer who even in his youth preferred the more aggressive King's Indian. The position on the board appears to have arisen via the opening moves: 1.d4 Nf6 2.c4 e6 3.Nf3 b6 4.g3 Bb7 5.Bg2 Be7 6.0-0 0-0 7.Nc3 Ne4 8.Qc2 Nxc3 9.Qxc3 f5 10.b3 Qe8 11.Ne1 Bxg2 12.Nxg2 Bf6 13.Bb2 Nc6 14.Qd2 and now Bobby is getting ready to move his queen.

During the subsequent seven months Bobby made a huge jump in strength—going from a 2300 player to world class. Among his victories during this stretch were the U.S. Junior in San Francisco, the U.S. Open in Cleveland and finally the U.S. Championship.

James Gore plays Black against Orest Popovych at the Marshall Chess Club circa 1965 (Photo: Beth Cassidy).

2
THE SENSATIONAL SUMMER OF 1957

Unlike today, when players can choose between several events every week, the 1950s offered few opportunities. There were no World Opens, National Opens, Chicago Opens, etc. Not only were there few national tournaments, but regional ones were also hard to find. Bobby got around this by playing training games and participating in specially arranged events like the Ruy Lopez Thematic. Unfortunately, few of his score sheets from this period have surfaced.

The Ruy Lopez Thematic Tournament, arranged and directed by Hans Kmoch, was held May–June 1957 at the Manhattan Chess Club with a flexible playing schedule. Four score sheets from the this tournament are in the possession of the Marshall Chess Club's Targ Collection but have not been made public:

1. Seropian–Fischer, Round 2, Steinitz Deferred, 0–1 in 25 moves.
2. Feuerstein–Fischer, Round 4, Mainline Chigorin, ½–½ in 51 moves
3. Fischer–Tamargo, Round 5, Mainline Chigorin, 1–0 in 35 moves.
4. Fischer–Gore, Round 6, Open Ruy Lopez, 6/9/57, ½–½ in 28 moves.

Hugh Myers offered the opening moves of a practice game he played with Bobby in the summer of 1957:[1]

> One of the game scores I most regret not being able to find is of one played in the summer of 1957. I was at the Manhattan Chess Club, just talking to Lombardy and a few other experts/masters. Bobby Fischer walked in, said he wanted some serious practice, and asked me for a game at tournament time controls (40 in 2, as I recall). This was okay, so we played, and I lost in about four hours. I'm only sure that it started 1.e4 e5 2.Nf3 Nc6 3.Bb5 a6 4.Ba4 Nf6 5.0-0 Be7 6.Re1 b5 7.Bb3 d6 8.c3 0-0 9.h3 Nb8, as in a 1992 Fischer–Spassky match game. I never played the Breyer Defense before or since, but Lombardy had just been talking to me about it. He watched the whole game ...and then berated me for losing it!

James Gore is one of a small group of individuals who are frequently mentioned as being close to Fischer—others include Jackie Beers, Jim Buff, Asa Hoffman,

[1] Hugh E. Myers, *A Chess Explorer: Life and Games*. Davenport, Iowa: MOB, 2002, (p. 40–41).

Sam Sloan, and Bernard Zuckerman. Not much is known about Gore, who was a few years older than Bobby and a strong master. Brady described him:

> A tall redheaded boy who dressed conservatively even as a teen and who adopted a condescending attitude towards anyone he defeated, had a great influence on Bobby.

There has been speculation that Fischer's interest in Hitler and the Third Reich had originally been kindled by Gore. Zuckerman, for one, believes this might have been the case. Gore stopped playing in tournaments in 1971, but still remained close with Bobby. When Mayor Lindsay gave Bobby the key to New York City, right next to him were his good friends Sloan, Zuckerman, and Gore. Not long after, Gore disappeared from the chess world and has not been heard from in nearly fifty years.

Another friend from Fischer's youth was Jackie Beers. Brady wrote of Beers:

> Since Bobby's suite had two bedrooms, he liked to have guests from time to time. Jackie Beers was his most frequent visitor. Bobby had known Jackie since childhood and they were an odd pair. Jackie was a rated expert, an excellent speed player, but he was always finding himself in trouble at chess clubs, usually because of his ferocious temper. Once, a fight at the Manhattan Chess Club resulted in a lawsuit against him that was eventually settled out of court, and there were stories of his chasing people in the street or their chasing him because of altercations. With Bobby, Jackie acted meekly and respectfully. He often stayed overnight in the Fischer apartment in Brooklyn and later was Bobby's houseguest when Fischer lived in California. Jackie was no sycophant or whipping boy, as he's been described by other writers. He recognized that Bobby was the "chief" of their friendship, but he wasn't afraid to speak up and disagree. While Bobby knew of Jackie's reputation for truculence and tolerated him nevertheless, he was careful not to include him in all areas of his life, knowing instinctively when Beers wouldn't be welcomed by others"

The poet and author Shaindel Beers wrote these words in 2012 about her uncle whom she met once in her early teens:

> You're writing about my Uncle Jack. I think the last time he contacted my parents was about a year ago. He has had mental illness issues and also leukemia.
>
> My dad and Uncle Jack grew up with Bobby. Their mothers took turns watching each other's kids, so I think it's natural they were best friends their entire lives. I don't think there was any "hanger on" status about it.

One curious thing to note about Beers is his late start playing tournament chess. He didn't appear on the USCF rating list until his early twenties, but that didn't stop him from making quick progress going from 1783 in 1964 to 2048 three years later. Eventually he became a master and was still playing into the mid-1990s.

NEW WESTERN OPEN (1957)

This was the summer that Bobby experienced his first taste of independence. He had made long trips before, but always accompanied by an adult. That July and August Bobby spent a month and a half away from his family and Brooklyn, playing in tournaments around the country and hanging out with newly-made friends.

The trip began with the New Western Open in Milwaukee. Today, the largest city in Wisconsin is a quiet town for chess, but from the 1930s to the 1960s it was one of the most important chess centers in the United States, particularly renowned for its scholastic program. During the Depression, the Milwaukee Municipal Recreation Department come up with the brilliant idea to teach chess to kids and adults through the city's recreational centers. The program, under the direction of Ernst Olfe (1898–1966), flourished and tens of thousands were introduced to the Royal Game. Among the well-known chess personalities that taught in the program were Arthur Dake and George Koltanowski.

Arpad Elo (1903–1992), inventor of the rating system that bears his name, was a master level player who won the Milwaukee city championship and Wisconsin state title on numerous occasions.

Elo was one of a number of Milwaukee organizers and tournament directors who had a national reputation. Pearl Mann (1922–1986) took over running the Milwaukee Municipal Recreation Department program in 1965 and served on the USCF Policy Board. She was a FIDE arbiter (the first woman to be awarded this title) and served as the Zonal president for the United States in FIDE. Mann also directed the 1963 Western Open in Bay City, Michigan, that Bobby played in.

Fred Cramer (1913–1989), best known for helping Fischer in Reykjavík, served as USCF president from 1960–1963. A U.S. delegate to FIDE and a FIDE vice-president, Cramer was the one who drafted the proposed regulations for the Fischer–Karpov match in Baguio that ultimately didn't happen.

Milwaukee also had a first-rate player in International Master William Martz. A participant in two U.S. Championships and several Student Olympiads, Martz also represented the United States in the 1972 Olympiad. The top player in Wisconsin for almost twenty years, he died of cancer in 1983 at the age of thirty-seven, less than a year after he had tied for first in the U.S. Open.

Fischer played in Milwaukee twice in 1957—the New Western Open over the July 4th weekend and the North Central Open over Thanksgiving. The fields

[left] Povilas Tautvaisas (Photo: Val Zemitis); [right] George Koltanowski circa 1990 (Photo: Richard Shorman).

in both events were quite strong by American standards of the time, in part due to the tournament's proximity to Chicago.

Fischer tied for sixth to twelfth in the summer event that was won by Donald Byrne and Larry Evans, with 6 from 8.

Later in the year Fischer returned to Milwaukee where he scored 5 from 7, tying for fifth. He lost to Charles Kalme in round five. This game was the last time Fischer lost in a Swiss system tournament.

Two of Fischer's games from events in Milwaukee are missing—the penultimate round of the New Western Open with Tautvaisas and the last round with Szedlacsek (North Central Open).

The game with Szedlacsek is in the Targ donation, but the chances of finding the one with Tautvaisas seems slim. This is a pity as he was known for his aggressive style of play and the game would likely have been lively. Povilas Tautvaisas (1916–1980) played twice for his native Lithuania in Chess Olympiads before settling in the United States after World War II. A fixture at Chicago tournaments in the 1950s and '60s, his resourcefulness in difficult positions earned him the nickname "The Old Fox."

Much less is known of the Hungarian born Szedlacsek (pronounced zed-la-chek). Tibor Weinberger, who like his countryman escaped after the Soviet invasion in 1956, recalls that Szedlacsek was known in Budapest as a formidable rapid player and a medium strength master. He was in his fifties and past his prime when he faced Fischer, but still strong enough to tie for thirteenth (out of 176 players) in the 1957 U.S. Open held in his new hometown of Cleveland.

Richard Fauber, who lost to Fischer in the first round of the New Western Open, commented on the two Eastern European refugees:[1]

> Tautvaisas was known as "Sausage" for his habit of taking bites of a large cylinder of lunch meat and saying with mouth full. "You want to go here and threaten...I cannot permit that so..." Clunk, he would move a piece with greasy hand. Delicatessen gamesmanship.
>
> Szedlacsek was a refugee from the abortive Hungarian revolution that brought Benko to our shores too. In Cleveland he was known for geniality (and his hands were grease free when he moved). A gentlemen of chess as my friend Ron Rosen recalls.
>
> One sidelight. My game with Fischer often includes a diagram. At the diagrammed position I was going to resign, but the room was full of players so I kept going until there were fewer to see me resign.

The New Western Open ended on July 7th and Bobby flew immediately to San Francisco to defend his U.S. Junior title.

U.S. JUNIOR (1957)

Chess Life reported on the U.S. Junior, held July 8–14 in San Francisco:[2]

> The Brooklyn master junior (or junior master) Robert Fischer gathered in the U.S. Junior title in stride at San Francisco with an 8½–½ score, drawing one game with California State Champion Gilbert Ramirez. Ramirez of San Francisco placed second with 7½–1½, losing no games but drawing with Richard Owen of Salt Lake City and Ronald Thacker of Richmond, in addition to Fischer. Stephen Sholomson of Los Angeles, who has recently shot into prominence on the Pacific Coast, was third with 6½–2½, losing to Fischer and Ramirez, and drawing with Leonard Hill of Mt. View. Thacker was fourth with 6–3, losing to Fischer and Hill while drawing with Ramirez and Ralph Clark of Long Beach.
>
> Fifth to tenth on Median points with 5½–3½ each were Mike Bredoff of Redwood City, Leonard Hill, Arthur Wang of Berkeley, Ralph Clark, Robert Walker of Portland, and Warren Miller of Albuquerque. Eleventh to fourteenth with 5–4 each were Rex Wilcox of Salinas, Andrew Schoene of Malaga, Thomas Heldt Jr. of Albuquerque, and David Krause of Palo Alto.
>
> Fred Wreden, aged ten, of San Francisco, won custody of the Independent-Press Telegraph Trophy for ranking players under thirteen years; the Milwaukee Journal Independent Press Telegram Trophy for ranking players under fifteen and the Hermann Dittman Trophy all went to fourteen-year-old Bobby Fischer.

---

[1] Letter to author dated June 17, 2012.

[2] *Chess Life*, August 5, 1957, (p. 1).

[right] Fischer plays Steven Sholomson while tournament directed George Koltanowski intently studies the action on a neighboring board. Roy Hoppe is playing Black in the game directly behind Bobby while John Blackstone is immediately behind Kolti;

[below] Bobby watches Ron Thacker (White) vs. Gil Ramirez in the 1957 U.S. Junior Open in San Francisco (Photos: California Chess Reporter archives).

San Francisco Chronicle

THE VOICE OF THE WEST

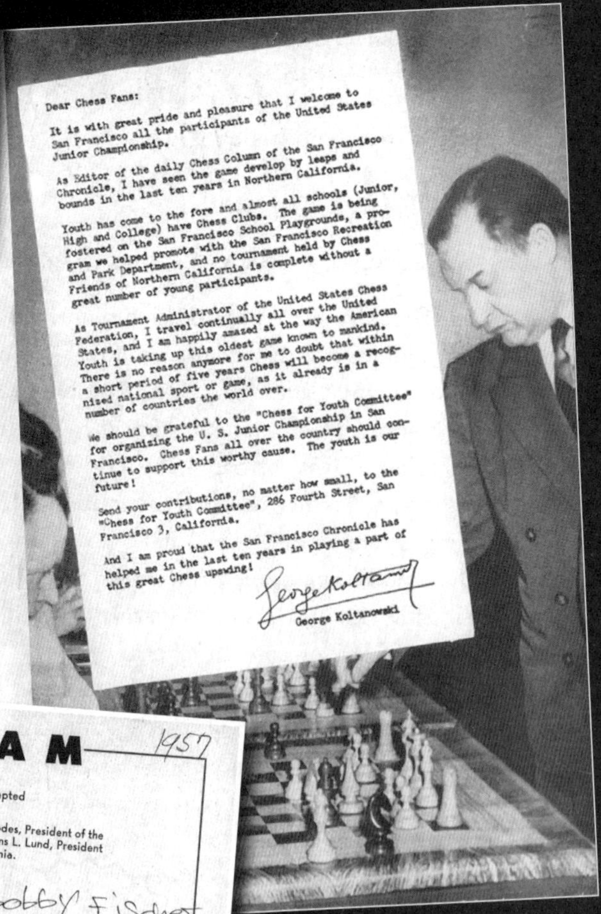

Dear Chess Fans:

It is with great pride and pleasure that I welcome to San Francisco all the participants of the United States Junior Championship.

As Editor of the daily Chess Column of the San Francisco Chronicle, I have seen the game develop by leaps and bounds in the last ten years in Northern California.

Youth has come to the fore and almost all schools (Junior, High and College) have Chess Clubs. The game is being fostered on the San Francisco School Playgrounds, a program we helped promote with the San Francisco Recreation and Park Department, and no tournament held by Chess Friends of Northern California is complete without a great number of young participants.

As Tournament Administrator of the United States Chess Federation, I travel continually all over the United States, and I am happily amazed at the way the American Youth is taking up this oldest game known to mankind. There is no reason anymore for me to doubt that within a short period of five years Chess will become a recognized national sport or game, as it already is in a number of countries the world over.

We should be grateful to the "Chess for Youth Committee" for organizing the U. S. Junior Championship in San Francisco. Chess Fans all over the country should continue to support this worthy cause. The youth is our future!

Send your contributions, no matter how small, to the "Chess for Youth Committee", 286 Fourth Street, San Francisco 3, California.

And I am proud that the San Francisco Chronicle has helped me in the last ten years in playing a part of this great Chess upswing!

George Koltanowski

George Koltanowski

PROGRAM 1957

MONDAY, JULY 8:
Doors open at 11 a. m. Registration accepted until 12:30 p. m.
12:45 p. m. Welcome address by Tom Tripodes, President of the Chess for Youth Committee and Jens L. Lund, President Chess Friends of Northern California.
1:00 p. m.-5 p. m. FIRST ROUND

TUESDAY, JULY 9:
9 a. m.-1 p. m. SECOND ROUND.
2-6 p. m. THIRD ROUND.

Bobby Fischer

WEDNESDAY, JULY 10:
9-1 p. m. FOURTH ROUND.
2 p. m. Sight seeing trip for all participants.

THURSDAY, JULY 11:
9-1 p. m. FIFTH ROUND.
2-6 p. m. SIXTH ROUND.

FRIDAY, JULY 12:
12-4 p. m. SEVENTH ROUND.

SATURDAY, JULY 13:
12-4 p. m. EIGHTH ROUND.

SUNDAY, JULY 14:
10 a. m.-2 p. m. NINTH and FINAL ROUND.
4 p. m. Prize distribution.

Special blindfold show by Howard Killough Jr., Russell, Kansas, 11-year-old participant. NOTICE TO ALL PARTICIPANTS: WATCH BULLETIN BOARD FOR ANY CHANGES IN THE PROGRAM. SILENCE MUST BE KEPT AT ALL TIMES IN THE TOURNAMENT HALL. (This rule will be strictly enforced — both for players as well as spectators, who are welcome to attend the sessions, free of charge.) Address yourself to the tournament director at all times if you are in doubt.

Tournament Director: George Koltanowski
International Chess Master

Assisted by: William S. Stevens
CNFC Tournament Director

Rare Chess Books display, courtesy of Dr. Norman Reider, San Francisco.
Use of Auditorium donated by Spreckles-Russell Dairy Co.

George Koltanowski's personal program from the 1957 U.S. Junior Open, signed by Bobby Fischer.

> In all, thirty-three juniors contested in the nine-round Swiss event directed by International Master George Koltanowski, held at the Spreckels Russell Dairy Co. auditorium located at 1717 Mission Street in San Francisco. While most of these were Californians, there was one from Brooklyn, NY (Fischer), one from Texas (James Bennett), one from Kansas (Howard Killough, Jr.), one from New Jersey (Andrew Schoene), one from Oregon (Robert Walker), one from Utah (Richard Owen), and two from New Mexico (Warren Miller and Thomas Heldt Jr.). California was ably represented by Ramirez and Sholomson although unfortunately Larry Remlinger could not participate.
>
> With George and Leah Koltanowski arranging matters, there was considerable outside activity for the players when they could be pried from the chessboards, including an evening as guests of the Fox Theater seeing the newest Pat Boone picture. Their hosts, the Spreckels Russell Dairy Co., served them chocolate milk and ice cream daily.

Roy Hoppe, who was equally proficient at chess and bridge, played in the 1957 U.S. Junior when he was thirteen, long before he became a USCF master. He shared his memories of Bobby with Eric Hicks in the *California Chess Journal* in the Fall of 2004.

> When the first round started, Fischer was still not present. The young players were kind of whispering to each other on how the defending champion did not even show up to defend his crown. Ten minutes after the clocks had started, Fischer burst into the room, with a dramatic entrance that few in the room will ever forget. Fischer stormed in, and walked with extreme confidence and arrogance as if he was on a grand mission. Kids who were standing near the door when he walked in clamored over to greet him. Fischer ignored them determinedly walking straight to the tournament Director's table. Bobby was wearing patched and holed Levis, two different colors of Converse tennis shoes, and a flannel shirt. His head was shaved; by all accounts an intimidating presence. George Koltanowski, world blindfold champion, and legendary California chess organizer was the tournament director for the event. He was stunned to see young Bobby storm across the room. Everyone in the quiet tournament hall heard Bobby ask, "What's first prize?!" Koltanowski walked Bobby to the prize table and showed him an electric typewriter, identical to the one he won the year before. Bobby stomped his feet and raised his voice and screeched, "I do not want another typewriter!" to the dismay of everyone in the room.

One of Bobby's victims in the tournament, Bill Haines of Vallejo, California, related that Fischer showed the other players in the tournament endgame studies. Here is one he remembered over forty years later.

U.S. JUNIOR CHAMPIONSHIP

SAN FRANCISCO, CALIFORNIA — **8–14 JULY 1957**

		1	2	3	4	5	6	7	8	9	
1. Robert Fischer	Brooklyn, NY	+19	+12	+4	+16	=2	+3	+5	+9	+6	**8.5**
2. Gilbert Ramirez	San Francisco, CA	=20	+18	+9	+3	=1	+6	+16	+8	=4	**7.5**
3. Stephen Sholomson	Santa Monica, CA	+22	+7	+14	−2	+24	−1	+12	=6	+5	**6.5**
4. Ronald Thacker	Richmond, CA	+29	+15	−1	−6	+28	=8	+17	+16	=2	**6.0**
5. Mike Bredoff	Redwood City, CA	−14	+20	+28	+11	=7	+10	−1	+12	−3	**5.5**
6. Leonard Hill	Mountain View, CA	+27	−11	+23	+4	+16	−2	+7	=3	−1	**5.5**
7. Arthur Wang	Berkeley, CA	+31	−3	+26	+9	=5	−12	−6	+18	+13	**5.5**
8. Ralph Clark	Long Beach, CA	+30	=26	−19	+22	=10	=4	+14	−2	+20	**5.5**
9. Robert Walker	Portland, OR	+17	+13	−2	−7	+29	+11	+24	−1	=10	**5.5**
10. Warren Miller	Albuquerque, NM	+28	−16	=22	+26	=8	−5	+27	+15	=9	**5.5**
11. Rex Wilcox	Salinas, CA	+33	+6	−16	−5	+21	−9	=13	+17	=12	**5.0**
12. Andrew Schoene	Malaga, NJ	+21	−1	+29	=14	+19	+7	−3	−5	=11	**5.0**
13. Thomas Heldt Jr.	Albuquerque, NM	+23	−9	−15	+33	=17	+26	=11	+19	−7	**5.0**
14. David Krause	Palo Alto, CA	+5	+X	−3	=12	=15	=24	−8	+23	=16	**5.0**
15. Leighton Allen	San Francisco, CA	bye	−4	+13	−24	=14	=28	+21	−10	=19	**4.5**
16. William Haines	Sacramento, CA	+25	+10	+11	−1	−6	+19	−2	−4	=14	**4.5**
17. Robert Dickinson	Redwood City, CA	−9	+21	−24	+23	=13	+20	−4	−11	+26	**4.5**
18. Fred Wreden	San Francisco, CA	=32	−2	−20	−21	+30	+22-	+29	−7	+24	**4.5**
19. James Bennett	Fort Worth, TX	−1	+27	+8	+32	−12	−16	+28	−13	=15	**4.5**
20. Richard Owen	Salt Lake City, UT	=2	−5	+18	−29	+22	−17	+26	+24	−8	**4.5**
21. Howard Killough Jr.	Russell, KS	−12	−17	+25	+18	−11	+23	−15	=27	+X	**4.5**
22. Ivan Vegvary	San Francisco, CA	−3	+X	=10	−8	−20	−18	+25	+31	+30	**4.5**
23. William Lee	San Francisco, CA	−13	bye	−6	−17	+25	−21	+30	−14	+31	**4.0**
24. James Schmerl	Piedmont, CA	−26	+30	+17	+15	−3	=14	−9	−20	−18	**3.5**
25. Don Sutherland	San Francisco, CA	−16	−29	−21	+31	−23	bye	−22	=30	+27	**3.5**
26. John Blackstone	San Jose, CA	+24	=8	−7	−10	+X	−13	−20	+28	−17	**3.5**
27. Allan Haley	Nevada City, NV	−6	−19	+31	−28	+X	+29	−10	=21	−25	**3.5**
28. Ray Hoppe	San Francisco, CA	−10	+31	−5	+27	−4	=15	−19	−26	bye	**3.5**
29. David Bogdanoff	Redwood City, CA	−4	+25	−12	+20	−9	−27	−18	bye	−F	**3.0**
30. Bruce Pohoriles	Larkspur, CA	−8	−24	−33	bye	−18	+31	−23	=25	−22	**2.5**
31. Jonathan Krug	San Rafael, CA	−7	−28	−27	−25	bye	−30	+X	−22	−23	**2.0**
32. Steve Joplin	Oakland, CA	=18	−F	bye	−19	−F	—	−F	—	—	**1.5**
33. Lincoln Fong	San Francisco, CA	−11	−F	+30	−13	−F	—	—	—	—	**1.0**

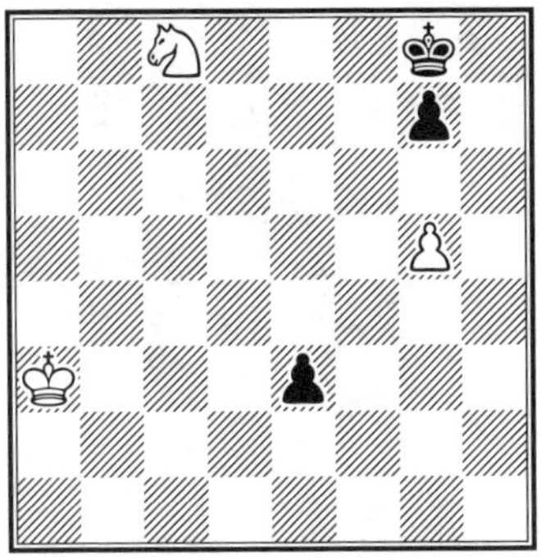

1.Ne7+ Kh7 (1...Kf7 2.Nc6 e2 3.Ne5+ Ke6 4.Nf3 Kf5 5.Kb3 Kg4 6.Ne1 Kxg5 7.Kc2 draws) 2.g6+ Kh8 3.Kb4 e2 4.Kc5 e1(Q) 5.Kd6 Draw, A lone queen can't give checkmate.

LINA GRUMETTE

The U.S. Junior ended on July 14th but the U.S. Open in Cleveland did not start until August 5th. With some time to spare, instead of returning home to Brooklyn, Bobby stayed in California. For over a week he hung out at the Mechanics' Chess Club in San Francisco in the company of Gil Ramirez. The *California Chess Reporter*[1] noted:

> His skill in move-on-move play has been demonstrated against fast company at MICC at several occasions since. Old timers gasp!

Bobby then took a side trip south to Los Angeles where he stayed at the home of Lina Grumette who would become a life-long friend and second mother.

During his stay in the Southland, Fischer hung out with John Rinaldo, Ron Gross, and Larry Remlinger—Bobby and Larry played at the Lincoln Park Chess and Checker Club in Long Beach. Today Long Beach is not considered an important chess center, though for a period of time in the 1950s it was, even hosting the 1955 U.S. Open. The club in many ways resembled the present home of the San Diego Chess Club that meets in Balboa Park.

Lina Grumette (1908–1988), was born Lina Futterman, on January 6, 1908, in Kaliningrad, then a part of East Prussia. She was a child when the Futtermans moved to New York, and there she learned to play chess, was a member of the Brooklyn Chess Club, and took lessons from Isaac Kashdan. She eventually reached 1900 and played in six U.S. Women's Championships (1948, 1951, 1955, 1957, 1959, and 1967). However, Lina Grumette is still remembered in the chess world for reasons beyond her play.

---

[1] *California Chess Reporter*, July 1957, (p. 2).

[left] Jacqueline Piatigorsky and Lina Grumette analyzing circa 1960 (Courtesy of the World Chess Hall of Fame); [right] The Manger Hotel, Cleveland, Ohio, site of the 1957 U.S. Open, played August 5–17. The hotel, located at E. 13th Street and Chester Avenue, is now the Parkview Apartments.

The activities that would put her on the map occurred after she and her husband Murray Grumette moved to Hollywood in the early 1950s. There they became friends with Herman Steiner and Jacqueline Piatigorsky. When Steiner died in 1955, Grumette was a key figure in the establishment and running of the Herman Steiner Chess Club. She served as the publicity director for the two Piatigorsky Cups, and in the 1970s and 1980s ran a chess club out of her West Hollywood home called the Chess Set which was the site for many master invitational tournaments. However, she will be best remembered as a devoted friend of Bobby Fischer.

The two first got to know each other in July 1957 when he stayed at her home. They met again in 1961 for the planning of Bobby's match with Sammy Reshevsky, and the Los Angeles leg of the event. Fischer was back in Los Angeles for the 1966 Piatigorsky Cup and it was Lina that Jacqueline Piatigorsky prevailed upon to get Bobby to leave the Miramar Hotel after he had overstayed his visit. Shortly afterwards she looked at apartments in Los Angeles with Bobby, and although he ultimately went back to New York, he did make the move to the Southland a few years later.

According to Irwin Fisk:[1]

> She was in Iceland [during the 1972 World Championship] when Fischer threatened to go home after the second game. Up to now, all that was known was the fact that Fischer was set to go home when Lina arrived and had a private dinner with him. When they emerged from the dining room, it was

[1] *Chess Life*, September 1989, (p. 11).

> thumbs up. The match continued. She would not divulge what she had said to change Fischer's mind and after her death it was reported she had taken the secret with her. However, before she died she told at least one close confidant that Garner Ted Armstrong, of the Pasadena-based Worldwide Church of God, was greatly admired by Fischer, and Armstrong had told Fischer that he was thinking of going to Iceland to watch him play. Lina reminded Fischer that Armstrong would be disappointed if he arrived in Iceland only to find that Fischer had given up and gone home. It was this reminder that convinced Fischer to continue the match.

Lina Grumette died of lung cancer on July 21, 1988.

U.S. OPEN 1957

The beginning of August marked the start of an epic road trip from San Francisco to Cleveland. Query MapQuest and you will be informed the 2462 mile journey should take around thirty-six hours of non-stop driving, traveling almost entirely on Interstate 80.

When Bobby made the trip in 1957 things were much different. The Interstate Highway System, first authorized in 1956, was only beginning to take shape. The carload of chess players consisting of Bobby, John Rinaldo, Gil Ramirez, William Rebold, and William Addison faced a tougher journey on the old Lincoln highway. The car, loaned to them by *California Chess Reporter* editor Guthrie McClain, broke down twice along the way, first in Wendover, Nevada, and then in Joliet, Illinois.

Gil Ramirez recalled that not only the car broke down, but so did the bus from Joliet to Chicago! In a letter written October 25, 2011, Ramirez confirms that the famous Fischer biting incident did occur, but not on the long road trip as some have claimed. The U.S. Open in Cleveland was actually the scene of the altercation. John Rinaldo repeatedly compared Bobby, then in the midst of a growth spurt, with the comic book figure Crusader Rabbit, who had big feet. Fischer did not like this, and finally cracked, going after Rinaldo. Ramirez tried to break it up and Fischer, perhaps thinking that he was taking Rinaldo's side, bit him in the arm and would not let go until he got punched in the face. Fischer started the U.S. Open with a black eye! [see pages 37 and 264 for other versions of this story].

Ramirez, who grew up in San Francisco, was a very talented player. He won the California Open in 1956 while only seventeen, and improved on his second-place finish in the 1957 U.S. Junior by tying for top honors with Robin Ault in 1959. Ault won on tiebreak and was given a spot in the 1959/60 U.S. Championship where he proceeded to go 0–11. This ended the practice of seeding the junior champion for several decades.

Arthur Bisguier, Anthony Saidy, and Pal Benko at the 1969 U.S. Championship in New York City. (Photo: Beth Cassidy).

Top ten finishes in the 1957 and 1959 U.S. Opens confirmed Ramirez as a serious talent, but his career was in fact nearing its end. One of his last major competitions was the 1961 Madrid International. Stationed in Spain during a stint in the U.S. Air Force, Ramirez found time to play a twelve-player round robin that was won by Robatsch and Milić ahead of O'Kelly and Pirc. Ramirez finished in the middle with a score of 5–6.

Ramirez remarked that when he left Madrid he traveled back to San Francisco by way of New York and paid a nice visit to Bobby. No mention was made of the altercation in Cleveland:[1]

> CLEVELAND 1957 — BOBBY FISCHER BECOMES YOUNGEST PLAYER TO WIN THE U.S. OPEN
>
> At fourteen years, Bobby Fischer, Erasmus [Hall] High student of Brooklyn, becomes the youngest master to win the U.S. Open title. Fischer scored 10–2 in a games-won tie with U.S. Champion Arthur Bisguier but gained the title on adjusted tie-breaking points, with Bisguier placing second. Donald Byrne, recent winner of the New Western Open, who was a strong contender throughout the race, finished in third place with 9½–2½.
>
> Tied for fourth with 9–3 were Walter Shipman, Robert Byrne (Donald's older brother), Edmar Mednis, and Anthony Santasiere. Scoring 8½–3½ were Anthony F. Saidy, Paul Brandts, and I. Theodorovich of Toronto, while 8–4 scores were completed by Hans Berliner, Attilio Di Camillo, Morton Siegel, Orest Popovych, Gerald Fielding of Regina, and William G. Addison. Scores of 7½–4½ were attained by Victor Guala, John W. Collins, and Dr. Erich W. Marchand.
>
> The event, which drew 175 players from twenty-three states, District of Columbia, Mexico, and Canada, was a thriller from the start. Donald Byrne climbed into the lead, showing the form that had won him the U.S. Open

[1] *Chess Life*, September 5, 1957, (p. 1).

Orest Popovych and Arthur Bisguier analyzing in the mid-1960s (Photo: Beth Cassidy).

title in Milwaukee in 1953. But in the ninth round, Byrne suffered his first defeat from Bobby Fischer, and the loss catapulted Fischer into first place with 8–1 (no losses) while Donald Byrne dropped into a second place tie with his brother Robert. Round ten, however, saw Donald Byrne climb to share the lead with Fischer, as Byrne defeated Walter Shipman, while Fischer was drawing with Robert Byrne. This gave Donald Byrne and Fischer 8½–1½ each, while Robert and Bisguier were close on their heels with 8–2. Still in contention with 7½–2½ each were Addison, Saidy, Guala, Siegel, Mednis, and Shipman. Round eleven saw the two leaders retain their place at the top as Bobby beat Addison and Bisguier defeated Saidy, but the final day of the competition saw Bisguier beat Byrne while Bobby drew with Shipman.

Bobby was declared the winner on tiebreak which produced some hard feelings, but he clearly faced stronger opposition than Bisguier who had lost to Addison in round six. Fischer drew with his co-winner, R. Byrne and Shipman, while beating D. Byrne, Mednis, and Addison! The two winners each received $750 for their efforts.

Arthur Bisguier's report on Fischer's last round opponent:[1]

> Walter Shipman, the last player to figure in the tie for fourth through seventh places, again demonstrated that he is an uncommonly difficult fellow to beat. He was the only player, other than Fischer, to finish undefeated in the tournament. Considering his stubborn and tenacious qualities and his excellent understanding of the positional precepts of chess, it becomes quite understandable why young Bobby accepted a draw against this formidable adversary. Unfortunately for Walter, sometimes his temperament is a little too placid and this style of play militates against him obtaining the very highest honors in a Swiss system tournament of this type.

Game anthologies give eleven of Bobby's twelve games from the U.S. Open played at the Manger Hotel (1802 E. 13th Street) in Cleveland. The twelfth

[1] *Chess Review*, October 1957, (p. 297).

William Addison at the Mechanics' Institute Chess Club in 1957 (Photo: Mechanics' Institute Chess Club Archives).

game will never be found, as it doesn't exist—Bobby won round one by forfeit when Horst Kemperer of Montreal, Canada failed to appear (he didn't show up for subsequent rounds, either).

Cleveland was the first great breakthrough for Bobby. While he had yet to fully mature both physically and mentally, Fischer was already a very sophisticated player as Robert Byrne explained:[1]

> Whereas most players have great trouble controlling their emotions during an important contest, either over optimistically evaluating their chances when on the attack, or over pessimistically giving up an inferior position as a certain loss, Fischer somehow manages to remain indefatigably objective. When I first met him as an opponent, in the United States Open Championship in Cleveland, 1957, he was only fourteen years old. Yet, throughout the twists and turns of our bitterly fought battle, he never allowed himself to become deceived about which way the wind was blowing. He knew he had the opening advantage, and he knew precisely when I struggled to equality, as well as the moment when he erred, giving me some winning chances. (The game ended in a draw). He has never found it necessary to give himself the silly pep talks that players with twice his experience indulge in.

Fischer entered the second half of the U.S. Open in Cleveland with a score of 5–1, just a half point behind the leaders. In the final five rounds he played many of the top players in the United States including Robert and Donald Byrne, Edmar Mednis, William Addison, and Walter Shipman, but before he met them he faced Latvian-American expert Igor (Igors) Garais who had started the event strongly with wins over Erich Marchand and Henry Gross.

1 Robert Byrne in Introduction, Edmar Mednis, *How to Beat Bobby Fischer*. New York: New York Times Book Co., 1974.

(23) Sicilian
Igors Garais – Fischer
Cleveland (7) 1957

1.e4 c5 2.Nf3 d6 3.d4 cxd4 4.Nxd4 Nf6 5.Nc3 a6 6.g3 e5 7.Nde2 Be7 8.Bg2 0-0 9.0-0 Nbd7 10.h3

10.a4 stopping ...b5 is the main alternative here.

10...b5 11.Be3

11.g4 is normally seen here and more consistent with White's previous play.

11...Bb7

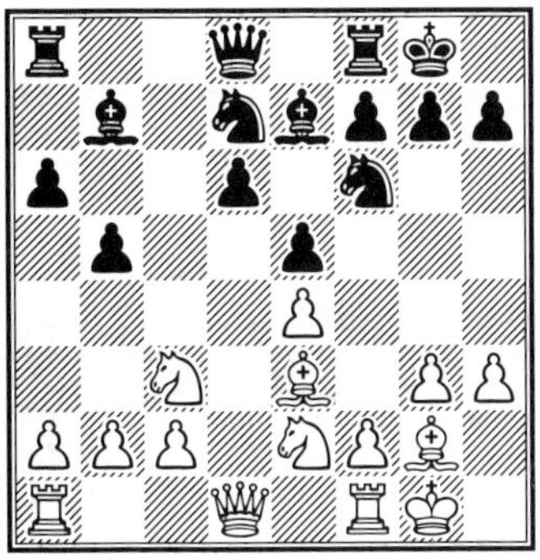

12.f4?!

Again, 12.g4 is more to the point.

12...Qc7 13.g4 b4 14.Nd5 Nxd5 15.exd5 exf4

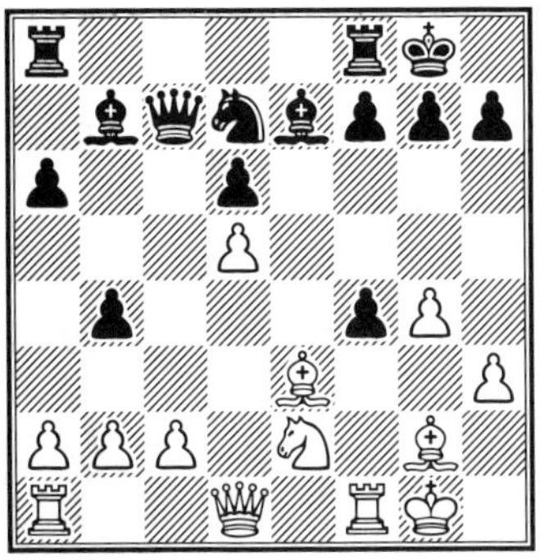

16.Rxf4?

16.Nxf4 or 16.Bxf4 should have been tried.

16...Bg5 17.Re4 Bxe3+ 18.Rxe3 Rae8 19.Rxe8 Rxe8 20.Qd2?

20.Nd4 was better although after 20...Qc5 White's d-pawn will soon fall.

20...Qc5+ 21.Kh1?

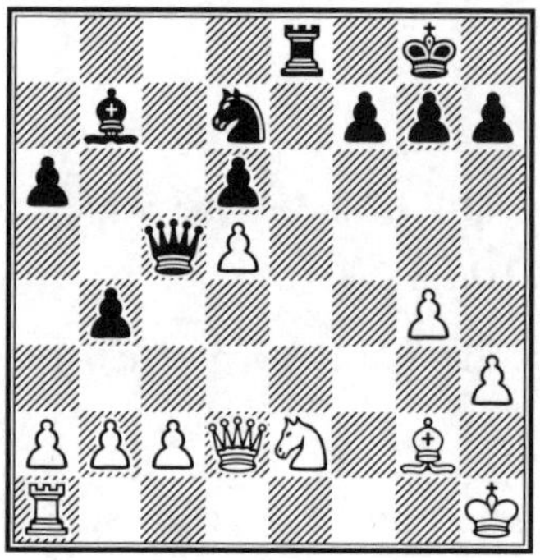

21...Qf2!, 0–1.

Bobby finished his highly successful summer by winning the New Jersey Open over Labor Day Weekend. His 6½–½ score included a draw with Dr. Ariel Mengarini and earned him $125.

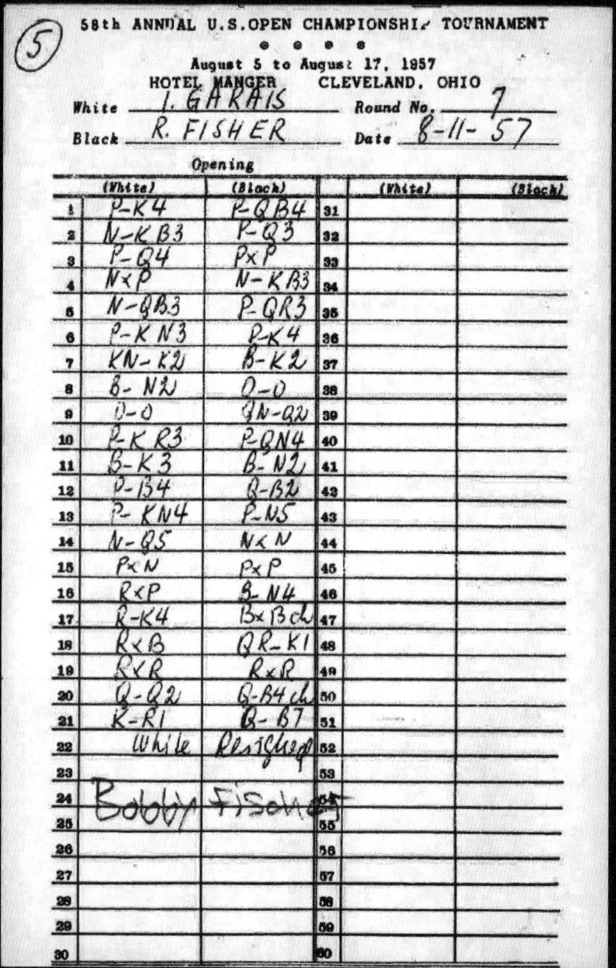

(5)

58th ANNUAL U.S.OPEN CHAMPIONSHIP TOURNAMENT

August 5 to August 17, 1957

HOTEL MANGER CLEVELAND, OHIO

White I. GARAIS Round No. 7

Black R. FISHER Date 8-11-57

Opening

	(White)	(Black)		(White)	(Black)
1	P-K4	P-QB4	31		
2	N-KB3	P-Q3	32		
3	P-Q4	PxP	33		
4	NxP	N-KB3	34		
5	N-QB3	P-QR3	35		
6	P-KN3	P-K4	36		
7	KN-K2	B-K2	37		
8	B-N2	0-0	38		
9	0-0	QN-Q2	39		
10	P-KR3	P-QN4	40		
11	B-K3	B-N2	41		
12	P-B4	Q-B2	42		
13	P-KN4	P-N5	43		
14	N-Q5	NxN	44		
15	PxN	PxP	45		
16	RxP	B-N4	46		
17	R-K4	BxB ch	47		
18	RxB	QR-K1	48		
19	RxR	RxR	49		
20	Q-Q2	Q-B4 ch	50		
21	K-R1	Q-B7	51		
22	White	Resigned	52		
23			53		
24	Bobby Fischer		54		
25			55		
26			56		
27			57		
28			58		
29			59		
30			60		

Igors Garais' score sheet, signed by Bobby Fischer, was found in the chess library of Peter Grey (1935-2016) of San Francisco. Grey was a noted chess archivist who helped George Koltanowski with his chess column in the San Francisco Chronicle *for many years. In return Kolti, who directed many U.S. Opens over three decades including Cleveland 1957, gave Peter many bulletins and score sheets from this annual event, including this one signed by the young Bobby (Score sheet: Mechanics' Institute Chess Club Archives).*

3
U.S. CHAMPIONSHIP 1957 (A Fitting End to a Great Year)

The most obscure match of Bobby's career was played in September of 1957 against Daniel Beninson. The Manhattan Chess Club was the venue for this forgotten encounter which Fischer briefly mention's in *Bobby Fischer's Chess Games*, giving the score as 3½–1½ in his favor. None of the games from this match are presently available, but all are in the Targ Collection.

Dr. Daniel Jacobo Beninson (1931–2003) was an Argentine radiation expert who lived in New York from 1956 to 1957, serving as the General Secretary of the United Nations Scientific Committee on the Effects of Atomic Radiation.

Bernard Taper profiled Fischer and Beninson in this 1957 "The Talk of the Town" piece:[1]

> We sat down to watch what was going on. Young Fischer, whom we discovered to be a lanky lad with a mischievous, rather faunlike face, was playing against a stout, elegant man in his middle twenties—an Argentine named Dr. Dan J. Beninson, who, we were told, is scientific secretary of the United Nations' Scientific Committee on the Effects of Atomic Radiation. They were playing chess such as we had never seen before—making their moves with split-second rapidity, while exchanging banter with each other and the kibitzers, most of whom were of college age. Within a few minutes, they had finished one game and were launched on another, and Fischer was asserting, with a triumphant grin, as he pushed his queen, "You're dead now."
>
> "That's what you think, Bobby, my boy," Dr. Beninson answered, instantly bringing his bishop across the board—an unexpected stroke, apparently, since it caused young Fischer to clap a hand to his head and brought a burst of laughter from the kibitzers. Everybody seemed to be having a high time. Once, when Dr. Beninson lingered over a move for perhaps three seconds, Fischer threw up his hands in feigned disgust and groaned, "It's no fun to play chess if you take all year over a move."

Beninson's responsibilities as a scientist never allowed him to realize his full potential as a player but his performance at Quilmes (a city in the province

[1] Bernard Taper, "The Talk of the Town—Prodigy," *The New Yorker*, September 7, 1957.

[top] Bobby, Daniel Beninson (glasses), and James Gore (White) analyzing Reshevsky–Lombardy live during the last round of the 1957/58 U.S. Championship. Bobby had already agreed to a quick draw with Abe Turner and Reshevsky went on to lose to Lombardy giving Bobby clear first;

[left] This shot of Bobby analyzing Reshevsky-Lombardy appeared twice on the cover of Chess Review *(the second time after he won the 1958/59 event);*

[bottom] William Lombardy.

of Buenos Aires) 1959 where he was second behind Foguelman but ahead of Sanguineti, Rossetto, Raimundo Garcia, Schweber, and Emma, show he was a strong 2300+ master. His performance against Bobby, a very creditable 1½–3½, just after Fischer had won the U.S. Open in Cleveland, is further evidence.

Journalist Michael "Mig" Greengard, who spoke with Beninson, offered:

> It was a training match, apparently one of several arranged for Fischer around this time. Neither player was paid. Beninson was one of the stronger players in the Manhattan Chess Club and was friends with others like Lombardy. He also puts the score at 3½–1½, Fischer. He doesn't remember the progressive score, but, is almost sure he didn't win any games. He said it was obvious to all that Fischer was going to be a star, that he was something special. He described him as "terribly strong" by then.
>
> They did stay in touch, Fischer's mother even calling ahead to ask Beninson to "take care" of Bobby while he was here on his first trip [to Argentina]. Beninson is pretty sure that he talked with Fischer on each of his trips[1] minus his recent 1996 visit to promote Fischer Random.

The following article was syndicated October 27, 1957:[2]

> **PRODIGY'S DEVOTION TO CHESS WORRIES MOTHER**
> **Fischer, Fourteen, Shows Little Interest in Other Pursuits**
> **What price child prodigy?**
>
> That question comes to mind regarding fourteen-year-old Bobby Fischer, an intense nail-biting youngster chess master in the United States.
>
> When the slender, sandy-haired boy won the United States open chess championship in Cleveland last August, triumphing over players. Al Horowitz, editor of *Chess Review*, was heard to remark; "Nobody in the world could have played better than Bobby on this occasion."
>
> And at the Manhattan Chess Club, where Bobby, the youngest member, plays several evenings a week, Hans Kmoch, the club's general manager, said:
>
> "He's so great that he shows the same potential as the immortals Paul Morphy and José Capablanca. He may someday become a World Champion."
>
> **Nervous at Table**
>
> It was at this club that young Bobby was observed while he sat at one of the tables. He was playing rapid transit, a kind of blitz chess in which moves must be made within ten seconds. On and on he played, never looking up, constantly biting his nails or drumming his long, thin fingers on the table. "Come on, hurry up and move," he kept saying to his opponents.
>
> Very shy as well as nervous, he paced restlessly about the room when a reporter talked to him. "All I want to do is to play," he said, and quickly returned to the table.

---

1 Fischer visited Argentina in 1959, 1960, 1970, 1971, and 1996.

2 Syndicated by North American Newspaper Alliance.

> One of the members said: "He's so sensitive that he used to go off and cry whenever he lost a game. He hates to lose and we sort of used to baby him around here. But he doesn't cry any more. He's growing up."
>
> Bobby lives with his mother and twenty-year-old sister in Brooklyn. His mother, a cheerful-looking visiting nurse, said the young chess genius, a high school sophomore, was precocious even as an infant. In nursery school, she said, he was a whiz at cutouts and other puzzle games.
>
> And at seven, he was a master of magic and card tricks. About the same age when he first learned to play chess, having become immediately fascinated when his sister Joan brought home a set she had picked up at a notion store. From then on, he's been practically living with the game.
>
> Mrs. Regina Fischer said, "By the time Bobby was eight, I had to take him out of public school and put him in a private school because he was so restless. In the private school he got along fine because the teachers understood him and encouraged him to develop his own personality.
>
> "Bobby has always been a nonconformist. He likes to wear dungarees and polo shirts because he considers good clothes sissy, and he doesn't like ties. He doesn't even own a tie."
>
> Mrs. Fischer has long been concerned over her son's total absorption in chess. Outside of a little tennis, which he plays at high school, where his grades are average, he doesn't appear to have any other interest, she said.
>
> "It's chess, chess, chess, from the minute he opens his eyes in the morning," she declared. Bobby has a chessboard at his bedside. He'll often play both sides of a game at breakfast. He has about forty manuals at home. Some of them are in foreign languages that he has learned sufficiently to follow the moves.
>
> The young wizard, though shy with strangers, is essential friendly and good natured, and gets along well with his classmates, according to his mother.
>
> "But he's not interested in anything else but chess," she said a bit forlornly. "Where's his future? He doesn't even want to go to college."
>
> She added hopefully, "Maybe when he gets older he'll change. I want my Bobby to develop like other boys."

Bobby ended 1957 in fine fashion winning the first of his eight U.S. Championships with an undefeated score of 10½ points in thirteen rounds. Note, he received a little help from his good friend Bill Lombardy who delivered in the last round by beating Sammy Reshevsky, for the only time in his career, giving Bobby clear first.

(24) King's Indian
Sammy Reshevsky – William Lombardy
New York (13) 1957/58

1.d4 Nf6 2.c4 g6 3.Nc3 Bg7 4.e4 d6 5.Be2 0-0 6.Nf3 e5 7.0-0 Nc6 8.d5 Ne7 9.Ne1 Nd7 10.Nd3 f5 11.f3 f4 12.Bd2 g5 13.Rc1 Ng6 14.Nb5 a6 15.Na3 Nf6 16.c5 g4 17.cxd6 cxd6 18.Nc4 g3 19.h3 Bxh3 20.gxh3 Qd7 21.Nf2 gxf2+ 22.Kh2 Qe7 23.Rxf2

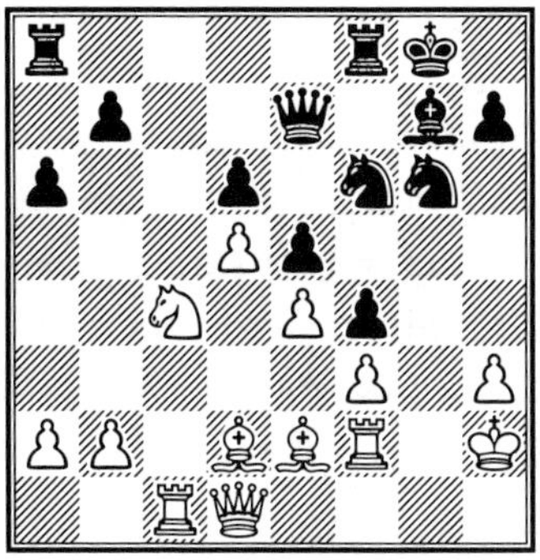

The photo (top of page 128) doesn't offer a clear view of the entire board, but it looks like Fischer, Gore, and Beninson are analyzing the position after 23.Rxf2 and examining 23...Nh4 instead of the stronger 23...Nh5 as played in the game.

23...Nh5 24.Bb4 Rad8 25.Qd3 Nh4 26.Rg1 Ng3 27.Bf1 Rf6 28.Rc2 Rg6 29.Be1 Bh6 30.Nb6 Kh8 31.Bg2 Rdg8 32.Rc8 Bf8 33.Rc2 Qg7 34.Na8 Qh6 35.Bf1 Nxf1+ 36.Rxf1

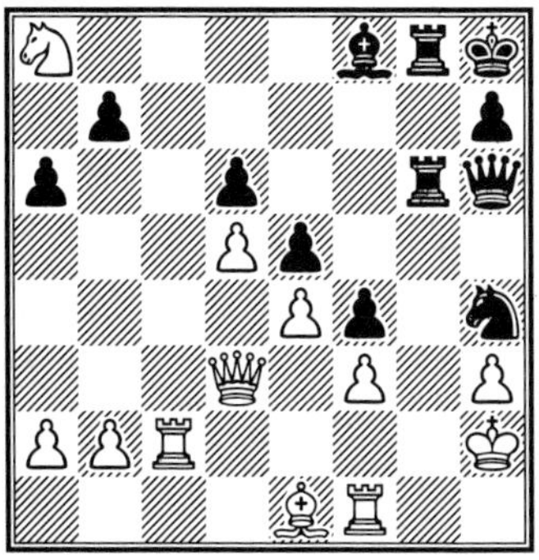

There are many roads to Rome, but here Black had a pretty finish in 36...Nf5! 37.exf5 Qxh3+ 38.Kxh3 Rh6+ 39.Bh4 Rg3+ 40.Kh2 Rxh4 mate!

36...Qg7 37.Qe2 Rg2+ 38.Qxg2 Nxg2 39.Rg1 Nxe1 40.Rxg7 Bxg7, 0–1.

Hugh Myers (1930–2008), best known for championing unorthodox openings through his magazine *MOB* (*Myers Openings Bulletin*), lived in New York for several years in the late 1950s and befriended Bobby. He gave his impressions of Bobby in his memoir, *A Chess Explorer*:[1]

> He won the U.S. Championship for the first time on January 7, 1958, clinching it with a short last-round draw against Abe Turner. It was a snowy evening. I was one of the few people he would listen to (Probably because he respected my taste in openings! I don't think he knew anyone else who owned and loved a 1956 Russian openings book by Lipnitsky, as we both did). So I was the only person to escort Fischer and his mother to the subway station. He was celebrating by throwing snowballs at passing busses! I got him to stop that, telling him he wouldn't want to see his name in the morning papers both for winning the championship and for getting arrested.
>
> I never believed the legend that Fischer had an IQ of 180—and I knew him a lot better than his biographer, Frank Brady, did. I never saw Brady at the Manhattan Chess Club, but I knew him as a quiet kibitzer in Greenwich Village coffee houses, where Fischer was rarely if ever seen.
>
> Except for his chess skill, largely a product of intensive book study (He was always carrying them.), I thought Fischer was an average boy. His strongest non-chess interests were things like New York Rangers ice hockey games and Tarzan comic books. He did study Russian—just to get more out of his Russian chess books. He was reasonably friendly with a small group of friends, mostly young experts and masters at the Manhattan Chess Club. I was the oldest of them, probably another reason he would pay attention to what I had to say (sometimes!).
>
> But in 1958–60 Fischer went from being somewhat self-centered to being more and more rebellious and antisocial. I blame that on feeling abandoned, along with his justifiable view that he was being maligned or ridiculed in the press. His mother always seemed to be going to some kind of activist demonstration, or he was embarrassed by things she tried to do for him—like asking the U.S. president to give him financial support—without his approval (His father had left him when he was two[2]). More than that, he was devastated when his sister Joan suddenly left New York, to get married. She was only four or five years older than Bobby, but she had a major role in raising him.
>
> My point in reciting all that here is I speculate that things might have been different except for my pneumonia. Maybe I could have influenced his behavior, but we disconnected in 1958–59; my interest in serious competition wasn't strong in those years.

---

1 Hugh E. Myers, *A Chess Explorer: Life and Games.* Davenport, IA: MOB, 2002, (pp. 43–44).

2 Myers seems to be alluding to Hans-Gerhardt Fischer who is listed on Bobby's birth certificate as his father. The information that Paul Felix Nemenyi, who died in 1952, was Bobby's actual biological father, did not become public knowledge until 2002.

One more Fischer story: A match that he played in 1957 has been something of a mystery, partly because its five games are not in the largest collection of his games (Hays 1992) but more because of conjecture as to why he would have played a match with an untitled and virtually unknown opponent.

Not a weak one, however. Fischer defeated Dr. Daniel Beninson ("Benninson" in the Brady and Hays books, but that's how I remember his name) by 3½–1½. From Argentina, he worked at the United Nations. After Carmine Nigro, who gave Fischer his first training, I believe Beninson came closest to being Fischer's coach. It seemed to me that he showed more respect for the chess opinions of Beninson than for those of anyone else (except his own!). Besides that, Beninson always wore expensive suits; Fischer didn't! His sartorial taste improved while associating with Beninson."

4

2626! BOBBY'S RATING SURGE

Much has been made of Bobby Fischer's meteoric rise to World Championship candidate while in his mid-teens. Unlike the prodigies who came before and after, Fischer is unusual in that he didn't show a special aptitude for the game when he first learned to play at the age of six. Half a dozen years later he was a low-class A player, and while this wasn't bad for a twelve-year-old American youngster in the summer of'55, it was nothing to write home about—by comparison with today's standards, Sergey Karjakin had earned the grandmaster title at the same age.

The USCF rating system was invented by USCF Business Manager Kenneth Harkness (1898–1972), and made its first appearance in the November 20, 1950 issue of *Chess Life*. To produce the first list Harkness had to retroactively rate tournaments from the 1930s and 1940s, which involved considerable guess work, and as a result, it took quite a while before the system stabilized and was statistically valid.

The newness and infrequency of the ratings, which only appeared annually until 1957, made it difficult to track a player's progress in those early years. When Bobby first started playing, ratings were done by hand and the results tabulated on index cards. Once a year Harkness would average the ratings written on the index cards and calculate the player's new rating.

A close examination of Fischer's USCF ratings card, which the U.S. Chess Federation still has, offers insights into his early progress from event to event. Bobby's first rating, achieved at the 1955 U.S. Amateur in Lake Mohegan, New York, was 1826 for his 2½–3½ score. His next event, the U.S. Junior Championship, did not go as well as his 5–5 score against weaker opposition was only good for a performance of 1625.These two events were averaged, and Bobby's first published rating of 1726 appeared in the May 20, 1956, issue of *Chess Life*.

During 1956 Bobby started to progress at an exceptional rate. He had a performance of 2357 in the New York City Open in January, but then performed miserably at the U.S. Amateur on Memorial Day weekend, with a 2003 performance. This would be his last failure for quite a while. Not long after this subpar performance he became a regular visitor to John Collin's home—aka the Hawthorne Chess Club—and soon began the climb that would take him to the chess heavens.

That summer he won the U.S. Junior Championship with a 2321 performance and followed that with an undefeated 8–4 score, his best achievement (2349) to date, in the U.S. Open. He dropped a little in the 3rd Rosenwald tournament, his first encounter with strong competition.

Bobby's fantastic leap in strength between the summer of 1956 and January of 1958 from 1726 to 2626—an improvement of 900 points—had never happened before and it's doubtful it will happen again.

5
A BREAK FROM TOURNAMENT PLAY

Several times in Bobby's career he took significant breaks from tournament play. The first occurred after his victory in the 1957/58 U.S. Championship. That event concluded on January 8, 1958, and Fischer did not play another tournament game until the first round of the Interzonal on August 5th. Bobby gave one of the reasons for this sabbatical in his first book of collected games:[1] "Writing this book was a big job, the annotations required practically every weekend from February to June and some time in between."

Originally, the break wasn't expected to last so long. Bobby was expected to play in the Manhattan Chess Club Championship (Spring 1958): *Chess Life*[2] stated that Arthur Bisguier and Bobby would be joined by eight qualifying players including George Kramer, George Shainswit, and Abe Turner in the final section of the Max Pavey Memorial Tournament for the Manhattan Championship.

On the day of the tournament, *The New York Times* reported:

> Bobby Fischer of Brooklyn, the new United States chess champion, will not compete in the annual Manhattan Chess Club championship scheduled to open at 2PM.
>
> The fourteen-year-old prodigy announced his withdrawal yesterday, but did not give his reason.
>
> His withdrawal left only nine entrants in the tourney, headed by Arthur B. Bisguier, the defending club champion. Bisguier will oppose George Kramer, a former New York State champion, in the opening round.
>
> The oldest entrant Harold M. Phillips, eighty-three, was champion and president of the club during the 1930s. He is known internationally as a leader in the chess activities in this country.

In retrospect, Bobby probably realized that he had outgrown events like the Manhattan Chess Club Championship. Henceforth he would play in only two American tournaments outside the national championship, the Western Open and the New York State Open, both in 1963.

---

1 Bobby Fischer, *Bobby Fischer's Games of Chess*. New York: Simon & Schuster, 1958.

2 *Chess Life*, March 20, 1958, (p. 35).

After a seventh month hiatus from tournament play, how did Bobby do so well in the 1958 Interzonal? Clearly his play in Yugoslavia was a definite step up from his performance in the U.S. Championship. The answer is, while he didn't play in tournaments the first half of 1958, he was still studying and getting plenty of practice with training games.

John Collins described a typical day for Bobby from June 1956 to June 1958:[1]

> Starting with that first afternoon in June, he became a regular too. Sometimes I would see him every day of the week. He began attending a junior high school and then Erasmus [Hall] High School, both of which were in my neighborhood. He would arrive at my home at a bit past noon. Being one who retires late and rises late, I would usually be just dressed and about and preparing my combination breakfast-luncheon when he came. We would sit down at the kitchen table, divide the packaged lunch his mother had made up and the brunch my sister had left me in the refrigerator before leaving for the office, and discuss chess and school while we ate rather hastily. Then we would hurry into the living room and play fast chess until almost one o'clock. Then he would jump up and, say, "I've got to go," and run the four blocks to Erasmus. When school was out at three o'clock, he would return, and we would play more fast games, analyze positions and go over several master games until Ethel came home from Dr. Walter V. Moore's office in the Fox Theater Building (Dr. Moore was a prominent ophthalmologist) and prepared dinner for us all. Finally, for the third time, it was back to the chessboard for more of the same, until around nine o'clock when Regina or his sister Joan would pick up Bobby and drive home. This was a typical day for us for something like two years.

This was the perfect environment for Bobby, who was living and breathing chess. The Hawthorne Chess Club offered him not only strong opposition but access to Collins' library which was first-rate. These were the necessary ingredients to help a talented young player become great in the 1950s, and if Bobby hadn't access to them things might well have turned out differently.

Collins may not have been Bobby's teacher in the sense that he gave him formal lessons, but there can be no doubt he really helped. One example concerned the problems Bobby had with the clock in 1955–57. Like many young players he sometimes lost his confidence when facing stronger opposition and would double or triple check his calculations. As a result, he'd end up in time pressure and lose some games because his flag fell—versus Pupols, Lincoln 1955; Reshevsky, 1955/56 Rosenwald; and Sherwin at a Log Cabin event in 1957 (the score of this game has not survived).

---

[1] John W. Collins, *My Seven Chess Prodigies*, New York: Simon & Schuster, 1975, (pp. 37–38).

To cure Bobby of this indecisiveness, Collins had him play games with his East German Alpha clock that was an all-purpose model. Besides serving as a regular chess clock it also offered the option to play bell games at five or ten seconds a move thanks to a built-in chime activated by turning a lever at the back of the clock. Fischer and Collins played thousands of ten-second games with this clock which now resides at the World Chess Hall of Fame in St. Louis. Fischer never lost a game on time after this training and was rarely in time pressure.

Collins and Bobby played endless practice games—exactly how many is unknown—right up until middle of July when he departed for Europe. There is no question these games wete invaluable to Bobby's development.

Collins wrote:[1]

> But the "last" one [visit] was somehow different. Sentimentally, in a way it was like a son's last night at home before going off to college, or a fledgling bird leaving the nest. He had arrived as usual about 3PM, and we had gotten right down to our usual series of fast games.
>
> A day or two before, we had played a training game, simulating tournament conditions with a clock and score keeping, now, once again, it was chess for fun. But there was something else in our thoughts. In a few hours Bobby would be flying to Europe, on his way to Moscow and Yugoslavia.

Game (25) is not published in any Fischer game collection, but is not completely unknown. A typed version was offered for sale online in combination with a copy of Max Euwe's book *Die Endspiellehre* dedicated and signed by Bobby Fischer to John Collins on May 26, 1966.

Played at a time control of forty moves in two hours, this game is also in the Marshall Chess Club's Targ donation.

---

(25) Ruy Lopez
Fischer – John Collins
New York (Training Game) May 26, 1958

1.e4 e5 2.Nf3 Nc6 3.Bb5 a6 4.Ba4 d6 5.c3

This was Fischer's preferred method of meeting the Steinitz Deferred throughout his career, his game with Geller (Bled 1961) where he played 5.0-0, a rare exception. One fine point of playing 5.c3 instead of 5.0-0 is that White can sometimes play d4 followed by Nd2-f1-e3 straight away where if he castles he must then play Re1 to allow this maneuver. Not only is a tempo saved with the 5.c3 move order, but the rook often stands better on f1 (supporting f2-f4) than e1.

5...Bd7 6.0-0

[1] John W. Collins, *My Seven Chess Prodigies*. New York: Simon & Schuster, 1975, (p. 43).

6.d4 Nge7 7.Bb3 h6 8.Qe2 Ng6 9.Qc4 Qf6 10.d5 b5 11.Qe2 Na5 12.Bd1 Be7 13.g3 0-0 14.h4 Rfc8?? 15.Bg5 and Black would likely have resigned immediately in Fischer–Ciocâltea, Varna Olympiad 1962 if it had not been a team tournament. Curiously Fischer had beaten Ciocâltea's countrymen Ghițescu in another miniature (fourteen moves) the previous Olympiad.

6...g6 7.d4 Bg7 8.Bg5 f6 9.Bh4

The more natural and common 9.Be3 leaves the bishop better placed for attack and defense.

9...Nh6 10.Nbd2 Nf7 11.Re1 0–0

Black could try to take advantage of the exposed position of the bishop with 11...g5 12.Bg3 h5.

12.Nf1 Qe8 13.Bb3 Kh8 14.Ne3 g5?!

14...exd4 15.Nd5 Qd8 16.Nxd4 (16.cxd4 Ng5=) offers White a small but durable advantage.

15.Bg3 Ne7 16.h4

White had a simpler path to advantage with 16.h3! Nh6 17.dxe5 dxe5 18.Nh2 stopping Black's attack with a clear positional edge.

16...g4 17.Nh2 h5 18.f3 Nh6?

18...gxf3 19.Nxf3 Nh6 followed by ...Ng4 and ...Qg6 would have offered Black reasonable counterplay. The text offers practical chances, but shouldn't hold up if White plays accurately.

19.fxg4 hxg4 20.Nhxg4 Nxg4 21.Nxg4 Qg6 22.Ne3 Bh6

22...Qxe4?? 23.Bc2 followed by Qh5+.

23.Bf2 Rad8 24.Bc2 Rg8 25.Qf3 Bf4 26.Kh1 Rg7 27.g3 Bh6

27...Bxg3?? 28.Rg1 wins material.

28.Nf5 Nxf5 29.exf5 Qe8 30.Be4 b6 31.dxe5 dxe5 32.g4

White is winning, but care is still required.

32... Rh7 33.Rad1 Qe7 34.Bc6?!

This trade costs White much of his advantage. The idea is right, but the timing is wrong. 34.Rd3, followed by Red1, would have left Collins hard-pressed to save his position.

34...Bxc6 35.Rxd8+?

Bobby would still have the better of it after 35.Qxc6. The text costs White control of the important d-file.

35...Qxd8 36.Qxc6 Bg5 37.h5 Rd7

The tide has turned and Black has full counterplay for the pawn. White needs to be careful.

38.Qe4 Rd2 39.Be3

The text holds the balance but 39.Re2 Rxe2 40.Qxe2 Qd5+ 41.Kh2 Qxa2 42.Qd3 Qxb2 43.Qd8+ Kg7 44.Qe7+ would have led to an immediate draw.

39...Bxe3 40.Qxe3?

40.Rxe3 Rd1+ 41.Kg2 Qd2+ 42.Re2 was still equal.

40...Qd5+ 41.Qe4 Qxa2?

41...Qxe4+! 42.Rxe4 Rxb2 43.g5 Rf2 44.gxf6 Rxf5 45.Kg2 Rxh5 46.Kg3 Rf5 47.Kg4 (47.Rc4! c5 48.a4 improves, only slightly better for Black) 47...Rxf6 48.Rxe5 Rc6 49.Re3 Kg7 50.Kf5 Kf7 with excellent winning chances for Black.

42.Qc6 Qd5+ 43.Qxd5 Rxd5 44.Kg2 Kg7

Collins alertly activates his king. The tempting 44...Rd2+ can easily lead to trouble after 45.Kg3 Rxb2 46.g5 fxg5?? (46...Rd2 should still draw after 47.gxf6 Kg8 48.Rxe5 Kf7) 47.f6 Kg8 (47...Rd2 48.Rxe5 Kg8 49.Re8+ Kf7 50.h6! wins) 48.h6, winning.

45.g5?

This is an example where active defense is not the right approach. White looks to be holding after 45.Kf3 Kh6 46.Rg1 Kg5 47.Ke4 Rd2 48.Rh1 Rd7 49.Kf3.

45...fxg5 46.Kf3 Kf6 47.Ke4 Rd7 48.Rh1 a5 49.h6 Rh7 50.c4 g4 51.Rg1 Kg5 52.Rf1 Rxh6 53.Kxe5 Rf6 54.Rf4?

This loses right away but after 54.b3 c6 (and not 54...g3?? 55.Rf3 drawing) the end is not far off.

54...Rf8 55.Rf1 Re8+ 56.Kd5 Kf6 57.Kc6 Re7 58.Kd5 Re5+ 59.Kc6 Rc5+ 60.Kd7 Rxc4 61.Rf2 Rc5 62.Rf4 Kg5 63.b4 axb4 64.f6 Kxf4, 0–1.

Game (26), made available for the first time by International Master Anthony Saidy, raises the question if more Fischer training games from the spring of 1958 might be out there.

---

(26) King's Indian
Anthony Saidy – Fischer
New York (Training Game) June 5, 1958

1.d4 Nf6 2.c4 g6 3.Nc3 Bg7 4.e4 d6 5.f3 e5

If Black wants to play ...e5 it needs to be played right away as 5...0-0 6.Bg5 e5? is met by 7.dxe5 dxe5 8.Qxd8 Rxd8 9.Nd5.

6.Nge2

6.dxe5 dxe5 7.Qxd8+ Kxd8 8.Bg5 c6 9.0–0-0+ Kc7 offers the first player no advantage. 6.d5 Nh5 7.Be3 0-0 8.Qd2 f5 9.0-0-0 f4 10.Bf2 Bf6 11.Qe1 gave White a very slight edge in Giri–Carlsen, Tata Steel 2013.

6...0-0 7.Bg5

7.d5 and 7.Be3 are the alternatives.

7...exd4 8.Nxd4 Nc6 9.Nc2 Ne5

9...Be6 10.Be2 h6 11.Bh4 g5 12.Bf2 Ne5 with equal chances in Benko–Fischer, Portorož (izt) 1958.

10.Qd2 Be6 11.b3

11.Na3 c6 12.Be2 a6 13.f4 Ned7 14.0-0 h6 15.f5 hxg5 16.fxe6 Ne5 17.exf7+ Rxf7 18.Kh1 b5 19.cxb5 axb5 20.Nc2 g4 with equal chances in Gurgenidze–Saidy, Varna (Student Olympiad) 1958.

11...a6

11...c6 12.Rd1 Qa5 13.Be2 Nfd7 14.Na4 Qxd2+ 15.Rxd2 Nb6 16.Nxb6 axb6 was balanced in Ding–J. Zhou, Beijing 2012.

12.Rd1 c6 13.Nd4?!

This costs valuable time as it isn't clear if capturing on e6 is a good idea. Better is 13.Be2 preparing to castle.

13...Qa5 14.Be2 c5 15.Nc2 b5 16.Bxf6?!

16.Nd5 Qxd2+ 17.Rxd2 Bxd5 18.Bxf6 Bxf6 19.Rxd5 Rfd8 20.Kf2 Nc6 21.Rhd1 should be enough to draw.

16...Bxf6 17.Nd5 Qxd2+ 18.Rxd2 Bg5 19.Rd1?!

19.f4 Bxd5 20.fxg5 Bxe4 21.Ne3 bxc4 22.Bxc4 Nxc4 23.Nxc4, when White's activity offers practical chances for the pawn.

19...bxc4 20.bxc4 Rab8

20...Bxd5! 21.Rxd5 Rfb8 22.Rxd6 Rb2 23.Bd1 Nxc4 was even stronger.

21.Nce3 Bh6 22.f4 Nc6 23.f5 gxf5 24.exf5 Bxd5 25.Nxd5 Nd4 26.Bd3 Rfe8+ 27.Kf1 Kh8 28.h4 Rb2 29.g4?

29.Rh3!

29...Be3 30.Rh3 Rf2+, 0–1.

The score of games 25, 27, and 28 and the result (1½–1½) of the available Fischer–Collins training games (and similar encounters with R. Weinstein and Lombardy), contradict Lombardy's assertion in *Understanding Chess*[1] that Collins was too weak a player to have helped him and Fischer.

---

[1] William Lombardy, *Understanding Chess: My System, My Games, My Life*. In association with Russell Enterprises, 2011, (p. 219).

(27) **Sicilian**
John Collins – Fischer
New York (Training Game) September 8, 1957

1.e4 c5 2.Nc3 Nc6 3.g3 g6 4.Bg2 Bg7 5.d3 d6 6.f4 Nd4

6...e6, 6...Nf6, 6...e5, 6...Rb8, 6...f5 and 6...Nh6 are all more commonly seen here, but the text is not completely unknown having been played by Grandmasters Hulak, Frolov, and Gutman.

7.Nf3 Bg4 8.h3 Bxf3 9.Bxf3 Nxf3+ 10.Qxf3 e6

10...Nf6 looks more natural and meets 11.e5 with 11...dxe5 12.fxe5 Nd7 13.e6 fxe6 14.Qxb7 0-0 and Black is doing fine.

11.0-0 Ne7 12.Be3 0-0 13.g4 Qd7 14.Rf2

14.f5

14...f5 15.Re1 b5 16.Rfe2 b4 17.Nd1 e5?

17...fxe4 18.dxe4 Nc6 was a better try for Black.

18.gxf5?

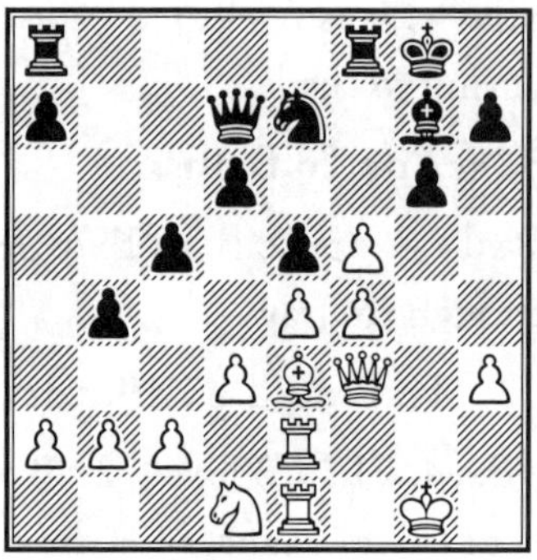

18.exf5! gxf5 19.fxe5 fxg4 (19...Bxe5 20.Bxc5) 20.Qxg4 Qxg4+ 21.hxg4 Bxe5 22.Bxc5 wins a pawn.

18...gxf5 19.Rg2 fxe4

19...exf4! 20.Bxf4 Ng6 21.Bg3 f4 22.Bf2 Rae8 and Black has a large, probably decisive advantage.

20.Qxe4 exf4

20...Ng6!

21.Bxf4

21.Bxc5!

21...Ng6 22.Bh2

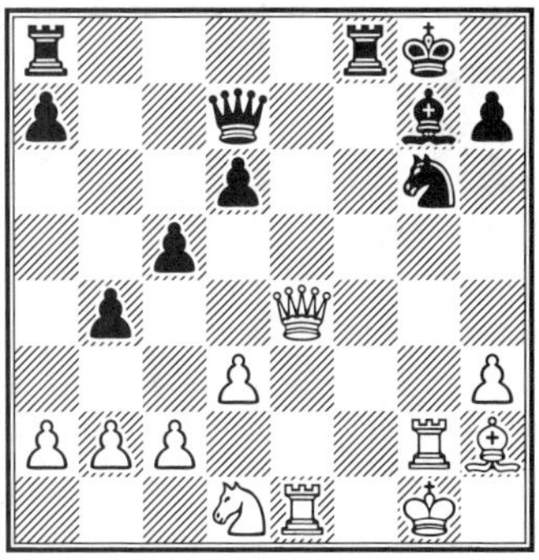

22...Qxh3

22...Rae8 23.Qd5+ Kh8 24.Re4 Rxe4 25.dxe4 Qxh3 should also win.

23.Qe6+ Qxe6 24.Rxe6 Bd4+ 25.Kh1 Rf1+ 26.Bg1 Rxd1 27.Rxd6 Re8 28.c3 bxc3 29.bxc3 Bxg1 30.Rxg1 Rxg1+, 0–1.

There were few international events in the years immediately after the end of World War II, and to compensate for this state of affairs various radio matches were organized. The best known is the 1945 event pitting the United States against the Soviet Union, but there were many others, including one between New York and Paris held Saturday, December 11, 1948, from 9AM to 6PM. John Collins was among those who played for the Marshall team.

The results of the match in board order were: Fine–O. Bernstein ½–½; E. Lasker–Tartakower ½–½; Horowitz–Rossolimo 0–1; Kashdan–Raizman 1–0; Hanauer–Betbeder ½–½; Collins–Bouteville ½–½; Faucher–Seneca ½–½; Gresser–de Silans ½–½.

(28) Sicilian
John Collins – Fischer
New York (Training Game) 1957 or 1958

1.e4 c5 2.Nf3 d6 3.d4 cxd4 4.Nxd4 Nf6 5.Nc3 a6 6.Bg5 e6 7.f4 Be7 8.Qf3 Qc7 9.Bd3

9.0-0-0 is the main move here.

9...Bd7 10.0-0-0 Nc6 11.Nxc6 Bxc6 12.Rhe1 h6

12...0-0

13.Bxf6 Bxf6

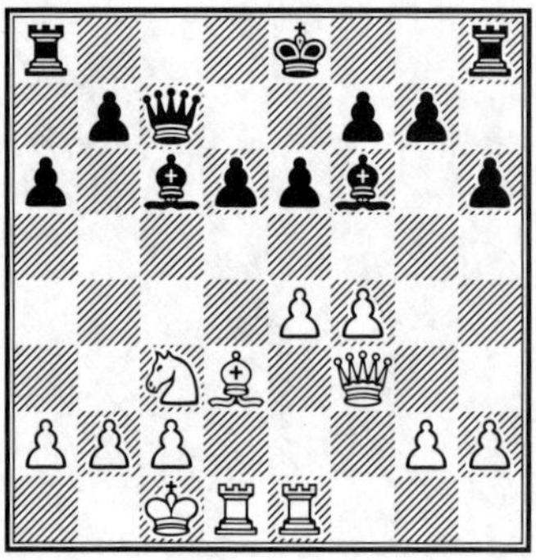

14.Nd5! exd5 15.exd5+ Kf8

15...Be7 16.dxc6 bxc6 17.Re2 and the king is still stuck in the center as 17...0-0 is met by 18.Qe4 winning a piece.

16.dxc6 bxc6 17.Bc4 d5

Black's strong pawn center compensates for the temporary displacement of his king.

18.Bb3 a5 19.Ba4 Rb8 20.c3

Anticipating ...Rb4.

20...g6 21.g3 Kg7 22.Re2 Rb6 23.h4 Rhb8 24.h5 g5 25.fxg5 Bxg5+ 26.Kb1 Qd6

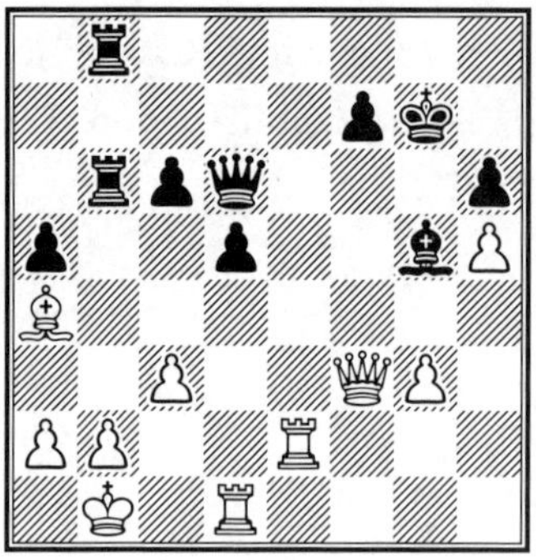

26...Qb7 followed by ...Bf6 looks more accurate.

27.Rf1

This leads to a draw. If White wants to try for more he needs to play 27.Ka1, intending Rb1, Qd3 and Bc2.

27...Qf6 28.Qxf6+ Bxf6 29.Rf3 c5 30.Rd3 Re6 31.Bd1 Rbe8 32.Rf2 d4 33.cxd4 cxd4 34.Rf5 Re3 35.Rf3 Re1 36.a3 R8e3 37.Kc2 a4 38.Kd2 Rg1 39.Rfxe3 dxe3+ 40.Kxe3 Rxg3+, ½–½.

PART THREE

Grandmaster *and* Candidate

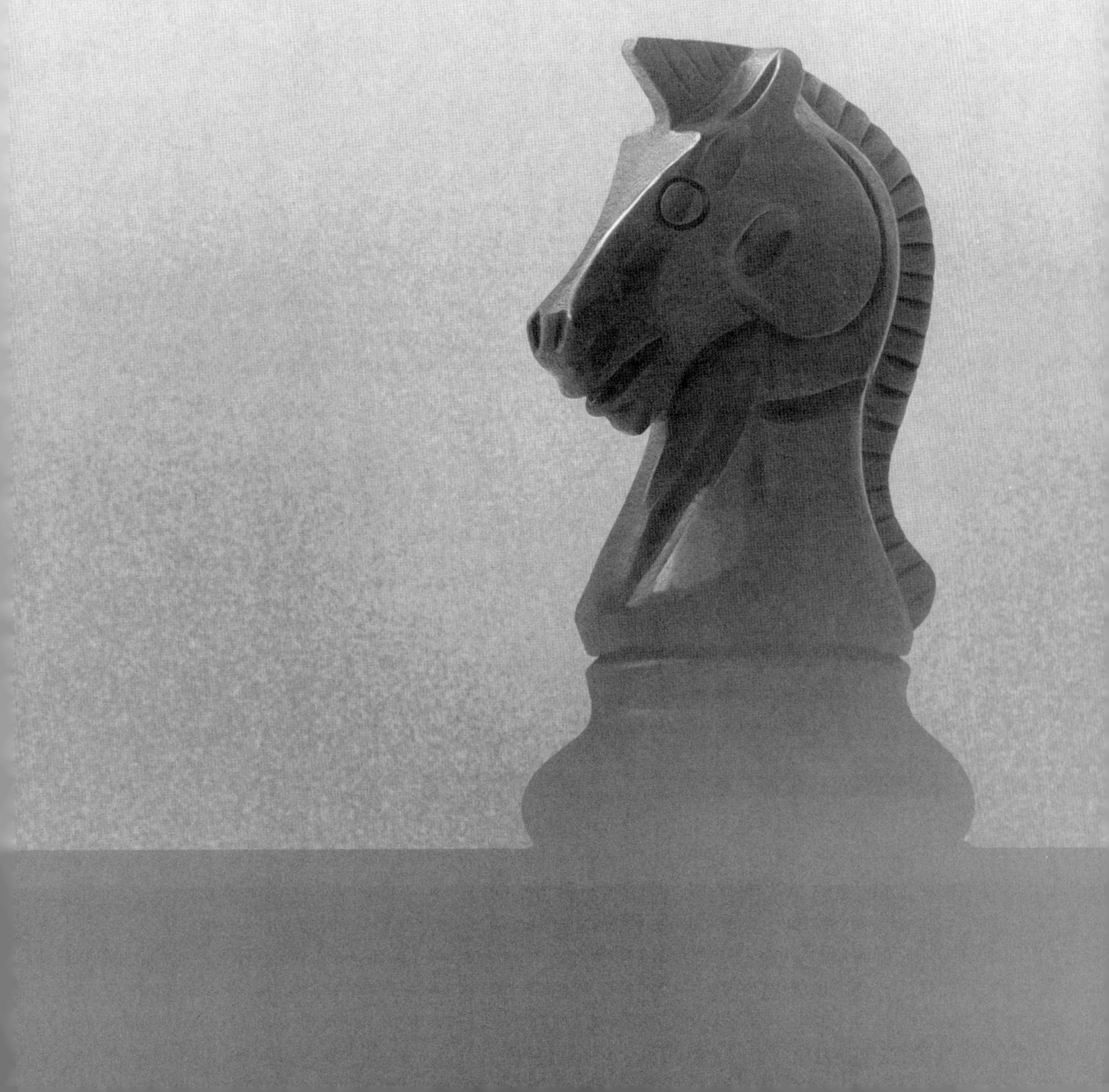

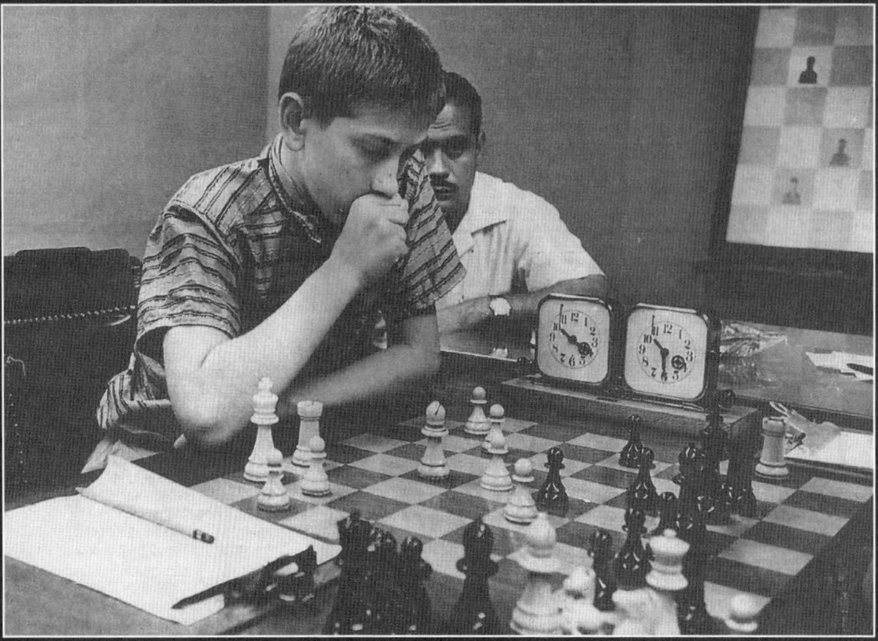

Bobby studies the position after Black's 23...Rc7 in game four of his 1957 match with Rodolfo Cardoso.

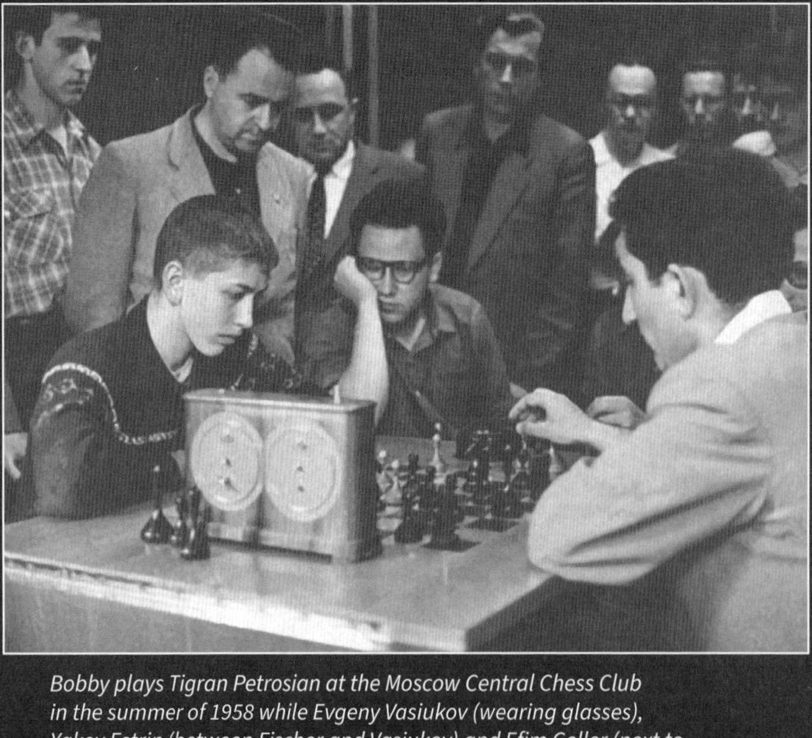

Bobby plays Tigran Petrosian at the Moscow Central Chess Club in the summer of 1958 while Evgeny Vasiukov (wearing glasses), Yakov Estrin (between Fischer and Vasiukov) and Efim Geller (next to Estrin) take in the action.

1
THE USSR AND YUGOSLAVIA

The summer of 1958 was the only time Bobby ever visited the Soviet Union. Sandwiched in between his jaunt to Brussels and his arrival in Yugoslavia for the Portorož Interzonal, his short stay in Moscow had a major impact on his life. Prior to his trip, Bobby thought of Soviet Chess in a positive way—his attitude completely changed within a week of setting foot in the USSR.

Bobby hit the Soviets' radar early on—before his extraordinary victory in the U.S. Championship in January 1958, even before he won the U.S. Open in August of 1957. This is evident from the letter below between two U.S. Chess Federation officers written prior to either event taking place:

> July 17, 1957
>
> Dear Mr. Mehwald,[1]
>
> The Chess Section of the USSR has expressed interest in having Bobby Fischer visit the Soviet Union on the basis that they would pay his expenses while there but not the transportation to and from the Soviet Union.
>
> Enclosed is a copy of a notice sent yesterday to a number of TV and radio stations as well as to chess columnists and chess clubs.
>
> Public interest in Bobby and in such a trip may make it possible to obtain national and radio coverage of the U.S. Open and also for the send-off if the trip materializes. Perhaps Mr. Cyrus Eaton would be interested in assisting financially.
>
> Please let me know your reaction and advise of any possibilities that occur to you and any action you want me to undertake.
>
> Sincerely
> Kenneth Harkness[2]

The press release mentioned was picked up by Frederick Chevalier, chess correspondent for *The Christian Science Monitor* and it ran July 27, 1957:

[1] Chairman, Financial Committee for the 1957 U.S. Open.

[2] Business Manager for the U.S. Chess Federation.

BOBBY FISCHER INVITED TO VISIT RUSSIA

Bobby Fischer, fourteen, has just retained his title as United States Junior Champion and is presently in California waiting for the 58th annual U.S. Open, to be played in Cleveland August 5–17.

An invitation to have Bobby visit Russia has been sent to the United States Chess Federation, according to Kenneth Harkness, Federation Business Manager. If this visit is to take place, since there is no government sponsorship of chess in this country, travel expenses must be raised. It would not be proper, of course, for the young Brooklyn boy to visit Russian alone, so it is hoped that some of our older chess experts can make the trip also. A fund of $2,500 for travel expenses for the group is necessary and must be raised in time for the trip to start on the closing day of the Open.

In the spring of 1958 the *Cleveland Chess Bulletin* published an open letter from Regina Fischer which is of interest as it touches upon two important points: First, Regina's attempt to organize a simul tour in the spring of 1958—the motivation was clearly to raise money for Fischer's participation in that summer's upcoming Interzonal in Yugoslavia. Second, it infers that as late as the end of March, Bobby had yet to sign the contract offered to him by Simon & Schuster for what eventually became *Bobby Fischer's Games of Chess*.

March 21, 1958

Dear Friends,

This is to inquire whether there would be any interest in having Bobby Fischer play one or more exhibitions games in your city during Easter vacation. He can leave here after school Thursday, April 3rd and is due back on April 9 or 10. The fee would be $100 per exhibition of twenty or twenty-five games, plus plane fare and expenses. If Bobby visits other cities en route your share of the plane fare would be prorated.

Also, Bobby hopes to complete by the end of the month his first attempt at writing. It is a booklet of full annotations of his thirteen games played in the U.S. Championship of December, 1957. It will probably be mimeographed without illustrations, and will probably cost about $2. Could you advise whether there would be any interest in individual or bulk purchases of this booklet among your chess players or clubs?

Trusting to hear from you as soon as possible, I am,

Sincerely yours,
Mrs. Regina Fischer

For some time, the issue of how to get the Fischers to Moscow was unresolved. Then on March 26, 1958, Bobby appeared on CBS's TV show *I've Got a Secret*. Emcee Gary Moore had a special surprise for Bobby: At the end of the show, after the experts failed to guess his secret (recently becoming the youngest U.S.

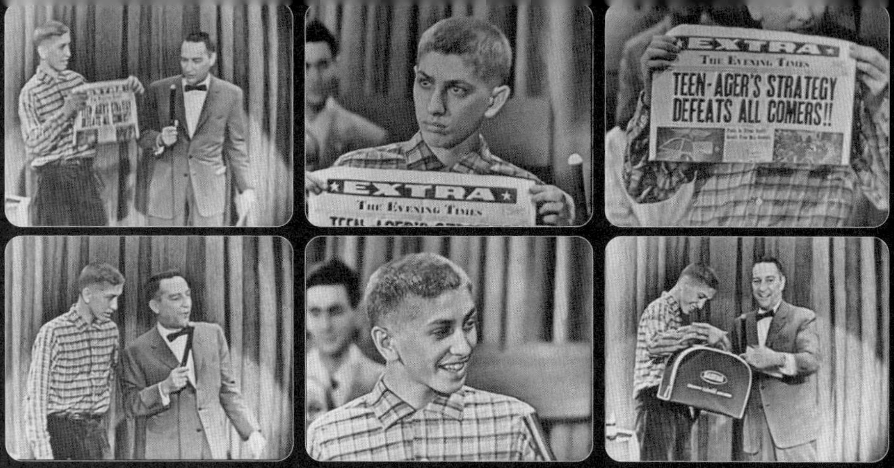

Bobby with Gary Moore on I've Got a Secret.

Chess Champion), Fischer was given two international airplane tickets that enabled him and his sister Joan to travel to Brussels, Moscow, and Belgrade.

The New York Times ran the following piece on May 25, 1958, shortly before Fischer left for the Soviet Union:

FISCHER EXPECTS TO MEET PRODIGY FIVE-YEAR-OLD IS LIKELY CHESS RIVAL FOR BOBBY, FIFTEEN, IN MATCHES AT MOSCOW

> Within one month of his departure for Moscow in response to an invitation from Soviet chess authorities, fifteen-year-old Bobby Fischer of Brooklyn, the United States chess champion was impressed by the news that Russia had a five-year-old chess prodigy named Ernest Kim. According to Soviet news sources, the World Champion Mikhail Botvinnik, speaks highly of the child's ability.
>
> Bobby believes that the Russians are planning to pit him against the five-year-old before matching him against some of the Russian grandmasters.

It's hard to know how much credence to give to the idea that Fischer was "...impressed by the news..." of such a rivalry when Bobby could have played fifty Ernest Kims at the same time in 1958 and beaten them all. Kim, like many exceptionally young prodigies, never realized his potential although he did become a 2300+ master. It appears the two never actually met.

En route to Moscow and Yugoslavia, Bobby made a short visit to Brussels. This overlooked stop-over was reported firsthand by Oregon high school student Larry Finley:[1]

OSWEGO BOY SPENDS DAY WITH AMERICAN WHIZ CHESS CHAMPION SEES FAIR

> Brussels, Belgium—1.e4 e5 2.Nf3 Nc6 3.Bb5 f5!? No, these are not the latest specifications for a new jet bomber or the performance record of a

[1] Larry Finley, "Chess Champion Sees Fair," *Oregon Journal*, July 11, 1958.

souped-up sports car. This is actually the beginning of a very interesting chess game, and one of the countless variations which Bobby Fischer, fifteen-year-old champion of the U.S.A. must analyze and understand. At fifteen Bobby is the youngest U.S. Champion and international master in history.

Being interested in chess myself, but also interested in how any fifteen-year-old could become champion of anything in this cut-throat game, I wanted very much to meet him. It happened in Brussels, Belgium, the site of the 1958 World's Exposition.

I was there on a vacation with my mother, and had heard from the local chess club that Bobby would be spending a weekend at the fair with his twenty-year-old sister, Joan.

Thinking that he might like another teenage boy to talk English with, I got in touch with him after he arrived. He was glad to talk with another American again and invited me right over.

My expectations mounted as I rode over to his room. At first I though he might have a long beard and smoke a pipe. Knowing that this was a little far-fetched, I thought he might wear a tweed jacket with horn-rimmed glasses and white tennis shoes. These thoughts all vanished, however, when I finally did meet him.

Bobby is tall and rather thin, which made me think he might be a lanky Texan, but Texas is rather far from his hometown of New York.

He and I hit it off very well together. That afternoon the three of us went to the fair, which they hadn't seen yet, and we all had a wonderful time. Bobby was particularly impressed with the huge size of the Atomium. We both realized that those puny little postcards didn't do the giant aluminum structure justice. I quickly found out that Bobby has a very keen mind, which he is not merely using in playing chess, but also to absorb the many things which the fair has to offer.

On our first day we spent three hours in the science hall, a giant wonderland of exhibitions, each depicting some phase of modern-day science. We saw the sections on the atom, the crystal, the molecule, and the living cell. Each was fascinating.

After visiting there, we proceeded to see the rest of the fair. Because I had worked there for a month I knew my way around and gave them a guided tour. I didn't know how much of the fair it was possible to see in the three days we had to spend there, but I quickly found out.

They both wanted to see everything and wanted me to show it to them. I also wanted to refresh my memory of the pavilions so I was glad to be with them.

Later in the day Bobby's sister grew tired of our boy-talk (chess, girls, cars, swimming, girls, cars, girls, etc.) so she left us and we were on our own the next two days.

There were many things at the fair that attracted our interests. First we saw the huge Russian Pavilion, with its Sputniks and heavy machinery. Fine arts seemed to be pushed into a corner in favor of scientific advances of the Russians in such fields as electronics, optics, etc. I must say, however, that all the exhibits were very interesting and somewhat thought provoking—to say the least.

We then crossed the way to see the highly controversial U.S. pavilion. We could see at once the reasons for controversy.

Aside from an ultra-modern "typical" American home and the "take it easy" theme of patio living, there are many objects of extremely abstract art throughout the pavilion. They are pleasing to the eye but I have heard Europeans asking, "Is America really like this?"

There are, however, some very good and interesting exhibits. The large computing machine always seems to attract attention. The atomic energy exhibit was somewhat overlooked in the beginning but it is now starting to attract spectators.

One exhibit has common approval. It was produced at a cost of millions of dollars and hundreds of years. This is the group of over 300 American college students who are acting as guides in the American pavilion. Each of them was handpicked and they all realize the responsibility put upon them to represent our country. Bobby and I noticed that nearly every state was represented – one student was even from Hawaii.

They all have an unending degree of patience, which is well needed when such questions as "Why doesn't the U.S. have a Sputnik?" are asked. All of them are proficient in two or more languages, and are also able to answer in five languages the two most asked questions of the day: "Where are the lavatories?" and "Where is Circarama?"

So although the American pavilion may raise a few questions as well as a few eyebrows, it still gives first place to the greatest pride of any country—its youth.

Bobby and I completely enjoyed our three days at the fair together. From viewing the fair from the top of the mighty Atomium to seeing a Netherlands' potato sorter in action, we had a continual ball.

The last day of our visit came, and I finally got up enough courage to ask for a game of chess. When he accepted I saw that he was going to be easy on me, but that wasn't what I wanted.

"Sure," he said, "I'll crush you, if that's what you want. You know," he continued, "I haven't crushed anyone for a long time, it might be fun at that!"

Well, I don't know if he enjoyed it or not, but he trounced me four games and it was real experience for me. His exact play quickly showed me why he was the champion of the United States. Not only did I enjoy the games, I also learned a great deal about chess strategy.

Invited by the Russian government to spend a few days in Moscow, Bobby and his sister had to leave the following day. I believe that in Moscow our chess champion will show the Russians that American kids have a lot on the ball, just as he showed me.

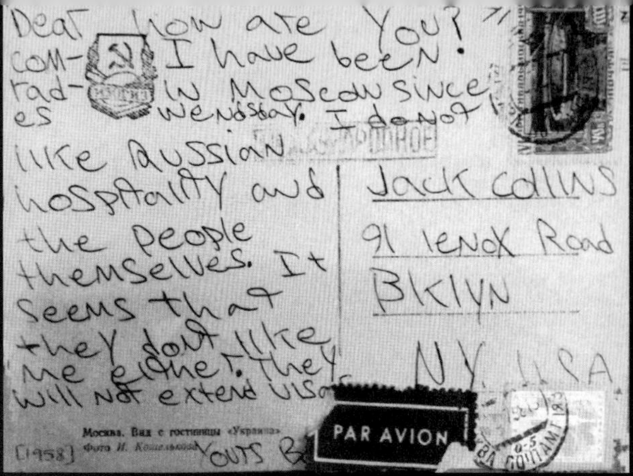

In a postcard from Moscow to John Collins, Bobby makes his feelings abundantly clear and his sense of humor ("Dear Comrades") is on full display. Kudos to Bobby for writing what he thought without fear of the potential consequences, to the Soviet censors for letting the postcard through, and to Collins for hanging on to it for over forty years (Postcard: Courtesy of the John Collins Collection at Indiana University's Lilly Library).

MOSCOW

Bobby arrived in Moscow with high expectations, a feeling that soon changed. Having grown up reading Soviet books and magazines he was full of admiration for its top players and their uncompromising and dynamic style of play. Looking back, it's not hard to see this one-time only visit poisoned Fischer's future relations with the "Russians"—like many Americans of the era he used this term exclusively despite the fact that few top Soviet players were ethnic Russians. Whether Fischer was justified in these feelings after his short visit is a complicated question that doesn't have an easy answer.

Bobby's hosts envisioned taking him to the Bolshoi Ballet and the Kremlin, but such cultural activities were anathema to the American teenager who was only interested in one thing—chess! Ideally, he wanted to play training matches against the best Soviet players, supplemented with a never-ending series of speed games. If given a choice, Fischer would have slept on a cot at the Moscow Central Chess Club and played 24/7. He had no idea why his request to play Botvinnik or Bronstein was not taken seriously, unable to appreciate the humiliation these two Grandmasters would have experienced if they lost to a fifteen-year-old boy.

How quickly Fischer soured on the USSR is evident from the postcard he sent to Jack Collins not long after he arrived in Moscow [see top of this page]. In the future Fischer would maintain good relations with many top Soviet players but grew to despise the apparatus that produced them. Bobby saw the Soviet Chess Federation as an evil organization that would do whatever it could to prevent him from winning the World Championship.

There is little to document Fischer's visit that dates back to the summer of 1958. Besides the postcard to Collins, a few iconic photographs have survived. The most famous one shows Bobby playing blitz against Tigran Petrosian at the Moscow Central Chess Club. Nothing seems to have been written in chess publications as to how Bobby fared against "Iron Tigran" and other Soviet players he met over the board (Nikitin and Vasiukov were two others he faced).

[left] David Bronstein;
[right] Mikhail Botvinnik, 1954.

One other surviving document, a letter from Regina Fischer to then USCF President Jerry Spann, dated June 29, 1958, suggests communication between the Soviets and Americans was far from optimal in the months leading up to Bobby and Joan's visit:[1]

> Dear Jerry,
>
> Many thanks for getting the cable out so promptly. At least they knew the federation was behind Bobby on this. I saw an item in the *NY Times* sports section today saying that it would be a big problem to extend the visa, so it was a good thing the Yugoslavs agreed to take them as of the second week in July in the meantime. The article also quoted the present hosts as not having expected Bobby for another month. At any rate, Bobby is going to play Petrosian on Monday, tomorrow, it said, so Bobby is satisfied with the chess practice he is getting I am sure. I have not had any letters from Bobby at all since he left. Joan dropped me a line twice, but not since they left Brussels. If they don't keep in touch any better than that I may take off myself – fly now, pay later, provided I could still get a visa, and my credit is OK'd.
>
> Thanks again.
>
> Regards,
>
> Regina Fischer

The theme of this letter—how poorly the visit was planned—is supported by newspaper accounts of the time. One paper reported that the Soviets only became aware of Bobby and Joan's imminent arrival when their plane had left Prague (they had flown there from Brussels) and was heading towards Moscow causing the hosts to rush to the airport at the last minute to greet them.

The Interzonal was scheduled to start on August 5 and the Soviets expected to host Bobby and Joan for the two weeks prior. They apparently had no idea the Fischer siblings would arrive six weeks before the event—fortunately the

[1] Letter from the USCF's Jerry Spann Collection currently housed at the World Chess Hall of Fame.

Yugoslavs were flexible and accommodating. It's understandable the Soviets wouldn't have wanted to host Bobby and Joan for an additional month and this, most likely, contributed to their visas not being extended.

Lev Abramov's (head of the Chess Section of the USSR Sports Committee at the time) explanation sounds like a propaganda piece:[1]

> A few days before Bobby and Joan's planned departure, they turned up at my office and said that they wanted to prolong their stay and play a few serious games. I was ready for this and I gave my agreement. A couple of days later the following incident occurred. In a restaurant, while awaiting the main course, Bobby was rocking about on this chair. Joan warned him, but he carried on doing it and fell over. When he got up, he immediately went to his room, growling "I'm fed up with these Russian pigs." This is what the interpreter passed on to her superiors, but I think it should have been "I'm fed up with this Russian pork". In short, I received a directive for them to leave Moscow. Unexpectedly, I received support from Bobby, who came into my room and asked: "What payment will I receive for these games?" I breathed a sigh of relief and replied: "None. You are our guest, and we don't pay fees to guests."

Mark Taimanov provided the first written account from the chess community of Bobby's blitz experiences in Moscow and it was corroborated by the Yugoslav arbiter Božidar Kažić (1921–1996) who was the referee for the 1971 Fischer–Taimanov Candidates match held in Vancouver. At the end of that match Kažić and the Soviet delegation (Taimanov and his seconds Evgeny Vasiukov and Yury Balashov) were taken to dinner by Bobby and Ed Edmondson (Fischer's acting manager). During the course of the meal a conversation came up about Bobby's performance in Moscow thirteen years before:

> At the closing of my infamous match against Fischer, Fischer and I were sitting with fellow grandmasters at a banquet and were talking peacefully after the preceding storms (curiously, we communicated in Serbian, which both of us knew). The conversation revolved around the match until my second, Evgeny Vasiukov, suddenly turned to Fischer. "Bobby, do you remember that in 1958 you spent several days in Moscow and played many blitz games against our chess players? I was one of your partners." "Of course, I remember," Fischer replied. "And the result?" Vasiukov asked. "Why only the result?" Fischer responded. "I remember the games. One was a French." And he rattled off all the moves!

Vasiukov, who died in 2018, remembered it differently, insisting that when Fischer offered to show their blitz games, he responded, "Bobby, I can show you

---

[1] Dimitry Plisetsky and Sergey Voronkov, *Russians versus Fischer*. London: Gloucester Publishers, 2005.

how we played." According to Vasiukov, Kažić only heard Bobby's side of things, and soon another story appeared heralding Fischer's magnificent memory.

Vasiukov recalled Fischer activities in Moscow with many more details:[1]

> The first time I met Fischer was in the summer of 1958, when the fifteen year-old Bobby came to Moscow as a result of an agreement between the USSR and the USCF, in order to play two training matches before the Interzonal tournament—with Spassky, the former world junior champion, and with the Moscow champion Vasiukov. But when he arrived in Moscow, he suddenly announced that he would only play the World Champion Botvinnik. This was received with a smile and he was courteously refused. Fischer then frequented the Central Chess Club, where for two weeks from morning till evening he tirelessly played blitz, crushing everyone right, left and center. And then they invited the three leading blitz players of that time: Bronstein, Petrosian, and me. But Bronstein did not come, saying: "What's the point of playing a boy." Petrosian won the first two games and then played with alternating success, retaining an advantage of two points. Before this I had played a blitz match with Geller. I didn't know that blitz was not his forte. With the score standing at 7–0 in my favor (without any draws!) we halted the match, and then I had to play Fischer. I thought that, if I had done so well against such a great grandmaster, I would also be successful against Fischer, but in the first five games he took a one-point lead. But then I adapted to his style of play and won by a big score. He reacted calmly to his defeats, except that each time he would set up the pieces for a new game with a discontented appearance.

Vasiukov's remembrances are of events that occurred over half a century prior, something which must be taken into consideration when examining their credibility. It's possible the results of the games are as he says as Vasiukov was always known as a strong blitz player. More interesting is his assertion that training matches were scheduled for Bobby during his Moscow visit, a claim not corroborated by other sources.

Spassky was already a huge talent by the summer of 1958—he had tied for third in the 1956 Candidates tournament at nineteen. Vasiukov had won the 33rd Moscow Championship in 1956, was second in 1957, and regained his title in 1958. He had also played on the winning Soviet student team at Uppsala in 1956, scoring 92% on first board.

It's hard to believe the Soviets would have arranged training matches for the benefit of a foreign competitor immediately prior to the Interzonal. The last-minute scheduling of Fischer's visit to Moscow, recounted by Yury Averbakh, also casts doubt on Vasiukov's account.[2]

---

[1] Dimitry Plisetsky and Sergey Voronkov, *Russians versus Fischer*. London: Gloucester Publishers, 2005, (pp. 238–239).

[2] Ibid.

Leonid Stein and Boris Spassky at the Tel Aviv Olympiad, 1964 (Photo: Beth Cassidy).

In 1957, on the eve of the World Youth and Student Festival in Moscow, Fischer's mother wrote a letter addressed to Khrushchev himself, if I'm not mistaken. In it she asked that her son be invited to the Festival. The wheels of bureaucracy turned slowly, and while the matter was being considered, the Festival ended. Nevertheless, an invitation was sent to the American to visit the following year, in 1958.

It was only after Bobby's appearance on *I've Got a Secret* earned him airline tickets on Sabena Airlines (with the routing New York–Brussels–Prague–Moscow–Belgrade–Munich–New York), that his participation in the Interzonal could be confirmed. The stopover in Moscow was finalized in late March of 1958 (three months before Fischer arrived in the Soviet Union). The bureaucracy in the Soviet Union always moved slowly, making it unlikely anything besides sightseeing and blitz were on the agenda for Bobby in late June of 1958.

Vladimir Bagirov's recollection rings true:[1]

> When the chess officials found yet another opponent for Bobby with a less familiar surname than the American expected, he got angry. They explained to him that there were hundreds of good chess players in the Soviet Union that could play decently. Bobby answered, "There are only about a dozen players in the Soviet Union that can play decently."

Boris Spassky on Bobby in Moscow:[2]

> I like to remember Bobby. He belonged to that category of tragic people. I felt that, observing him back in 1958 when he came to Moscow with his sister. Yes, I was in the Central Chess Club then and I saw him playing blitz, and Bronstein also watched. I remember Petrosian was there too... For Bobby that was a sad experience, since he saw nothing at all of Moscow. He sat for days on end in the CCC and just played. And then he was asked to leave Moscow... Yes, it was a sad experience for him. And there was one thing he never grasped: that he had a huge number of fans in Russia! During the match in Reykjavík, as I well know, many rooted for him...

[1] Vladimir Bagirov, *White Fischer*. Riga: 1991.

[2] From a 2015 interview at Chess 24.com.

Seated Theo Schuster, Yury Averbakh, and Miguel Najdorf. Standing (far left) Alexander Roshal, Viktor Kupreichik and Yury Bogadanov medical doctor for the Soviet Delegation. FIDE Candidates matches, London 1983.

The report from Larry Finley, the date of Regina's letter, and newspaper accounts provide a rough timeline that suggest that Bobby and Joan left New York around June 19, spent a long weekend in Brussels (June 20–22), flew to Moscow (June 23), and then onward to Belgrade on July 9.

JANOŠEVIĆ AND MATULOVIĆ

Unlike Fischer's sojourn in Moscow, his time in Belgrade was documented in detail. Yugoslavia's leading paper, *Politika,* ran a regular chess column giving excellent coverage of Bobby's activities prior to the Portorož Interzonal. This is not surprising as the 1950s to the early 1980s were a golden time for the game's popularity in the Balkan nation. This could partially be attributed to the individual success of Gligorić and Ivkov, who both played in Candidates matches. The excellence of the national teams, which finished in the top three in almost every Olympiad during this period, was another contributor.

The first mention of Fischer in *Politika* occurred on July 10 where it was reported that Bobby and his sister arrived in the Yugoslav capital the day before from Moscow. The article states that during his visit to the Soviet capital, he played some blitz games and gave simultaneous displays. That Bobby played blitz is an acknowledged fact, but it's doubtful he gave simuls—it's never been mentioned anywhere else.

More interesting is the following statement in *Politika*:

> Until the Interzonal tournament begins, Fischer will be playing a few matches in Yugoslavia, but he has stated that he wants to play as few games as possible so that he does not tire before the start of the Interzonal in Portorož.

A few days later Bobby gave an in-depth interview to Miro Radojčić where he reiterated not only his desire to get some practice, but also mentioned his prospective opponents and the conditions he wished to play under:[1]

[1] Chess Notes http://www.chesshistory.com/winter/winter97.html

> He informed the Yugoslav Chess Federation that while he is here, he does not wish to play any public matches in front of an audience, and he is very pleased that he found complete understanding.
>
> Why does he not want to play public matches?
>
> "I would like to be as well prepared as possible for the tournament in Portorož, and not to be physically tired. Matches played in front of an audience are too exhausting, and there is too much unnecessary nervousness. Besides, I would not like to play too much chess. I would like to play about six serious games, one every other day, in some quiet place, without much noise. Two games have already been arranged with Janošević, the next two most probably will be with Matulović, and the last two I should like to play with Ivkov, if he has the time and is available. The rest of the time I have I would like to spend on physical training, sports like tennis and swimming if it is possible."

Miro Radojčić (1920–2000), was a well-known foreign correspondent who covered the United Nations for *Politika* for several decades. Radojčić was also a strong chess master who played in the Yugoslav Championship. While stationed in the United States he took time off from his journalistic activities to play in tournaments and tied for second with Robert Byrne and James Sherwin, behind Pal Benko, in the 1964 U.S. Open. His undefeated score of 9½–2½ included a win over William Lombardy and draws with Benko, Byrne, and Sherwin. A year before he lost to Fischer in the New York State Open, a game which sadly has not been preserved.

Bobby's desire for practice games was understandable—the only over-the-board training he had since the end of the U.S. Championship (early January) were a handful of games with John Collins and Tony Saidy. There was a definite need to get the rust off prior to the Interzonal.

The games with Dragoljub Janošević, published in *Politika* on July 19 and played sometime between July 10 and 18, were both drawn. Fischer as White didn't get anything in a correctly played Ruy Lopez, but he was winning for the last few moves of their second encounter, whose final result was probably influenced by mutual time pressure.

Janošević (1923–1993) was a respected master who had played in over a half dozen Yugoslav Championships before his match with Fischer—he played his best chess in his forties and earned the Grandmaster title in 1965. He defeated Fischer at Skopje 1967, making him one of a handful of players who faced Bobby three or more times and had plus scores—Yefim Geller, Mikhail Tal, and Abe Turner are three others.

Fischer's second opponent, Milan Matulović (1935–2013), is remembered for his personal failings as much as his abilities as a chess player. A two-time

Yugoslav Champion, Matulović is one of the most successful Olympiad team members of all time winning 77% of sixty games played. In 1958, though not yet at the peak of his powers, he had already finished fifth in the previous two Yugoslav Championships—mammoth twenty-player round robins which at the time were among the strongest annual events in the world.

Matulović earned the nickname "J'adoubovic" for his habit of taking back moves—one well publicized incident was his game against the Hungarian Grandmaster István Bilek at the 1967 Sousse Interzonal where at move thirty-eight he played 38. Bf3??, quickly said "j'adoube", and then placed his king on g1.

There were allegations throughout Matulović's career that he bought and sold games—one example was his last round encounter with Taimanov at the 1970 Interzonal where he was purported to have been paid to throw the game. His habit of playing on in lost positions didn't endear him to his colleagues, nor did his notorious personal life where he posed as a doctor, using the alias Dr. Marinelli, as a means to seduce young women.

Details surrounding the Fischer–Matulović match were initially slow to surface. For many years only the moves to Matulović's win in the first game and the final result of the match, 2½–1½ for Fischer, were known. Matulović victory was published in a number of places, most prominently in *How to Beat Bobby Fischer*, where it is the first of sixty-one games.

In his preface to the game Mednis wrote:[1]

> To get use to Yugoslavia, as well as international chess, [Bobby] arrived in Belgrade early in July and played a two game (two draws) match against Janošević before defeating the promising young master Matulović 2½–1½, despite the loss of the first game. The match progress and the result were the first indication of Fischer's iron resolve to succeed and to ignore any immediate roadblocks. Thus, in the first game, he was simply positionally crushed, but undaunted, came back to score 2½ points out of the next three games.
>
> At that time, I was returning from the World Student Championship in Varna, Bulgaria, and had to spend the better part of a day in Belgrade waiting for the train to Paris. Wandering onto the streets of Belgrade, I inquired about a chess club. Instead, I was led to a hotel where Fischer was known to be staying and as I entered his room, I found him studying (what else?) chess! His joy was great at seeing the unexpected visitor and he showed me immediately how he had "killed" Matulović. That afternoon was spent touring the parks of Belgrade with Mr. Fischer as my guide. Already he was a celebrity to the people of Belgrade—everywhere he went he was ogled and stopped. As I bid him good-bye and good luck in the afternoon at the train station, I felt optimistic about his chances at Portorož. He had the kind of

---

[1] Edmar Mednis, *How to Beat Bobby Fischer*. New York: Random House, 1974, (pp. 3–4).

> healthy confidence that is so valuable, but showed no signs of dangerous overconfidence.

In 2001, not long before he died from complications from pneumonia, Mednis spoke about the Matulović match. He distinctly remembered Fischer showing him the games in Belgrade, but unfortunately could not remember the moves to any of them.

Boris Ivkov was intended to be Bobby's third opponent, but the two never played (Ivkov confirmed this in his book *Povratak Bobija Fišera*[1]) and this could explain why the match with Matulović was four games instead of the originally planned two. In any event, Bobby was able to get the six training games he desired.

Judging from Ivkov's comments it appears he witnessed all four games.

> Before the 1958 training match with Matulović, Fischer—as a fifteen-year-old—analyzed forty of Matulović's games. And he played four wild, fierce games—convincingly losing one, winning one convincingly and one luckily. And the drawn game was not a calm between two storms.

Ivkov believed that fortune favored Bobby, and wrote he was lucky to beat Matulović as he was not only losing in the first game (which he lost) but also the fourth and final game of the match. This assessment of the final game is corroborated by a report in *Politika* on July 26 where a brief note stated that the fourth game of the Fischer–Matulović match had been adjourned, with Fischer standing better and holding winning chances. Matulović played the French Defense, achieved a better position and turned down a draw offer. However, in time-trouble he played so poorly, that in the adjourned position Fischer had three pawns for the exchange and winning chances. The next day *Politika* reported Fischer won the adjournment forcing Matulović to resign at move fifty. Despite winning the match Bobby came away impressed by his opponent's combative play. According to Ivkov Fischer remarked:

> He [Matulović] plays the strangest chess I have ever encountered, fierce, almost wild in the daring of the combinations in all types of positions.

The match was played July 18–26 (until recently the dates were thought to be July 20–26). Per Fischer's wishes, games were played every other day except when there were adjournments which was the case for games two and four. The site of play was the Chess Club Slavia in Belgrade. Božidar Kažić served as the arbiter.

Only the first game is currently in the public domain. The scores of Bobby's two wins are in the Marshall Chess Club's Targ Collection and hopefully will be made public soon.

---

[1] Borislav Ivkov, *Povratak Bobija Fišera*. Novi Sad, Serbia: Chess Press, 1993

Fischer 2½ – Matulović 1½ (0, 1, ½, 1). July 18–26 Belgrade, Yugoslavia

Game 1 July 18 Matulović–Fischer King's Indian 1–0 (41 moves)

Game 2 July 20 Fischer–Matulović Caro-Kann, 1–0 (50 moves)
Opened **1.e4 c6 2.Nc3 d5 3.Nf3 dxe4 4.Nxe4 Nf6 5.Nxf6+ gxf6**, and was likely adjourned at move forty-one and resumed the following day (July 21) with Bobby winning a queen ending.

Game 3 July 23 Matulović–Fischer ½–½ (no other details are available)

Game 4 July 25 Fischer–Matulović French 1–0 (50 moves)
Opened **1.e4 e6 2.d4 d5 3.Nc3 Bb4 4.e5 Ne7 5.a3 Bxc3+ 6.bxc3 b6** and was likely adjourned at move forty-one and resumed the following day (July 26).

Fischer's collective performance (3½–2½) in the two matches could not be considered a great competitive success, but six tough games got the rust off and, as Mednis noted, gave Bobby a healthy dose of confidence heading into the Interzonal.

Regina's letter of August 3, two days prior the start of the Interzonal, is a good example of her involvement, more precisely, her meddling in her son's career:[1]

> Dear Jerry,
>
> I am very upset about Bobby and Lombardy switching around the way it seems they are and feel it can only result in antagonizing both Sherwin and the Yugoslavs. It seems that Radojčić had arranged to be Bobby's second, and Lombardy to be Sherwin's. Now it seems Lombardy will be Bobby's instead, and whether Radojčić will be Sherwin's I don't know. Apparently, Lombardy and Bobby are not worrying about that. Leave it to these kids to put their foot in it whenever possible. It is too bad there is no official there from the USCF.
>
> Best Regards,
>
> Mrs. Regina Fischer

William Lombardy did indeed serve as Bobby's second at the Portorož Interzonal although he also did double duty as the USCF Delegate at the concurrent FIDE Congress as a cost-saving measure. Miro Radojčić did not serve as James Sherwin's second, so the other American representative did not have a coach for the event.[2]

---

1 Letter from the USCF's Jerry Spann Collection currently housed at the World Chess Hall of Fame.

2 Email exchange with James Sherwin January 31· 2020.

A WORLD CLASS PLAYER

It's difficult to pinpoint exactly when in his rise to world class grandmaster Bobby considered himself to be the best player in the United States. Definitely not at the beginning of 1958. Interviewed shortly after the 1957 U.S. Championship, Fischer was asked point blank if he was the best player in the United States:

> "No," he said humbly, "one tournament doesn't mean that much. Maybe," he paused, "maybe Reshevsky is better."

But by the fall of 1958 Bobby had probably changed his opinion. Frank Brady wrote:[1]

> Bobby had pulled rank on the displaced sovereign almost immediately after winning the Championship, refusing to participate in the 1958 Olympiad unless he, rather than Reshevsky, played first board.

Fifty years after the fact, Larry Evans stated (this could be Evans' own recollection or one influenced by Brady's earlier account.):[2]

> In 1958, Bobby insisted on his rights as U.S. Champion to play first board ahead of Reshevsky, disappointing his fans by refusing to play on our team at the Munich Olympiad.

It's not 100% certain why Bobby didn't play in Munich, but missing school appears to have been a bigger consideration than what board he would have played. Accounts in the August issue of *Chess Review* never mention Fischer as a potential participant at Munich until after Portorož:[3]

> Though the full membership of the team has not yet been settled, it is expected to include international grandmasters Sammy Reshevsky, Arthur Bisguier and Larry Evans, and William Lombardy, World Junior Champion, and Robert Byrne, international master and fourth ranking U.S. player.

And in November:[4]

> Bobby Fischer, really on merit, should be on the team but says he cannot spare the time from school.

Brady again:

> Bobby could have taken a month off from Erasmus, but he would have gotten in trouble, and at that point in his life, believe it or not, he was not

---

1 Frank Brady, *Profile of a Prodigy: The Life and Games of Bobby Fischer,* 2nd edition. New York: David McKay, 1973, (p. 43).

2 Karsten Müller, *Bobby Fischer: The Complete Games of the American World Chess Campion,* Russell Enterprises, 2009. Larry Evans in the Introduction, (p. 7).

3 *Chess Review,* August 1958, (p. 227).

4 *Chess Review,* November 1958, (p. 328).

Bobby Fischer, Raymond Weinstein, and Walter Browne all attended Erasmus Hall High School, Brooklyn, NY.

thinking of dropping out of school. He was a full week late in starting school after Portorož, and he had a number of Regents exams with which to contend. After that grueling semester, and then the U.S. Championship, he began to have doubts whether he should finish high school. As soon as he reached sixteen, March 1959, he dropped out (much to the rue of Regina). When he was in Mar Del Plata, Regina was trying to get him to enter an Argentinean school, but to no avail.

Brady's assessment is supported by Regina Fischer's statement in a July 12, 1958 letter to Jerry Spann:[1]

> I have no objection to Bobby playing in the Olympiad, but he says he is coming back on September 14th.

> **BOY CHESS MASTER STRANDED IN EUROPE**[2]
>
> Bobby Fischer, the fifteen-year-old Brooklyn boy who moved into the top rank of the world chess players last week, may be stranded in Yugoslavia without money.

Bobby had sent Regina a cable from Portorož, Yugoslavia saying he wasn't able to get a plane home until Oct. 4. He was scheduled to start his junior year at Erasmus Hall High School in Brooklyn on Sept. 8, but had received a week's grace to finish the tournament.

> "Bobby was anxious to get back to start school, and was concerned about the work he was missing," Mrs. Fischer said yesterday. "He certainly isn't playing hooky."

[1] Letter from the USCF's Jerry Spann Collection at the World Chess Hall of Fame.
[2] *The New York Times*, "Boy Chess Master Stranded in Europe," September 14, 1958.

> [Regina] was most concerned that her son might be stranded without money and with no one to help him.
>
> "He only had about $10 or $15 the last time I talked to him by telephone," [Bobby left the United States in June and] visited the Soviet Union as a guest of the Soviet Government... In Portorož his hotel room and meals were paid for by the arrangement of the tournament.
>
> "He was playing chess all the time and didn't have any occasion to spend much money," Mrs. Fischer said, "so he had very little money with him."
>
> Bobby had traveler's checks with him, she said, but these were stolen, along with a transistor radio she had given him as a gift.

Fortunately there was a happy ending: Bobby tied for fifth place in the Interzonal and the prize money more than covered the cost of a train ticket from Belgrade to Munich and a flight from Munich to Brussels where he used the last part of his Sabena Airlines ticket he won on *I've Got a Secret* to get back home.

William Lombardy's account of events (written half a century after the Interzonal) got some of the facts right (he and Bobby traveled to Munich from Belgrade and Bobby flew out of Munich), but after so much time he forgets Bobby was barely in Munich, much less had several days to debate whether or not to play in the Olympiad. Fischer was only fifteen, and felt that school still had a place in his life. That would change soon.

William Lombardy on leaving Portorož:[1]

> After Portorož, Bobby and I traveled by train to Munich, where in a few days his seat to New York was reserved. On the train from Portorož via Ljubljana I learned that Bobby wasn't sure where his passport and Yugoslav visa might be. Perhaps they were in his huge bag, perhaps not! I was not going to sift through his dirty laundry to find out.
>
> When we arrived at the Yugoslov border I told him to "sit tight." Eventually a border agent entered our coach compartment. I handed him my own passport and visa for review. As he was returning my papers, I suddenly pointed to Bobby and said, "Fischer, Fischer!" The man was delighted and said, "Da, da!" He left the compartment without demanding Bobby's papers!
>
> In Yugoslavia, unlike the USA, Fischer was a national hero, possible because of the opinions and writings of Svetozar Gligorić and Belgarde-born United Nations journalist Miro Radojčić...
>
> I intended to spend those few days in Munich to convince Bobby to play on the team. I was also intending to convince USCF President Jerry Spann to put Fischer on first board (which was not very difficult). But Bobby himself was adamant. He was tired of all the political wrangling and was bent on leaving. He used as excuse that he "had to get back to school." But we both

[1] William Lombardy, *Understanding Chess: My System, My Games, My Life*. In association with Russell Enterprises, 2011, (pp. 94, 95, 96)

> knew that school meant nothing to him. We spent a few days at Munich' Hotel Torbräu and then I accompanied him to the airport. *Bon voyage*!

On the subject of Reshevsky, Lombardy wrote:

> After all these years, I still conclude that Sammy was unable to do his part as a team player...
>
> No matter how many U.S. Championships Bobby won, or what his result in the World Championship cycle, the USCF officials and those at ACF (the monetary arm of U.S. chess that felt it deserved absolute decision-making power) both for their selfish reasons always accommodated Sammy. Whenever Fischer was not on the team, it was because Sammy was illegitimately accorded first board.

Bobby's outstanding performance in Portorož gave him a spot in the following year's Candidates tournament and earned him the grandmaster title at the unprecedented age of fifteen!

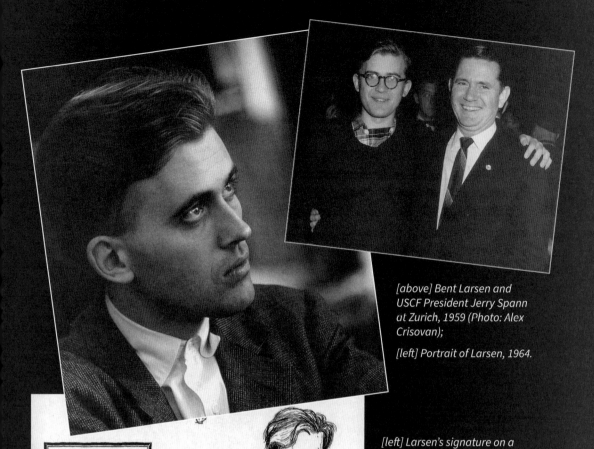

[above] Bent Larsen and USCF President Jerry Spann at Zurich, 1959 (Photo: Alex Crisovan);

[left] Portrait of Larsen, 1964.

INTERNATIONAL TEAM TOURNAMENT
MOSCOW, 1956

WHITE: Bent Larsen	BLACK: Harry Golombek
1) P-Q4	N-KB3
2) P-QB4	P-K3
3) N-QB3	B-N5
4) Q-N3	N-B3
5) P-K3	O-O
6) N-B3	P-Q3
7) P-QR3	BxN ch.
8) QxB	R-K1
9) B-K2	P-K4
10) PxP	PxP
11) P-QN4	P-K5
12) N-Q4	NxN
13) PxN	B-N5
14) BxB	NxB
15) P-R3	Q-R5
16) O-O	N-B3
17) B-K3!	P-KR3
18) P-Q5	N-Q2
19) B-Q4	P-KB3
20) P-B5!	N-K4
21) BxN	RxB
22) P-Q6	Q-R4
23) P-B6!	BPxP
24) PxP	R-N1
25) Q-B7	Q-K1
26) QR-B1	K-R2
27) Q-B8	R-K2
28) QxQ	R/2xQ
29) R-B7	R-K4
30) P-QR4	P-QR4
31) R-N1	PxP
32) RxNP	R-QB4
33) RxR	PxR
34) R-N6	Resigns

Bent Larsen — **DENMARK**

BENT LARSEN

Bent Larsen was born in Odensk, Denmark on March 4, 1935. At the age of sixteen he was awarded the title of Danish Master and at the age of nineteen became the Champion of Denmark.

Larsen's great year was 1956. In January, he played a match for the Championship of the Northern Countries with Fridrik Olafsson, which Larsen won with a score of 4½-3½. In June, he tied for first at Hanko, Finland. In July, he garnered First Prize at Gijon, Spain. In August, Larsen took First Prize at Copenhagen. In September, Larsen participated in the Team Tournament at Moscow where he obtained the highest percentage of all first position players. In his game against the then ex-World Champion, Mikhail Botwinnik, he had the better of the game but allowed Botwinnik to escape with a draw. Larsen also played well against Svetozar Gligoric and succeeded in winning.

At the conclusion of the Moscow Team Tournament, Larsen was awarded the title of Grandmaster by the International Chess Federation whose headquarters are in Stockholm, Sweden.

In Hastings 1956, Larsen tied for first place with Gligoric ahead of Olafsson and Szabo, among others.

Larsen is an engineering student at the Technical University of Denmark at Copenhagen, and he finally decided to take a rest from chess for a while and make a little progress with his studies.

Now Larsen is competing in the Inter-zonal Championship Tournament at Wageningen, Holland. The chances are very good that Larsen in company with Olafsson and Szabo will walk away with the top three prizes which will qualify them all for the next World Championship Candidates' Tournament. The tournament at Wageningen will conclude on November 27 and on November 30 they will be making their first moves here at Dallas 1957.

[left] Larsen's signature on a program from Dallas 1957;

[below] Bent Larsen celebrates his win at Palma de Mallorca, 1967.

2
THE GREAT DANE

The first time Bobby met Bent Larsen over-the-board was round eight of the 1958 Portorož Interzonal. Bobby was +2 at that point in the tournament, while Larsen—who had been awarded the grandmaster title in 1956 in part for making the best score on board one in the Olympiad that year—was at 50%. The Dane was looking to get on the plus side of the ledger at the expense of the young American, but things didn't go his way. Their match years later in the 1971 Candidates semifinal has created the false impression that Bobby always dominated Larsen, which isn't true. Prior to their meeting in Denver the score was 3½–2½ in Bobby's favor. Larsen described their first meeting:[1]

> Of course I knew about the best game in chess history that had ever been played by a thirteen year old: Donald Byrne–Bobby Fischer, and I was familiar with a few more games of the young genius. Nevertheless, in our first meeting I would have been disappointed with a draw against a fifteen-year-old boy by choosing a forced variation, which would have led to an equal endgame. That was at the Interzonal in Portorož, Yugoslavia in 1958, one of the worst tournaments of my entire career! This game against Fischer was certainly the main reason for my poor showing in the tournament. At the fifteenth move of a Sicilian Dragon I didn't want to play the best move, because White could force a drawish endgame. Because of this he got a decisive mating attack, and the game is today adorned in his book *My 60 Memorable Games*.

Notes by Fischer and Larsen are incorporated into the annotations of Game (29). Modern computers don't overturn the verdict that 15...Rac8 was in effect the losing move, but point out Black could have defended better.

---

(29) Sicilian
Fischer – Bent Larsen
Portorož Interzonal 1958 (8)

1.e4 c5 2.Nf3 d6 3.d4 cxd4 4.Nxd4 Nf6 5.Nc3 g6

[Fischer]: "Larsen was one of the diehards who refused to abandon the Dragon until recently. White's attack almost plays itself ...weak players

[1] Translated by Eric Tangborn from Bent Larsen, *Alle Figuren greifen an* (*Attack with all Pieces*). Stuttgart: SchachDepot Verlag, 2009.

even beat Grandmasters with it. I once thumbed through several issues of *Shakhmatny Bulletin*, when the Yugoslav Attack was making its debut, and found the ratio was something like nine wins of ten in White's favor. Will Black succeed in reinforcing the variation? Time will tell."

So, wrote Bobby Fischer in his notes to his game with Bent Larsen, number two in *My 60 Memorable Games*. The verdict is still out. The Dragon was Garry Kasparov's secret weapon in his 1995 World Championship match with Viswanathan Anand and its theoretical standing in 2018 is as good as it has ever been with no refutation in sight.

It's not uncommon for opening variations to be misnamed and the Yugoslav Attack against the Dragon is one of them. It was actually the Soviet master Vsevolod Rauzer (1908–1941), who shares the invention of the variation 1.e4 c5 2.Nf3 d6 3.d4 cxd4 4.Nxd4 Nf6 5.Nc3 Nc6 6.Bg5 with the German master Kurt Richter, who is the true originator of the setup with f3, Qd2 and queenside castling against the Dragon—over fifteen years before the Yugoslavs started analyzing it.

[Larsen] "The Dragon Variation. Its popularity at that time was fading, and my losses to Averbach and Matanović in Portorož also didn't contribute to winning more followers."

6.Be3 Bg7 7.f3 0-0 8.Qd2 Nc6 9.Bc4

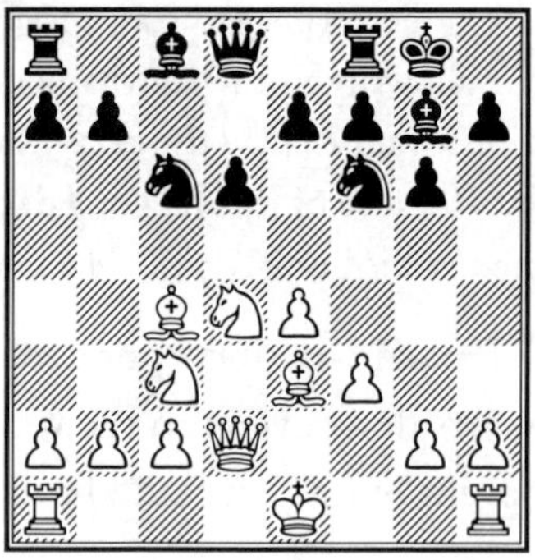

9...Nxd4

9...Bd7 normally leads to the main lines of the Dragon, but Black has intriguing sidelines. After 10.Bb3, an old favorite of the Chinese Grandmaster Bu, is 10... Na5 11.0-0-0 Nxb3+ 12.cxb3 Qa5 13.Kb1 Rfc8, which he used successfully on several occasions. Grandmaster Khalifman in his *Opening for White According to Anand* series (2009 analyzes 14.g4 as better for the first player, although after Bu's 14...Rc7, play is still complicated.

This may all be academic, as Grandmaster Negi in his *1.e4 vs. the Sicilian II* (2015) points out Black can dispense with 12...Qa5 and instead play the immediate 12...b5!?. After 13.Ndxb5 Qb8 14.Nd4 a5 Black had plenty of open lines to compensate for the pawn in Strengell–Skarba, email 2008. Negi's solution is to defer castling and play 11.g4!

Like its cousin 1.e4 c5 2.Nf3 Nc6 3.d4 cxd4 4.Nxd4 g6 5.Nc3 Bg7 6.Be3 Nf6 7.Bc4 0-0 8.Bb3 d6 9.Qd2 Bd7 10.0-0-0 Nxd4 11.Bxd4 b5, this variation typically arises from an Accelerated Dragon move order—White not playing Bb3 so early in a regular Dragon. This commitment to an early Bb3 gives Black extra options from the 4...g6 move-order (1.e4 c5 2.Nf3 Nc6 3.d4 cxd4 4.Nxd4) but there is no free lunch—White has the possibility of playing the Maróczy Bind starting with 5.c4. At the very top level the Accelerated Dragon most often arises via 1.e4 c5 2.Nf3 Nc6 3.Nc3 g6 4.d4—with White trying to dodge the Sveshnikov with 3.Nc3 and Black finding the Accelerated Dragon more attractive when the Maróczy Bind is no longer an option.

The Russian Grandmaster Vadim Zvjaginsev reaches the game continuation via 9...Qa5 10.0-0-0 Nxd4 11.Bxd4 Be6.

10.Bxd4 Be6

This was one of the first ways of countering the Yugoslav Attack and is still played today. The Soviet International Master and theoretician Georgy Lisitsin (1909–1972), who was an early Dragon pioneer in the 1930s, played this variation extensively in the 1950s. Lisitsin, for whom the gambit 1.Nf3 f5 2.e4 is named, played in ten Soviet Championships and wrote well known books on the endgame and middlegame. The latter, *Strategiya taktika shakmat* (*Strategy and Tactics in Chess*) is justly regarded as a classic.

Khalifman explains the motivation for the knight trade followed by ...Be6; "In general, the system we are analyzing has a sound positional basis. Black develops all his pieces to maximally active positions in harmony with the principles in the opening and then he advances his b-pawn. Still, the simple strategy has its drawbacks as well. The exchange on d4 is a position concession for Black. White's bishop is dominant on d4 and he has additional possibilities because of this (like for example the possibility to capture Bxf6 at an appropriate moment). Secondly, Black's possible chances of organizing counterplay along the a1-h8 diagonal diminish considerably. White's plan is in fact tremendously simple. He needs some prophylactic moves (Bb3, Kb1), later he advances his kingside pawns, then he opens files on the kingside etc. Black must play very energetically and purposefully; otherwise he will soon be in a very difficult position."

11.Bb3

Trading on e6 leads to a different type of game. Although the Chinese star Yu Yangyi has tried it, Black should be doing fine: 11.Bxe6 fxe6 12.0-0-0 Qa5 13.h4 (13.Kb1 Rac8 14.h4 Rc4 Calzetta Ruiz–Andersson, Villarrobledo (rapid) 1998, or perhaps even simpler 14...Nh5) 13...Nh5 and Black had already equalized in Yu Yangyi–Édouard, Gibraltar 2016.

11...Qa5

11...Rc8 12.0-0-0 Bxb3 13.cxb3 (13.axb3 should also favor White despite good practical results for the second player.) 13...d5 is another little tested Dragon/Accelerated Dragon variation used with success by Grandmasters Evgeny Pigusov and Viacheslav Eingorn.

12.0-0-0

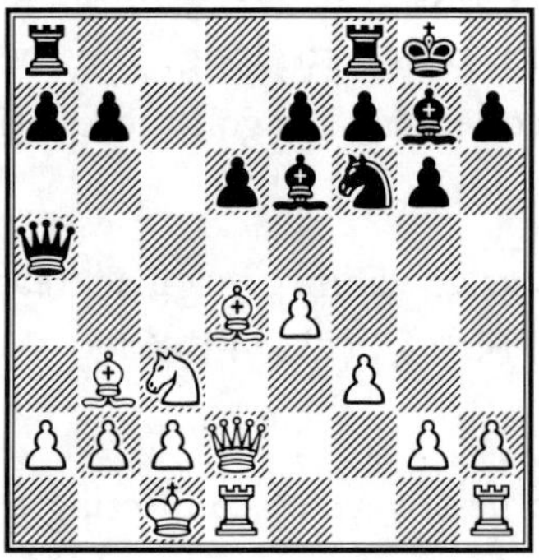

12.0-0 Rfc8 13.Rad1 Bc4 14.Rfe1 Rc6 gave Black an easy game in Blehm–Markowski, Warsaw 2001. Now the second player has to make an important decision.

12...b5

One of Black two main choices.

12...Bxb3 13.cxb3! (13.axb3 is met by 13...Qa1+ 14.Nb1 Rfc8 15.h4 when 15...Rc6, followed by doubling on the c-file, gives Black strong counterplay.) may seem counterintuitive, but as Fischer explains; "Black cannot make any attacking headway against this particular pawn configuration. White is lost in the king and pawn ending, it's true, but Black usually gets mated long before then, As Tarrasch put it: "Before the endgame the gods have placed the middlegame." 13...Rfc8 14.Kb1 Rc6 15.g4 Rac8 16.h4 and the dangerous attack down the h-file, so characteristic of the Yugoslav Attack, is in full swing.

The main alternative to the text is 12...Rfc8 13.Kb1 b5 when critical is 14.Rhe1 Bxb3 (14...b4 15.Nd5 Bxd5 16.exd5 favors White) 15.cxb3

Rab8 16.Rc1 a6 17.g4 Rc6 18.h4 Rbc8 19.a3 b4 20.Na2 Rxc1+ 21.Rxc1 Rxc1+ 22.Nxc1 and Black equalized with 22...h5 in Grischuk–Nakamura, London 2012.

13.Kb1 b4

Black prefers to dispense with 13...Rfc8 which would transpose to Grischuk–Nakamura.

14.Nd5

Weaker is 14.Ne2 Bxb3 15.cxb3 Rfd8 (Fischer). Black would be threatening ...e5 followed by ...d5.

14...Bxd5

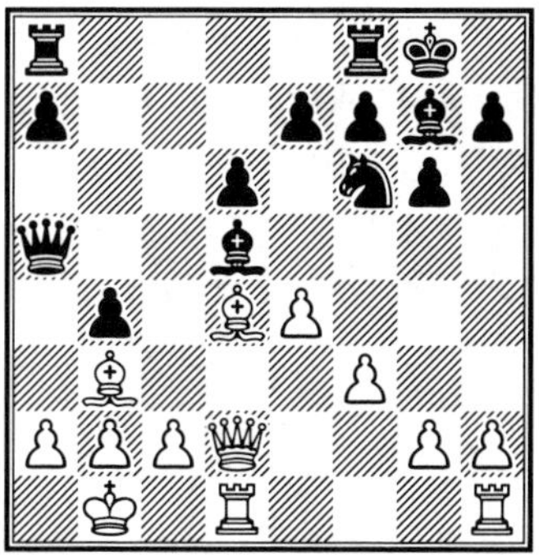

[Fischer] "Bad judgment is 14...Nxd5? 15.Bxg7 Kxg7 16.exd5 Bd7 17.Rde1 with a clear advantage for White, Suetin–Korchnoi, USSR Championship prelims 1953." White is not only attacking e7, but also threatening Re4–h4.

15.Bxd5

Stronger is 15.exd5. Now Black plays 15...Qb5 threatening ...a5-a4 which forces White to head for an endgame with either 16.Rhe1 a5 17.Qe2 or the immediate 16.Qd3. The evaluation of these two variations is critical for an objective assessment of the health of the ...Nxd4, ...Be6 variation against the Yugoslav Attack. Do White's two bishops and space advantage promise nothing but suffering for Black who is confined to playing for two results? Conventional wisdom holds this position, but tournament results don't back it up. Let's look at the two variations.

(A) 16.Rhe1 a5 17.Qe2 Qxe2 18.Rxe2 a4 19.Bc4 Rfc8 20.b3 Rc7.

[Khalifman] "White's pawn-structure is slightly compromised with the move b2-b3 and his bishop is placed awkwardly on c4, so he cannot attack effectively Black's only real weakness on the queenside—his b4 pawn. Neither 21.c3 nor 21.Bb5 has yielded White any advantage."

(B) 16.Qd3, recommended by both Khalifman and Negi, is more precise as White avoids having to play b3. After 16...Qxd3 17.Rxd3 Black has two choices:

(B1) 17... Rfc8 (most commonly seen) 18. Re1 Rc7 19. c3 a5 20. cxb4 axb4 21.Rdd1 (21.Rc1 Rxc1+ 22.Kxc1 allowed Black to play 22...Nd7 with no problems in Inarkiev–Zvaginsev, Kazan 2005) when 21...Bh6 22.g3 Kf8 and the immediate 21...Kf8 are both solid but neither seems to fully equalize.

(B2) 17...Nd7 (If Black wants to get his knight to e5 or c5 this is the time to do it.) After 18.Re1 (18.f4 Nc5?! 19. Bxc5 dxc5 20.Re3 Bf6 21.g4 favored White in Karthikeyan–Vallejo Pons, Tbilisi 2017) the most precise move looks to be 18...Bf6! (18...Ne5 19.Rdd1 g5 Szeląg–Kanarek, Poland (ch) 2013 is also worth considering) 19.Bxf6 exf6 20.Rde3 a5 21.Ba4 Ne5 22.f4 Ng4 23.Re7 Nxh2 24.Bc6 Rab8 25.Ra7 Ng4 26.Rxa5 f5. Black is fine with ...Nf2-e4 or ...Nf6-e4 coming up fast.

15...Rac8?

[Fischer] "The losing move. After the game Larsen explained he was playing for a win, and therefore rejected the forced draw with 15...Nxd5 16.Bxg7 Nc3+ 17.bxc3 (17.Bxc3 bxc3 18.Qxc3 Qxc3 19.bxc3 Rfc8 renders White's extra pawn useless.) 17...Rab8! 18.cxb4 Qxb4+! 19.Qxb4 Rxb4+ 20.Bb2 Rfb8, etc. After 15...Nxd5, however, I intended simply 16.exd5 Qxd5 17.Qxb4, keeping the game alive."

While this does keep the game alive, Black has a number of choices that offer equal chances including 17...Rfb8, 17...Qc6, 17...a5 and 17...Bxd4.

[Larsen] "In the current game the decisive moment lies somewhere else; for example, here I could have played 15...Nxd5 16.Bxg7 Nc3+! 17.Bxc3 bxc3 18.Qxc3 Qxc3 19.bxc3 Rfc8 with an attractive endgame with good expectations of a draw. Fischer however admitted to me after the game that he intended to play 16.exd5 Qxd5 17.Qxb4, which would have given Black excellent prospects."

16.Bb3!

[Fischer] "He won't get a second chance to snap off the bishop! Now I felt the game was in the bag if I didn't botch it. I'd won dozens of skittles games in analogous positions and had it down to a science: pry open the h-file, sac, sac...mate!"

16...Rc7

This loss of time is necessary if Black is ever to advance his a-pawn.

[Fischer] "16...Qb5? is refuted by 17.Bxa7."

17.h4

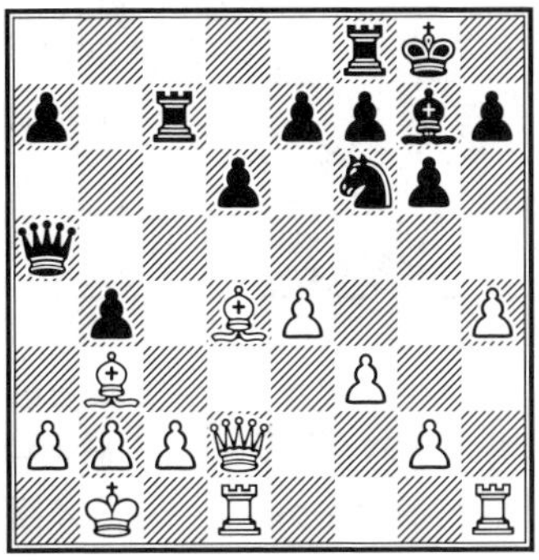

17...Qb5

[Fischer] "There is no slowing down White's attack: 17...h5 18.g4! hxg4 (18...Rfc8 19.Rdg1 hxg4 20.h5 gxh5 21.fxg4 Nxe4 22.Qf4 e5 23.Qxe4 exd4 24.gxh5 Kh8 25.h6 Bf6 26.Rg7 with mate to follow.) 19.h5 gxh5 (19...Nxh5 20.Bxg7 Kxg7 21.fxg4 Nf6 22.Qh6+ and mate the next move.) 20.fxg4 Nxe4 (20...hxg4 21.Rdg1 e5 22.Be3 Rd8 23.Bh6 is crushing; 20...Nxg4 21.Rdg1 Bxd4 22.Rxg4+ hxg4 23.Qh6 with mate to follow.) 21.Qe3 Nf6 (21...Bxd4 22.Qxe4 Bg7 23.Rxh5 wins.) 22.gxh5 e5 23.h6 and Black can resign."

With the text Black hopes for ...a7–a5–a4 harassing White's bishop, but Fischer never gives him the opportunity.

18.h5!

Fischer notes there was no need to lose a tempo playing the preparatory g4 in support of h4–h5. The middlegames arising from the Dragon Sicilian are often perfect examples of the importance of the initiative when opponents castle on opposite wings. As the Confederate General Nathan Bedford Forrest so clearly stated: the way to win is "to get there first with the most men."

18...Rfc8

[Fischer] "18...gxh5 19.g4! hxg4 20.fxg4 Nxe4 21.Qh2 Ng5 22.Bxg7 Kxg7 23.Rd5 Rc5 24.Qh6+ Kg8 25.Rxg5+ Rxg5 26.Qxh7 mate."

19.hxg6 hxg6

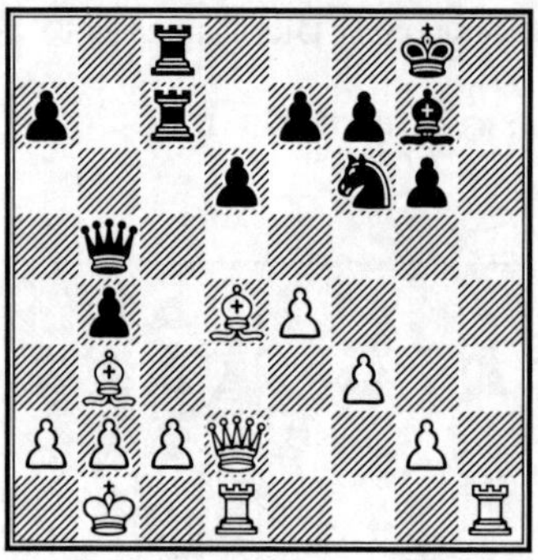

20.g4

Fischer] "Not the impatient 20.Bxf6? Bxf6 21.Qh6 e6!= (threatening ...Qe5) and Black holds everything."

20.Rh6, threatening Rxg6, is a computer idea that deserves to be remembered. White's compensation for the exchange is evident after 20...Bxh6 21.Qxh6 Qh5 22.Qc1 g5 (anticipating White's plan of Rh1 followed by Qh6). 23.Rh1 Qg6 24.g4, but it is not clear how he can make progress.

20...a5 21.g5 Nh5

This is definitely Black's best try and matters are not quite so clear as Fischer thought, as we shall soon see. *My 60 Memorable Games* quotes analysis by Vasiukov which shows that the alternative, 21...Ne8, loses on the spot to: 22.Bxg7 Nxg7 (22...Kxg7? 23.Qh2 mates.) 23.Rh6! (threatening to double on the h-file as well as capture on g6). 23...e6 (or 23...a4 24.Qh2 Nh5 25.Rxg6+) 24.Qh2 Nh5 25.Bxe6! fxe6 (25...Qxg5 26.Rxg6+! Qxg6 27.Bxc8) 26.Rxg6+ Ng7 27.Rh1 winning. The counterattack 21...a4? is met by 22.gxf6 axb3 23.fxg7! bxc2+ 24.Qxc2! e5 25.Qh2.

22.Rxh5!

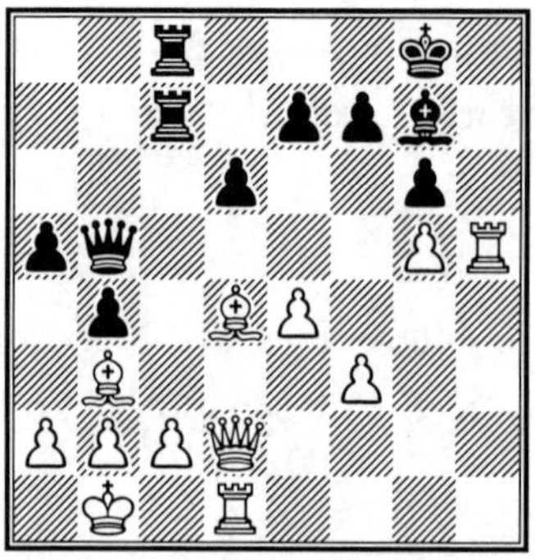

22...gxh5

After this everything is pretty clear, but Black had a chance to offer stiffer resistance which is not mentioned in Fischer's analysis. He gives 22...Bxd4

23.Qxd4 gxh5 24.g6 Qe5 (24...e6 25.Qxd6) 25.gxf7+ Kh7 (25...Kf8 26.Qxe5 dxe5 27.Rg1 e6 28.Bxe6 Ke7 29.Bxc8 Rxc8 30.Rg5 winning.) 26.Qd3+ (intending f4) should be decisive. However the computer move 24...Rc4, blocking the bishop's diagonal, allows Black to keep fighting with a king run: 25.Qe3 (25.Qd2 should transpose while Black is fine after 25.Bxc4 Qxc4 26.gxf7+ Kxf7 27.Qd2 Rc5) 25...fxg6 26.Qh6 Kf7 27.f4 Ke8 28.e5 Kd7. White, of course, has other choices, and it's hard to believe Black is completely okay after 24...Rc4, but it had to be tried.

23.g6 e5

23...e6 24.gxf7+ Kxf7 (24...Rxf7 25.Bxe6) 25.Bxg7 Kxg7 26.Rg1+ Kh7 27.Qg2 Qe5 28.Qg6+ Kh8 29.Rg5 Rg7 30.Rxh5+ Kg8 31.Bxe6+ Kf8 32.Rf5+ Ke7 33.Rf7+ mates – Fischer.

24.gxf7+ Kf8 25.Be3 d5

25...a4 26.Qxd6+ Re7 27.Qd8+! Rxd8 28.Rxd8+ Re8 29.Bc5+ Qxc5 30.fxe8Q mate; 25...Rd8 26.Bh6 winning.

26.exd5

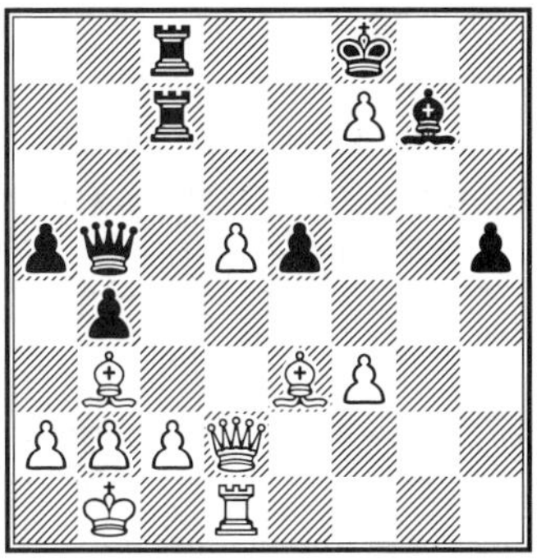

White still has to be alert as 26.Bxd5 is met by 26...Rxc2! when the tables have turned. After 27.Qxc2 Rxc2 28.Kxc2 Qe2+ 29.Bd2 Bh6 Black's h-pawn has suddenly become very dangerous.

26...Rxf7

26...a4 27.d6! axb3 28.dxc7 wins.

27.d6 Rf6

After 27...Rd7 28.Be6 and 28.Bh6 both win. 27...Rxf3 is answered by 28.d7.

28.Bg5 Qb7

28...Qd7 29.Qd5! Qf7 (29...Rf7 30.Be7+!) 30.Bxf6 winning.

29.Bxf6 Bxf6 30.d7 Rd8 31.Qd6+, 1–0.

Fischer points out a faster win with 31.Qh6+.

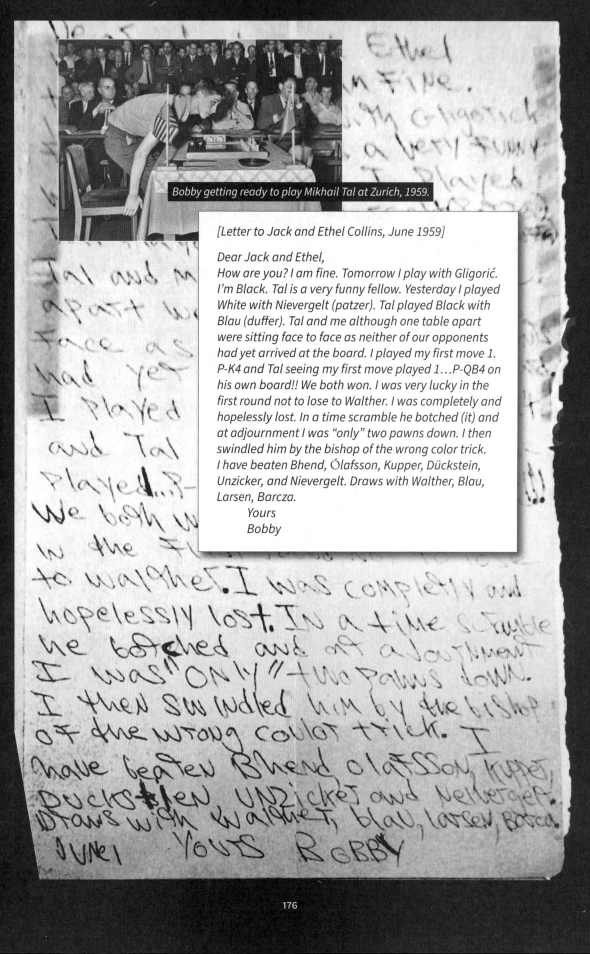

Bobby getting ready to play Mikhail Tal at Zurich, 1959.

[Letter to Jack and Ethel Collins, June 1959]

Dear Jack and Ethel,
How are you? I am fine. Tomorrow I play with Gligorić. I'm Black. Tal is a very funny fellow. Yesterday I played White with Nievergelt (patzer). Tal played Black with Blau (duffer). Tal and me although one table apart were sitting face to face as neither of our opponents had yet arrived at the board. I played my first move 1. P-K4 and Tal seeing my first move played 1…P-QB4 on his own board!! We both won. I was very lucky in the first round not to lose to Walther. I was completely and hopelessly lost. In a time scramble he botched (it) and at adjournment I was "only" two pawns down. I then swindled him by the bishop of the wrong color trick. I have beaten Bhend, Ólafsson, Kupper, Dückstein, Unzicker, and Nievergelt. Draws with Walther, Blau, Larsen, Barcza.

Yours
Bobby

Larsen:

> A year later in Zurich I played the Caro–Kann Defense. Bobby secured the bishop pair. In the endgame I had good defensive opportunities, exchanging off all the pawns on the queenside. In a position with two bishops versus two knights and both sides having three kingside pawns, I offered a draw, but Fischer wanted to play on. Consequently, we played almost another forty moves, and only when Bobby was threatened with the loss of a bishop, was peace agreed on. Unfortunately, one cannot checkmate with only two knights...
>
> In this phase Fischer overrates the power of the bishop pair; this appears to be an American tradition since the time of Fine and Kashdan.

A letter dated June 1959 to Jack Collins and his sister Ethel is shown on page 176. Written from Zurich before round eleven, Bobby's use of words such as "patzer" and "duffer" condescending terms for weaker players (i.e. he drew the "duffer") reveal the sixteen-year-old's personality! The story Fischer relates, when Black played 1...c5 before White has arrived to play his first move, is classic Tal.

Fischer would lose to Gligorić in round eleven, but still had one of the best results of his career to date, sharing third with Keres behind Tal and Gligorić.

Anthony Saidy, then a twenty-two-year-old medical student, was on a holiday break and volunteered to be Fischer's chaperone. As soon as they arrived in Zurich they split up as Bobby decided to stay in an expensive hotel, seemingly oblivious to the plight of Saidy who was given no money for his lodging and as a "starving student" ending up staying at a budget accommodation. Saidy visited the tournament every day but he and Bobby had no contact, surprising as just a few years before the two were close, Fischer even vacationing with the Saidy clan on Martha's Vineyard.

---

(30) Caro-Kann
Fischer – Bent Larsen
Zurich 1959

1.e4 c6 2.Nf3 d5 3.Nc3 Bg4 4.h3 Bxf3 5.Qxf3 Nf6 6.d3 e6 7.a3 Bc5 8.Be2 0-0 9.0-0 Nbd7 10.Qg3 Bd4 11.Bh6 Ne8 12.Bg5 Ndf6 13.Bf3 Qd6 14.Bf4 Qc5 15.Rab1 dxe4 16.dxe4 e517.Bg5 Bxc3 18.bxc3 b5 19.c4 a6 20.Bd2 Qe7 21.Bb4 Nd6 22.Rfd1 Rfd8 23.cxb5 cxb5 24.Rd3 Qe6 25.Rbd1 Nb7 26.Bc3 Rxd3 27.cxd3 Re8 28.Kh2 h6 29.d4 Nd6 30.Re1 Nc4 31.dxe5 Nxe5 32.Bd1 Ng6 33.e5 Nd5 34.Bb3 Qc6 35.Bb2 Ndf4 36.Rd1 a5 37.Rd6 Qe4 38.Rd7 Ne6 39.Bd5 Qe2 40.Bc3 b4 41.axb4 axb4 42.Bxb4 Qxe5 43.Ba5 Qxg3+ 44.Kxg3 Re7 45.Rd6 Nef4 46.Bf3 Ne6 47.Bb6 Ne5 48.Bd5 Rd7 49.Rxd7 Nxd7 50.Be3

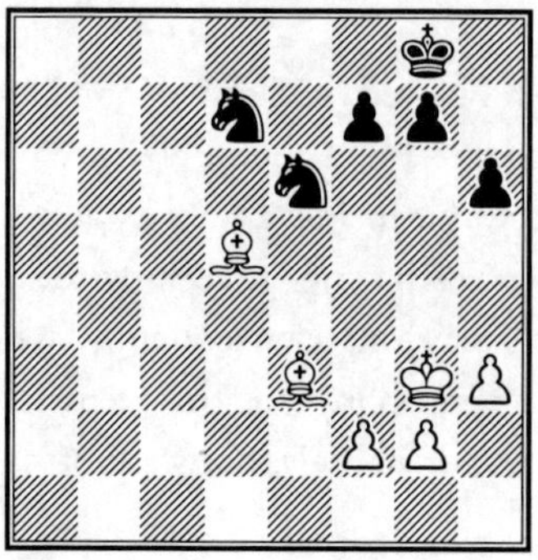

Top players today, not bothered by the possibility of an adjournment, would not hesitate to play this position to the bitter end. White risks nothing and there are practical chances to win with a few mistakes by Black. Strong computer engines evaluate the position as between a half and two-thirds of a pawn better for White.

50...Nf6 51.Bc6

Maybe 51.Ba2 was more accurate, preserving the option to exchange on e6. One hypothetical line that shows Black has to stay alert goes 51...g5 52.Kf3 Kf8?! 53.Bxe6 fxe6 54.h4 g4??+ 55.Kf4 Kf7 56.Bd4 winning.

51...g5!

With no worries about a trade on e6 this space-grabbing move makes perfect sense, anticipating White attempts to expand on the kingside with f4 and g4.

52.Kf3 Kg7 53.Ba4 Nd5 54.Bc1 h5 55.Bb2+ Kh6 56.Bb3 Ndf4 57.Bc2 Ng6 58.Kg3 Nef4 59.Be4 Nh4 60.Bf6 Nhg6 61.Kf3 Nh4+ 62.Kg3 Nhg6 63.Kh2 h4 64.Kg1 Nh5 65.Bc3 Ngf4 66.Kf1 Ng7 67.Bf6 Nfh5 68.Be5 f6 69.Bd6 f5 70.Bf3 Nf4 71.Ke1 Kg6 72.Kd2 Nge6 73.Be5 Nc5 74.Ke3 Nce6 75.Bc6 Kf7 76.Kf3 Ke7 77.Bb7 Ng6 78.Bc3 Ngf4 79.Ba6 Nd5 80.Be5 Nf6 81.Bd3 g4+ 82.Ke2 Nd7 83.Bh2 gxh3 84.gxh3 Kf6 85.Ke3 Ne5 86.Be2 Ng6 87.Bf1 f4+ 88.Kf3 Ne5+ 89.Ke4 Ng5+ 90.Kxf4 Nef3 91.Bg3 hxg3 92.fxg3. ½–½.

The Zurich tournament ended in early June, three months before the 1959 Candidates tournament. At the beginning of the summer, funding for the American players scheduled to compete[1] looked bleak. The situation changed markedly at the beginning of August, the catalyst being a letter from Regina Fischer to the editor of *The New York Times* that ran on August 6th. This was

[1] This reference is to Fischer, and the new U.S. player Pal Benko who during the 1957 World Student Team Championship in Reykjavík defected from Hungary and sought asylum in the United States.

followed on August 17 with an appeal in *Sports Illustrated,* and culminated on August 21 with a piece by Eleanor Roosevelt in her syndicated column "My Day":[1]

> HYDE PARK—One mother who is doing her very best to help her son is Mrs. Regina Fischer of Brooklyn, New York. Her son is Bobby Fischer, the sixteen-year-old United States chess champion, and his current predicament is a shortage of funds.
>
> As our national champion, Bobby is the official U.S. entry to the coming Candidates tournament, which will take place in Yugoslavia September 6 to October 31.[2] Winner of this eight-man competition will become the new challenger in 1960 for the World Championship title, now held by Mikhail Botvinnik of Russia. Mrs. Fischer is calling on all she can reach in her search for money to send her son to this tournament.
>
> For some reason the United States Chess Federation does not seem to be strong enough to give our champion the money needed for participation in the various tournaments. Other countries back their representatives in these events. In the Candidates tournament there will be four Russian players, well provided with seconds, physical trainers and every moral and financial backing.
>
> Chess is a game that holds world interest, and though we in this country have not adopted it in the way some other countries have, still we have a considerable number of enthusiasts here. I don't know why we shouldn't be able to raise the $2,000 needed to send our representative and a second to this tournament in Yugoslavia. It would seem to me that many people who consider this game educational would be willing to send in small sums.
>
> Bobby Fischer is young to be carrying the responsibility of representing the U.S., and I hope he will not also be asked to carry the responsibility of raising the money for travel and living expenses. I hope many of my readers will send contributions to: Bobby Fischer, care of the U.S. Chess Federation, 80 East 11th Street, New York 3, New York earmarked for use in representing the U.S. in the Yugoslavia tournament.

The money soon began to pour in, *Sports Illustrated* alone gave $2,000. Enough money was raised to pay for the travel of Fischer and Benko, Larsen's stipend as second, plus $1,000 was leftover to kick start the funding for the 1960 U.S. Olympiad team. Why wasn't Lombardy offered the job as Bobby's second—he knew Bobby much better than Larsen and had ably seconded him at the 1958 Portorož Interzonal? Larsen explained why he got the job instead of Lombardy:[3]

---

1 United Feature Syndicate, Inc, August 21, 1959.

2 The actual dates of the Candidates tournament were September 7–October 29, 1959.

3 Bent Larsen, *Alle Figuren greifen an* (*Attack with all Pieces*). Stuttgart: SchachDepot Verlag, 2009.

> I received a letter from his mother, Regina Fischer asking if I was willing to act as second to her son for the upcoming Candidates tournament (later I learned that she had earlier made the same offer to Albéric O'Kelly, however without consulting Bobby). She was seeking a grandmaster from Europe simply to save on travel costs.
>
> I accepted the offer. Bobby arrived in Yugoslavia and called me from Dubrovnik. He suggested that in ten days we meet in Venice and do opening preparations. Alright. I arrived in Venice, but... where was Bobby? This lasted almost a week, until I learned that he was in Munich. He did not like Venice. Munich was better, but then he got homesick and wanted to return to New York. His mother wanted him to stay in Europe. A few days later I accompanied him to the airport with the instructions to send his mother a telegram after his departure, so that she wouldn't be able to persuade him to remain. The next time we saw each other was in Bled (in what is today Slovenia), right before the start of the tournament."

To economize at a time when the U.S. Chess Federation provided only minimal support, and the American Chess Foundation backed Sammy Reshevsky almost exclusively, was quite understandable. The money saved on air fare was substantial—adjusting for inflation, air fare to Europe was five to six times higher in the 1950s than it is today.

Albéric O'Kelly was likely the second foreign grandmaster Bobby encountered (after Max Euwe) and the two reportedly got along well during Bobby's stopover in Brussels on the way to Moscow in 1958. Considering this and the fact there were very few West European grandmasters in the late 1950s, it's not so surprising the Belgian number one would have been considered for the job.

Larsen, who was eight years older than Fischer, had plenty of things to say about Bobby's behavior during the Candidates:

> Fischer had a poor start, likely due to a cold that he had caught. I insisted every day that he consult with the tournament doctor, but he didn't want to. Eventually he allowed himself to be persuaded, perhaps because at this time he had just a half point out of four rounds. Why did he not want to consult the tournament doctor? His anti-communist feelings and convictions were so dominating, that he could not imagine that the training in such a country could produce a competent doctor. One time he had a vehement dispute with a waiter in the hotel. I said to him: "Bobby, you're only making unnecessary enemies." He merely answered: "I want all communists to be my enemy." One must of course understand that these were the years of the cold war—only a few years before Senator Joe McCarthy had started his notorious campaign against "anti-American activities."
>
> The doctor prescribed him three different medications. Bobby took two of them without a grumble, the third however did not appeal to him—something that had to be dissolved in boiling water and then inhaled for ten

Albéric O'Kelly and Boris Spassky at the Tel Aviv Olympiad (Photo: Beth Cassidy).

minutes. Ten minutes sitting bent over a sink with a towel over his head and inhaling the steam was for Bobby simply a waste of time. I could not persuade him to read a book while doing this so that his time would not remain idle. So, it came to me to read *Tarzan's New Adventures* to a candidate for the World Championship!

My relations with Bobby during the tournament were completely fine. In any case the experience I had with Bobby was probably better than Lombardy in Portorož and Saidy in Zurich—there Bobby was not satisfied with the hotel that was designated for the participants, and the one that he found and met his expectations would turn out to be more expensive. Saidy, who had to pay for all his own expenses, simply could not afford the new hotel, but Bobby seemed completely indifferent to the "stupid" financial problem.

Brady paints a somewhat different picture of the relationship between Larsen and Fischer and attributes several harsh comments to Larsen. Brady wrote:[1]

> Bobby's second, the great Danish player Bent Larsen, who was there to help him as a trainer and mentor, instead criticized his charge, perhaps smarting from the rout he'd suffered at Fischer's hands in Portorož. Not one to keep his thoughts to himself, Larsen told Bobby, "Most people think you are unpleasant to play against." He then added, "You walk funny"—a reference, perhaps, to Fischer's athletic swagger from years of tennis, swimming, and basketball. Declining to leave any slur unvoiced, he concluded, "And you are ugly." Bobby insisted that Larsen wasn't joking and that the insults "hurt." His self-esteem and confidence seemed to have slipped a notch.

Larsen continued:

> Perhaps my job was somewhat easier as Bobby realized early on that he could not win the tournament. Only once did we engage in an extensive analysis session—completely for nothing, in my opinion. In one of his games against Benko, Bobby had a very poor position, until as always, the

[1] Frank Brady, *Endgame: Bobby Fischer's Remarkable Rise and fall—from America's Brightest Prodigy to the Edge of Madness*. New York: Crown Trade, 2010, (pp. 110–111).

Hungarian-American got into time trouble, and committed a blunder. The game was adjourned, but the position didn't offer much. Bobby could reach various rook endings with three versus two pawns on the queenside. He certainly had one pawn more, but it was completely drawn. The whole night I had to analyze this position that offered no prospects with him. Of course, this is somewhat silly from the point of view of the second. However, it is thankful that the work of the second is also at least partially psychological in nature. [Larsen is referring to Benko–Fischer from round seventeen, which indeed was dead drawn at adjournment.]

Concerning opening theory, the young Bobby simply knew everything! I have to say though that he was really determined and stubborn. The best example of this was how he played against the Caro-Kann. As White, he played the Two Knights variation (1.e4 c6 2.Nc3 d5 3.Nf3), but without any success. I tried to persuade him to instead play the "Panov-Attack", because in my opinion that would have fit his style much better. However, he wanted to stay with "his" variation and also gave me a reason, which I agreed with: "I can't give up this variation without winning at least one game with it.

It was a dreadful tournament. There were eight players, with everyone playing everyone else four games, thus twenty-eight games in all. There were two passages in Bled, one in Zagreb, and one in Belgrade. When we met in Zagreb, he found something wrong with the—brand new and ultra-modern—hotel. Gligorić and the other Yugoslavians found him other lodgings. Bobby believed this other one would be much better. And so we moved, and the other hotel did please him much more, although the old house and room were much less comfortable. The restaurant and the services were especially acceptable to him.

Different businesses in Zagreb offered gifts to the players. In every round packages were laid on the tables. Once there were two bottles, a liqueur and a brandy, made from plums. That same evening I came into Bobby's room and surprised him as he was trying to open one of the bottles, however without an opener or corkscrew. He asked: "Where can I get a corkscrew?" "Maid service, I think", I answered. He called room service. "But what will you drink it with?"—"I don't want to drink it, I want to pour it down the toilet!"

Alcohol was after all a poison to him, and the contents of the other bottle seemed to have already disappeared in the drain. He also did not want to give away his Slivovitz (plum brandy made in Slavic countries), as he did not want to be guilty of poisoning other people! Later I was able to take his bottle. He probably accepted that because it relieved him of the responsibility, or perhaps because he admired people with such determination, as I do to this day.

I do not know what his reason was for rejecting alcohol, but with time he became more flexible with this matter—that applied also to communism, the Caro-Kann, and the bishop pair.

3
UNDER SURVEILLANCE

Regina Fischer first attracted the attention of the FBI in the 1940s and she remained under surveillance through 1973—the last entry in her file noted her opposition to the Vietnam War. Because of his mother, Bobby's movements were also scrutinized. Surveillance started with his 1958 trip to the USSR as the FBI suspected the Soviet's invitation was an attempt to recruit him as an operative.

The FBI files on Regina and Bobby's 1959 visit to Mexico City raise suspicions, but come to no definitive judgment. When reading these transcripts, it's important to keep in mind that 1959 was the year Fidel Castro overthrew the Cuban dictator Fulgencio Batista and subsequently established strong ties with the USSR. The Cold War was very much alive, and understandably, the FBI was interested in individuals who had spent significant time in the Soviet Union.

Regina Fischer fit the bill. In the early 1930s, still in her teens, she moved from the United States to Berlin. There she met her future husband Hans-Gerhardt Fischer. Fearing the rise of the Nazis, and having a desire to further their careers, in 1933 Regina and Hans moved to the Soviet Union where he secured employment at the Moscow Brain Institute and she attended medical school at the I.M. Sechenov First Moscow State Medical University. They were married the same year, and in 1938 their daughter Joan was born.

The Great Depression prompted thousands of Americans to relocate to the Soviet Union. Some, desperate for work, were lured by the propaganda of a worker's paradise with plentiful jobs and good pay. Others were idealists who naively believed that the Soviet experiment was a nation free of the sexism and racism that was prevalent in the United States. What the majority of those "dreamers" soon had in common was disillusionment, and most ended up leaving within a few years. By 1938, with war in Europe on the horizon, foreign nationals who still lived in the USSR risked being imprisoned (many of those who remained were sent to labor camps). Regina and her baby daughter Joan were among the last Westerners to leave, escaping to Paris in 1938.

Regina Fischer was unquestionably a highly intelligent and energetic woman who was ahead of her time. The question of "why" she chose to study medicine in the Soviet Union is easily explained—it was her only opportunity. Medical schools in the United States had quotas limiting not only the number of women who could enroll, but the number of Jews who could study. The likelihood of a Jewish woman of modest means becoming a doctor there during the 1930s was little or none, rendering medical school in Moscow an obvious choice. Her decision to study there is hardly proof she was a Soviet agent.

The heating up of the Cold War in the late 1950s and Regina's having lived in the Soviet Union led to increased attention by the FBI. And, to add fuel to the fire, it was known to the agency that Regina joined the Communist Party in 1945 while living in Portland, Oregon—the FBI had kept a close watch on the Soviet trade mission aka "the Red Fort" at 931 SW King, where Regina had applied to work.[1] It's not clear whether her joining the party was an act of expediency by someone needing a job or a sign of true commitment. Later FBI files indicate she was expelled from the party sometime prior to April 1953 for not being a "faithful party member."

Questions remain: Was Bobby Fischer's mother ever a true believer in communism? Was she a spy for the Soviet Union as the FBI tried to prove for many years? Was she a socialist? Or, had she simply believed strongly in unilateral disarmament at a time when fear of nuclear annihilation was widespread?

The visit to Mexico, which appears to have been Regina's first trip outside of the United States since her return in the late 1930s, worried the FBI, which may have harbored suspicions she planned to meet her former husband, Hans-Gerhardt Fischer, in Mexico City. Hans had fought in the Spanish Civil war and later settled in Chile, and was, according to the FBI, an active member of the Chilean Communist Party.

One can imagine the FBI fearing some sort of clandestine meeting between Regina and Hans where secrets would be exchanged. Hans-Gerhardt Fischer may well have worked for the Soviet intelligence services. However, looking at Regina's life it's hard to picture her as a spy—the poverty she endured upon returning to the United States as she struggled to support two children as a single mother doesn't appear to be the best cover story for a secret agent, nor does the public attention generated by her campaigning for her son and her very public political views.

The FBI never came up with any proof Regina was a Soviet spy despite three decades of surveillance and a file close to 800 pages thick, produced at a cost to American tax payers of hundreds of thousands of dollars. Bobby's sister Joan probably had it right when she called her mother "a professional protester."

---

[1] Michael Munk, *The Portland Red Guide: Sites & Stories of Our Radical Past*. Portland, Oregon: Ooligan Press, 2007.

Al Horowitz shakes hands with Marshall Tito at the 1950 Dubrovnik Olympiad while teammates George Shainswit (partly hidden), Larry Evans, George Kramer, and Herman Steiner look on (Photo: Piatigorsky Collection, courtesy of the World Chess Hall of Fame).

The Fischer family was under FBI surveillance throughout Bobby's formative years, and the effect this had on him cannot be underestimated—particularly jarring was one occasion when he witnessed agents interviewing his mother at 560 Lincoln Place.

Excerpts from the transcripts below show how thorough (and repetitive) the FBI information gathering was. The files are redacted and the names of agents and informants removed and replaced with ***. It seems obvious that someone in the Fischer's apartment building kept an eye on the family. The contact at *Chess Review* had to be either I.A. Horowitz or Jack Straley Battell (later the U.S. Chess Federation's long serving head of Correspondence Chess). Others supplying information were people Regina worked with.

- On January 30, 1959 *** 560 Lincoln Place, Brooklyn, New York, telephonically advised Special Agent *** that subject and her son ROBERT had been out of town for about a week but she did not know where they had gone.

- On February 10, 1959, *** advised that the subject and her son Robert had reservations to depart for Mexico City on January 21, 1959, aboard Aeronaves Flight Number 401. The informant stated they planned to return to New York City on February 1, 1959, aboard Aeronaves Flight Number 400, but that this reservation had not yet been confirmed. The informant stated as far as he knew, ROBERT FISCHER, the well-known fifteen-year-old chess player was not competing in a chess tournament in Mexico City. The informant stated he learned from the subject, that the trip was being made "for a little vacation."

- On February 11, 1959, *** *Chess Review* 134 West 72nd Street, New York City, advised he knew of no chess tournament which had been held recently in Mexico City in which ROBERT had participated. He stated he knew nothing of the activities of ROBERT FISCHER or his mother REGINA FISCHER.

- On February 11, 1959, *** Reservation Manager, Aeronaves, 500 Fifth Avenue, New York City, advised that REGINA FISCHER and BOBBY FISCHER had reservations on their Flight Number 401, on January 20, 1959, for Mexico City, but this was canceled, and they actually left on January 21, 1959, on the same flight. He stated they had tentative reservations on their Flight Number 400 from Mexico City to New York City on February 1, 1959, but he had no record that these reservations had been kept.

- On February 12, 1959, *** advised that the subject and her son ROBERT had returned to their residence at 560 Lincoln Place, on what she believed to be February 11, 1959. She stated they could possibly have returned on February 10, 1959, but that February 11, 1959, was the first day she had seen them at the apartment building. *** stated she still did not know where subject had been and had no information concerning her recent activities.

- On February 11, 1959, *** American Red Cross, advised that the subject taught first aid and nursing courses in the Kingsborough Housing Project during the following period of time: September, 1958, to October 14, 1958, and November, 1958, to December 18, 1958.

- *** stated the subject is a very intelligent, but "peculiar" person. *** stated she could not explain exactly what she meant by peculiar but stated she received this impression inasmuch as the subject is a flighty, unconventional individual. She stated she felt she had received this impression inasmuch as the subject has "big ideas" but never accomplishes with her ideas. *** stated that although the American Red Cross has a prescribed course of teaching in their nursing services, the subject was always inserting her own plans of teaching which often ran counter to those courses planned by the American Red Cross. *** stated the subject is a strong willed individual who would be most capable of most anything she might set her mind to.

- *** stated she learned from ***, Erasmus Hall High School, Brooklyn, New York, that ROBERT FISCHER had taken a trip with his mother but she did not learn where they had gone.

- She stated *** had advised her the high school had received a telegram during the early part of February, 1959, from the subject in Chicago, advising them ROBERT could not return to school at that time inasmuch as she, the subject, was ill. ***stated she did not learn the nature of the subject's illness or if she was actually in Chicago at the time this telegram was sent.

- *** advised she has talked with the subject, but has never received any impression that the subject was either pro-Communist or pro-Soviet. She stated their discussions have dealt only with nursing and the methods of teaching the American Red Cross courses.
- On March 2, 1959, *** 27 Crook Street, Brooklyn, New York, telephonically advised that she had recently been in personal contact with the subject in and attempted to question the subject about her recent trip to Mexico, but that the subject's son ROBERT was present and continually interrupted their conversation.
- *** again commented that he attempted to avoid any contact with REGINA FISCHER inasmuch as he considered her to be a "pain in the neck."
- *** stated she did not learn from the subject that had ROBERT had his school books with him in Mexico City, that he would have stayed there and gone to high school. The subject told **** that ROBERT would be moving in what she believed to be the next two weeks to Mexico City to attend high school.
- *** stated the subject told her she was in the hospital twice in Mexico City for treatment of stomach trouble and while they were there they stayed in a hotel. The subject told *** that her trip could have been a lot better except for the trouble ROBERT caused her while they were in Mexico City. *** stated denied having a boyfriend in Mexico City and in fact, did not mention anyone she might have visited while there.
- *** stated the subject advised her that after ROBERT left for Mexico City she could see no reason why she should stay in New York City and was planning on moving in a few weeks but did not indicate where she would go. *** stated that she did not think it was odd for the subject to pick up and move inasmuch as she has been on the move most of her life.
- *** stated she still has not received any indication that the subject is either pro-Communist or pro-Soviet.
- March 9, 1959, The subject and subject's son ROBERT went to Mexico City, 1/21/59, and returned to NYC about 2/11/59. *** advised he knew of no chess tournaments subject's son scheduled to play in Mexico City. Subject taught first aid and nursing courses for the American Red Cross, Brooklyn, N.Y. *** advised subject's son ROBERT, moving to Mexico City to go to high school and subject also leaving NYC but future residence unknown. Subject in hospital in Mexico City on recent trip to that city. Subject's bank accounts reflect no pertinent information.

[top] A street scene of Leningrad pictured on the front of a postcard mailed to Alex Liepnieks in 1960. "Greetings from Leningrad" wrote the two Latvian-Americans (Mednis and Kalme) and their Soviet-Latvian counterpart Janis Klovans. Note: Kalme uses his Latvian given name Ivars in place of the Americanized Charles.

[right]Julius Szabo of Romania faces Raymond Weinstein of the United States in round three of the 7th World Student Team Championship held in Leningrad.

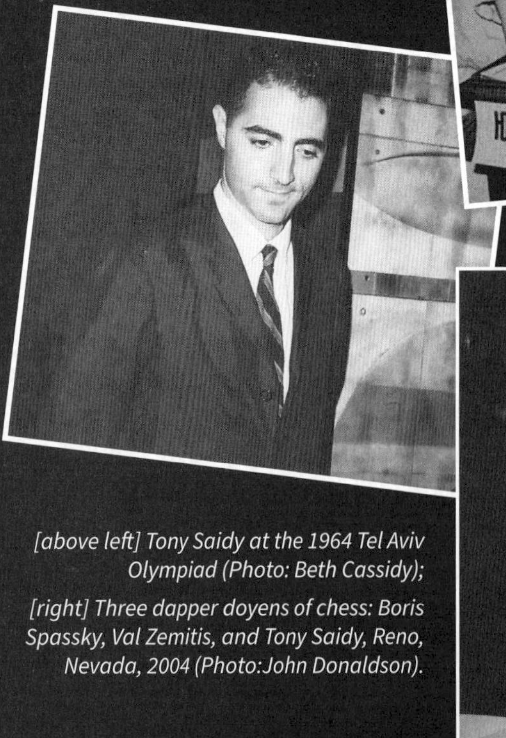

[above left] Tony Saidy at the 1964 Tel Aviv Olympiad (Photo: Beth Cassidy);

[right] Three dapper doyens of chess: Boris Spassky, Val Zemitis, and Tony Saidy, Reno, Nevada, 2004 (Photo:John Donaldson).

4
TEAM TOURNAMENTS

WORLD STUDENT TEAM CHAMPIONSHIP

Bobby started off the new decade by winning his third U.S. Championship title in convincing fashion with an undefeated score of 9–2, a point ahead of Robert Byrne. His next event, in Mar del Plata, was another great success—he tied for first with Boris Spassky. The return trip to Argentina a few months later did not go as well—his performance at Buenos Aires was his worst result as a grandmaster scoring only 8½ from 19. Curiously he did fine against the top six finishers (+2). Supporters of Sammy Reshevsky pointed to his first place tie with Viktor Korchnoi in Buenos Aires, 4½ points ahead of Bobby, as evidence their man still had a claim to being the strongest American player. Bobby didn't play again until just before the Olympiad that fall.

The summer of 1960 was an historic time for American chess—the United States beat the Soviets, and they did it in the Soviet Union at the World Student Team Championship[1] held in Leningrad.

The USSR was the dominant country in the World Student Team Championships of the 1950s and 1960s by virtue of their superior depth and top-rate coaching. However, they didn't fare as well in the World Junior Championships with a fourteen year gap between Boris Spassky (1955) and Anatoly Karpov (1969).

The 1959 World Student Team Championship in Budapest, which the United States sat out, was won by Bulgaria with 40½ points to the Soviet Union's 39. Future grandmasters Padevski and Tringov of Bulgaria won the individual silver and gold medals on boards one and two, while the Soviet team performed very well lower down. Fourth board Yury Nikolaevsky and second reserve Vladimir Liberzon won gold medals, and first reserve Anatoly Volovich took the silver. However, boards one through three—Bukhuiti Gurgenidze (6–4), Alexander Nikitin (6½–3½) and Aivars Ģipslis (7½–2½)—couldn't keep pace with their Bulgarian counterparts.

---

1 Sometimes referred to as the Student Olympiad.

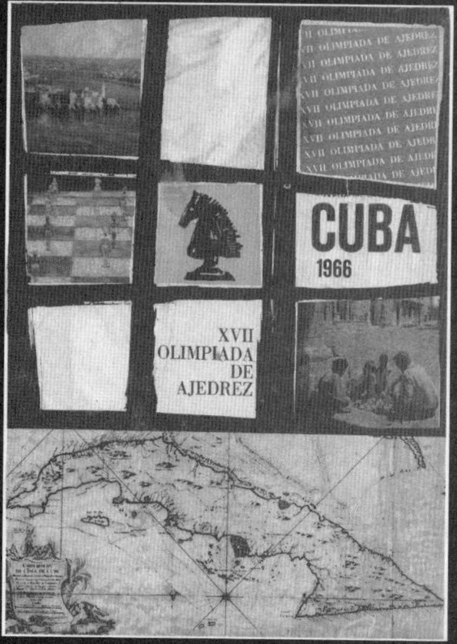

[top left] Fischer watches William Lombardy consider his 15th move in his game against Romanian master Corvin Radovici in round one of the A group final at Leipzig, 1960. Lombardy represented the United States in seven Olympiads between 1958 and 1978 scoring 69% in 91 games and winning four team and two individual medals;

[top right] This massive (475 page) book on the Havana Olympiad was published in several languages by the organizers;

[left] Jiménez vs. Fischer, Leipzig 1960. Eleazar Jiménez, Cuba's top player for many years, did well against Bobby with three draws in four games.

The bronze medal winning United States team at the 1982 Lucerne Olympiad : (left to right) Larry Evans (team captain), Walter Browne, Lev Alburt, Larry Christiansen, Jim Tarjan, Yasser Seirawan, and Lubomir Kavalek.

The Summer of 1960 witnessed an even greater disgrace for the Soviets as they lost on home ground to the Americans at the height of the Cold War. The United States student team of William Lombardy, Charles Kalme, Raymond Weinstein, Anthony Saidy, Edmar Mednis, and Eliot Hearst was in outstanding form and scored 41 points from 52. The USSR finished second with 39½, while Yugoslavia was third at 37 (Cleveland's late Milan Vukcevich playing a key role), and the Czechs, fourth with 31½—imagine what would have happened if Bobby had been playing! He couldn't, of course, no longer being a student. As it was, Lombardy beat Spassky (with Black) in their individual matchup and won the gold medal on board one with 12 out of 13. Kalme (11½–1½) and Weinstein (7½–2½) tied for gold medals on their respective boards.

This was truly an exceptional performance. To put things into perspective, a United States team has finished first ahead of the Soviets/Russians only two other times—the 1993 World Team Championship in Lucerne, Switzerland, and the Baku Olympiad in 2016.

The Soviets got their revenge the following year in Helsinki: (1st) USSR 39½, (2nd) USA 34½, (3rd–4th). East Germany and Czechoslovakia 31. The Soviets showed up with a new team, while the Americans were only missing Saidy. The United States, who lost to the Soviets 3–1, again had great results from Lombardy and Weinstein on the first and second boards (each won silver medals for 9/11 scores). Fourth board Kalme had 7½/10, Mednis, the first reserve had 5½/8, and second reserve Larry Gilden won both his games. Unfortunately, third board James Sherwin, an Interzonalist in 1958, was in uncharacteristic form and scored only one and a half points from six games.

Bobby never played in a World Student Team Championship. He wasn't strong enough to make the team in 1956 or 1957 and the United States didn't participate in 1959. The one year he might have played was 1958, but that event in Varna, Bulgaria, was held right before the twenty-round Portorož Interzonal—playing thirty games in a little over a month was too much chess, even for Bobby.

World Student Team Chess Championship tournaments, which officially started in 1954, were an important annual event for several decades, in many cases offering young players their first opportunity to gain international experience.

The U.S. Chess Federation started sending players to these events in 1956, but until Jacqueline Piatigorsky stepped in to fund the teams in the late '60s, sponsorship was challenging to say the least. Often the job of scraping up enough money to field a team fell on the team captain who would make appeals to individual donors. Those who gave money would later receive a small booklet on the tournament by the Czech arbiter and International Master Jaroslav Šajtar, who was closely associated with these events.

United States Student Team

TO MY AMERICAN CHESS FIRENDS

Once again after a seven year lapse, the burden of raising funds for the United States Student Team is mine. Before, the task was not easy — it is no less difficult now. Your help is urgently needed.

You have probably been called upon in the past to lend your support to this worthy cause. Whether or not you have, however, you are most urgently asked to lend your support now.

In our students lies the future and seccess of American Chess. From past events have emerged grandmasters and international masters. The need to insure continued United States participation in these international events is apparent. We were world champions in 1960, but winning itselt is not necessarily the major objective. We must first afford our players the vital experience in international tournaments, for these players are certain one day to represent us on our Olympic Team, International tournament experience is particularly important if the United States is to complete with subsidized foreign players, particularly those of the Soviet Untion.

Individual contributions in amy amount will be greatly appreciated. If, however, you are a chess organizer or a member of a chess club in your area, why not assign yourself the job of raising a minimum of twenty-five dollars? Even one dollar contribution from those with large hearts but small purses add up. All contributions are tax deductible. Please send in yours N O W ! In anticipation of your assistance, please accept my personal thanks.

Cordially in the cause of American Chess
WILLIAM LOMBARDY
International Grandmaster and Director, U.S.C.F.

Please make all checks payable to AMERICAN CHESS FOUNDATION STUDENT FUND, and mail to Willaim Lombardy. 1600 University Avenue, Bronx 53, New York.

READ WHAT THE PHENOMENAL, 6-TIME U.S. CHESS CHAMPION BOBBY FISCHER, and the runner-up for the 1963-64, LARRY EVANS, think abou the U.S. Student Team of 1964.

"We cannot improve or hope to contest Soviet superiority unless we give our young players a chance to hone their play in international competition such as this." *Larry Evans, Former U.S. Chess Champion.*

"When the U.S. Student Team won the world championship of Leningrad in 1960, I remember the great pleasure I felt when I read in a Russiam magazine the devious twisting to find an excuse for the failure of the Russian team to win the championship. First, it was stated that their failure to win was due to a lack of preparation, and then the writer of the article complained bitterly that some of the team players had the gall to 'take a boat to a Ball!' prior to the game with the Americans. I hope that I again have the pleasure to read a similar Russian complaint when our U.S. Student Team repeats its brilliant performance this summer" *Bobby Fischer, U. S. Chess Champion.*

The backcover of the 1964 winter issue of American Chess Quarterly *with Bobby's appeal for funds.*

By 1964 the responsibility to raise funds had fallen on perennial first board William Lombardy, who played for the team seven times between 1956 and 1964. To help him get the ball rolling *American Chess Quarterly* devoted its entire backcover as an appeal for support for the Student Team. The appeal featured team captain Lombardy, the magazine's editor Larry Evans, and a third individual not known for his philanthropic work—Bobby. Fischer was adamant throughout his life that no one should make money off of him. He held this position with such conviction that he would rather forgo $99,000 in a $100,000 deal if he thought someone else was going to receive $1,000. Why did Fischer made the exception in this case? Was he more flexible on this issue early in his career? Or, was it because the appeal was simply to raise money to cover expenses and no profit was involved, the players not receiving honorariums? Whatever the reason, Bobby's participation was a rare occurrence. Bobby's appeal:

> When the U.S. Student Team won the World Championship at Leningrad in 1960, I remember the great pleasure I felt when I read in a Russian magazine the devious twisting to find an excuse for the failure of the Russian team to win the championship. First, it was stated that their failure to win was due to a lack of preparation, and then the article complained bitterly that some of the team players had the gall to 'take a boat to a Ball' prior to the game with the Americans. I hope that I again have the pleasure to read a similar Russian complaint when our U.S. Student Team repeats its brilliant performance this summer.
> —Bobby Fischer, U.S. Chess Champion

This was written only two years after the Candidates tournament in Curaçao and Fischer was still upset by what he alleged was collusion between Soviet players. His article, "The Russians Have Fixed World Chess,"[1] started a war of words that continued for several years. [see pages 269–271 "There Was Open Collusion." Curaçao 1962.]

Fischer expressed his on going anger with the Soviet chess bureaucracy on national television during his 1971 appearance on *The Dick Cavett Show*:[2]

> When I first started playing chess, to me the Russians were heroes...and they still are as chessplayers. I used to study all their literature and most of the first chess books I read were Russian. But the first time the Russians ever mentioned me—I was thirteen—they said, "Well, he's a very fine talented young player, but all this publicity he's getting is sure to do damage to his character." And sure enough, from then on they started attacking my character. And they had never met me or knew anything about me.

---

[1] Bobby Fischer, *Sports Illustrated*, August 20, 1962, "The Russians Have Fixed World Chess," (pp. 18–19, 64–65).

[2] *The Dick Cavett Show*, Summer 1971.

British Columbia master Dan Scoones, a longtime student of the Russian language and the history and culture of the Soviet Union, believes Bobby may have misunderstood early Soviet write-ups about him. He points to an article on Fischer, which appeared in the February 1957 issue of *Shakhmaty v SSSR*, translated here by Scoones:

> **YOUNG CHESS PLAYER'S SUCCESS**
>
> Amongst the participants in the New York tournament, the thirteen-year-old schoolboy R. Fischer attracted special attention. One of his games, in which he defeated D. Byrne, was awarded a special prize as the most beautiful in the tournament. R. Fischer was born in 1943 and learned to play chess at an early age. Fischer was the youngest player in the U.S. Junior Championship, which took place last summer. Despite this, he led from start to finish and in the end captured the title. Next, Fischer took part in two adult tournaments: the "open" championships of the USA and Canada. In both tournaments, the young player came ahead of many well-known masters. It should be noted, though, that in the United States a great deal of publicity has arisen around Fischer's name. There have been newspaper articles, radio and television programs about him; and Fischer is traveling around the country giving simultaneous exhibitions. This can hardly contribute to the normal development of an undoubtedly talented young chess player.

It's easy to see how Fischer could have taken this as a personal attack. However, as Scoones explained, if you knew something about the Soviet Union at the time, you would understand the comments were not directed at Fischer himself:

> I don't agree that the statement about the "normal development of the... young chess player" is a personal attack on Fischer's character. Instead it expresses the Soviet view that the development of chess players (and other sportsmen) in bourgeois cultures was always negatively affected by the constant need to earn a living. That meant making chess into a public spectacle, with exhibition tours and special publicity, when the young player should be making a proper study of the game. Of course in Fischer's case they were wrong in the end. But I often think that he might not have contracted such a strong case of Russophobia if he had read this passage slightly differently.

Future International Master Anthony Saidy, who played such an important role in Fischer's life in both his formative years and his 1972 bid for the World Championship, was making his own mark in 1960. That year Saidy played on the winning World Student team, took first in the Canadian Open, and nearly won the U.S. Open. Charles Henin's 1961 *Chess Life*[1] portrait introduces a figure who is still active in chess today, sixty years later.

---

[1] *Chess Life*, September 1961, (p. 258).

One of the finest young players in the country is Anthony Saidy, a twenty-four-year-old medical student from New York. The current Canadian Open champion, Saidy has long been considered a threat in any event in which he competes. He has placed high several times in the U.S. Open, and last year at St. Louis Tony defeated both the winner (Byrne) and the runner-up (Benko) and seemed headed for the title when a loss to Poschel in the eleventh round ruined his chances and brought him down to a tie for fourth prize. Undaunted, Tony a month later scored his first major tournament win at the Canadian Open at Kitchener, Ontario.

Saidy has competed on the U.S. Student Team no less than four times, with consistently fine results. He was high scorer for the team in Iceland (1957) and Bulgaria (1958) and scored 4½–2½ on board four in the team's victory last year at Leningrad. Against Soviet opposition Tony holds an even score, despite a loss to a comparative unknown in 1956—M. Tal.

Tony was born in Los Angeles, but has lived in New York since age ten. His family is involved in the rather offbeat world of the theatre, his father Fred Saidy, being a well-known playwright who has penned many fine shows including the delightful *Finian's Rainbow*. Tony learned chess from his father, whom he says is a poor player but good at bridge. At eleven he joined the Marshall Chess Club and was one of the "Marshall Juniors," whose past ranks have included many of the country's leading players. Tony obtained his B.S. at Fordham, is currently in his fourth year at Cornell University Medical College in New York and will soon be Dr. Saidy.

Saidy is husky and rugged looking, appears poised and confident both on and off the chessboard. He captained the U.S. Student Team twice, and was a key organizer as ICIA president, which involved the not inconsiderable task of collecting the funds necessary for the team's existence.

Saidy has an aggressive, positional chess style, which together with a fine knowledge of openings and a sharp eye for combinational possibilities, make him a very dangerous opponent. He generally thinks deeply in the early stages of the game and as a result often gets into time trouble. Though a fine blitz player and an expert at "time pressure swindles," Tony often pays the penalty for trying to cheat the clock. In the recent U.S. Championship, Saidy came tantalizing close to being the first American in four years to defeat Fischer, when a blunder just before the time control cost him the game.

LEIPZIG OLYMPIAD

At a time when the peak age for a player was considered thirty-five, the emphasis at the 1960 Olympiad in Leipzig was on youth. The World Champion and Soviet first board Mikhail Tal was only twenty-three years of age. Even more remarkable was the composition of the United States team. Bobby, making his debut for the U.S. national team on board one, was only seventeen(!), second board William Lombardy was twenty-two, and second reserve Raymond Weinstein was nineteen.

Leipzig was a great success, as youth (Fischer, Lombardy, and Weinstein) combined with experience (Robert Byrne, Bisguier, and Rossolimo) and the team triumphantly finished second. Robert Byrne won the individual silver medal on board three and Bobby received a bronze medal for his first board finish. This was the first team medal for the United States since the glory days of the 1930s when U.S. chess dominated the Olympiads—the 1960 team's captain, Isaac Kashdan, played on three of those winning teams.

One of the tragedies of American chess is that Raymond Weinstein's career was so brief. The cousin of Arthur Bisguier (and no relation to International Master Norman Weinstein), Raymond had a breakout year in 1960. He not only starred in Leipzig (6½/8), but also played a key role in the U.S. team's victory in the Student Team Championship in Leningrad. Arguably even more impressive was his third place finish in the U.S. Championship at the end of the year, behind Fischer and Lombardy, but ahead of Reshevsky, R. Byrne, Benko, and several other strong players. Sadly, just a few years later, Weinstein was diagnosed with a serious mental illness and his chess career came to a close.

Prior to the event it was questionable if the U.S. would even send a team—money was tight and the U.S. Chess Federation barely had enough to run its day-to-day operations. Due to a lack of funds the United States was unable to send a team to the 1954 and 1956 Olympiads, and in 1960 it was touch and go right up to the event.

Bobby did his part to remedy the team's plight. He gave a well-publicized simul at the prison on Riker's Island playing twenty prisoners while another 2400 inmates watched. His mother got into the effort as well, protesting in front of the White House wearing a sign that read "Ike Says Yes. The American Chess Foundation Says No"—a reference to President Eisenhower's encouragement to send a team albeit with no government funding, and the American Chess Foundation's refusal to provide full support (probably influenced by Sammy Reshevsky's decision not to play).

Regina's well-intentioned actions drew Bobby's ire–he hated it when she publicly campaigned for him or the team he was playing on. Early on he made it very clear to his mother that he didn't want to be beholden to anyone. This trait of Bobby's strained their relationship.

The American Chess Foundation was founded in 1955 to assist Sammy Reshevsky, the unquestioned U.S. top player at the time, who was trying to support his wife and three kids on a chess professional's income. The emergence of Bobby, a few years later, caused the ACF to reconsider their objectives. Eventually, they expanded financial support beyond Sammy, but this didn't happen until the 1961 Fischer–Reshevsky match when Jacqueline Piatigorsky emerged as a major and much-needed donor. Her subsequent support of the U.S. Olympiad teams put U.S. participation on much firmer ground.

One of the chief expenses for U.S. Olympiad teams (and World Student teams) was airfare. Compared with today, transatlantic flights in the '50s and '60s were not cheap—for example, in 1955 the least expensive ticket to fly round trip from New York to Frankfurt cost $330 ($3,200 in 2020 dollars).

Regardless of Bobby's feelings, Regina certainly knew how to generate publicity as the following two *New York Times* articles attest.

Reported September 28, 1960:

> **CHESS OFFICE PICKETED**
> **FISCHER'S MOTHER WANTS U.S. TEAM IN WORLD OLYMPICS**
>
> Mrs. Regina Fischer continued to picket the headquarters of the American Chess Foundation at 1372 Broadway to get it to send a team to the World Chess Olympics opening at Leipzig, East Germany, on October 14. She is the mother of the seventeen-year-old national champion from Brooklyn.
>
> Mrs. Fischer carried a sign saying that President Eisenhower favored having an American team at the Olympics and the foundation had the money to send one.
>
> A spokesman for the foundation said yesterday that the responsibility for sending a team abroad rested with the United States Chess Federation. He said the federation had not acted to send a team because the State Department was not in favor of it.
>
> A spokesman for the federation said it was awaiting word from the State Department whether a team should be sent.

And on October 12, 1960:

> **CHESS PROTEST IS OVER**
> **BOBBY FISCHER'S MOTHER ENDS 6-DAY HUNGER STRIKE**
>
> The mother of seventeen-year-old Bobby Fischer, the United States chess champion, said yesterday that she had ended her hunger strike Monday afternoon after six days without food.
>
> She had stopped eating in an effort to persuade the American Chess Foundation to provide more money for the United States team in the 1960 Chess Olympics.
>
> The mother, Mrs. Regina Fischer, has also been picketing the foundation at 1372 Broadway. She said it had provided only $2,000 for the games in Leipzig, East Germany this year, compared with $6,318 given for the American team expenses for the 1958 Olympics in Munich.

The upshot of Regina's protests was that the ACF increased its funding, and induced other sponsors to come forward. It also brought about a dramatic change in her life when her picketing caught the eye of Ammon Hennacy, a noted social activist. Hennacy suggested a hunger strike for chess as a means to get the media's attention, and was also the one who proposed she join the San Francisco to Moscow walk for peace, a move that led her to leave New York at the end of the year.

Jonathan Penrose scored a famous victory over reigning World Champion Mikhail Tal at the Leipzig Olympiad and almost defeated Bobby as well. Annotations to Game (31) includes notes by Penrose.[1] This is one of several Fischer tournament games that standard sources give incorrectly (see the note after 31...Qxd5).

(31) Sicilian
Jonathan Penrose – Fischer
Leipzig 1960

[Penrose] "When I sat down to play Bobby Fischer in the second round of the Olympiad Final, I was terrified at the thought of playing this outstanding genius."

1.e4 c5 2.Nf3 d6 3.d4 cxd4 4.Nxd4 Nf6 5.Nc3 a6 6.f4 e5 7.Nf3 Nbd7 8.a4 b6 9.Bc4 Qc7 10.Qe2 Be7 11.0-0 Bb7 12.fxe5 dxe5 13.Bg5 h6 14.Bh4

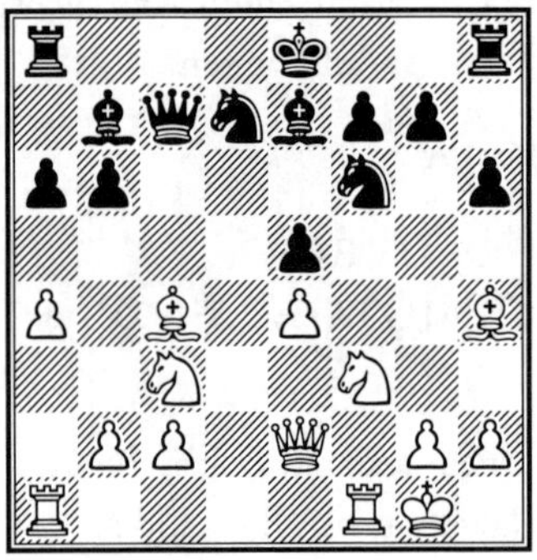

14...Bb4?

[Penrose] "After the game Fischer criticized this over-ambitious move. Much better was 14...0-0."

This move is quite playable if followed up correctly.

15.Bxf6

[1] Penrose's annotations originally published in *Chess*, August 1988 (pp. 35–36).

[Penrose] "'Why did you think so long after this move?' Fischer asked me after the game, 'I saw it right away!' He had a point. I was playing too slowly and later got into serious time trouble."

15...Nxf6 16.Nh4 Rc8

Better is 16...Bxc3 17.bxc3 Bc8, covering the f5–square, and then ...0-0 when Black has no problems. After 18.Rxf6 gxf6 19.Bd5 Rb8 20.Qh5 Rh7 21.Rf1 Qd6 White has compensation for the exchange, but not more.

17.Bb5+

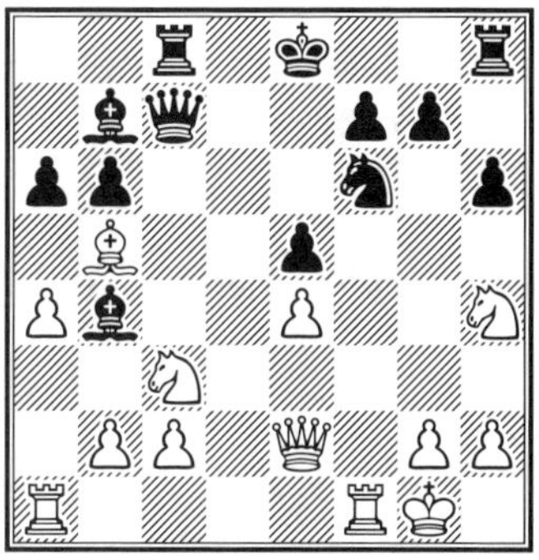

Penrose gives this move an exclamation mark, criticizing Black's last move, but in fact Fischer's position is fine if followed up correctly.

[Penrose] "Note 17.Bxa6 Bxa6 18.Qxa6 Qc5+ 19.Kh1 Bxc3 20.bxc3 0-0 favors Black."

17...Nd7?

This move looks to be the start of Black's troubles. 17...Kf8 is not considered by Penrose, but appears quite playable: 18.Bxa6 Bxa6 19.Qxa6 Bxc3 20.bxc3 Kg8 followed by ...Kh7 connecting rooks.

[Penrose] "White was hoping for 17...axb5 18.Qxb5+ Qc6 19.Qxb4 Nxe4 20.Nf5."

18.Bxd7+ Qxd7 19.Rad1

19.Nf5 0-0?? 20.Qg4 wins, but as Penrose points out Black has an adequate defense in 19...g6.

19...Bc5+

19...Qe6 20.Nd5 Bc5+ 21.Kh1 0-0 22.Rf6! Bxd5 (22...gxf6 23.Nf5 is even worse) 23.Rxe6 Bxe6 24.Nf3 a5 25.Nxe5 Rfe8 when Black doesn't have enough compensation for his material deficit.

20.Kh1 Bd4 21.Nf5 g6

Again 21...0-0?? loses to 22.Qg4.

22.Nxd4 exd4 23.Nd5 Bxd5 24.exd5+ Qe7 25.Qf2 0-0 26.Rxd4 Qc5

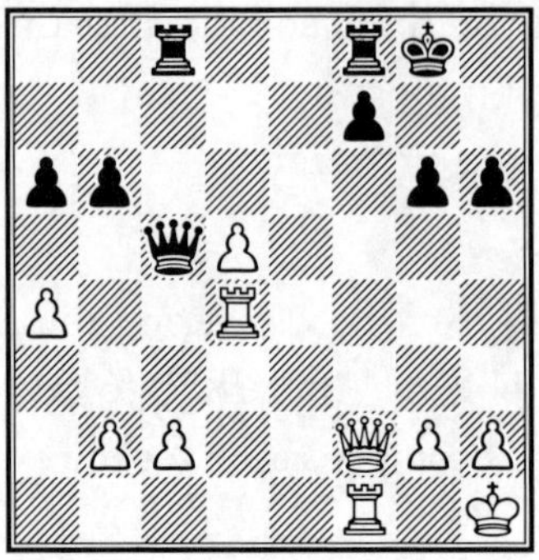

[Penrose] "The position is clearly a technical win but Fischer was playing fast and I was getting short of time."

27.Rd2?!

[Penrose] "The rook is already where it needs to be. Therefore 27.c3 is correct."

27...Qb4 28.c3 Qb3 29.Rd4

[Penrose] "29.d6 also looks good."

29...Rc4 30.Rxc4

[Penrose] "More incisive is 30.d6 Rxd4 31.Qxd4 Qxb2 32.d7"

32.Re1!, preparing d7 while taking away ...Qe2, is decisive.

[Penrose] "32...Rd8 (32...Qe2! 33.Rd1 Rd8 and the way forward for White is not clear) 33.Qd5."

30...Qxc4 31.Kg1

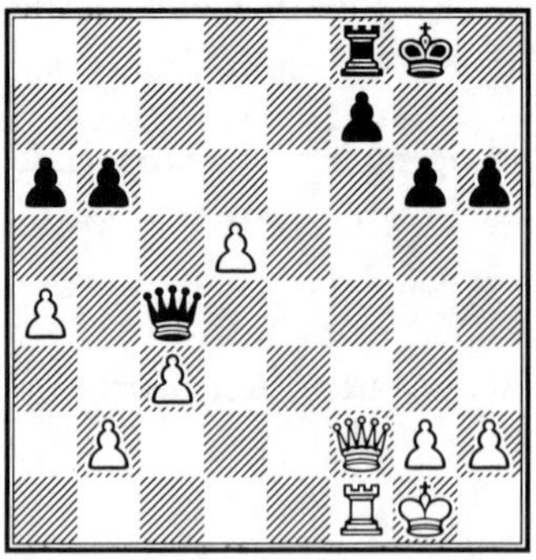

[Penrose] "Now it's already slightly more difficult. If 31.Rd1 then 31... Qxa4."

31...Qxd5

Mega Database and many other Fischer collections give the game ending in a draw after 31...Qxa4 32.Qxb6 Qc4 33.Qb4 Qxb4 (33.d6 is winning)

34.cxb4 Rb8 35.Rf4 Rd8, but as Penrose writes in *Chess* that is not how the game went!

32.Qxb6 Qc4 33.Qb4 Qxb4?

Quite possibly Fischer had not yet seen the idea of b5 and a5.

[Penrose] "33...Qd5, which centralizes the queen, keeps f7 protected and prepares to activate the rook on e8, was much better and offered decent chances to hold."

34.cxb4 Rb8

[Penrose] "34...Rc8 35.b5! axb5 36.a5 is similar to the game."

35.Rf4

[Penrose] "35.b5! axb5 36.a5 was more direct."

35...Rd8, ½–½.

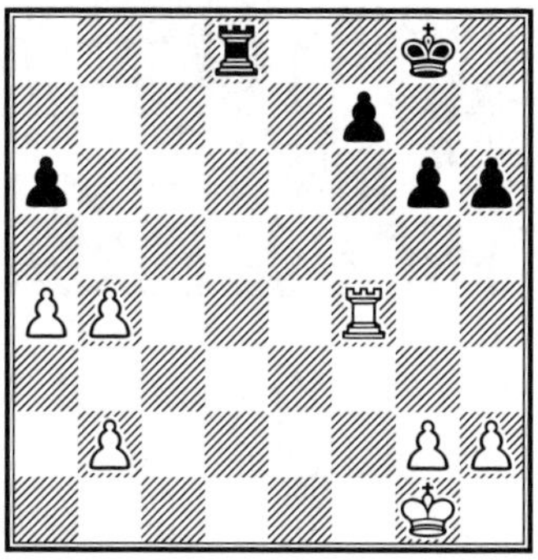

[Penrose] "Still in time trouble, here I offered a draw to which Fischer gave the instant reply 'SURE!' American grandmaster Robert Byrne, spectating, was the first to comment, quizzing Bobby 'How did you get so busted?' but Bobby was already busy demonstrating to me the line 35...Rd8 36.b5! axb5 37.a5! followed by 38.b4 when White will advance his king to c5, capture the b-pawn and win with two connected passed pawns—a view confirmed by another interested onlooker Viktor Korchnoi. I didn't see this idea—probably because I didn't want to give up my extra pawn. Later I heard that Botvinnik had also taken an interest in the game, remarking: 'In the first half of the game Penrose played very well—in the second half he didn't play!'"

The evaluation that White is winning after b5 and a5 looks to be correct. The following variations are not conclusive but give an idea of the difficulties Black is facing. 37...Kf8 38.b4 Ke7 39.Re4+ (the immediate attempt to activate the king with 39.Kf2 leads to a drawn king and pawn ending after 39...Rd2+ 40.Ke3 Rxg2 41.Rf2 Rxf2 42.Kxf2) 39...Kf6 40.Kf2 Kf5

[left] "The Seven Invaders." Team Captain Eliot Hearst gives inspiration to his troops before the Battle of Varna. The U.S. team 1962 (left to right) Larry Evans, Pal Benko, Edmar Mednis, Eliot Hearst (captain), Robert Byrne, Bobby Fischer, Donald Byrne (Drawing courtesy of Chess Life*);*

[right] Mr. Dependable, Grandmaster Larry Christiansen (circa late-1970s) played on nine U.S. Olympiad teams and three World Team Championships from 1990 to 2002, collecting seven team medals of all colors plus three individual board prizes. He also captained the U.S. team that took second at the 1998 Elista Olympiad (Photo Jerry Hanken).

41.Ke3 Rd1 42.g4+ Kf6 (42...Kg5 43.Re5+ Kxg4 44.Rxb5) 43.h4 Rh1 (43...Rb1 44.Kd4 Rxb4+ 45.Kd5 Rb1 46.Kc5 Kg7 [46...g5 47.h5] 47.a6 f5 48.gxf5 gxf5 49.Rb4 Ra1 50.Kb6 winning.) 44.Kd4 Rc1 (44...Rxh4 45.g5+ hxg5 46.Rxh4 gxh4 47.a6) 45.Kd5 Rc2 46.Re8 Rc4 47.a6 and again White is winning.

Besides the four Olympiads Fischer played for the United States, he also represented his country in team matches in 1960 and 1962. The first, against a strong German team (Darga, Lehmann, and Bialas all played in the 1960 Olympiad), was held at the Cumberland House in Berlin on November 10, 1960, the day after the Leipzig Olympiad ended. It was organized by Alfred Seppelt, longtime head of the Berlin Chess Federation. Seppelt would later make news in 1978 when, after a private visit with Fischer in West Germany, he sold a photo of Fischer to the *Berlin Morgenpost*. Their friendship was immediately terminated.

USA		West Berlin
1. Fischer (W)	1–0	Klaus Darga
2. William Lombardy	½–½	Dr. Heinz Lehmann
3. Robert Byrne	1–0	Rudolf Teschner
4. Arthur Bisguier	1–0	Alfred Seppelt
5. Raymond Weinstein	1–0	Wolfram Bialas
	4½–½	

Ingi Jóhannsson of Iceland vs. Mikhail Tal (Boris Spassky is on Tal's right) at the 1966 Havana Olympiad.

Bobby's win over Darga is featured in *My 60 Memorable Games*. Losses to Ivkov, Uhlmann, Mednis, and Kovacevic have sometimes given the impression the French Winawer was Fischer's Achilles' heel, but he also played some of his most brilliant games against it. The win over Darga and later defeats of Schweber and Larsen are classics.

FISCHER'S RECORD IN THE CHESS OLYMPIADS

Fischer played in the 1960, 1962, 1966, and 1970 Olympiads with outstanding results. He scored 49 points from 65 games (+40, –7, =18), winning two team silver medals (and two fourth place finishes) and two silver and one bronze individual medals. His career win record of 75.4% is outstanding and behind only Isaac Kashdan (79.7%), Sam Shankland (76.8%), and James Tarjan (75.5 %) among American players who have played in more than one Olympiad.

The United States has had only two World Champions (Steinitz and Fischer), but since 1928 it has consistently been among the top finishing teams at the Chess Olympiads. The U. S. dominated in the 1930s—finishing first in 1931, 1933, 1935, and 1937. Attracting less attention have been the steady results posted since World War II, when the Soviets first started competing. This is particularly true for the period since 1974. During the stretch from 1974 to 2018 (leaving out the boycott year of 1976) the U.S. has finished first once, second three times, and third on no fewer than eight occasions. That is a dozen team medals in twenty-two tries.

Considering that in most of these competitions, particularly after the breakup of the Soviet Union in 1990, the American teams were rarely ranked in the top three by rating, you have a tradition that deserves more recognition. Below is the record of the U.S. team from 1950 to 2018.

U.S. TEAM PERFORMANCE 1950–2018

(c) = team captain

1950 (Dubrovnik) 4th—Reshevsky, Steiner, Horowitz (playing captain), Shainswit, Kramer, Evans

1952 (Helsinki) 5th—Reshevsky, Evans, R. Byrne, Bisguier, Koltanowski (playing captain), Berliner

1954 (Amsterdam) The U.S. did not participate.

1956 (Moscow) The U.S. did not participate.

1958 (Munich) 4th—Reshevsky, Lombardy, Bisguier, Evans, Rossolimo, Spann (c)

1960 (Leipzig) 2nd—Fischer, Lombardy, R. Byrne, Bisguier, Rossolimo, Weinstein, Kashdan (c)

1962 (Varna) 4th—Fischer, Benko, Evans, R. Byrne, D. Byrne, Mednis, Hearst (c)

1964 (Tel Aviv) 6th—Reshevsky, Benko, Saidy, Bisguier, D. Byrne, Addison, Kashdan (c)

1966 (Havana) 2nd—Fischer, R. Byrne, Benko, Evans, Addison, Rossolimo, D. Byrne (c)

1968 (Lugano) 4th—Reshevsky, Evans, Benko, R. Byrne, Lombardy, D. Byrne (playing captain)

1970 (Siegen) 4th—Fischer, Reshevsky, Evans, Benko, Lombardy, Mednis, Edmondson (c)

1972 (Skopje) 8th–9th—Kavalek, R. Byrne, Benko, Bisguier, Martz, Kane, D. Byrne (c)

1974 (Nice) 3rd—Kavalek, R. Byrne, Browne, Reshevsky, Lombardy, Tarjan, Benko (c) and Koltanowski (c)

1976 (Haifa) 1st—R. Byrne, Kavalek, Evans, Tarjan, Lombardy, Commons, Goichberg (c) Note: there was a boycott of this Olympiad by the Soviet Union and the East Bloc.

1978 (Buenos Aires) 3rd—Kavalek, Browne, Lein, R. Byrne, Tarjan, Lombardy, Benko (c)

1980 (Malta) 4th—Alburt, Seirawan, Christiansen, Tarjan, de Firmian, Shamkovich, Benko (c)

1982 (Lucerne) 3rd—Browne, Seirawan, Alburt, Kavalek, Tarjan, Christiansen, Evans (c)

1984 (Thessaloniki) 3rd—Dzindzichashvili, Kavalek, Christiansen, Browne, Alburt, de Firmian, R. Byrne (c) and Fedorowicz (c)

1986 (Dubai) 3rd—Seirawan, Christiansen, Kavalek, Fedorowicz, de Firmian, Dlugy, Donaldson (c)

1988 (Thessaloniki) 4th—Seirawan, Gulko, Benjamin, Christiansen, Kudrin, de Firmian, Donaldson (c)

1990 (Novi Sad) 2nd—Seirawan, Gulko, Christiansen, Benjamin, Fedorowicz, de Firmian, Donaldson (c)

1992 (Manila) 4th—Kamsky, Yermolinsky, Seirawan, Christiansen, Gulko, Benjamin, Donaldson (c)

1994 (Moscow) 5th–7th—Gulko, Yermolinsky, Benjamin, Seirawan, Shabalov, Kudrin, Donaldson (c)

1996 (Yerevan) 3rd—Gulko, Yermolinsky, de Firmian, Kaidanov, Benjamin, Christiansen, Donaldson (c)

1998 (Elista) 2nd—Yermolinsky, Shabalov, Seirawan, Gulko, de Firmian, Kaidanov, Christiansen (c)

2000 (Istanbul) 26th–32nd—Seirawan, Gulko, Shabalov, Kaidanov, Yermolinsky, de Firmian, Christiansen (c)

2002 (Bled) 37th–45th—Kaidanov, Seirawan, Gulko, Benjamin, Christiansen, A. Ivanov, de Firmian (c)

2004 (Calvia) 4th—Onischuk, Shabalov, Goldin, Kaidanov, Novikov, Gulko, Postovsky (c)

2006 (Turin) 3rd—Kamsky, Onischuk, Nakamura, Ibragimov, Kaidanov, Akobian, Donaldson (c)

2008 (Dresden) 3rd—Kamsky, Nakamura, Onischuk, Shulman, Akobian, Donaldson (c)

2010 (Khanty Mansiysk) 5th–10th—Nakamura, Kamsky, Onischuk, Shulman, Hess, Donaldson (c)

2012 (Istanbul) 4th–5th—Nakamura, Kamsky, Onischuk, Akobian, Robson, Donaldson (c)

2014 (Tromso) 12th–23rd—Nakamura, Kamsky, Onischuk, Akobian, Shankland, Donaldson (c)

2016 (Baku) 1st—Caruana, Nakamura, So, Shankland, Robson, Donaldson (c)

2018 (Batumi) 2nd—Caruana, So, Nakamura, Shankland, Robson, Donaldson (c)

[Note: Starting in 2008 the Olympiads have been played on four boards with one reserve player, down from the traditional two reserves. The number of countries competing has increased dramatically in the past sixty years from sixteen countries in 1950 to sixty in 1970, one hundred and eight in 1990, one hundred and forty-nine in 2010 and one hundred and eighty in 2016.]

BOARD MEDALS WON BY U.S. PLAYERS – 1950–2018

1st board – Reshevsky (bronze) 1950, Fischer (bronze) 1960, Fischer (silver) 1966, Fischer (silver) 1970, Caruana (bronze) 2016 , Caruana (silver) 2018

2nd board – Benko (silver) 1962, Seirawan (silver) 1980, Yermolinsky (silver) 1996, Seirawan (silver) 2002, Kamsky (bronze) 2012

3rd board – R. Byrne (bronze) 1952, R. Byrne (silver) 1960, Evans (bronze) 1976, So (gold) 2016

4th board – Evans (silver) 1958, Seirawan (gold) 1994

1st Reserve – D. Byrne (silver) 1962, Lombardy (gold) 1970, Lombardy (silver) 1976, Tarjan (gold) 1978, Tarjan (bronze) 1982, deFirmian (bronze) 1998, Shankland (gold) 2014

2nd Reserve – Evans (gold) 1950, Rossolimo (bronze) 1958, D. Byrne (bronze) 1968, Tarjan (gold) 1974, Commons (gold) 1976, de Firmian (bronze) 1984

MOST BOARD MEDALS BY A U.S. PLAYER 1950–2018

3 medals – Evans, Fischer, Seirawan, and Tarjan

2 medals – D. Byrne and R. Byrne, Caruana, deFirmian, and Lombardy

Note: The method of determining board prizewinners has changed with time. For many years the best percentage score was used regardless of strength of opposition. For example, Yermolinsky had the third best rating performance of the entire 1996 Olympiad, but took home the silver medal on board 2 as Richard Robinson of Bermuda had a higher percentage score. The former had an outstanding personal result of 2334 but his performance rating was well behind Yermolinsky's 2760.

Another example is Yasser Seirawan's result in 2002. Losing in the last round he fell behind a player from Monaco (7 from 9 compared to 6½ from 9) although his performance rating for the event was still several hundred points higher. The switch from best percentage score to highest rating performance was made in 2008 and with it any chance for successful players on lower ranked teams to fight for individual board medals.

5
BBC CONSULTATION GAME

Bobby never played in a tournament in England. He was signed up to play at Hastings in 1957, but changed his plans when it was announced, late-in-the-day, that the concurrent 1957/58 U.S. Championship would be a Zonal. However Fischer did play chess in London. His best-known activity there was a consultation game played and taped in the fall of 1960 as part of a series of radio programs the BBC produced on chess, Game (32).

Two teams—Leonard Barden and Fischer on one, and Jonathan Penrose and Peter Clarke on the other—were set up in separate studios. The game lasted eight hours and only stopped when the studio time ran out. Bobby was annoyed at the end when Penrose and Clarke would not resign and the game was adjudicated:

> At Broadcasting House, no agreement could be reached on the proper result. Penrose and Clarke were claiming a draw, which was flatly rejected by Fischer: "What's the matter with you guys–are you dreaming or something?" So an independent adjudicator was sought—no less a player than former World Champion Dr. Euwe. In the meantime, Jonathan perhaps remembering the adjudication that went against him as a junior in the Glorney Cup put in some serious homework. "'I spent a lot of time on it, wrote it all down and sent it to Dr. Euwe. I wondered if, today, computers would find something wrong with my analysis."[1]

The teams discussions were edited to remove dead air space. The result was a most interesting program.

Unfortunately, the original recording no longer exists. According to Barden (long-time chess columnist for *The Guardian*), when he asked the BBC, they responded, "the tape has been wiped and used for another program." This is a shame, as Fischer's comments were not included when the game eventually appeared in print in *Chess Treasury of the Air*,[2] and are seemingly lost forever.

The game and comments by the players were originally broadcast over the BBC's Third Network (now BBC Radio 3) every Sunday afternoon at the rate

[1] "Jonathan Penrose Last of the Great Amateurs?" *Chess*, August 1988, (p 30–37).

[2] Terence Tiller (ed.), *Chess Treasury of the Air*, (pp. 124–132).

of several moves per show starting in early January 1961 and finished with Max Euwe's adjudication on May 7 that year.

According to Barden—who says his true function as Fischer's consultation partner was "to encourage the sometimes-taciturn Bobby to verbalise his ideas"—Fischer's visit to London was partly motivated by a desire to visit Savile Row and expand his wardrobe; the £50 fee he received for agreeing to take part in the consultation game covered the cost of a new suit:[1]

> Handsome and over six feet tall, he was friendly, talkative, and took pride in his growing collection of suits... After Leipzig he decided to visit London and Saville Row, and agreed to take part in a consultation game on BBC's Network Three weekly half-hour radio chess programme.
>
> The next day, after being fitted for his suit, Fischer visited my home. He had a prodigious appetite and ate most of the contents of my mother's well-stocked fridge. We played five-minute blitz at which, although I was then British lightning champion, he trounced me: "You're just a British weakie," he taunted. Fischer's deep-set eyes, large hands and talon-like fingers had a charismatic, even hypnotic effect. During Leipzig I also gave the top grandmasters memory tests for the BBC programme, with revealing results. Tal, prompted with some obscure game, rattled off the opening and the occasion, and when it was his own game, gave me a resume of the pre-game banter and the post-mortem analysis. Fischer's memory, by contrast, was excellent only for his own wins.

Trying to establish when the consultation game was played is a challenge. When asked the date by fellow British journalist David Spanier, Barden's answer was less than helpful: "The broadcast was recorded in September or October 1960." This seems unlikely, as the consultation game was played after the Leipzig Olympiad, held October 17–November 9 which all four players participated in. The day after it ended, the U.S. team met a strong Berlin team in an exhibition match, so that accounts for Bobby's whereabouts on November 10. Before Leipzig, Fischer warmed up with a small round robin in Reykjavík (October 5–10). Conceivably the consultation game could have been squeezed between the two events, but it seems unlikely. Bobby was back in New York in time for the December 18 start of the 1960/61 U.S. Championship. These events form a basic timeline, but it's difficult to get more specific than that.

Fischer's partner in the BBC game, Leonard Barden, was joint British Champion in 1963 and represented England in several Olympiads. Jonathan

[1] Leonard Barden in his obituary of Bobby Fischer. *The Guardian*, January 18, 2008.

Penrose was for many years England's best player and nearly beat Bobby in the Leipzig Olympiad. In his later years he was among the world's best correspondence chessplayers. His teammate, Peter Clarke, was one of England's top players in the 1960s, and the author of excellent game collections of Tal and Petrosian.

Game (32) was annotated by Grandmaster Alejandro Ramirez for ChessBase in 2014 and he concluded that it was a solidly played technical game, slightly better for White throughout, but with a draw a fair result.

After move 46 and eight hours of play, the recording tape ended and the game was stopped. Listeners were encouraged to send in their analysis of the position. Some of the material that follows first appeared in *Chess Treasury of the Air*.

Former World Champion Max Euwe, in his role as adjudicator, wrote the analysis that follows.

---

(32) Sicilian
Fischer and Leonard Barden – Jonathan Penrose and Peter Clarke
London 1960

1.e4 c5 2.Nf3 e6 3.d4 cxd4 4.Nxd4 Nf6 5.Nc3 d6 6.g4 h6 7.h3 Nc6 8.Be3 Bd7 9.Qd2 Nxd4 10.Qxd4 Qa5 11.0-0-0 Bc6 12.Kb1 Be7 13.Bg2 0-0 14.Qd2 Rfd8 15.Nd5 Qxd2 16.Nxe7+ Kf8 17.Bxd2 Kxe7 18.Rhe1 Rac8 19.c4 Nd7 20.b3 e5 21.Be3 Nc5 22.f3 b6 23.h4 Ne6 24.Bf1 f6 25.h5 Be8 26.Kb2 Bf7 27.a4 Rb8 28.a5 Nc5 29.Ra1 Rd7 30.Kc3 bxa5 31.Bxc5 dxc5 32.Rxa5 Rc7 33.Rea1 Rbb7 34.Rb1 Be8 35.b4 cxb4+ 36.Rxb4 Rxb4 37.Kxb4 Rb7+ 38.Kc3 Bf7 39.Bd3 Kd7 40.c5 Rb3+ 41.Kc2 Rb7 42.Bb5+ Kd8 43.Bc6 Rc7 44.Bd5 Be8 45.Kb3 Bd7 46.Kc4 Ke7

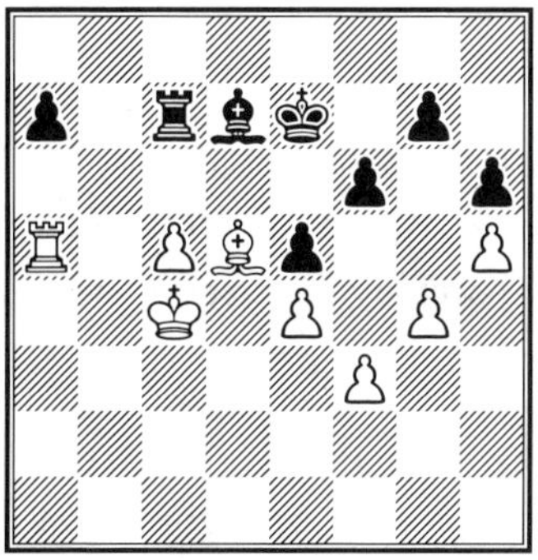

There are two types of chess positions. In the first it is possible to prove a clear win or draw within reasonable time. In the second type this is not possible.

One should not worry if the term "reasonable" is a little vague. For the time required for such a proof increases, after a certain limit, at an inordinate rate. If the mathematical proof for a win or draw cannot be supplied within two weeks, it may take years or even a century. An extreme case is the starting point of the game of chess. This "problem" would take more than a million years to solve mathematically.

The adjourned game Fischer and Barden v. Penrose and Clarke belongs to the second category of positions. This could be expected. If four strong players, at least two of them world class, cannot come to a mutual understanding about the given position, one may be sure that the position does not contain a clear win or a clear draw.

All this may sound disappointing to you, and there is certainly reason to ask: "If there is no proof of the result, what can you offer us instead?"

No more than a presumption, an appraisal, and evaluation which is based on an overall view of the position and on a number of variations. Further, naturally, on my experience as a chess player.

I cannot avoid my judgment being subjective; it is certainly debatable, but, can hardly be refuted. For others one can no more *disprove* my adjudication than I can *prove* it. I hope there are no serious mistakes in my illustrative variations, but even if I have made any they should not necessarily affect my general considerations of the result.

You certainly have a right to consider all this very unsatisfactory, but please do not blame me; I cannot alter the nature of chess.

Let us now look at the position. I need hardly say there are only two possible results: either White wins or Black reaches a draw. A loss for White, of course, may be ruled out.

I begin with a few general remarks. The first is that should White succeed in bringing his c-pawn to c6 and his King to c5, the game must be won for him. An example: 47.Ra6 Kd8 48.c6 Ke7 49.Kc5. The position now reached is not worth analyzing. It is a clear win for White. I trust you agree. But of course, Black should not permit this.

I have one more general remark. Should the White rook succeed in definitely reaching the seventh or eighth rank, Black is lost in that case too. By "definitely," I mean "without Black's being able to oppose the White rook with his own rook." An example: 47.Ra1 Kd8 48.Rb1 Ke7 49.Rb8, etc. Perhaps this is a little more complicated. White threatens 50.Rg8; and should Black close the eighth rank by playing 49...Be8, he soon comes into *Zugzwang* after White's 50.Ra8. On the other hand, if Black (after the penetration) tries to oppose the White rook by ...Rc8, then White answers Rb7 thus occupying the seventh rank, which is equally fatal for Black. Again: Black is not forced to accept any of these possibilities. A last general remark has to be made. Should White at some moment exchange rooks, a dead draw will result in almost all cases.

With these three remarks in mind, we try the following variations, starting from our initial position: 47.Ra6 Bc8 48.Ra2 Bd7 (stopping the advance of the c-pawn) 49.Rb2 (threatening to penetrate to the eighth rank) 49...Kd8 (meeting 50.Rb8+ with 50...Rc8 and if 51.Rb7 then 50...Rc7) 50.Rf2 (angling for the advance f3-f4) 50...Ke7 51.f4 Bxg4? 52.Rg2 Bxh5 53.Rxg7+ Kd8 54.Rg8+ Ke7 55.fxe5 fxe5 56.c6! Kd6 57.Rd8+ Ke7 58.Rh8 followed by Kc5 with a winning position.

Does this mean that White is winning? No! The culprit was the capture of the g-pawn, which allowed White's rook to become incredibly active. Black can improve his position greatly by substituting 50...Rc8 for 50...Ke7.

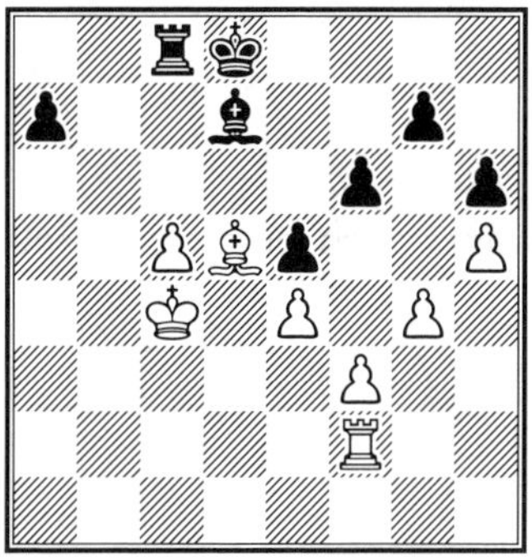

Now 51.f4 exf4 52.Rxf4 a5 53.Rf2 Kc7 54.e5 Bxg4 55.exf6 gxf6 56.Rxf6 Bxh5 57.Rxh6 Be2+ 58.Kd4 Rd8 with a draw.

It was a pleasure to go over the different entries for the final adjudication of the game Fischer and Barden versus Penrose and Clarke. I have found in these entries many more possibilities than I had seen myself, and especially in the analysis sent in hors concours by Penrose and Clarke.

Having studied the position again and again, I have returned to the conclusion already given in my first talk: Black with best play will manage to reach a draw. However, there are still a few difficult points to treat.

One of the listeners came up with an interesting winning attempt for White... After 47.Ra6 Bc8 he varies with 48.Rc6 and after 48...Rxc6

49.Bxc6 Ba6+ 50.Kd5 Black's position is not so easy, but he can hold with 50...Be2 51.Ba4 Bxf3 52.c6 Bxg4 53.c7 Bc8 54.Kc6 f5 55.exf5 Bxf5 with a draw due to White's wrong-colored rook-pawn.

Another tricky try is the pawn sacrifice g5 followed by h6. For example: 47.Kb4 (instead of 47.Ra6) 47...Ke8 48.Ra2 Ke7 49.Rc2 Be8 50.Rc1 Bc6 (50...Bd7? 51.c6! followed by 52.Kc5) 51.Bxc6 Rxc6 52.Rd1 a6 53.Rd5 Ke8 54.Kc4 Ke7 55.Rd1 Ke8

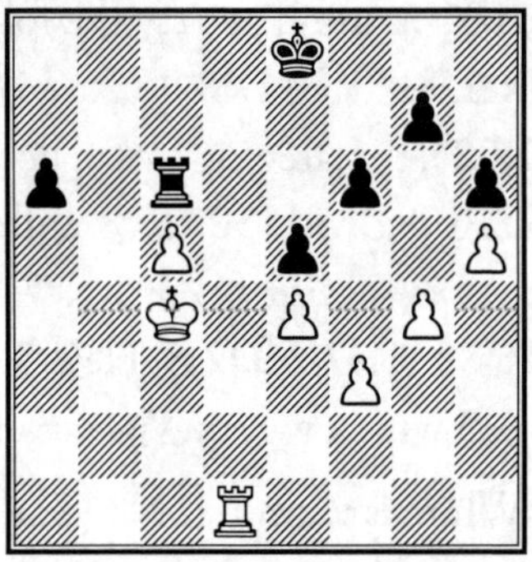

56.g5!? hxg5 (56...fxg5? 57.Kd5) 57.Rh1 Ke7 58.h6 gxh6 59.Rxh6 Rc7! 60.Rh7+ Kd8 61.Rh8+ Ke7 62.Ra8 Rd7 63.Rxa6 Rd4+ 64.Kb5 Rd3 65.Kb6 Rxf3 66.Ra7+ Ke6 67.c6 Rb3+ and White cannot win. A narrow escape for Black!

I repeat my adjudication: with best counterplay by Black, a draw must result.

PART FOUR

the Early Sixties

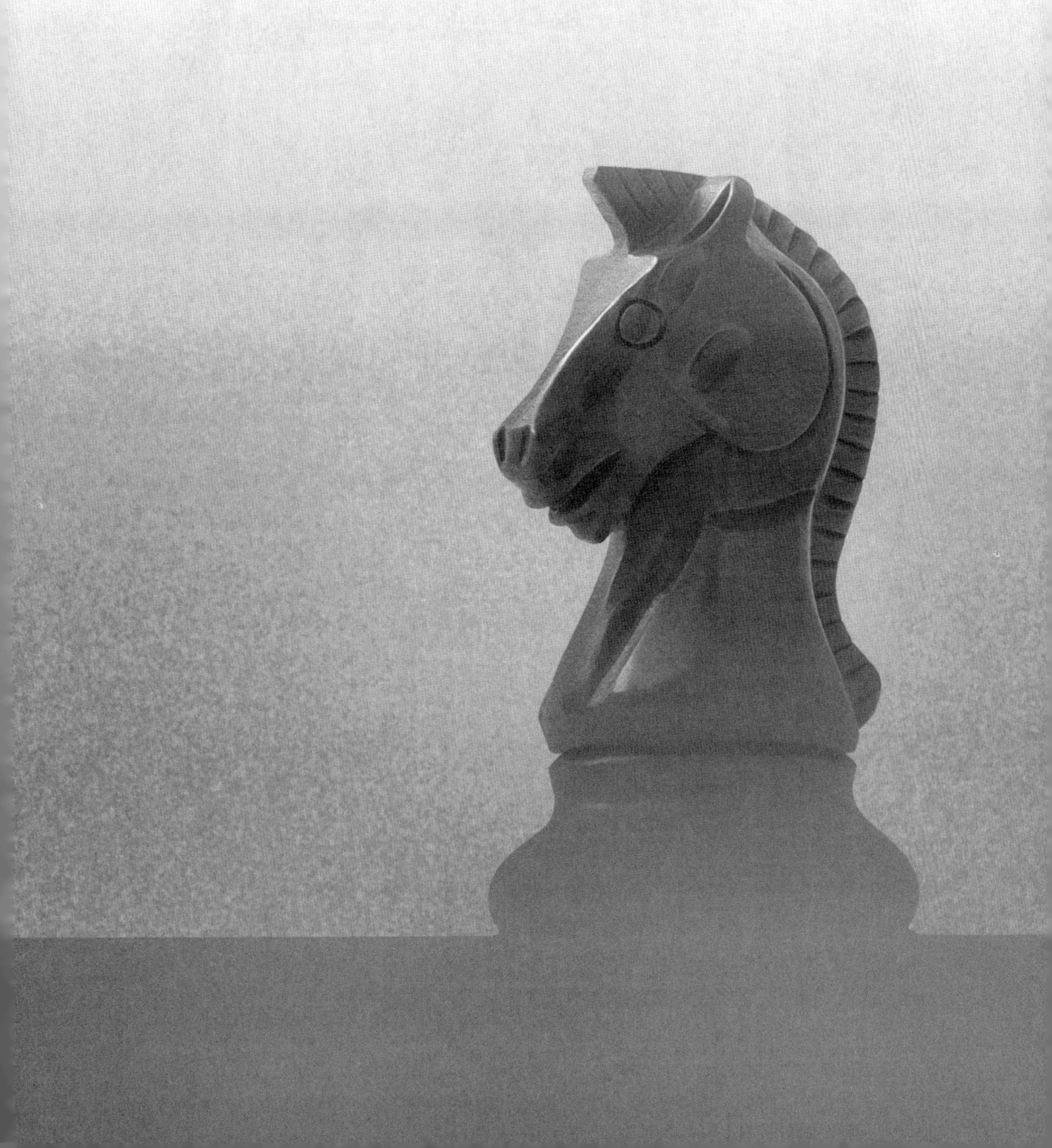

From CNVA Bulletin, 5/8/61

Photo by Waddell Studio, LaGrange, Indiana

[top] Barton Stone, Regina Fischer, Jerry Lehmann, Mardy Rich, Dave Rich, and Bea Burnette on U.S. 66 in Illinois;

[middle] Red Square: Regina Fischer looking up; Patrick Proctor between Scott Herrick and David Rich;

[bottom] During the walk across the United States the core group was sometimes joined by local supporters, but for the most part, it was just the original ten marchers.

1
ON HIS OWN

REGINA AND THE WALK FOR PEACE

Those looking for Bobby's haunts from the 1950s to the 1970s will be disappointed when they find there is not much left to see. Sure, it's possible to walk by locations of the now defunct Manhattan Chess Club, including 100 Central Park South (1940–1957), Hotel Woodrow, 35 West 64th Street (1957–1962), Henry Hudson Hotel, West 57th Street (1962–1971) and East 60th Street (1971–1974); however it takes a good imagination to feel their connection with important events from Fischer's career.

The Four Continents Bookstore (822 Broadway), where Bobby picked up Soviet chess literature, is long gone, as is Walter Goldwater's University Place Bookshop (821 Broadway) which was right next door. The two were just a block away from 80 East 11th Street, where the U.S. Chess Federation had an office from the late 1950s to the early 1960s and the great chess booksellers Albrecht Buschke and Fred Wilson had their stores.

Fortunately, some historic spots remain. The Marshall Chess Club at 23 West 10th Street, scene of the "Game of the Century" and where Bobby played the 1965 Capablanca Memorial by telex, is the most prominent public location. Not far away is Washington Square Park, which Bobby frequented in the 1950s, even playing a tournament there. Made famous by the movie *Searching for Bobby Fischer*, it's still home to chess players, as is the Chess and Checkers House in Central Park which was a short walk from the Manhattan Chess Club when it was located on Central Park South.

These sites all bring back memories, but the one location documentary film crews always make sure to capture on film is 560 Lincoln Place in Brooklyn, where Bobby lived with his mother and sister in apartment Q in the 1950s. Located close to the Brooklyn Public Library and the Hawthorne Chess Club, this was home when Bobby was progressing from promising beginner to world class grandmaster and it was where he did much of the work on the book that would ultimately be called *My 60 Memorable Games*.

The fall of 1960 marked a major change in Bobby's life when his mother moved out of the apartment they had shared for close to a decade, to travel from New York to San Francisco. Bobby was now on his own—his sister Joan moved out when she married Russell Targ in 1958.

Before she left New York, Regina made sure Bobby was on solid financial footing. Thanks to a $14,000 ($122,000 in 2020 dollars) bequest from his maternal grandfather Jacob Wender, she was able to set up a trust that gave Bobby $175 each month, which covered the rent, gas and electric, with a small amount left over. This took a lot of pressure off Fischer as he did not have to depend solely on prize money, which was minimal in the early 1960s. Bobby was seventeen-years-old and free to devote himself entirely to chess.

It was around this time that Bobby started what was to become a lifelong habit of listening to the radio, particularly late at night. Most likely the first broadcast he heard of Herbert W. Armstrong's Radio Church of God (renamed Worldwide Church of God in 1968) was during the time he was living alone at Lincoln Place. Armstrong's broadcasts were the beginning of a relationship that would last over a decade and have a major impact on Fischer's life.

Regina Fischer was a force to be reckoned with. Not only did she talk the talk of a peace activist, she literally walked the walk. When ten members of the Committee for Non-Violent Action departed from Union Square in San Francisco on December 1, 1960, Regina was among them. At age forty-seven (by far the oldest), she was the only one who had been to the Soviet Union before, albeit back in the 1930s.

Leaving the city, they followed the El Camino Real south on the first leg of their march to New York City. As they made their way across the United States handing out leaflets advocating disarmament, they were sometimes joined by local supporters, and other times threatened with violence. Averaging twenty-five to thirty-five miles a day (on foot), they made it to the East Coast by summer.

When they reached New York City the group boarded a plane and flew to London, where their numbers were bolstered by a large group of Europeans at Trafalgar Square. They resumed their walk, heading south to the ferries that crossed the English Channel. Due to the ongoing conflict with Algeria their arrival in Le Havre was not welcomed by French officials. Several of the group, including Regina, attempted to evade the authorities by jumping from the ferry before it docked and swimming to shore only to be arrested by waiting gendarme and sent back to England. The next attempt to land on the Continent worked better as they caught a ferry to Belgium and then walked to Moscow via West Germany, East Germany, and Poland. Regina was one of a group of female supporters who had tea with Mrs. Khrushchev.

While Regina didn't leave a record of the trip, there remains a good witness in David Rich, who at nineteen was the youngest member of the Walk for Peace. David walked the entire route to New York, and said he believed Regina walked two-thirds of the distance. The walkers were supported by a station wagon containing their gear and most took turns behind the wheel. David Rich spoke of his experience in May 2015:

> When a small group of people spends half a year walking twenty-five to thirty-five miles a day they are going to devote a fair amount of time talking with each other. Such was the case with those who made the trek from San Francisco to New York in late 1960. Rich remembered that politically Regina was furthest to the left of the small group, but not an ideologue. She was objective when comparing the merits of capitalism and communism and didn't feel what was practiced in the Soviet Union was real communism. Rich said that if forced to characterize her beliefs he would categorize her as a socialist. He recalls that "she was not that hard to get along with" despite their different beliefs (Regina was an atheist and Rich a Christian pacifist). Despite their age difference (almost thirty years) she was never condescending. Rich remembers that Regina was proud of her son's chess accomplishments, but, saddened by his self-absorption and disdain for other people.

Regina's obituary, published in the *Palo Alto Times*, on August 13, 1997, offered a snapshot of her later years:

> While abroad, she married her second husband, Cyril Pustan, in England. For the next fifteen years, she practiced pediatric medicine in London, Germany, and Portugal, where she and her husband wrote a book about the coffee cooperatives in the northern part of that country, and another on using English and American folk songs to teach English.
>
> When her husband died, she returned to the United States to live near her daughter's family in Palo Alto. In her mid-70s, she traveled to Central America, where she volunteered as a reporter and a physician in Nicaragua and helped run a United Nations refugee camp in Honduras. In her 80s, she translated a book by the prize-winning Costa Rican author, Luisa Gonzáles, *Life at the Bottom*, which was later made into a play.
>
> In her final years, she took language and computer classes at Foothill and Cañada colleges. She also volunteered in support of the Linus Pauling Institute and tutored students in English.

ON THE BEACH

International Master Jeremy Silman:

One of the most delightful Fischer anecdotes I've ever heard was from my friend Swami Shankarananda ("Shanks"), a master, who met Fischer in the early '60s when he was attending Columbia University.[1] What makes the following tale so endearing is that male chess players usually have no idea how to speak to women. One famous grandmaster, in an effort to be alone with a young lady playing in the same tournament, asked her, "Would you like to go up to my room and study mating patterns?" Has there ever been a more pathetic line? Yet, many players actually think this will work.

The grandmaster's moronic pickup line was a case of low-level lechery, but Fischer's was one of innocence mixed with a complete lack of experience.

Here's what Shankarananda told me:

"One time we were at the beach and Bobby saw a pretty girl sitting by herself. He went up to her and said:

'I'm Bobby Fischer, the great chess player.'

It was a good opening gambit, but she had never heard of him. Her reply made him realize she was foreign, so he asked where she was from.

'Holland' she replied.

'Do you know Max Euwe?' (the Dutch former World Champion), Bobby asked

She'd never heard of him. Now Bobby had run out of ideas. He shrugged his shoulders and walked away."

Shankarananda:

I met Bobby in 1960 because of a chance encounter my father had with Bobby's mother. My father[2] was an artist who did performances called 'chalk talks' at schools and various organizations, and he created a brochure to advertise his performance. He was visiting his printer for that purpose when a woman overheard a conversation that Pop had with the printer to the effect that his son (me) was attending Columbia and playing chess on the chess team there.

The woman told my father, "My son only wants to play chess all the time too... Maybe you've heard of him. He is Bobby Fischer."

Of course, Bobby was quite famous by then, especially in a chess playing family. He was about seventeen at this point and had been U.S. Champion since he was fourteen.

---

1 Shanks (born Russell Kruckman), along with Michael Valvo, and Robin Ault, was a member of the Columbia University chess club in the early 1960s. He was top scorer on the Columbia team that tied for first in the 1962 Intercollegiate Championship and later earned the title of national master,

2 Renowned artist (painter, cartoonist, illustrator, teacher, and author) Herbert Kruckman (1904–1998).

"A Painting of Bobby that my father did inspired by his visit to our house." Fischer is on the left and James Sherwin (probably) is on the right (Painting by Herbert Kruckman courtesy of Swami Shankarananda).

Regina confided that she was worried about Bobby and that he didn't have many friends. Pop said that I would certainly be excited to hear he had met Bobby's mother and he was sure I'd be happy to call Bobby and get together with him. On that note, she gave Pop their phone number.

When I called Bobby, I was as nervous as I had ever been calling up a girl to ask for a date. I invited him over to my parents' brownstone in Williamsburg. I said I could have some members of the Columbia chess team there. He said, "That could be interesting..."

On the appointed day, my teammates gathered at my parents' home. We were all playing blitz on the living room floor with chess clocks. Finally, there was a knock on the door and Bobby walked in. We were quite star struck.

My father and I had a long conversation with him about many things, including palmistry and Caryl Chessman, a criminal who had recently been executed for kidnapping and rape. Bobby was fascinated by Chessman, maybe because of his name.

Bobby read some of our palms. He told me, "You're intuitive," and he told one of my friends bluntly, "You're gonna die soon.'"

Bobby averted his eyes from the chess games at his feet. He told us, "Watching weak players screws up my game.'" But at one point our team captain Gus, who is a very strong blitz player, played a nice combination including the sacrifice of an exchange. Bobby, who didn't look like he was watching said, "Ohhh, very good. I thought you were a weaky!" Gus hasn't forgotten that remark, I can assure you.

The meeting was successful and we saw each other quite a few times during the next few years.

Early in our friendship, Bobby invited me to visit him at his apartment in Brooklyn. I visited him with a friend. The apartment was noticeably messy, with clothing strewn around and a broken table. Bobby offered us an apology, "My mother hid money on me so I had to break up the place looking for it."

We settled down for some chess analysis, which consisted of watching in awe as Bobby played over games from *Schachmaty Bulletin*. His fingers flew and he pointed out variations at a speed that was well beyond my comprehension. One time, he had to pull back about five to seven moves because he had assumed that the game would go down a certain line which it didn't.

Bobby was getting ready to go to a tournament in Mar del Plata, Argentina, at which Boris Spassky (who was not yet World Champion) would compete. Recently, Spassky had been experimenting with the old romantic opening, the King's Gambit.

Bobby said, "If I have Black, I think Spassky will play the King's Gambit against me. I'll take the pawn and win." He showed us the lines of his new defense. Since Bobby was studying nineteenth-century sources at that time, particularly Steinitz, he must have found an old line and polished it up. He showed us a number of variations.

Later that evening we took the subway over to Greenwich Village and had dinner. Then we went to the Marshall Chess Club where Bobby played rapid chess with Bernard Zuckerman at the odds of five minutes for Zuckerman to a half minute for Bobby. Zuckerman later became an international master, but at the time his rating had not yet reached 2000.

Bobby won game after game and heckled Zuckerman good naturally, as blitz players do: "Don't you see anything, Zuckerman?" And when Zuckerman made a decent move, Bobby would say, "Even a blind chicken can find a kernel of corn."

And, oh yes, Mar del Plata. Spassky played White, and after 1.e4 e5, he offered the gambit. Bobby took the pawn with gusto and built up what he called a 'winning position', only to have Spassky's attack break through. That was his only loss, however, and he and Spassky tied for first place.

During the winter of 1960–61, I visited the U.S. Championship as often as I could to give Bobby support. Not that he needed any, this would be his fourth U.S. title in a row!

On December 23, 1960, my Columbia friend Nick and I sat just outside the ropes watching Bobby's game with Hans Berliner. I think the Championship was held in the Henry Hudson Hotel in midtown New York in those days. Berliner set up Alekhine's Defense and on his seventeenth move Bobby played BxN(f5), giving up the two bishops. When Bobby took the knight, Nick, who was a very expressive person, said to me in a loud whisper, "Why did he do that!?" I said, whispering softly, "I think maybe he didn't want the knight to blockade at d6." Nick considered this for a moment and then 'whispered' even more loudly, "He's a genius!"

Bobby won a nice game. We went out afterwards to get something to eat and play tabletop soccer. Bobby had long legs and he walked very fast. As we walked through the city he turned to us and said with gusto, "You liked bishop takes knight, didn't you?" He had heard Nick's stage whisper. Like a great performer he really enjoyed the appreciation of his audience.

2
RESHEVSKY VS. FISCHER

THE BATTLE OF THE GENERATIONS

The battle of the generations pitted the forty-nine-year-old Sammy Reshevsky against the eighteen-year-old Bobby Fischer. The match may not have found either player at his peak—Sammy's best years were behind him and Bobby's yet to come—but both players were among the best in the West and top dozen in the World. While Fischer would eventually dominate his older rival, with a life time record of +9, −4, =13 (including 7 points from their last nine games), they were closely matched in the summer of 1961. Never has there been a match involving two American players that drew as much attention as this one.

The rivalry was already well established by the time of the match. Fischer entered it having won four consecutive U.S. Championships, while Reshevsky had a magnificent result at Buenos Aires 1960 where he tied for first with Viktor Korchnoi.

The unchallenged American number one since the end of the Second World War, Reshevsky was not ready to step aside for the young generation of stars coming up in the 1950s and early 1960s. He still saw himself as the best American player, and as such, entitled to play first board for the United States in the Olympiads.

The rivalry between Bobby and Sammy was beneficial to the extent it motivated them to be at their best, but it was detrimental in that Fischer and Reshevsky were Olympiad teammates only once. Money, principally the lack of it, sometimes contributed to Reshevsky's failing to play, but the rivalry also played a role. The two only joined forces at Siegen 1970, by which time even Reshevsky had to admit that Fischer was clearly better.

Along with the huge age disparity, there were other stark differences between the two titans of American chess: Bobby was over a foot taller than Sammy who stood barely over five feet. Both players were of Jewish ethnicity, but Reshevsky was Orthodox (his refusal to play on the Sabbath and religious holidays created scheduling difficulties during the match) whereas Bobby was non-practicing. Reshevsky was married with three children. Bobby was a bachelor.

[top left] A young Sammy Reshevsky with Douglas Fairbanks and Charlie Chaplin in 1921;

[top right] Reshevsky in 1942;

[middle] Pasadena 1932 Sammy Reshevsky, Arthur Dake, and Herman Steiner being awarded their prizes by Henry McMahon secretary for the organizing committee;

[below] Sammy Reshevsky, "breathing fire," considers his 10th move in his round nine game against Robin Ault in the 1959 U.S. Championship.

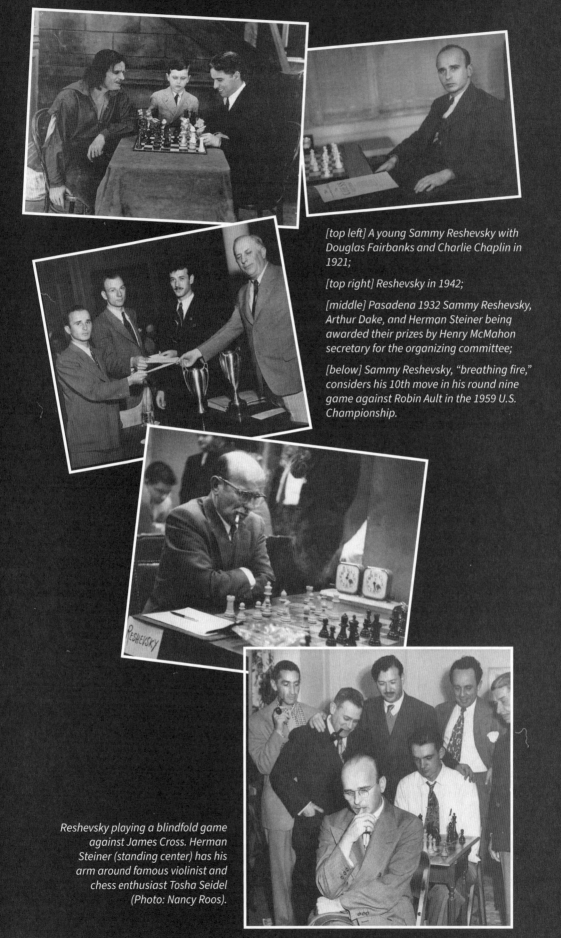

Reshevsky playing a blindfold game against James Cross. Herman Steiner (standing center) has his arm around famous violinist and chess enthusiast Tosha Seidel (Photo: Nancy Roos).

Historically, a large number of the top players in the world have been Jewish and many would not play on high holidays such as Yom Kippur and Rosh Hashanah. Reshevsky went further, unilaterally refusing to play on the Sabbath, believing it to be a violation of the Talmudic prohibition against work. This strict interpretation made Sammy unique among chess masters—fellow Orthodox Jewish Grandmasters Boris Gulko and Leonid Yudasin would play on the Sabbath, albeit with an assistant to keep score and punch the clock for them. Years later, when he followed the practices of the Worldwide Church of God, Bobby also would not play from sundown Friday to sundown Saturday, but that wasn't the case in 1961.

Fischer and Reshevsky had their differences, but they also shared much in common. Beneath their bitter rivalry was a grudging mutual respect borne from being among the best in the world, yet having to struggle to earn a living in a country that had no understanding of what it meant to be a top chess player.

Both players were prodigies, although only Sammy met the definition as a pre-teen. Both had unconventional childhoods. Much has been said of Fischer's difficult childhood, but an argument can be made that Reshevsky's situation was worse. Neither followed a traditional academic path. Fischer dropped out of high school at sixteen while Reshevsky had little formal schooling in his youth—starting at the age of eight he supported his large family for four years by giving endless simultaneous exhibitions.

Reshevsky looked back upon his early years in *Reshevsky on Chess*[1] (a book rumored to have been ghostwritten by Fred Reinfeld):

> Wherever I went, great crowds turned out to see me play. For four years, I was on public view. People stared at me, poked at me, tried to hug me, asked me questions. Professors measured my cranium and psychoanalyzed me. Reporters interviewed me and wrote fanciful stories about my future. Photographers were forever aiming their cameras at me. It was, of course, an unnatural life for a child, but it had its compensations and I cannot truthfully say that I did not enjoy it. There was the thrill of traveling from city to city with my family, the excitement of playing hundreds of games of chess and winning most of them, the knowledge that there was something "special" about the way I played chess, although I didn't know why.

This abuse came to an end when Sammy was twelve and his parents wound up in District Court in Manhattan, charged with improper guardianship for not providing an adequate education for their son—they claimed that as a young boy Sammy had attended a rabbinical school in New York. The case was dismissed, and soon afterwards chess enthusiast Julius Rosenwald, the wealthy co-owner

[1] Sammy Reshevsky, *Reshevsky on Chess: The U.S. Champion Tells How He Wins*. New York: Chess Review, 1948.

of Sears, Roebuck & Company in Chicago, stepped in and became Reshevsky's benefactor, taking care of his education.

Sammy took a sabbatical from chess the second half of 1924 to the fall of 1931, playing in only one serious tournament, the 28th Western Championship in Kalamazoo. It's doubtful any other top player has taken such a long break from the game in their formative years.

Reshevsky graduated with a degree in accounting from the University of Chicago in 1934 and later specialized in tax preparation. Accounts suggest that Sammy didn't have any special aptitude for this type of work, nor did he enjoy it. He was probably frustrated knowing his state-supported rivals from the Soviet Union and Eastern Europe didn't have to worry about supporting their families.

In the early 1950s, at a time when the economic necessities of supporting a family threatened to overwhelm him, a fund was raised among chess lovers by Maurice Wertheim, a wealthy investment banker, which gave Reshevsky some $3,000 a year to supplement the $6,000 to $7,000 a year he made in tournaments and exhibitions.

This stipend made it possible for Reshevsky to give up his accounting job for good and concentrate solely on chess. And having the additional time, he played in more tournaments and gave transcontinental exhibition tours—both of which upped his income. Thanks to this backing he continued to play at an elite level in his forties and into his early fifties.

Wertheim died in 1950 and a few years later a more formal arrangement of assistance was established with the founding of the American Chess Foundation (the original members were Alexander Bisno, Jacques Coe, Walter Fried, Morris Kasper, Rosser Reeves, Lessing Rosenwald, and Maurice's widow Cecile Wertheim). This organization made it possible for Reshevsky to play in important tournaments that had meager prizes, and not suffer financially. This was a welcome change, albeit small, from the amateur-first mentality that had dominated American chess to that point. Unfortunately, it seems the ACF didn't have enough money to support other American players a few years down the line—namely Fischer and Lombardy—which undoubtedly led to bad feelings.

Before the start of the match, prominent grandmasters were almost unanimous in predicting a victory for Reshevsky. Gligorić, Larsen, Keres, and Petrosian all chose Sammy, with Petrosian even predicting the final score to be a lop-sided 9½–6½. Only Kashdan backed Bobby, writing in his column in the *Los Angeles Times*:

> Your editor will go out on a limb with the prediction that Fischer will win two games through superior knowledge of the openings and win by the margin of 9–7.

Kashdan knew Sammy from way back having been a teammate on the 1937 U.S. Olympiad team which won gold. He also had firsthand knowledge of Bobby's capabilities, having captained him at the 1960 Olympiad where the Americans finished second, medaling for the first time in twenty-three years.

Why did so many favor Reshevsky when Fischer had won the last four U.S. Championships? Clearly, this was because of Sammy's incredible record in matches—he was undefeated at that point in his career having defeated Kashdan, Horowitz, Lombardy, Bisguier, D. Byrne, Najdorf (twice), Benko, and Gligorić!

Why was Reshevsky so successful? It definitely was *not* because of his sometimes indifferent opening play—blamed at one time on a lack of study, we now know this was the not the case. Pal Benko, who seconded Reshevsky in his 1968 Candidates match against Viktor Korchnoi, spent a month prior to the event training with him and attributed Sammy's opening difficulties to a poor memory, making it difficult for him to remember long opening variations.

Reshevsky was often in time pressure, a result of spending too much time on the opening, but handled *zeitnot* well, aided by a good eye for tactics and excellent calculating ability. He was also a fine positional player, but what he really had going for him was tremendous fighting spirit.

William Lombardy remarked:[1]

> In my initiation to the Manhattan Chess Club, various masters would observe a game in progress and then opine,"Don't worry, Sammy's (Reshevsky) lost, but that's when he is the most dangerous! There have been and are top players who make a habit of winning hopeless positions. In this respect Reshevsky was at the head of the list of miracle workers. Despite the fact that he was one of the worlds' truly great chess geniuses, the little toupéed man still found himself in lost positions.
>
> Why? His physical stature was that of the smallest ape. But he had the heart, the courage and determination of a gorilla protecting his turf and family. Sammy took risks and mostly played relentlessly for the win. This policy often put him in trouble in which genius did not help. His determined focus to fight in the process of playing the game he loved was at the heart of success. Such a personality rarely fails. Even as a budding master I analytically observed the "little" man like grim death glued with iron will to his seat! If such were his sole contribution to chess that would have been enough, particularly in verification of the iron will to follow Emanuel Lasker's observation. "Chess is a struggle!"

Lombardy is right on the mark in his assessment of Sammy, especially that of family protector. Reshevsky was very much a family man devoted to his wife

1 William Lombardy, *Understanding Chess: My System, My Games, My Life*. In association with Russell Enterprises, 2011, (p. 232).

Norma and their three children Malke, Joel, and Sylvia. Outside of his faith they were everything to Sammy, and when he played tournaments and matches he would do whatever it took to take home the prize money.

Reshevsky played with "sharp elbows" and he was involved in a number of controversies during his career. Some of them were minor (participants in blitz tournaments in New York, played with a ten second timer instead of clocks, expected Reshevsky to move around the twelfth second), but others were more serious. Two that come readily to mind are the incidents with Denker at the 1942 U.S. Championship and his taking back a draw offer against John Fedorowicz at Lone Pine 1981, which saw some karmic justice as the "Fed" went on to win. One could also mention the various matches Reshevsky played against significantly lower-rated players in the late 1970s and early 1980s to earn rating points to qualify for the U.S. Championship. This was technically legal but definitely against the spirit of the regulations.

An international master's eyewitness account confirms that Reshevsky's competitive instincts were still strong as he neared eighty:[1]

> We met in the 1990 U.S. Open in Jacksonville, Florida, and had a wild game in which first White (Reshevsky) and later Black had the better of it. The time control was 50/150 and I got in bad time pressure in an interesting ending in which I had three minor pieces and a pawn against White's rook and four pawns. Reshevsky noticed after playing his fifty-first move that my flag was down and tried to claim a win on time. I replied that we were in a new time control. Reshevsky continued to maintain he had won on time at which point I suggested we call a tournament director over to make a ruling. At this point Sammy finally agreed to the draw. Reshevsky may have looked like a kindly old grandfather but his will to win no matter what was still there.

Reshevsky's wife Norma often accompanied him to tournaments, helping him keep to the strict kosher diet he adhered to. While he had a professional relationship with Benko, who was perhaps closest to him of the American players, calling them friends would have been a stretch. It's not clear if Reshevsky had any real friends among top American players with the possible exception being I. A. "Al" Horowitz. Sammy was very much a "lone wolf." He was respected but not loved by his colleagues.

A 1955 vivid portrait of Sammy that appeared in *Sports Illustrated*, captures him well:[2]

> At forty-three, Reshevsky, despite his smallness, is an imposing figure whose icy boardside manner is a weapon which powerfully complements his wits. Barely five feet two inches tall, with a wide, bulging brow and

[1] John Donaldson commenting on the 1990 U.S. Open.

[2] John Kobler, "Icy Wizard of the Royal Game." *Sports Illustrated*, October 17, 1955, (p. 46).

> steely eyes, he sits unmovingly erect for hours on end, his head in his cupped hands, his mouth pursed in an expression of ineffable hauteur. Most players nibble and sip at something at intervals during a game; Reshevsky eats nothing and only seldom drinks a glass of water. He chain-smokes, but in him even this habit betrays no sign of nerves. "Sammy," a colleague once observed, "plays chess like a man eating fish. First he removes the bones, then he swallows the fish." His self-confidence is so boundless that in tournament play, where forty moves must be made within two and a half hours, he will spend half that time pondering a single move, feeling sure of finding one that will make the next moves virtually automatic. On rare occasions only does he leave himself so little time that he blunders through sheer haste.

And what did Bobby think of Sammy? We have no written record until three years after their match when the first issue of Frank Brady's classic but short lived magazine, *Chessworld*, ran Bobby's article "The Ten Greatest Masters in History."[1] Bobby wrote of his fellow countryman:

> For a period of ten years—between 1946 and 1956 Reshevsky was probably the best chess player in the world. I feel sure that had he played a match with Botvinnik during that time, he would have won and been World Champion.
>
> His chess knowledge is probably less than that of any leading chess player; many B players have greater opening knowledge than he. Had he really studied instead of settling for knowledge of a few main columns in *Modern Chess Openings*, he would have a lot easier time of it today.
>
> He is like a machine calculating every variation, and has to find every move over-the-board by a process of elimination. He can see more variations in a shorter period of time than most players who ever lived. Occasionally, in fact he comes up with new moves—spontaneous ideas he has fabricated from no knowledge.
>
> Still, he gets into fantastic time pressure, and sometimes has to make twenty moves in a minute; but he has emerged from such lapses dozens of times to win.
>
> Reshevsky seems to know the openings better today than at any previous times in his career, but his powers of concentration have fallen off a bit. At fifty-two, he is the oldest of the leading American players (he was once the youngest), and by reason of his tenacity and ability to fight overwhelming odds deserves a place on this list.

The two major omissions from Fischer's "Ten Greatest Masters" list were Lasker and Botvinnik. So, when Fischer writes that Sammy could have beaten

[1] *Chessworld*, "The Ten Greatest Masters in History," Bobby Fischer as told to Neil Hickey, v. 1, #1, January–February 1964, (pp. 56–61).

Botvinnik, it is important to keep in mind that Fischer might have been somewhat prejudiced as he found the "Patriarch's" style too boring. As he expressed in his well-known mantra, "The players have gotten soft on the Botvinnik–Barcza–Benko diet", he had no warm feelings for players who opened 1.Nf3 or 1.c4 and fianchettoed one or more bishops. Back in 1964 Bobby only believed in 1.e4! International Master Anthony Saidy believes he expresses Fischer's sentiment about Reshevsky more accurately: "SR would have been world champ if he'd lived in the USSR."

The final word goes to Lombardy:[1]

> Reshevsky was neither a tactician nor a positional player. He was a complete player who combined and applied pertinent principles with flawless execution. Reshevsky knew how to wait, and how and when to advance.

THE MATCH

The Fischer–Reshevsky match was set for sixteen games, with the first four in New York, the next eight in Los Angeles, and the final four to be played in New York. The full sixteen games would be played regardless of one player reaching 8½ points prior.

New York City:
July 16 (2PM), July 18 (5PM), July 20 (5PM), July 24 (5PM)

Los Angeles :
July 27 (7:30PM), July 30 (7:30PM), Aug. 1 (7:30PM), Aug. 3 (7:30PM), Aug. 6 (7:30PM), Aug. 8 (7:30PM), Aug. 10 (7:30PM), Aug. 12 (7:30PM)

New York City:
Aug. 15 (5PM), Aug. 17 (5PM), Aug. 20 (2PM), Aug. 22 (5PM)

Games one through four were played at the Empire Hotel in New York (44 West 63rd Street, near Lincoln Center), starting on Sunday, July 16,1961. Why the games were played there instead of the Henry Hudson Hotel at West 57th street, where the Manhattan Chess Club was headquartered at the time, is not clear. It is but one unanswered question in a match that would have undoubtedly benefited from stricter regulations.

The Fischer–Reshevsky match was sponsored by the American Chess Foundation and Jacqueline Piatigorsky. This was the first of several world class events that Piatigorsky would be involved with in the 1960s—the 1963 Interzonal playoff, the two Piatigorsky Cups, and the three-player playoff for the last spot in the 1968 Candidates matches being the others.

The first leg of the match went smoothly with no controversies on or off the board. The first two games were dramatic, Fischer and Reshevsky trading wins.

---

[1] William Lombardy, *Understanding Chess: My System, My Games, My Life*. In association with Russell Enterprises, 2011, (p. 21).

Games three and four were draws, leaving the match tied when they left New York for Los Angeles.

Neither player had an official second, but International Master Bernard Zuckerman helped Bobby analyze his adjournment from game one:[1]

> We found a draw in the rook and pawn ending (50...Kg7), but he saw a ghost and deviated at the board and ended up losing.
>
> Incidentally Fischer's lapses in the endgame during the match led Reshevsky to claim the endgame was Bobby's weakness. He might have been weaker than Reshevsky in this phase of the game in 1961, but that certainly wasn't true later.
>
> One thing that does stand out is how few Queen endings Fischer had during his career—only the games with Berliner (1957/58 U.S. Championship), Barcza (Zurich 1959) and Spassky (game nineteen of the 1992 match) come to mind.

After the fourth game on July 24, the players traveled to Los Angeles and resumed the match on July 27 at the brand new Herman Steiner Chess Club. Located at 8801 Cashio Street in West Los Angeles (not far from Beverly Hills), the Steiner Chess Club flourished in the 1960s and early 1970s. Frank Lloyd Wright Jr., who had designed an addition to the Piatigorsky's home at 400 S. Bundy Drive, was the architect for the building that housed the Steiner Club.

This was the first public event at the club named for International Master Herman Steiner (1905–1955), a strong player and outstanding promoter of the game. Steiner was a good friend and chess teacher to Jacqueline Piatigorsky and raised her game from near-beginner to close to 2000 in just a few years.

The games in the Los Angeles stage of the match were held at two different locations—the Steiner Chess Club sharing honors with the Beverly Hilton Hotel. Games were adjourned after five hours of play, and all adjournments were played at the Steiner Chess Club, which would also have been the venue for the ill-fated twelfth game of the match. A pass to see the eight games of the match in Los Angeles cost $10 ($86 in 2020 dollars).

The referee for the Los Angeles leg was National Master Irving Rivise (1918–1976). A former USCF vice-president, Rivise grew up in New York but moved to Los Angeles after World War II. Well-liked and respected and a strong player to boot, Rivise was a natural to be the referee for the most important chess event held in southern California since Pasadena 1932. Alas, he would soon have his hands full.

The match provided many surprises. Contrary to Kashdan's prediction, Fischer did not win any games out of the opening. Reshevsky's adoption of the

---

[1] From an interview Zuckerman gave to the World Chess Hall of Fame in 2014.

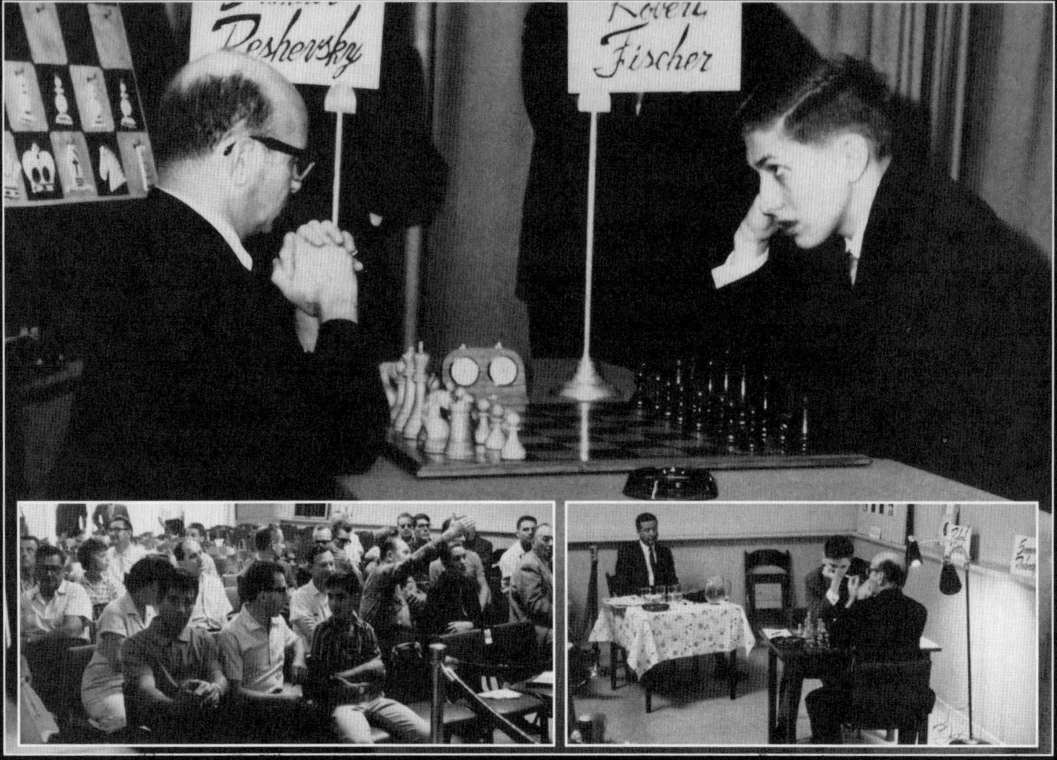

[top] Reshevsky and Fischer; [bottom left] Spectators watching the match; [bottom right] Referee Irving Rivise at table on left.

Accelerated Dragon variation of the Sicilian in the five games in which he played Black served him well. He willingly accepted slightly worse positions (as did Kramnik against Kasparov with his Berlin in their 2000 World Championship match) confident that he could hold. Sammy did lose a sharply played game that transposed into a Dragon in game two, but after that Bobby got little out of the openings and all four encounters were drawn. Clearly Fischer must have feared an improvement from the opening of game two, but giving up a sharp weapon might have been a mistake.

While Reshevsky stuck to his guns as Black, Fischer varied between the King's Indian and 1...Nf6 with 2...e6 against Sammy's habitual 1.d4. Examining the games more than five decades later, Fischer should have been one or two points ahead after eleven games, but he didn't take advantage of his opportunities.

Reshevsky was undoubtedly upset when he lost game five after achieving a winning position, but that was a full fight where the win was never simple and Fischer had to outplay his rival step-by-step to turn the game around. While it is true that had the match continued, Fischer would have had White in three of the five remaining games, the momentum had probably shifted a little to Reshevsky's side after the near death save in game eleven.

Round 8, Game (33), was arguably the biggest missed opportunity of the match.

[top] Jacqueline Piatigorsky and Bobby, 1961;

[bottom] Senior Master James Cross, one of the strongest southern California players of the 1950s and early 1960s, analyzes game six of the match live on the patio of the Steiner Chess Club. Spectators divided their time between watching the game and listening to commentary.

(33) Sicilian
Fischer – Sammy Reshevsky
New York/Los Angeles (8) 1961

1.e4 c5

Reshevsky answered 1.e4 throughout his career by either the Sicilian or 1...e5. One might have thought in this match Sammy would have chosen the supposedly more solid 1...e5 aiming to defend against the Ruy Lopez. The only problem with this is that he would have been playing into one of Bobby's greatest strengths. Sure enough, when Reshevsky made the switch to 1...e5 at the Second Piatigorsky Cup in 1966 and at Sousse the following year, he paid the price and was dutifully ground down.

2.Nf3 Nc6 3.d4 cxd4 4.Nxd4 g6

The adoption of the Accelerated Dragon was an excellent practical choice by Reshevsky who was a firm believer in a "win with White and draw with Black philosophy" when facing strong opposition. The successful implementation of this strategy was one of the things that made Sammy such a strong match player.

Reshevsky toyed with the Accelerated Dragon and Dragon during his career, but his main Sicilian weapon was the Taimanov (4...e6). Maybe he should have played the Accelerated more often. Everyone remembers his famous loss to Bobby (1.e4 c5 2.Nf3 Nc6 3.d4 cxd4 4.Nxd4 g6 5.Nc3 Bg7 6.Be3 Nf6 7.Bc4 0-0 8.Bb3 Na5? 9.e5 Ne8? 10.Bxf7+! Kxf7 11.Ne6), but in sixteen games with this opening (including Maróczy Binds via English opening move orders) he lost only twice against very strong opposition! Of course, he only won once, but such results were in keeping with Reshevsky's strategy.

5.c4

This move requires some explanation. Fischer's usual choice was 5.Nc3, but Reshevsky had held him twice quite easily with the offbeat 5...Bg7 6.Be3 Nf6 7.Bc4 0-0 8.Bb3 Ng4 9.Qxg4 Nxd4 with Bobby trying 10.Qd1 in game four and 10.Qh4 in game six.

Fischer definitely found this line frustrating to meet as in his only other encounter with it, against Ballard at a simultaneous in Wichita in 1964, he lost in the main line after 10.Qd1 Nxb3 11.axb3 b6 12.Bd4 (12.Qd5 Bxc3+! 13.bxc3 Qc7! was game four of the match) 12...f6.

While Fischer was skilled at playing the Black side of the Maróczy, his performances with White (three draws) were less impressive.

5...Nf6 6.Nc3 Nxd4 7.Qxd4 d6 8.Be2 Bg7 9.Be3 0–0 10.Qd2

Fischer varied with the inferior 10.Qd1 in game 10. Bobby later started playing this variation as Black, reaching it from English opening move orders. One wonders if Sammy's play in this match had an influence on him.

10... Be6 11.0–0 Qa5 12.Rac1

12.f4 Rfc8, ½–½ was Fischer–Benko, U.S. Championship 1960/61. Played in the tenth round, it clinched Bobby's 4th title with a round to go.

Interesting is 12...Rac8 13.b3 b5 14.f5 and now either 14...Bd7 or 14...b4 gives Black an improved version of the normal line as Black has managed to play ...b5 without the preparatory ...a6, which means White is missing Rac1. Also ...Rac8 may be better than the routine ...Rfc8 as the f7 square is not protected by only the king.

12...Rfc8

This move order is often considered an inaccuracy, but it's not clear this is actually true. The correct move is held to be 12...a6 meeting 13. f4 with 13...b5, as 14.f5 allows 14...Bxc4.

13.b3 a6 14.f4 Bg4

This looks like over-the-board improvisation by Reshevsky who borrows a well-known idea from the Dragon Sicilian—1.e4 c5 2.Nf3 d6 3.d4 cxd4 4.Nxd4 Nf6 5.Nc3 g6 6.Be2 Bg7 7.Be3 0–0 8.0–0 Nc6 9.Nb3 Be6 10.f4 Qc8 11.Kh1 Bg4 is one example.

The more common played move, 14...b5, is answered by 15.f5 and Black has to retreat as c4 is protected. The standard "refutation" goes 15...Bd7 16.e5, but it is not at all clear White is better after 16...b4.

15.Bd3 Bd7

White appears to have achieved what he was aiming for, but Black's position is still very resilient.

16.h3

This does not look very impressive. Possibly Bobby would have done better with the more direct 16.b4 Qd8 17.Nd5 Nxd5 18.exd5 with a solid advantage.

16...Bc6 17.Qf2 Nd7 18.Nd5 Bxd5 19.exd5

The structure reached after 19.exd5 is known to favor White if Black cannot achieve ...b5 (for example if he is already committed to ...a5). This is particularly true with the queens exchanged. Two good examples of White's chances in such positions are Gelfand–Mališauskas, Moskow 1989 and Gelfand–Andersson, Polanica-Zdrój 1997.

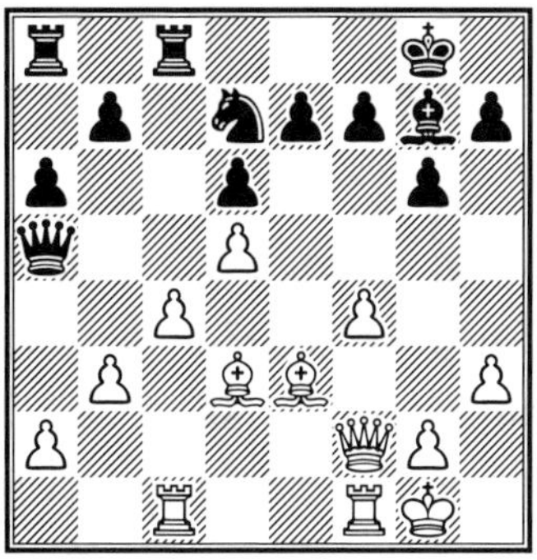

19...b5

Black has achieved a better version of the position reached at the end of the line starting with 16.b4.

20.Rfe1 Nc5

Black could have also tried 20...Rab8.

One move that is almost always useful in such positions is ...Bf6 protecting the backward e-pawn and not fearing a trade of bishops, as after ...exf6 the damaged pawn structure is compensated by increased king safety and play on the dark squares.

21.Bb1 bxc4 22.Rxc4 Nd7 23.Bd2 Qb6

Reshevsky's shows excellent judgment here as 23...Qd8 24.Rc6 would have been unpleasant.

24.Rxc8+ Rxc8 25.Qxb6 Nxb6 26.Rxe7 Bc3!

This was all nicely timed by Reshevsky who heads for a drawn ending. 26...Nxd5 27.Rd7 Bc3 28.Bxc3 Nxc3 transposes.

27.Bxc3 Nxd5 28.Rd7 Nxc3?

28...Rxc3! 29.Rxd6 Rc1+ 30.Kh2 Ne3 31.Bd3 Rd1 32.g4 Nc2 33.Rc6 Rd2+ 34.Kg1 Nd4 35. Rc8+ Kg7 36.Bxa6 Nf3+ 37.Kf1 Nh2+ 38.Ke1 Nf3+ forces the well-known rook and knight drawing sequence. Reshevsky, in his customary time pressure misses this, and now things start to go bad.

29.Bd3 d5

29...Nxa2 30.Bc4 would have been just what Fischer, later famous for his skill in rook and bishop versus rook and knight endings, was looking for.

30.Bxa6 Ra8 31.Rd6 Nxa2

31...Rb8! was more accurate and very close to equal.

32.Bb7 Rb8

Reshevsky correctly decides his only drawing chances are with pawns on one side of the board. Instead 32...Ra7 33.Bxd5 Nc3 34.Bc4 leaves White with a queenside passed pawn in addition to extra material and a better minor piece.

33.Bxd5 Nc1

Run this game on a strong engine and you will see that White's advantage has increased substantially the last few moves. Fear not Reshevsky fans. Sammy knows exactly what he is doing. Winning chances for White require pawns on both sides of the board.

34.f5

34.Rd7 Nxb3 35.Rxf7 was an important alternative, as after the forced 35...Kh8, White gets a position very similar to the game, but with an extra pair of pawns on the board, which typically favors the side trying to win. While the player with the advantage normally tries to avoid pawn trades, here matters are not clear—in the game continuation Fischer benefits from Black's h-pawn becoming a target.

Normally this sort of ending would be drawn (remember White's rook pawn is of the wrong color) if Black's knight were on the kingside, but the question for him is how to get it there. Bobby wants to keep it off sides while advancing his king and pawns.

Objectively, Black should be able to hold, but in view of the torture he will endure the practical chances are more like 50/50 that White win or Black draws.

34...gxf5 35.Rf6 Nxb3 36.Rxf5 Kh8 37.Rxf7 Nc5

This is what Sammy has been aiming for. He is a pawn down, but all the action is on one side of the board. It doesn't help White that his h-pawn is the wrong color for his bishop.

38.Rc7 Na6 39.Rc4

This continues the campaign to keep the knight under house arrest. The more direct 39.Ra7 allows it to escape: for example 39...Nc5 40.Kf2 Rd8 41.Bf3 Nd3+ 42.Ke3 Ne5 43.Be4 Rd7 and Black draws comfortably.

39...Rd8 40.Be6 Rd6 41.Bf5 Rf6 42.Bd3 h6 43.Kh2 Kg7 44.Kg3 Nb8?!

Reshevsky's understandable desire to get his knight back into play should have cost him the game. He had to continue to tread water with 44...Rd6 or 40...Rb6.

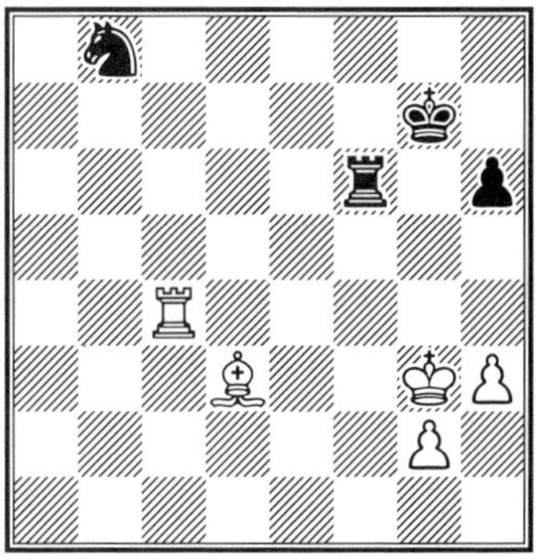

45.Be4?!

"An incredible post-adjournment lapse. Fischer told me he had arrived at this position in analysis, and had concluded that 45.Rc7+ Rf7 46.Rxf7+ Kxf7 47.Bb5! – stalemating the knight – lead to an easy win in the remaining king and pawn ending." [Larry Evans in *Chess Life*, October 1961, p. 295]

This is hard to understand, not only because Bobby had seen this in his adjournment analysis, but also because he had used exactly this idea to beat William Addison at the 1957 U.S. Open.

45...Rf7 46.Bd5 Rd7 47.Bf3 Rf7 48.Bh5 Ra7 49.Rg4+ Kh8 50.Re4 Kg7

Reshevsky still has to be careful. Consider that on the natural 50...Nd7? White has 51.Re8+ and Black must either allow a nasty pin or drop his h-pawn: 51...Kg7 52.Re7+ and now 52...Kf8 is met by 53.Rh7 while 52...Kh8 leaves Black totally paralyzed. In both cases White wins easily.

51.Re6 Na6 52.Rg6+ Kh7 53.Rd6 Nc5 54.Bg6+ Kg7 55.Bf5 Ra6 56.Rd5 Ne6

Finally Black's knight has reconnected with the rest of his army.

57.Re5 Ra3+ 58.Kf2 Nf4 59.Re4 Nd5 60.Rg4+ Kf6 61.Be4 Ne7

This is the perfect square for the knight where it is easily protected and guards the g6 square.

62.Rf4+ Kg7 63.Bf3 Ra5 64.Rc4 Re5 65.Kg3 Re6 66.Rc7 Kf6 67.Kg4 Re5 68.h4 Rb5 69.Rc4 Rb6 70.Be4 Kf7 71.Rc7 Kf6 72.Kh5 Rb5+ 73.Kg4 Rb4 74.Kf3 Rb3+ 75.Kf2 Rb4 76.Ke3 Rb3+ 77.Kf4 Ng6+ 78.Kg4 Rb4 79.Rc6+ Kf7, ½–½.

This had to be a bitter disappointment for Fischer who was better the entire game and missed a clear win.

Fischer tied for first in the 1957 U.S. Open. To achieve this, in Game (34) he didn't miss his chance to force a winning pawns and bishop endgame, while Addison had a knight and pawns.

---

(34) Caro-Kann
Fischer – William Addison
Cleveland (11) 1957

1.e4 c6 2.Nc3 d5 3.Nf3 dxe4 4.Nxe4 Nf6 5.Nxf6+ exf6 6.Bc4 Bd6 7.Qe2+ Qe7 8.Qxe7+ Kxe7 9.d4 Bf5 10.Bb3 Re8 11.Be3 Kf8 12.0–0–0 Nd7 13.c4 Rad8 14.Bc2 Bxc2 15.Kxc2 f5 16.Rhe1 f4 17.Bd2 Nf6 18.Ne5 g5 19.f3 Nh5 20.Ng4 Kg7 21.Bc3 Kg6 22.Rxe8 Rxe8 23.c5 Bb8 24.d5 cxd5 25.Rxd5 f5 26.Ne5+ Bxe5 27.Rxe5 Nf6

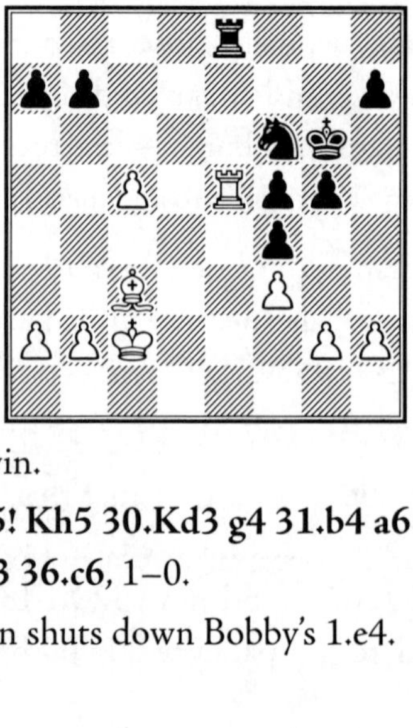

White to play and win.

28.Rxe8 Nxe8 29.Be5! Kh5 30.Kd3 g4 31.b4 a6 32.a4 gxf3 33.gxf3 Kh4 34.b5 axb5 35.a5 Kh3 36.c6, 1–0.

Reshevsky once again shuts down Bobby's 1.e4.

(35) Sicilian
Fischer – Sammy Reshevsky
New York/Los Angeles (10) 1961

1.e4 c5 2.Nf3 Nc6 3.d4 cxd4 4.Nxd4 g6 5.c4 Nf6 6.Nc3 Nxd4 7.Qxd4 d6 8.Be2 Bg7 9.Be3 0–0 10.Qd1

This seemingly anti-developing move is never going to replace 10.Qd2 as the main try in this position but it has a certain logic. White wants to play Nd5 without the trade of queens, which would occur after Qd2 and ...Qa5.

10...Bd7

Black can also stick to the traditional development scheme (...Be6, ...Qa5, ...a6, ...Rfc8) aiming for ...b5. One example of this is Haznedaroğlu–Malakhov, Tripoli 2004, which continued 10...Be6 11.Rc1 Qa5 12.0–0 Rfc8 (12... a6 meeting 13.f4 with 13...b5 looks a tad more accurate–Black wants to be able to capture on c4 in the event of f5) 13.b3 a6 14.f4 Bg4 (14...b5 15.f5) 15.Bxg4 Nxg4 16.Qxg4 Bxc3 17.f5 Bd2 with a very slight advantage for White.

11.0–0 Bc6 12.f3 Nd7 13.Qd2 Rc8

The modern way to play this position is 13...a5. Grandmasters Bent Larsen and Margeir Pétursson were pioneers in demonstrating the viability of Black's dark-square strategy to combat the Bind. The problem with Reshevsky's move is that the rook is better placed on a8 where it supports ...a5-a4. After the text Black has a cramped position with no clear counterplay, but his position is still tough to crack.

14.Rac1 a5 15.Kh1?!

This move isn't necessary and leaves the king poorly placed for the endgame. The correct approach was 15.b3 meeting ...a4 with b4. White will gradually prepare the advance b4 to drive away the knight, which will soon be landing on c5.

15...Nc5 16.b3 Qb6

Another plan is 16...Be5 followed by ...e6 and sometimes ...Qh4. One possible continuation is 17.Rfd1 e6 18.Bg5 f6 19.Be3 f5 with double-edged play that offers chances for both sides.

17.Nd5 Bxd5 18.cxd5

The alternative 18.exd5 leads to similar play: 18...Qb4 19.Qxb4 (19.Rfd1 Qa3 possibly followed by ...Na6-b4 is a plan to remember.) 19...axb4 20.Bd2 (this is the only move that offers White chances.) 20...Ra8 21.Rc2 Bc3, as in the game.

An alternative plan is 21...Ra7 22.Bxb4 Rfa8 23.Bxc5 Rxa2 24.Rxa2 Rxa2 25.Bxd6 exd6 and it is hard to imagine White winning this position with opposite colored bishops. That said, Reshevsky's way of playing with ...Bc3 as in the game looks more natural and forcing.

18...Qb4 19.Qxb4

This move is not normally played in this variation (when the black rook is on a8) but here Fischer seeks to take advantage of the fact that the rook is not attacking the pawn on a2 after the exchange on b4. Paradoxically the rook on c8 makes White's traditional handling of the position (again with the rook on a8) ineffective here. For example after 19.Rfd1 Qa3 20.Rc4 Rc7 21.Rdc1 Rfc8 it turns out that 13...Rc8 was quite useful after all.

Even worse for White is 19.Rc2 as after 19...Qxd2 20.Bxd2 a4 there is a nasty trick after 21.b4? in 21...Nxe4!. After 22.Rxc8 Rxc8 23.fxe4 Rc2 24.Rd1 a3 25.Kg1 Rxa2 Black soon recovers his piece and leaves White struggling to draw after 26.Kf1 Rb2 27.Ke1 a2 28.Bc4 b5 29.Bxa2 Rxa2.

19...axb4 20.Bd2 Ra8 21.Rc2 Bc3

Once again Black had a viable alternative in 21...Ra7, as after 22.Bxb4 Rfa8 23.Bxc5 Rxa2 24.Rxa2 Rxa2 25.Bxd6 exd6 he should hold the pawn-down ending comfortably.

22.Bxc3 bxc3 23.b4 Na4 24.a3

24.Bb5 Rfc8 25.Rfc1 Nb2 26.Rxc3 Rxc3 27.Rxc3 Rxa2 28.Rc1 Ra3 29.Kg1 Rb3 30.Rc7 Rxb4 31.Rxb7 Nd3 and the upcoming bishop versus knight ending with all the pawns on one side of the board can only offer Black chances.

24...f5 25.Bb5 fxe4 26.fxe4 Rxf1+ 27.Bxf1 Kg7 28.Bb5 Kf6 29.Bxa4 Rxa4 30.Rxc3 Ke5

The contrast in king activity is tremendous and completely compensates for the pawn minus—it's Bobby who has to be careful here.

31.Rc7 Kf6 32.Rc3 Ke5 33.Kg1 Kxe4 34.Rc7 Kxd5 35.Rxe7 b5 36.Rxh7 Rxa3 37.Rg7 Rb3 38.Rxg6 Rxb4 39.Rg5+ Ke6 40.Kf2 d5, ½–½.

(36)
Sammy Reshevsky – Fischer
New York/Los Angeles (11) 1961

What would turn out to be the last game of the match was arguably the most dramatic. Fischer, using his favorite King's Indian, played sharply from the beginning and quickly obtained a highly advantageous position. Reshevsky defended tenaciously, but through excellent play Bobby increased his advantage, until both sides started to bobble the ball after the adjournment with Fischer missing several easy wins. The final critical moment was reached after 52...Ra2+:

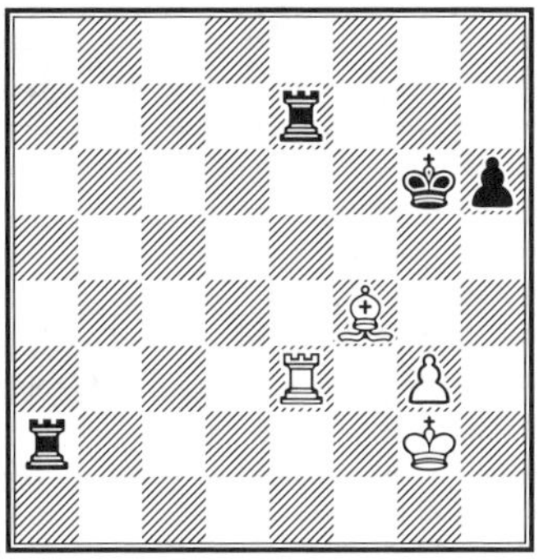

53.Kf3?

Fischer, in *My 60 Memorable Games*, points out "correct was 53.Kh3! in order to keep Black's king out of g4 after the exchange of rooks: e.g., 53...Rxe3 54.Bxe3 h5 55.Bf4 Ra1 56.Bc7 Kf5 57.Bf4 Rb1 58.Bc7! Rh1+ 59.Kg2 Rc1 60.Bf4! (gaining a vital tempo by hitting the rook), 60...R (any); 61.Kh3! maintaining the blockade."

53...Rb7?

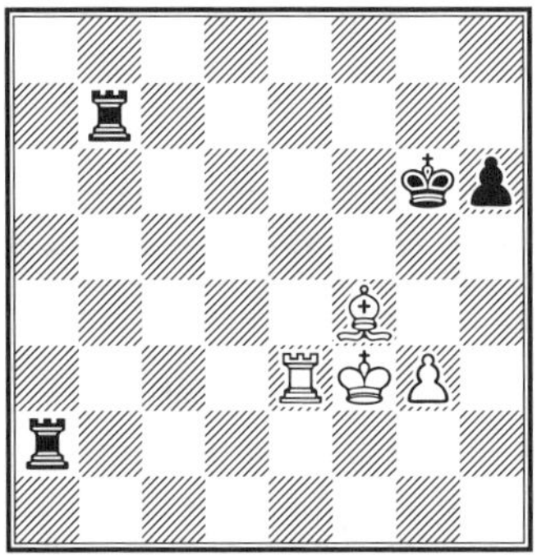

"Returning the favor" says Fischer who claims Black wins, giving the beautiful line:

53...Rxe3+ 54.Bxe3 h5 55.Bf4 Kf5 56.Bd6 Rb2 57.Bf4 Rb3+ 58.Kg2 Kg4 59.Bd6 Rb2+ 60.Kg1 Kh3 61.Be5 Rb4! 62.Bc7 Rg4! 63.Kf2 Kh2 64.Be5 Kh1 65.Kf3 Rg8 66.Bf4 Rf8 67.Kf2 (67.Ke3 Kg2) 67...h4 68.Kf3 h3 69.Kf2 h2 70.Kf1 Ra8 71.Kf2 Ra2+ 72.Kf1 Ra3! 73.Kf2

73..Rf3+!! 74.Kxf3 Kg1 75.Be3+ Kf1 winning.

This looks very convincing and suggests that all Black needs to do is bring his king to h1 and he wins. Unfortunately there is a flaw.

Going back to the position reached after 66...Rf8.

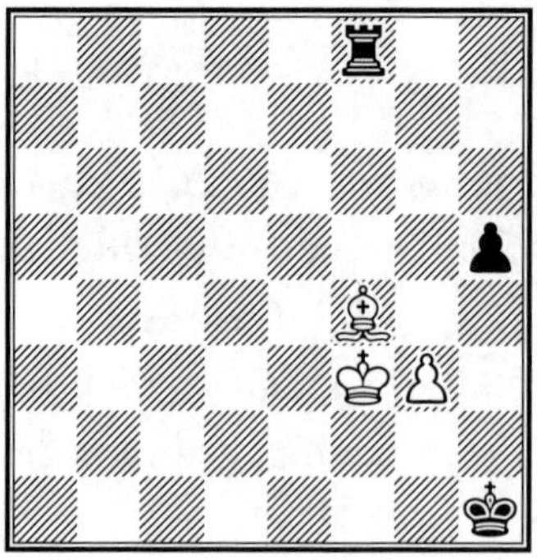

White does not have to retreat his king but can draw with 67.g4 h4 68.g5 h3 69.Kg4 h2 70.g6 Kg2 71.Bxh2 Kxh2 72.Kg5.

Is the position reached after 54..h5 really a draw? No! It turns out Black made a mistake by moving his rook away from the g-file (allowing the possibility of g4) before his king reached f1. Substitute 66...Kg1! (for 66...Rf8?) and the win can be had after 67.Be3+ Kf1 68. Bf4 Ra8 (the rook activates itself but in such a way that g4 is not possible) 69.Be3 (threatening g4) 69...Rf8+ (only now when the Black king is on f1 freeing the way for h-pawn in the event of g4) 70.Bf4 Rf7 (zugzwang) 71.g4 (71. Ke4 Kg2) 71...h4 72.g5 h3 73.g6 (73.Kg3 Rxf4 74.Kxh3 Kf2) 73...h2 74.gxf7 h1 (Q) 75.Ke3 Qg1+ 76. Kf3 Qg7 wins.

Credit goes to Grandmaster Jacob Murey who discovered the win working on his own in the days when chess players had to actually analyze such endings and not reply on a silicon oracle.

Now, of course, this six-piece endgame has been worked out by computers. One wonders if Bobby ever consulted the Nalimov Endgame Tablebases and if so what he thought of them. Fischer Random Chess is all about forcing players to think from move one to avoid computer preparation in the opening, but here the silicon oracle is working from another direction. Would Fischer have loved the possibility to learn the absolute truth about endgame positions or would he have been horrified by computers creeping ever deeper into his beloved game?

54.Re6+ Kf5 55.Re5+ Kf6 56.Rd5 Rb3+ 57.Kg4, ½–½.

The Fischer–Reshevsky match came to a controversial end when Fischer forfeited the twelfth game. Originally scheduled to be played August 12th in the evening, the game was rescheduled to eleven in the morning, primarily to accommodate Mrs. Piatigorsky who wished to hear her husband, cellist Gregor Piatigorsky, perform for the first time with the celebrated violinist Jascha Heifetz. Other reasons were given for the time change, but none of them overrode the fact that the players and organizers had a signed contact that stipulated game twelve was to be played at 7:30PM (this time printed in the press release issued by the American Chess Foundation). Fischer was willing to play in the afternoon, but definitely not in the morning as he was known to be a late riser.

Remarkably, Fischer, only eighteen at the time and far from his friends and supporters in New York, stood his ground. Irving Rivise, in his five-page report on the match, mentioned that Bobby spent the afternoon, the day before game twelve was to be played, as a guest at the Piatigorsky home. Tremendous pressure must have been put upon him to agree to play the next morning, and yet he didn't cave in. Even at a young age Bobby couldn't be pushed around.

The forfeit win gave Reshevsky the match, 6½–5½, and 60% of the purse. This was unacceptable to Fischer who took legal action in what may have been the first of many lawsuits he initiated during his life.

A deep division ran through the American chess community when the match was prematurely concluded with many letters of support for each player published in *Chess Life* and *Chess Review*. At the same time private correspondence between cooler heads worked hard to mend fences recognizing sponsors for American chess were in short supply. Following are two letters that provide an example of the fence mending operations being conducted at the time. The first is from U.S. Chess Federation business manager and *Chess Life* editor Frank Brady. The other is from Marshall Chess Club President Saul Rubin.

The Chess 'Kings' Collide: Fischer Sues Reshevsky

Bobby Fischer, 19-year-old U. S. chess champion, made a legal move yesterday after due deliberation against an opponent, Samuel Reshevsky, once a boy prodigy himself. Mr. Reshevsky is 50.

Young Fischer asked the State Supreme Court to bar Mr. Reshevsky, former U. S. chess champion and a grand master, from engaging in any public chess exhibition until the completion of a series of matches started between them last year.

According to the youth's complaint, he entered into a contract with Mr. Reshevsky on March 15, 1961, for a series of 16 matches. The purse was to be about $8,000, with the winner to get a 55 per cent cut, the loser 45. After 11 games, the players were tied at 5½ points each.

Subsequently, the teen-ager alleged, Mr. Reshevsky claimed the 12th game and the match on the ground the young man failed to appear. Bobby maintained he had never agreed to the time scheduled for the 12th game, that he was ready to go ahead with the match, but Mr. Reshevsky refused.

Bobby, through his lawyer, Harold Davis, of 76 Beaver St., advised the court, "My reputation as the most skillful and proficient chess player in the United States will be irreparably damaged and tarnished unless Mr. Reshevsky fulfills the terms of the contract."

Bobby also said it was the general custom among chess pros that "forfeited games are not declared or accepted because of a temporary failure between two players to agree upon a mutually satisfactory date and time."

Therefore, according to Bobby, Mr. Reshevsky improperly claimed the 12th game of the 16-game series and he wants the older player to be directed to continue the series "from the end of the eleventh game."

Bobby lives at 560 Lincoln Place, Brooklyn, while Mr. Reshevsky lives in Spring Valley, N. Y. He could not be reached there yesterday. Mr. Reshevsky has 30 days in which to answer the suit.

Herald Tribune photo by DON RICE

Herald Tribune photo by JAMES KAVALLINES

FROM CHESSBOARD TO COURTROOM—Samuel Reshevsky (left) and Bobby Fischer.

[right] The final position from game five of the Reshevsky-Fischer match after 57…Kf5. Referee Irving Rivise and promoter Alex Bisno are there to watch Bobby grab a 3-2 lead;

[below left] Reshevsky posing before game six with his customary cigarette;

[below right] Jacqueline Piatigorsky (Photo: Piatigorsky Collection, courtesy of the World Chess Hall of Fame).

November 7, 1961

Mr. Samuel Reshevsky
5 Hadassah Lane
Spring Valley, NY

Dear Mr. Reshevsky,

I would like to refer to my letter to you of October 24th, in which I ask for your comments on whether you are agreeable to continuing your match with Fischer from the twelfth game on. As to date I have not received an acknowledgment from you.

Since that time I have received over 200 letters and postcards from every part of the United States, from chessplayers who feel that Fischer was improperly forfeited and sincerely believe that the match ought to continue. There seems to be no end to the public interest in the controversy—and no let-up of mail coming in supporting the continuance of the match.

I sincerely believe that the existing situation of the enraged chess public could be alleviated by your returning your share of the prize fund to the American Chess Foundation and informing them and the public press that you are ready, willing and able to continue the march from the twelfth game on, with conditions as to the percentage of prize money being distributed, rate of play, referees, etc., remaining the same. The prize money would be increased, of course, to an additional $1,000, which I have previously mentioned to you and published in *Chess Life*.

Not only do I believe that this will straighten the matter out in the eyes of the chess world, but I believe that spectator interest will be so keen to see the final outcome of the remaining five games, that there is an opportunity for both you and Fischer to realize even greater remunerations from gate receipts than you have before.

You have the prestige and the respect of the chessworld to gain by the continuance of the match. You have nothing to lose.

Sincerely,
Frank R. Brady

Written on Marshall Chess Club stationary:

November 24, 1961

Dear Mrs. Piatigorsky,

It has been brought to my attention that you had intended to make a substantial contribution to American chess through the American Chess Foundation, but that you have changed your mind because of the "unfair" manner in which *Chess Life* has handled the Fischer–Reshevsky story. Three of us who have expressed views on the matter in *Chess Life* are disturbed and troubled that you should deem our attitude unfair, and would be extremely pleased if you and your husband would favor us with an opportunity to discuss this matter in a most friendly manner.

> On behalf of Harvey Breit, Frank Brady, and myself, I cordially invite you and your husband to be our guests at luncheon at your early convenience. If you will telephone me (Worth 2–3555) and let me know when it will be convenient for you to have luncheon with us, I shall gladly make the necessary arrangements.
>
> Very sincerely yours,
> Saul Rubin

The match was never resumed, leaving Bobby in an unhappy state, so much so that he declined his invitation to play in the U.S. Championship a few months later, the only one he missed in a nine-year period.

Bobby filed a lawsuit in 1962, but not against Jacqueline Piatigorsky—surprisingly it was Sammy Reshevsky who was his target. The matter was settled out of court and there are no public records, so it's unclear exactly what transpired. In all probability Jacqueline paid Bobby the difference between the 40% loser's share and the 50% due for a drawn match.

The conclusion could be drawn that after their bitter dispute Bobby and Jacqueline never had anything to do with each other. Fortunately, such was not the case. It was Jacqueline who first extended the olive branch by inviting Bobby to play in the First Piatigorsky Cup scheduled to start July 2,1963. He declined (Pal Benko took his place), citing her refusal to meet his demand for a $2,000 ($17,000 in 2020 dollars) honorarium. But this might have been a smoke screen as no one in the event received an honorarium; the large prize fund of $10,000 ($85,000 in 2020 dollars) provided enough incentive. Most likely, Fischer's ongoing feud with the Soviets after Curaçao 1962 [see pages 269–271] contributed to his decision not to play—two of the players he accused of cheating there, Petrosian and Keres, had accepted invitations to play in the Piatigorsky event.

Fischer did have an indirect association with the event, providing deep (and humorous) annotations in *American Chess Quarterly* to the game Keres–Reshevsky, won in fine style by Sammy. Bobby's commentary included a fictitious game where Sammy was defeated in a King's Gambit in less than ten moves.

Jacqueline sweetened the offer for the Second Piatigorsky Cup. Not only was Bobby the first player to be invited, but in correspondence that can be found at the World Chess Hall of Fame, she proposed he author the tournament book. Fischer accepted the invitation to play but did not agree to write the book. In fact, he annotated only his game with Najdorf, while all other players except Donner provided comments to each of their eighteen games. As it turned out, even though Fischer didn't have much to do with it, the *Second Piatigorsky Cup* is considered one of the greatest tournament books ever. The unique format, where both players provided independent notes to each game, proved to be a successful formula.

The relationship between Jacqueline and Bobby did not end with the Second Piatigorsky Cup. Her financial support for Bobby's World Championship run, starting with the 1970 Interzonal and extending all the way to Reykjavík, was considerable. The U.S. Chess Federation, American Chess Foundation, and Jacqueline (through her Piatigorsky Chess Foundation) were equal partners in providing not only expense money but also honorarium as the prize money offered by FIDE for many of the events was minimal.

Reshevsky also benefited from Piatigorsky's generosity. The two struck up a friendship after the 1961 match. There are dozens of letters, in the collection of the World Chess Hall of Fame, from Sammy to Jacqueline that contain (in addition to friendly chit chat) Sammy's analysis of her games—Jacqueline was a high A player/low expert at the time who would finish second in the 1965 U.S. Women's Championship. Piatigorsky did not pay Reshevsky for these "lessons." Instead, a quid pro quo of a kind existed—she always responded favorably to requests by the American Chess Foundation and U.S. Chess Federation to support Sammy. By the late 1960s this assistance became more formalized.

The Piatigorsky Foundation, U.S. Chess Federation, and American Chess Foundation provided Reshevsky with first-rate financial support for 1967 Sousse Interzonal and the playoff, and Candidates' match with Korchnoi the following year. This was impressive considering the U. S. Chess Federation had only around 10,000 members at the time.

In 1968 this support included:

Four months' living expenses for Reshevsky and family prior to the Interzonal Playoff = $4,000

Benko's fee for the Reshevsky–Benko warm-up match = $400

Second's fee for Benko for the Korchnoi match = $600

Reshevsky honorarium for the Korchnoi match = $5,000

In addition, Reshevsky, Mrs. Reshevsky, and Benko came to Amsterdam several weeks early for the match with Korchnoi, an additional expense that was fully covered. All told, the three benefactors spent over $14,000 ($121,000 in 2020 dollars) supporting Reshevsky.

Keep in mind that in 1968 the only American players keeping themselves afloat as chess professionals were Reshevsky, Pal Benko (the King of the American Swiss in the 1960s), and Bobby. Everyone else had another job.

It's worth noting that when Reshevsky played Korchnoi in the 1968 quarterfinals at the age of fifty-six, it was the only the third time he had played in a Candidates level event—he was equal third in the five player 1948 World Championship tournament, and equal second at the Zurich 1953 Candidates tournament. For various reasons (unsuitable venues, not qualifying from U.S. Championships/Zonals, and choosing not to play), after Zurich he did not appear again in the middle stages of the World Championship cycle until the 1964 Interzonal where he finished tied for eighth in a field of twenty-four. Due to a rule in place at the time restricting the number of qualifiers from any one country, Reshevsky played a three game playoff with Lajos Portisch for the last spot in the Candidates. He was beaten 2½–½, the first match he lost in his career.

Three years later, at the Sousse Interzonal (1967), Reshevsky tied with Leonid Stein and Vlastimil Hort for sixth place and the last qualifying spot for the Candidates' matches. The three met in a playoff match held February 18–March 3, 1968, at the Herman Steiner Chess Club in Los Angeles with Jacqueline Piatigorsky handling all the arrangements. The three players all scored 50% and Reshevsky advanced due to a better tiebreak from the Interzonal. His reward was to meet Viktor Korchnoi, almost twenty years his junior, who destroyed him 6½–2½.

Unlike Fischer, Reshevsky was an active player his entire life, playing at a high level until the very end. Emanuel Lasker's third place finish at Moscow 1935 at the age of sixty-six, just half a point behind Botvinnik and Flohr, was considered a miracle at the time. Later, Vassily Smyslov raised the bar, reaching the finals of the Candidates matches in 1984 at age sixty-three. But in the history of chess, Reshevsky and Viktor Korchnoi are the only two who continued to play at a high level into their seventies.

Although Sammy's results were not up to Viktor's, he did finish equal third in the 1981 U.S. Championship, tied for first in the 1984 Reykjavík Open, and narrowly lost (3½–4½) a match in 1984 to Larry Christiansen, close to five decades his junior. Sammy Reshevsky was truly one of the giants of modern chess.

3
ANTISEMITISM

The origins of Fischer's rabid antisemitism have long been a subject of discussion. Exactly when it started is difficult to pinpoint, but there is evidence to suggest that the premature ending of the match with Reshevsky may have been a catalyst—after being forfeited Bobby felt that the American chess establishment was against him.

Jerry Hanken, who had shown Fischer around Los Angeles in early 1961 while conditions for the Fischer–Reshevsky match were being worked out, was also Bobby's chauffeur for the Los Angeles leg of the match. Hanken drove Bobby daily from his lodgings at the Miramar Hotel in Santa Monica to the Herman Steiner Chess Club and Beverly Hilton Hotel allowing much time for conversation. According to Hanken:

> All of the Los Angeles contingent were Reshevsky supporters. Jacqueline herself thought of Fischer as an upstart brat... [Fischer's sense that this match was stolen from him was] absolutely the origin of his vicious antisemitism.

Grandmaster Lubos Kavalek is of the opinion that the Reshevsky match combined later with the failed lawsuit against Brad Darrach—Bobby thought he had an iron-clad case that would prevent *Bobby Fischer vs. the Rest of the World* from being published—caused Fischer to lose his faith in the U.S. Chess Federation and the U.S. government.

Garry Kasparov offered his insight:[1]

> We must not forget that after the match with Reshevsky there was a lot of ballyhoo in the American press. Everyone accused Fischer, the radio, and newspapers were not sparing in their epithets, condemning the spoiled 'brat', who disgraced the title of USA Champion with his behavior. The USCF also took Reshevsky's side. It is not surprising that Bobby felt wronged, abandoned by everyone, driven into a corner...
>
> But everyone could not have taken up arms against him just like that, surely there must be a reason?! And Fischer found it. They were all Jews: Reshevsky, the Piatigorskys, leaders of the Federation, journalists, arbiters...

[1] Garry Kasparov, *My Great Predecessors: Part IV.* London: Everyman Chess, 2004, (p. 280).

> And so they were supporting one another! In addition, he was irritated by the fact that he, Bobby the genius, was dependent on the whims of patrons, who like this Rothschild descendant, were also largely Jews. "For golf tournaments millionaires are happy to give $300,000, whereas for chess they throw in a measly thousand or two—and even boast about this! The tournaments bear their names, everyone has to bow before them, play when they want—and all for a couple of thousand dollars, which means nothing to them and which they deduct from their income tax!"
>
> For a little-educated, extremely egocentric youth from Brooklyn, such a "simplified" view on the world was understandable. Grandmaster O'Kelly commented very aptly: "Fischer's behavior resembles that of a savage: everything that happens around him he perceives as a threat." As he grew older, Bobby could have got rid of his complexes, but he was unlucky: on top of all the unpleasantness in his homeland, the Soviet "steam-roller" also drove over him, and this, generally speaking, broke his identity. He grew up like a dwarf birch, in the suffocating atmosphere that filled the chess world from the moment that the Soviet Union entered FIDE, with the total domination of Soviet players and, hence, of the Soviet political and sports machine. At times the pressure assumed ugly forms (as, for example, in the Candidates tournament on Curaçao). And I think Fischer's antisemitism, which increased with the years, was largely associated with the domination of "Soviet-Jewish" players. It seemed to him that they were all united against him with the aim of preventing him from becoming World Champion. I remember Reshevsky telling me how, during the Interzonal tournament on Mallorca, with burning eyes Fischer informed him that he was reading a "very interesting book." "What is it?" Sammy asked innocently. "*Mein Kampf*" Bobby replied.

Undoubtedly there is some truth in what Hanken, Kavalek, and Kasparov have to say about the bitter ending of the Reshevsky match marking the start of Fischer's antisemitism. Still, it is not so clear that this was the beginning.

Pal Benko has a different opinion on this and said in a 2016 interview[1] that Fischer showed paranoia towards Jews when he first met him at the Portorož Interzonal when Bobby was just fifteen years old:

> I liked the way he played chess. And he was correct at the chessboard. Of course he had his stupid ideas, he was a hopeless case, but he hardly talked about them at the time. His mental problems already showed when he was very young. He was sixteen when we were training at Grossinger's, a luxurious hotel with all facilities outside New York. And he showed me a photo of Hitler and said he thought he was a great guy. Look at the map of Europe and see how Germany is divided, what a great guy that he achieved that. Then later he got his doubts and was no longer convinced that Hitler was such a great guy. And he believed that maybe he was a Jew. Some people think he

1 *New In Chess*, #2, 2016, (p. 59).

> picked up these ideas later, but it was already then. He could not escape from the stuff he had in his head. I have no idea where it came from, I am not a psychiatrist. I told him, you are paranoid, and he said, yes, but sometimes paranoids are right.

Hans Ree, in his article "At the Kibbutz with Bobby" describes a much different Fischer than usually portrayed:[1]

> At the end of the tournament [Netanya, 1968] the two of us were invited by one of the participants, Yaacov Bernstein, to spend a few days on the kibbutz where he lived. Considering Bobby's later views the idea of his spending time on a kibbutz may seem strange, and in fact during the tournament I had asked him about his views on Jewry.
>
> I had heard from a Dutchman involved with the Candidates tournament on Curaçao in 1962 that Bobby had made strong antisemitic statements. If this were true, what was he doing in Israel now? Bobby said that indeed he had been antisemitic and that this had been stupid. "Besides, I'm half-Jewish myself, so how can I be antisemitic?" As we know, this insight was subsequently lost.
>
> At the kibbutz we played some blitz. In our tournament game I had collapsed as soon as Bobby had uncorked an opening novelty. Playing blitz I hoped for... well, not really revenge, but maybe one draw out of a series of games, was that too much? But no way. After a while he wanted to give me knight odds. I protested, but I had to oblige. That game he won also, and then he refused to go on. "No challenge," he said.
>
> "Fischer is Fischer, but a knight is a knight," said Mikhail Tal when Bobby had claimed that he could give knight odds to any woman player. But for me, a knight was not enough.
>
> Afterwards we were looking at the games from the recent Candidates matches, Tal–Gligorić and Korchnoi–Reshevsky. About the latter match I could contribute some insights, as it had been played in Amsterdam and Dutch masters had been analyzing the games. Our days at Bernstein's kibbutz were pleasant and I'll always remember the sight of Bobby embracing a horse and whispering sweet little words into its ears.

And so the discrepancy.

---

[1] ChessCafe.com.

[left] Bobby analyzing at the Marshall with club president Saul Rubin in 1962. William Slater (husband of many-time U.S. Women's Championship participant Kathryn Slater) is in the background. The Slaters operated the teletype machine that received and sent moves for Bobby Fischer when he played in the 1965 Capablanca Memorial from the Marshall Chess Club (Photo: Carl Mydans).

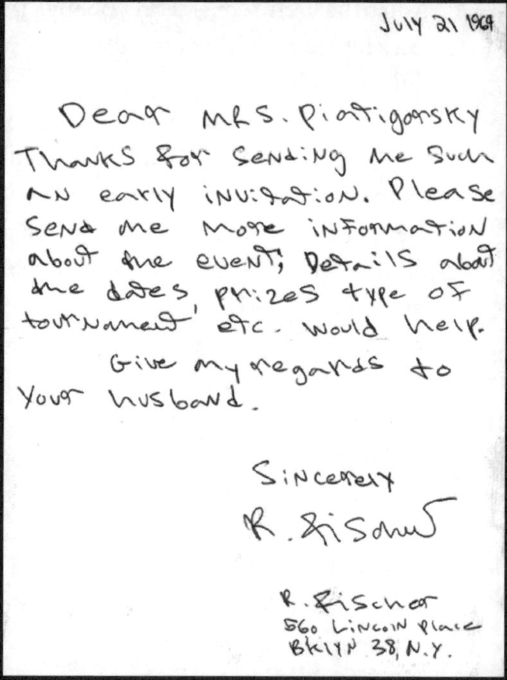

July 21 1964

Dear Mrs. Piatigorsky
Thanks for sending me such an early invitation. Please send me more information about the event; Details about the dates, prizes type of tournament etc. would help.
Give my regards to your husband.

Sincerely
R. Fischer

R. Fischer
560 Lincoln Place
Bklyn 38, N.Y.

[above] Jacqueline and Gregor Piatigorsky;

[right] Yury Averbakh, Jacqueline Piatigorsky, and Pal Benko (Photo: Piatigorsky collection, courtesy of the World Chess Hall of Fame).

[left] Jacqueline Piatigorsky watches Fischer and Spassky play;

[middle] Spassky, Piatigorsky, and Fischer;

[bottom] Jacqueline Piatigorsky.

Players in the First Piatigorsky Cup: Pal Benko, Svetozar Gligorić, Friðrik Ólafsson, Miguel Najdorf, Tigran Petrosian, Sammy Reshevsky, Paul Keres, and Oscar Panno (July 1963).

Players in the Second Piatigorsky Cup held August and July 1966: Lajos Portisch, Fischer, Boris Spassky, Jan Hein Donner, *(continued on opposite page)* *Bent Larsen, Miguel Najdorf, Borislav Ivkov, Tigran Petrosian, Wolfgang Unzicker. Though not in photo, Sammy Reshevsky also played.*

Kashdan, Petrosian, Najdorf, Ivkov, Rona Petrosian, Portisch, Fischer, and Helen Kashdan.

4

PORTRAIT OF A GENIUS AS A YOUNG CHESS MASTER

Ralph Ginzburg's article on Bobby Fischer, "Portrait of a Genius as a Young Chess Master," had a profound impact on the eighteen-year-old. Based on an interview with Bobby, conducted by Ginzburg in late August 1961 (a few weeks after the Reshevsky match ended), it was published in the January 1962 issue of *Harper's Magazine* and subsequently received worldwide attention when the British magazine *Chess* reprinted it a few months later.

Questions have been raised as to the article's accuracy. Bobby disavowed it immediately upon publication, claiming whole pages were fabricated—however, he didn't take legal action. Frank Brady has suggested the interview belongs in the realm of "creative non-fiction," and that Ginzburg made up quotes that he attributed to Fischer. In *Endgame* he wrote:[1]

> One can never know the full truth, of course, but even if Ginzburg merely reported verbatim what Bobby had said, it was a cruel piece of journalism, a penned mugging, in that it made a vulnerable teenager appear uneducated, homophobic, and misogynistic, none of which was a true portrait.

Ralph Ginzburg (1929–2006) is perhaps best remembered as the publisher of *Eros*, a high end artsy magazine of erotica which landed him a short-term prison sentence in the '70s when the U.S. Supreme Court found him guilty of violating obscenity laws. Exactly how he met Fischer is not clear as Ginzburg's work as a writer and photographer dealt primarily with his social activism, and there is no instance of him writing about chess before or after the interview. Ginzburg was never a tournament player yet reading the interview it's clear that he was familiar with the game as the mistakes mainstream journalists often make in writing about chess are nowhere to be found. Ginzburg's byline stated that he played lots of chess, but Bobby Fischer beat him "in three seconds flat."

In all probability, Ginzburg interviewed Fischer on spec without a commitment from *Harper's*. What was his motivation? Was it money? If it was attention he craved, he received plenty of that after the interview.

---

[1] Frank Brady, *Endgame: Bobby Fischer's Remarkable Rise and Fall—from America's Brightest Prodigy to the Edge of Madness*. New York: Crown Trade, 2011, (p. 139).

What induced Bobby to sit down to be interviewed? Maybe he saw it as his chance to talk about what happened in the Reshevsky match. More likely he didn't give it much thought. After all, how many eighteen-year-olds carefully think through what they're doing?

Fischer was devastated by the article, and would shy away from journalists for the next decade only to be burned again in 1974—this time by Brad Darrach's tome *Bobby Fischer vs. the Rest of the World*. The truth will never be known in either instance, proving or disproving the authenticity of Fischer's statements is impossible as Ginzburg and Darrach both destroyed their notes.

Ginzburg's seven-page interview, which covered all aspects of Fischer's life, became primary source material for journalists and other researchers. This, despite the fact Fischer repeatedly claimed much of what was attributed to him was made up. While parts of the interview are hard to stomach, other sections offer valuable insights into the young Bobby. Ginzburg put a lot of work into this interview and reached out to important members of the American chess community including John Collins, Frank Brady, Lisa Lane, and Al Horowitz.

Following are some excerpts from Ginzburg's article. Author's comments are in brackets [ ]:

> [Ginzburg's description of Bobby,"Fischer is handsome, over six feet tall, with broad shoulders, intense hazel eyes, and sharp features," and his behavior in the summer of 1961 ring true. He starts the interview with Fischer acting like a typical teenager.]
>
> Bobby came to my office in midtown Manhattan last August 25. The date had been made for the day before at three o'clock, but at four he had phoned to say that he just didn't feel like coming. When he did appear, he was again an hour late. Without knocking, he flung open the door, strode halfway across the room, and greeted me with the words, "Hey, do you have some food up here or something?"
>
> I said I would phone for some food and asked what he wanted.
>
> "A turkey white meat on rye, two celery sodas (still available today as Dr. Brown's Cel-Ray soda), some tea, and a couple plums," he said.
>
> "How does one make a living at chess?" I asked.
>
> "Reshevsky and I are the only ones in America who try. We don't make much. The other masters have outside jobs. Like Rossolimo, he drives a cab. Evans, he works for the movies. The Russians, they get money from the government. We have to depend on tournament prizes. And they're lousy. Maybe a couple hundred bucks. Millionaires back this game, but they're all cheap. Look what they do for golf: $30,000 for a tournament is nothing. But for chess they give $1,000 or $2,000 and they think it's a big deal. The tournament has to be named after them, everybody has to bow down to them, play when they want, everything for a couple thousand dollars which is

nothing to them anyhow. They take it off their income tax. These people are cheap. It's ridiculous."

A reliable estimate which I later received fixed Fischer's and Reshevsky's average yearly prize winnings at $5,000 each. This just about covers their chess-playing expenses. In short, they earn no surplus directly from playing. Reshevsky, aged forty-nine, a married man with a family, receives a stipend from the American Chess Foundation. Bobby, who lives alone in a Brooklyn flat, has his rent, food, and clothing bills paid by his mother.

[Fischer wrote for *Chess Life* and *American Chess Quarterly*, but not Al Horowitz's *Chess Review*. Could the following comments by Horowitz, as reported by Ginzburg, have burned his bridges with Bobby?]

It is safe to say that Bobby Fischer has aroused greater admiration for his chess-playing skill than any young player has ever before enjoyed. It is also a painfully well-known fact in the chess world, however, that never before has a young player aroused so much personal antipathy. This ill will seems to stem from what Al Horowitz, former U.S. Open Champion, has described as Fischer's "colossal egotism." Horowitz says: "The huge egos of great chess players are legendary. Psychologists have been amazed by their vanity, have studied it, and anecdotes concerning it are abundant. But never before has there been such a prima-donna as Bobby. ...Already he has managed to alienate and offend almost everybody in the chess world. That includes officials, patrons, writers, almost everybody and anybody who might be in a position to help him in his career."

[One of the most controversial and best remembered part of the interview was Fischer's remarks about women in chess.]

"Lisa Lane has said—and lots of other people agree—that you're probably the greatest chess player alive."

[Fischer is alleged to have responded]

"That statement is accurate, but Lisa Lane really wouldn't be in a position to know. They're all weak, all women. They're stupid compared to men. They shouldn't play chess, you know. They're like beginners. They lose every single game against a man. There isn't a woman player in the world I can't give knight-odds to and still beat."

[Lisa Lane was a pioneering figure in American women's chess. At a time when there were possibly less than a hundred women tournament players in the country, she was one of the very best. At her peak Lane was rated around 2100 USCF, which was a considerable achievement at the time. However, Fischer was correct, she was not a strong enough player to make an accurate assessment of who the best player in the world was. No player rated 2100, male or female, would have had the needed chess knowledge. Fischer's claim that he could give any woman in the world knight odds sounds outrageous until you examine it more closely. The Women's World Champions in the 1950s and early 1960s (Bykova, Rudenko, and Rubtsova) were, at best, strong experts. Fischer in 1961 was one of the top ten players in the world. At minimum, there was a 500 rating point gap between the top woman player and Bobby—a huge difference. The lopsided situation would soon change with the emergence of Nona Gaprindashvili (who, in 1978 was the first woman to earn the grandmaster title), and more recently the likes of Judit Polgar and Hou Yifan. It is noteworthy Bobby never chose to respond to Mikhail Tal's offer to back Nona in a friendly match.]

"How about the men champions, like the Russians, Botvinnik, Tal, Keres, Smyslov, can you beat them?"

"They have nothing on me, those guys. They can't even touch me. Some people rate them better than me. That really bugs me. They think that no Americans play chess. When I meet those Russian potzers[1] I'll put them in their place." ("Potzer," an ugly and insulting word in its original Yiddish, means an inferior player in chess parlance, where it is used without insulting connotation.[2] Bobby's English is entirely free of profanity.)

"Would you consider yourself the greatest player that ever lived, even better, say, than Capablanca, Steinitz, or Morphy?"

"Well, I don't like to put things like that in print, it sounds so egotistical. But to answer your question, Yes."

"Do you have any one or two closest friends?"

"No. I don't keep any close friends. I don't keep any secrets. I don't need friends. I just tell everybody everything, that's all."

I asked him if this policy of 100% honesty toward everybody at all times wasn't perhaps at the core of his difficulty in dealing with people. That is, if his forthrightness hadn't perhaps sometimes been misinterpreted as tactlessness. Bobby said that might have been the case.

[The parts of the interview that sound authentic and provide a glimpse of what the young Bobby was like follow.]

I asked him to describe a typical day in his life."Lots of the time I'm traveling around. Europe, South America, Iceland. But when I'm home, I don't know, I don't do much. I get up eleven o'clock maybe. I'll get dressed and all, look at some chess books, go downstairs and eat. I never cook my own meals. I don't believe in that stuff. I don't eat in luncheonettes or automats, either. I like a waiter to wait on me. Good restaurants. After I eat I usually call up some of my chess friends, go over and analyze a game or something. Maybe I'll go to a chess club. Then maybe I'll see a movie or something. There's really nothing for me to do. Maybe I'll study some chess book."

---

1 More common is "patzers."

2 Patzer: "Also potzer. [Origin uncertain: cf. G. patzen to bungle.]. Although said to be from the Yiddish, there is no Yiddish, German, or Hebrew word or word combination to suggest it. Prob. from 'patsy' with the familiar '-er' ending added." —The *Oxford English Dictionary, Second Edition* (1989).

[And]

> We drove to Bobby's house located on the edge of Brooklyn's Bedford-Stuyvesant district where the homicide and general crime rate is among the highest in the city. The house is a four-story walk-up with a barber shop and a candy store on the ground floor. He told me that his four-room apartment has a library of some two hundred chess books, piles of chess magazines, and an inlaid chess table made to order for him in Switzerland. There are three beds in the apartment, each with a chessboard beside it, and Bobby sleeps in them in rotation.

[The number of chess books (200) might seem like a small library for an elite player, but keep in mind very few were available in 1961, particularly in English. The other beds in the apartment had previously been those of Bobby's sister and his mother. The inlaid table from Switzerland that Bobby had specially shipped to him was later sold to Bernard Zuckerman when Fischer moved to Los Angeles.]

[Ginzburg's final conclusions were sure to have offended Fischer, and cruel to write about someone so young, but in retrospect, over half a century later, some of them ring true.]

> The interview ended. Several things about him had become clear. First of all, whereas chess is just a game for most people, a diversion from life, for Bobby Fischer chess is life and everything that happens off the chessboard is a distraction. Second, though Bobby is possibly the greatest chess player of all time, he is not a genius in other respects (nor, incidentally, are most other chess masters of the world). Third, though Fischer is eighteen years old, he shows some traits of much younger children, who behave that the world is centered around filling their needs. Finally, though it was easy to see how Bobby could offend people with his sweeping statements, he does not show malice. Concerned with his own feelings, he is gentle, shy, almost timid. Bobby is, as his sister later told me, "a boy who requires an extra amount of understanding." Perhaps this is inevitable for a boy who has grown up without a father.
>
> ...
>
> On the way to my car after leaving my office, we made two stops. The first was at a paperback bookstore where Bobby wanted to buy a book. He examined *Commandant of Auschwitz* and *The Bridge Over the River Kwai* and finally selected the store's last copy of Bernard Baruch's *My Own Story*. He seemed particularly impressed by the photographs of old Wall Street tycoons. "They were pretty snazzy in the old days," he said. "Look how elegant and gentlemanly they are."
>
> We next stopped at a posh espresso house for a bite to eat. Bobby ordered a slice of pecan cream pie, a side order of butter cookies, and an elaborate frozen pineapple drink. When he had finished his pie, I mentioned that the place

was reputed to be owned and operated by homosexuals. Bobby was horrified and eyed the waiters narrowly. "Gee, you'd think the place would die off with a reputation like that." Returning his attention to his drink. "Maybe they put something in here. I better not drink it." He didn't touch it again. Nor did he eat any more of his cookies.

...

I asked him what he planned to do if and when he managed to beat Botvinnik and become the World Champion.

"First of all," he said, "I'll make a tour of the whole world, giving exhibitions. I'll charge unprecedented prices. I'll set new standards. I'll make them pay thousands. Then I'll come home on a luxury liner. First-class. I'll have a tuxedo made for me in England to wear to dinner. When I come home I'll write a couple chess books and start to reorganize the whole game. I'll have my own club. The Bobby Fischer ... uh, the Robert J. Fischer Chess Club. It'll be class. Tournaments in full dress. No bums in there. You're gonna have to be over eighteen to get in, unless like you have special permission because you have like special talent. It'll be in a part of the city that's still decent, like the upper East Side.

"And I'll hold big international tournaments in my club with big cash prizes. And I'm going to kick all the millionaires out of chess unless they kick in more money. Then I'll buy a car so I don't have to take the subway any more. That subway makes me sick. It'll be a Mercedes-Benz. Better, a Rolls-Royce, one of those fifty-thousand dollar custom jobs, made to my own measure. Maybe I'll buy one of those jets they advertise for businessmen. And a yacht. Flynn had a yacht. Then I'll have some more suits made. I'd like to be one of the Ten Best-dressed Men. That would really be something. I read that Duke Snyder made the list.

"Then I'll build me a house. I don't know where but it won't be in Greenwich Village. They're all dirty, filthy animals down there. Maybe I'll build it in Hong Kong. Everybody who's been there says it's great. Art Linkletter said so on the radio. And they've got suits there, beauties, for only twenty dollars. Or maybe I'll build it in Beverly Hills. The people there are sort of square, but like the climate is nice and it's close to Vegas, Mexico, Hawaii, and those places. I got strong ideas about my house. I'm going to hire the best architect and have him build it in the shape of a rook. Yeh, that's for me. Class. Spiral staircases, parapets, everything. I want to live the rest of my life in a house built exactly like a rook."

• • •

A quick revisit to Ralph Ginzburg's claim that Fischer said:

> They're all weak, all women. They're stupid compared to men. They shouldn't play chess, you know. They're like beginners. They lose every single game against a man. There isn't a woman player in the world I can't give knight-odds to and still beat.

Fischer is on record stating Ginzburg misquoted him, took things out of context, and in some instances simply made things up. Nona Gaprindashvili's star was already on the rise in early 1962 and Fischer, never one to make false claims concerning chess, certainly would have realized he couldn't give Nona "knight odds." Or would he? In 1968 he gave Dutch International Master Hans Ree knights odds at blitz and beat him.

Fischer wasn't so negative about women players in the late '60s. Cleveland master David Presser tells a story he heard several decades ago by an individual long forgotten. Presser remembers being told:

> Back in the late 1960s or early 1970s, Marilyn Koput, one of America's top women players, was in New York City playing in (I believe) the U.S. Women's Closed. She had an adjournment, a rook and pawn ending, and had spent several hours analyzing the adjourned position. She was sitting in an automat eating and analyzing the endgame when Bobby walked in and sat down at her table. She showed him the adjourned position; Bobby made a suggestion which Marilyn refuted. There followed another suggestion and another refutation by Marilyn. This went on for a while. Of course, Marilyn had investigated the position at length, but still it is impressive that she kept refuting Bobby's quick suggestions.

Born in Milwaukee, Marilyn Koput (1948–2018), later Braun and Simmons, is best remembered for tying for first with Eva Aronson in the 1972 U.S. Women's Championship, earning her the Woman International Master title.

The first U.S. Women's Championship Koput played in was held June 15–29, 1969, at the Hotel McAlpine in New York City. If the meeting between Bobby and Marilyn happened, this would have been the time and place (no bulletin exists, so it's unknown whether Marilyn had any adjourned games).

Marilyn's sister Cindy, an accomplished tournament player in her own right (she was rated in the top twenty-five women in the U.S. in 1975) never heard her sister talk about crossing paths with Bobby. However, a newspaper article published in the *Austin American* on August 10, 1972, stated:

> Mrs. Braun said she met Fischer in New York in 1969 and went to lunch with him. He was "very polite, friendly and sociable," she said, but she wouldn't want to play against him, adding, "I don't want to humiliate myself."

It seems quite possible that they met. Did they analyze her adjournment? Could be. That sounds like it might have been Bobby's idea of a perfect date! That said, even taking into account that Marilyn was close to expert strength by today's standards and she was good friends with fellow Milwaukeean Bill Martz (who might have been in New York as her second), the idea that she repeatedly shot down Bobby's analysis is a bit of a stretch.

5

BOBBY FISCHER AT EIGHTEEN (A PERSONAL RECOLLECTION)

by Jerry Hanken

National Master Jerome "Jerry" B. Hanken (1934–2009) was an important figure in American chess for half a century. In the early 1960s he was one of the best players in southern California, and later became a prominent organizer and tournament director. Hanken, who grew up in Cincinnati, didn't learn the game until studying for a master's degree at the University of Kansas in the late 1950s. The late start didn't stop him from making rapid progress and by the time he moved to California he was already an expert, soon to become a Master.

Hanken, who lived in Los Angeles most of his life, became well acquainted with Fischer when he visited there in 1961, 1964, and 1966.

Hanken's memoir was originally written in 1972. Twenty years later, he added a preface to bring his portrait of Bobby up to date.

Authors notes are in brackets [ ]:

> The following personal memoir was written exactly twenty years ago (i.e. 1972), at the time that Bobby Fischer won the World Chess Championship. Most of this article covered the period of time during the match in Los Angeles in 1961 between Fischer and the late Samuel Reshevsky. Fischer was eighteen at the time (i.e. in 1961), and my fascination with him as a chess player comes through pretty clearly.
>
> A lot of water has passed "under the dam" since that time, and if I actually chose to rewrite the story at this time I would be a lot more blunt. I would probably include some of Fischer's remarks attacking Jews and praising Hitler, as well as his occasional foul and abusive language toward his opponent.
>
> Fischer's two recent press conferences in Yugoslavia, and the fact that he has undertaken to play the current match in violation of United Nation sanctions under a government which can only be described as neo-fascist, sadly confirm that he has not outgrown these unpleasant attitudes.
>
> I would certainly not be the first person to observe the tragic irony of the current situation. As a director of the U.S. Chess Federation and as president

of the Southern California Chess Federation, I had hopes that a Fischer comeback would mean another great chess boom as there was in the 1970s.

I still believe that Bobby Fischer was the greatest chess player in the history of the game. Over the chessboard Bobby sought and found greater truth than any other player in history. Even at forty-nine, after twenty years away from the game, his play against the aging and burned-out Spassky is strikingly good. Unfortunately, the image of chess he is presenting to the world is embarrassing to every chess player.

Will Fischer play again after this match? Or will he return to hibernation? It is clear that he still believes himself to be World Champion, and unless dethroned by Spassky (unlikely), he will continue to claim the title. I can't imagine Gary Kasparov's ego allowing Bobby to dictate the terms of any match, particularly in view of the derogatory terms in which Fischer has described his successor—no matter how great the financial stakes.

In any case, I present the following memoir as a historical oddity. The incidents, anecdotes, and descriptions given here are essentially accurate. My memory was clearer at the time, but perhaps somewhat clouded by my determination to admire Bobby Fischer no matter what. I am older and wiser now.

• • •

[October 1972] There are about seventy-five or eighty chess players in the world who have achieved the rank of "grandmaster." These can be roughly divided in three categories.

The first category would include the really competent and talented players who have, with a good deal of hard work and experience, gained the pinnacle of chess fame. They don't win many tournaments, but they perform successfully over a period of time and have an occasional brilliant outing. These could be called "ordinary grandmasters."

The next category might be classified as "super grandmasters." There are no more than fifteen in this category, and probably closer to ten. These players are often referred to as being of "world class" because they are in direct competition for the World Championship of chess. Among this group are the present World Champion Boris Spassky, and his immediate predecessor, Tigran Petrosian. Also, one would have to consider Michael Tal, Vassily Smyslov, Michael Botvinnik, all former World Champions, and Viktor Korchnoi of the Soviet Union.

The third category of grandmaster is Bobby Fischer.

I first met Bobby Fischer in Cleveland, Ohio, at the United States Open chess championship in the summer of 1957. He was somewhat small for his fourteen years of age, but even then, he possessed the confidence and tenacity which were later to characterize his approach to life, as well as to chess. I had just completed two rather futile years as a graduate student at the University of Kansas and was returning to my native Ohio to teach High School. It was

[left] Hanken at the Steiner Chess Club around the time of the Fischer–Reshevsky match in the summer of 1961;

[above] Jerry Hanken with Isaac Kashdan. Kashdan directed the famous Lone Pine tournaments (held not far from Death Valley) from 1971–1981 and Hanken was his man Friday who, among other duties, would arrange to have the foreign players picked up at LAX and driven 200-plus miles to the small high desert town.

during this summer that the game of chess had become almost an obsession to me. Having learned the game only the year before, I immediately plunged into the icy waters of tournament play only to be battered and beaten about in a rather unpromising manner. However, persistence, at the expense of my graduate work, had brought me to the point where I was becoming an almost competent tournament player.

Perhaps it was the fact that I was a schoolteacher which made it so easy for me to relate to the rather taciturn and closemouthed young Bobby at the time. He was always surrounded by other young players and older chess masters with whom he continually indulged in so-called "rapid transit" or five-minute chess. The stream of New York toned invective which passes back and forth between the players in such matches is familiar to all serious chess buffs, but it was my first introduction to it. "Patzer!" or "Bread" were two of the nicer epithets applied by Fischer to his usually hapless opponents. Bobby's "rapid transit" chess has always been almost superior to his tournament play. His amazing quick insight and fantastic physical responses have placed him in a class by himself in this form of chess as well as tournament play.

At the time, there was very little, other than chess, which I found in common with Bobby. He expressed rather negative feelings about teachers in general, but never went into this in any detail. During this tournament, my first United States Open and Bobby's first major victory in a national chess tournament, the jealousy and rancor which Bobby had aroused in his fellow players was already becoming evident. A strange incident occurred during that tournament which I recall very vividly. Bobby came down to the tournament room one day with a noticeable black eye. He refused to talk about it with anyone, but, later on, I heard that he had been the object of some considerable teasing among his peers. Bobby was being sponsored at Cleveland because of his victory in the United States Junior which came the month before and he was housed with other young players in a special hotel suite. The story was, that one of the young men had been mercilessly annoying Bobby and that, in a fit of rage, Bobby had sunk his teeth into the boy's arm. He refused to let go and the other boy was finally forced to punch him in the eye in order to reclaim his somewhat chewed up arm. [Hanken is referring to an incident that occurred during the 1957 U.S. Open, see pages 37 and 121]. There were no further reports of anyone seriously teasing or bothering Bobby Fischer.

I did not see Bobby again for four years. In that time, there were lots of changes in my life and in his also. I had moved from Ohio to Los Angeles, California, in 1960 and started working for the Los Angeles County probation department as a counselor in one of their probation camps. I had achieved some moderate success in the game of chess, having won the Cincinnati Championship in 1959 and having scored some victories over local masters in Los Angeles in the year that I had been there. I was officially rated as an "expert."

Bobby's success during that time was no less than fantastic. He had qualified to play in the Candidate's tournament to determine the challenger for the World Championship, and was awarded the grandmaster title at the age of fifteen. He had won the United States Championship three times during that period and was then the youngest grandmaster in the world. In the same way that Bobby's genius had flowered over the chessboard, his personality seemed to have grown and broadened also.

The occasion of our meeting again was the now famous Fischer–Reshevsky match which ended in such a fiasco here in Los Angeles. I renewed our acquaintance as soon as he came to town and I was struck by both physical and personality changes he had undergone over the past four years. Bobby was now a tall, thin, almost gangly young man, who was rather expansive in his manner of expressing himself. He had the same New York brashness, but seemed to have lost a lot of the shyness and reticence which characterized his discussions of anything outside of chess. It is true that Bobby had dropped out of High School in his sophomore year and he freely stated that he did so because he felt that the Public School System had nothing to offer him. He was a professional chess player and knew that this was to be his life's work. Many people who met Bobby casually at chess tournaments or became acquainted with him in business situations came away with the feeling that his concerns were limited to chess and money. However, at this stage in Bobby's life, he had other interests. When a subject appealed to him, he plunged into it with the same fanaticism and single-mindedness with which he approached the game of chess itself. Bobby was fascinated by gangsters. He read everything that he could get his hands on about Dillinger, Baby Face Nelson, Ma Barker, and the FBI. His admiration was equally distributed among the good guys and the bad guys. What Bobby really admired was power, the naked force that allows one person to dominate another. He was, of course, preoccupied with this concept at the time because he was trying to dominate the older, established Grandmaster Reshevsky and establish himself as the lone star on the American chess horizon. He often talked of Reshevsky in the gangland terms which he learned in his reading of what might be called "American Social History" of the '20s and '30s. He thought of a victory on the chessboard as a "hit" in the classic gangster sense.

Another interest which Bobby had at the time was palmistry. He had done some rather extensive reading in this area and prided himself on being able to trace a lifeline. This was, perhaps, a foreshadowing of his later total involvement in fundamentalist Christian religion. On the lighter side, Bobby loved to sing. When he felt good, he would burst forth with a chorus of "Tonight" from *Westside Story*. He told me that Vassily Smyslov, the former World Champion chess player, who was also a professional opera singer, has complimented him on his voice and told him that it had promise. I must be forgiven for always having felt that Smyslov was putting Bobby on a bit.

Bobby's knowledge and interest in poetry were limited to the narrative variety. However, he could quote almost the entire length of Robert Service's "Shooting of Dan McGrew" and very much enjoyed listening to my rendition of Service's other famous pot boiler, which I had memorized when I was in High School, "The Cremation of Sam McGee."

We went to a couple of movies and a play together. I don't recall the movies, but I do remember the play was Jean Genet's *The Balcony* which is a rather satirical approach to politics and kinky sex. Bobby's reaction to this play was blunt. He didn't understand it. In fact, he considered it a waste of time and very dull. None of the raucous gross humor of the play seemed to touch him at all. His taste in movies ran more to the action adventure genre.

He was also very interested in the whole correction system and prevailed upon me to introduce him to some, what he called "inmates." He had given some simultaneous exhibitions in the East at real prisons. [Bobby gave an exhibition at Riker's Island in 1960.] I took him to the probation camp where I worked and he was gracious and highly instructive with the court wards who were placed in the camp. He showed honest compassion toward them and he also showed a great flare for showmanship in presenting some games and instruction. During these times, Bobby's good humor was infectious. But as the tension grew in the match with Reshevsky and Bobby unable to gain any substantial advantage over the older grandmaster, he because less easygoing and displayed occasional outbursts of temper.

Every now and then, I was able to talk Bobby into playing a few offhand games. He spotted me one minute to five on the clock and beat me every time. It was obvious that he did not really want to play with someone whose strength was so much lower, so I seldom asked him. He did, on occasion, show me games which he had played in recent years in which he took some pride. Of course I understood that Bobby was an exceptional chess player. However, the occasion when it first dawned upon me that Bobby was something more than just a really outstanding player, but a chess phenomenon, stands out very vividly in my mind. I had won a game in a local match which was published in the *Los Angeles Times* chess column. The game went something like twenty-six moves and, as it is seldom that I have games published, I was somewhat proud of the achievement. I showed the paper to Bobby and pointed out the game, at the same time asking if he would play it over and give me his comments. He picked up the newspaper, glanced at it for approximately ten seconds, handed it back to me with a kind of casual offhand "Yeah, good game." I was rather hurt. I presumed that he was just putting me off and was really not interested. So I said, "Come on Bobby, just take a few minutes and play it over." He didn't say another word, but took out his wallet chess set, which he carried everywhere he went, and began moving the pieces into the original positions. Then, more swiftly than my eyes could follow and without again even glancing at the paper, he ran through the moves of the game, pausing briefly at the twenty-second move to demonstrate a quicker way to win. He then put away his pocket set. At that moment I really felt that I was in the presence of a true genius.

It was during this time that I became aware of a somewhat odd quirk of mind which, in later years, emerged as the characteristic which made communication with Bobby so difficult and misunderstanding so easy. He has a mental tenacity, and a stubborn refusal to confront some aspects of reality. The following story is an illustration. Until Bobby was sixteen, he had been a notoriously sloppy dresser. He often wore old clothing, rather shaggy pullovers, blue jeans, and tennis shoes, and could by no stretch of the imagination be classed as a sharp dresser. Sometime around his sixteenth birthday, as is true with many adolescents, he did a complete about face. By the time I met him again in 1961, he might be called a real fashion plate. He often bragged of his expensive shoes and was careful to point out that his shirts were made by the same tailors who did custom service for President John Kennedy. His suits were always pressed and he would never be seen in public without a tie.

I have never been much of a dresser myself, suffering from chronic obesity which leads me to favor rather baggy, comfortable clothing. In the days when it was necessary to wear a tie on my job, I often loosened the top button of my shirt. Bobby was politely critical of my mode of dress and constantly urged me to take more pride in my appearance. On one occasion I pointed out to him that he had not always been such a careful and fastidious dresser himself. As soon as I made this remark, a veil seemed to descend over his eyes. "No," he said, "I always dressed good." I was of a particular perverse frame of mind at the time so I dug out an old *Chess Review* magazine which had a picture of him at the Interzonal tournament in 1958. He was wearing a sloppy white long-sleeved pullover which was somewhat baggy at the elbows and a pair of blue jeans. He glanced at the picture, gave a slight wave of his right hand,

and dismissed this totally damaging evidence as if it did not exist. I could almost see his mind closing to the reality of the picture. It did not fit in with his present self-image and, therefore, it did not exist. [This observation is right on the money. Consider Fischer's later antisemitic remarks and failure to acknowledge that the *Protocols of the Elders of Zion* is completely made-up.]

Bobby was only eighteen years old at the time, but the patterns of his life seemed already set. His attitude toward other human beings was dominated by his obsessive involvement with chess. To Bobby, at that time, women were "patzers." He stated, more than once, that he could easily give knight odds to any woman in the world and beat her at chess. It never seemed to occur to Bobby to think of women in any other terms. For that matter, he never thought of anyone in any real terms. Money and power had great meaning to Bobby, but they were rather intricately interwoven with the game of chess itself. Chess, at its root, is a power struggle between two human minds. I had a German friend who used to refer to it as "ritual murder." I think that Bobby always understood chess in these terms. Grandmaster Reuben Fine, who is also a psychoanalyst, once wrote a fascinating treatise in which he theorized the game of chess as a complete working out of the traditional Oedipal situation.

Except for his rather expensive taste in clothes, which I am told he still retains to some extent to this day, Bobby's concern with money can also be seen as the other side of the power coin. In most ways, Bobby lives like Ralph Nader. Money has always been symbolic, in that it represented power over other people in the way that chess strength does.

In reading about the problems which Bobby caused in the present World Championship match, I had a déjà vu feeling. As the match between Fischer and Reshevsky progressed, it became obvious that Bobby was doing battle, not only with Reshevsky, but also with himself. He made several nervous mistakes, allowing a win to get away during an adjournment at one time and blundering in another game. He began to complain about the lighting and the noise of the crowd. He seemed to be building up a very personal resentment toward Reshevsky. He referred to him in rather derogatory terms and showed open hostility on at least one occasion when he agreed to a draw by shoving all of the pieces toward the center of the board in a gesture of disgust and contempt. [This stands in sharp contrast to the almost universal view that while Fischer's behavior away from the board might have been less than perfect, he was always a gentleman while playing.]

When the time for the start of the twelfth game was changed a week ahead of time, from two o'clock to eleven o'clock, Bobby became very stubborn and, despite attempts at persuasion on the part of various people, he refused to play. Very much like the situation in Reykjavík in the second game, Bobby was duly forfeited. He protested the forfeit which would have given Reshevsky a one point lead in the match at the time, and refused to play until the forfeit was removed. This the local match committee refused to consider and the match ended in a true fiasco with lawsuits and counter suits. After the second game of the World Championship this year, I was convinced that the same course would be followed. Of course, I was delighted when Bobby did agree to play, even with the forfeit, which seems to show that he is less inflexible than he was eleven years ago.

Bobby left town rather hastily after the end of the match and I did not see him again until the Piatigorsky Cup tournament of 1966. We had dinner together on one occasion early in the tournament, but I did not feel very comfortable with him, nor it seems did he with me. In that five years, he seemed to have closed in upon himself. The volatility and occasional raucous good humor did not seem to be there. The suspicion and paranoia had grown significantly. He had his good moments. Once we were able to prevail upon him to come to the backroom where we local experts attempted to analyze the games as they were in progress. He had won a particularly neat game against the Hungarian Grandmaster Portisch and, in demonstrating the game and discussing it, he showed a little of what I recall as his flair for showmanship. However, the crowd seemed to intimidate him and he left as quickly as he could after the presentation. It may be recalled that Fischer had a very bad start in that tournament and made a miraculous recovery by which he almost caught Boris Spassky in the last round but fell a point short.

To most expert chess players, Bobby Fischer's genius at the chessboard has never been surpassed or even equaled in the history of the royal game. His achievements are overwhelming. Whether he can gain enough control over his own emotions to meet the responsibility of his vast and awesome talent is a moot point at the time of this writing. Bobby is the best player in the World. He should be World Champion.

6

"THERE WAS OPEN COLLUSION."

CURAÇAO 1962

Fischer's result at the 1962 Stockholm Interzonal—an undefeated 2½ points ahead of the field at the age of only eighteen—started talk of Bobby as a potential World Champion and to this day is still a performance to be remembered. Coming on the heels of his second-place result at Bled, it meant he had racked up forty-one consecutive games without a loss against some of the best players in the world. The only caveat about Bobby's performance in Stockholm was that he beat only two players among the top ten finishers (by contrast Geller was plus four) and achieved his huge score by defeating players who would not be playing in the upcoming Candidates tournament. This was the first time a non-Soviet player had won an Interzonal. *Chess Review*[1] reported:

> According to our correspondent Zandor Nilsson, Bobby made a great hit in Sweden in TV and radio appearances, in feature articles, and he was applauded by Nilsson for quiet, modest, and sportsmanlike conduct throughout the tournament.

Fischer's accusations that the Soviet players cheated at the 1962 Candidates tournament are widely known. Fischer aired those accusations in *Sports Illustrated*[2] soon after the Curaçao tournament ended. Fischer wrote:

> Russian control of chess has reached a point where there can be no honest competition for the World Championship...anything I say about Russian dominance...is bound to look like an alibi for not having beaten the Russians in the Curaçao tournament...
>
> Well I know better. And if these reasons sound like sour grapes, I hope a statement of the facts will change the impression... At Curaçao it was flagrant. There was open collusion between the Russian players. They agreed ahead of time to draw the games they played against each other. Each time they drew they gave each other half a point... They consulted during the games, and

[1] *Chess Review*, April 1962, (p. 104).

[2] Bobby Fischer, *Sports Illustrated*, August 20 1962, "The Russians Have Fixed World Chess," (pp. 18–19, 64–65).

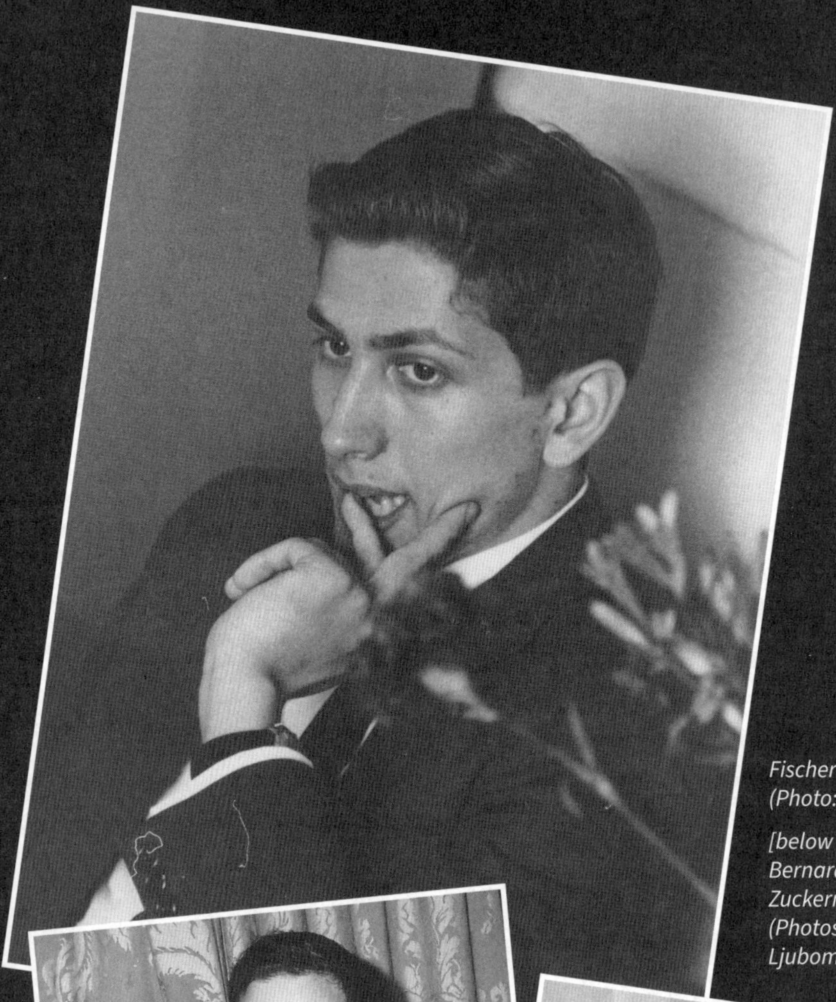

Fischer at Curaçao, 1962 (Photo: Dr. Richard Cantwell);

[below clockwise from left] Bernard “Zook the Book” Zuckerman; Pal Benko 1965 (Photos: Beth Cassidy); Ljubomir Ljubojević.

> commented on my moves in my hearing. Then they ridiculed my protests to officials. They worked as a team. …

It's true Petrosian, Keres, and Geller drew all twelve games they played against each other in an average of nineteen moves, but whether prearranging a draw is cheating is a question best left to debate. However, it's a moot point, because it wouldn't have been an effective strategy against Bobby if he had gotten off to a good start.

The Soviet players certainly did not throw a game in Curaçao—neither, of course, did Bobby. But Bernard Zuckerman pointed out that those with suspicious minds might have wondered about one of Bobby's games:[1]

> I wasn't there, but of course what is best remembered is Bobby's claim that the Soviet players made prearranged draws. What is a bit strange is that after losing to Benko in the first round of Curaçao Bobby complained "you ruined my chances" implying that Benko was not supposed to beat him. Later, in round twenty-two, Bobby won against Benko in a position in which he could have resigned for many moves. Not a dumped game of course, and one which is easily explained by Benko's chronic time pressure, but the Soviets could have said it looked suspicious.

(37) French
Fischer – Pal Benko
Curaçao (22) 1962

1.e4 e6 2.d4 d5 3.Nc3 Nf6 4.e5 Nfd7 5.f4 c5 6.dxc5 Bxc5 7.Qg4 0–0 8.Bd3 f5 9.Qh3 Bxg1 10.Rxg1 Nc5 11.Bd2 Nc6 12.Nb5 Qb6 13.0–0–0 Bd7 14.Nd6 Na4 15.Bb5 Nd4 16.Be3 Ne2+

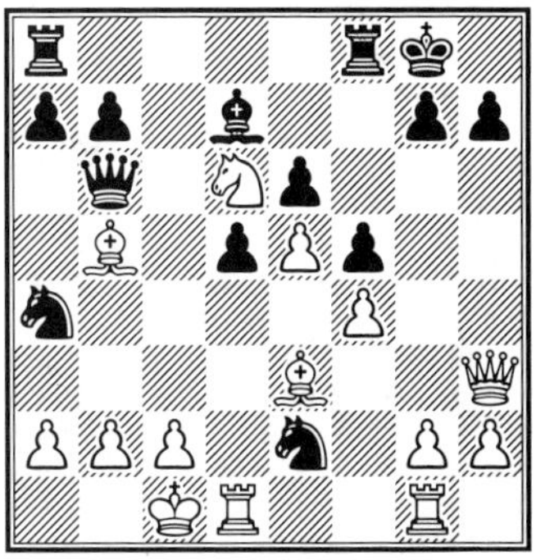

17.Bxe2??

This should lose on the spot. 17.Kb1 d4 18.Bxa4 Bxa4 19.Bf2 Nxg1 20.Bxg1 Qa6 21.Bxd4 Qe2 22.Rc1 Bc6 leaves Black with only a small advantage.

[1] From an interview Zuckerman gave to the World Chess Hall of Fame in 2014.

Robert Fischer

Here the author must be careful, otherwise the superlatives might roll like marbles from the stairs. Let's begin at the "beginning". A beginning which scores of very great men never reach. At the age of 14 champion of the U.S.A. Please realize that then grandmasters as Reshevsky, Evans and Byrnes also lived in the U.S.A. and please remember that a 15-year-old in Portoroz 1958 obtained admission to the Candidates' Tournament 1959 before Bronstein, Szabo, Pachman and Panno, with "en passant" the title of grandmaster to his credit. After that - for instance winner of the Interzonal Tournament Stockholm 1962 without one game lost, before Petrosyan, Geller, Kortchnoi, Filip, Stein, Benko and Gligoric. In the "Losbladige Schaakberichten" the well-known theoretical periodical by Dr. Euwe, they speak about the "American Giant" these days. One can certainly stick to this appellation, for Bobby (Robert James according to his birth-certificate) is a giant, a super-giant.

Now he is 19 and more than mature as a chess artist. Maybe this maturity was the most amazing of his achievements in Stockholm. No fireworks on h7 like many "young talents" are apt to demonstrate, no, a certainty, a vision, a patience and a technique for the end game like Rubinstein, like Lasker, like Smyslov, like . . . . you go on.

With this youth all styles, all positions, all emotions are collected in one master's hand. The experts of modern chess predict a growth until the 45th year; on the other hand we find the idea: playing very strong chess is learned young and quickly. As one does not exclude the other we might stop "gazing the crystal". Bobby Fischer will come far, still farther than now. Maybe he becomes worldchampion, now or later, in ten years. Nobody need be surprised.

Birth date: March 9, 1943 - Place: Chicago.

Fischer's page from the Curaçao 1962 program.

Fischer being interviewed by Lars-Gunnar Björklund for Swedish radio, 1962.

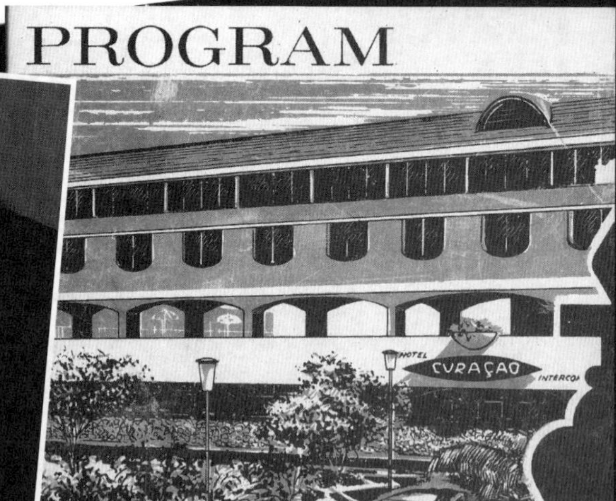

17...Qxb2+ 18.Kd2 Qb4+ 19.Kc1

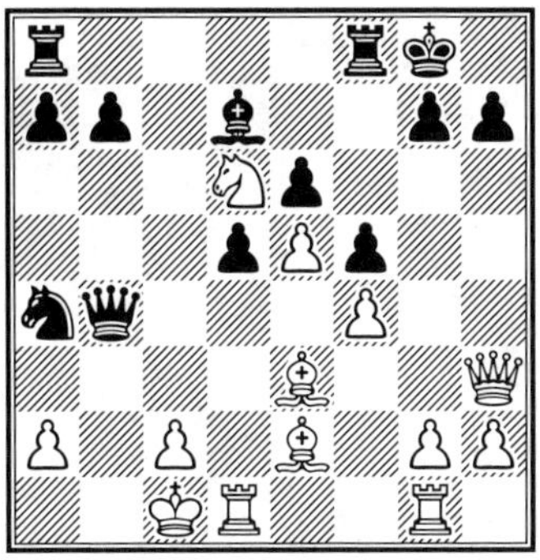

19...Nc3! 20.Rde1 Nxa2+ 21.Kd1 Nc3+ 22.Kc1 d4 23.Bf2 Rfc8

23...Rac8 is a little more precise because in some lines it is helpful to have f7 defended.

24.Bd3

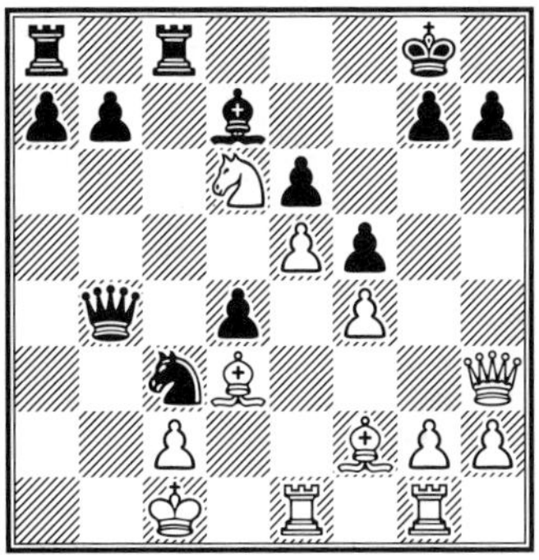

24...Na2+

24...Ba4 25.Nxc8 Rxc8 26.Bh4 Nd5 27.Qf3 Qa3+ 28.Kd2 Bxc2 29.Bxc2 Rxc2+ 30.Kxc2 d3+ 31.Kd2 Qb2+ 32.Kd1 Qc2 mate; 24...Rc5 intending ...Ra5 was another clear-cut win.

25.Kd1 Nc3+

Black was still winning, albeit in a more complicated fashion with 25...Ba4 26.Ke2 Bxc2 27.g4 (27.Bxc2 Rxc2+ 28.Kf1) 27...Rc3 28.Rg3 Bxd3+ 29.Rxd3 Nc1+ 30.Rxc1 Qb2+ 31.Rd2 Qxc1 32.Qg2 d3+ 33.Rxd3 Rc2+ 34.Kf3 Qb1 35.Qh3 (35.gxf5 Rxf2+ 36.Kxf2 Qc2+) 35...Qa2 36.Bg1 Qa6 37.Qf1 Rc3 38.Ke3 fxg4 winning. The text should also bring Black victory.

26.Kc1 Rc5

Or 26...Ba4.

27.Qh4 Ra5

27...Ba4 was still strong.

[top] Tal and Benko (Photo: Dr. Richard Cantwell).;

[middle] Bobby visits Tal in the hospital during the Curaçao tournament. Tal withdrew after round 21 due to illiness (Photo: Dr. Richard Cantwell);

[bottom] (left foreground) Tigran Petrosian, (standing left to right) Nathan Divinsky, Unknown, Yefim Geller, Mikhail Tal, and (looking over Tal's shoulder) Pal Benko.

28.Kd2

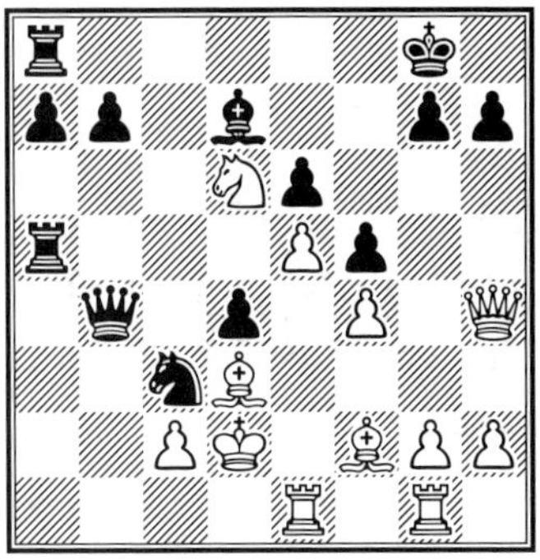

28...h6??

28...Ra3! Wins quickly, e.g., 29.g4 (29.Nc4 Ne4+ 30 Ke2 Rc3!) 29...Ne4+ 30.Ke2 Rxd3! 31.cxd3 Qd2+ 32.Kf3 Qxd3+ 33.Kg2 Nxd6 34.exd6 Bc6+.

29.g4!

The tables have turned. Fischer doesn't hesitate to grab his chance and takes the point.

29...fxg4

29...Ne4+ 30.Ke2 Qd2+ 31.Kf1 and the attack has ended or 29...Nd5+ 30.Ke2 Nxf4+ 31.Kf1 Nxd3 32.gxf5 Nxe1 33.Rxg7+ with mate soon to follow.

30.Rxg4 Kh8

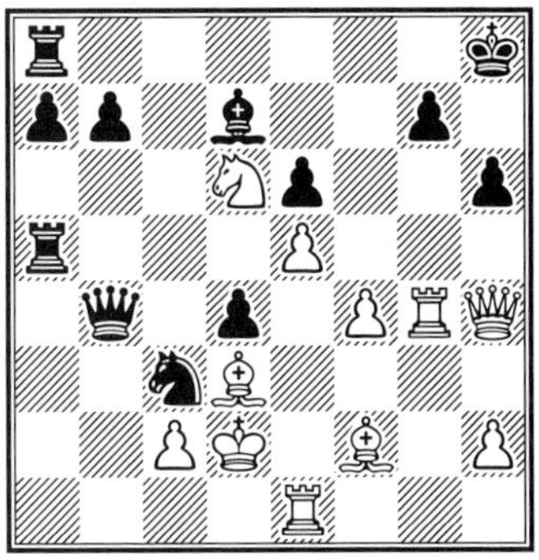

31.Qxh6+!, 1–0.

Zuckerman continues on his theme and draws attention to Game (38):

> The Soviets did make noise when Bobby beat James Sherwin in the 1958 Interzonal winning a completely drawn rook and pawn ending when the defender failed to use the frontal defense in a rook and pawn versus rook ending. I remember Ljubojević also failed to defend this ending against Ehlvest (Rotterdam 1989).

(38) Ruy Lopez
Fischer – James Sherwin
Portorož (14) 1958

1.e4 e5 2.Nf3 Nc6 3.Bb5 a6 4.Ba4 Nf6 5.0–0 Be7 6.Re1 b5 7.Bb3 d6 8.c3 0–0 9.h3 a5 10.d3 Bb7 11.Nbd2 a4 12.Bc2 Nb8 13.Nf1 c5 14.d4 cxd4 15.cxd4 Nc6 16.Ng3 g6 17.Bd2 Re8 18.d5 Na5 19.b3 Bc8 20.bxa4 bxa4 21.Bxa4 Bd7 22.Bxd7 Nxd7

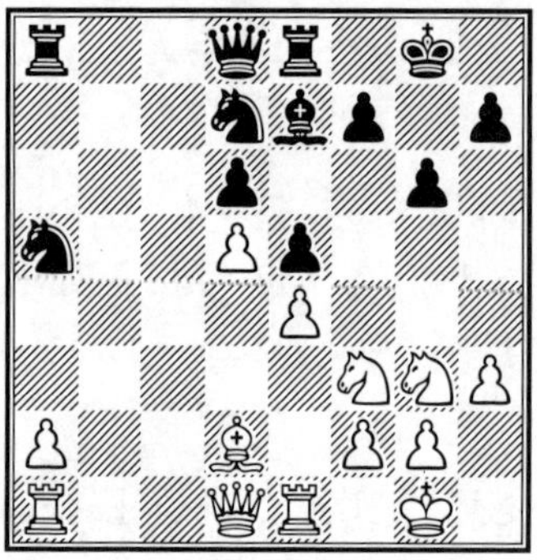

Black has some compensation for the pawn.

23.Bb4 Qb6 24.a3 Nc5 25.Qe2 Reb8 26.Nd2 Nab3 27.Nxb3 Nxb3 28.Rab1 Nd4 29.Qd3 Qa6 30.Qxa6 Rxa6 31.Rb2

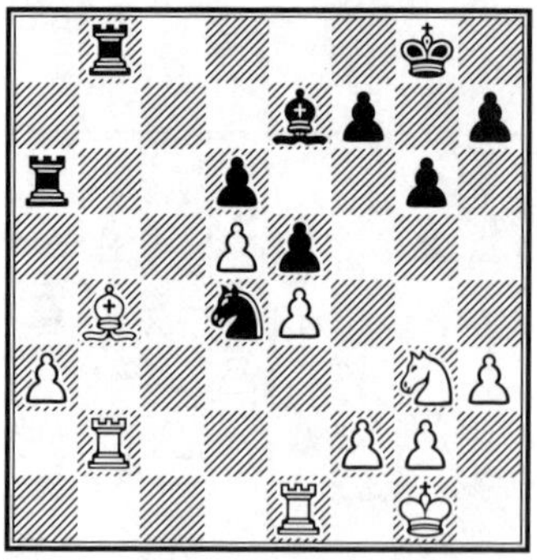

31...Rba8 32.Ra1 Ra4 33.Nf1 Nb5 34.Bd2 Rxa3 35.Rxa3 Nxa3 36.Rb7 Kf8 37.Ne3 Rc8 38.f3 h5 39.Bb4 Nc2

39...Rc1+ 40.Kf2 Rb1 would have avoided the difficult pawn down ending that ensues.

40.Nxc2 Rxc2 41.Rb6 Ke8 42.Bxd6 Bxd6 43.Rxd6 h4 44.Ra6 Rc1+ 45.Kh2 g5 46.Ra2 Rf1 47.Ra6 Rd1 48.Rb6 Ke7 49.Rb2

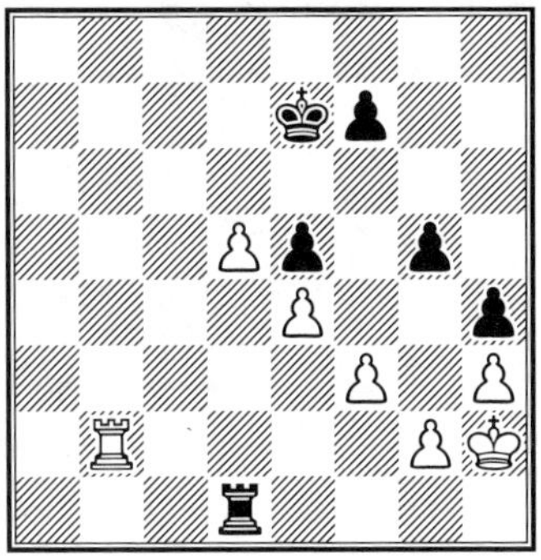

49...Rf1 50.Rb3 Rd1 51.g4 Rd2+ 52.Kg1 Rd1+ 53.Kf2 Rd2+ 54.Ke3 Rh2 55.Rb7+ Kf6 56.Rb6+ Ke7 57.Rb7+ Kf6 58.Rb6+ Ke7 59.Rh6 Rxh3

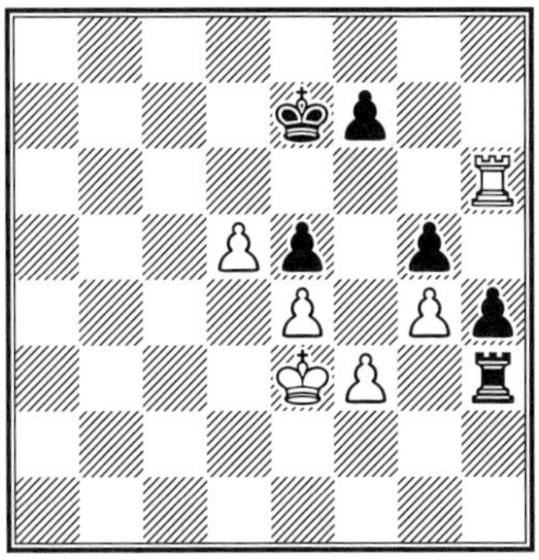

60.d6+ Kd7 61.Rf6 Rh2 62.Rxf7+ Kxd6 63.Rf6+ Ke7 64.Rg6 h3 65.Rxg5 Ke6 66.Rh5 Kf6 67.Kd3 Kg6 68.Rh8 Kg7

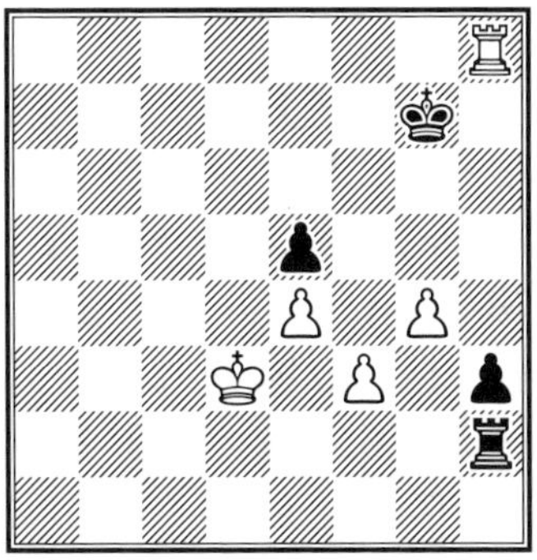

69.Rh4 Kg6 70.Rh5 Kf6 71.Ke3 Ke6 72.f4 exf4+ 73.Kxf4 Rh1 74.Kg3 Re1 75.Kxh3 Rxe4 76.Rf5 Ra4 77.Rf8 Ke7 78.Rf3

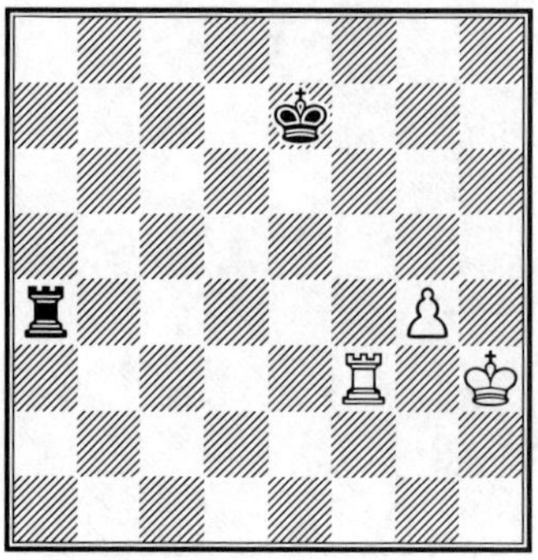

78...Ke6⁇

Frontal defense is the saving grace when the defender's king is cut off and the side with the extra pawn has not advanced their king and pawn past the fourth rank. 78...Ra8 79.Kh4 Rh8+ 80.Kg5 Rg8+ 81.Kh5 Rh8+ 82.Kg6 Rg8+ with a draw.

Sherwin knew this of course, but after a long and tiring defense it's not uncommon for even strong players to make inexplicable mistakes.

79.Kh4 Ra8

Too late.

80.g5 Rh8+ 81.Kg4 Ke7 82.g6 Rf8 83.Rf5 Rh8 84.Kg5 Rh1 85.Rf2 Rh3 86.g7 Rg3+ 87.Kh6 Rh3+ 88.Kg6 Rg3+ 89.Kh7 Rh3+ 90.Kg8, 1–0.

(39) French
Jaan Ehlvest – Ljubomir Ljubojević
Rotterdam 1989

1.e4 e6 2.d4 d5 3.Nc3 Be7 4.Bd3 dxe4 5.Nxe4 Nf6 6.Nf3 Bd7 7.0–0 Nxe4 8.Bxe4 Bc6 9.Bd3 Nd7 10.Re1 0–0 11.Bf4 Bd6 12.Ne5 Nxe5 13.dxe5 Bc5 14.Qg4 Qd4 15.Qh4 h6 16.Rad1 g5 17.Bxg5 Qxf2+ 18.Qxf2 Bxf2+ 19.Kxf2 hxg5 20.b4 b5 21.Re3 a5 22.a3 axb4 23.axb4 Ra4 24.Rb1 Kg7 25.Rg3 f6 26.exf6+ Kxf6 27.Ke3 Rh8 28.h3 Rh4 29.Rf1+ Rf4 30.Rxf4+ gxf4+ 31.Kxf4 Rxb4+ 32.Ke3 Bd5 33.Rg8 Kf7 34.Rc8 Bxg2 35.Rxc7+ Kg8 36.Rh7 Bf1 37.Bg6 Rc4 38.h4 Bh3 39.Bd3 Rb4 40.Rh5 Bf5 41.Bxf5 exf5 42.Rxf5 Rxh4 43.Rxb5 Kf7 44.Re5

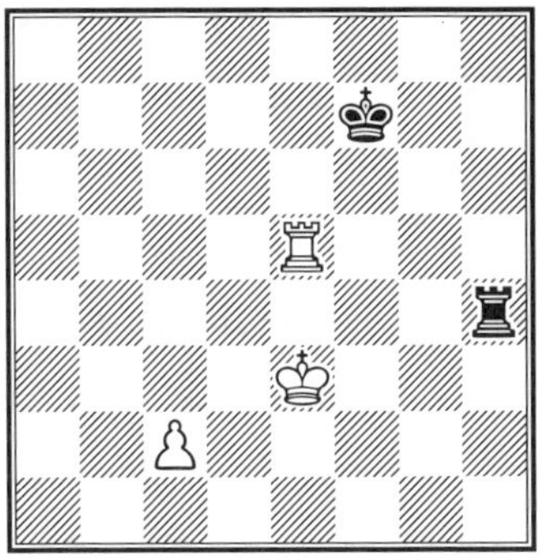

44...Rc4?

44...Rh8! leads to a classical frontal defense draw.

45.Kd3

Now White is winning, aided in part because his pawn is still far back.

45...Rc8 46.c3 Kf6 47.Re3

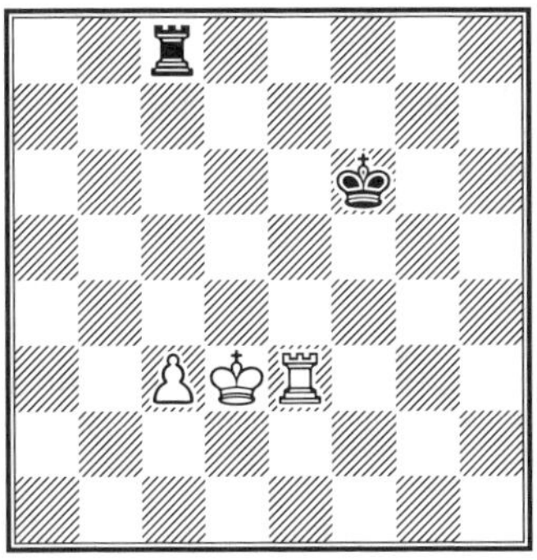

Textbook technique by Ehlvest. Now that the pawn is protected the king can safely approach the enemy rook.

47...Rd8+ 48.Kc2 Kf7 49.Kb3 Rb8+ 50.Kc4 Rc8+ 51.Kb5 Rb8+ 52.Kc6 Rc8+ 53.Kd7 Rc4 54.Kd6 Rc8

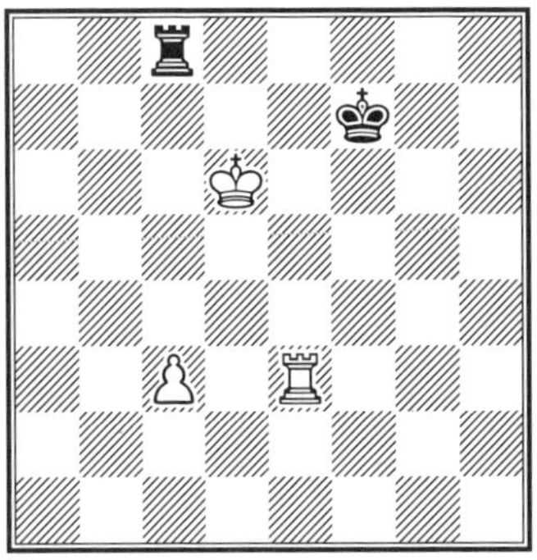

55.Re7+! Kf6 56.Rc7 Rd8+ 57.Kc6 Ke6 58.c4 Ke5 59.c5 Kd4 60.Kb7 Rd5 61.Kb6 Kc4, 1–0.

Black resigned in view of 62.Rh7 Rd3 63.c6.

International Master Bernard Zuckerman, famous for his encyclopedic opening knowledge (hence his nickname "Zook the book" or "Zuckerbook"), as well as his terrific understanding of endgame theory, started the game quite late (not until age fifteen).

[Donaldson]: Can you tell us how you started to play?

[Zuckerman]: Bobby and I were born the same month of the same year (March 1943) although he was a little older being born on the 9th and myself the 31st. Although we were the same age we did not start to play at the same time. Bobby began when he was six but I didn't until I was fifteen. By then he was already U.S. Champion.

[Donaldson]: Did you go to Erasmus Hall High School like Bobby and Raymond Weinstein and frequent the Hawthorne Chess Club?

[Zuckerman]: No, I grew up in a different part of Brooklyn and went to Thomas Jefferson High School. I never went to the Hawthorne Chess Club on Lennox Avenue in Brooklyn. By the time I started playing it had either ended or was about to. I did visit John "Jack" Collins at his new home in Stuyvesant Town in Manhattan. Speaking of Collins, Bobby never referred to him as his coach although he sometimes talked of Carmine Nigro as his teacher.

[Donaldson]: Where did you first start playing and what sort of progress did you make beginning at the late age of fifteen?

[Zuckerman]: I first started playing at the Marshall Chess Club but before joining thought it a good idea to read a few books first. These included Capablanca's *Primer of Chess*, Botvinnik's *One Hundred Selected Games*, and a few Reinfeld books (that even then I understood were not for stronger players). Despite the late start my progress was pretty fast. My first USCF rating, which was published in February 1959, was 1850. By the end of 1965 I was playing in the U.S. Championship where I scored 6½ from 11, tying for fourth place.

INCIDENT WITH BENKO

The incident: Pal Benko hit Bobby Fischer. The dispute was over the services of Arthur Bisguier, whom Benko believed was there to help both Americans participants and not just Fischer. Fortunately, the incident had no lasting effects on the relationship between Bobby and Benko who remained close friends until Fischer's death.

Pal Benko told his side of the story:

> It was at Curaçao that Fischer and I had our one and only altercation, and I've always felt that the USCF was, at least partially to blame...[1]

Benko continued:[2]

> Look, actually it was a misunderstanding. There was this great guy in the Federation, Morris Kasper, who was giving money, as the U.S. government was giving us nothing. But he had money for only one second. He told me, if Fischer has an adjourned game, Bisguier will work with him. But if Bobby doesn't need him, you can use him. That was OK with me, Bobby was the big star. But Kasper didn't tell Bobby about this arrangement. So the tournament starts. I beat Fischer, Tal, and I am in first place after the first leg and I have an adjourned game with Petrosian. And I ask Bisguier, come on let's analyze my game.
>
> "No!" Bobby said, "I forbid it. No way Bisguier is going to help you."
>
> I called him a selfish pig and he said some nasty things to me. And I told him, don't repeat that, but he repeated it and I hit him. The next day I regretted it and from that moment onwards I could not play against him anymore. I knew that he was mentally ill and I should not have hit him.

Fischer sent a letter to the tournament committee in Curaçao asking (in vain) that Pal Benko be expelled from the tournament:

> May 10, 1962
>
> To the tournament committee of the 1962 Curaçao Candidates tournament.
>
> This is an official protest of the behavior of Pal Benko on the night of May 9, a little before midnight, Benko entered my room without my permission. He had followed Bisguier in. I immediately asked him to leave and he refused. I repeatedly asked him to leave and he refused each time. He became angry when I refused to allow my second, Arthur Bisguier, to help him (Benko) analyze his adjournment with Petrosian. He insulted me and when I answered him he struck me while I was seated in a chair. I did not strike him back. Then he finally left the room.
>
> I suggest that Benko be fined and/or expelled from the tournament.
>
> The above episode was witnessed by Arthur Bisguier.
>
> Respectfully,
>
> Robert Fischer

1 Pal Benko and Jeremy Silman, *Pal Benko: My Life, Games, and Compositions*. Los Angeles: Siles Press, 2003, (p. 127).

2 *New In Chess*, 2016 #2, (p. 58).

[above] Fischer, Bay City 1963;

[left] The historic Wenonah Hotel, site of the 1963 Western Open. The hotel was closed after a horrible fire in 1977 which claimed ten lives.

7
GOODBYE TO THE SWISS

WESTERN OPEN (1963)

Bay City, Michigan, located near the base of Saginaw Bay on Lake Huron—about a two-hour drive from Detroit on Interstate 7—was a popular summer resort town and a fine setting for the Western Open, a strong tournament which was held at the historic Wenonah Hotel.

The Western Open featured a prize fund of $2,500 and attracted 161 players (which was outstanding for the time). Remarkably, the same weekend, the Eastern Open in Washington, D.C. smashed the American tournament attendance record with 224 players. This topped the previous record of 197 set by the 1961 U.S. Open in San Francisco. The new figure did not last long as a month later in Chicago the 1963 U.S. Open, with no competing tournaments, had 266 participants

Master Richard Verber, one of the giants of Chicago chess, marked the 1963 U.S. Open as the beginning of a new era for chess in the Windy City. Previously, Chicago had played second fiddle in the Midwest to Milwaukee. Though significantly smaller in population than Chicago, Wisconsin's largest city held many important tournaments and produced a number of prominent figures who played an important role in the history of U.S. chess This list includes Arpad Elo, Fred Cramer, Pearl Mann, and Ernest Olfe. Mann and Olfe were well-known tournament directors and officiated in Bay City.

The 1963 Western Open was the next-to-last Swiss system tournament Bobby ever played in. The New York State Open, held shortly after over the Labor Day weekend, was his last—from then on it was only round-robin or match events. The truth was that Bobby was close to outgrowing United States tournaments altogether as he was already head and shoulders above other American players.

Bobby was the overwhelming favorite to win the Western Open, but there was competition for him in the Byrne brothers, Arthur Bisguier, and Hans Berliner, not to mention many national masters looking for a chance to collect the scalp of the five-time U.S. Champion.

Bobby hadn't played in a Swiss system tournament since Thanksgiving weekend 1957 (North Central Open in Milwaukee). In short events there's always the risk one mistake can prove fatal in the battle for first place, and this is likely the reason Bobby stopped playing in the U.S. Championship after collecting his eighth title in eight tries in the 1966/67 tournament. He had a close call in the 1965/66 event when he lost consecutive games to Robert Byrne and Sammy Reshevsky near the end and felt that a longer tournament, ideally twenty-two rounds like the Soviet Championship, was the solution to ensure the best player won. Keep in mind that Bobby lost only a total of three games in eight U.S. Championships—the third was to Edmar Mednis.

Apparently, Bobby had no doubts he would win the Western Open, despite there being only eight rounds to separate the 161 player field. When he was nicked for a draw in round four by Michigan master Paul Poschel (=2nd in the 1960 U.S. Open with Pal Benko), Bobby found himself in a tough battle for first, resolved only when he defeated Hans Berliner in the last round with Black. His final score of 7½ from 8 put him a half a point ahead of Robert Byrne and Stephan Popel, both of whom had the good fortune of not playing the winner.

Bobby took home $750 ($6,400 in 2020 dollars) for his first place finish and appeared to have thoroughly enjoyed the event. *Chess Life* editor J.F. Reinhardt, who played in the tournament, wrote about the rare tournament appearance by Bobby outside New York City:[1]

> Fischer, whose very appearance at the tournament caused a sensation, was, not unexpectedly, the center of attention. Playing with extraordinary rapidity, he won some of his games while other, more pedestrian, competitors were still completing their opening moves. In addition to playing two rounds of tournament chess a day, the youthful champion signed countless autographs, indulged in five-minute games until all hours of the night, and offered free (and sometimes bewildering) advice to wood-pushers bogged down in postmortems. In a gracious speech at the awards banquet following the tournament, Fischer expressed himself as quite pleased with the tournament conditions, saying that the lighting and conditions of play were superior to many of the international tournaments in which he has competed.

Fischer commented about his opposition in Bay City in the September 1963 issue of *Chess Life*—this was only a year after Curaçao and Bobby was still having a war of words with the Soviets:

> The players at the Open were surprisingly strong. I was expecting twenty move-crushers, but it didn't happen. In fact, the opposition was keen enough that I consider five or six of eight of my games played there to be superior

[1] *Chess Life*, July–August 1963, (p. 163).

to any games played in the Piatigorsky Tournament, with the exception of Najdorf's win over Keres.

Many familiar, if not famous, names can be found in the Bay City crosstable. The list of strong players included many European masters who settled in the Midwest after World War II. These immigrants proved to be a tremendous stimulus for chess in the American heartland, raising the level of play immensely.

Among those playing in Bay City from the Baltic States were:

Leonids Dreibergs (Saginaw). Latvian master who finished sixth at Riga 1930 and ninth at Kemeri 1939. He later won the Michigan Championship twice (1954 and 1955).

Andrew Karklins (Chicago). The child of Latvians, but born in Germany in 1947, Karklins was still on his way up in 1963 and wouldn't become a master until four years later. He competed in the 1973 and 1974 U.S. Championships and wrote the excellent book *Modern Grandmaster Chess*[1] about the 1964 Soviet Zonal. Karklins' father Erik played strong expert level chess into his late 90s.

Kazys Skema (Michigan). After World War II this Lithuanian master played in many tournaments in Germany with fellow displaced chessplayers. He came to the United States in the early 1950s, his first home being in Massachusetts, later settling in Michigan where he won the 1962 state championship. Skema spent the last years of his life near Harrisburg, Pennsylvania where he died in 1991.

Povilas Tautvaisas (Chicago) was another Lithuanian master who played twice for his country in chess Olympiads. He was one of the best Illinois players of the '50s and '60s. Tautvaisas was a devotee of aggressive play, particularly his favorite Schliemann variation (3...f5) and deferred Schliemann (3...a6 4.Ba4 f5) against the Ruy Lopez.

Arguably the strongest of the foreign-born players was Ivan Theodorovich. Born in Ukraine as Ivan Suk, he immigrated to Toronto, Canada in 1949 and changed his name to Theodorovich sometime in the mid-50s—International Master Lawrence Day, who also lived in Toronto, believed one reason for the name change was that the Ukrainian got tired of having his name pronounced "suck." Rated over 2400 USCF in the 1950s, he was the winner of the 1964 New York State Championship (along with a young Duncan Suttles), and four-time Ontario champion (1955, 1960, 1964, 1968). Theodorovich, who was an early pioneer of the Kalashnikov variation (1.e4 c5 2.Nf3 Nc6 3.d4 cxd4 4.Nxd4 e5 5.Ndb5 d6), is remembered by Toronto players as an optimist who believed, "There is always a move."

1 Andrew Karklins, *Modern Grandmaster Chess: As Exemplified in the 1964 USSR Zonal Tournament*. Chicago: Chicago Chess Books, 1974.

There was also plenty of native-born talent:

Future International Master Edward Formanek was only twenty-one when the 1963 Western Open was held, but already a strong player. Formanek is associated with Pennsylvania (where he was a math professor at Penn State for many years), but originally from Illinois where he lived until he went to Houston in the mid-1960s to study for his doctorate at Rice University. Today he lives in retirement in Las Vegas and continues to play in tournaments.

William "Bill" Bills was one of the best players in Texas in the 1950s and 1960s (state champion in 1954 and 1959) before moving to San Francisco in the late 1960s.

Joseph Pundy (Chicago), Richard Verber (Chicago), Angelo Sandrin (Chicago), Kajeta Czerniecki (Chicago), Erich Marchand (Rochester), Ronald Finegold (Michigan), Morrie Weidenbaum (Detroit), Thomas Wozney (Cleveland), Richard Kause (Cleveland), Charles Weldon (Milwaukee), and Mitchell Saltzberg (New York) were all rated masters when they played in Bay City.

Another master who competed was Paul Poschel (1929–2017) of Ann Arbor Michigan, the only player to take a half point from Bobby in Bay City, and in so doing, stopped what could have been the greatest winning streak in chess history. Fischer had two near record consecutive win series in his career. The second, and better known one, started at the end of the Palma Interzonal and continued through several Candidates matches until Tigran Petrosian ended it. That was nineteen games (twenty if you count the forfeit win over Panno), and remarkable in that almost all Fischer's victims were world class players.

The second and lesser known streak began after the draw with Poschel and included the last four rounds of the 1963 Western Open, the 7–0 score in the New York State Open, and 11–0 result in the 1963/64 U.S. Championship plus the first two rounds of the Capablanca Memorial, where it ended with the draw to Ciocâltea. Throw out the draw with Poschel and the streak extends another four games to twenty-eight (the last round win against Bisguier in the 1962/63 U.S. Championship and the first three rounds of the Western Open), enough to break the all-time consecutive win record of twenty-five set by Wilhelm Steinitz.

Paul Poschel was born in New York in 1929, but at some point in his formative years his family moved to Chicago. He first made a name for himself by winning the 1945 Illinois Junior Championship, and the same year he and his father played in the U.S. Open in Peoria. A few years later he finished thirteenth out of twenty in the U.S. Championship in South Fallsburg, New York, and in 1949 was =4th in the U.S. Open in Omaha.

During the 1950s Poschel got married and received a PhD in Psychology from the University of Illinois. This left him little time for chess until he moved to Michigan, first living in Royal Oak and by 1960 in Ann Arbor. That year he had a performance that put him on the map big time—a share of second place in the 1960 U.S. Open with Pal Benko behind Robert Byrne, but ahead of Larry Evans, Arthur Bisguier, Raymond Weinstein, James Sherwin, Anthony Saidy, and Robert Steinmeyer. This outstanding tournament raised his rating from 2252 to 2318, putting Poschel in the top twenty-five players in the country, but he never had the opportunity to realize his full potential as a player. His job as a research psychologist and family responsibilities limited his opportunities for playing outside Michigan. Instead he played locally and was recognized as one of the best players in his adopted home state for three decades.

The many strong players who competed in Bay City were joined by U.S. Chess Federation administrators Fred Cramer and Donald Schultz, as well as *Chess Life* editor and USCF business manager Joe Reinhardt and his right-hand man David Daniels. Cramer is remembered for his role in helping Bobby Fischer on his road to the World Championship, and Schultz was a key player in the USCF and FIDE for over thirty years.

Reinhardt and Daniels worked in the USCF office when it was located at 80 East 11th St. in New York City. This was at a time when the organization was just beginning to recover from the deficits it ran in the 1950s. Money was tight, but despite limited resources the two did excellent work during a period in which the USCF experienced steady growth.

David Daniels was a member of the Brooklyn College Team that won the 1962 National Intercollegiate Team Championship and in a few years his rating would cross 2200, but his greatest contribution to the game was as a writer. He is perhaps best known for the books he co-authored with William Lombardy (*U.S. Championship Chess*, *Chess Panorama*, and *A Guide to Tournament Chess*) and for pinch-hitting for Fischer's column in *Boys' Life* when Bobby was off playing in international tournaments.

In an email to the author Daniels recalled:

> I wrote about chess a great deal in the '70s, but mostly as a ghost. I still feel contractually obligated to withhold information about what I wrote under other people's names. I did publish a few articles for *Chess Life & Review* under my own name, mostly obituaries. I stopped writing about chess when I moved to South Jersey to take up a teaching job, from which I am now retired.
>
> Fischer and I both participated in his next to last weekend tournament: the Western Open in Bay City in 1963. In the fourth round on Friday I played a local master named Ron Feingold [father of Grandmaster Ben Finegold and National Master Mark Finegold and grandfather of National Master Spencer Finegold]. Having made several small errors in the opening, after about twenty moves I found myself virtually restricted to the last two ranks of the chessboard, and Feingold spent the next two hours trying to convert his enormous space advantage into something more tangible. I defended as best I

could, and after about sixty more moves had repaired the damage sufficiently to eke out a draw. We were among the last to finish and decided to forego what would have been a dreary post-mortem in favor of a late dinner.

We went to the only joint open in Bay City at that hour, a cafeteria called the Red Lion. We took trays and went to the back of a long line, consisting almost entirely of chessplayers. As we stood waiting our turn, I heard a familiar voice bellowing from the vicinity of the cashier on the other side of the restaurant: "Hey, Daniels." It was Fischer. "Your opponent played like a horse's ass."

The wonder of this story consists less in Bobby's lack of restraint than in his grasp of the more than eighty games taking place simultaneously with his own. He had no reason to keep track of either Feingold's play or mine; we were certainly no threat to him. But where chess was concerned, he never missed a thing. [Funnily enough, Fischer's next opponent was Finegold who he beat in a long technical ending]

Another incident I remember from that weekend was a seemingly endless series of five-minute games (each player has five minutes, timed by a clock, to complete his moves or he loses) he played against a Midwesterner who, for reasons that will soon become obvious, I'll refer to only as L. L wasn't as good a player as I was, and I wouldn't have wagered a dime on myself in a five-minute game with Fischer, who was one of the five best speed players in the world. Nevertheless, L played Bobby for about six hours at ten dollars a game, providing him what looked like a nice bonus to the few hundred dollars he took home for winning the tournament. I was told later that about five in the morning, L wrote Fischer a check for $3,000—after which he returned home and promptly stopped payment.

There are different accounts of the legendary blitz session(s) played between Fischer and Leopoldi and the details vary. Frank Brady summed up the affair:[1]

The night before the final round, Fischer played a bout of five-minute chess with Norbert Leopoldi, Chicago advertising man known as a strong Midwest master.

Word spread throughout the tournament hall that Fischer had won $250. The next morning, after playing all night without sleep, the figure had risen to $3,500 with Fischer giving odds of Pawn and move and Pawn and two moves. Out of hundreds of games played, Leopoldi managed to win three games.

Eyewitness Don Schultz had a slightly different account of the marathon blitz session:[2]

I wanted to play in as many rated tournaments as possible, so Teresa and I hit the tournament trail. We went all the way to Bay City, Michigan to play

---

1 Frank Brady, *Profile of a Prodigy: The Life and Games of Bobby Fischer*, 2nd edition. New York: David McKay, 1973, (p. 70).

2 Don Schultz, *Chessdon*. Boca Raton, FL: Chessdon Publishing, 1999, (pp.16–17).

> in the 1963 Western Open… Fischer and Grandmaster Arthur Bisguier were tied for first …[and] they were scheduled to play against each other the next morning in a game that would likely determine the tournament winner.
>
> That evening, after finishing my fourth round game, I was on my way out to dinner with Teresa when we noticed a large crowd watching Fischer playing twenty-minute games with Chicago Master Norbert Leopoldi. Fischer and Leopoldi were betting on the games starting at five dollars a game, later doubling the amount bet and continuing to increase the stakes in subsequent games. Fischer was spotting Leopoldi the amazing odds of playing Black, giving the king bishop pawn and allowing Leopoldi to play the first four moves as long as he did not move any of his pieces beyond the fourth rank.
>
> After watching them for a while, we left for dinner. When we returned to the hotel we were surprised to find Fischer and Leopoldi still playing, though not as surprised as I was the next morning, when on my way to play my fifth-round game, I saw Fischer and Leopoldi finally ending their marathon match. Fischer immediately went to the tournament hall, arriving slightly late for his game with Bisguier.
>
> The match had taken its toll on Bobby and after only a few moves he fell fast asleep at the board. All Arthur had to do to beat Bobby and win the tournament was to let Bobby sleep through the game then Arthur would win on time. Bisguier, being the gentleman he is, awoke Fischer. A rested Fischer quickly disposed of his opponent. As for the outcome of the Leopoldi match, Fischer won about $3,500.

Schultz wrote this from memory, over thirty-five years after the fact, so it's inevitable that some inaccuracies and exaggeration have crept into his telling—certainly, he has the time control wrong—but perhaps this is how legends grow.

Another source[1] after Leopoldi's death wrote:

> On the weekend of July 4, 1963, while he was president of the Chicago Chess Club, he played Fischer through one entire night of the Western Open Championship. He recalled that they both fell asleep at the board the next day.

Fischer never mentioned the incident in print and it is unclear what sum changed hands—it's been said the two settled on $500. This was far from the amount owed, but still a large sum ($4,000 in 2020 dollars).

The Austrian born Norbert Leopoldi (1912–1992), a decent player who several times nearly reached a USCF rating of 2200, was a devotee of blitz chess. He played tens of thousands of games over the years with his good friend and fellow Chicago expert Daniel Fischeimer at the Lincoln Park Chess Pavilion. That said, he was no match for Bobby who could give even some international masters 5–1 time-odds.

---

1 *Illinois Chess Bulletin, 1992.*

Three Lithuanian Chess Masters: Romanis Arlauskas, Povilas Tautvaisas, and Kazys Skema in Germany, late 1940s (Photo: Val Zemitis).

Leopoldi was good friends with many famous players over the decades including Alekhine, Flohr, Koltanowski, and Dzindzichashvili. A successful businessman, Leopoldi liked to give back to the game which gave him so much pleasure and in 1982 he sponsored the Cloverline International Chess Tournament, a six-player double round robin featuring two of the strongest players in the world at the time—Viktor Korchnoi and Robert Hübner. Leopoldi is also remembered for sponsoring chess instruction for inner-city youth in Chicago long before such programs became popular.

It's possible that Fischer and Leopoldi first met when they sat across from each other in round three of the Western Open. Bobby won their tournament game quickly and convincingly after an opening which began 1.e4 c5 2.Nf3 Nc6 3.d4 cxd4 4.Nxd4 g6 5.Nc3 Bg7 6.Be3 Nf6 7.Bc4 Na5?!. This eccentric move was played quite a bit in the 1960s, particularly by the Yugoslav Grandmaster Vasja Pirc. Bobby had already faced this move at Bled 1961 where he played 8.Be2 against Bertok. Against Leopoldi he preferred 8.Bb3 choosing not to play 8.Bxf7+ ala his game with Reshevsky from the 1958/59 U.S. Championship—7.Bc4 0-0 8.Bb3 Na5? 9.e5 Ne8 10.Bxf7+!. The reason is after 7...Na5 8.Bxf7+ Kxf7 9.e5 Black is not obliged to try to hang on to his extra piece and can return the extra booty with 9...Nc4 or 9...d5 or even the untested 9...Nh5, which might be best.

Truth lurks at the bottom of all legends and the Fischer–Leopoldi all-night blitz session that ended with Bobby falling asleep at the board helps to clear up an inconsistency. In his 2013 autobiography,[1] published forty years after the fact, Bisguier wrote:

---

[1] Arthur Bisguier, *The Art of Bisguier: Selected Games 1961–2003*. Milford, CT: Russell Enterprises, 2008, (p. 69).

Norbert Leopoldi playing at the Illinois Open, May 1965 (Photo: Larry Nocerino, Chicago Sun Times).

> Paired against Bobby in the New York State Open[1] that year, I noticed that he was taking a long time to move. Then I saw he'd fallen asleep. In a few minutes the flag on his clock would fall. That's not the way I like to win games, tourneys or titles. So I made what some called my biggest blunder of the tournament. I awakened Fischer. Bobby yawned, made a move, punched his clock and proceeded to beat me. It ended up as Game 45 in his *My 60 Memorable Games*. Later I heard that Fischer had stayed up late the previous night playing speed chess for money.

American Chess Quarterly[2] was the only magazine to publish all of Fischer's games from the 1963 Western Open—there was no bulletin. ACQ editor Larry Evans made an error and listed Bobby's opponents as Arthur Bisguier in round six and Donald Byrne in round seven, and unfortunately, this error has been repeated in every source from Wade and O'Connell's monumental *Bobby Fischer's Chess Games* to Mega Database. Evans' blunder is understandable in that such pairings would have Bobby alternating colors perfectly. This is normally the case for the top-rated player in a Swiss event, but top-ranked takes precedence over top-rated and due to Fischer's round four draw with Poschel he didn't catch up to Hans Berliner until round seven was completed. This meant Bobby actually had White in rounds five and six and Black in rounds seven and eight.

1 The New York State Open? Did Fischer fall asleep at the board in two consecutive tournaments against Bisguier? This seems highly unlikely. Fischer and Bisguier did play in round five of the New York State Open, however, all the evidence confirms the incident occurred at the Western Open.

2 *American Chess Quarterly*, volume 3, no. 2 (Fall 1963).

Game (40) is important for helping to develop the theory of the King's Indian Attack. Fischer was noted for his habitual use of the King's Indian Attack around 1956–57 via 1.Nf3 and 2.g3. Ten years later he started playing it again, but selectively via 1.e4 and only then after 1...e6, 1...c6 and 1...c5/2...e6.

He won several famous games—Panno, Myagmarsuren, U. Geller, and E. Nikolić (as Black)—that remain model examples of how to attack using this formation.

The game with Myagmarsuren from the Sousse Interzonal in 1967 was particularly noteworthy as White played the groundbreaking 13.a3 to stop Black's ...a4-a3. Previously to this game, White played exclusively on the kingside on the theory that any action on the other side of the board would only accelerate Black's play. Fischer's genius was to realize this position was an exception to the rule that one shouldn't play on the side of the board where the opponent is stronger.

When Fischer played 13.a3 against Myagmarsuren, it was not only a theoretical novelty, but also a completely new way of handling the position. What wasn't common knowledge was that Fischer not only knew about this idea but also had already played it—with colors reversed—in the following game. Admittedly, the first time out it was a less complicated decision, but the idea to advance the a-pawn against Myagmarsuren did not come out of thin air.

(40) King's Indian
Arthur Bisguier – Fischer
Bay City (7) 1963

1.d4 Nf6 2.c4 g6 3.Nc3 Bg7 4.Nf3 0–0 5.e3 d6 6.Be2 Nbd7 7.0–0 e5 8.b4 Re8

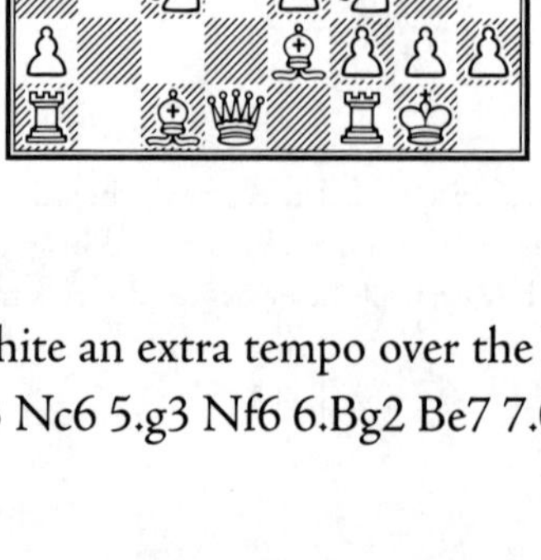

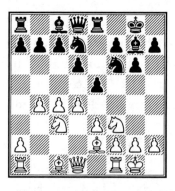

9.Bb2

9.a4 aims to give White an extra tempo over the French line (1.e4 e6 2.d3 d5 3.Nd2 c5 4.Ngf3 Nc6 5.g3 Nf6 6.Bg2 Be7 7.0–0 0–0 8.e5 Nd7 9.Re1 b5 10.Nf1 a5. Besides 9...e4 (which might justify White's last move), Black can also play 9...exd4 as Karpov did when he faced Rivas at Dos Hermanas in 1991.

9...e4 10.Nd2 Nf8 11.Qc2 Bf5

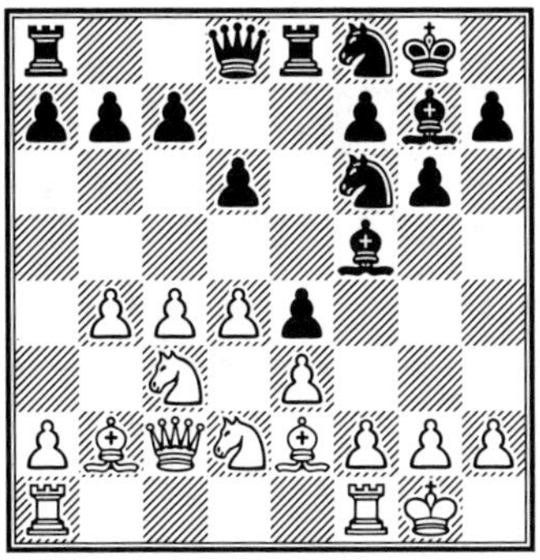

12.d5

White plays to post a knight on d4. An alternative idea to make use of his extra move (with colors reversed) is 12.Rfc1 h5 13.Nd5.

12...h5 13.Nb5 h4

An alternative plan was 13...N8h7 14.Nd4 Bg4.

14.Nd4 Bd7 15.a3

This might seem a little slow, especially as White moves this pawn again just four moves later, but it isn't completely clear how he should proceed here and Bisguier wants to keep his options open. The immediate 15.a4 would be met by 15...a5 when 16.bxa5 Rxa5 17.Bc3 Ra6 18.a5 h3 leads to a position which promises a sharp fight with chances for both sides.

15...h3

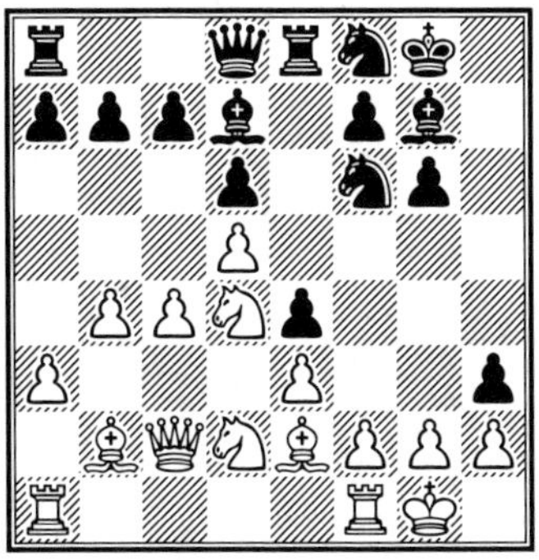

The plan of advancing the h-pawn down the board has proven successful in many games. Kamsky–Lenderman, U.S. Championship 2014, is a recent example where White won a fine game.

16.g3 Qe7 17.Rfc1 Bg4 18.Bf1 N8h7 19.a4 Ng5 20.a5

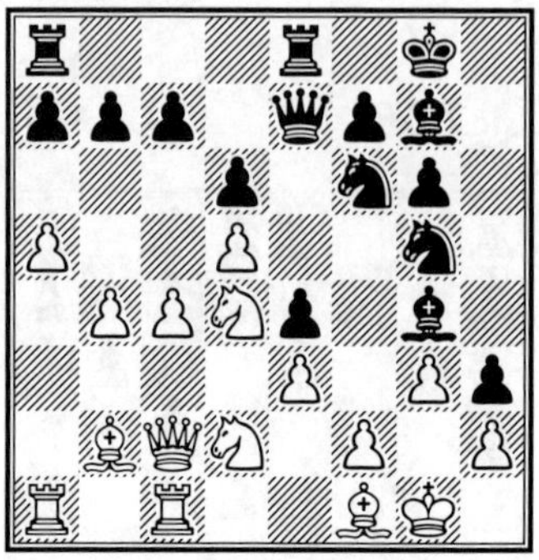

20...a6

Just like Fischer–Myagmarsuren, Black wants to stop White from playing a6 and posting a knight on c6. The advance of the rook pawn is more or less forced here, unlike Bobby's game against the Mongolian where it was a more complicated strategical decision.

21.Rab1 Nd7 22.c5 Bxd4

Concrete play from Black who wants to increase his control of f3. The trade of pieces here and on move twenty-four removes pressure on White's king so there will be no spectacular piece sacrifices that feature in Fischer's most famous King's Indian Attack brilliancies—23.Bf6! Myagmarsuren, 19...Bg4! E. Nikolić and 28.Be4! Panno.

23.Bxd4 Ne5 24.Bxe5 Qxe5 25.Nc4 Qe7 26.b5 axb5 27.Rxb5

White's play on the queenside is proceeding smoothly and Bobby is not able to focus his attention exclusively on Bisguier's king.

27...dxc5 28.Rxb7 Qd8 29.Qc3 Bc8 30.Rb5 Qxd5 31.Qa3 Qd8

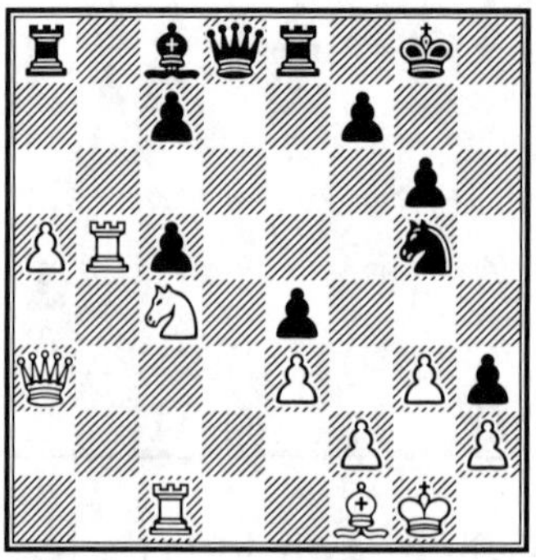

32.Qxc5?!

32.Rxc5 was better, meeting 32...Nf3+ 33.Kh1 Qf6 with 34.Qc3; but 33...Qe7! is still very strong.

32...Nf3+ 33.Kh1 Qf6?

33...Ba6! gives a winning advantage, for example, 34.Bxh3 (34.Rb2 Qf6) 34...Kg7 35.Rb2 Rh8, etc.

34.Qxc7?

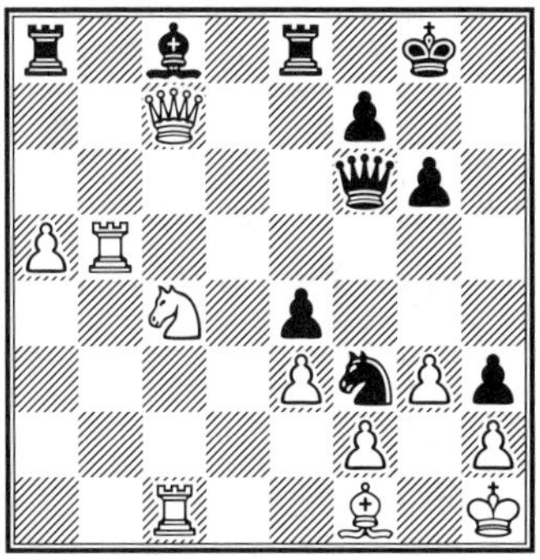

Not 34.Rb2? Ba6! 35.Rbc2 Red8! and White is in big trouble.

34...Nxh2! 35.Kxh2?!?

This loses on the spot. 35.Qf4! justifies Bisguier's active defensive strategy, for example, 25...Qxf4 36.gxf4 Nxf1 37.Rxf1 Ba6 38.Rc5 Rec8 39.Rxc8+ Rxc8 40.Nd6 Rc6 41.Rd1 Bd3 42.Nb7 Kf8 43.Kh2 Rc7 44.a6 Bxa6 45.Na5! and White will very likely hold the resulting ending.

35...Qxf2+ 36.Kh1 Bg4, 0–1

Bobby annotated all of his games from the Western Open for *Chess Life* in his column "Bobby Talks Chess."

POUGHKEEPSIE (1963)

The 1963 New York State Open (not to be confused with the annual New York State Championship, the longest running tournament in the United States) was the last Swiss system event Bobby Fischer played in. Strangely enough, the most basic facts about his participation are not certain fifty-seven years later, despite his having been a world class player since 1958. The list of uncertainties includes who his opponents were, the order in which he played them and even some of the moves of his game with the Yugoslav journalist Miro Radojčić.

Organized by Don Schultz and held at the IBM Country Club in Poughkeepsie, the First Annual New York State Open was held over seven rounds from August 30 to September 2. Looking at the advertisement in *Chess Life*, it doesn't appear to be that impressive of a tournament—the place prizes of $200 for first, $100 for second, and $50 for third, were more typical of a regional event in the early 1960s. Why Bobby Fischer and Arthur Bisguier played can be answered in two words—appearance money.

Schultz wrote in his memoir *Chessdon*,[1] that after the Western Open he talked to Frank Brady about what it would take to bring Bobby to Poughkeepsie—he was told a $500 appearance fee. Fischer's participation was confirmed when Schultz got IBM to come up with the not inconsequential sum ($4,000 in 2020 dollars). When Arthur Bisguier heard about Bobby's participation, he also asked for an honorarium and a deal was struck that he would receive a guarantee equivalent to second prize. This didn't end up costing Schultz much as Bisguier in fact tied for second with International Master James Sherwin, National Master Matthew Green, and expert Joseph Richman at 5½ from 7.

Bobby traveled to the event on the New York Central Railroad with Brady, who directed and reported on the event.

Trying to find all of Bobby's games from this event is surprisingly difficult considering that by 1963 he was already a two-time World Champion candidate and five-time U.S. Champion. Four of the games (Oster, Beach, Greenwald, and Bisguier) appeared in *Chess Life* with Bobby's notes. The games against Richman and Green were published soon after the tournament in *The New York Times*. So far so good, but what of the game with Radojčić? For this we have but a fragment.[2]

No bulletin or crosstable was produced for this event, nor was it given much coverage in *American Chess Quarterly*, or *Chess Review*, or the New York state chess federation publication of the time. Frank Brady did report on it for the *Poughkeepsie Journal*, as did Al Horowitz in *The New York Times*.

The event must have been submitted too late for the October USCF rating list, as it was only rated in January (ratings given below). Taking these calculations into account and a few other clues including conversations with some of the participants (Andy Soltis and the Meyer brothers John and Eugene) and Brady's newspaper reports, it appears the order in which Fischer played his games was the following (Fischer's colors are in parentheses).

Roy Oster	(B) round 1	(1819)
Winthrop Beach	(W) round 2	(1999)
Ben Greenwald	(B) round 3	(2181)
Matthew Green	(W) round 4	(2354)
Joseph Richman	(B) round 5	(2215)
Arthur Bisguier	(W) round 6	(2507)
Miro Radojčić	(W) round 7	(2262)

[1] Don Schultz, *Chessdon*. Boca Raton, FL: Chessdon Publishing, 1999.

[2] Included in the annotations to Fischer–Bisguier, game 45 in *My 60 Memorable Games*.

The double White in rounds six and seven is the result of Fischer–Radojčić being a forced pairing. Likely Radojčić had 5–1 going into the last round and was White his two previous games. Bisguier, Sherwin, Green, and Richman, who ended up tied for second at 5½–1½, must have had 4½ going into the last game. Almost certainly Radojčić was ahead of Sherwin (who played Soltis in the final round) in the standings after round six, or Bobby would have played the latter.

Brady mentions Fischer played Bisguier in round six and Radojčić in round seven, with the round seven game lasting thirty-three moves.

Some clarity is required on two details: A photo of Fischer sitting across from his first-round opponent was published in Schultz's memoir[1] with a caption that identified the player as John Otis. Fischer wrote that his first round opponent was Roy Oster and Andy Soltis remembers the same. FIDE Master Frank Thornally, National Master Alan Benson, and Sam Sloan all knew Roy Oster when he played in California in the late 1960s and are all but 100% certain Oster is the person pictured. Also, at 1557, Otis seems too low-rated to have been Bobby's first round opponent.

On the second point, Brady wrote in the *Poughkeepsie Journal* that Fischer played Hy Wallach in round two—presumably instead of Beach. Wallach appears on the January 1964 USCF rating list at 1980—a rating similar to Beach's. Brady wrote Fischer won the game in twenty-five moves—Fischer's game with Beach ends after White's twenty-fourth move.

Fischer wrote of his round two game:

> Before this game began, when I asked Mr. Beach how to spell his name, he remarked that we had met over the board on a previous occasion some years ago and that I had beaten him on the white side of a Pirc Defense. I had absolutely no recollection of that game.[2]

It seems prudent to go with Fischer—it's doubtful he would have made this sort of mistake—if he had it seems pretty certain someone would have written to *Chess Life* with a correction.

Game (41) with Green was first published in I.A. Horowitz's *New York Times* chess column[3] and later republished in Yasser Seirawan's magazine *Inside Chess*.[4]

Matthew Green (1915–2006) was born in Cleveland but moved to New York in his formative years. There he benefited from living at the epicenter of American chess and by the mid-1930s he was good enough to play in the Marshall Chess Club Championship. A few years later he graduated to competing in several U.S.

[1] Photo published in Don Schultz, *Chessdon*. Boca Raton, FL: Chessdon Publishing, 1999.

[2] Fischer and Winthrop Beach played in round three of the 1956 Greater New York City Open Championship.

[3] *The New York Times*, September 16, 1963.

[4] *Inside Chess*, September 4, 1995, issue 17.

Championships. New Jersey champion in 1957 and 1962, Green was still among the top thirty players in the United States when he faced Bobby for the second time in the last round of the New York State Open—their first encounter was the 1957 New Jersey Open, won by Bobby.

(41) Sicilian
Fischer – Matthew Green
Poughkeepsie (4) 1963

1.e4 c5 2.Nf3 e6 3.d4 cxd4 4.Nxd4 a6 5.Bd3 Nc6 6.Nxc6 bxc6 7.0–0 d5 8.exd5 cxd5 9.c4 Nf6 10.cxd5

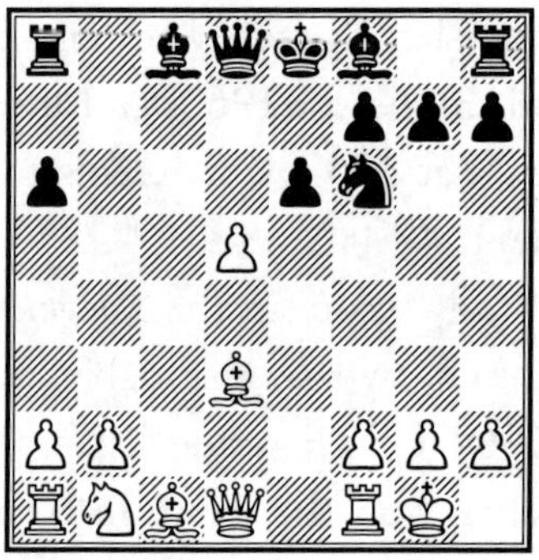

10...Nxd5

Black is able to develop his pieces more easily after 10...exd5 but takes on a weakness. White's realized his chances in the classic positional tour de force Fischer–Petrosian, from game 7 of their 1971 match—11.Nc3 Be7 12.Qa4+ Qd7 13.Re1 Qxa4 14.Nxa4 Be6 15.Be3 0–0 16.Bc5 Rfe8 17.Bxe7 Rxe7 18.b4 Kf8 19.Nc5 Bc8 20.f3 Rea7 21.Re5 Bd7 22.Nxd7+ Rxd7 23.Rc1 Rd6 24.Rc7 Nd7 25.Re2 g6 26.Kf2 h5 27.f4 h4 28.Kf3 f5 29.Ke3 d4+ 30.Kd2 Nb6 31.Ree7 Nd5 32.Rf7+ Ke8 33.Rb7 Nxf4 34.Bc4 1–0. One can imagine Petrosian would have loved knowing about Fischer's game with Green, but it seems unlikely he did.

The third capture, 10...Qxd5, allows White to obtain an advantage by making natural moves: 11.Nc3 Qd7 12.Bf4 Be7 13.Qe2 Bb7 14.Rac1 0–0 15.Rfd1.

11.Be4

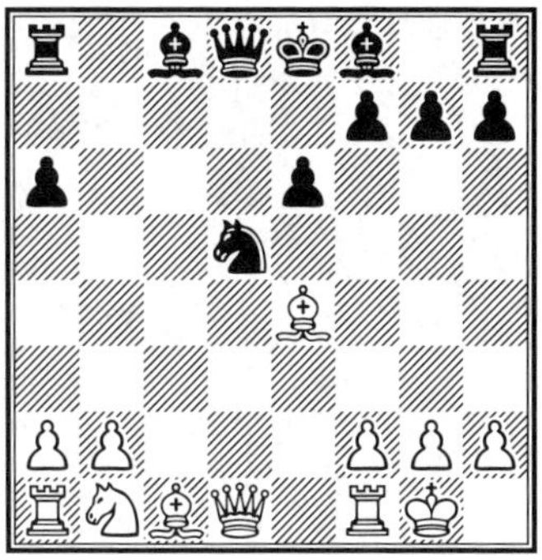

11.Nc3!? might be stronger: 11...Nxc3 12.bxc3 Bd6 (12...Be7 13.Rb1 0–0 14.Qf3 Bd7 15.Rd1 Qc8 16.Be4 Ra7 17.Bb7 winning) 13.Qh5 Bb7 14.Rd1 Qc7 15.Rb1 h6 16.Be3 and Black can't castle as 16...0–0 is met by 17.Bxh6!.

11...Bd6

Black had an important alternative:

11...Bb7 12.Nc3 (12.Qa4+ Qd7 13.Qxd7+ Kxd7 14.Rd1 Bd6 15.Bxd5 exd5 16.Nc3 Ke6=; 12.Qb3 Rb8 13.Na3 Bd6 14.Nc4 0–0 15.Nxd6 Qxd6=) 12...Nxc3 13.Qxd8+ Rxd8 14.Bxb7 Ne2+ 15.Kh1 Nxc1 16.Raxc1 a5 with only a small advantage for White.

12.Nc3! Nxc3 13.Bc6+

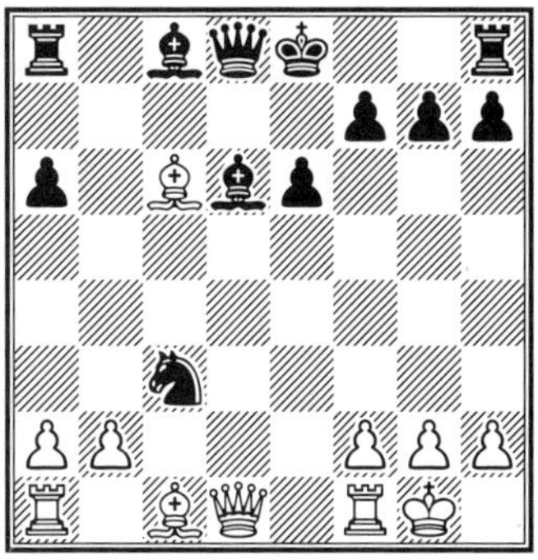

13...Ke7?

13...Bd7 14.Qxd6 Nb5 15.Bxd7+ Qxd7 16.Qxd7+ (16.Qb4 Qd4 17.Bd2 Qxb4 18.Bxb4 Nc7 with equal chances as the knight returns to its powerful outpost on d5) 16...Kxd7, with only a small advantage to White, was much better.

14.bxc3

The sharper 14.Qg4 or 14.Qh5 were definitely stronger, but the text is also quite good as Black's king insecurity is a problem not easily resolved.

14...Rb8 15.Qg4

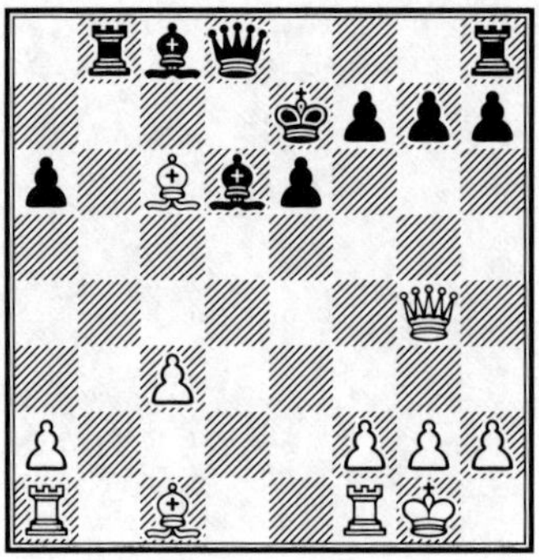

15...Rg8?

Black had to play 15...Kf8, although after 16.Rd1 Qc7 17.Qd4 Qxc6 18.Bf4 Bxf4 (18...Be7 19.Bxb8 Bb7 20.Qg4 h5 21.Qh3 g5 isn't completely correct but might offer better practical chances.) 19.Qxf4, White is in command, but not to the extent as the game continuation.

16.Qh4+ f6 17.Qxh7 Bb7 18.Bxb7 Rxb7 19.Re1 Qc8

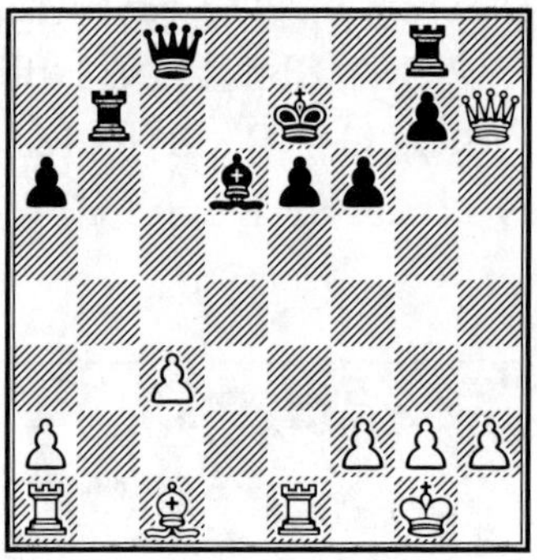

20.h3

20.Be3 and 20.Qg6 were good alternatives.

20...Kf7 21.Qh5+ g6 22.Qf3 Rb5 23.a4 Rf5 24.Qe2 Bc5

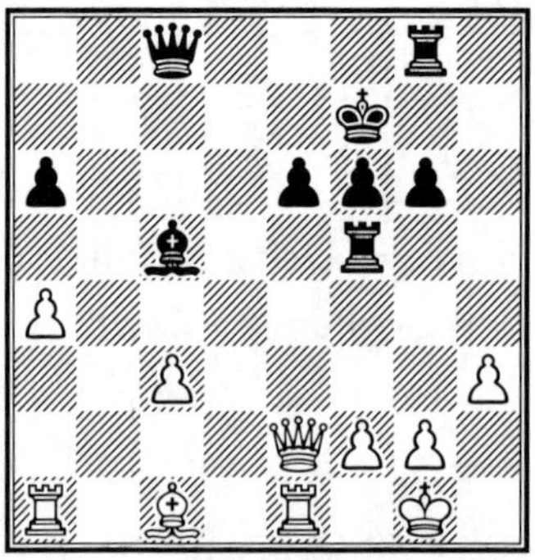

25.Be3 Re5 26.Qf3 Rd8 27.Rab1 Bxe3 28.Rxe3 Rxe3 29.Qxe3

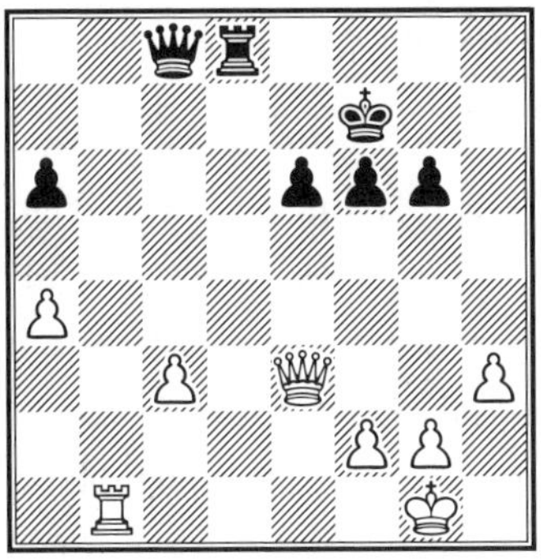

29...Rd7 30.Qh6 f5 31.c4! Qd8 32.Kh2 a5 33.f4 Kf6 34.Rb7! Re7 35.c5, 1–0.

One curiosity from Poughkeepsie which has been alluded to earlier, is Fischer's game with the Yugoslav journalist and chess master Miroslav Radojčić. During the 1960s Radojčić lived in New York and was the U.S. foreign correspondent for the Yugoslav newspaper *Politika*. He also wrote a long-running column for *Chess Life* called "Observation Point," and found time to play in many American tournaments, most notably tying for second with Robert Byrne and James Sherwin in the 1964 U.S. Open in Boston behind Pal Benko.

When Fischer annotated his famous game with Bisguier in the Two Knights Defense (9.Nh3!?) for *Chess Life*, he did not mention that he had another game in the same line with Radojčić and we would have never known if Bobby hadn't included a note in his revised annotations, which appeared as game 45 in *My 60 Memorable Games*. There, after 1.e4 e5 2.Nf3 Nc6 3.Bc4 Nf6 4.Ng5 d5 5.exd5 Na5 6.Bb5+ c6 7.dxc6 bxc6 8.Be2 h6 9.Nh3!? Bc5 10.0-0, he writes:

> Played by Steinitz in the sixth game of his second match with Tchigorin in 1892. Better is 10.d3! 0-0 11.Nc3 Re8 12.0-0 Bxh3 13.gxh3 Qd7 14.Bg4 Nxg4 15.hxg4, etc. as I played versus Radojčić here in a later round.

In fact, it was the very next round. White is a clear pawn up and winning when Bobby stops his note, but wouldn't it be nice to have the remaining moves? Fischer never had the preservationist instincts of other greats, most notably Garry Kasparov.

For a final word on Bobby's last Swiss, Don Schultz reported[1] that Fischer was a model of decorum throughout the tournament and didn't complain when housed in substandard lodging. Bobby wrote Schultz after the event praising his organization and stating that he was looking forward to future events in Poughkeepsie.

---

1 Don Schultz, *Chessdon*. Boca Raton, FL: Chessdon Publishing, 1999.

A CHESS GOD PASSES JUDGEMENT

Bobby Fischer is unique among his contemporaries for many reasons. His love and appreciation of great players of the past and his interest and intense study of antiquarian chess literature definitely set him apart. Did any other great player after 1900, besides Lasker, make a careful study of Steinitz? The simul tour around North America Bobby made in the first half of 1964, with the exhilaration expressed by fans, echoed earlier journeys by Lasker, Capablanca, and Alekhine, and is another example of his honoring the past. Serving as an adjudicator was another link between Bobby and his predecessors. Like great players of the past Fischer earned money evaluating positions, in his case making quick assessments of games in weekend Swiss events. Two-time Candidate Pal Benko got $50 for doing this, but Bobby demanded and received $100!

Fred Wilson, in a letter to the editor of *New In Chess*,[1] recalled what it was like to have a chess god pass judgment on them. During a Greater New York Open in early December 1963, Wilson had a game with Walter Browne that had to be adjudicated—there were no sudden death time controls in those days. With the next round fast approaching the tournament director would have a strong grandmaster make a quick assessment of the position and render a verdict.

Heaven help those who disputed Bobby's decisions. Wilson recalled Browne disagreeing with Bobby, trying one variation after another to prove he was winning, and Fischer refuting them all:

> Finally, Bobby said to Walter "If you keep this up, I will give the win to him," pointing at me! Others that challenged Fischer were met with, "You wanna play this out for a hundred bucks?" This instantly ended the conversation.

Walter Browne gave Wilson–Browne as the first game in his book, *The Stress of Chess... and its Infinite Finesse*,[2] with comprehensive annotations. He prefaced his notes to the game with the following comments:

> ...In those days with three games in one day, adjudication was the only option. Naturally, with perhaps five to ten games still going, Bobby had his work cut out to do it in a relatively short amount of time. Despite this, he hired himself out for a modest sum to be the adjudicator for the tournament. Although Bobby took his time before declaring the game a draw, I now know beyond the shadow of a doubt that he came to the wrong conclusion, as the post-game analysis thirty-two years later proves.

It's not certain if the adjudicated position is actually drawn with best play, but the analysis Browne presents to show he was winning is mistaken.

---

1 *New In Chess*, 2013, issue #1.

2 Walter Browne, *The Stress of Chess ...and its Infinite Finesse*. Netherlands: New In Chess, 2012.

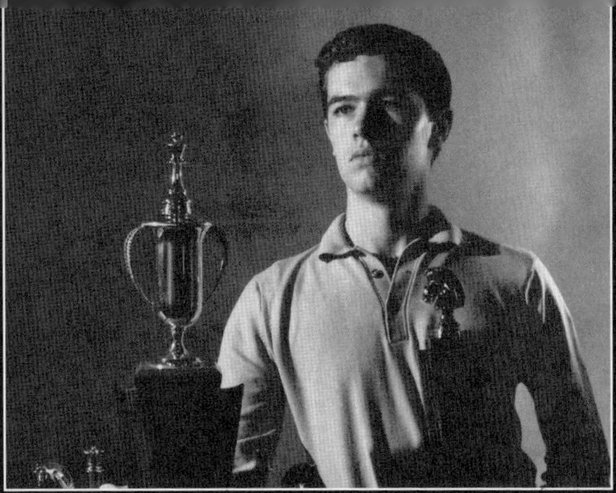

[left] Fred Wilson with the Hamilton-Russell Cup in his shop near Union Square, NYC (Photo: Eduardo Bauzá Mercére;

[right] Walter Browne after winning the first U.S.Junior Closed (1966).

(42) Göring Gambit
Fred Wilson – Walter Browne
New York 1963

1.e4 e5 2.d4 exd4 3.c3 dxc3 4.Nxc3 d6 5.Bc4 Nc6 6.Nf3 Be6 7.Bxe6 fxe6 8.Qb3 Qd7 9.Qxb7 Rb8 10.Qa6 Nf6 11.0–0 Be7 12.e5 dxe5 13.Rd1 Bd6 14.Kh1 0–0 15.Qe2 h6 16.b3 Qf7 17.Ne4 Nd5 18.Be3 Rb4 19.Qd3 Qf5 20.Nfd2 Nd4 21.Nc4 Be7 22.Ng3 Qxd3 23.Rxd3 Bf6 24.Ne4 Nc2 25.Rad1 Ncxe3 26.fxe3 Nb6 27.Nxf6+ gxf6 28.Nxb6 Rxb6 29.Rd7 Rc6 30.Kg1 Rf7 31.Rd8+ Kg7 32.Ra8 Ra6 33.Rd2 f5 34.Kf2 Rd6?! 35.Rc2 Ra6 36.Rc8 Kf6 37.a4 Rb6 38.R8xc7 Rxb3 39.Rxf7+ Kxf7 40.Rc7+ Kf6 41.Rxa7 Rb2+ 42.Kg3 e4 43.a5 Re2 44.a6 Rxe3+ 45.Kf2 Ra3 46.Ra8 Ke5 47.a7 f4 48.Ke2 Ra2+ 49.Kf1 e3 50.Ke1 Ra1+ 51.Ke2 Ra2+

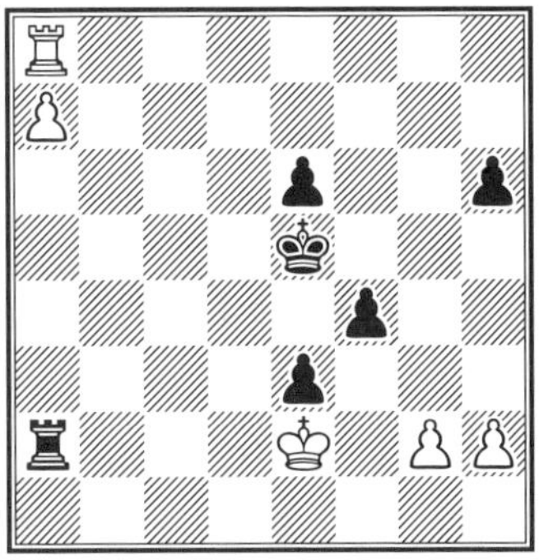

[Browne] "Here the game was adjudicated a draw by R.J. Fischer, and he took quite a while to decide! Actually Black is winning. I extensively analyzed it around 1995 in *Blitz Chess*."

52.Kf1 h5! 53.h3

[Browne] "53.Rh8 Rxa7 54.Rxh5+ Ke4 55.Rb5 Ra1+ 56.Ke2 Ra2+ 57.Kf1 f3 58.Rb4+ Kd3 59.gxf3 Ra1+ wins."

53...Ke4 54.Re8 Rxa7 55.Rxe6+ Kf5 56.Re8 Ra1+ 57.Ke2 Ra2+ 58.Kf1 Kg5 59.Rf8 Ra1+ 60.Ke2 Rg1 61.Rg8+ Kh4

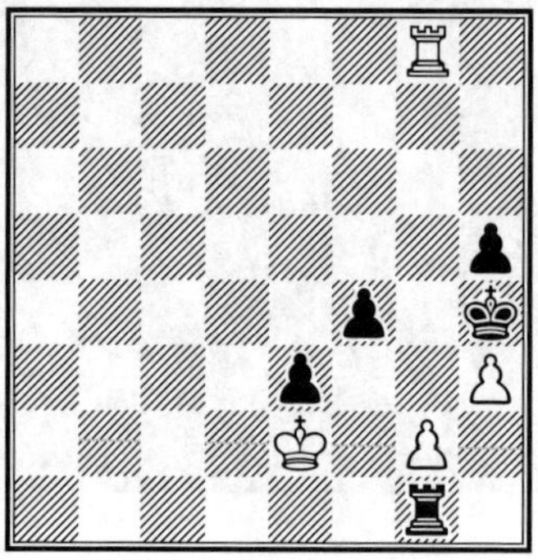

62.Kf3

[Browne] "62.Rg7 Rb1 63.Rg6 Rb2+ 64.Kf1 f3 65.gxf3 Kxh3 66.Re6 Rf2+ 67.Kg1 Rxf3 wins."

62...Rf1+ 63.Ke2 Rf2+ 64.Ke1 f3 65.gxf3 Kxh3 66.Re8 Rxf3 67.Ke2 Rg3 68.Kf1 h4 69.Re4 Rf3+ 70.Ke2 Rf6 71.Rxe3+ Kg2

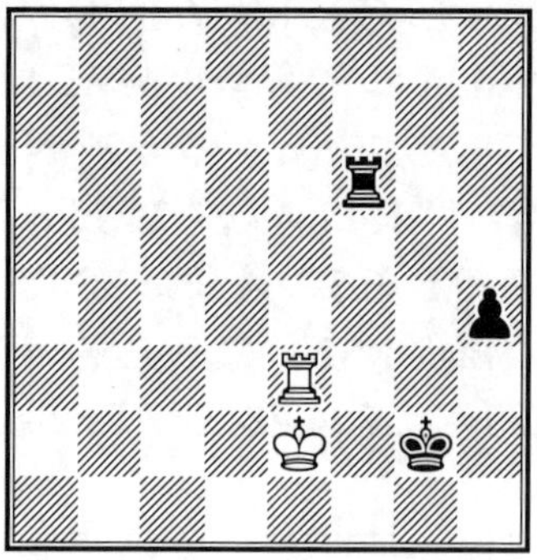

72.Re8??

White draws with 72.Re4!, leaving Black three choices:

(A) 72...Kg3 73.Re3+ and Black has made no progress.

(B) 72...Rf2+ 73.Ke1 h3 74.Rg4+ Kf3 75.Rf4+ with a drawn king and pawn ending.

(C) 72...h3 73.Rg4+ Kh1 74.Rg7 Ra6 75.Kf2 with a well-known theoretical draw. White's king is too close to allow Black to free his king.

72...Rf2+ 73.Ke1 Rf3 and Black wins.

Most likely, Bobby stopped serving as an adjudicator shortly after Wilson–Browne. He probably didn't need the money after his 1964 tour and time controls were starting to speed up, allowing most games to be played to a finish.

U.S. CHAMPIONSHIP 1963/64

Bobby Fischer's performance in the 1963/64 U.S. Championship was sensational—never before (or since) has someone made a perfect score (11–0!) in a U.S. Championship. Fischer thought highly enough of his play that four of his eleven victories are included in *My 60 Memorable Games*—among these are the well-known brilliancies against Robert Byrne and Pal Benko. But things didn't always go smoothly for Bobby in this event—in fact he was in trouble in the very first round against Edmar Mednis.

Many strong players came to the United States after World War II, particularly from Latvia. Among those who emigrated from this small Baltic nation were Elmars Zemgalis (whose performances in Germany from 1946–49 earned him the Grandmaster Emeritus title from FIDE), and strong national masters Ivars Dahlbergs, Erik and Andrew Karklins, Leonid Dreibergs, John Pamiljens, John Tums, Val Zemitis, and Viktors Pupols.

Note: Latvian first and last names typically end in the letter "s", but most Latvian-American chess players removed the "s" from their first name when they came to the United States. In the case of Valdemars Zemitis the change included shortening his first name to Val.

The Latvian born players that achieved the most in American chess were Charles Kalme and Edmar Mednis, both members of the U.S. gold-medal winning team in the 1960 Student Chess Olympiad held in Leningrad.

Kalme would retire from tournament play by the mid-1960s to pursue a career in academia as a mathematician, while Mednis stayed involved with chess the rest of his life, representing the United States in two Olympiads and an Interzonal. He wrote many books on all aspects of the game, particularly the endgame, where he was a well-respected expert.

One contribution of Mednis that is not well known was his annotations to his 1963 loss to Fischer, Game (43), that were published in the obscure American magazine *The Chess Courier*[1] The annotations were written for a tournament book on the 1963–64 U.S. Championship which was advertised but never published. The editor's note to the Mednis–Fischer game read:

> Burt Hochberg has turned his talents to the promotion of chess for the benefit of the American Chess Foundation. To be more exact, Burt is preparing a tournament book of the 1963 United States Championship, which was won by Bobby Fischer with a clean sweep. Games will be annotated by the players and the notes will not appear anywhere else but in the book, except in the case of the sample game herein. Proceeds from the sale of the book will be donated to the American Chess Foundation for the furtherance of the cause of chess.

[1] *The Chess Courier*, February 1964, (pp. 3–4).

Edmar Mednis at work

Edmar and the well-known organizer Alex Liepnieks

Evidently the desire to produce a book on the U.S. Championship was a strong ambition for Burt Hochberg (1933–2006), the long-serving editor of *Chess Life* (later *Chess Life and Review*). Hochberg edited the USCF house publication from 1966 to 1979, but also found time for other projects, producing bulletins for the 1966/67 U.S. Championship (with Michael Valvo) and writing *Title Chess*, a tournament book on the 1972 U.S. Championship. He also served as editor-in-chief and later executive editor of RHM, which published many outstanding books in the 1970s including *How to Open a Chess Game*, *San Antonio 1972*, and *Wijk aan Zee 1975*.

American chess publisher and bookseller Dale Brandreth (1931–2019), once noted that no other country has produced so many state and regional publications as the United States. Some, such as *Northwest Chess* which covers the Pacific Northwest, have been around forever (founded in 1947 and still going strong), but most last only a short time. Printed cheaply and in small quantities, their content not properly valued, issues were thrown out without much thought. Years later, copies of these publications are scarce.

EDMAR MEDNIS
Edmar – NY State and Intercollegiate Champion 1956
Edmars Mednis

Edmar Mednis as a young man (Photos: Archive of Val Zemitis).

(43) Guioco Piano
Edmar Mednis – Fischer
New York (1) 1963/64

Annotations by Edmar Mednis unless otherwise noted.

1.e4 e5

[Author]: Curiously Fischer didn't have a single Sicilian as White or Black in this event. He did have five games that opened 1.e4 e5, playing Black twice. In the two other games he had as White, his opponents answered with the Caro-Kann and Pirc.

2.Nf3 Nc6 3.Bc4 Bc5 4.c3 Nf6 5.d4 exd4 6.cxd4 Bb4+ 7.Bd2 Bxd2+ 8.Nbxd2 Nxe4

A move typical of Fischer's present play. The move is no better than 8...d5 9.exd5 Nxd5 10.Qb3 Nce7, but it has the advantage of being less known.

[Author]: This remains the case today with only a handful of tests at the grandmaster level. The German Woman Grandmaster Bettina Trabert, with three games as Black in Mega Database, has played it more often than anyone else.

9.Qe2

For those looking for more aggressive play for White, Grandmaster Rossolimo recommends 9.Nxe4 d5 10.Bxd5 Qxd5 11.Nc3 Qh5

[Author]: Rossolimo–Dunkelblum, Dubrovnik (ol) 1950, continued 12.d5 Ne7 13.Qb3 0-0 14.0-0 and White's space advantage and lead in development more than compensated for the isolated d-pawn.

Those looking for even more aggressive play for White may wish to try the gambit approach with 9.d5 Nxd2 10.Qxd2 Ne7 11.d6 though it shouldn't lead to more than equal chances.

9...d5 10.Nxe4 0–0

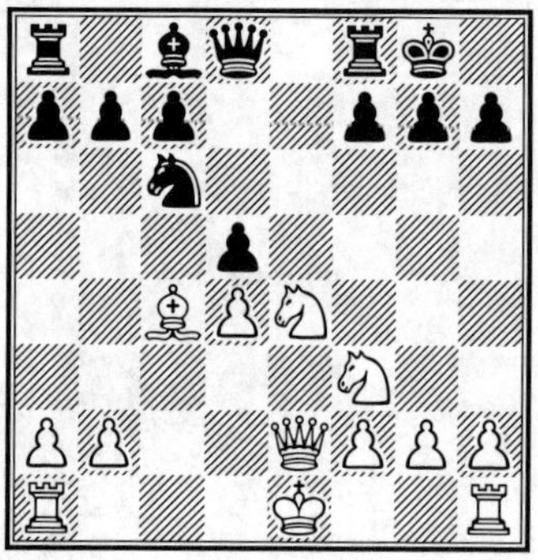

11.0–0–0

After 11.0–0 Bg4! is too strong.

11...Bg4

If 11...Re8, White can gain a clear advantage with 12.Bxd5 Qxd5 13.Nf6+ or obtain a powerful attack with 12.Nfg5!

12.h3 Bxf3 13.gxf3 dxc4?

[Author]: This natural looking move is imprecise. Correct is 13...dxe4 14.Qxe4 Qd6 15.Rhe1 Rad8 with a slight advantage for Black according to Stockfish.

14.Qxc4 Qh4 15.Kb1 Qf4 16.d5

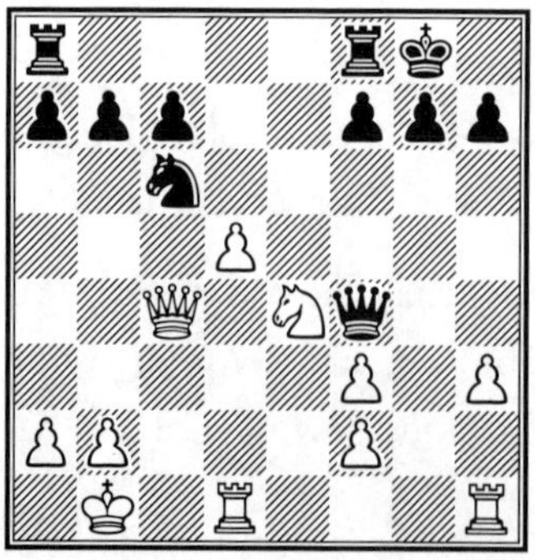

The position is about even here, White's active position compensating for his pawn weaknesses.

16...Ne5

I was expecting 16...Ne7 after which White would have played 17.Qc3. The text is just playable, but should force Black to settle for a draw by repetition of moves.

17.Qxc7 Rac8 18.Qd6

[Author]: 18. Qxb7 Rb8 19.Qxa7 Nc4 with equal chances (Stockfish).

18...Rcd8 19.Qc7 Rc8 20.Qd6

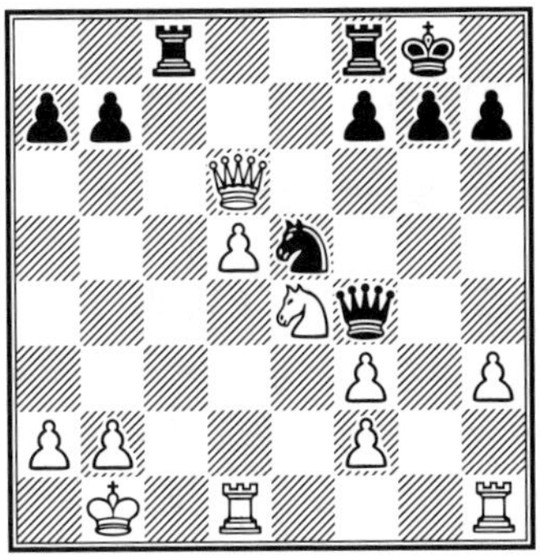

20...Rfd8

But this act of bravery should have cost Black dearly. Required was 20... Rcd8 with repetition of moves.

21.Qe7 Nxf3 22.d6! Ne5

With Black's rooks on c8 and d8 22...Re8 loses to 23.d7.

[Author]: This is where Black starts to get into trouble. Stockfish gives 22...Qe5 with equal chances.

23.Rhe1

A slight inaccuracy. With the simple 23.Qxb7 White would have won a pawn and kept a superior position.

23...Rd7

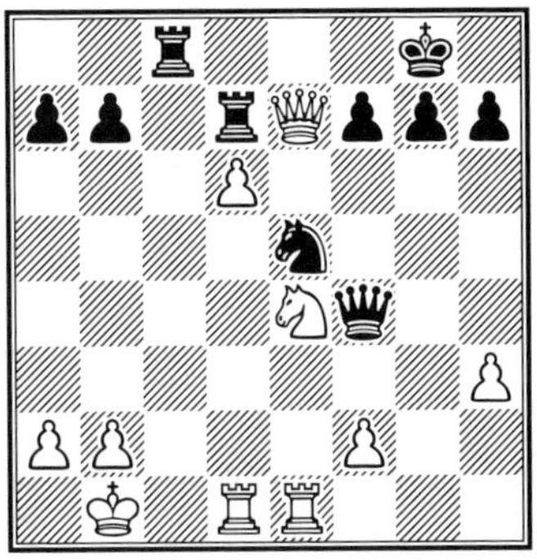

24.Qg5?

But this is definitely inferior. A definite edge could have been kept with 24.Nc5!! as Black has nothing better than to allow 24...Rxe7 25.dxe7 Re8 26.Rd8 f6 27.Rxe8+ Kf7 28.Rg8! Instead, after the text, White has a slightly inferior game, although, of course, it should still be a draw.

[Author]: Even stronger is 24.Rd5! Rxe7 25.dxe7 Nc6 26.Nd6 Nxe7 27.Nxc8 winning—Stockfish.

24...Qxg5 25.Nxg5 f6 26.Ne4 Ng6 27.Rc1 Rxc1+ 28.Rxc1 b6

A later Nc5 must be prevented.

29.Rc7 Nf8 30.Kc2 Kf7 31.Kc3 Ke6 32.Rc8 Ng6 33.Kd4 h6 34.Re8+ Kf7 35.Rc8 Nf4 36.h4 g6 37.Rh8 f5

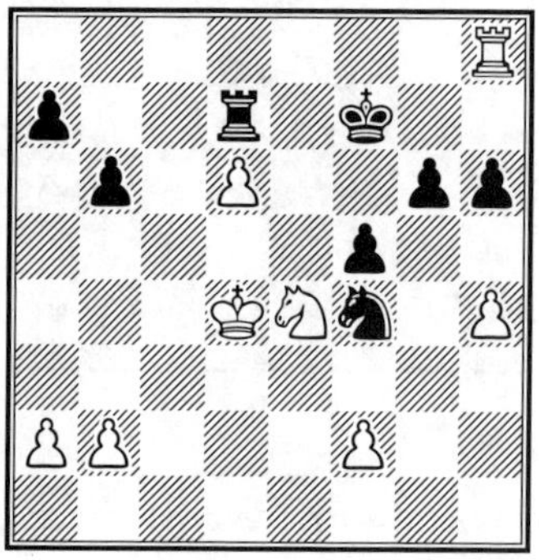

38.Rh7+?

It appears that Black has made progress, but exactly here White could have forced a draw with 38.Ke5!, as Black has nothing better than to allow perpetual check with 38...fxe4 39.Rh7+ Ke8 40.Rh8+, as the attempt to win with 38...Nd3+ 39.Kd5 Nb4+ 40.Ke5 Nc6+ 41.Kd5 Ne7+ 42.Ke5 fxe4 loses to 43.Rh7+ Ke8 44.Ke6!. Similarly, 38...Kg7 loses to 39.Rh7+!

38...Ke6 39.Rxd7 Kxd7 40.Nc3 Kxd6 41.Nb5+ Kd7

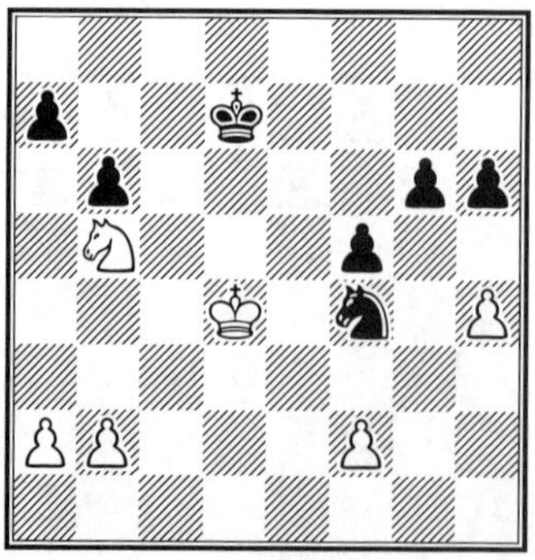

42.Nxa7?

But to play this move, with time pressure being over, without even considering the thematic 42.Ke5, is inexcusable. Instead, it appears this would still be satisfactory for a draw (if 42...Ng2 43.h5!). From now on Fischer plays the game perfectly.

42...Ng2! 43.Ke5

One move too late! Unfortunately, 43.h5 fails to 43...gxh5 44.Ke5 h4 and the pawn queens.

43...Nxh4 44.Kf4 g5+ 45.Kg3 Ng6 46.a4 f4+ 47.Kg2 g4 48.Nb5

White's sealed move.

48...Ne5! 49.Nc3

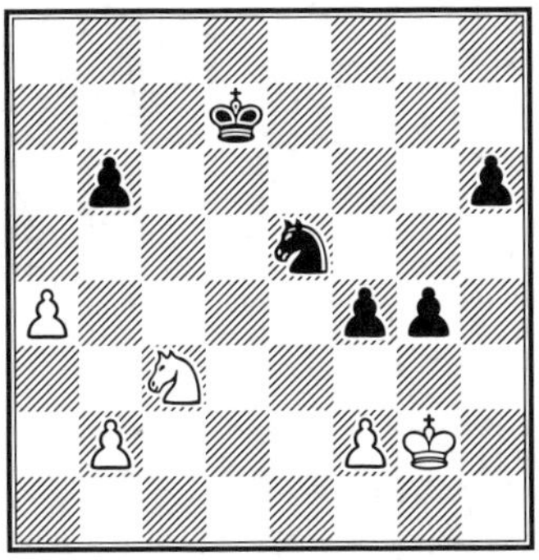

49...Ke6!!

This is the winning idea. Black's kingside pawns need protection by the king. The knight takes care of the queenside very well. During analysis I had only considered 49...Kc6, 49...Nd3 and 49...Nc4, all of which give White excellent drawing chances, if not a forced draw!

50.b4

There is nothing better, but now Black clearly wins.

50...Nc6! 51.f3 h5 52.b5 Ne5 53.fxg4 hxg4 54.Kf2 Nd3+ 55.Kg2 Nc5 56.Kf1 Kf5 57.Kg2 Ke5 58.Kf2 Nd3+ 59.Ke2 g3 60.Kf3 Ne1+ 61.Ke2 g2 62.Kf2 f3, 0–1

This was not the only time Mednis missed a chance to beat Fischer in a U.S. Championship—he was also completely winning in their game in the 1959/60 event. While Edmar did defeat Bobby in the 1962/63 U.S. Championship, their overall score in tournament games was 5½–1½ in Bobby's favor.

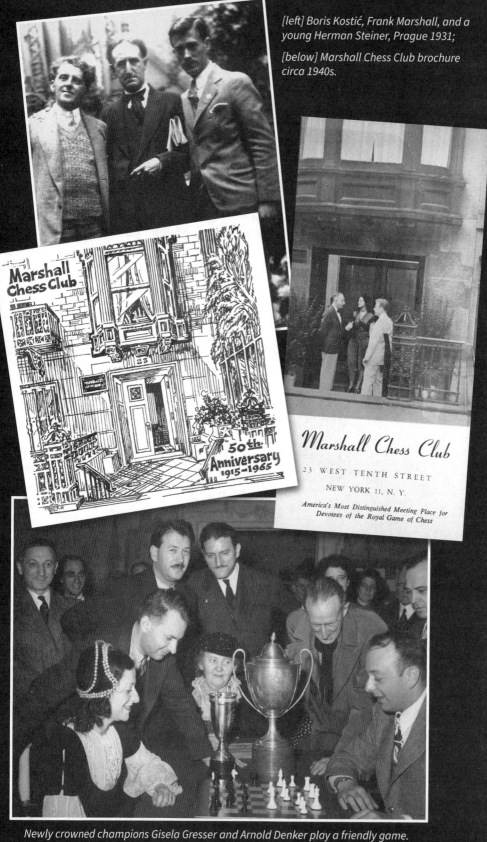

[left] Boris Kostić, Frank Marshall, and a young Herman Steiner, Prague 1931;

[below] Marshall Chess Club brochure circa 1940s.

Marshall Chess Club
23 WEST TENTH STREET
NEW YORK 11, N. Y.
America's Most Distinguished Meeting Place for Devotees of the Royal Game of Chess

Newly crowned champions Gisela Gresser and Arnold Denker play a friendly game. Leaning on the table are Reuben Fine (left) and Frank Marshall (right) with an unknown women sitting between them. Standing are Edward Lasker, Herman Steiner, and I.A. Horowitz. U.S. Championships, New York City, 1944. Frank Marshall died roughly half a year after this photo was taken (Photo: Nancy Roos).

8
FISCHER LECTURES

Since the U.S. Chess Federation was unable to raise his requested honorarium, Fischer didn't participate in the 1964 Tel Aviv Olympiad. Instead he gave a series of six lectures at the Marshall Chess Club starting October 28. This was announced in Frederic Chevalier chess column in *The Christian Science Monitor* and Sam Sloan confirms it took place:

> Yes. It did happen and I took the class. This is how I got to know Bobby Fischer well because after each lecture we would walk around Manhattan together until the early morning. The class cost $20 for six lectures at the Marshall Chess Club and only about twenty people attended. I was the only strong player. The others were rank beginners with some just learning the legal moves of chess.

Sadly, no one thought to record the lectures or take notes—as would also be the case for another Fischer talk in Los Angeles five years later. This was given to a much stronger group of players with several masters and experts in attendance—including Bruce Antman who would later become a top-ranked poker player. John Blackstone and Art Drucker remember that Fischer, a long-time comic book fan, loved Antman's name.

Art Drucker, who served as the right-hand man for the Piatigorsky Foundation for over twenty years, recorded the following event in his January 1970 notes for the organization:

> Grandmaster Robert J. Fischer gave a 2½-hour lecture to the Student Chess Club. Nearly forty youngsters filled the room to participate in this lively lecture/discussion. Mr. Fischer didn't work from a prepared text but spent the entire time answering questions about current chess theory. This is the only such lecture Mr. Fischer intends to give during his stay in California. Our sponsorship of the event gave these youngsters a unique opportunity to see the greatest American chessplayer.

This was not the only time Bobby spoke to a group of southern California juniors. Andy Sacks remembered Fischer giving a lecture and game analysis to the Juniors section of the Herman Steiner Chess Club (a predecessor of the

Rodolfo Cardoso, Toronto World Junior 1957.

Student Chess Club), when it was on Beverly Boulevard in West Hollywood in early 1961. Bobby was in town for the planning for his match with Reshevsky. Sacks said the game Fischer analyzed (using a large demonstration board) was his win against Rodolfo Cardoso from the 1958 Portorož Interzonal.

It's interesting that Fischer chose this game to show, as the endgame is an excellent demonstration of the fight between bishop and knight. It must also have been associated with good memories as the win played a key role in Bobby's qualification for the Candidates, but did Fischer realize he was lost after only thirteen moves? Fortunately for him Cardoso did not find 13...Nd5.

(44) Caro-Kann
Fischer – Rodolfo Cardoso
Portorož (20) 1958

1.e4 c6 2.Nc3 d5 3.Nf3 dxe4 4.Nxe4 Bg4 5.h3 Bxf3 6.Qxf3 Nd7 7.Ng5?!

7.d4 is much more natural. Occasionally Fischer's love of material could cause him to play artificially. This game is one example. His draw with Matulović from the Palma Interzonal is another.

7...Ngf6 8.Qb3?!

The logical follow-up to White's previous move, but 8.d4 was still the better move.

8...e6 9.Qxb7?!

Again 9.d4 was to be preferred

9...Nd5 10.Ne4

10.d4 was still relatively best, although after 10...Nb4 11.Kd1 Black's compensation for the sacrificed pawn is obvious.

10...Nb4 11.Kd1

The influence of Steinitz, who was noted for his king moves in the opening and middlegame, is felt. The only modern player with similar habits that comes readily to mind is the young Yasser Seirawan.

11...f5 12.c3

12.a3 Rb8 13.Qxa7 Nd5 also lands White's queen in big trouble.

12...Rb8 13.Qxa7

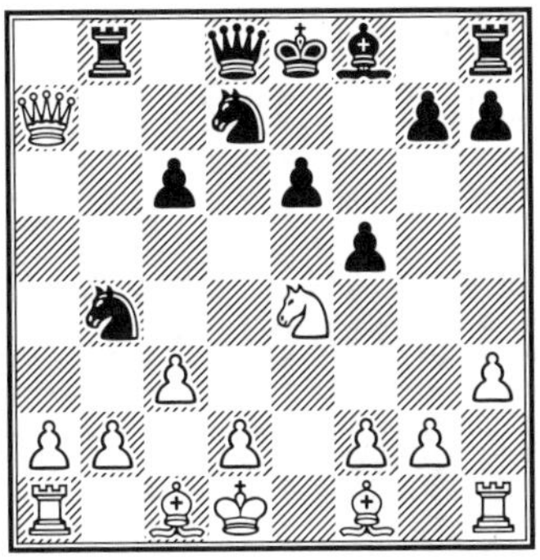

13...fxe4?

13...Nd5! 14.Ng3 (14.c4 Nb4 15.a3 Ra8 wins a piece) 14...Nc5 and White's queen is in mortal danger.

Fischer's performance in Portorož is remembered as pretty convincing. Although he never challenged for first, he was always in the hunt to qualify for the Candidates by virtue of beating up on the lower half of the field. Here, in the penultimate round, one of the tailenders could have dashed his hopes to advance.

14.cxb4 Bxb4 15.Qd4 0–0 16.Bc4 Nc5 17.Qxd8 Rbxd8 18.Rf1

Things have settled and Fischer now went on to defeat Cardoso in a well-played bishop versus knight endgame.

18...Rd4 19.b3 Bxd2 20.Ke2 Bxc1 21.Raxc1 Rfd8 22.Rfd1 Kf8 23.Rxd4 Rxd4 24.Rd1 Rxd1 25.Kxd1 Ke7 26.Kd2 Kd6 27.Kc3 Nd7 28.Kd4 Nf6 29.a4 c5+ 30.Ke3 g5 31.Be2 Kc6 32.Bc4 e5 33.a5 h6 34.Kd2 h5 35.Ke3 h4 36.Be2 Kb7 37.Bc4 Kc6 38.Ke2 Kb7 39.Kd2 Kc6 40.Ke3 Kb7 41.Kd2 Kc7 42.g4 Kc6 43.Kc3 Ne8 44.b4 Nd6 45.Bf1 cxb4+ 46.Kxb4 Nc8 47.Bg2 Kd5 48.a6 Na7 49.Ka5 Kc5 50.Bxe4 Nb5 51.Bg2 Na7 52.Ka4 Nb5 53.Kb3 Kb6 54.Kc4 Kxa6 55.Kd5 Kb6 56.Kxe5 Kc7 57.Kf6 Nc3 58.Kxg5 Nd1 59.f4 Kd6 60.Kxh4 Ke6 61.Kg5 Kf7 62.f5, 1–0.

Fischer did a series of talks on famous players with Dimitrije Bjelica for Yugoslav television in 1970, which may be his only recorded lectures.

The following fragment was published inside the notes to Fischer–Beach, New York State Open 1963 in the February 1964 issue of *Chess Review*. It is not clear exactly when this game was played—1963 is an educated guess.

(45) Pirc
Fischer – N.N.
1963

1.e4 g6 2.d4 Bg7 3.Nc3 d6 4.h4

An interesting possibility is 4.h4, which I have played in some skittles games.

4...h5?

4...Nf6 5.Be2 c5 6.dxc5 Qa5 7.Kf1! Qxc5 8.h5

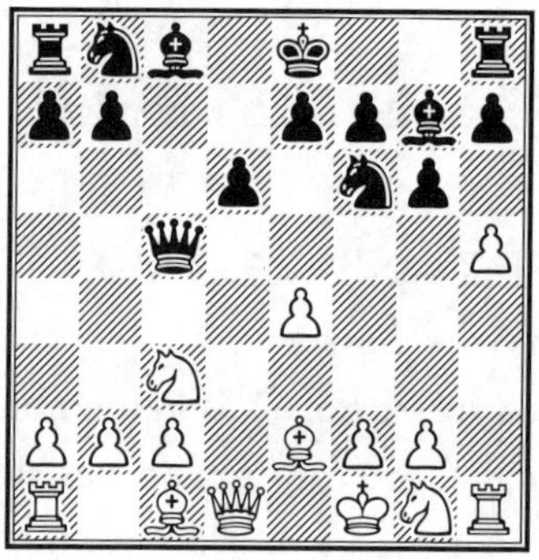

with a double-edged game. I beat Tal in a 5–minute game with this line.

5.Nh3! Bxh3?

A common mistake in this line.

6.Rxh3 c5 7.dxc5 dxc5 8.Bb5+ Nc6 9.Rd3 Qa5 10.Bd2

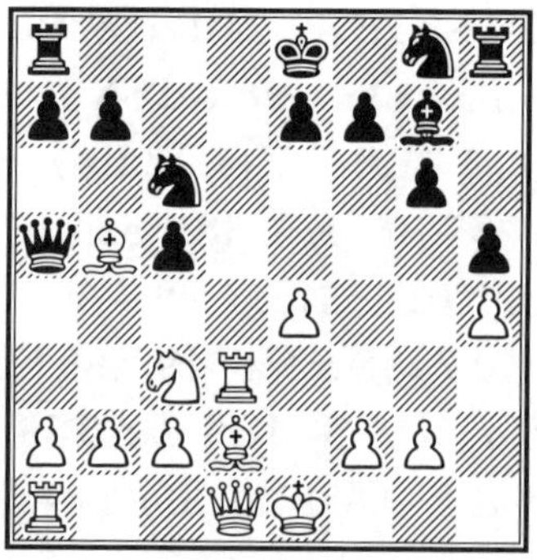

with a won game for White.

9
1965 CAPABLANCA MEMORIAL

Bobby Fischer will be remembered as not only one of the strongest chess players of all time, but also as one of its greatest innovators. The increment clock (David Bronstein also deserves some of the credit for this idea), Fischer Random chess (the pieces are placed on different squares in the starting position), and the rule change forbidding writing down a move before playing it (Fischer hated this practice that was the norm for many Soviet players) are three of his ideas that have been adopted.

Fischer was one of the first world-class players to challenge a computer—the Greenblatt Program in 1977. Twelve years earlier, in the summer of 1965, he played an entire tournament without sight of his opponents.

Chess by telegraph dates back to the 19th century, and normally is associated with team events, but the experiment Bobby engaged in was a first and stretched the idea of two opponents playing at a distance to the limit.

Bobby's acceptance of his invitation to play in the 1965 Capablanca Memorial, to be held in the Cuban capital of Havana, was well received in the chess world. Fischer had not played in an international tournament since the Curaçao Candidates tournament and there was much curiosity about how he would do in this mammoth twenty-two-player round robin. Then politics intruded and it looked as if Bobby would not be able to play, as the U.S. State Department refused to give permission to travel to Cuba.

In early 1964, Frank Meyer, senior editor of *National Review* (and father of International Master Eugene Meyer and FIDE Master John Meyer), and former USCF president Jerry Spann, held a debate at the Marshall Chess Club on the subject of whether or not the United States should compete with the Soviet Union over the chessboard.[1] Meyer held the position that the United States should not be fraternizing with the enemy, while Spann maintained it was important to have contact between the Soviet and American people. This was not a theoretical issue for Spann. A high-ranking member of FIDE, he had

[1] The transcript of this debate was published in *Chessworld*, March–April 1964.

experienced this interaction first-hand when he captained the American team to victory in the 1960 World Student Team Championship in Leningrad.

The viewpoints of the two men mirrored that of the nation. The concern wasn't only the Soviet Union, but other communist countries as well, particularly nearby Cuba. The official position of the U.S. government in 1964 was that travel to the island nation was not permitted for ordinary citizens, however, it allowed for some exceptions, including journalists.

When Larry Evans played in the 1964 Capablanca Memorial he didn't use his journalistic cover. As editor of *American Chess Quarterly* and a frequent contributor to *Chess Life*, he could have, but didn't. Evans led the event much of the way and his fourth place finish was one of the better results of his career, but he wrote next to nothing about the tournament or his visit. He flew to and from Cuba via a third country, and in hindsight it seems like he thought he could get away with the trip if he kept a low profile.

Evans considered his Cuban trip a matter of principle. When he arrived in Havana he was asked if he would be punished for defying his government, and he responded, that American citizens—unlike Cubans—had the right to travel wherever they pleased in peacetime. When he returned home to the United States he was interviewed several times by the FBI.

The next year, Fischer, likely influenced by Evans' unpleasant FBI experience and the risk he too might be interrogated or even prosecuted, made the decision not to make the trip to Cuba.

The Cubans really wanted Bobby in the tournament, so when the USCF came up with the idea for him to play from New York via teletype they were game. Just how badly they wanted him to participate can be seen in the Cuban government being prepared to spend $13,000–$3,000 appearance fee for Bobby and $10,000 for the open phone line and teletype machine at the Marshall Chess Club ($106,000 in 2020 dollars). The financial arrangements explain in part why Fischer was willing to suffer through a marathon tournament under difficult circumstances—the hunger to play again was definitely a factor, but the equivalent of a $24,000 honorarium probably didn't hurt.

Despite Bobby's willingness to play under novel circumstances, his participation was still up in the air as the Cuban government tried to score propaganda points that Fischer would not accept:

> I WOULD ONLY BE ABLE TO TAKE PART IN THE TOURNAMENT IN THE EVENT THAT YOU IMMEDIATELY SENT ME A TELEGRAM DECLARING THAT NEITHER YOU NOR YOUR GOVERNMENT WILL ATTEMPT TO MAKE POLITICAL CAPITAL OUT OF MY PARTICIPATION IN THE TOURNEY, AND THAT IN THE FUTURE NO POLITICAL COMMENTARIES ON THIS SCORE WILL BE MADE.

Castro then cabled back denying claims he had called Fischer's participation a propaganda coup for Cuba. Perhaps more importantly he challenged Bobby's courage:

> OUR LAND NEEDS NO SUCH "PROPAGANDA VICTORIES." IT IS YOUR PERSONAL AFFAIR WHETHER YOU WILL TAKE PART IN THE TOURNAMENT OR NOT. HENCE YOUR WORDS ARE UNJUST. IF YOU ARE FRIGHTENED AND REPENT YOUR PREVIOUS DECISION, THEN IT WOULD BE BETTER TO FIND ANOTHER EXCUSE OR TO HAVE THE COURAGE TO REMAIN HONEST.

This verbal jousting finished, Bobby and the organizers were set for him to play, but there were still more hurdles to clear. Grandmaster Jan Hein Donner, who played in the 1965 Capablanca Memorial, wrote an article that described how the Soviet participants, no doubt egged on by their government, tried to get Bobby to sign a paper denouncing the U.S. government for its failure to allow him to travel to Cuba.[1]

This was a bit tricky as most of the participants in the event, sympathetic though they might be to Bobby, were from communist countries and had no wish to stick their necks out. Fortunately, the Cuban organizer Barreras found the perfect solution to the impasse—more and more glasses of Bacardi rum. Soon the large crowd splintered into many happy small groups who had a hard time remembering what they were talking about. Not long after, the organizers announced that everyone agreed Fischer was playing!

One last detail remained to be solved—under what rules would Bobby play? There had been important events in the past that were not contested face to face—the 1945 USA–USSR match the best remembered—but nothing like a month-long event involving just one player playing from a distance. The technical commission of Grandmasters Donner, Geller, O'Kelly, and Pachman had their work cut out for them, particularly as the Soviets were convinced Bobby would find some way to try to cheat. Eventually this last obstacle was dealt with, chiefly by the ever-practical Barreras wisely ignoring the committee's recommendations!

The pre-tournament hullabaloo led to the 1965 Capablanca Memorial getting considerable attention in non-chess publications with *The New York Times* reporting on the event throughout—this included devoting the better part of a page on August 28 to the tournament. Alongside a write-up of Fischer's victory over Smyslov, there was a lengthy article on Bobby, dubbed the "Chess Virtuoso," that traced Fischer's development as a player, and concluded by noting Fischer earned $12,000 ($98,000 in 2020 dollars) a year from chess tournaments and

[1] Dimitry Plisetsky and Sergey Voronkov, *Russian's versus Fischer.* London: Gloucester Publishers, 2005, (pp. 128–130).

magazine articles, and still lived in the walk-up apartment on Lincoln Place in Brooklyn that he was brought up in.

Fischer had a strong start, defeating Lehmann in round one and then winning a beautiful game against the eventual tournament winner Smyslov. This would later become game 51 in *My 60 Memorable Games* and is characterized by Fischer's magnificent positional performance in which he slowly outplays his opponent step by step, taking advantage of his queenside pressure and Smyslov's doubled e-pawns

Black's doubled e-pawns turned out to be a key factor in another Ruy Lopez from the same event, where Fischer was White against Soviet Grandmaster Ratmir Kholmov. The difference in this game was the pawns were a source of strength, covering key central squares, and not a weakness.

Played near the end, in round eighteen when Fischer was starting to feel the effects of a long tournament, this game features a beautiful move (19...Nd4!!) that caught Bobby completely off guard. This temporary sacrifice (the back-up threat of ...d4-d3 guarantees the piece will be won back) didn't win material, but instead led to a large positional advantage.

David Bronstein once remarked, "When you play the Ruy, it's like milking a cow." Fischer was a first-rate dairyman losing only ten games in the Ruy Lopez out of more than 100 he played as White, with most defeats occurring in the early stages of his career. His only losses after this game with Kholmov were to Bent Larsen (Second Piatigorsky Cup) and Boris Spassky (game five of their 1992 match).

Grandmaster Ratmir Kholmov (1925–2006), known in Soviet chess circles as "The Central Defender" for his resourcefulness in saving difficult positions, was one of the top ten to fifteen players in the world from the mid-1950s to the late 1960s. He is one of a handful of players to have defeated both Fischer and Kasparov—Petrosian, Spassky, and Korchnoi are three others in this exclusive club.

Kholmov never played in the West during his prime and there has been speculation he was considered a security risk. According to Grandmaster Gregory Serper, in a wonderful article published at chess.com, while Kholmov was serving as a sailor in the Soviet Merchant Marine during World War II his ship was captured by the Japanese and he became a POW.

If this is true, Kholmov may have been lucky to only have been prevented from playing in the West. Many Soviet soldiers who were taken prisoner during World War II were considered "contaminated" when repatriated.

Most of the top fifteen players in the world during Kholmov's prime were citizens of the Soviet Union. There were few strong tournaments in the West and invitations to play in these infrequent events were prized being hard to come by. This might account for Kholmov's playing exclusively in socialist countries..

However, there's likely another explanation why Kholmov never played in the West: He was "no enemy of the bottle" and the Soviet authorities worried his fondness for alcohol was a potential source of embarrassment. There is support for this in a well-known story in which Kholmov plays the leading role. In the version given by Serper, the game was played in a Soviet Team Championship, another has it taking place place in a simul.

In both cases a very drunk Kholmov, as Black, plays the sequence 1.e4 Nc6 2.f4 b6 3.Nf3 e5. Here, after 4.fxe5, he realizes at the last second he cannot play his intended 4...Nxe5? and with clear amazement on his face, says loudly: "That's weird! I've been playing the Grünfeld my whole life and never had such a horrible position after just four moves!" The reference is to the well-known variation 1.d4 Nf6 2.c4 g6 3.Nc3 d5 4.cxd5.[1]

(46) Ruy Lopez
Fischer – Ratmir Kholmov
Havana (18) 1965

Commentary by Ratmir Kholmov.[2]

Until now I had not had an opportunity to cross swords with the young and already-famous American champion and I was therefore looking forward to this encounter with particular interest. The first concern was: which opening variation to play against him? There was no doubt that I was going to meet 1.e4 with 1...e5. The main thing that troubled me was the fact that all of the lines in the Spanish Game that I had used in the Havana tournament had already come to Fischer's attention. Here I received some friendly advice from Vassily Smyslov. He recommended the move 9...Na5, which I had not employed in practice for a long time. As the course of the game demonstrated, this turned out to be a psychological surprise for the American champion, one that contributed to my success. And so...

1. e4

As far as I know, Fischer never plays anything else! However, despite his restricted opening repertoire, he achieved real success in this very strong event. If one considers that he has not taken part in many big tournaments in recent years, then his result in the Havana tournament must be acknowledged as exceptional.

1 While this is a great story, with a fundamental truth at its core, it should be pointed out that Kholmov rarely played the Grünfeld, preferring to meet 1.d4 with 1...Nf6 and 2...e6.

2 Ratmir Kholmov, Translated by Dan Scoones, *Shakhmatny Riga*, #3/1966.

1...e5 2.Nf3 Nc6 3.Bb5 a6 4.Ba4 Nf6 5.0–0 Be7 6.Re1 b5 7.Bb3 0–0 8.c3 d6 9.h3

Here is the position in which Black stands at the crossroads. He has many different continuations, but not everyone has the ability to choose a variation that suits his own specific tastes. For a long time I used to get playable positions with the line 9...Be6, but after losing a game to Alexey Suetin my willingness to play this variation suffered a sharp decline.

9...Na5

The oldest and most well respected continuation!

10.Bc2 c5 11.d4 Qc7 12.Nbd2 Nc6 13.dxc5 dxc5 14.Nf1 Be6

The game Suetin–Averbakh, 32nd USSR Championship 1964/65, took a different course: 14...Rd8 15.Qe2 Rb8 16.Ne3 g6 17.Ng5 Bb7 18.Bb3 Rf8! 19.Nd5 Nxd5 20.Bxd5, and White had the advantage. In the present game Black boldly accepts the doubling of his pawns, based on the idea that White will find it hard to get at them.

15.Ne3 Rad8 16.Qe2 c4 17.Ng5 h6

Clearly not 17...Bc8?, because of 18.Nd5 Nxd5 19.exd5 Bxg5 20.Bxg5 Rxd5 21.Qe4! and White wins.

18.Nxe6 fxe6 19.b4?

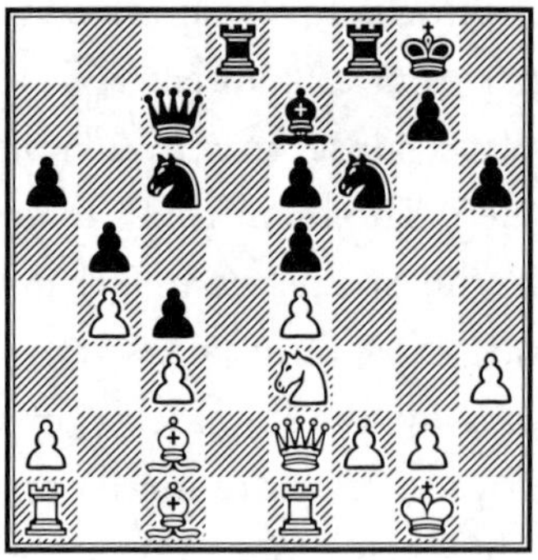

The result of a miscalculation, or just a common oversight? I still do not know, because after the game there was no opportunity for a post-mortem with my unseen opponent. [Translator's note: Fischer was playing by telex from New York.] Stronger was 19.a4. Also possible was 19.b3, but for the time being Black can ignore the threat of 20.bxc4 because of the reply 20...b4! with excellent play for the pawn.

19...Nd4!

With this move Black takes over the initiative.

20.cxd4 exd4 21.a3

In making his nineteenth move, Black had to take into account the dangerous possibility 21.e5!? Now 21...Qxe5 is no good because of the shot 22.Nf5! However, on 21.e5?! Black had prepared the stronger reply 21...d3! Now on 22.exf6 there follows 22...Bxf6! 23.Qg4 Bxa1 24.Qxe6+ Qf7 25.Qxf7+ Kxf7! 26.Bd1 d2 27.Bxd2 Rxd2 28.Bh5+ g6 29.Rxa1 gxh5 with a winning position for Black. Of course, if White had played 19.a4 then 19...Nd4 would not have worked.

21...d3 22.Bxd3 Rxd3!

More solid than 22...cxd3, after which White can play 23.Qa2!, and Black in some difficulties. For example, on 23...Qc6 there can follow 24.Nf5.

23.Ng4 Kh7

Of course not 23...Nxg4 because of 24.Qxg4 with a double attack on e6 and h6.

24.e5 Nxg4 25.Qe4+ g6 26.Qxg4 Rf5

Black has emerged with an indisputable positional advantage. His pieces are excellently placed, while the White pawn on e5 requires continuous defense.

27.Qe4 Qd7 28.Be3 Qd5 29.Qxd5

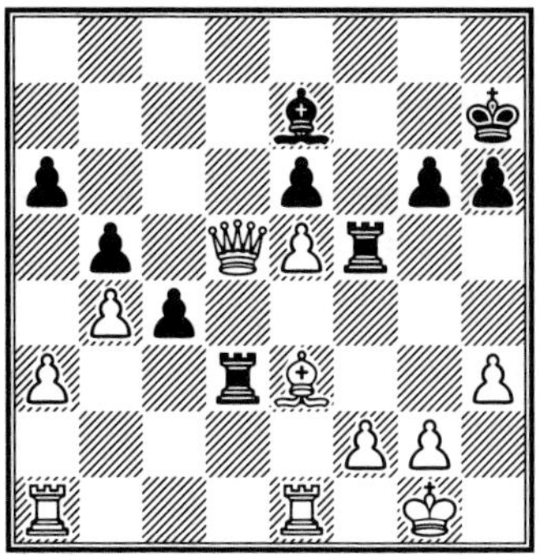

At this juncture I very much wanted to play 29...exd5, creating two connected passed pawns. However, the reply 30.Bc5! would be very unpleasant for Black, so after long thought I refrained from capturing with the pawn.

29...Rxd5 30.f4 g5?

Here Black misses the very strong continuation 30...Bh4! After this it would be very difficult for White to defend himself; for example, 31.Rd1 Bg3 32.Rxd5 exd5 33.Rd1 Bxf4 34.Bxf4 Rxf4 35.Rxd5 c3! 36.Rc5 Rc4. Or 33.Rf1 g5! 34.e6 (34.fxg5 Bh2+) 34...gxf4 35.e7 Re5 and Black wins. It is possible that White may do better with the immediate 31.Rf1, but after 31...g5 he cannot play 32.g3.

31.g3 gxf4 32.gxf4 Rf8 33.Kg2 Kg6 34.Rg1 Rd3 35.Kf3+ Kf5!

In playing this move Black had to take many possibilities into account. The position of the Black king looks threatening for White, but at the same time there are certain hidden dangers for Black. For example, after 36.Rg7 Bd8 37.Rag1, the move 37...Bb6 is impossible due to mate on g5.

36.Rg7 Bd8! 37.Rb7

White must prevent 37...Bb6. After 37.Rag1 Rxe3+! 38.Kxe3 Bb6+ 39.Ke2 Bxg1 40.Rxg1 Rd8 Black would obtain a won endgame.

37...Rg8

This creates threats of ...h5-h4 or ...Bh4.

38.Rb8!

If 38.Rf7+ then 38...Kg6 39.Rb7 Kh5! and the threat of ...Bh4 cannot be prevented.

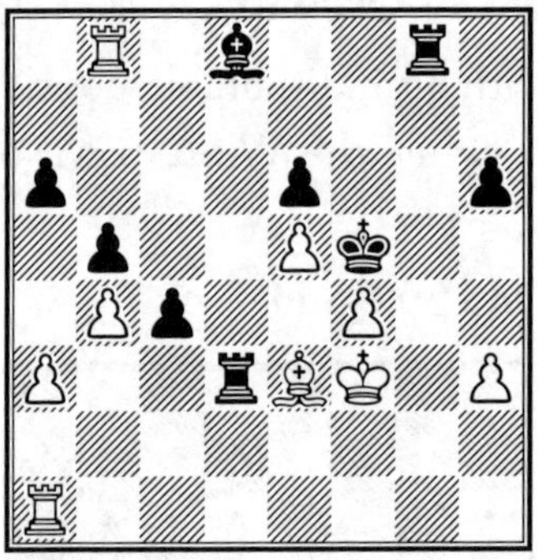

Black has a won position. However, wearied by the previous struggle, I simply could not calculate all of the possibilities for both sides and therefore decided to play more quietly. Black wins after 38...h5; for example, 39.Rb7 Bh4 40.Rf7+ Kg6 41.Ra7 Kh6 42.f5+ Bg5 43.Re1 exf5 44.h4 Bxe3 45.Rxe3 Rxe3+ 46.Kxe3 Rg6 47.Kd4 Rc6 48.Kd5 c3!, etc.

38...Rg7 39.a4

Perhaps better was 39.Ra2 h5 40.Rd2 Rxd2 41.Bxd2 Rd7 42.Be3 Rd3. White has exchanged a pair of rooks, but his position has not become any easier because he still must concede the square e4. If now 43.h4, then 43...c3 44.Ke2 Ke4 45.Bc1 Bxh4 46.Re8 Rh3!, etc.

39...h5 40.axb5 axb5 41.Rxb5

There does not seem to be anything better. True, I was somewhat afraid of 41.R1a8, but here Black wins after 41...h4 42.Rxd8 Rg3+ 43.Kf2 Rdxe3 44.Rd4 Ref3+ 45.Ke2 Rxh3 46.Rf8+ Kg4 47.Rg8+ Kh5 48.Rg5+ Kh6, etc. Black also must win after 43...Rgxe3.

41...Bh4

Now Black's coordination and White's scattered pieces quickly decide the game in Black's favor.

42.Ke2 Rg2+ 43.Kf1 Rh2 44.Kg1 Re2 45.Bb6 c3 46.Kf1 Rh2, 0–1.

What was it like for Fischer to play twenty-one games in a small room with the only company for eight to twelve hours a referee that never spoke? In one word—DIFFICULT! Brady elaborated on this:[1]

> The arrangement was certainly not easy for Bobby, however. To avoid any hint of cheating, he had to be isolated from everyone except the referee. It was a sterile, feedback-barren experience with no chance to read his opponent's body language. ...
>
> A typical four-hour game was transformed by the teletype process into an eight—or nine-hour affair. Some games stretched to twelve hours. The tournament became a test of endurance and stamina. Bobby grew exhausted. His opponents have the same problem, but each only had to submit to the process once—when playing Fischer. Bobby had to play this strange, isolated form of chess every single game. In the midst of the tournament, someone asked how well he thought he'd do and he answered, "It's question of when I'll crack up."

Brady had a first-hand taste of what Fischer was going through. He was the referee for the first two games but got the axe before round three—Brady's biography of Bobby, *Profile of a Prodigy*, had just been published and Fischer did not like the way he was depicted, and that was that.

As reported in the *Reading Eagle*:[2]

> **CHESS CHAMPION FIRES REFEREE**
>
> U.S. Chess Champion Bobby Fischer, overseen by a new referee, was to resume long-distance play this morning in the Capablanca Memorial Chess tournament in Havana.
>
> Fischer, twenty-two, fired his original referee yesterday, only an hour before beginning a match via teletype to Cuba with Romania's Victor Ciocâltea.
>
> The ousted referee, Frank Brady, thirty-one, said that he received a long-distance call from Fischer's attorney in Massachusetts, who said the young chess master didn't want him around.
>
> "I talked to Bobby later and he said he felt it would disturb his concentration if I was in the room with him," Brady said. "The problem is with the book I wrote about him. He didn't like it."

---

1 Frank Brady, *Endgame: Bobby Fischer's Remarkable Rise and Fall—from America's Brightest Prodigy to the Edge of Madness*. New York: Crown Trade, 2011, (p. 159).

2 *Reading Eagle*, August 30, 1965.

And *The New York Times*[1] stated:

> [Fischer] pulled two surprises yesterday in his third game of the Capablanca Memorial tourney: He adopted an unusual defense, and he discharged his referee.

There's no reason to doubt Brady's recollection, but there are contradictory reports surrounding who the referees and runners were and when they served in these capacities. This caption accompanied a photo published in *Chess Life.*[2]

> Photo caption: J. F. Reinhardt, who was New York referee in the first two games of the Capablanca Memorial, makes White's second move in round one. Bill Goichberg, who relayed the moves from the teletype room is in the foreground. (Photo: Robert Parent).

In the photograph it appears that Reinhardt is in the act of playing 2.Nf3 with White's pawn on e4 and Black's on c5. These moves match those played in Lehmann–Fischer, round one. Had Brady and Reinhardt shared the duties of referee for the first two games? This looks to be a mystery without an answer. What is known for sure is that Reinhardt served as the referee for a good portion of the tournament.

Then there's the long standing question surrounding the first move of the Ciocâltea–Fischer round three game. This is the famous game where Fischer essayed Alekhine's Defense for this first time in his career.

Since Fischer was past his temporary infatuation with meeting 1.e4 with 1...e5, and back to his habitual Najdorf Sicilian (which he played the other four times he met 1.e4 in the tournament), there has long been a question if Ciocâltea's first move was garbled by the teletype machine and was in fact mistakenly relayed as 1.d4 to Fischer.

Grandmaster Victor Ciocâltea (1932–1983) won the Romanian Championship eight times between 1952 and 1979. A participant in eleven Olympiads between 1956 and 1982, he was one of a select group of players who defeated Fischer (Varna 1962).

The nagging question of the first move:[3]

> All went well until Fischer played Victor Ciocâltea of Romania. Ciocâltea's first move, 1.d4, was played on the Marshall Club board by a FIDE judge. Fischer replied with his usual 1...Nf6. Then came the remarkable reply, 2.e5!? There was considerable consternation on West 10th Street as the officials realized that White's first move had been 1.e4 and not 1.d4. Could

---

1 *The New York Times*, August 29,1965, (p. 22).

2 *Chess Life*, September 1965, (p. 191).

3 Arthur Bisguier and Andrew Soltis, *American Chess Masters from Morphy to Fischer*. New York: Macmillian, 1974, (p. 213).

> Fischer take his move back? Could the error in transmission be explained? It didn't matter because Fischer waved aside the fears by playing 2...Nd5. He was willing to play Alekhine's Defense, an opening he had never played before in tournament chess and was not to play again for five years. But he was sufficiently prepared to hold Ciocâltea to a draw in an unfamiliar opening.

Chess historian Edward Winter asked the question:[1]

> Do contemporary reports corroborate this account? We see nothing in *Chess Life*, *Chess Review*, or the tournament book (published in Buenos Aires later in 1965).

Winter's question is an excellent one as there was no discussion of the matter in magazines at that time. Fortunately, some of the individuals who were present that day are still with us and remember what actually happened.

Paul M. Albert, best known for his sponsorships of the Albert Brilliancy prizes at U.S. Championships from 1983 to 2003, gave one account:[2]

> On the question of how Fischer wound up playing Alekhine's Defense in this game, let me comment as someone who was present at the Marshall Chess Club this game; in fact I was running the wall-board for spectators in the front of the club while Bobby was playing behind the closed sliding doors in the rear of the club.
>
> The teletype machine was in the club office just adjacent to where the wall-board was located. On the first move when the runner emerged from the office he told me what I heard as 1.e4 (probably 1.PK4 in those days), which I put on the board. In other words, I got the moves from Havana before Bobby got them in the back room a few seconds later by being played on his board. When the runner returned he told me 1...Nf6 (1...NKB3), which I posted, on the board.
>
> I was immediately berated by all the spectators that the MOVE was impossible because Bobby never played Alekhine's Defense. I responded that I merely posted what I had been given. I do not know what actually happened in the back room. I do not remember who the referee, runner, and teletype operator were; I did not know any of them. I do know that Frank Brady was not present, because I have asked him about it, and I have told this story at a couple of Fischer oriented events in which I participated at the Marshall.
>
> From the picture in the Winter article, Bill Goichberg may have been the runner. I'll have to ask him what he remembers, if he in fact was the runner for this game. Obviously from when I was told 1.e4 (apparently the correct move) until it got to the back room and was apparently played as d4, somehow someone got confused. I don't know what happened in the office/teletype room when 1...e5 (1...PK4) was received. I remember a sort of confused

[1] Edward Winter, *Chess Notes 6194*, https://www.chesshistory.com.

[2] Paul M. Albert, Chessgames.com.

FIDE Master Sameer Sursock, three-time Champion of Lebanon, playing against Grandmaster Victor Ciocâltea in round eleven of the 1972 Vrnjačka Banja Zonal.

ambiance including the spectators thinking I was incompetent as wall-board operator. I'd love to know definitively what actually happened.

The definitive insider account is offered by Peter Sepulveda and it clears up the matter once and for all—Ciocâltea did play 1.e4:[1]

> As to your first question. It is true. I was there in the office that day. As you can imagine the teletype communications using analog transmission was not the most reliable. We had set up in the office, a small space, the teletype machine inside and just to the right of the doorway. We also had a small table in the office with a chessboard and pieces set up for the current game so that we could make sure that we were receiving correct moves and were transmitting them correctly. The door was kept closed so that whoever was operating the teletype would not be disturbed and besides the machine made so much noise as to wake up the dead. The first move from Havana was 1.d4. This was given to Fischer via the referee. I can't recall who was in charge. Fischer replied 1...Nf6. This move was transmitted by Bill Slater (Kathryn's husband). The second move received was 2.e5. At this point there was great consternation, as you can imagine given Fischer's temperament. So we asked for confirmation stating that we had received d4 as the first move. Back came the reply that it was 1. e4 and not 1. d4. So Mr. Goldwater (the club president) decided to go to Fischer and explain the situation. Everyone in the office expected Fischer to blow up. However, to the delighted surprise of everyone Fischer calmly accepted the facts and played on. I remember Mr. Goldwater saying how much relief he felt. Everyone in the office was smiling. As to your second

[1] Email to author, November 7, 2016.

[left] Kathryn Slater played in seven U.S. Women's Championship stretching from 1937 to 1974. She and her husband William who served as managers of the Marshall Chess Club for many years, put in long hours at the teletype machine;

[right] Russ Garber manning the teletype machine at the Marshall Chess Club during the 1965 Capablanca Memorial (Photos: Beth Cassidy).

question of who were the operators of the teletype. The late Bill Slater was the main operator helped by Russ Garber and Kathryn Slater. I even transmitted once in Spanish to Havana (it was brief). I was never a runner (except for one move) and I don't recall who they were.

I'm sorry, but I can't help you as to who were the referees.

Attendance was always high, but not as large as the 1972 World Championship match. I recall that ABC sent a television crew the first day of the match. The AP sent a correspondent and photographer once.

Fischer played upstairs in the back room from the Great Hall. The doors were kept closed so that he wouldn't be disturbed by the crowds during play. There is a plaque on the table today commemorating the event.

Here is an amusing story from the event: Fischer was scheduled to resume an adjourned game with International Master Wade. It was early in the morning and Mr. Goldwater came to me with a list of items that Fischer wanted for breakfast. Among them was orange juice. So I went as directed to Bigelow's drugstore, which had a luncheonette. They had everything Fischer wanted but the orange juice. So I went looking for a store that was open so that I could buy the orange juice. However, being early morning everything was closed. So I went back to the club and told Mr. Goldwater that I couldn't find any orange juice. He told me not to worry and went to deliver the breakfast to Fischer. Fischer blew up. He started screaming at Mr. Goldwater, calling him among other things an idiot. Contrast this with what happened in the Ciocâltea incident.

There seems to be something about the third game that makes it the best remembered of this strange experiment never again to be repeated. It could be because it was played on a weekend early in the tournament and spectator attendance might well have reached its peak.

Dr. Arthur S. Antler recalled what a special occasion it was to see Bobby in action:[1]

> I remember clearly being taken to the Marshall Chess Club one Sunday afternoon to see Bobby Fischer play chess by teletype in the Capablanca Memorial Tournament at Havana, Cuba. The State Department refused to allow Fischer to play in person, as we didn't have diplomatic relations with this communist country. Fischer was allowed to play against his opponents by teletype, and he made his moves from the Marshall Club. He was isolated in a private room, but the main hall was crowded with spectators viewing a large demonstration board. I remember how excited I was watching the moves unfold. That Sunday, Fischer's opponent was the Rumanian Master Victor Ciocâltea. The game was adjourned after the first playing session in a double-edged position. It was finally drawn after play resumed the next day.

If that isn't enough about Ciocâltea–Fischer, consider one last fact—it ended Fischer's longest winning streak.

1 Arthur S. Antler, *AVRO 1938: The Ultimate Chess Tournament*. Dallas: Chess Digest, 1993, (from the Introduction).

PART FIVE

the Late Sixties

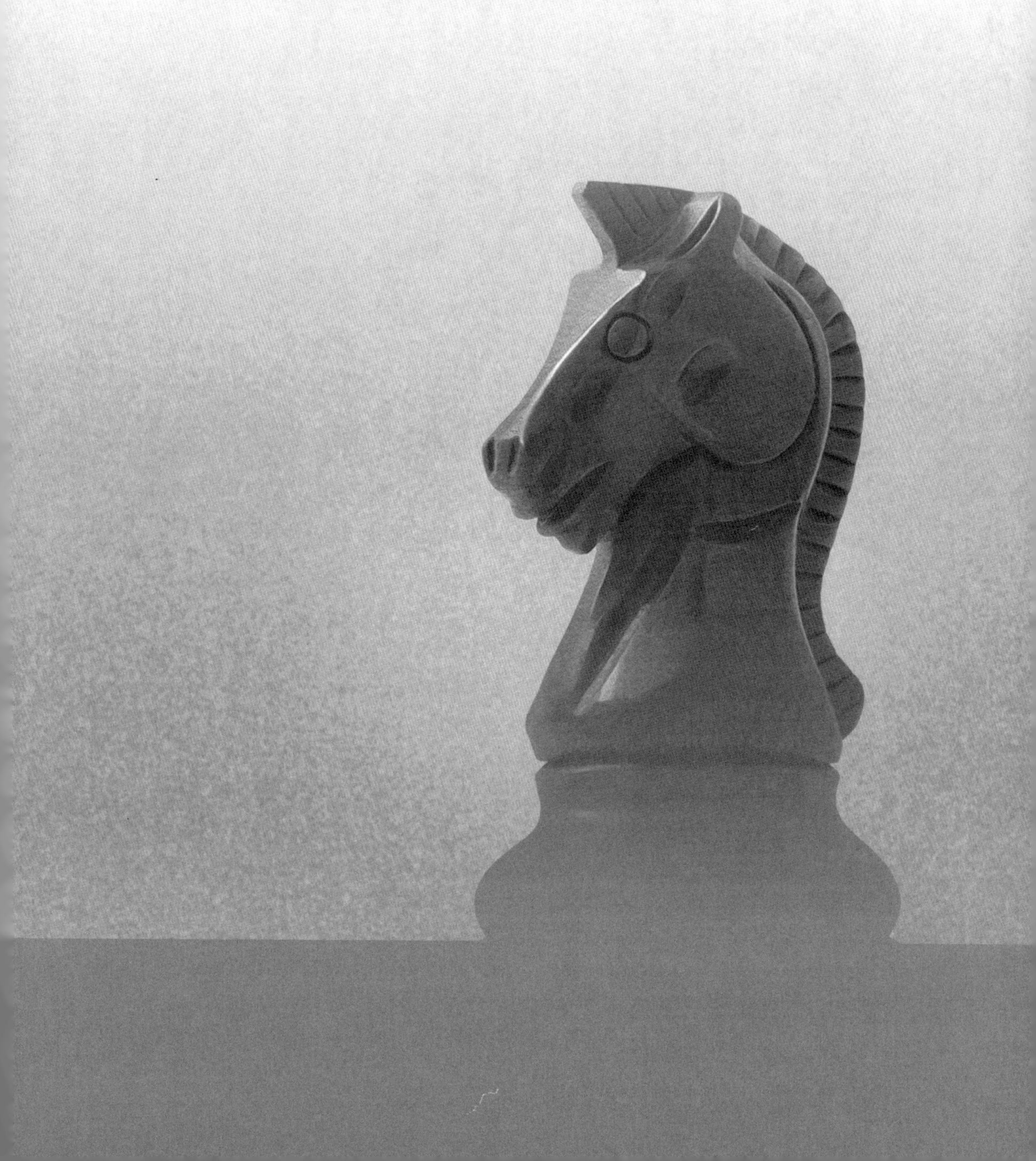

(from left) Jacqueline Piatigorsky, Tigran Petrosian, Gregor Piatigorsky, (unidentified), Ed Edmondson, Friðrik Ólafsson, Isaac Kashdan, Pal Benko at the First Piatigorsky Cup 1963 (Photo: Piatigorsky collection, courtesy of the World Chess Hall of Fame).

1
THE HEDGEHOG

Bobby Fischer's contributions to chess include countless opening innovations and original middlegame plans. His pioneering use of the King's Indian Attack is an example of how he seamlessly combined the two. Wins against Ivkov (Second Piatigorsky Cup 1966), Myagmarsuren (Sousse Interzonal 1967), and Panno (Buenos Aires 1970) are still model games half a century later.

Fischer is also one of the founding fathers of the Hedgehog. Grandmasters Ulf Andersson and Ljubomir Ljubojević played it extensively in the 1970s and 1980s, but they did not create it.

García Soruco–Fischer, Havana Olympiad 1966, is credited as the game where the plan ...Kh8, ...Rg8, ...g5, ...Rg6 and ...Rag8 was first seen, but this may not be true. Andy Soltis, in his introduction to *Morphy's Chess Masterpieces*, points out Bobby may have been influenced by Paulsen–Morphy, New York 1857, where Black played ...Kh8, ...Rg8 and ...g5. The pawn structure is different, but there is some similarity.

Here is how the Hedgehog may have developed.

Both players were blindfolded in Game (47).

(47) Ruy Lopez
Louis Paulsen – Paul Morphy
New York 1857

1.e4 e5 2.Nf3 Nc6 3.Nc3 Bc5 4.Bb5 d6 5.d4 exd4 6.Nxd4 Bd7 7.Nxc6 bxc6 8.Ba4 Qf6 9.0-0 Ne7 10.Be3 Bxe3 11.fxe3 Qh6 12.Qd3 Ng6 13.Rae1 Ne5 14.Qe2 0-0 15.h3 Kh8

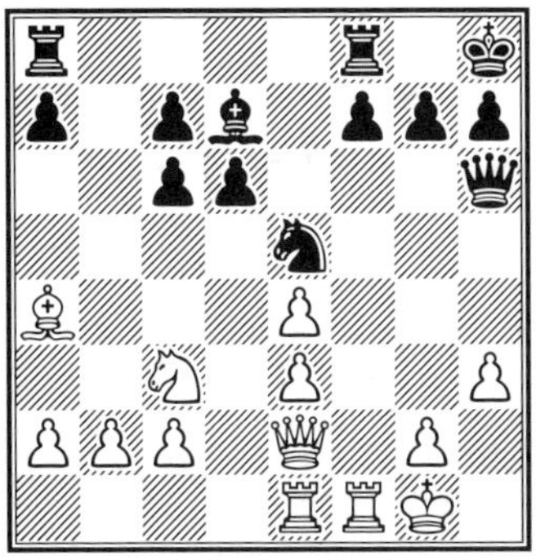

16.Nd1 g5 17.Nf2 Rg8 18.Nd3 g4 19.Nxe5 dxe5 20.hxg4 Bxg4 21.Qf2 Rg6 22.Qxf7 Be6 23.Qxc7

Morphy now announced mate in five starting with 23...Rxg2+, 0–1.

Game (48) is considered the first example of the plan being executed in its entirety.

---

(48) Sicilian Najdorf
Julio García Soruco – Fischer
Havana (ol) 1966

1.e4 c5 2.Nf3 d6 3.d4 cxd4 4.Nxd4 Nf6 5.Nc3 a6 6.Bc4 e6 7.Bb3 b5 8.a3 Be7 9.Be3 0-0 10.0-0 Bb7 11.f3 Nbd7 12.Qd2 Ne5 13.Qf2 Qc7 14.Rac1 Kh8

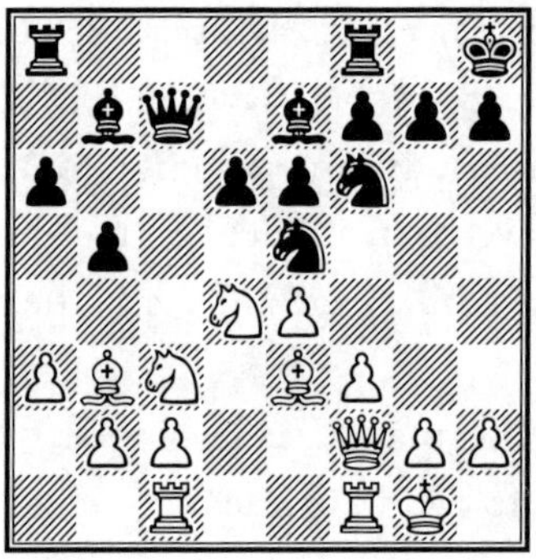

Passive moves (a3, f3 and Rac1) by the Bolivian Olympiad team member are just the encouragement Fischer needs to implement what Kasparov calls the "compressed spring" strategy.

15.Nce2 Rg8 16.Kh1 g5 17.h3 Rg6

17...d5 is a good move, but it reduces the tension. The text gives White more problems to solve.

18.Ng3?

White cannot just sit. He had to try something active like 18.Rfd1 Rag8 19.c4, with the idea 19...bxc4 20.Bxc4 Nxc4 21.b3.

18...Rag8

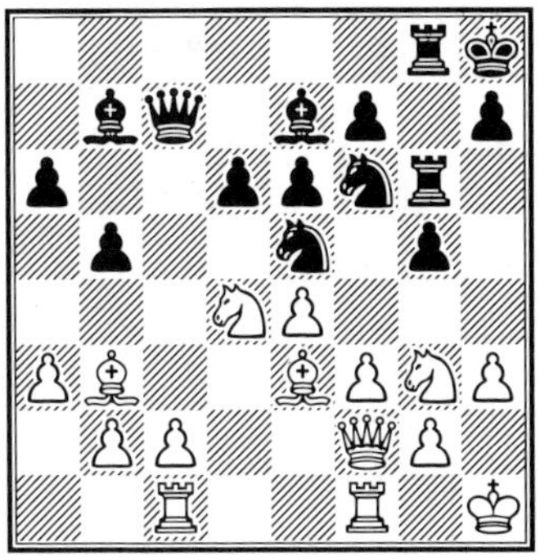

18...d5 was again quite good for Black, but Bobby sticks with his strategy and is soon rewarded.

19.Nxe6?

This just loses, but it is hard to suggest a satisfactory defense.

19...fxe6 20.Bxe6 Nxe4 21.Nxe4 Rxe6, 0–1.

Fischer's first try with the variation worked like a charm, his opponent allowing him to do everything he wanted. The second time around things were not so simple. The nineteen-year-old Andersson was not yet a world-class grandmaster, but still a strong player rated 2480 on the July 1970 FIDE rating list, placing him in the top 100 players in the world at the time.

This game was played in a hotel room the day after the Olympiad. Fischer was paid a fee by a Swedish newspaper which published the game score a move a day over several months.

---

(49) Larsen's Opening
Fischer – Ulf Andersson
Siegen September 28, 1970

1.b3

This was not the first time Bobby opened 1.b3, as he had played it a few months before against Tukmakov in Buenos Aires. Fischer stated 1.e4! is "best by test", but he had a much better career record with 1.b3; in fact, he was a perfect 4–0. All the games were played against quality opponents (Mecking and Filip were the two others) and were interesting fights where Bobby introduced new ideas.

1...e5 2.Bb2 Nc6 3.c4 Nf6 4.e3 Be7 5.a3 0-0 6.Qc2

6.d3 d5 7.cxd5 Qxd5 8.Nc3 Qd6 9.Nf3 Bf5 10.Qc2 Rfd8 11.Rd1 h6 12.h3 Qe6 13.Nd2 Nd7 14.Be2 Kh8?! (14...Qg6 –Kasparov) 15.0-0 Bg6

16.b4 a6 17.Rc1 Rac8 18.Rfd1 f5 19.Na4 Na7 20.Nb3 b6 21.d4 f4 22.e4 and White soon won in Fischer–Tukmakov, Buenos Aires 1970.

6...Re8

6...d5 7.cxd5 (7.d3) 7...Nxd5 8.Nf3 Bf6 9.d3 g6 10.Nbd2 Bg7 11.Rc1 was a dream Sicilian for White in Petrosian–Sosonko, Tilburg 1981. Black is actually two tempi down on normal lines in the Scheveningen (colors reversed) as he has spent three moves with his king bishop instead of one.

7.d3 Bf8 8.Nf3 a5 9.Be2 d5 10.cxd5 Nxd5 11.Nbd2 f6

Andersson supports his e-pawn with the text, but step by step he is drifting into a passive position where he will soon have no constructive plan.

Soltis suggests 11...g6 followed by ...Bg7 as Sosonko played, but wouldn't ...g6, ...Bg7 and ...d5 in the opening save a couple moves over ...Be7-f8-g7?

12.0-0 Be6 13.Kh1!!

[Alex Fishbein] "The exclamation points are not awarded to this move, but rather Fischer's entire plan. It is the originality of the plan that merits praise. Later, this plan became popular in Hedgehog positions, where (with colors reversed), White's c-pawn is on the fourth rank."[1]

13...Qd7 14.Rg1 Rad8 15.Ne4!

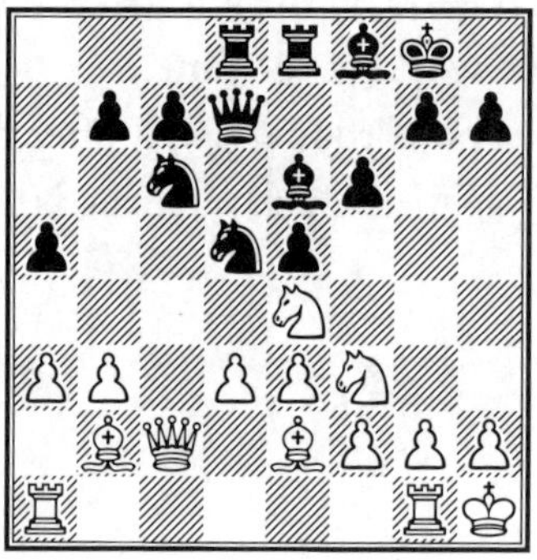

15...Qf7

If 15...h5, then 16.h3 with g4 to follow. In fact Black has no way to stop g4 as noted Hedgehog expert Russian Grandmaster Sergey Shipov points out:

15...Kh8 16.g4! Bxg4 17.Rxg4! Qxg4 18.Nxe5 Qe6 19.Bg4 Qg8 20.Nxc6 bxc6 21.Rg1! with powerful compensation for the exchange.

15...Nb6 16.g4! Bxg4 17.Nh4 f5 18.Nxf5 Qxf5 (or 18...Bxe2 19.Nf6+ Kh8 20.Nxd7 Bf3+ 21.Rg2 Rxd7 22.Nh4 Bxg2+ 23.Kxg2) 19.Bxg4 Qf7 20.d4 exd4 21.Ng5. In both cases White is winning.

16.g4! g6?!

---

[1] Alex Fishbein, *Fischer!: The Chess Career of Bobby Fischer.* Manasquan, NJ: R&D,1996.

This unforced weakening increases the strength of g4–g5.

16...Nb6 17.Nfd2 Be7 (Shipov) or 17...Bd5 (Kasparov) would have offered complicated play.

17.Rg3 Bg7 18.Rag1!

[Kasparov] "A remarkable attacking construction! The original source, with reversed colors, was the game Soruco–Fischer (Havana Olympiad 1966)."[1] [2]

18...Nb6 19.Nc5! Bc8 20.Nh4 Nd7?

[Shipov] "Black had to sacrifice the exchange for a pawn: 20...Rd5 21.Bf3 Rxc5 22.Qxc5 Qxb3 with chances for both sides."

21.Ne4!

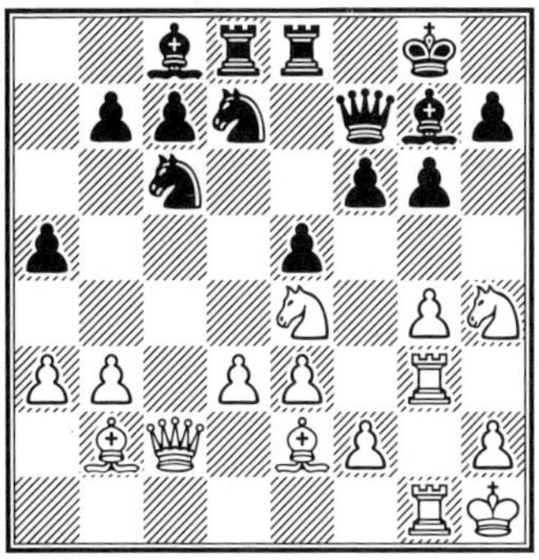

[Kasparov] "An amazing paradox: with the board full of pieces, practically without coming into contact with the enemy army and not straying beyond his own half of the board, White has imperceptibly achieved a winning position."

21...Nf8 22.Nf5! Be6 23.Nc5 Ne7 24.Nxg7! Kxg7 25.g5! Nf5 26.Rf3 b6 27.gxf6+ Kh8 28.Nxe6 Rxe6

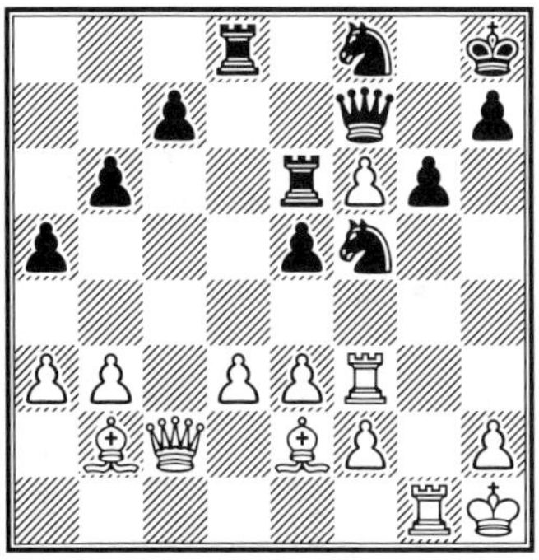

---

[1] *Garry Kasparov on Fischer: Volume IV My Great Predecessors*. London: Everyman Chess, 2004.

[2] Arthur Van De Oudeweetering, in *Improve Your Chess Pattern Recognition* (pages 219-220), points out Nievergelt-Keres, Zurich 1959, saw a similar plan of g4, doubling rooks on the g-file and after Nf3-h4 playing the sacrifice Nf5. The sixteen-year-old Bobby Fischer was a participant at Zurich 1959.

29.d4! exd4 30.Bc4 d3 31.Bxd3 Rxd3 32.Qxd3 Rd6 33.Qc4 Ne6 34.Be5 Rd8 35.h4 Nd6 36.Qg4 Nf8 37.h5 Ne8 38.e4 Rd2 39.Rh3 Kg8 40.hxg6 Nxg6 41.f4 Kf8 42.Qg5 Nd6 43.Bxd6+, 1–0.

> [Kasparov] "This game made such a great impression on Ulf Andersson, that in the 1970s the talented Swedish grandmaster, who is well known for his skill in defense, became one of the main ideologists of the "Hedgehog" set-up and the "compressed spring" method when playing Black! That is how the chess revolution of the 1970s began."[1]

Just a day after the game with Andersson, Fischer got the opportunity to use his plan once again, this time in a simul. White's fate is similar to what would have happened to García Soruco if had hadn't self-destructed with 19.Nxe6?.

---

(50) Sicilian
Michels – Fischer
Münster (simul), September 27, 1970

1.e4 c5 2.Nf3 d6 3.d4 cxd4 4.Nxd4 Nf6 5.Nc3 a6 6.Bd3 e6 7.Nb3 Be7 8.0-0 Qc7 9.Qe2

9.Be3 Nbd7 10.f4 0-0 11.Qf3 is a popular main line.

9...Nbd7 10.Be3 0-0 11.f3?!

11.f4 is necessary as the text is too passive.

11...b6 12.Qf2 Bb7 13.Rfd1 Rac8 14.Rac1

White has no constructive plan.

14...b5 15.a3 Ne5 16.Kh1 Kh8

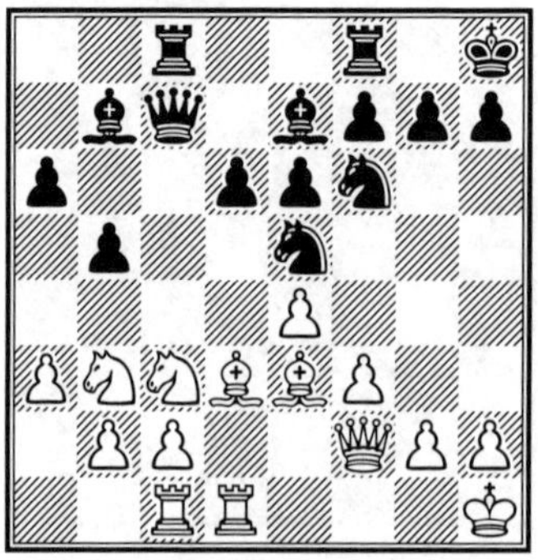

17.Bb6 Qb8 18.Rd2 Rg8 19.Rcd1 g5 20.Bd4 Rg6 21.Qf1 Rcg8 22.a4

White decides he can't wait forever.

[1] *Garry Kasparov on Fischer: Volume IV My Great Predecessors*. London: Everyman Chess, 2004.

22.Qe1 Bd8 23.Qf1 Bc7 followed by breaking with ...d5 is another idea at Black's disposal. If 22.Qg1 then 22...Nxd3 23.cxd3 e5 24.Be3 d5.

22...bxa4 23.Nxa4

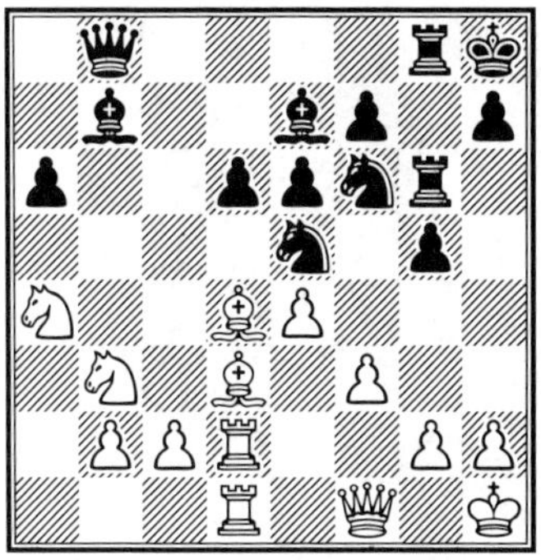

23.Na5 had to be tried.

23...Rh6

23...g4! 24.f4 Nxd3 25.cxd3 g3! 26.h3 e5! 27.f5 Rg4! 28.hxg4 exd4 29.Nxd4 Qf8 wins even more quickly.

24.Bxe5 dxe5 25.Nac5 g4! 26.Nxb7 Qxb7

26...Nh5! would have ended things faster.

27.Bxa6?

27.g3 had to be played.

27...Qa7 28.Qd3 gxf3 29.Na5

As 29.gxf3 is met by 29...Nh5.

29...Ng4 30.gxf3 Qf2, 0–1.

Having seen these games, should Fischer be considered the father of the Hedgehog? That's a difficult question to answer. He certainly discovered the key setup with ...Kh8, ...Rg8, ...g5, ...Rg6 and Rag8. We also know he was very conscious of Black's ability to break with ...d5 (or when to avoid it). What we don't know for sure, since none of his opponents had their c-pawn on c4 or ...c5, is if he was aware of the ...b5 break played independently or in conjunction with ...d5. It does seem likely. Less clear is the maneuver ...Bf8-e7-d8-c7, a now standard Hedgehog maneuver, that was only employed regularly after Fischer became World Champion and stopped playing.[1] All in all, it seems fairest to credit Fischer as the originator of the kingside plan in the Hedgehog.

[1] Opočenský–Sämisch, Pieštany 1922, appears to be the first game where ...Bf8-e7-d8-c7 was played and K. Treybal–Flohr, Budapest 1934, is another earlier example. For more on this see Grandmaster Lubomir Kavalek's article at https://www.huffpost.com/entry/baseline-chess-hedgehog-a_b_4409302.

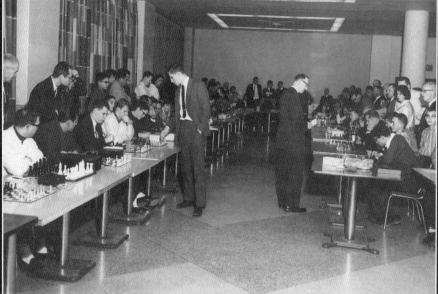

[top] Bobby faces an unknown opponent during his exhibition in Rochester, New York, February 15, 1964 , sponsored by the Eastman Kodak Company;

[bottom] Standing with his back to Fischer is Dr. Erich Marchand a strong master who worked for Kodak. Rochester was an early stop on Fischer's 1964 tour. (Photos: Courtesy of Ron and Shelby Lohrman).

2
MY 60 MEMORABLE GAMES

What would become one of the all-time classic game collections, *My 60 Memorable Games,* was published in 1969. Larry Evans wrote on more than one occasion about the difficulties in getting Bobby to let Simon & Schuster go ahead with publication. For much of the project, which started sometime in 1964, Fischer was torn between his desire to write as perfect a book as possible, (which led to never ending revisions) and the fear of giving the Soviets (and other competitors) too many of his trade secrets.

The working title of *My Life in Chess* and/or *My 52 Memorable Games* appeared on drafts.[1] When the book was initially completed it ended with Bobby's victory over Nicolas Rossolimo from the 1965/66 U.S. Championship (game 52 in the published book). At that point, the project was shelved.

When Bobby eventually allowed Simon & Schuster to go ahead with publication, a decision was made to bring the book up to date, adding eight additional games covering 1966 and 1967. Evans suggested that Bobby's decision to go forward was a pragmatic one:

> He was feeling depressed about the world and there was an excellent chance that there would be a nuclear holocaust soon. He felt he should enjoy whatever money he could get before it was too late.

As a member of the Worldwide Church, Fischer's fear of a nuclear holocaust was quite understandable as it was part of Herbert W. Armstrong's prophecies.

One eighteen-page working draft dated 1966[2] contains two fully annotated games (Fischer–Smyslov, Havana 1965 and Fischer–Rossolimo, U.S. Championship 1965/66) that appear as games 51 and 52 (with a few minor changes) in the published book. However, the other material in the draft, seven game fragments from the 1965/66 U.S. Championship, didn't make it into *My 60 Memorable Games.*

---

[1] The collections of both David DeLucia and the World Chess Hall of Fame in St. Louis hold manuscript of early drafts.

[2] This eighteen-page draft is in David DeLucia's collection.

The games and fragments in this working draft were prefaced by an introduction:

> "AMERICA"
>
> BOBBY FISCHER TALKS CHESS
>
> Probably my best game of 1965 was against Vassily Smyslov, former World Champion and winner of the Capablanca Memorial Tournament in Havana, where I was enabled to compete by relaying chess moves via telephone. Smyslov permitted me to double his wing pawns after 11...Be6; but his judgment seemed justified since the pawns controlled important squares and rendered it difficult, if not impossible, for White to penetrate successfully. However, Smyslov failed to fight back with his customary energy and drifted into a passive ending. Missing the best defense, he gradually got squeezed to death.
>
> The second game, against Rossolimo in the recently concluded U.S. Championship, is a good example of sustaining the initiative in what would appear to be an equal position. In this event, after drawing with Addison in the first round, I won six in a row and it looked like clear sailing since I remained a point and a half ahead of the field with only four rounds to go. But then came a rude awakening—two consecutive losses. Against Robert Byrne I blundered in the opening and lost the exchange without compensation. Then against Reshevsky I played the opening listlessly and he obtained a crushing bind after a handful of moves. Luckily, I still had a half point lead even after these two losses. Pulling myself together, I won my last two games (against Rossolimo and Burger) to clinch the title. Byrne and Reshevsky tied for 2–3, trailing by a point.

Stamped on the cover of this manuscript was a potential clue to its story:

> THERON RAINES
> 207 East 37th Street
> NEW YORK, NY 10016
> YU 6–2412.

Contacted in 2011, literary agent Theron Raines responded:

> No, I didn't sell the book that you mention. I knew Bobby for a couple of years, sold something by him to *Sports Illustrated*, but then he put everything in the hands of a lawyer whose name I don't recall.
>
> I met Bobby very early—recall watching two exhibition games he played against Max Euwe—lost one, tied one, but he made Euwe VERY uncomfortable in the second game. With regard to the *Sports Illustrated* article[1]: When Bobby came to see me, I talked to him about the Russians

[1] Raines was referring to the only article Fischer ever wrote for *Sports Illustrated*—the piece in which he accused the Russians of fixing games at Curaçao 1962. "The Russians Have Fixed World Chess," *Sports illustrated*, August 20, 1962.

> and he said they would cheat by throwing games to each other, then all playing very hard against him. I asked how he would cope with that, and he said, with a little smile, "I'll beat 'em." This was probably on the second occasion we met. On the third occasion, a Saturday morning, I went with him to talk to Bob Creamer at *Sports Illustrated*. We had to sign in downstairs, and I signed first, then Bobby signed with a big grin—"M. Tal."

The working title "Bobby Fischer Talks Chess" was an obvious choice as that was what he used for his *Chess Life* column, but why "America"—that is a mystery.

The annotated games with Smyslov and Rossolimo are known, but the light annotations to the others are new and revealing. Characteristically Fischer takes the high road, praising his opponents and accepting the blame for his poor play.

The notes to Fischer–Zuckerman make it clear that many standard sources got Black's forty-third move wrong when they translated the game from English Descriptive to Algebraic notation—it's definitely 43...Qc6 and not 43...Qc3.

Games (51) thru (57), all annotated by Fischer, are presented exactly as he wrote them with these exceptions: 1. English Descriptive notation has been changed to Algebraic; 2. The moves preceding the diagram (where Fischer's notes start) have been added; 3. The games are presented in chronological order.

(51) Nimzo-Indian
Larry Evans – Fischer
New York (3) 1965/66

1.d4 Nf6 2.c4 e6 3.Nc3 Bb4 4.e3 b6 5.Nge2 Ba6 6.a3 Bxc3+ 7.Nxc3 d5 8.b3 Nc6 9.Be2 0-0 10.a4 dxc4 11.Ba3 Re8 12.b4 Ne7 13.0-0 Ned5 14.Rc1 c6 15.Bf3 b5 16.a5 Qc7 17.Qc2 Rad8 18.Rfd1 Bb7 19.Rd2 Nxc3 20.Qxc3

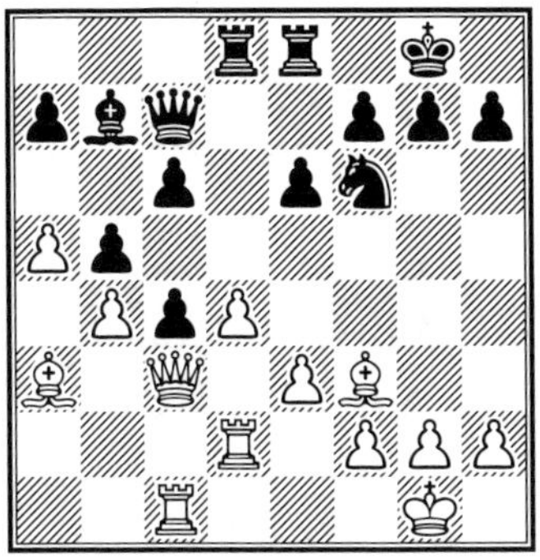

Evans dropped a pawn in the opening by a careless transposition of moves, but the win looked difficult.

20...c5!

A shot which shatters all White's hopes for prolonging resistance.

21.dxc5

Equally futile is 21.bxc5 Bxf3 22.gxf3 Nd5, etc.

21...Bxf3 22.gxf3 Rxd2 23.Qxd2 Rd8 24.Qe1 Rd3 25.Bb2 Nd5 26.Bc3 f6 27.Ba1

White has no moves.

27...e5 28.Kg2 Qd7 29.Rc2 e4! 30.Rc1

If 30.fxe4 Qg4+ 31.Kf1 Nxe3+! 32.fxe3 Rd1.

30...exf3+ 31.Kh1

31.Kxf3 Qh3+ 32.Ke2 (32.Ke4 Ne7! forces mate.) 32...Nxe3!

31...Nxb4

Black wins easily.

32.Qg1 Kf7 33.Bd4 Nc6 34.Qg3 Nxd4 35.exd4 Rxd4 36.Rg1 g5 37.c6 Qxc6 38.Qb8 Rd7 39.h3 Qe6 40.Rg3 c3 41.Qh8 Qf5 42.Kh2 Rd2 43.Rxf3 Rxf2+ 44.Rxf2 Qxf2+ 45.Kh1 Qf3+ 46.Kh2 Qf4+ 47.Kg1 Qe3+ 48.Kf1 Qxh3+ 49.Ke2 g4 50.a6 Qf3+ 51.Ke1 Qe3+ 52.Kf1 Qd3+ 53.Kf2 g3+ 54.Kg2 Qe4+ 55.Kxg3 Qg6+, 0–1.

(52) Ruy Lopez
Fischer – Pal Benko
New York (4) 1965/66

1.e4 e5 2.Nf3 Nc6 3.Bb5 a6 4.Ba4 Nf6 5.0-0 Be7 6.Re1 b5 7.Bb3 d6 8.c3 0-0 9.h3 Nb8 10.d4 Nbd7 11.Nh4 Nb6 12.Nd2 c5 13.dxc5 dxc5 14.Nf5 Bxf5 15.exf5 Qc7 16.g4 h6 17.h4 c4 18.Bc2 Nh7 19.Nf3 f6 20.Nd2 Rad8 21.Qf3

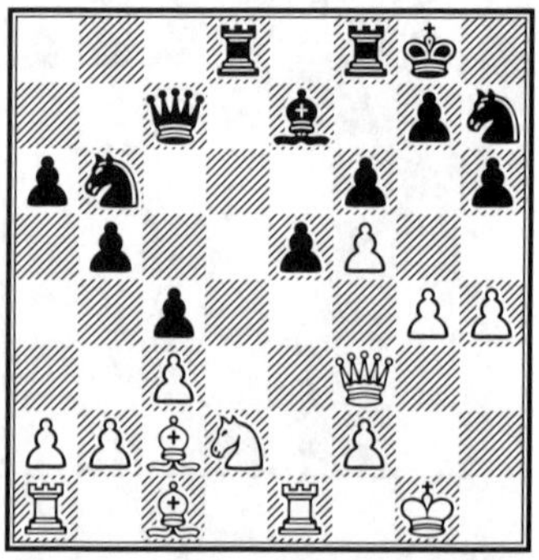

Sometimes your greatest ally is your opponent, who sees ghosts.

21...h5?

A difficult-to-explain blunder. With this suicidal nervous reflex, Benko opens up the position—which of course is just what White wants. After a normal defensive move such as 21...Rd7 or 21...Nd5 White, although better, certainly has no clear win in view.

22.gxh5 Nd5 23.Ne4 Nf4 24.Bxf4 exf4 25.Kh1 Kh8 26.Rg1 Rf7 27.Rg6

And White piled up on the g-file and broke through with h6 etc.

27...Bd6 28.Rag1 Bf8 29.h6 Qe5 30.Qg4 Rdd7 31.f3 Bc5 32.Nxc5 Qxc5 33.Rxg7 Rxg7 34.hxg7+ Kg8 35.Qg6 Rd8 36.Be4 Qc8 37.Qe8+, 1–0.

---

(53) Torre
Arthur Bisguier – Fischer
New York (5) 1965/66

1.d4 Nf6 2.Nf3 g6 3.Bg5 Bg7 4.Nbd2 c5 5.c3 cxd4 6.cxd4 Nc6 7.e3 0-0 8.a3 h6 9.Bh4 d6 10.Bc4 Bf5 11.h3 Rc8 12.0-0 e5 13.e4 Bd7 14.dxe5 dxe5 15.Ba2 g5 16.Bg3 Qe7 17.Re1 Rcd8 18.Nh2 Be6 19.Bxe6 Qxe6 20.Nhf1 Rd3 21.Re3 Rd7 22.Qb3 Qe7 23.Nf3 Rfd8 24.Rae1 Nh5 25.Rc3 Qf6 26.Ne3 Nd4 27.Nxd4 exd4 28.Ng4 Qg6 29.Rd3 Nxg3 30.fxg3 Rc7 31.Nf2 Rdc8 32.Re2 Rc1+ 33.Kh2 h5 34.Qxb7 Be5 35.Qd5 R1c5 36.Qd7 h4 37.Nh1 Rc1 38.Rf3 g4 39.Qxg4 Qxg4 40.hxg4

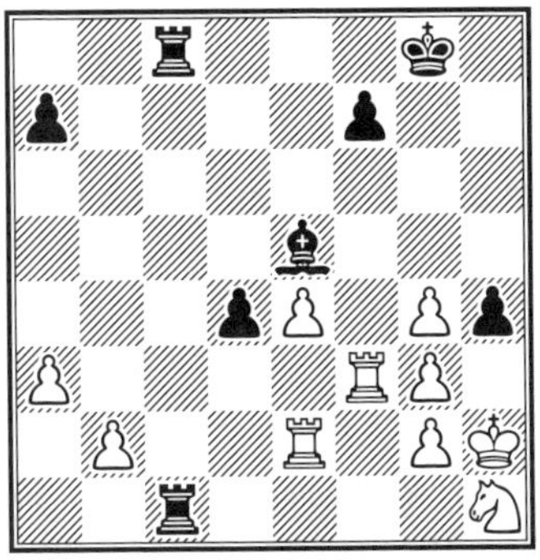

40...Kg7!

Threatening ...hxg3+ and ...Rh8 mate.

41.Rf5

41.Rf5 Rxh1+ 42.Kxh1 Rc1+ 43.Kh2 hxg3+ 44.Kh3 Rh1 mate.

41...Rxh1+!, 0–1.

(54) Sicilian
Fischer – Bernard Zuckerman
New York (6) 1965/66

1.e4 c5 2.Nf3 d6 3.d4 cxd4 4.Nxd4 Nf6 5.Nc3 a6 6.Bc4 e6 7.Bb3 b5 8.f4 Bb7 9.f5 e5 10.Nde2 Nbd7 11.Bg5 Be7 12.Bxf6 Nxf6 13.Qd3 Rc8 14.0-0 0-0 15.Ng3 Rc5 16.Nd5 Bxd5 17.exd5 a5 18.a4 b4 19.Ne4 Nxe4 20.Qxe4 Qb6 21.Kh1 Bf6 22.g3 Rfc8 23.Kg2 Kf8 24.Rae1 Ke7 25.Qd3 Kd8 26.Re4 Kc7 27.Bc4 Kb8 28.Rf2 Ka7 29.h4 Qd8 30.Ba6 Rb8 31.Bb5 Rbc8 32.Rd2 Qb6 33.Kh2 h6 34.Bc6 Be7 35.Qe2 R8xc6 36.dxc6 Qxc6 37.b3 f6 38.Qg4 Bf8 39.Rc4 d5 40.Rxc5 Qxc5 41.Qg6 d4 42.Qe8 Kb7

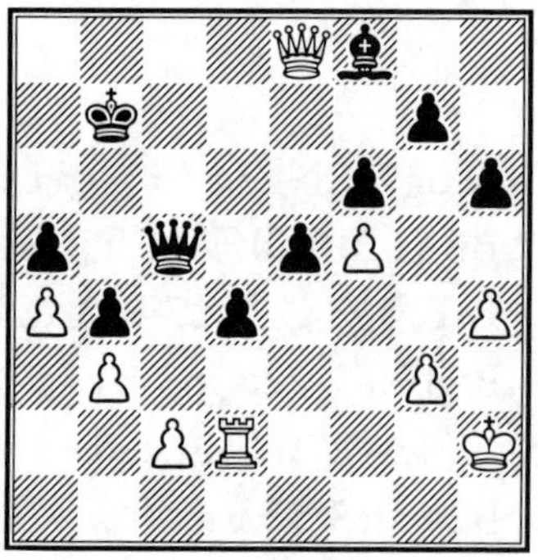

This adjournment looked difficult, but turned out to be unexpectedly easy when Zuckerman failed to offer resistance.

43.Kh3!? Qc6?

Better was 43...Qd5! and if 44.Rg2 (44.Kh2) 44...Bc5! with active play. White's best would be to play his king back with 44.Kh2.

44.Qf7+

44.Qxf8 Qh1+ forces a draw by perpetual check.
[Author] This variation is clear evidence that Black played 43...Qc6 and not 43...Qc3 as given in many sources—MegaDatabase 2016 and Karsten Müller's book on Bobby Fischer, to name two.

44...Kb6 45.Rg2 Qc5 46.Re2 Qd6 47.Qe8 Qc5 48.Kg4! Be7 49.Kh5 Bd6 50.Kg6 Bc7 51.Kxg7 Qc3 52.Qb5+ Ka7 53.Qd3 Qc6 54.Kxh6 Qe8? 55.Qxd4+! Bb6 56.Qd5, 1–0.

(55) Nimzo-Indian
Anthony Saidy – Fischer
New York (7) 1965/66

1.c4 Nf6 2.Nc3 e6 3.d4 Bb4 4.e3 b6 5.Nge2 Ba6 6.Ng3 Bxc3+ 7.bxc3 d5 8.Qf3 0-0 9.e4 dxc4 10.Bg5 h6

One of the tense moments occurred in the following position. A buzz hummed through the tournament hall, as it did whenever it looked like I might be in trouble.

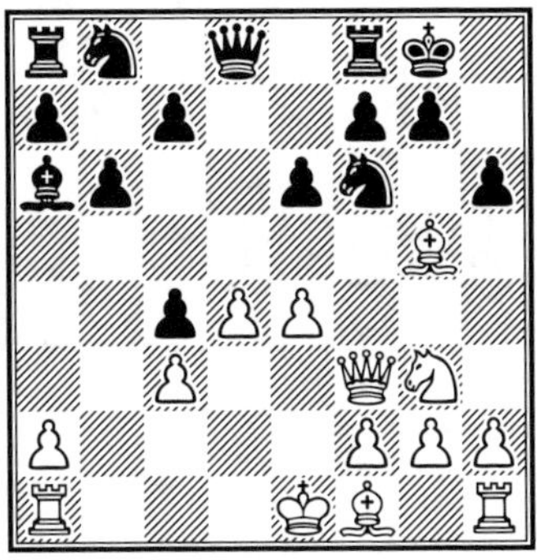

11.Bd2

This brought a groan of disappointment from the audience. Everyone had expected 11.h4 (threatening 12.e5). After 11...hxg5 12.hxg5 Re8 13.gxf6 Qxf6 14.Qh5 g6 15.Qh7+ Kf8 16.e5 Qg7 17.Qh4 threatens Ne4 with a crushing attack.
However, Black can secure equality simply by 11...Bb7! 12.Bxf6 (12.Bxc4 Nbd7) 12...Qxf6 13.Qxf6 gxf6 14.Bxc4.

[Author] Modern computer engines (Komodo, Stockfish and Houdini) all give White a clear advantage in the position after 14.Bxc4.

Anthony Saidy wrote a two-page article ("Old Hat!") for *Chess Life* (March 1966) analyzing 11.h4, but only examined 11...hxg5 and not 11...Bb7.

11...Nbd7 12.e5 Nd5 13.Nf5

If 13.Nh5 Qh4! 14.g3 Qe7 ends the attack; 15.Qg4 f5.

13...exf5 14.Qxd5 Re8! 15.Bxc4

If 15.Be2 Nxe5 16.Qxd8 Nd3+.

15...Nxe5! 16.Qxd8 Nxc4+ 17.Qxe8+ Rxe8+ 18.Kd1 Nxd2 19.Kxd2 Re2+ 20.Kc1 Rxf2 21.g3 Bb7 22.Re1 Be4 23.Re3 Rxh2

The rest is agony. Black mopped up.

24.a4 h5 25.Ra3 g5 26.Rb3 f6 27.a5 h4 28.gxh4 Rxh4 29.Ra3 Rh7 30.axb6 axb6 31.Ra7 Re7 32.d5 Kf7 33.Kd2 f4 34.Re1 f5 35.c4 g4 36.Rb7 g3 37.d6 cxd6 38.Rxb6 f3, 0–1.

(56) French
Fischer – Robert Byrne
New York (8) 1965/66

1.e4 e6 2.d4 d5 3.Nd2 Nc6 4.c3 e5 5.exd5 Qxd5 6.Ngf3 exd4 7.Bc4 Qh5 8.0-0 Nf6 9.Qe1+ Be7 10.Nxd4 0-0 11.Be2 Bg4 12.Nxc6 Bd6!

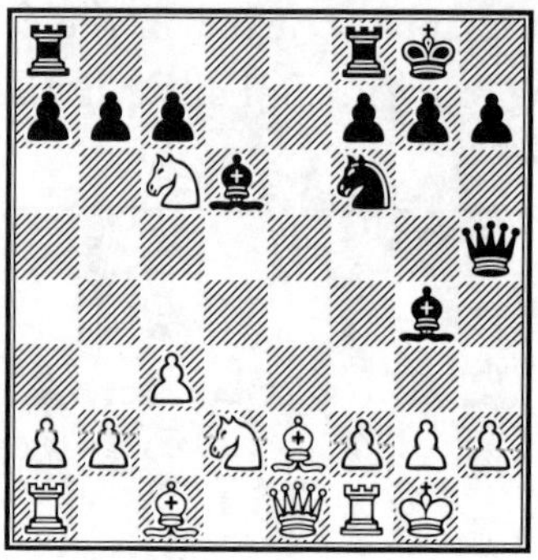

I had calculated only on 12...Bxe2 13.Nxe7+ Kh8 14.Nf5! Bxf1 15.Ng3.

13.h3

White must lose material. 13.f4 Bxe2 14.Rf2? Ng4!

13...Bxe2 14.Nd4 Bxf1 15.Qxf1 Rfe8 16.N2f3 a6 17.Bg5 Qg6 18.Rd1 Re4 19.Be3

The rest, being a matter of technique, was concluded by Byrne with dispatch.

19...Nd5 20.Bc1 Rae8 21.Nd2 R4e7 22.Nc4 Bf4 23.Nf3 c6 24.Nb6 Bxc1 25.Nxd5 cxd5 26.Rxc1 Re2 27.Rb1 Qc2 28.Rc1 Qxb2 29.Rb1 Qxc3 30.Rxb7 Rxa2 31.Kh2 h6 32.Qb1 Rxf2 33.Qf5 Qxf3 34.Qxf3 Rxf3 35.gxf3 Rd8 36.Rb6 d4, 0–1.

(57) Nimzo-Indian
Sammy Reshevsky – Fischer
New York (9) 1965/66

1.d4 Nf6 2.c4 e6 3.Nc3 Bb4 4.e3 b6 5.Bd3 Bb7 6.Nf3 0-0 7.0-0 Bxc3 8.bxc3 Be4 9.Qc2 Bxd3 10.Qxd3 d6 11.e4 e5 12.Bg5 Nbd7 13.Nh4 h6 14.Bd2 Re8 15.Rae1 Nf8 16.Nf5 Ng6 17.f4 exd4 18.cxd4 c6 19.d5 cxd5 20.cxd5 Ne7 21.Ng3 Rc8 22.Bc3 Ng6 23.Bd4 Kh7 24.Nf5 Rc7 25.Kh1 Rg8 26.Re3 Nh5 27.Ref3 Nf6 28.Rh3 b5 29.g4 Nxg4 30.Qg3 Qe8 31.Nxd6 Qe7 32.e5 Nf6 33.f5 Nxd5 34.fxg6+ fxg6 35.Nf7 Qxf7 36.Rxf7 Rxf7 37.e6 Rf1+ 38.Kg2 Rf5 39.Rh4 Re8 40.Qd6 Ref8 41.h3 Rc8 42.Re4 Rc2+ 43.Kg3 Rd2 44.e7 Rg5+ 45.Rg4 Nxe7 46.Rxg5 hxg5 47.Qxe7 Rxd4 48.Qxa7 Rf4 49.Qe7 Rf5

Reshevsky had me paralyzed in the mid-game, missed several mates, sealed a lemon, but just managed to win anyway in the adjournment!

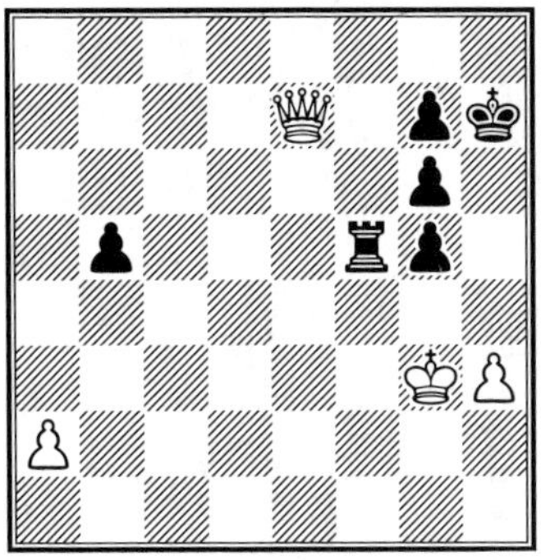

50.Qe8! Rc5

50...b4 51.Qa4! Rf4 52.Qa5 Kh6 53.Qd8! etc.

51.Kf3 Rc2 52.Qe6 Rc1 53.Qb3 Rc5 54.Ke4 Rf5 55.Kd4 Kh8 56.Kc3! Kh7

56...Rf3+ 57.Kb4 Rxb3+ 58.Kxb3! wins neatly.

57.Kb4 Re5 58.a3

Pointless.

58...Kh6

58...Kh8 59.Qd3 Kh7 60.Qxb5 wins.

59.Qg8! g4 60.h4! g5

60...g5 61.h5 Kxh5 62.Qh7 mate.

61.h5!, 1–0.

Fischer's first book, *Bobby Fischer Teaches Chess,* was published in hardcover in 1966 by Basic Systems (a subsidiary of Xerox Corporation). Initial sales were decent, but gave no indication that it would become the best-selling beginner's chess book of all time with over one million copies sold.

At roughly the same time the book was published, the games manufacturer Milton-Bradley came out with *Beginners Chess by Bobby Fischer an American Champion,* an inexpensive chess set. Aimed at the novice player it was endorsed by Bobby and came with instructions on how to play based on those that appeared in *Bobby Fischer Teaches Chess.* Large "board-like printed sheets" explained everything in the simplest manner. Also included were a set of red and ivory colored plastic chess pieces and a folding board. Everything was placed in a cardboard shell. Very likely Bobby's only involvement with this product was his endorsement.

Milton-Bradley came out with Beginners Chess by Bobby Fischer an American Champion *an inexpensive chess set featuring red and ivory plastic pieces. Very likely Bobby's only involvement with this product was his endorsement.*

Since the 1970s the colors black and white have been the standard for chess pieces in the United States, but that wasn't always the case. Back in the 1950s and 1960s, red and white was not an uncommon combination and Windsor Castle sets containing these colors were in daily use at the Steiner Chess Club in Los Angeles. The Mechanics' Institute Chess Club of San Francisco, the oldest in the United States (founded in 1854), still has a half dozen of these sets in regular use in its skittles/analysis room.

Lajos Portisch recalled[1] that during the 1966 Piatigorsky Cup Fischer suggested they switch to a Windsor Castle set for their second game. Fischer was dissatisfied with the Herman Steiner-designed pieces used for the tournament and may have felt they were unlucky. A three-game losing streak in the first half of the tournament and missed opportunities in the Los Angeles leg of the 1961 Reshevsky match may have contributed to these feelings. In both instances he played with a Steiner set.

Portisch, the traditionalist, was horrified at the idea of playing with red pieces, but in retrospect felt maybe he should have given them a try as he was crushed by Bobby using a conventional set (game 53 in *My 60 Memorable Games*).

[1] From a 2014 interview Portisch gave as part of a Bobby Fischer exhibition at the World Chess Hall of Fame in St. Louis.

3
U.S. CHAMPIONSHIP 1966/67

Bulgarian International Master Nikolay Minev (1931–2017) reminisced:[1]

> Olympiad, 1966. I was in my best form. I played in the final against Petrosian, Gligorić, Szabó, Fischer, Najdorf, Larsen, Uhlmann, and Pomar. They gave me the day off against Johannessen of Norway, a weaker player. Against all these guys, I drew six, won one, and lost five. I lost almost all my games with the Black pieces, and saved two, I think. One of these games was against Bobby Fischer. I had prepared a rare continuation in the French Defense, and at the moment I played the characteristic move, I tried to see how Bobby would react to it. I was not able to see his reaction because he played immediately the best move available. This meant that he had studied that variation. After that, it was a very interesting game. I missed one move. He had a bishop on g2 and a pawn on g3. I missed the move, pawn to g4. After g4, I was in bad shape. I was able to make an interesting move which held some chances for him to go wrong tactically. Even Yasser when he saw the game said,"Oh, you have this move now!" I said,"I have this move; I made this move, but I lost immediately." Bobby thought a little bit, and found two or three moves in a row, very accurate moves which finished the game. It's possible that against anybody else, I would have had some success. Against Bobby, it was not possible.
>
> My impression of him was that he was interested only in chess. Nothing else. One evening they took the American team, the Bulgarian team, and others to the Tropicana, which is the best nightclub in Havana. On the stage were fifty women who were almost naked. Everybody was watching the show except Bobby Fischer, who had his pocket chess set out and was showing Benko some position from that day.
>
> As a doctor, I will tell you that even at the Olympiad in Varna, in '62, I started to see that something was wrong with him. In the first round, there was a power failure for twenty minutes. Everyone was talking, milling around, going here and there. Bobby took his chair, went to the corner, and with his back to the wall, stayed there for twenty minutes without moving. Clearly scared. This is the first symptom of schizophrenia.

[1] From a 2011 interview with Derrick Robinson.

[left] Nikolay Minev at work in his study in 2011 (Photo: Derrick Robinson);
[right] Rossolimo playing blitz with Miroslav "Miro" Radojčić respected Yugoslav political journalist and strong master, to Rossolimo's left is Dr. Edward Epp (Photo: Beth Cassidy).

(58) French
Fischer – Nikolay Minev
Havana 1966

Notes by Minev.

1.e4 e6 2.d4 d5 3.Nc3 Nf6 4.Bg5 dxe4 5.Nxe4 Be7 6.Bxf6 gxf6 7.g3 Bd7 8.Nf3 Bc6 9.Qe2 f5 10.Ned2 Bf6 11.c3 Qe7 12.Bg2 Nd7 13.0-0 0-0 14.Rfe1 Rfe8 15.b4 a6 16.a4 b6 17.Nc4 Be4 18.Rad1 Red8

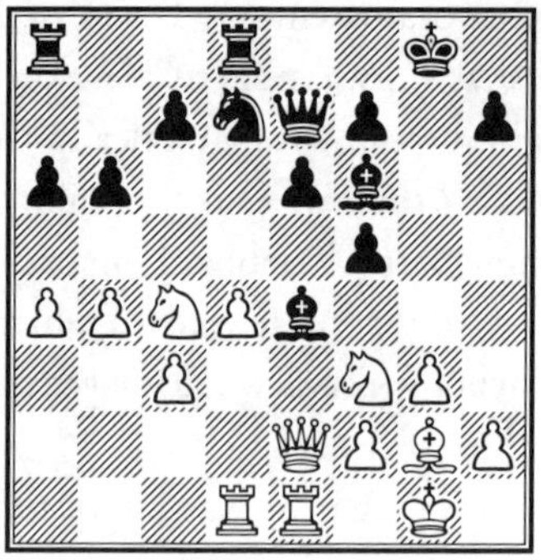

19.g4! Kh8 20.Ncd2 fxg4

Worth considering is 20...Bc2 21.Rc1 fxg4 22.Rxc2 gxf3 23.Bxf3 Rg8+ 24.Kh1 Rad8 25.Qxa6 c5.

21.Nxe4 gxf3 22.Bxf3 Rg8+ 23.Kh1 c6?

23...Bg7 avoids giving up a pawn.

24.Nxf6 Nxf6 25.Bxc6 Rac8 26.b5 axb5 27.axb5 Rg5 28.d5 Qc5 29.dxe6 Rxc6?

29...fxe6 30.Qxe6 Rf8 offered more resistance.

30.bxc6 Ng4 31.Rd4 Qxc6+ 32.f3 Re5 33.exf7 Qf6 34.Rxg4, 1–0.

Rossolimo, who spoke five languages, was a man of many talents including a rich baritone voice. He recorded an album of Russian folk songs, the cover of which was designed by Marcel Duchamp who frequented the Nicolas Rossolimo Chess Studio at 217 Thompson Street in Greenwich Village, NYC.

The 1966 U.S. Championship was to be Bobby's last. Unlike the previous year, where he lost in consecutive rounds to Robert Byrne and Sammy Reshevsky (and only finished a point ahead of them) he steamrolled the field, scoring 9½ from 11 (two points ahead of Larry Evans and three and a half points ahead of the rest of the field).

Russian-born (of Greek ancestry) Grandmaster Nicolas Rossolimo (1910–1975) lived in France from 1929 until he immigrated to the United States in 1952. He played with Bobby on two silver medal winning U.S. Olympiad teams (1960 and 1966). Rossolimo is best remembered for the variation of the Sicilian that bears his name (1.e4 c5 2.Nf3 Nc6 3.Bb5).

Rossolimo won many brilliancy prize games featuring brilliant combinations. A true chess artist, he once wrote:

> What am I supposed to do? Trade in my romantic combinative style for "today's style" and become a hunter of points at any price? No, I will not do so. I will fight for the art of chess. I will not become a monster.

Chess played an important role in the life of Dada artist Marcel Duchamp. A master strength player who was a teammate of Alexander Alekhine on the French Olympiad team in the early 1930s, Duchamp moved to United States in 1942 and settled in Manhattan.

In the late '50s Duchamp lived at 28 West 10th—across the street from the Marshall Chess Club (23 West 10th). He also had a strong affiliation and loyalty to the London Terrace Chess Club (located a little further from his home on West 23rd Street) where he won the club championship in 1958 and 1959.

Duchamp was a big fan of Bobby:[1]

> Duchamp and Teeny [Duchamp's wife Alexina] followed with great interest the development of Bobby Fischer, whom they had first met when he was a

[1] Calvin Tomkins, *Duchamp: A Biography*. New York: Henry Holt, 1996, (p. 428).

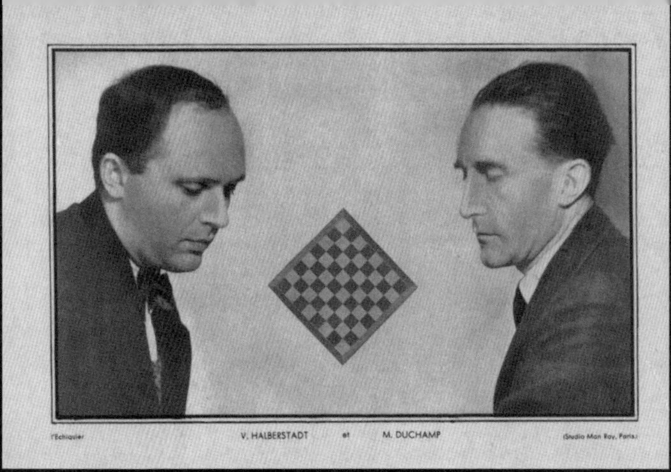

Marcel Duchamp (right) with French player and endgame theorist Vitaly Halberstadt. Together they authored 'L'Opposition et les cases conjuguées sont réconciliées *(Montage by Man Ray).*

> twelve-year-old phenomenon playing at the Manhattan chess club. Fischer use to take the subway from Brooklyn every day after school and go home the same way several hours later. In 1967 the president of the Manhattan Chess Club asked the Duchamps to go along as "chaperons"when Fischer, who was twenty-four by then, played in and won a major tournament in Monte Carlo. They had to wake him up every morning, which was not easy, but aside from that they found him well behaved, respectful, and quite likable.

Duchamp served on the Board of the American Chess Foundation and spent a lot of time raising money for them. A benefit auction at the Parke-Bernet Galleries in 1961, arranged by Duchamp and his wife brought in $37,000. The 1966 exhibition *Hommage á Caïssa* was also a success.

At least once (and possibly at other times) Duchamp served as a tournament director for the London Terrace Chess Club. Long-time Mechanics' Chess Club member Peter Stevens recalled one such incident in 1960 or 1961, where Duchamp was a last-minute substitute for the regular director Joe Pandolfini (the step-father of Bruce, who also worked as a manager at the Marshall Chess Club). Peter had a good result in the tournament, and regrets to this day cashing the five dollar prize check, signed by the renowned artist.

Duchamp definitely qualifies as the most famous tournament director of all time! George R. Martin, author of the *Game of Thrones* series, would be another contender for this title. When Martin was starting out as a writer in the mid-1970s, he needed a job to pay the bills until he got established. Directing tournaments for Bill Goichberg's Continental Chess Association for several years kept his weekdays free to write. Martin had a rating over 2000 in the 1970s.

International Master Michael Valvo (1942–2004) was recognized as a strong blitz player at an early age. He won the 1963 U.S. Intercollegiate while a student at Columbia University and played on the 1964 U.S. Student Olympiad team

Michael Valvo (smoking a cigarette), Pal Benko, and Bernard Zuckerman at the 1964 US Open in Boston (Photo: Beth Cassidy).

at Krakow, which placed fourth. Valvo was the proofreader for *Bobby Fischer Teaches Chess* along with International Master Raymond Weinstein. A noted expert on computer chess, he was heavily involved with every World Computer Chess Championship from the early 1980s up until his death.

Notes to Game (59) are by Michael Valvo, who provided the annotations for the 1966–1967 U.S. Championship bulletins.

(59) Sicilian
Nicolas Rossolimo – Fischer
New York (3) 1966/67

1.e4 c5 2.Nf3 d6 3.d4 cxd4 4.Nxd4 Nf6 5.Nc3 a6 6.Be3 e5 7.Nde2 Be7 8.h3 Be6 9.Ng3 g6 10.Bd3 Nbd7 11.0-0 0-0 12.Qf3 Kh8 13.Rad1 b5 14.Qe2 Qa5 15.a3 Rab8 16.Rfe1 Qc7 17.Nf1 Nb6 18.Bxb6 Rxb6 19.Ne3 b4 20.Na4 Rbb8 21.axb4 Rxb4 22.Ra1 Qc6 23.Nc3 Rxb2 24.Ned1 Rb6 25.Rxa6 Bd8 26.Rxb6 Bxb6 27.Nb5 Nh5 28.Qd2 Nf4 29.Bf1 Bc5 30.c4 f5 31.g3 Nh5 32.exf5 gxf5 33.Qh6 Ng7 34.Qd2 f4 35.Kh2 Nf5 36.Bg2 Qd7 37.g4

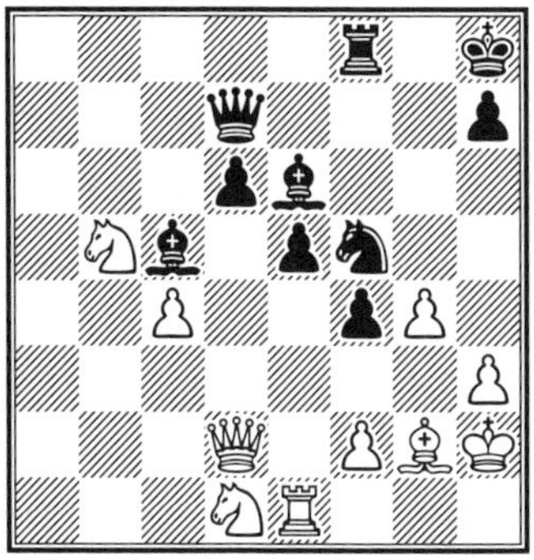

37...Bxc4

Fischer has informed us that his thirty-seventh move was an error. He gives 37...Nh4 as correct, with a probable win.

38.Rxe5 Nd4 39.Re4 Bxb5 40.Rxd4 Qg7 41.Rd5 Bc4

The sealed move.

42.Rh5 f3 43.Bh1 Bd4 44.Ne3 Be2 45.h4 Qa7 46.Bg2 Be5+ 47.Rxe5 dxe5 48.Qd6 Qb8 49.Qxb8 Rxb8 50.Bh3 h6 51.Kg3 Kg7 52.Nf5+ Kg6 53.Ne7+ Kf7 54.Nf5 Rb6 55.h5?

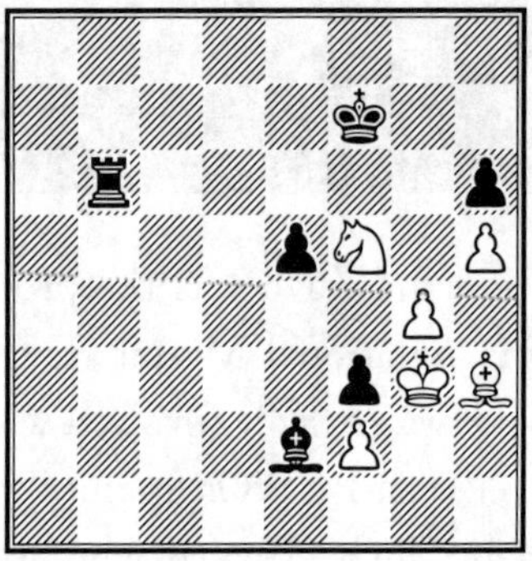

A bad move, losing the game. Both Fischer and Rossolimo agreed after the game that if White simply temporizes by shifting his knight or bishop, Black can make no significant progress, since his king must stay near White's 2–1 pawn majority. The likely outcome would be a draw. The text move loses because Black's king now has access to g5.

55...Ra6 56.Kh4 Bd3 57.Ne3 Ra2 58.Kg3 Be4 59.Bf1 Re2! 60.Nc4 Kf6 61.Nd6 Bc6 62.Bh3 Bd5 63.Nf5 Kg5 64.Ne3 Bc6 65.Bf1 Re1 66.Bh3 e4

The noose tightens; White is getting into zugzwang.

67.Nf5 Bd7 68.Nxh6?!

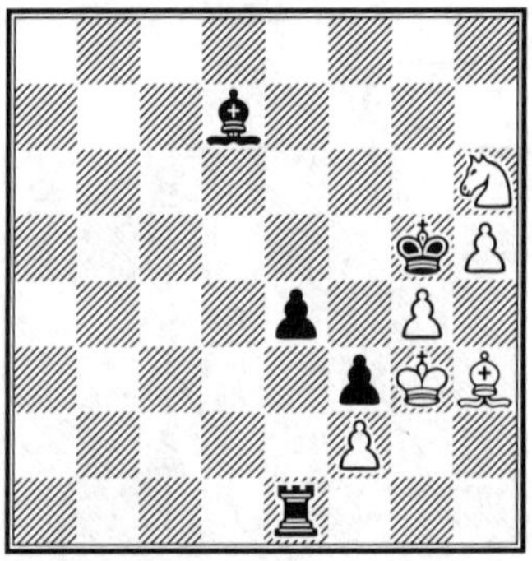

A swindle—see the next note.

68...Kxh6 69.g5+ Kxg5 70.h6??, 0–1.

The point—if Black now tries to keep the piece with 70...Bf5, then 71.Bxf5 Kxf5 72.h7 Rh1 73.h8Q Rxh8 Stalemate!

White resigned without waiting for Black's reply, which would have been 70...Kxh6! 71.Bxd7 Kg5 72.Bh3 Rg1+ 73.Kh2 e3! and wins as if 74.fxe3 f2.

Dr. Arthur S. Antler[1] shared some anecdotes about two mid-1960s U.S. Championships and how they inspired him to become a life-long chess player:

> Later that year I was eyewitness to the brilliancy Robert Byrne played against Larry Evans in the last round of the 1965/66 U.S. Championship, played in the Henry Hudson Hotel in Manhattan. I had never seen so many sacrifices and counter-sacrifices in a chess game. I was particularly impressed with the relaxed way Byrne made his moves, never rushing them, even when his replies appeared forced or obvious. When the game ended, the entire audience, myself included, gave Byrne a richly deserved standing ovation. After this game there was no question about my interest in chess; I was hooked!

(60) Sicilian
Robert Byrne – Larry Evans
New York (11) 1965/66

1.e4 c5 2.Nf3 a6 3.Nc3 d6 4.d4 cxd4 5.Nxd4 Nf6 6.Bg5 e6 7.f4 Qb6 8.Qd2 Qxb2 9.Rb1 Qa3 10.e5 dxe5 11.fxe5 Nfd7 12.Bc4 Bb4 13.Rb3 Qa5 14.0-0 0-0 15.Bf6 gxf6

The following U.S. Championship Zuckerman defeated Byrne with 15...Nxf6 16.exf6 Rd8.

16.Qh6 Qxe5

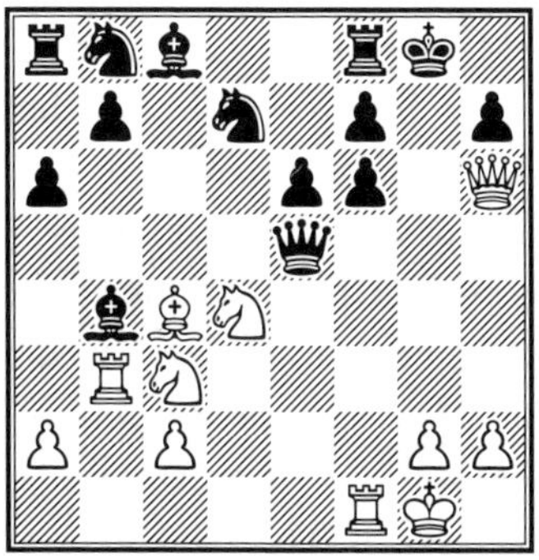

[1] Arthur S. Antler, *AVRO 1938: The Ultimate Chess Tournament.* Dallas: Chess Digest, 1993, (from the Introduction).

17.Nf5! exf5 18.Ne4! Bd2 19.Nxd2 Qd4+ 20.Kh1 Ne5 21.Rg3+ Ng4 22.h3 Qe5 23.Rf4 Qe1+ 24.Nf1 Qxg3 25.Rxg4+ Qxg4 26.hxg4 Nd7 27.Ng3 Kh8 28.Bd3 Rg8 29.Bxf5 Rg6 30.Bxg6 fxg6 31.Ne4 b5 32.g5 Bb7 33.Nxf6 Nf8 34.Qh2 Bc8 35.Qe5 Ne6 36.Nd7+, 1–0.

Antler continues:

> The following year I attended every round of the U.S. Chess Championship, again held at the Henry Hudson Hotel. This time, however, I was not in the audience, but on stage with the players, moving the pieces on the large demonstration boards. I remember vividly how excited I was on the day a round was to be played. I was not yet seventeen years old, and would leave my house after returning from high school and take the train, alone, from Canarsie, Brooklyn to New York City. When the round ended at 1AM I would return home by the same route. Traveling by the subway system had a certain risk involved, but my parents, seeing how important this event was for me, allowed me to do it. Fortunately, there were no incidents. Although I was not formally paid for my services, I was given a free tournament bulletin for each round (which I own to this day) as well as free admission to each round. Adjourned games were played during the day, and because of my academic responsibilities I was unable to attend them; I had to rely on the published bulletins for the continuation of each game. Several months after the championship ended, Ed Edmondson, then president of the USCF, gave me a chess clock for all my hard work and effort. The tournament allowed me to literally sit next to all the players, including Bobby Fischer. I have one Fischer anecdote to relate.
>
> During the U.S. Championship of 1966/67, I was given several responsibilities. Since there were six games in progress simultaneously and only a few volunteers to make the moves on the wall-boards, I would sit in a chair on stage between two games. Not only was I asked to make the moves for both games on the demonstration boards, I was also required to keep score of each game for the tournament bulletin the next day. You can well imagine that at times things could get quite hectic recording and demonstrating two games simultaneously. I would often sit in my chair with my pen in hand poised for the next move. During one game I noticed that Fischer kept staring at me uncomfortably, despite my silence and otherwise good manners. I had no idea what was bothering him, but continued to hold my pen ready for the next move. Finally he walked over to me and asked me to put the pen down. I did, of course, since I didn't want to antagonize him or otherwise make a scene. I would put the pen in my pocket, take it out for each move and the return it to my pocket. After the game I went over to Fischer and asked him what the problem was. He told me that the way I was holding the pen, anticipating the next move, made him nervous, and that's why he asked me to put it away. That was the one and only conversation I had with probably the greatest chess player of all time.

Robert Byrne and Larry Evans analyzing their last round game from the 1965-1966 U.S. Championship. Robert's brother Donald is to his immediate left.) The position on the board appears to be the line 15... Nxf6 16.exf6 Rd8 17.Qg5 g6, which did not occur in the game (Photo: Beth Cassidy).

Antler was but one of many young players who had the honorable job of serving as a wall-boy at a U.S. Championship. Andy Soltis, Bruce Pandolfini, and Stephen Brandwein are three of the best-known players who performed this task in the 1960s. This is yet another job made obsolete by technological advances. A pity, as many promising young players were stimulated to get better after their close interaction with top players.

Few American players have as distinguished a record in U.S. Championships as James Sherwin (born in 1933). Among non-grandmasters only Sherwin and fellow International Master William Addison have achieved lifetime plus scores (five events or more) in the most prestigious annual competition in the United States. Addison did it in five tournaments in the 1960s while Sherwin achieved his record in eight tournaments during the '50s and '60s.

A close look at Sherwin's consistent performance, all the more remarkable in that he was never a professional player, shows that only Fischer, Sammy Reshevsky, Larry Evans, and Robert Byrne had better records in the U.S. Championships held in the 1950s and 1960s.

1954 (14 players) 1. Bisguier 10; 2. Evans 9; 3. Seidman 8; 4. Sherwin and Pavey 7½

1957/58 (14 players) 1. Fischer 10½; 2. Reshevsky 9½; 3. Sherwin 9

1958/59 (12 players) 1. Fischer 8½; 2. Reshevsky 7½; 3. Sherwin 6½

1959/60 (12 players) 1. Fischer; 8. Sherwin 5

1960/61 (12 players) 1. Fischer 9; 2. Lombardy 7; 3. R. Weinstein 6½; 4–6. Sherwin, Bisguier and Reshevsky 6

1961/62 (12 players) 1. Evans 7½; 2. R.Byrne 7; 3–6. Sherwin, Benko, Mednis, Seidman 6 ½

1962/63 (12 players) 1. Fischer 8; 12. Sherwin 2½

1963/64 (12 players) Did not play

1965/66 (12 players) Did not play

1966/67 (12 players) 1. Fischer 8; 2. Evans 7½; 3–4. Sherwin and Benko 6

In eight U.S. Championships Sherwin finished in third place four times, and fourth place two times. Sherwin's overall score was 49 from 92 games, or 53%. Remove the one bad result (1962/63) and it's 46½ from 81 games, over 57%.

Sherwin who was ten years older than Bobby, first met him when Bobby was around nine or ten. A few years later his mother would bring Fischer over to Sherwin's home where he and Bobby would play blitz.

The two played ten tournament games with their lifetime score +7, -2,=1 in Bobby's favor. Two of their early games, which Sherwin won, were played in E. Forry Lauck's Log Cabin Chess Club's 50/50 tournaments. These one-day tournaments were an easy commute for New York players who only had a half hour to forty-five-minute drive from central Manhattan to 30 Collamore Terrace, in West Orange, New Jersey. The score of one of Sherwin's two wins as White in a King's Indian Samisch is known, but the other, which he won on time in a drawn queen and pawn ending, is not.

The famous game Fischer–Sherwin, New Jersey Open (played at Edgar McCormick's Independent Chess Club in East Orange, NJ) is the first game in Bobby's *My 60 Memorable Games*. The game was played in the seventh and final round of the eighty-one-player New Jersey Open, which Fischer won two weeks after his victory in the 1957 U.S. Open in Cleveland.

The highlight of Sherwin's career was finishing third in the 1957/58 U.S. Championship behind Bobby Fischer and Samuel Reshevsky. This qualified him to play in the 1958 Interzonal where he scored 50% against the six qualifiers for the Candidates tournament, beating Gligorić and Ólafsson.

Sherwin first attracted widespread attention when he won the 1951 New York State Championship at the age of seventeen. Two years later he qualified for the A group of the World Junior where he defeated Boris Ivkov and Bent Larsen. Sherwin's first major national success was tying for first with Arthur Bisguier in the 1956 U.S. Open in Oklahoma City.

While Sherwin will be remembered as a strong player he also made a very important contribution as the president of the American Chess Foundation from 1979–1990. This was during its golden period when it gave strong support to top American players including offering $10,000 apiece for each of the 1985 American Interzonalists.

4
MOVE WEST YOUNG MAN

THE APARTMENT

The spring of 1968 found Fischer in California living on Ambrose Avenue in Los Feliz, a section of Los Angeles near Griffith Park. Like many a New Yorker before him, he was attracted to southern California by the weather, and it didn't hurt that his friend Lina Grumette lived only a few miles from his new home. The desire to study chess without distractions also played a role in his relocation.

The first major move of Fischer's adult life raises questions half a century later: When did Bobby give up his Brooklyn apartment, the place he called home for roughly eighteen years? What was the fate of his pre-1968 books, score sheets, and chess-related ephemera that possibly never made it to Los Angeles? Are there Fischer treasures long packed away and forgotten, waiting to be recovered—for example, where are Fischer's score sheets from the 1963 New York State Open?

In 1967 Fischer divided his time from the beginning of April to the end of September and parts of October and November, between Monaco, Yugoslavia, Tunisia, and the Philippines. Sometime during the year he moved out of 460 Lincoln Place, but appeared to have kept the apartment for another year and lived at the Tudor Hotel when not traveling. Brady suggests Fischer may have been out of the apartment by early 1967:[1]

> Fischer returned from Monaco [the Grand Prix International held March 24–April 4, 1967] to New York and his suite at the Tudor Hotel on East 42nd Street, close to the United Nations. He had given up the family apartment in Brooklyn, mainly because it had grown too unwieldy for his careless bachelor habits. No neatnik he, the apartment began to show the wear and clutter of a home without a housekeeper. He had lived in Brooklyn for more than seventeen years, grown up there, learned chess there, and dazzled five continents with his exploits, would always go back to his home in Crown Heights. He was used to Brooklyn and in some ways was sorry to

[1] Frank Brady, *Profile of a Prodigy: The Life and Games of Bobby Fischer*, 2nd edition. New York: David McKay, 1973, (pp. 128 and 142).

> leave it. Also, it was necessary for him to travel into Manhattan almost daily, mainly by taxicab, so that he could get to the Manhattan and Marshall Chess Clubs, and to be more readily available to see his publisher, his friends and his growing legion of chess contacts. ...
>
> In the spring of 1968, Bobby gave up his suite at the Tudor Hotel and moved to Los Angeles, leasing a small house on Ambrose Avenue. He didn't take all of his possessions across the continent, however, storing many of his books, records and clothes in Manhattan, with Burt Hochberg and Harry Evans (Larry's father), indicating perhaps that he was not sure he would stay permanently.

Sam Sloan is of another opinion, believing Bobby left much earlier:

> Fischer had moved out of the apartment on 560 Lincoln Place Apt 4Q by September, 1964 and complained to me "I should never have given up that apartment." He was living at the YMCA on West 23rd Street by that time, the same YMCA that later became famous with the song named YMCA.

Sam Sloan has written and spoken about being Bobby's constant companion for the second half of 1964. While prone to exaggeration and at times wildly inaccurate, Sloan can also be a valuable source, having been active in American chess for over sixty years. However, caveat emptor to those who quote him without having a second source—Sloan's internet post of December 2002 is an example of what awaits those who don't:

> Péter Lékó was killed in a car accident today in Budapest. It has been reported that Lékó died in a car crash while analyzing a game he had played against Shirov on a pocket set. Shirov is in Spain now and was not in the accident. Lékó, twenty-three, recently won a qualification tournament and was scheduled to play a match for the World Chess Championship. He was once the world's youngest grandmaster and has consistently been rated in the top ten players in the world.

All this was a surprise to Lékó's wife Sofia when she was called to the phone with the sad news, especially so as she had just left her husband in good spirits in the next room! That said, a second source, Nenad Nesh Stanković, Bobby's assistant for non-chess matters during his stays in Yugoslavia and Hungary in the early 1990s, confirmed Sloan's claim, quoting Fischer in his memoir:[1]

> "You know, Nesh," that's what he called me, "you're the only person to spend so much time with me." Then he looked over at Philippine Grandmaster Eugene Torre and Hungarian-American player of the old school Pal Benko who were keeping us company that evening, and he burst into laughter and

[1] Nenad Nesh Stanković, *The Greatest Secret of Bobby Fischer: The Truth About the Greatest Chess Player of All Time*. 2012, (p. 7).

added, "I mean, the only one who lasted that long." He continued by adding the story of his "strange" friend Sam Sloan with whom he cruised Manhattan for six months, every inch of the heart of Manhattan. They spent time together every day during that period, but then "poor Sam" disappeared without a trace.

Recently, Sloan spoke of the time he spent with Bobby:

> This would have been from the beginning of September 1964 after the U.S. Open in Boston until the end of January 1965 when I returned to study at the University of California at Berkeley. Not quite a full six months but almost that much.
>
> I first met Bobby at the 1956 Eastern States Open in Washington, D.C. The next time I met him was at the Manhattan Chess Club at the Henry Hudson Hotel in 1964 where he was analyzing various Kevitz Defenses with Alexander Kevitz. He said to Kevitz, "Would you play this in a tournament game, I mean against a strong player?" He must have already known the answer to that question. This was after the U.S. Open in Boston.

Bernard Zuckerman remembered the timing of Bobby's move to Los Angeles differently than Sloan and his account is closer to Brady's. Well-known for his phenomenal memory and encyclopedic opening knowledge, "Zook the Book," aka "Zuckerbook," recalled events from over forty years earlier like yesterday:[1]

> I'm not certain of the very first time [I met Bobby] but I certainly got to know him in 1958 and visited his home many times over the years up until May or June 1968 when Bobby moved to Los Angeles.
>
> That date is fixed in my mind because he had to sell his library and chess table when he went to California. I bought the table and still use it today. Bobby had purchased it after the Zurich tournament in 1959 and it took six months to arrive in New York from Switzerland. It wasn't cheap at $150 when Drueke tables were selling for $50.
>
> When I first received the table, it was not in the best shape as Bobby was often tough on his possessions. There were a lot of stains on the table, but my father, who was a craftsman, was able to refinish it.
>
> I remember Bobby picking up my copy of the Zurich 1959 tournament book and handling it so roughly that a page dropped out.
>
> By the way the table I picked up was not the only nice one Bobby had. He received a beautiful one after the Havana Olympiad along with all the other first boards. Burt Hochberg, the long-time editor of *Chess Life*, bought it for $500 from Bobby.
>
> Bobby sold his library to the well-known book dealer Walter Goldwater. He had quite a collection by this point and I remember part of his motivation in selling was a fear that he was becoming a compulsive book buyer. Selling

[1] Interview by John Donaldson, summer 2014, for the World Chess Hall of Fame's 2014–2015 exhibition devoted to Fischer.

> them certainly solved the problem of what to do with them when he moved to the West Coast, but later Bobby missed them quite acutely and ended up buying many of the books a second time.

While these accounts vary, it's clear that Fischer spent much of 1969 in Los Angeles studying and working on *My 60 Memorable Games*, which was published that year. He was in New York in June and paid a visit to the U.S. Junior Closed and U.S. Women's Championship (the events were held concurrently at the Hotel McAlpin). He appeared to have been in New York in the fall as well.

THE LIBRARY

Around early 1970, Fischer sold some of his books to antiquarian book dealer Walter Goldwater. Fischer continued to be based in Los Angeles on Ambrose Avenue—Serbian Master Dimitrije Bjelica wrote of visiting Fischer there in 1970.[1]

As it turned out, Bobby wished he hadn't sold his library as his letter to Goldwater, owner of the University Place Book Shop in Manhattan, confirms:

> January 9, 1971
>
> Dear Mr. Goldwater,
>
> I hope you got my first letter about my wanting to buy back any remaining books, magazines and tournament bulletins, etc. from my collection that you have left. Please do not sell anymore until I get back to the States and discuss this. I know we will agree on the price.
>
> Also, if you sold some of my books in relatively large blocks maybe you could contact the people you sold them to and tell them that I would really like to buy them back. I really miss those books. You never know what you've got 'till it's gone, I guess. Also, in any event I hope you have a list written out of my books, magazines, etc. So, I can try to rebuild my library from it. I'm not sure when I'll be back to the States. Maybe a few days or a month or two. I don't know my plans. But I hope you'll get to work on this right away so when I get back, we can take care of business. If you can get the books—I've got the money—so we understand each other.
>
> Sincerely
>
> Bobby Fischer
> c/o the USCF
> 479 Broadway,
> Newburgh, New York

Goldwater, a one-time president of the Marshall Chess Club and a long-time book dealer specializing in radical literature (like Regina Fischer he had visited

[1] Dimitrije Bjelica, *Grandmasters in Profile*. Zavod za izdavanje udzbenika, 1973.

the Soviet Union in the 1930s), donated the books he bought from Bobby to the New York Public Library, which in turn put them up for auction.

Over the years, many of Fischer's pre-1970 books and letters have passed through different hands. Chess historian and book dealer Fred Wilson was one of the curators of a chess book exhibition organized by the Grolier Club in New York City in 1975. Wilson wrote: [1]

> Finally, of course, there was Bobby Fischer. We had several important original game scores and interesting letters on view. Unfortunately, I am advised that I cannot quote directly from these letters. I will, however, remark that in one letter Fischer expresses regret that he sold his entire chess library to a book dealer (not me, unfortunately!) in 1970 as he had begun to miss some of his volumes.

It should be emphasized that financial need was not the motivation for Fischer selling his chess library. By this stage in his life with decent royalties coming in from *Bobby Fischer Teaches Chess* and *My 60 Memorable Games,* plus income from his *Boys' Life* column that ran from December 1966 to January 1970, the days of just getting by were long gone. Appearance fees (something Bobby was always a tough negotiator for) and prize money were on the rise. When he won the 1962 Stockholm Interzonal, he received only $750 for a tournament that lasted over a month, but later that year received $5,000 honorarium for playing for the U.S. team at the Varna Olympiad. Granted he did have to take care of his own travel expenses, but this sum ($42,000 in 2020 dollars), is over double what Fabiano Caruana, Hikaru Nakamura, and Wesley So each received for leading the United States to first place in the 2016 Olympiad in Baku.

Fischer had an even bigger payday in 1964 with his transcontinental exhibition tour of North America. Charging $250 an exhibition (even more in a few cases when he played over fifty boards), he grossed around $10,000 ($83,000 in 2020 dollars). Many chess fans were not only glad to host Bobby but also happy to drive him to his next exhibition, so expenses were for the most part limited to a few flights and compensating Larry Evans' father, Harry, who organized the tour. In 1965 *The New York Times*[2] gave his yearly earnings as $12,000 ($100,000 in 2020 dollars).

Larry Evans once asked Fischer why he sold his books when he didn't need the money. Fischer told him, as he had Zuckerman, that he felt he was in danger of becoming a collector. Many have suffered from the pleasant disease of buying more books than they could read, but that wasn't a malady Bobby suffered from—he was a reader! Zuckerman's description of Fischer's rough handling

1 *Chess Life and Review*, February 1976, (p. 71).
2 *The New York Times*, August 28, 1965.

of books suggests Fischer loved them for the information they contained, but nothing beyond that.

The chess teacher and writer Bruce Pandolfini, who grew up in New York and is four years younger than Bobby, worked for Walter Goldwater. Pandolfini had a Fischer moment in 1964:

> When I was a teenager, I worked one summer at Walter Goldwater's University Place Bookshop in Greenwich Village. Walter was then president of the Marshall Chess Club and an expert book dealer in a number of subjects. One day Bobby Fischer came in needing some money. Fischer wound up selling a bunch of his books to Walter for a song. I think there were about fifty books, and I don't recall what Walter eventually did with the lot. But Walter did let me buy a few of them, though he didn't sell them cheaply. I believe it cost me an entire week's salary. The books I got I wanted for two reasons. For one, with all the magical power they conveyed, those books had been owned and read by Fischer, the chess god. But, also, they were wonderful books no matter who had previously possessed them. There were Polish endgame books by [Stanisław] Gawlikowski, a magnificent book on tactics by Lisitsin, and several other foreign language delights.
>
> One of them was a book by Lipnitsky in Russian. It was threadbare, but it looked intriguing. Nevertheless, I didn't realize how fully intriguing it was until a few weeks later. Having put it aside for a bit, I thought I'd drag it to the Marshall and look it over more intently. Or maybe I was just trying to show it off and tell people from whom I had gotten it. When Raymond Weinstein saw me looking at it, he immediately identified it as Fischer's copy. He claimed (and since others have backed this fact up), that Fischer had carried it around with him on his travels for a full year. Furthermore, as Weinstein asserted, that was the very book that Fischer himself had said helped him become a grandmaster. That revelation (whether true or not) was both astonishing and thrilling to hear. But there was one more surprise yet to come (I guess I hadn't looked at the book as carefully as I should have—and I surmise neither had Walter Goldwater). Leafing through its first pages, Weinstein found what I had unfathomably missed: Fischer's actual printed signature (that's how he signed in those days). Probably, to this very day, that's the one book I prize the most.
>
> After that summer, though I did see Walter around the Marshall, I never went into his bookstore again. (Frankly, though I liked Walter, I couldn't stand his venue, which was horribly dusty and triggered my allergies. Moreover, his main libraries were not on chess but on black and radical literature, which I did not particularly read or collect.)
>
> What Brady and Wilson apparently are referring to is another sale altogether, a much later sale than my 1964 purchase. It's surely possible that Walter bought books from Bobby a couple of times, even if Bobby only refers to such a sale once. Fischer may also have sold books to Abe Buschke,

> because he did go into Buschke's shop. I definitely saw Bobby there on at least one occasion. Also, the later sale seems to be more extensive than the sale I recollect. Fischer's actual library would have been much larger than just two shopping bags.

Note: The works by Lipnitsky[1] and Lisitsin have been translated into English,[2] but Gawlikowski's works are only available in the original Polish.

What became of Fischer's pre-1970 treasures? Good question. Some items can be found in the collection of David DeLucia, but most of it is either in the hands of many smaller enthusiasts or is unaccounted for.

The move to Los Angeles turned out to be permanent, with Fischer living there for the better part of a quarter century before leaving in the summer of 1992 for Serbia, never to return to the United States.

---

1 Isaac Lipnitsky, translated by John Sugden, *Questions of Modern Chess Theory*. Glasgow: Quality Chess, 2008.

2 A greatly condensed English translation by the *Chess Player* in the 1970s.

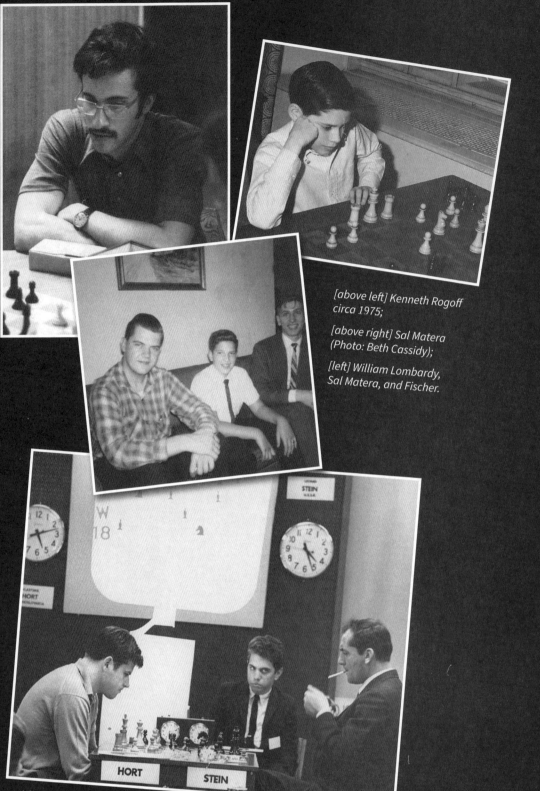

[above left] Kenneth Rogoff circa 1975;

[above right] Sal Matera (Photo: Beth Cassidy);

[left] William Lombardy, Sal Matera, and Fischer.

Vlastimil Hort and Leonid Stein at move 18 of their first game in the three-player playoff with Sammy Reshevsky for the last spot in the 1968 Candidates. Wall-boy and future Grandmaster James Tarjan watches intently (Photo: Art Zeller).

5

"HE WALKED INTO THE ROOM, AND EVERYTHING CHANGED."

Readers of the August 1989 issue of *Chess Life*[1] were treated to an article by Richard Fireman that drew a vivid picture of Bobby in the late '60s, just a few years before fame would take away his privacy. The setting for this trip down memory lane was the 1969 U.S. Junior Closed, held in New York City at the McAlpin Hotel (34th and Broadway). Those lucky few who were present for Bobby's visit were the eight contestants, tournament director Bill Goichberg, and the sole spectator—Fireman. When originally published, Fireman was not credited as author. This was corrected when a slightly revised version was posted online in 2007. What appears here is the later version:

FISH TO FISCHER BY RICHARD FIREMAN

Back in those years, it seemed, just about everything was strange; the craziness of Woodstock, the craziness of Vietnam, and just plain life. It was, I believe, 1970,[2] and I was a college student and A-player invited by my friend Steve Spencer, a rising young master, to come see him play in the U.S. Junior Invitational Championship. The top eight under-twenty-one-year-olds in the country were to be slugging it out: Tarjan, Rogoff, DeFotis (Greg), Weinstein (Norman), Matera, Deutsch, Jacobs (the Texan one, I think), and my friend. It was a weekend or a holiday (Christmas?!) or maybe it wasn't (what were classes in Existentialism worth compared to living it?), so I said sure and came into New York to the old McAlpin Hotel where the tournament was being held.

For a while everything seemed normal (too quiet, I would've said if I were a cowboy in an old Western movie just before the Indians attacked); the games seemed to be progressing normally—Steve, who was destined to finish last, was trying to hold off the inevitable attack after grabbing a pawn—and aside from tournament director William Goichberg I was the only spectator.

---

[1] *Chess Life*, August 1989, (pp. 49–50).

[2] Fischer attended more than one U.S. Junior Closed tournaments that were held in New York in the late '60s. Fireman was actually at the 1969 U.S. Junior Closed (not 1970), which meant that Randy Mills was playing, not Anthony Deutsch who was second the following year. The eight player round robin was held in late June and Fischer was twenty-six, not twenty-seven.

Nobody seemed to care whether I was there or not, and I sat quietly by in a nearby chair and read my book and occasionally glanced over at the boards to see what was happening.

Time passed, and then HE walked into the room, and everything changed.

A tall young (twenty-seven) man in a sports jacket carrying some papers under his arm, with an abstracted look and an aura of energy radiating from him you could feel across the room. As though in a movie caught in the projector, everything stopped. Hands with pieces about to descend were poised in mid-air, head-scratchings were suspended, twitchings froze. Then, as though they'd been caught staring at a woman they were attracted to, everyone suddenly resumed their actions as though nothing had happened, and the movie started up once again. It seemed nonchalant (does anything ever seem chalant?!), but it wasn't. For, miraculously, ten or fifteen minutes later all the games were finished, even though it hadn't been anywhere close to the time control.

Because everyone wanted to meet Bobby.

He'd been quiet, nodding hello to Goichberg and casually walking about the room, glancing at each of the boards and hardly seeming to study, or even notice, the positions. Then he returned to the corner of the room and just sort of hung around until the inevitable gathering, the flocking to the waterhole.

"Let's go look at some games," he said, and heads wordlessly bobbed up and down. Since the room was reserved for use only for the duration of each day's tournament, we had to go to another room, Goichberg explained. Fischer—he asked us all to call him Bobby—nodded and turned around and started walking, with Bill and the players following. I tagged along, not quite believing it was happening. Hell, this man was a legend. But he seemed as normal as the next guy, at least till then...

So we went into a room and sat down and set up a board and Bobby took one of a bunch of Russian magazines from under his arm and started moving the pieces around, and we stared. At some point he stopped after making a move and, with a slightly puzzled look—as though he were a novice who wasn't quite comprehending the underlying reasons behind the strategies—said, to no one in particular, "I wonder why he did that?" One of the young masters, naturally eager to impress, offered a plausible explanation: maybe he wanted to do such-and-such and was afraid his opponent would do this-and-that, so he first prepared it by playing this move. Fischer shrugged it off: "No, that doesn't work, because..." and reached out for the pieces...

...and you could barely see what the sequence was, his hands moved so fast. If before when he entered it was like in that old *Twilight Zone* episode where time is frozen, this was like the Keystone Cops where the action is speeded up to an unnatural, ludicrous extent. Everyone just stared, jaws literally agape, mental tongues hanging. An eternity (well, twenty seconds or so) passed before us. Bobby was long since finished exhibiting that particular variation. "Right?" he inquired. Yeah, sure, Bobby, anything you say. Nobody was about to dispute him. Hell, we barely saw what it was he had just shown us. And, except for myself, these were Masters, the cream of the crop of America's rising young talent, superstars of the future, paralyzed in disbelief by what they had just witnessed. You'd think we'd asked for a daffodil and he'd pulled out the Burning Bush, we were so stunned. It wasn't just the sheer speed of his action—though that was certainly impressive enough—but the seeming effortlessness of it, the naturalness which he exhibited; it was as though it were as normal as breathing to him, as though it were all simple and straightforward and of-course-this-is-what-happens-if-you-do-that, isn't it obvious? That's what was so stunning, as though his mind were a computer, as though anything we could have thought of had already been considered and incorporated and analyzed and dismissed, all in one simple algorithm. As though he were just on a whole other level. I've since met and analyzed with a number of grandmasters, and they weren't even close, so it's not just the difference in playing strength. Sure, they exhibit a natural feel for the game and understanding beyond that of the rest of us mortals, but they're still in the same order of things, the same part of the universe: they fumble around with this idea and that, and they're more likely to come to the right conclusions because of their talent and experience and insight. But they still have to work at it. With Bobby it wasn't like that. With him it was like he had a key to the door containing the mystery, a special pass. With him it was as simple as going into that room with all the answers, looking for what you wanted, finding it and taking it out. Maybe he had to clear a couple of things off the shelves before he found what he wanted, but he didn't have to hire the A-Team to break down the door.

Well, I'm sure *he* knew what he would've done in that position we'd stopped at, but the move the Russian had made evidently wasn't it, and even Bobby couldn't read minds, and nobody else, after his little display, was about to offer any other suggestions, so he sort of shrugged and proceeded with the game. Ten or so moves later—uh oh—he paused again. "Hmmm...," he hmmmed, and we held our collective breath. You could've heard an atom drop. "Why did he do that?" Aww, come on, Bobby, you've gotta be kidding. But he wasn't. Please, give us a break. But he didn't. He just sat there and waited, looking, interminably. Finally we had to breathe, but shallowly. And, finally, someone had to say something...

"Uhh...well..."

Heads snapped, eyes staring in wonder and admiration at the voluntary sacrifice. What courage. What fortitude. What a jerk. Doesn't he know there be dragons in those parts?

"Errr, maybe, I don't know, uh, maybe he wanted to do *that*?" He sort of half-gestured at a move, then pulled his hand away quickly as though he didn't really mean it, he had just said it because his mother had made him promise he would do it. He put his hand back into his pocket and stood frozen, neck tensed, awaiting the axe.

It came. "No, no, that wouldn't work..." and, I swear, I don't know how it was possible but his hands moved even faster. Swish, swish, chop-chop-chop, and the resulting mangled position was something a two-year-old might have gotten into against the Prussian Army. "Oh, yeah, right," mumbled the recalcitrant offerer/offering, "Sorry, Bobby."

"Okay," came the voice from the Mount, his hands resetting the pieces, and the tension broke, and we all started breathing normally. One of the guys next to the last suggester elbowed him in the ribs and smiled, and we all glanced at each other, grinning. It was okay to be mortal. Hell, it was even fun. Next time Bobby paused the delay wasn't so great, the fear absent. Sure, the same process ensued, but we expected it to, even wanted it to. It wasn't competitive, as though we stood a chance of seeing something he didn't; it was constructive, a learning experience for all of us (most of all, for me, since I was the weakest player); the challenge in it was to see how long your move would last before being proved absolutely worthless, and we all took turns being good-naturedly pummeled. Bobby expected it, invited it, encouraged us to participate. Go ahead, bob for apples. Eat of the tree of knowledge. We did, and later went to a nearby Japanese restaurant with him and talked of everything but chess—I remember he mentioned he was learning how to drive a car, for instance—and then, smiling, he departed. Who *was* that masked man...?

He had been nothing like the image I'd expected of him, the media depiction of the crazed recluse, the impossible boy wonder who made life impossible for everyone he met. In fact, he'd been downright friendly. Piecing it together later—after the shock wore of—I concluded that he'd probably felt much more comfortable among us, who were not only not of the media but not even his peers, and who looked up to him rather than down or suspiciously; that we made him feel not only admired but, more importantly, welcome. And that, I felt, was something he rarely felt, and something he appreciated. Perhaps even yearned for. I don't know; I can't pretend to really know the man. But if you're out there, Bobby, and by some chance read this, I want you to know that, yes, you were welcome that day. And that we would welcome you back.

Fischer annotated the game Rogoff–Spencer for his *Boys' Life* column[1] and shared his opinion about Rogoff's future prospects:

The other day I dropped over to the U.S. Junior championship at the McAlpin Hotel in New York City and saw some very talented young players in action, struggling for the title. It brought back memories of years ago when I used to be in those events. The player that impressed me the most was sixteen-year-old Ken Rogoff from Rochester, N.Y. What I liked best about Ken—who won the championship—was his self-assured style and his knowing exactly what he wanted over the chessboard. I'm told he's only been

1 *Boys' Life*, October 1969.

> playing chess two or three years and it should encourage each of you young fellows who read this column to know that by applying yourself, as Ken did, you can become a fine player in a relatively short time, too."

What happened to the participants in 1969 U.S. Junior Closed? Almost the entire group—soon to be eclipsed by the upcoming Fischer boomers Grandmasters Seirawan, Benjamin, Christiansen, de Firmian, Fedorowicz, Henley, Rohde, and Tisdall—stopped playing by their early thirties, achieving success in other careers.

The most well known of the group, Ken Rogoff, would earn the grandmaster title and play in an Interzonal, but soon afterward leave the game to pursue a career in academia. Currently a Professor of Economics at Harvard University, Rogoff served as the Chief Economist at the International Monetary Fund from 2001 to 2003. His early departure from the game was typical of the group who started playing when chess professionals were almost non-existent.

Norman Weinstein became a strong international master and would certainly have become a grandmaster had he kept playing. Like Rogoff he went into finance, in his case not academia but as an investment banker on Wall Street.

In 1990 Weinstein convinced his firm (Bankers Trust) to put an ad in *Chess Life* inviting strong chess players to apply for commercial banking positions. Among the hires were Grandmasters Max Dlugy and David Norwood, Woman Grandmaster Anna Akhsharumova, and Senior Master Girome Bono. Weinstein's thought was some of the skills that make for strong players—quick decision-making under pressure being one of them—were transferable. That definitely proved to be the case with Norwood, who despite having no prior background in finance, has had an extremely successful career.

Another of the Bankers Trust hires was Sal Matera. Like Weinstein he reached the level of strong international master and won a gold medal on board two in leading the United States to a second place finish in the 1974 World Sudent Team Championship. Matera was also a noted chess teacher, with the young Joel Benjamin among his pupils, but again like most of the others in this group was out of chess by the late 1970s.

James Tarjan, who became the strongest player among the 1969 U.S. Junior Closed alumni, was also the youngest (born 1952). He developed into a strong grandmaster who played on five U.S. Olympiad teams including the one that took gold in 1976, but again (!) retired at an early age, switching to a career as a librarian in his early thirties.

Tarjan returned to the arena in 2014 and three years later shocked the chess world by defeating former World Champion Vladimir Kramnik while scoring 5½–3½ against nine grandmasters at the Isle of Man. His performance rating

[clockwise from top] Larry Christiansen , Yasser Seirawan, and actor Peter Falk; Peter Biyiasas and Nick de Firmian; Joel Benjamin, Ken Rogoff, John Fedorowicz; Ronald Henley; and Jonathan Tisdall (Photos of de Firmian , Benjamin, and Fedorowicz: Alan Benson).

for the event (2671 FIDE) is one of the best ever achieved by a U.S. player age sixty-five or older—matched only by Sammy Reshevsky.

FIDE Master Jon Jacobs of Dallas was a teammate of Matera's on the silver-medal-winning U.S. entry in the 1974 World Student Team Championship. A two-time Texas state champion, he worked for Ken Smith's Chess Digest organization throughout the 1970s, writing books, and articles, before going into a career in business.

Two of the participants in the 1969 U.S. Junior Closed are no longer with us. FIDE Master Greg DeFotis (1951–2017) was a very promising chess talent who could have gone far had he not decided to pursue a career as a professional games player, equally adept at bridge, backgammon, and gin rummy. DeFotis shared sixth place in the 1972 U.S. Closed Championship, scoring +3 =9–1 and tied for first in the 1973 U.S. Open held in his hometown of Chicago.

National Master Randy Mills (1949–2014)—not to be confused with Indiana Master Jim Mills—is the least known of the group. A three-time Kansas state champion (1967–1969), he was the only competitor in the 1969 Closed coming from a chess desert, but had a respectable finish scoring 2½ from 7. Little is known about Mills' life, but an obituary mentions he was an accomplished pianist with a deep love of classical music.

Not all participants in the 1969 U.S. Junior Closed chose conventional paths. Fireman's friend, National Master Steve Spencer of New York—not to be confused with the San Diego master of the same name who was close in age—become one of the most colorful characters American chess has ever seen.

A promising junior player, who participated in the 1968 and 1969 U.S. Junior Closed Championships, Spencer moved to Berkeley, California, after graduating from high school in the mid-1960s. While in Berkeley, Spencer was a member of the University California, Berkeley team (along with Master Frank Thornally, Richard Laver, Mike Morris, and Sam Sloan) that won the 1967 Pan American Intercollegiate. He attended UCB (or was in the Bay Area) from roughly 1967 to 1969.

Spencer appears to have played no tournament chess from 1970–73. He reappeared in the Bay Area for a short time in 1974, but soon after moved to a commune in Willow Springs, Missouri, supporting himself for several years by playing tournaments around the country. Spencer kept expenses down by hitchhiking, crashing on floors, and performing surgery on half-eaten pizza using a knife to remove portions chewed by previous eaters.

Seeing Spencer in action convinced one seventeen-year-old future international master that it might be prudent to attend college before attempting to become a professional chess player.

Spencer intentionally played openings that avoided drawish positions and was fond of the Veresov (1.d4 Nf6 2.Nc3 d5 3.Bg5) and meeting 1.e4 with 1...Nc6. He also played the Modern Defense in provocative fashion—for example 1.d4 g6 2.e4 Bg7 3.Nc3 a6 4.a4 d6 5.Be2 Nc6 6.Be3 f5 7.d5 Nb4 and now 8.a5 (intending Ra4) led to sharp complications in Donaldson–Spencer, Vancouver 1976.

International Master Elliott Winslow recalled attending an event in Woodstock, New York, in the summer of 1977 where he ran into Spencer who had stop playing chess, become a born-again Christian, and worked as an insurance salesman.

Sal Matera won the 1967 U.S. Junior Closed. Fischer was in attendence and the article Matera wrote[1] included Fischer's comment on a position Matera showed him on the last day of the tournament.

(61)

James Tarjan – Sal Matera

New York (1) 1967

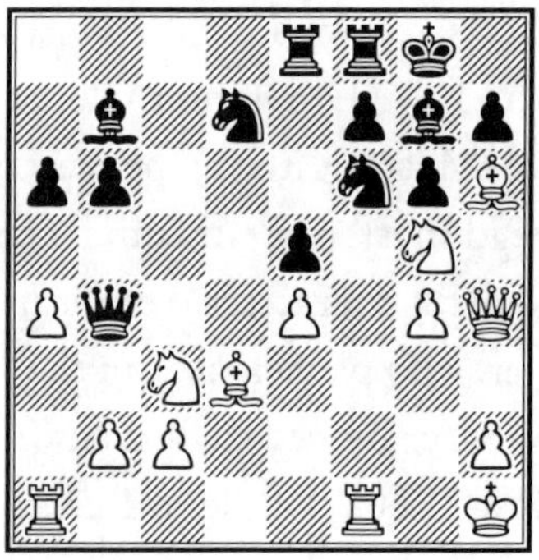

Here the game continued:

1.Ra3 Nc5! 2.Rxf6!

2.Bxg7 Kxg7 3.Rxf6 Kxf6 4.Nxh7+ Kg7 5.Nxf8 Rxf8 and Black stands much better due to his threats to the e and b pawns.[2]

2...Bxf6 3.Bxf8 Bxg5 4.Qxg5

4.Bxc5? Qxa3!

4...Kxf8 5.Qf6 Re6 6.Qh8+ Ke7 7.Kg2 Rf6

Black had a winning position (Matera).

[1] *Chess Life*, October 1967

[2] Stockfish recognizes the variation starting as 1.Ra3 as White's best and confirms Fischer's analysis beginning with 1.Rf3. Here, after 2.Bxg7 Kxg7 3.Rxf6 Kxf6 4.Nxh7+, the move 4...Kg7 is a mistake due to 5.g5!. Instead 4...Ke6 would offer equal chances.

After the game I (Matera) suggested the possibility of 1.Rf3!? which I feared during the game 1...Qxb2 2.Rd1!! Qxc3 3.Rh3

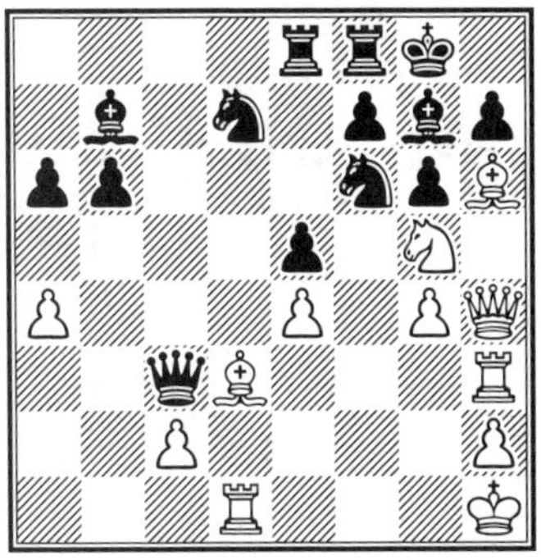

If White had played 2.Raf1 Black would now have 3...Bxh6 4.Qxh6 Qd2!. White now threatens 4.Bxg7 Kxg7 5.Qh6+ Kg8 6. Nxh7 followed by 7.Nf6+ with a mate. Tarjan and I worked out the following lines:

(A) 3...Nxe4 4.Bxe4 Bxe4+ 5.Nxe4 Qxc2 6.Re1 etc.

(B) 3...Nc5 4.Bxg7 Ncxe4 5.Bxe4 Bxe4+ 6.Nxe4 etc.

(C) 3...Nh5 4.gxh5 Bxh6 5.hxg6 etc.

(D) 3....Bh8 4.Nxh7 followed by 5.Bd2 etc.

I (Matera) showed this analysis to a number of masters who unanimously agreed that White wins.

On the day the tournament ended, I showed the position to Bobby Fischer, who immediately said the whole idea was unsound. Ten minutes later he had the answer: 3...Bh8 4.Nxh7 Nxe4 5.Bxe4 Qxc2! or 5...Bxe4+ 6.Kg1 Qxc2.

White can make things more complicated by 5.Kg1, but then Black wins with 5...Qc6, threatening 6...Ng5. What intuition the U.S. Champion has!

6
THINK AHEAD, BE AGGRESSIVE, TAKE ADVANTAGE

Sports journalist Phil Elderkin:[1]

> Barnett [Dick Barnett was a basketball player for the New York Knicks] has been a chess buff for either thirteen or fourteen years. He can't remember which. But he's played in tournaments, he's played by mail and he even offered to go against Bobby Fischer.
>
> "Earlier this season Fischer was in New York to watch us against Milwaukee." Dick explained, "I met him when he came into our dressing room after the game. We had some conversation and I told him I'd play him in chess if he'd play me one-on-one in basketball. My ambition is to be in the room with Bobby sometime when he's got an important match.
>
> "In my opinion, chess is a game you can relate to almost anything that's important, including basketball," he continued. "Nobody plays it well unless he thinks ahead, learns to be aggressive and is able to take advantage of his opponent's mistakes."

Today it's commonly accepted that elite chess players need to be in good physical condition to deal with the stress of top-level competition, but that has not always been the case. Arguably the first World Champion who understood the importance of a regular fitness program was Mikhail Botvinnik, famous for his fifteen minute walks before each game. Botvinnik practiced the Müller workout, emphasizing body-weight exercises, dynamic stretching and proper breathing, for much of his life.

Most of the other Soviet World Champions in the 1950s and '60s, particularly Tal and Petrosian, were not as keen on sport as "the Patriarch" and it would take Bobby Fischer to move physical training and chess into the modern era.

The first sport Bobby took to, like many a young boy growing up in Brooklyn, was baseball. He played not only in his youth, but also in his adult years when he had the opportunity. Walter Browne remembered meeting up with Fischer and Jim Buff in Central Park after Buff, a former semi-pro baseball player, had

1 Phil Elderkin, "Barnett's World," April 29, 1972.

tutored Bobby on some of the finer points of the game. Northern California expert Joe Tracy recalls Bobby and Buff playing catch in Golden Gate Park when Fischer stayed with his old friend in San Francisco in 1980.

During his youth Bobby learned to swim and this was one of his main forms of exercise when preparing for the 1972 match in Reykjavík. The other sport that was a staple of Fischer's adult life was tennis—there were numerous sightings of Bobby playing during his Candidates match with Bent Larsen in Denver.

What isn't well known is that Bobby competed in the second annual Dewar's Sports Celebrity Tennis Tournament at La Costa Country Club in Carlsbad, California (just outside San Diego), in early June of 1972. This is probably the only instance where a world chess champion (or soon-to-be World Champion) competed with sports professional in an athletic competition. Bobby was either a pretty good tennis player or very brave.

The roughly sixty athletes in the Dewar's Sports Celebrity Tennis Tournament played doubles with alternating partners. Baseball Hall of Famer Hank Greenberg was the winner. Other legends competing included: basketball players Rick Barry, Gail Goodrich, and Elgin Baylor; runners Marty Liquori and Gerry Lindgren; boxer Joe Frazier; and football players Deacon Jones and O.J. Simpson, but it was Bobby that was the center of attention. Newspaper accounts of the time mention Barry, Jones, and Baylor asking Fischer for his autograph.

Lubos Kavalek recalled a somewhat similar event combining doubles tennis and alternate move chess organized by Dimitrije Bjelica in Italy. Three top-level chess players were partnered with three top tennis pros: Karpov/Mulligan, Andersson/Lundquist, and Spassky/Šmíd, with the latter winning.

Tennis was not the only racket sport Bobby played. He was also a keen table-tennis player, as was noted on several occasions. Aben Rudy stated:[1]

> Fischer, let it be known, is a very proficient tennis and table-tennis player, as any one of his many victims will reluctantly testify.

In his wanderings around Manhattan, Bobby would stop on occasion at Marty "The Needle" Reisman's table tennis parlor on Manhattan's Upper West Side. Reisman offers this impression of the competitive drive of the young Fischer in his autobiography *The Money Player*:[2]

> Fischer played table tennis the way he played chess: fiercely, ferociously, going for his opponent's jugular. He was a killer, a remorseless, conscienceless, ice-blooded castrator.

---

1 *Chess Life*, December 5, 1957, (p.3).

2 Marty Reisman, *The Money Player: The Confessions of America's Greatest Table Tennis Champion and Hustler*. New York: Morrow, 1974.

Brad Darrach offered more evidence of Bobby's hyper-competitive spirit:[1]

> I am also a very ordinary Ping Pong player, and though Fischer is quite faster he really isn't much better. But when we played he attacked me with such icy concentration that I lost by an embarrassing score."Did you see those Chinese players on TV?" he crowed. "Don't you think I could beat them? I mean, they're little guys and look at my reach!" He stretched his arms out wide. "How about that reach! Don't you think with a little training I could beat them?"

Bobby always had this overwhelming urge to be the best. As a nine-year-old grade-school student, he elicited the following appraisal by a teacher:

> Whatever he played, baseball in the yard or tennis, he had to come ahead of everybody. If he had been born next to a swimming pool he would have been a swimming champion. It just happened to be chess.

Garry Kasparov and Magnus Carlsen have also shown this level of competitiveness outside the 64 squares on numerous occasions.

Allyn Kahn, who was assigned by Donald Byrne to accompany Bobby during his visit to State College, Pennsylvania, in 1964, offers a glimpse at just how badly Bobby wanted to win at everything:

> Fischer and I walked around the campus while I pointed out the key buildings, some very old stately structures and some newer brick buildings with classrooms and lecture halls. We both laughed at the posters plastered on the walls—Penn State is an Architectural Disaster!
>
> Then we came to The Hub, which was the name for the modern-looking student union building, the center for all kinds of non-academic events from impromptu folk concerts to collegiate chess tournaments.
>
> We didn't spend much time in any one place until we came to a ping-pong table in an out of the way hall in the Hub. Without a word we started a game. I was confident I could beat him, because that entire semester I played every night with my roommate as a break from studying. In what seemed like just a few minutes I was winning 11–7.
>
> Then I really hit my stride. I played some excellent volleys, deftly combining attack and defense, returning shots with lightning fast reflexes, keeping Fischer off balance. At one point during our ping-pong game, Fischer and I came to the sudden mutual realization that I was about to win! The score was 19–11.
>
> Now it was his serve, and Fischer did something so strange and remarkable that I remember it vividly even fifty years later. He held the ball in one hand and his paddle in the other. He was standing with his knees slightly bent, arms at his side as if ready to serve. Then he just stopped.
>
> He didn't look at me, but, had a far off stare as his demeanor completely changed. For a fraction of a second it seemed like all the muscles in his face

[1] Brad Darrach, *Life*, May 19, 1972.

> and body tensed at the same time, and then completely relaxed again as he took a deep breath and quickly let it out. There was a complete sense of focus and seriousness that came over him. Although Fischer didn't move, it was as if a new person instantaneously entered the room, something like when someone is beamed down into the Star Trek transporter room. This all took place in a just a few seconds.
>
> From that moment on Fischer was a different player. After a few more minutes the score was 20–18 in my favor. I was able to get one more point due to a lucky slam that hit the edge of the table and went in an unpredictable direction. I still felt confident that I could win. But that is not what happened. I could not win another point. Fischer became invincible. A few more volleys and Fischer won the game.
>
> It never occurred to me at the time to ask Fischer what just happened. It is well known that an essential quality of all top chess players is a tremendous "will to win." But I think I witnessed something truly unique.
>
> Years later a similar pattern could be seen in some of Fischer's tournaments and matches, including his 1972 World Championship match with Spassky. Fischer would start off badly and be facing insurmountable odds. Yet he would come from behind and suddenly appear unbeatable. I have read a lot about Bobby Fischer, but I have never seen any discussion of his ability to make such spectacular comebacks.

Bobby's strong "will to win" was still intact in the early 1990s where he often played racquetball against Dodd Darin, son of the crooner Bobby Darin. Dodd, roughly twenty years younger and a former intercollegiate tennis player beat Fischer "like a drum". No surprise there, but what's interesting was how Bobby failed to acknowledge that Darin was a much better player. Bobby's competitiveness did not allow him to recognize the obvious.

During Fischer's stays in Reston, Virginia, in 1977 and 1978, he played soccer with Grandmaster Lubos Kavalek. It's unknown if Bobby showed any talent for the game, but it is clear what his worst sport was: bowling (he was doing very well if he bowled over 100).

Fischer was probably his fittest the year after the match in Reykjavík. During that time, he worked out regularly at the Ambassador College gym under the watchful eye of Harry Sneider, a world class weight lifter (he bench-pressed 450 pounds at age sixty-one). Sneider had trained Olympic high jumper Dwight Stones, a two-time bronze medalist and former three-time world record holder in the event. Sneider became a good friend of Bobby and was involved in the effort to rescue Fischer's possessions after they were seized in late 1998 [see pages 609–619].

7
TIDBITS AND CHATS

In the early 1970s, American readers who wanted inside information on Bobby Fischer would have to look beyond the pages of *Chess Life & Review* and turn to the independent monthly *Chess Digest Magazine*.

Ken Smith (1930–1999), a master at chess and even better at poker, ran a successful general contracting firm in Dallas for several decades. But if that wasn't enough to keep him busy, in the late 1960s the ten-time Texas Chess Champion founded Chess Digest Inc., and soon became a major force in American chess. The mail order book and equipment business also published books and two magazines—the biweekly *Chess Newsletter* and the more substantial monthly *Chess Digest Magazine*.

Bobby had many helpers on his road to the crown: Grandmasters Robert Byrne, Larry Evans, Lubos Kavalek, William Lombardy, and International Master Bernard Zuckerman assisted (at different times) with the chess preparation; Ed Edmondson, Fred Cramer, and Frank Skoff dealt with administrative details, as did lawyer Paul Marshall; Robert Wade and Les Blackstock had the labor intensive job of preparing index cards containing the games of Fischer's opponents.

Ken Smith's role was as the go-to man for new books and bulletins. Smith had the European contacts to quickly obtain materials in all languages, which made him the the perfect person for this task, so important in the pre-computer days. It didn't hurt that Smith, who was well-off, didn't charge Bobby.

Smith's pro-bono work came with its own perk: This enabled him to offer his readers a glimpse of what it was like to be in Bobby's inner circle, offering juicy tidbits while keeping trade secrets at the same time. Sometimes Smith and Fischer's conversations touched on topics dealt with nowhere else, as in the following chats:[1]

· MIDNIGHT CALL TO KEN SMITH

At 12:01 AM, Tuesday, Feb. 3, my personal phone rang—it was Bobby Fischer and he was in California.

[1] *Chess Digest*, May 1970, (p. 98).

Fischer: Do you have the address of the Denmark book dealer?

Smith: No, it's at the office. What do you need?

Fischer: I am looking for a book on [Adolf] Anderssen with pictures and sketches.

Smith: The only one I have is the German with diagrams, call me tomorrow.

Then some small talk—

At 6:45PM, Wednesday, Feb 4, Fischer called again. After giving him the address he wanted, I asked him about his plans. Yes, he had received the invitation to play in the "World Match," but he had not answered it and probably wouldn't play. Also, he had other invitations but he had not accepted them as yet. I remarked that I hoped he would play in Yugoslavia and then went on to discuss a proposed booklet on the Fischer–Sozin Attack versus the Sicilian.

ANOTHER PHONE CALL FROM BOBBY FISCHER

At 6:30PM, Friday, Feb. 20, my personal phone rang.

Fischer: Hello, Bobby, here again.

Smith (quickly): You are going to play in the World match?!?

Fischer: Yes, I have decided to play

Smith: Versus Spassky—that will be a good match.

Fischer: Not necessarily, the Russians reserve the right to pull him and put in, maybe, Petrosian when they want to.

Smith: Surely, they wouldn't do that, they should keep their strongest team. I think the World will win, especially now that you will play—moving everybody down a notch means a lot.

Fischer: If the match is over eighteen boards as originally proposed then the World side would have a good chance—over ten boards Russia will be the favorite.

Smith: Since the Yugoslavs followed Euwe's directive and invited eighteen maybe if everyone accepted they would have to play the eighteen boards, we will see! Now what do you want? I have everything—games and theory and what I don't we will have air-mailed in.

One wonders why Bobby felt the World had a better chance against the USSR if more boards had been added. Did he not believe in the Soviets' deep bench?

The next interview took place at the USSR vs. the Rest of the World tournament held in Belgrade, Yugoslavia March 29–April 5, 1970. The other person in the conversation is Dimitry Postnikov, team captain of the USSR Chess Federation.

TALKING TO BOBBY FISCHER

Fischer: I knew that we would lose the match but if we had played on fifteen boards it would be different. We would have chances.

Question: What about your opponent Petrosian?

Fischer: He was not in good form, but neither was I, after all I have not played for one and a half years, and I feel it.

Question; Do you regret not having played Spassky?

Fischer: No, because I beat Petrosian.

Question: Would you like to play a match with Spassky?

Fischer: Yes, but only under the condition that the first man who wins six games is the winner.

Question to Postnikov: Do you see the possibility of a match in the near future between Spassky and Fischer, even an unofficial one in which the title would not be at stake?

Postnikov: No. Spassky in losing, even if it is an unofficial match, would lose everything. Fischer in losing would lose nothing. Everyone wants to play Spassky. Don't you think we have plenty of masters in our country who would jump on the opportunity to play Spassky a match? Petrosian would like nothing better. But that would not be right. Why did Fischer not play the match which was organized by the Dutch, between him and Botvinnik? Spassky says that if he does play a match then the formula FIDE now has of playing Zonals and Interzonals to find a challenger for the title would have no value, and he cannot go above FIDE.

Question to Fischer: What do you think of Spassky's strength?

Fischer: He is a very strong player, but he made many mistakes in his match with Petrosian for the World title. Here, too, he blundered against Larsen in the third game. True, it could happen to anyone. Chess has become a very tough game nowadays.

Question: Why did you give your first board to Larsen?

Fischer: I know that I am better than he is, but frankly speaking, it was fair to give him first board because he played in many tournaments and he won most of them. Also, I had not played for a year and a half.

Question: Who are the best players in the World today?

Fischer: Spassky, Petrosian, Korchnoi, me, and Larsen.

Question: Who do you think will play Spassky for the World title in 1972?

Fischer: It could be either Korchnoi or Larsen.[1]

Question: Your plans?

Fischer: I might play in the rapids at Herceg-Novi, and then go to the Zagreb event that starts on April 12. I don't know yet. I am really tired physically. I am going to Sarajevo, they are planning to make a film about me there. I have many offers for simultaneous exhibitions, but am turning them all down."

Question: The future of chess?

Fischer: The machines will take over. Waiter, two glasses of milk. (Fischer drinks milk all the time, especially when in action over the chess board. You may see him eat fruit as well.)

Question for Postnikov: How about allowing Fischer into the next Interzonal at Palma de Mallorca next November, thus allowing him to become a qualifier for the challenger of the world title?

Postnikov: Nyet...Both Dr. Euwe and I are opposed to the breaking of FIDE rules!

1 At that point in time Fischer didn't know he would play in the Interzonal.

8
FISCHER AS BLACK AGAINST THE MARÓCZY BIND

Bobby's life underwent a major transformation when he defeated Tigran Petrosian in the Candidates final, earning the right to play Boris Spassky for the World Championship. Overnight he went from private citizen to public figure, the likes of which the chess world had never seen before or since. Fischer appeared on the covers of both *Life* magazine (November 12, 1971) and *Time* (July 31, 1972), and he was interviewed by Mike Wallace on the television show *60 Minutes* (April 9, 1972).

Shortly after becoming World Champion, Bobby had a rude awaking as to the cost of being a worldwide celebrity. Thanksgiving weekend in 1972 he visited the American Open. Upon his entering the venue every player in the room, whether their clock was ticking or not, started moving towards him. The event, held in Santa Monica at the Miramar Hotel, attracted a large number of participants including celebrities such as Joni Mitchell (who played) and Peter Falk (who was gathering backstory for his character in an upcoming chess theme episode of *Columbo*, "The Most Dangerous Match"), but Bobby attracted more attention than any of them. Horrified by the limelight, Bobby promptly fled. The days when Fischer could venture into public without being recognized were over [see page 478 for more on this event].

Contrast this with Bobby's appearance just two years earlier at the 1970 Atlantic Open, held in New York City over the July 4th weekend. International Master Elliott Winslow remarked, while Fischer's arrival at the tournament caused spectators and players to take notice, the pause was momentary, and things quickly returned to normal. In those days, before his march to the title, Bobby could analyze a game, for example with the young talent Paul Jackyln, while a large crowd of spectators respectfully watched in silence, but once he took the crown this was no longer so.

In the years leading up to the 1972 match, Bobby was private, even shy at times, but he could also be quite friendly if he felt comfortable.

New Jersey expert Mark Wieder recalled an incident during the 1970 Palma de Mallorca Interzonal where his friend and college teammate, future Master Allan Savage, decided to call Bobby. Wieder related:

> We called Bobby person to person at the hotel in Palma de Mallorca and he answered. After confirming with the operator that he wasn't being charged for the call, he accepted. I told him we were college students in New England and wanted to congratulate him for clinching the Interzonal and asked about that day's game—I think versus Gligorić [The game was after round twenty-two, December 19, 1970]. He asked me my rating so he would know at what level to talk to me. Then he rattled off the game (which he had won—this was the next to last round). At the end of the call, which ran twenty minutes, I said, "Well, beat Panno for us tomorrow." To which he answered, "Well, I'll beat him for myself!" As you know the score of that game goes 1. c4, 1–0. [Panno refused to play in protest over the game being rescheduled to accommodate Fischer's religious beliefs.]

What other world-class player would have accepted this call from a complete stranger? Who else would have taken the time to ascertain his listener's playing strength to adjust his commentary to the right level? Only Bobby. During his 1964 simul tour Fischer gave lectures before his exhibitions and was noted for neither talking up or down to audiences of varying strength.

Wieder ran into Bobby in person at the blitz tournament held August 1971 to honor Fischer's match victories over Taimanov and Larsen, and the opening of the Manhattan Chess Club at its new home on E. 60th St. just off Fifth Avenue.

He added:

> After the Manhattan speed event, I went up and told Bobby it was me on that call. He said, "What'd that cost you?" I said eighteen dollars. He said, "Oh, well that was worth it!"

Bobby Fischer was never noted for a wide repertoire. Most of his career he opened 1.e4, defended it with the Najdorf Sicilian and met 1.d4 with the King's Indian and sometimes the Grünfeld and Modern Benoni. There was also some early experimentation with classical chess, opening 1.e4 e5 and 1.d4 d5 as Black.

Bobby began his career meeting 1.c4 and 1.Nf3 with King's Indian formations, then moved on to Queen's Gambit Declined setups before finally settling on 1...c5 followed by ...g6 in his peak years. The latter served him well, leading to impressive wins over Petrosian and Smyslov where he met the English with ...e6 and ...Nge7, but there was a price to pay—White could force him to play against the Maróczy Bind.

The position reached after 1.c4 c5 2.Nf3 g6 3.d4 cxd4 4.Nxd4 Nc6 5.e4 (or 1.e4 c5 2.Nf3 g6 3.d4 cxd4 4.Nxd4 Nc6 5.c4), where White has an unquestioned advantage in space, is not one many World Champions of the twentieth century were willing to defend. Besides Bobby, only Tigran Petrosian comes to mind. Fischer's score fighting the Maróczy was excellent, but he really struggled in several of the games.

First comes Fischer's most famous win on the Black side of the Maróczy.

(62) Sicilian
Bent Larsen – Fischer
Denver (2) 1971

1.c4 c5 2.Nf3 g6 3.d4 cxd4 4.Nxd4 Nc6 5.e4

This is an interesting moment as Larsen transposes into the Maróczy Bind, an opening that he was an acknowledged expert on—as Black! While he rarely faced one of his all-time favorite opening systems, Larsen did win a beautiful game against Petrosian on the White of this structure in the Second Piatigorsky Cup, Santa Monica 1966.

5...Nf6 6.Nc3 d6

The game between Larsen and Petrosian continued 6...Bg7 7.Be3 Ng4 8.Qxg4 Nxg4 9.Qd1 Ne6 with Black concentrating his play on the dark-squares.

The text is the start of a different variation named after the Georgian Grandmaster Bukhuti Gurgenidze. Black trades a pair of knights as in the 7...Ng4 line, but instead of playing on the dark squares with ...a7-a5, opts for ...a7-a6 aiming for ...b7-b5 to break down one of the two pillars of the Bind.

Garry Kasparov writing in Volume 4 of *My Great Predecessors*[1] has this to say about the position reached after 6...d6:

"Fischer liked to fianchetto his dark-squared bishop and was not afraid of the Maróczy Bind, believing in the solidity of Black's rather passive position. This was in the nature of a challenge to Botvinnik, who considered that with the pawn wedge on e4 and c4 White had a stable positional advantage. Under the influence of Fischer, there was a rapid growth in the employment of this set-up for Black in the 1970s, and then it again abated, before appearing in the arsenals of Anand and Ivanchuk in the 1990s. They still play this, as though demanding that White demonstrate the evidence of his advantage."

7.Be2

[1] Garry Kasparov, *Garry Kasparov on Fischer: My Great Predecessors Part IV*. London: Everyman Chess, 2004, (p. 401).

7.Nc2, avoiding the trade on d4, might be more testing. Peter Heine Nielsen, in his excellent chapter on the Accelerated Dragon in *Experts vs. the Sicilian,* makes the point that White generally does best in Maróczy structures with all four minor pieces on the board or none at all.

7...Nxd4 8.Qxd4 Bg7 9.Bg5

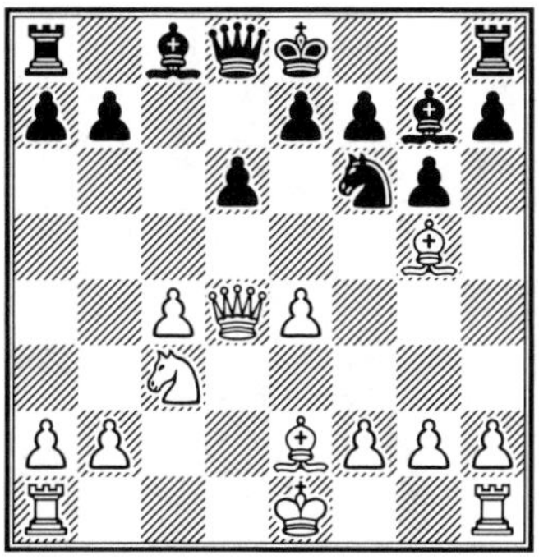

9...h6

This move has never been as popular as 9...0-0 and 9...Qa5; still, it is significant that two World Champions (Fischer and Petrosian) chose to meet 9.Bg5 with 9...h6. International Master Jeremy Silman points out that one important point behind ...h6/...Kh7 is that Black avoids tricks based on Nd5, meeting ...Qxd2 with Nxe7+. This means Black can play ...Rac8 (instead of the almost automatic ...Rfc8) in certain positions, leaving his other rook on f8 for the defense of his king.

Kasparov gives 9...h6 a dubious mark (?!).

10.Be3

This is invariably played, but there is nothing wrong with 10.Bd2. The move looks modest but contains plenty of venom as the bishop discourages ...Qa5 and gives extra support to the knight on c3.

One nice example of White's possibilities in this line can be seen in the following win by a young American star: 10.Bd2 0-0 11.0-0 Be6 12.Qd3 Nd7 13.b3 Nc5 14.Qe3 Bd7 15.Rad1 a5 16.f4 Bc6 17.e5 Nd7 18.exd6 exd6 19.Qg3 Re8 20.Bf3 Nf6 21.f5 Kh7 22.fxg6+ fxg6 23.Bf4 Qb6+ 24.Kh1 Rad8 25.Qh3 Bxf3 26.Qxf3 Re6 27.Bxh6 Bxh6 28.Nd5 Nxd5 29.Qf7+ Bg7 30.Qxe6 Ne3 31.Rd3 Nf5 32.Rxf5 1–0 Robson–Belous, Moscow 2012.

10...0-0 11.Qd2 Kh7 12.0-0

It seems natural to castle and prepare f2-f4 but there is also something to be said for the more restrained 12.f3 Be6 13.Rc1 when Black has two principle choices:

(A) 13...Qa5 14.0-0 Rfc8 15.b3 a6 16.f4 b5 17.f5 b4 18.fxe6 bxc3 19.Qxc3 Qxc3 20.Rxc3 and White has a slight edge after both recaptures.

(B) 13...Rc8 14.Nb5 a6 15.Nd4 Bd7 16.0-0 with a small pull for White in Seirawan–I. Ivanov, Durango (US ch.) 1992.

12...Be6

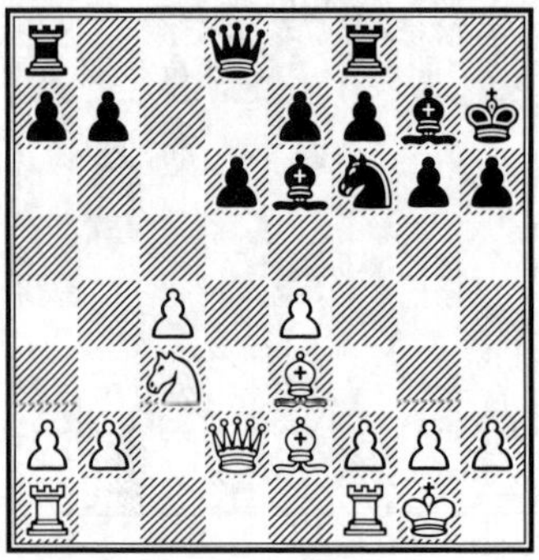

13.f4

13.Rac1 Qa5 14.f4 Rac8 15.b3 a6 16.f5 Bd7 17.h3 Bc6 18.Bd3 Nd7 19.Nd5 Qxd2 20.Bxd2 Rfe8 21.Bb1 Bd4+ 22.Kh1 Kg7 23.fxg6 fxg6 24.Nf4 Bf6 25.Be3 ½–½ Gulko–Petrosian, Biel Interzonal 1976.

This game is a good illustration of the difficulties White faces in obtaining a tangible advantage against this line of the Maróczy. Gulko was able to kick the bishop with f5 but it easily succeeded in finding a good home on c6 while Black's pieces obtained use of the e5 square.

[Kasparov]: "Timman's move 13.Bd4!? was possibly more unpleasant for Black—after the inevitable exchange of the dark-squared bishops the weakness of the enemy kingside will begin to tell"

The dark-side of ...h6 is that it can weaken Black's kingside if the bishop on g7 is exchanged

13...Rc8 14.b3 Qa5 15.a3

The immediate 15.f5 might be better. After 15...Bd7 16.Qd3 Bc6 17.a3 Nd7 18.b4 Qe5 (The queen needs to be on e5—18...Qc7 19.b5 Ne5 20.Qd2 Bd7 21.Nd5 Qd8 22.Rac1 b6 23.a4 is clearly better for White besides being an easy-to-play position.) 19.Rac1 Nb6 (19...a6!? and 19...a5!? are alternatives) 20.Kh1 Na4 21.Nd5 Bxd5 22.exd5 leaves White with a small but stable advantage.

[Kasparov]: "15.Bf3 Bg4 16.Rad1 Bxf3 17.Rxf3 b5! with equality."

15.Rac1 will likely transpose to the aforementioned Gulko–Petrosian game.

15...a6 16.f5 Bd7 17.b4

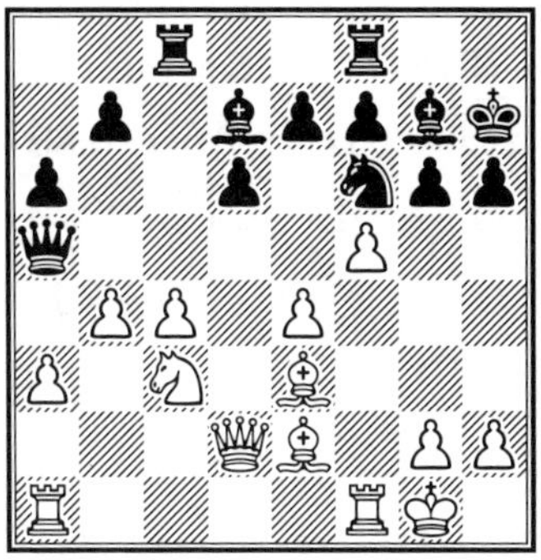

17...Qe5!

This is the right square for the queen, just like Bobby's game with Naranja from the 1970 Interzonal, which we will see later. The queen is very active here and it's not easy to exploit its seemingly exposed position. Fischer liked to play with his queen so this move was typical for him. The queen also ends up on e5 on a full board in an old main line of the Yugoslav Attack in the Dragon Sicilian.

This fascination with moving the queen to where it seems to be in danger appears to have been part of Bobby's bag of tricks well before the 1970s. John Blackstone had a discussion with the Canadian International Master Zvonko who recalled that Fischer's lecture preceding his 1964 simul in Toronto was filled with profound thoughts and ideas. One of them was "...that the queen's real prowess could only be realized by drawing upon her the firepower of the enemy, and just when it seems she is about to be captured, she uses her power to jump to the other side of the board!"

18.Rae1

Black answers 18.Rac1 with the thematic 18...b5 while on 18.Rad1 Nxe4 works well. For example, 19.Nxe4 Qxe4 20.c5 (20.Rf4 Qc6 21.Bf3 Qc7 22.Be4 Bf6 23.fxg6+ fxg6) 20...Bxf5 21.Bf3 Qe6 22.Bxb7 Rc7 23.Bd5 Qc8 24.cxd6 exd6 when White has enough activity for the pawn but nothing more.

18...Bc6

Here 18...Nxe4? runs into 19.Nxe4 Qxe4 20.Bd3, but 18...b5! (Kasparov) was probably simpler.

19.Bf4

19.Bf3 might be better, but again Black can get away with capturing on e4: 19...Nxe4 20.Nxe4 Bxe4 21.Bxe4 Qxe4 22.Rf4 Qc6 23.Rh4 h5 24.Qd3

(24.Bd4 keeps some advantage) 24...d5 25.fxg6+ fxg6 26.Rxh5+ Kg8 27.Rxd5 Qxc4 28.Bc5 Qxd3 29.Rxd3 Bf6 30.Rd7 .b6 31.Bxb6 Rc3 32.a4 Ra3 33.a5 Bc3 34.Rb1 Bxb4. This long but important analysis by Houdini supports Fischer's decision to centralize his queen.

19...Nxe4 20.Nxe4 Qxe4 21.Bd3 Qd4+ 22.Kh1

Alternatively 22.Be3 is met by 22...Qc3 23.Bxh6 Bd4+ 24.Kh1 Qxd2 25.Bxd2 Be5 with equality.

22...Rce8

22...b5! (Kasparov) as 23.Rxe7 is met by 23...bxc4.

23.Be3 Qc3 24.Bxh6

Larsen recovers his pawn, but now Fischer has no problems and long-term potential in his central pawn mass.

24...Qxd2 25.Bxd2 Be5 26.Bf4 Bxf4

[Kasparov]: "26...Bf6 was simpler."

27.Rxf4

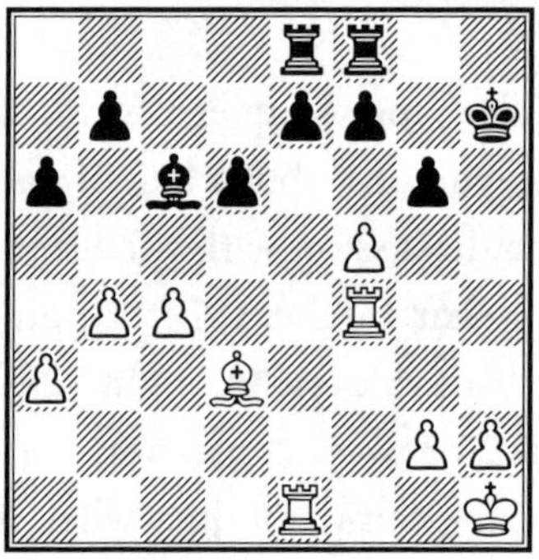

27...gxf5!

{Kasparov]: "An accurate and timely exchange—instead 27...Kh6 28.Re3 allows White a serious initiative."

It is not clear who is the hunter and hunted. Larsen is trying desperately to win to recover from his loss in game one of the match while Fischer is eager to go two up and break his opponent's spirit.

28.Rxf5

The tricky 28.Re3 is met by 28...Rg8 (and not 28...e6?? 29.Rg3 with mate soon to follow) 29.Bxf5+ Kh6 30.Bh3 d5 with equal play.

28...Kg7 29.Rg5+ Kh6 30.h4!

Kasparov approves of White continuing to fight for the initiative and gives this move an exclamation mark.

30...e6

He also likes this move which signals that Fischer is finally ready to mobilize his central pawns

31.Rf1

31.Kh2 Rg8 32.Rxg8 Rxg8 33.g3 Rg4 would likely lead to a draw.

31...f5! 32.Re1!

Both players' last moves receive exclamation marks from Garry who writes: "For the moment a tough struggle between two worthy opponents is in progress. White is pressing on the weaknesses and skillfully maintaining the tension."

32...Rf7 33.b5

Larsen succeeds in chasing the bishop off its powerful diagonal but not for free. Fischer now has three connected passed pawns and the use of the a-file. The latter will prove to be a major factor in deciding the final result.

33...axb5 34.cxb5 Bd7 35.g4

[Kasparov]: "Fischer has achieved his aim: White has come out of cover and begun pressing over the entire board. In reply Black is prepared for a counterattack."

35...Ra8!

35...Rg7 36.Rxg7 Kxg7 37.gxf5 Rh8 is a drawing attempt. Bobby is hoping for more.

36.gxf5 exf5

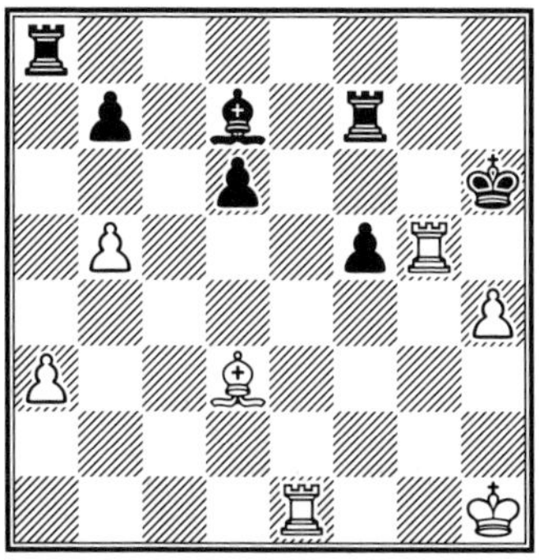

37.Bc4??

This blunder in time pressure effectively decides the match as Larsen lost game three horribly, a shell of his normal self after losing two tough fights that could have gone either way.

Correct was 37.Reg1 when 37...Ra4 (37...Rxa3?? 38.Rg6+ Kh7 39.Bc4) 38.Rg6+ Kh7 39.Rxd6 Rxh4+ 40.Kg2 Bxb5 41.Bxb5 Rg7+ 42.Kf2 Rf4+

43.Ke3 Re4+ 44.Kf2 Rf4+ would have been the fair result for this titanic battle.

37...Ra4! 38.Rc1?

[Kasparov]: "Another blunder, but even after the better 38.Bxf7 Rxh4+ 39.Kg2 Kxg5 40.Be8 White's position, in all probability, would have been lost."

38...Bxb5! 39.Bxf7 Rxh4+ 40.Kg2 Kxg5 41.Bd5 Ba6 42.Rd1 Ra4 43.Bf3 Rxa3 44.Rxd6 Ra2+ 45.Kg1 Kf4 46.Bg2 Rb2 47.Rd7 b6 48.Rd8

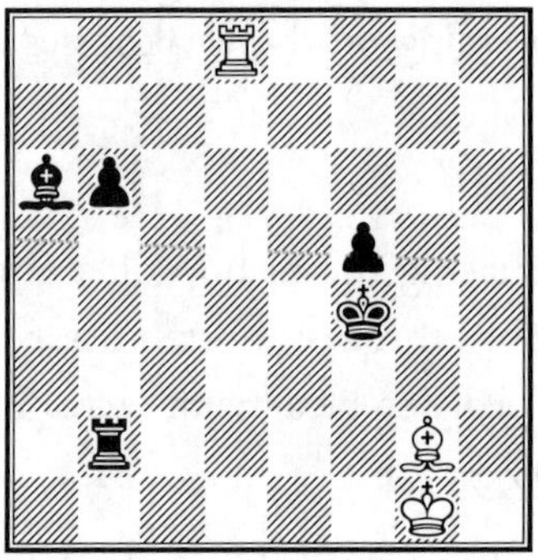

48...Be2 49.Bh3 Bg4 50.Bf1 Bf3 51.Rb8 Be4 52.Ba6 Ke3 53.Rc8 Rb1+ 54.Kh2 Kf4, 0–1.

Mato Damjanović (not to be confused with fellow Grandmaster Branko Damljanović) was one of the better Yugoslav players of the 1960s–1970s, winning individual silver and team bronze in the 1960 Olympiad at Leipzig.

Damjanović–Fischer was originally scheduled for round two but rescheduled due to Fischer's late arrival in Argentina. It was played sometime in the first half of what would turn out to be a runaway victory for Bobby, who finished 3½ points ahead of the field.

Why did Fischer, rated over 250 points higher than his opponent, choose to defend the Maróczy Bind which is known to provide few winning chances for Black unless White is ambitious? We saw Bobby get plenty of opportunities when Larsen went after him, Game (62), but here Damjanović is much more respectful—what was to have been a hundred-question exam has now been turned into to a short multiple choice test.

Game (63), though hardly Fischer's best, is one of his most instructive. It's a perfect example of an "ugly" fighting grind out victory. Magazines like to print short, flashy wins, but the following game is the type that so often makes the difference between finishing first or second.

One of the qualities that made Fischer so exceptional was his tremendous fighting spirit in which he makes use of every last opportunity. Damjanović–Fischer, Buenos Aires 1970, is a perfect example.

(63) Sicilian
Mato Damjanović – Fischer
Buenos Aires (2) 1970

1.d4 Nf6 2.c4 c5 3.Nf3 cxd4 4.Nxd4 Nc6

Bobby learned his lesson from this game and later in the year at the Palma de Mallorca Interzonal played 4...e6 against Reshevsky.

5.Nc3 g6 6.e4 d6 7.Be2 Nxd4 8.Qxd4 Bg7 9.Be3 0-0 10.Qd2 Be6 11.f3

This move, which strengthens the e4 pawn and is often a prelude to Nd5, is commonly played in the Maróczy Bind, but here it looks imprecise. Better and more flexible are 11.Rc1 or 11.0-0.

11...Rc8

This move is a clear indication that Black wants to fight and is not content with a quick draw which Damjanović could easily force after the normal set up with ...Qa5.

One example of the drawing variation from Bobby's practice was his game with Petrosian from their Candidates match. 11...Qa5 12.Rc1 Rfc8 13.b3 a6 14.Nd5 Qxd2+ 15.Kxd2 Nxd5 16.cxd5 Bd7 17.Rxc8+ Rxc8 18.Rc1 Rxc1 19.Kxc1 Kf8 20.Kc2 e6 ½–½ Petrosian–Fischer Buenos Aires (4) 1971.

Drawing Petrosian with Black was good match strategy, but Bobby was not about to give Damjanović an easy half point.

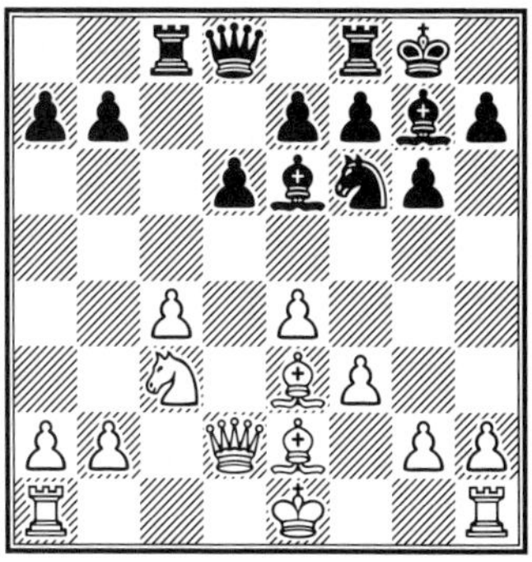

12.Nd5

White doesn't have a satisfactory way to defend his c-pawn which promises an advantage. The alternative to the text, 12.b3, is met by 12... b5 (...Be6, ...Rc8 doesn't have the theoretical seal of approval of the main line with ...Be6, ...a6, ...Qa5 and ...Rfc8), but here it allows this thematic break without the preparatory ...a6) 13.e5 Nd7 14.Nxb5 Nxe5 15.Rd1 a6 16.Nc3 Qa5 17.Nd5 Qxd2+ 18.Rxd2 Nc6 19.Kf2 a5, which offered equal chances in Zubov–Kuzubov, Alushta 2004.

12...Nd7

12...Nxd5 is a quick equalizer which illustrates why 11.f3 was not the most challenging continuation: 13.cxd5 Bd7 14.0-0 e6 15.dxe6 Bxe6 16.Rfd1 Qf6 17.Bxa7 Qxb2 18.Qxb2 ½–½ Gulko–Ivanchuk, Novgorod 1995. Bobby wants more and aims for a "good knight versus bad bishop" scenario.

13.0-0 Nc5 14.Rac1 a5

The players have reached a position similar to one that arises in Larsen's favorite Anti-Bind line 1.e4 c5 2.Nf3 Nc6 3.d4 cxd4 4.Nxd4 g6 5.c4 Bg7 6.Be3 Nf6 7.Nc3 0-0 8.Be2 d6 9.0-0 Bd7 10.Rc1 Nxd4 11.Bxd4 Bc6 12.f3 Nd7 13.Be3 a5.

Some differences are easy to spot: ...Be6 instead of ...Bc6 and ...Rac8 (instead of ...Rfc8), but the most important factor is that White's knight has been drawn to d5. This allows Black the opportunity to create a minor piece imbalance in the position with ...Bxd5. On the other hand he has lost the option to try ideas based on ...Be5 and ...e6, sometimes with ...b6 and ...Ra7-d7, when if everything goes perfectly Black will be able to play...f5.

This thematic advance can break the Maróczy Bind (see Keres–Petrosian, 1959 Candidates), but it demands precise timing and energetic play for it to work. When White is playing well against the Maróczy ...f5 is normally hard to achieve without creating serious weaknesses in Black's position.

15.b3

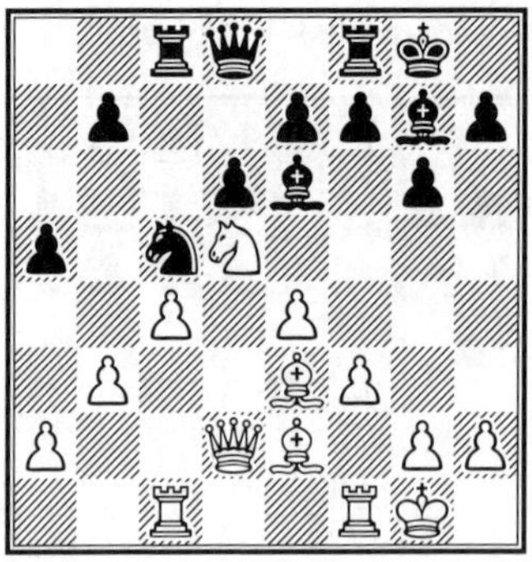

15...Bxd5(!)

The exclamation mark is not because Black will have the better of it after the trade—not at all! In fact, if anything, White has a small advantage. So why did Bobby trade on d5? Because now he has better chances to fight for a win as the position is imbalanced. One key question that will dictate play henceforth is which minor piece will be stronger—White's light-squared bishop or Black's knight?

First timers playing the Black side of the Maróczy often have the mistaken impression that when they trade their light-squared bishop for a White knight on d5 they are doing well but it depends on what else is going on in the position: i.e. are the dark squared bishops off the board?, does Black have in ...b4 and ...a5 to secure the knight on c5 or has he done even better and anchored his horse on d4 with ...e5. If none of the above is true, particularly the exchange of dark-squared bishops, White is very likely going to have an edge—his space advantage should count for something.

16.cxd5 Qb6 17.Rc4!

Damjanović stops Bobby from any ideas based on ...Qb4. 17.Rc2? allows the trick 17...Bh6 with the point that 18. Bxh6?? is met by 18...Nxe4+ 20. Be3 Nxd2 21. Bxa7 Rxc2.

Of course White would never dream of capturing on h6, but he has made a concession allowing Black to trade on e3. Unlike the Dragon Sicilian lines in the Yugoslav Attack, where White goes out of his way to trade dark-squared bishops, here the exchange often helps Black, as almost all of White's pawns are on the same color as his remaining bishop.

17...Qa7 18.Rc2

The text was played to stop ...b5, but maybe White doesn't need to. 18.Rfc1!? b5 19.R4c2 Cvetković–Banikas, Patras 1998, is a bigger test of Black's resources. White meets 19...b4 with 20.Bb5

18...Bh6!?

Fischer unbalances the position to create more potential problems for his opponent but also himself. The text costs time as the bishop will have to return to g7, but White is now forced to come out and fight.

19.f4!

This removes the support of White's e-pawn but is clearly the right decision. The alternatives 19.Bxh6? Nxe4+ 20.Qe3 Qxe3+ 21.Bxe3 Rxc2 22.Bd3 Rc3 and 19.Kh1? Nxe4! 20.Bxa7 Nxd2 21.Rfc1 Nxb3! 22.Rxc8 (22.axb3 Bxc1) 22...Nxc1 23.Rxf8+ Kxf8 24.Bc4 b5! leave Black with a winning position.

19...Rc7 20.g3

This unnecessarily softens up the kingside. More natural was 20.Rfc1, when 20...Rfc8 21.Bg4 Rd8 22.a3 Qa6 23.Be2 Qa8 24.Qe1 Rdc8 25.Qh4 Bg7 26.Bg4 Rf8 was Malakhov–Banikas, Menorca 1996. White has a large advantage if he had played 27.e5.

20...b6 21.Rfc1 Bg7 22.Bb5 Qa8!

Black tries to lure White's bishop to c6. After 22...Rfc8 23.Qg2 Black is suffering with no opportunities for active play.

23.Qe2

Fischer's idea was 23.Bc6 Qa6 (23...Rxc6 24.dxc6 Qxc6 25.e5 and Black doesn't have any compensation for the sacrificed material) 24.Qg2 (24.Rc4 is better) and now 24...Qd3! with active play as Elie Agur points out in his outstanding book *Bobby Fischer: His Approach to Chess.*

Note that 23.Bxc5 bxc5 is pleasant for Black as his dark-squared bishop has become a powerhouse.

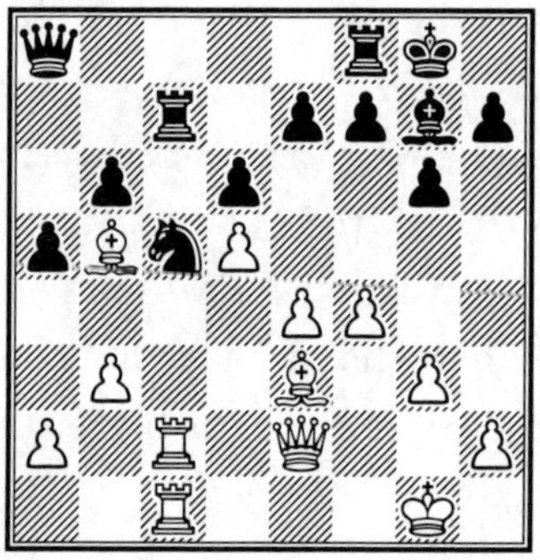

23...e5?

This move has been given an exclamation mark by several annotators and indeed at first glance it looks good as Black challenges White for space and sharpens the game. Unfortunately it's just not good. Holding still with 23...Qb8 was objectively the better choice although it would mean a passive position with little counterplay.

Jeremy Silman, in his insightful notes to this game at chess.com (part of his series "My Favorite Classic Games") explains the motivation behind Fischer's twenty-third move. "Very risky, but other (solid) moves would have given Black a draw at best. So, playing the role of chess psychologist, Bobby complicates the position, hoping to outplay his opponent in the resulting chaos."

24.dxe6 fxe6 25.Rd1 Rd8 26.Bd4

This is another hard move to annotate. It's not White's best try but it should leave him with some advantage if followed up correctly.

Silman points out the shortcomings of 26.Bd4 in no uncertain terms. "A terrible move! By giving up his bishop pair, White creates a situation where the knight, if it finds a permanent home (meaning a pawn can't eventually chase it away), can end up as the dominant minor piece. And, as things went, that's exactly what happened."

Silman's assessment of the position is correct, but only if White plays passively. As we shall soon see 26.Bd4 maintains White's advantage, as does Agur and Psakhis suggestion of 26.Bc4. Incidentally, both of them join Silman in giving 26.Bd4 a question mark.

There is another candidate move for White to consider and it only takes strong computer engines seconds to find it. Had Damjanović found 26.f5! Fischer would have been in big trouble. The move is certainly thematic (open the position for the two bishops), but it takes a human a moment to realize that the position that arises after 26...Qxe4 27.fxe6 Qxe6 28.Bg5 Qxe2 29.Rxe2 followed by Rxd6 recovering the pawn leads to a winning ending. White's bishops are very active while the b6 pawn and Black's weak back rank are vulnerable as can be seen in the following variations:

(A) 29...Rb8 30.Rxd6 Rcc8 (30...Bc3 31.Bd8) 31.Re7

(B) 29...Rf8 30.Rxd6 Nb7 31.Rd1 Nc5 32.Bc4+ Kh8 33.Be7 Rfc8 34.Bd8

26...Bxd4+ 27.Rxd4

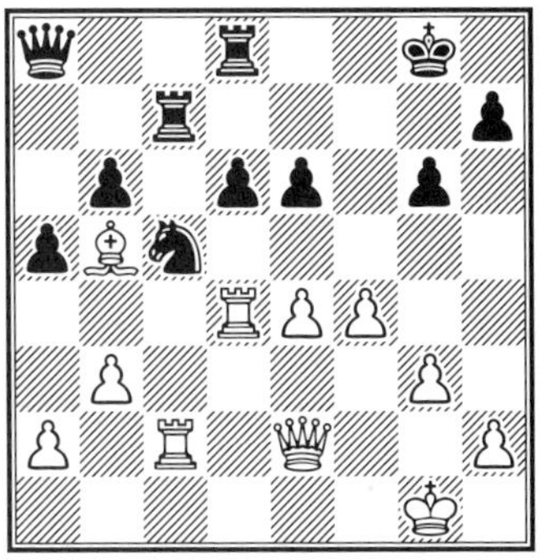

27...e5?

This is the thematic follow-up fixing the pawn structure. In an endgame this structure could be in Black's favor but we are still in the middlegame. Objectively Fischer should sit with 27...Qb8 leaving White with a large advantage. Instead Bobby chose a very risky (bad) continuation. Why? Silman explains the pros and cons behind 27...e5.

[Silman]: "Fischer keeps standing on the razor's edge. His dream: get his pawns on dark-squares. Why? Because the bishop can't threaten them and dark-squares like d4 and c5 can be occupied by the knight. The negative side is that the d5-square is open for White's pieces and the bishop has control over many cleared out diagonals. Placing the pawns on dark-squares makes them safe from the bishop but at the cost of opening the board for the bishop."

28.fxe5 dxe5 29.Rxd8+?

Agur, Psakhis, and Silman all question the text (rightly) and point out that 29.Rd5! is better, but fail to appreciate just how much. Try to find a move for Black! Trading on d5 only creates a dangerous passed pawn and exposes the e-pawn to attack. The steadier looking 29…Re7 is met by 30.Qd2! when 30…Rxd5 31.exd5 Ne4 (aiming to blockade on d6) is met by 32.Qe3. Bobby definitely dodged a bullet!

Black is finally close to equality after the exchange of rooks and Fischer was likely growing more confident by the moment. Silman writes of White's last move: "Damjanović is exhibiting "Fischer fear" and suddenly plays to draw. Not too wise since the prime Fischer was one of history's greatest endgame masters."

We would add that Damjanović, having lost in round one to Gheorghiu with White, was understandably hoping to keep the bleeding to a minimum. That said the best way to draw (or beat!) a stronger player is with the better position.

29...Qxd8 30.Bc4+ Kg7 31.Bd5 Nd7!

From this point on Fischer plays wonderfully and makes the most of his chances, first in the queen and knight versus queen and bishop ending and later with knight versus bishop.

32.Qf2

32.a4 Nf6 33.Rd2 (33.Rxc7+ Qxc7) 33...Rc1+ 34.Kg2 Qc7(Agur) offers Black, who controls the c-file, slightly the better of it.

32...Rxc2 33.Qxc2

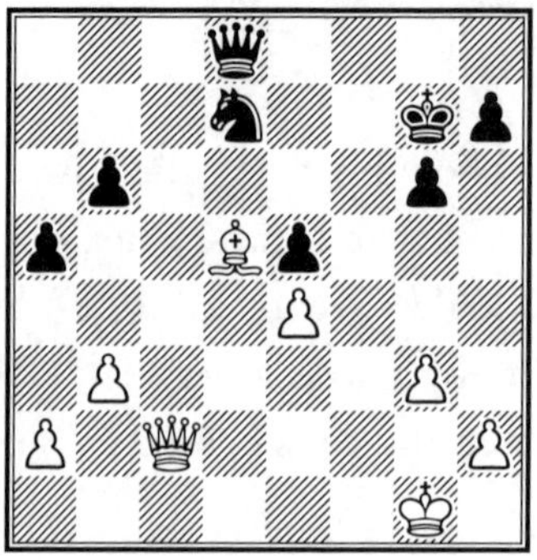

33…b5!

Fischer continues to transform the pawn structure to favor his knight versus the bishop. The text plans …b4 to fix the White pawns on a2 and b3. Black dreams of …a5-a4-a3 when a2 become a huge target vulnerable to…Nxb3 if the queens come off. Should the knight manage to get to c3, White would also be lost.

34.Kg2

Damjanović activates his king but there was much to say for Agur's suggestion of 34.Qc6!? b4 (34...Qb6+? 35.Kg2! Qxc6 36.Bxc6 Nc5 37.Bxb5 Nxe4 38.Bc6 with a slight edge to White in the ending.) 35.Kg2 Nf6 36.Qe6 when it's hard to see Black winning the game.

34...b4

Black continues his plan. Objectively he may not yet have anything concrete, but he does have a plan.

35.Qc6

Staying active is the right course of action.

35... Nf6 36.Kf3?!

This is yet another move that is hard to annotate. White prepares his king for the upcoming endgame and to be fair it should be drawn, but it's easier to hold with queens on the board. It's hard to see how Black can play for a win with his exposed king after 36.Qe6 Qc7 37.Bc4 Qb7 38.Bd5.

36...Qd7! 37.Qxd7+

Taking into account Damjanović's previous moves it is unlikely that he would have avoided the trade of queens, but if he had Fischer was ready for him: 37.Qc5!? Qh3 38.Qe7+ Kh6 as 39.Qxf6?? is met by 39...Qf1+.

37...Nxd7 38.Ke3 Kf6 39.Kd3 Nb6

This was absolutely necessary as White would be winning if allowed to play Kc4.

40.Bc6 Ke7 41.h4 h6

Silman is spot on when he writes: "The position is, with best play, drawn, but if anyone is going to win, it's Black. The reason is that White's king can't penetrate into the queenside and White doesn't have any long-range targets to attack. Black's knight, on the other hand, will be able to attack anything it wants since it has access to both light and dark squares."

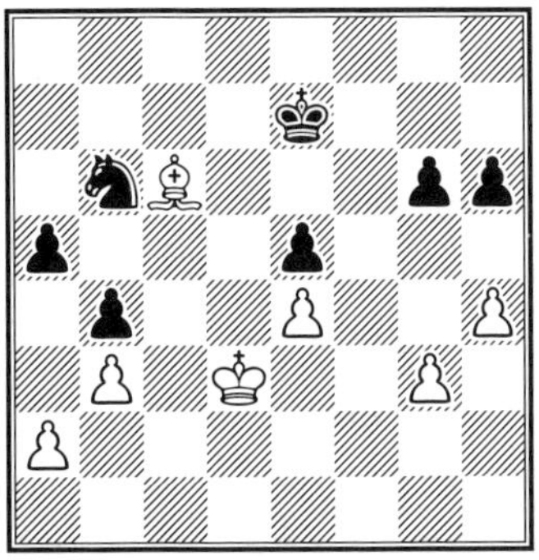

42.Ke3

Psakhis points out if White gets too aggressive it will rebound: 42.Bb5?! Nc8 43.Kc4 Nd6+ 44.Kc5 Nxe4+ 45.Kb6 Kd6! or 45...Nc3!? 46.Kxa5 e4. In both cases Black is winning.

42...Nc8 43.Kd3 Nd6

Black has succeeded in bringing his knight to the golden square d6 where it denies White's king entry to the queenside, attacks e4, and is positioned to head to c3 (via b5) if given a chance. Note that he has kept his king on e7 to avoid allowing White the chance to play Be8. Fischer wants to be very careful about advancing his pawn to g5 as this could potentially provide White's king a target to attack and access to the f5 and h5 squares.

44.Ke3 Kd8 45.Kd3 Kc7 46.Ba4 Kb6 47.Ke3 Kc5

This feint with the king doesn't produce any immediate results but it reminds White that Black has all the time in the world. White can only sit back and defend, which is psychologically difficult. Many a defender has made an unforced error in such positions.

48.Bd7 Kb6 49.Ba4 Kc7 50.Kd3 Kd8 51.Bc6 Ke7 52.Ke3 Ke6 53.Kf3

53.Ba4 Nb7 54.Be8 Kf6

53...Kf6

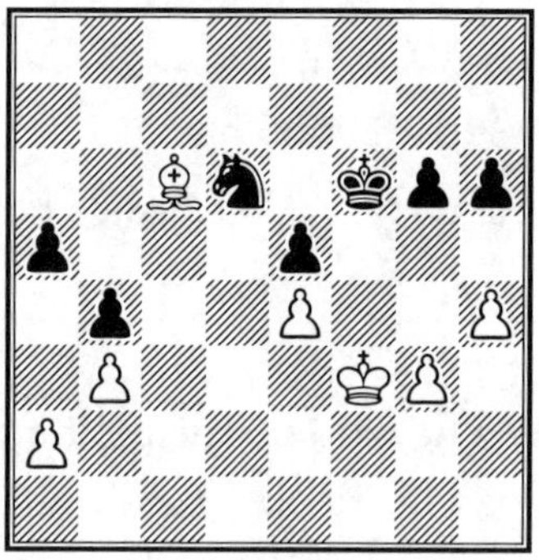

54.g4

This move violates the principle not to put pawns on the same color of the bishop and eliminates the possibility of White obtaining counterplay on the kingside with Kg4. Agur, Psakhis, Müller, and Silman all understandably query this move.

[Silman]: "A mistake! Damjanović thought that by closing the kingside and then bringing his King to the queenside, Fischer would be out of tricks and a draw would occur. But in reality this move takes away his own king's sting, which was the ability to move to g4 and penetrate into Black's position. Now that the doors to the kingside are shut, Fischer is able to give maximum attention to the queenside, while also forcing White's bishop to attend to the loose e4- and g4-pawns."

So why did an experienced grandmaster like Damjanović play it? Because it draws. Rules are rules, but here the position is closed enough that White can defend against the threats of a Black king invasion or a deadly knight foray.

54...g5 55.h5 Ke7 56.Ke3 Kd8 57.Kd3 Kc7 58.Ba4 Kb6 59.Bd7 Kc5 60.Ba4

60.Ke3 Nb7 61.Bc8 Nd8 62.Bd7 Kd6

60...Nc8 61.Be8 Ne7 62.Ke3 Ng8 63.Bd7 Nf6 64.Bf5 Kb5 65.Kd3 a4

Black has brought his king and knight to their optimum squares and makes the key advance. Will Fischer be able to win or can Damjanović hold?

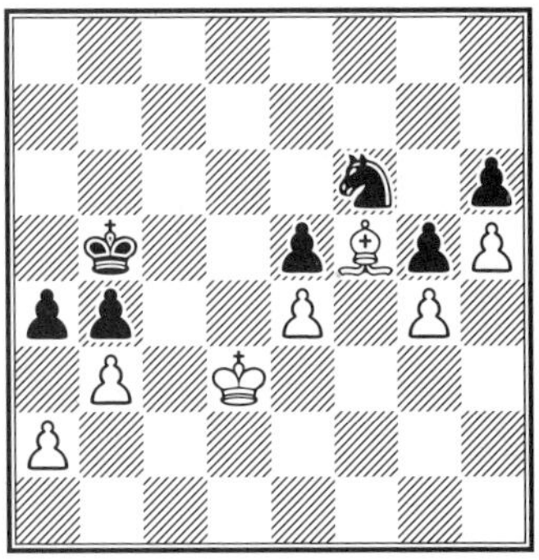

66.bxa4+??

Only this loses! Damjanović made several imprecise moves in this game but only this move leads to a zero in the crosstable.

Grandmaster Matanović gives the following winning line if White does not capture: 66.Ke3 a3 67.Kd3 Kc5 68.Ke3 Ne8 69.Kd3 Nd6 70.Bd7 Nc4! 71.Be8 (71.bxc4 b3) 71...Nb2+ 72.Kd2 (72.Ke3 Nd1+ 73.Kd3 Nc3 wins) 72...Kd4 winning. What this variation demonstrates is that White must guard against three threats. The first two are pretty easy to see: a king invasion via d4 or ...Nb5-c3 followed by capturing on a2. The third, ...Nc4, is more subtle and emphasizes the importance of playing ...a7-a5-a4-a3.

Damjanović claimed after the game he was drawing, but no one believed him until recently. Agur, Psakhis, and Silman in his *Silman's Complete Endgame Course* (2006) all agreed with the assessment White was lost whether he captured on a4 or not. However it turns out Damjanović was right, as Müller and Silman have more recently pointed out. In 2010 Silman wrote: "White, tired and depressed, finally cracks. He should have held fast with 66. Kc2 a3 67. Kd3 Kc5 68. Ke3 and used his bishop to keep the knight off the various key light-squares that would enable Black to do queenside damage."

It turns out the losing move in Matanović analysis is 69.Kd3?? Instead White had two ways to draw by keeping the threats of ...Nb5 and ...Nc4 under control. For example: 69.Bd7 Nd6 70.Ba4 and 69.Bc8 Nd6 70.Ba6 both stop Black's threats.

66...Kxa4

Fischer is finally winning after almost seventy moves of hard work.

67.Kc4

67.Kc2 Ka3 68.Kb1 b3 69.axb3 Kxb3 70.Kc1 Kc3 71.Kd1 Kd3 is an easy win for Black.

More challenging is 67.Ke3!? but here Black also comes out on top. 67... Ka3 68.Be6 Kb2! (68...Nxg4+? 69.Bxg4 Kxa2 70.Kd2 b3 71.Be6 g4 72.Ke3 (72.Kc3? g3–+) 72...Ka3 73.Bc4 b2 74.Bd3 Ka2 75.Kf2 b1Q 76.Bxb1+ Kxb1 77.Kg3 Kc2 78.Kxg4 Kd3 79.Kf5 Kd4 80.Kg6 Kxe4 81.Kxh6 Kf5 82.Kg7 e4=) 69.Kd3 Kb1 70.Ke3 (70.Kc4 Kxa2 71.Kxb4+ Kb2 72.Kc5 (72.Bf5 Kc2) 72...Kc3 73.Bf5 Kd3 74.Kd6 Kd4–+) 70...Kc2 71.Bb3+ Kc3 72.Be6 Ne8 73.Bc8 Nd6 74.Bd7 Nc4+ 75.Ke2 Kd4 76.Bf5 Nd6 77.Kf3 Nb5.

67...Ka3 68.Kc5 Kxa2 69.Kxb4 Kb2 70.Kc5 Kc3 71.Kd6 Kd4 72.Ke6 Nxe4 73.Kf7 Nf2 74.Kg6 e4

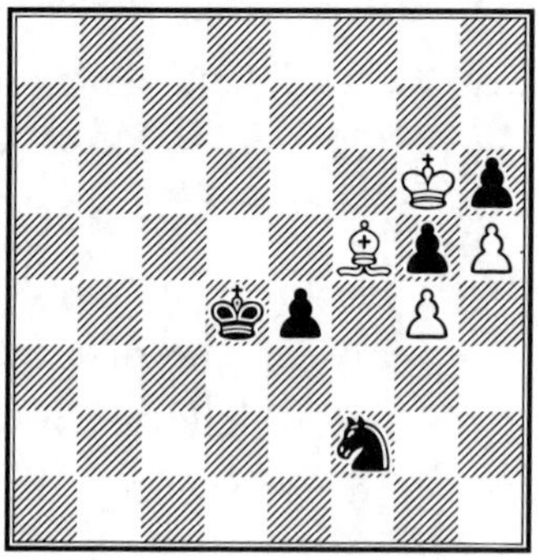

75.Kxh6

75.Bxe4 doesn't change the result: 75...Kxe4 76.Kxh6 Kf4 77.Kg6 Nxg4 wins.

75...e3 76.Kg7 e2 77.h6 e1Q 78.h7 Qe7+ 79.Kg8 Ne4!, 0–1.

White resigns because of the variation 80.Bxe4 (80.h8Q+ Nf6+) 80... Kxe4 81.h8Q Qe8+ 82.Kg7 Qxh8+ 83.Kxh8 Kf4 winning.

Game (64) was the last-time Petrosian and Fischer met before their Candidates match the following year. Played in the last round this game had no major importance for Fischer as he had already won the tournament, but for the "Iron Tiger" a win could have potentially given him a share of second instead of sixth place.

(64) Sicilian
Tigran Petrosian – Fischer
Rovinj/Zagreb (17) 1970

1.c4 c5 2.Nf3 g6 3.e4 Bg7 4.d4 Nc6

Many strong players do not like to give their opponent the clear advantage in space the Maróczy Bind affords. This explains the attempts to complicate matters with the text as well as 4...Qa5+ and 4...Qb6.

5.dxc5

5.Be3 should not offer much after 5...Qb6 6.Nc3 cxd4 7.Nd5 Qa5+ 8.b4 Qd8 9.Nxd4 Nf6.

Besides the text White has another strong continuation in 5.d5. After 5...Nd4 6.Nxd4 Black has two ways to capture, but neither promise equality:

(A) 6...Bxd4 7.Bd3 d6 8.0-0 Nf6 9.Nd2 gives White a favorable Benoni where Black loses time due to the awkward position of the bishop on d4. White can play for both e4-e5 and b2-b4.

(B) 6...cxd4 is more often seen, but after 7.Bd3 d6 8.0-0 Nf6 9.Nd2 0-0 10.b4 and later f4 White has a free hand on both wings and the pawn on d4 gets in Black's way. Smyslov and Stein both tried this variation despite these drawbacks.

5...Qa5+ 6.Nfd2

6.Bd2 Qxc5 7.Nc3 Nf6 8.Be2 0-0 9.0-0 is also possible and almost transposes to the King's Indian Averbakh variation line 1.d4 Nf6 2.c4 g6 3.Nc3 Bg7 4.e4 d6 5.Be2 0-0 6.Bg5 c5 7.dxc5 Qa5 8.Bd2 Qxc5 9.Nf3 Nc6 10.0-0 except that White has an extra tempo (Bd2 in one move and not Bg5-d2).

6.Nc3 Bxc3+ creates precisely the sort of imbalanced position Fischer was looking for.

6...Qxc5 7.Nb3 Qb6 8.Be2 d6 9.0-0

Again White avoids 9.Nc3 Bxc3+.

9...Nf6

The problem for Black is he can't force White to play Nc3 which would allow him to capture on c3. If he continues to delay developing his king knight, White works around him: 9...Be6 10.Be3 Qc7 11.Qd2 Nf6 12.Nc3 and Black has a bad version of the Maróczy Bind—just as he ends up with in the game continuation.

10.Nc3 0-0 11.Be3

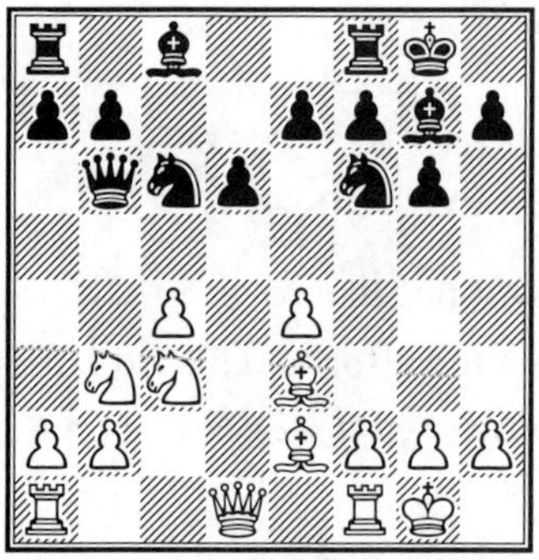

11...Qd8

Fischer's seemingly dynamic opening choice has landed him a lifeless position where he has no counterplay. White is at least one tempo ahead of typical Maróczy Bind positions plus he has his knight on b3 instead of d4, although the latter is a mixed blessing. On the plus side it prevents a trade of knights keeping Black cramped. The other side of the coin is that b3 is not a particularly great square for the piece (c2 would be better where it can go to e3 eyeing d5).

12.Rc1 Be6

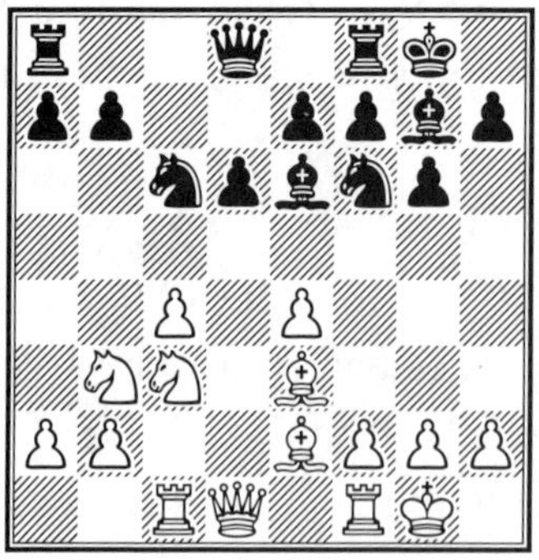

13.Nd4?!

Petrosian was one of the greatest positional players in the history of the game but the text does not look right. Possibly he was influenced in his decision to make this move by his successful usage of Nb3-d4 in a similar position against Ģipslis at Zagreb 1965.

More to the point is 13.f3 followed by Qd2 and Rfd1. White may choose to meet ...Nf6-d7-c5 with Na1!, preparing b4 and planning to bring the knight into the game via c2. This plan was used in a similar position to great effect in Serper–Ruban, Novosibirsk 1993.

Black might meet 13.f3 with 13...a5 intending ...a4 followed by ...Qa5. His position isn't brilliant but it's not easy to crack.

White also has another promising possibility in the ambitious 13.f4.

It's interesting to hear what Garry Kasparov, who gives 13.Nd4 as dubious, has to say about this position in his volume on Bobby in the *My Great Predecessors*[1] series.

[Kasparov]: "What for? After 13.f3! Black has a difficult position: he does not have the usual knight exchange on d4 and his queen cannot move out from d8. For example: 13...Ne5 14.Nd5, or 13...Rc8 14.Nd5 Nd7 15.Qd2 b6 16.Nd4 with persistent pressure. But, apparently, Petrosian was thinking only of a draw."

We can't argue with Kasparov's assessment of the position on the board, but as to Petrosian's ambitions the situation might have been a little more complicated than he hypothesizes.

Looking at the crosstable after the event everything appears quite clear with Fischer first with 13 from 17, Hort, Korchnoi, Smyslov, and Gligorić tying for second with 11 points, Petrosian a half point back and Minić and Ivkov sharing seventh with 9 points. This would suggest that Petrosian had everything to gain by a win and nothing to lose if he lost. This is mostly true, but with Smyslov and Hort drawing in the last round while Korchnoi and Gligorić were winning there were many possible scenarios—it just happened that for Petrosian one of the least favorable transpired.

It's also important to note the previous month Petrosian had lost to Fischer four times, more losses than he suffered in entire years in his heyday. True, two were in the blitz tournament that preceded this event, but the 3–1 defeat in their individual match in the USSR versus the World contest had to hurt.

Finally we would point out that Rovinj/Zagreb was a seventeen round event. This was the final game and Petrosian, fourteen years older than Fischer and on the wrong side of forty, had to be feeling the fatigue more than his younger and more physically fit rival.

---

[1] Garry Kasparov, *Garry Kasparov on Fischer: My Great Predecessors Part IV*. London: Everyman Chess, 2004, (p. 342).j352

All this said, Petrosian's move still retains a slight edge. His choice may not be the most precise, but it does lead to an easy position to handle where he is only playing for two results, albeit a draw is considerably more likely. This fits perfectly into Petrosian's "safety first" motto.

13...Nxd4 14.Bxd4 Qa5

Now we are in a known position—Black's queen moves being canceled out by White's extra usage of his knight.

15.f4

Another way to handle the position is 15.f3 but not 15.Qd2? Nxe4 winning a pawn—this trick often occurs when the bishop is on d4 instead of e3.

Kasparov writes about 15.f4:

"Not a bad move, but one that demands very concrete, energetic play: it nevertheless weakens the pawn structure (one recalls a similar attempt by Larsen in their Candidates match in Denver). 15.Nd5?! Nxe4 16.Bxg7 Kxg7 17.Qd4+ Nf6 did not work, but 15.Qd3!? and then b2-b3 came into consideration."

15...a6

15...Rfc8 16.b3 b5 doesn't quite work: 17.Nxb5 (17.cxb5 Nxe4!) 17...Nxe4 18.Bxg7 Kxg7 19.Bf3 and neither 19...Qb6+ or 19...Nd2 is satisfactory.

16.f5

16.Qd3 b5!? 17.cxb5 axb5 18.Qxb5 Rfb8 19.Qxa5 Rxa5 20.b3 Rb4 gave Black great Benko Gambit like play in Bogner–Chadaev, Neustadt 2008.

[Kasparov]:"Petrosian probably did not even consider the variation 16.b4!? Qxb4 17.Rb1 Qa5 18.Rxb7 as after 18...Rfe8 the weakness of the c4-pawn promises Black sufficient counterplay."

16...Bd7

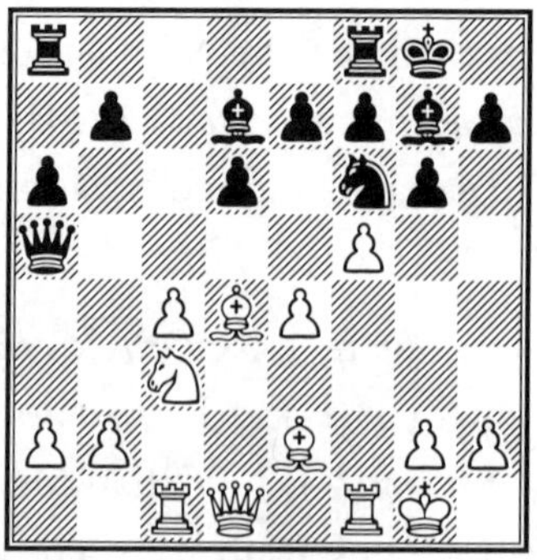

17.c5!

This is the thematic way to handle the position but White's advantage is still small. Kasparov gives 17.c5 an exclamation mark accompanied with the comment: "White has nevertheless pushed forward."

17...Bc6!

Kasparov gives this move an exclamation mark as well.

18.cxd6

18.fxg6 fxg6 19.Nd5 is Houdini's suggestion of how to handle the position, but it still evaluates the position as only slightly better for White.

18...exd6 19.fxg6

This is where White lost his advantage according to Kasparov who writes: "Of course 19.Bc4! was stronger, but for Petrosian, especially against Fischer, it was an excessively complicated, unclear continuation."

Garry Kimovich then gives the following line: 19...Kh8! 20.Rf4!? Rae8 21.Qd3 and White has some advantage.

He dismisses the variation starting with 19...Nxe4 on account of 20.fxg6 hxg6 21.Bxg7 Kxg7 22.Nxe4 Bxe4 23.Qxd6 Bf5 24.Bd5! when White has a dangerous initiative.

However, after 24...Rae8, with ideas like...Be6 and ...Qa5-b5-d7, Black looks fine. One critical line, given by Stockfish, is 25.Bxb7 Re2 26.Qd4+ Kg8 27.Bd5 Qd2 28.Qxd2 Rxd2 and Black recovers his pawn.

19...fxg6 20.Bc4+ Kh8 21.Bd5

21.Qd3 Rae8 22.Rce1 Ng4 23.Nd5 Ne5 is equal according to Kasparov.

21...Rae8 22.h3 Bxd5 23.Nxd5 Nxd5 24.Rxf8+ Rxf8 25.exd5

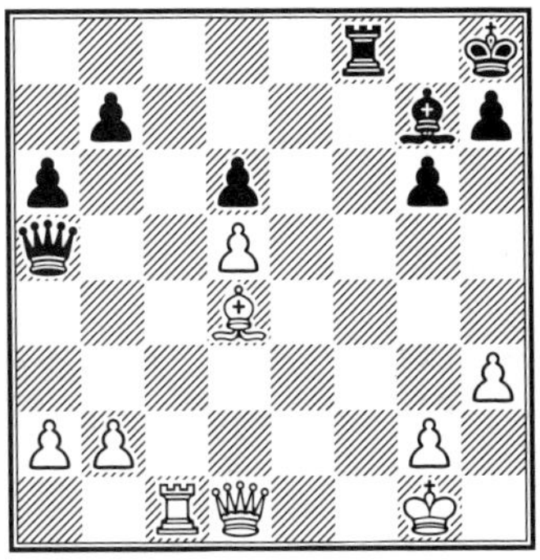

25...Qb4

Whatever advantage Petrosian had is long gone.

26.Bxg7+ Kxg7 27.b3 Qf4 28.Rc3 Qf2+ 29.Kh2 Rf7 30.a4 h5 31.Rc4 Re7 32.Qa1+ Qf6 33.Qc3 Qxc3 34.Rxc3 Kf6 35.Rf3+ Kg5 36.Rf8 Re3 37.g3

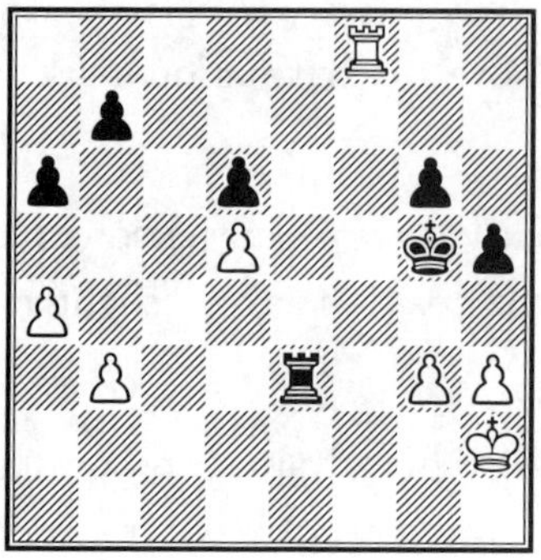

37...Re2+

Petrosian wanted to force Black's king back. Fischer declined to take the pawn as after 37...Rxb3 38.h4+ Kh6 39.Rh8+ Kg7 40. Rd8 Rb6 41.a5 Rb5 42.Rxd6 Rxa5 43.Rd7+ Kh6 44.Rxb7 Rxd5 45.Kg2 Black's extra pawn is meaningless due to his poor king position, White's active rook and the simplified material.

38.Kg1 Rb2 39.h4+ Kg4 40.Rf6 Kxg3 41.Rxg6+ Kxh4 42.Rxd6 Rxb3 43.Rg6 Rb4 44.Rg7, ½–½.

White does not establish the Maróczy Bind until the middlegame in the following battle, but the risks Fischer takes in trying to create winning chances are similar to his game with Damjanović examined earlier.

(65) English
Renato Naranja – Fischer
Palma de Mallorca Interzonal (8) 1970

1.c4 c5 2.Nc3 g6 3.Nf3 Bg7 4.d4

4.g3 Nc6 5.Bg2 e6 was Fischer's anti-English variation, which he used to defeat Petrosian in a famous battle during the 1970 USSR versus the World match. Bobby also won a nice game with it against Smyslov six rounds before this game.

4...cxd4 5.Nxd4 Nc6

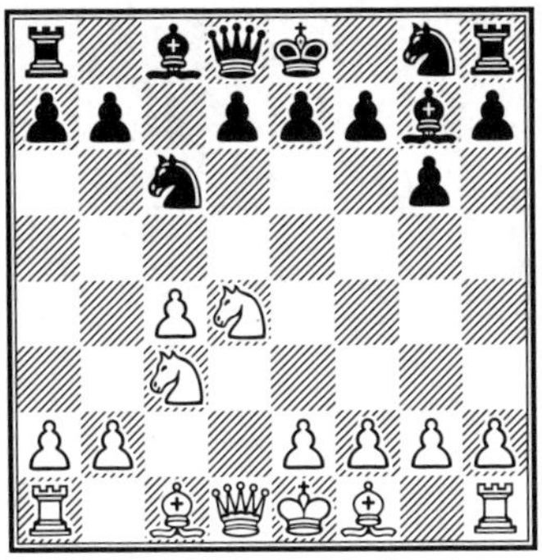

6.e3

6.Nc2 is not as attractive as Black has yet to play ...Nf6. This gives him the opportunity to play the unbalancing 6...Bxc3+ creating an interesting position in which play against the doubled pawns compensates for White's two bishops. Such situations were Fischer's cup of tea with his game against Quinteros (Buenos Aires 1970) a perfect example of his skill: 7.bxc3 Nf6 8.f3 d6 9.e4 Be6 10.Be2 Rc8 11.Ne3 Qa5 12.Bd2 Ne5 13.Qb3 Nfd7 14.f4 Nc5 15.Qc2 Nc6 16.0-0 Qa4 and Black was already doing well and went on to win.

6...Nf6 7.Be2 0-0 8.0-0 Nxd4

Black has many good choices against White's passive setup—8...b6, 8...d5 and 8...d6 are all playable alternatives.

9.Qxd4 d6 10.Qh4

This is more natural than the awkward looking 10.Qd2?! which quickly landed White in trouble in Danov–Fischer, Skopje 1967, after 10...Be6 11.Qc2 a6 12.Bd2 Rc8 13.Qa4 (13.b3 d5!) 13...Nd7 14.Qb4 a5 15.Qb3 Ne5 16.Nd5 b5!.

10...Be6 11.Rd1 Qb6

Fischer wants to interrupt White's ultra-solid development scheme of Bd2, Rac1 and b3. The more natural 11...Rc8 would have been met by 12.Bd2 when 12...d5 13.Be1 Qb6 would likely lead to a draw before move thirty after 14.cxd5 Nxd5 15.Nxd5 Bxd5 16.Rxd5 Qxb2 17.Rad1 Qxe2 18.Qxe7.

12.Rb1

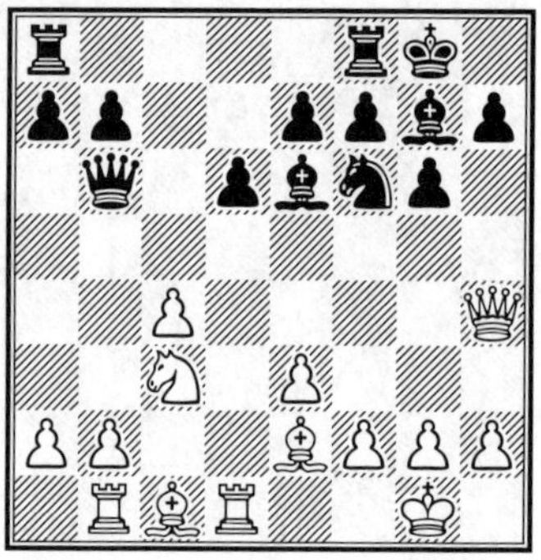

12...Qc5

Botvinnik, in the report he wrote to help Taimanov prepare for his match with Fischer, noted that the Fischer was fond of long queen moves. One might go further and state that if Steinitz is remembered for a fondness for moving his king in the opening and early middlegame then Fischer should be partly remembered for his willingness to move his queen into the enemy camp early in the game.

Sometimes, like game 2 of his match with Larsen (17...Qe5), placing the queen in close proximity to the enemy forces was definitely the right idea. Here the situation is more complicated. The next few queen moves are fine but then Bobby misses his way and soon lands in big trouble. 12...Rac8 and 12...Nd7 are both reasonable moves, but do nothing to stop White from completing his development.

13.b4 Qf5 14.e4

White sets up the "Bind" with this move.

14...Qe5! 15.Rb3

15.Bb2 g5 16.Qg3 Qxg3 17.hxg3 Rfc8 18.Nd5 Nxd5 19.cxd5 Bd7 20.Bxg7 Kxg7 21.Rdc1 looks very drawish but the Filipino International Master Naranja is more ambitious.

15...Bd7?!

Here Bobby had to bail out with 15...Bxc4! and after the forcing sequence 16.Bxc4 Rac8 17.Bd3 Rxc3 18.Bb2 Rxd3 19.Rdxd3 Qxe4 20.Qxe4 Nxe4 21.Bxg7 Kxg7 an interesting ending is reached in which Black has a knight and two pawns for the exchange. Tactics hold his position together—for example, 22.f3 Ng5 23.b5 Ne6 24.Ra3 a6 and Black avoids dropping a pawn, while his knight will soon be anchored on c5.

16.f4 Qe6 17.f5! gxf5 18.exf5 Qxf5

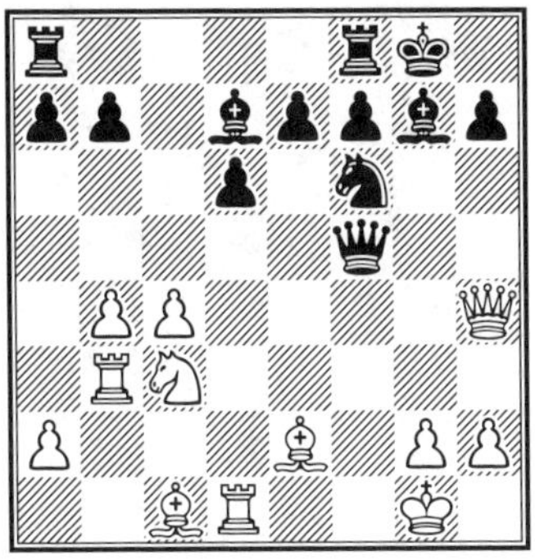

19.Bg5?

19.Nd5! bring the rook on b3 into the attack, or19.Bb2 each would have given White a significant advantage.

19...h6!

Fischer was always one for active defense. Here he uses simplification to save the day.

20.Bxh6 Qh7 21.Bg5 Qxh4 22.Bxh4 Be6 23.Bxf6

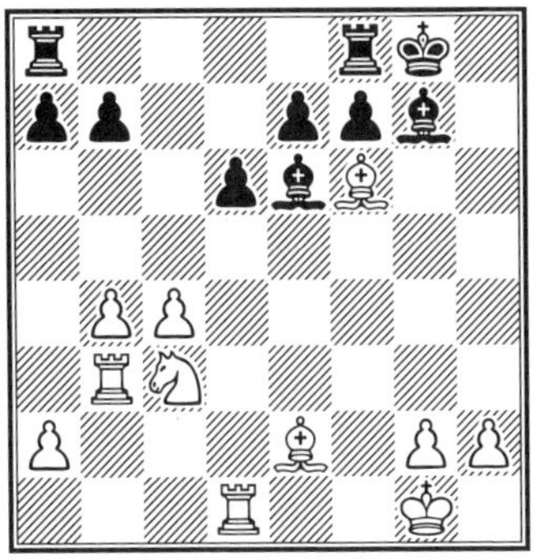

23...exf6?!

This might not be needed as 23...Bxf6 24.Nd5 Bxd5 25.Rg3+ Kh7 26.Rxd5 (26.Rh3+ draws.) 26...Be5 looks fine for Black.

24.Nd5 Rfd8 25.Rf3 Kf8 26.Nxf6

There was no hurry to recover the pawn. White could have tried to keep up the pressure with 26.Ra3, but it's hard to imagine Bobby not being able to defend this position.

26...Rac8 27.Nh7+ Kg8 28.Nf6+

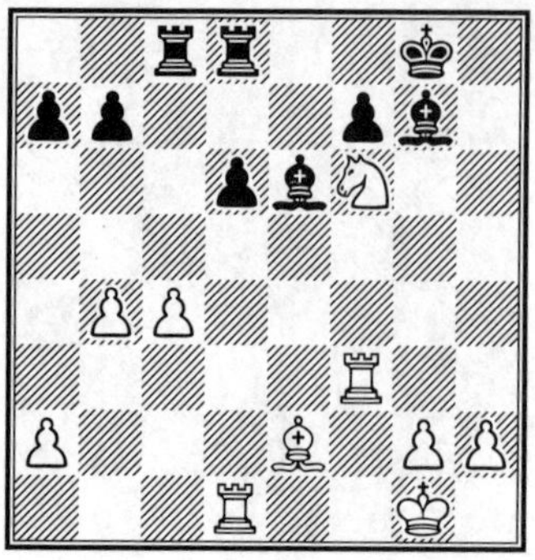

28...Bxf6

Now all the pieces come off the board and a draw is no longer in doubt.

29.Rxf6 Bxc4 30.Bxc4 Rxc4 31.Rfxd6 Rxd6 32.Rxd6 Rxb4 33.Rd2 b5 34.Kf2 Ra4 35.Ke3 Kg7 36.Kd3 Ra3+ 37.Kd4 a5 38.Kc5 b4 39.Kb5 f5 40.g3 Kf6 41.Re2 Kg5 42.Rf2 Kg6 43.Rd2 Kf7 44.Re2 Kf6 45.Kc4 Kg5 46.Kb5 Kg4 47.Rf2 Kh3 48.Rd2, ½–½.

FISCHER AS BLACK VERSUS THE ENGLISH / KING'S INDIAN

Games (66) and (67) don't feature the Maróczy Bind, but are relevant to the repertoire (...c5 with ...g6 versus 1.Nf3/1.c4) that Bobby used in his World Championship run-up in 1970–71.

(66) English
Julio Saadi – Fischer
Mar del Plata (4) 1960

1.c4 Nf6 2.Nc3 g6 3.d4 Bg7 4.g3 0-0 5.Bg2 c5 6.Nf3 cxd4 7.Nxd4 Nc6 8.0-0

White can also try to avoid the trade of knights with 8.Nc2, a line that more commonly arises after 8.0-0 d6 when White wants to avoid the complications of capturing on c6.

While 8.Nc2 isn't played nearly as often as 8.0-0, it merits special attention as it was Garry Kasparov's choice when he faced Péter Lékó at Horgen in 1994. The former World Champion handled the early middlegame in instructive fashion.

After 8...d6 9.0-0 Be6 10.b3 Qd7 11.Bb2 Bh3 12.Ne3 Bxg2 13.Kxg2 Ne4 14.Qc2 Nxc3 15.Bxc3 Bxc3 16.Qxc3 White had achieved just the sort of position he was aiming for—a small but stable advantage with Black having only limited counterplay.

Noteworthy was Kasparov's decision on whether to preserve his king bishop. He could have saved it with 11. Re1 Bh3 12.Bh1, but after 12...Ng4 13.Bd2 Qf5! Fominyh–Ovseevich, Alushta 1994) Black is doing well as White has no convenient way to guard the f2 square.

The young Fischer went out of his way to avoid the sort of position Lékó reached against Kasparov—one in which Black is playing for only two results (draw or loss)—when he faced Donner at Bled 1961. That game continued 8...Ng4 9.Bd2 a6 10.0-0 b5 11.h3 Nge5 12.cxb5 axb5 13.b3 (13.Nxb5 Nc4 14.Bc3 Nxb2 15.Qc1 Bxc3 16.Nxc3 Na4 would have offered both sides equal chances) 13...d5 14.Nxb5 (as 14.Nxd5 is met by 14...Bxh3) 14...Ba6 15.a4 Bxb5 16.axb5 Rxa1 17.Nxa1 Na7 18.Bb4 d4 19.f4 Nd7 20.Qd3 Qb6 21.Rc1 Nxb5 22.Rc6 with a small edge for White and his two bishops.

8...Ng4

This unbalancing move experienced a burst of popularity in the late 1980s as an attempt to generate more fighting possibilities for Black.

Bobby had a famous game on the White side of this position after the more routine 8...Nxd4.

8...Nxd4 9.Qxd4 d6 10.Bg5 (10.Qd3) 10...Be6 11.Qf4 (This was Fischer's novelty. Normally the queen would go to h4 in such positions but Bobby preserves the option of retreating to d2.) 11...Qa5 12.Rac1 Rab8 13.b3 Rfc8 14.Qd2 a6 15.Be3 b5 (This is the natural follow-up to all of Black's previous moves, but playing this thematic advance costs Black material. More prudent was something like 15...Rd8 16.Rfd1 b5 17.Nd5 Qxd2 18.Bxd2 Nxd5 19.cxd5 Bd7 20.Rc7 Rbc8 21.Rdc1 Kf8 when only White can be better, but how to make progress is not clear.) 16.Ba7 bxc4 (Black would like to have the other bishop, but unfortunately after 16...Ra8 17.Bxa8 Rxa8 18.Bd4 bxc4 19.bxc4 the capture of the critical c-pawn by 19...Bxc4 is met with 20.Rfd1 with the very strong threat of capturing on f6 followed by Ne4. Black has no good answer to this.) 17.Bxb8 Rxb8 18.bxc4 Bxc4 19.Rfd1 Nd7? (19...Qh5) 20.Nd5 and White went on to win in Fischer–Spassky, Reykjavík (8) 1972.

8...d6 is a similar gambit to the game continuation, but as we will see Fischer's version works better for Black as White is committed to e3 which creates weaknesses on the light squares.

9.e3 d6 10.Nxc6?

10.b3 is the main line, with 10.h3 and 10.Nde2 worthy alternatives. If 10.Bxc6 bxc6 11.Nxc6 Black has 11...Qd7 followed by ...Bb7 with good play for the pawn.

10...bxc6 11.Bxc6 Rb8 12.Bf3

12.Bg2 Ne5 13.Nb5 Ba6 14.Nd4 Bxc4 and Black was already better in Taimanov–Solozhenkin, St. Petersburg 1998.

12...Ne5 13.Be2 Ba6

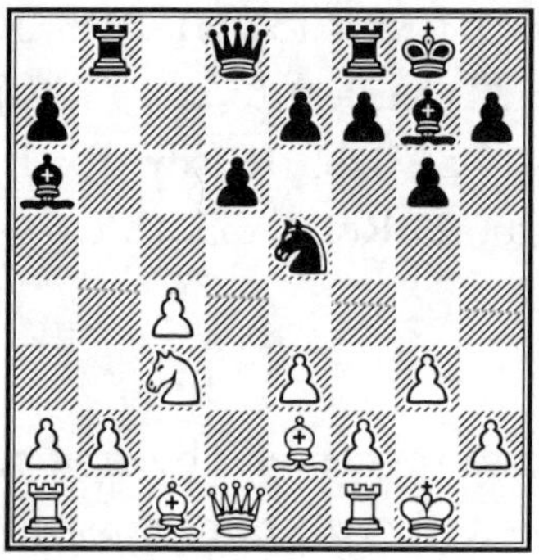

14.b3?

Either 14.Qa4 or 14.Qc2 were obligatory.

14...Nxc4 15.Qc2 Qa5

Black is already winning.

16.Nd5 Qxd5 17.bxc4 Qb7 18.Ba3 Bxa1 19.Rxa1 Rfc8 20.e4 Rc7 21.Bd3 Qc6 22.Rc1 Rbc8 23.Qb3 Qd7 24.Bb2 Qe6 25.Qc3 f6 26.Qa5 Bxc4 27.Bd4 Rc6 28.Qa4 Bb5 29.Qxb5 Rxc1+ 30.Kg2 Rd1 31.Be3 Rxd3 32.Qxd3 Qxa2 33.Qb5 Qe6 34.Qb7 a5, 0–1.

---

(67) English
Zbigniew Doda – Fischer
Havana (19) 1965

1.Nf3 c5 2.g3 g6 3.Bg2 Bg7 4.0-0 Nc6 5.c4 e6 6.Nc3 Nge7 7.e3 0-0 8.d4

This line has a well-known reputation for producing quick draws and was clearly what the Polish International Master was hoping for.

8...cxd4 9.Nxd4

9.exd4 d5 also leads to drawish positions but Black can try to muddy the waters ala Fischer with 9...d6.

9...Nxd4

Playing 9...d5 is tantamount to offering a draw. If Black wants to make a game of it 9...a6 and 9...Qb6 are also playable.

10.exd4

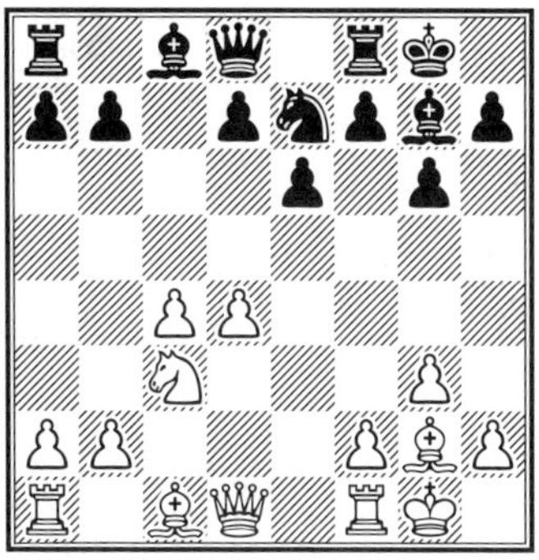

10...d6

Doda could not have expected Bobby to play 10...d5 11.cxd5 Nxd5 with a quick handshake to follow for two reasons. First, making quick draws was not Bobby's normal practice. Second, he had just lost back to back games in rounds seventeen and eighteen to Geller and Kholmov and desperately needed to win his three remaining games against outsiders to have a chance to finish at the top (which in fact he did to share second with Geller and Ivkov, half a point behind Smyslov).

11.d5

Fischer hopes to gradually outplay his opponent, but after the text move there can be no doubt that White, with more space, is already slightly better.

11...e5 12.b3 e4

An alternative was 12...f5 but sooner or later Black will be forced to play ...e4, as ...f4 is not playable as White would be handed over the e4 square on a silver platter.

13.Bb2 f5 14.Qd2 h6

Bobby could have stopped Nb5 with 14...a6 but after 15.a4 followed by Ne2 and Nd4 (or Nf4) the knight will reach e6 nonetheless. 15.Ne2 allows Black counterplay by 15...Bxb2 16.Qxb2 b5.

15.Nb5! Bxb2 16.Qxb2 a6 17.Nd4 g5 18.f3!

Doda increases his advantage with simple but effective moves

18...exf3

18...Ng6 19.fxe4 f4 to secure the e5 square for the knight is a typical plan in similar positions, but the pawn sacrifice is not sufficient here as White is well positioned to play b4 and c5 undermining the knight.

19.Bxf3 Ng6

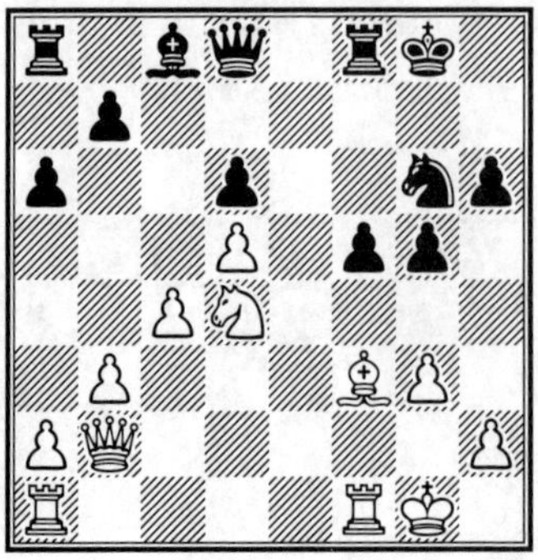

20.Ne6!

Doda, an experienced competitor who played seven times for the Polish Olympiad team, does not fall into the trap of playing safely. Once Fischer declined the unspoken offer of a draw in the opening he has played aggressively, taking advantage of the opportunities Bobby has given him (chiefly not contesting the center with ...d5). Being able to play Ne6 in a King's Indian structures is often a very good sign for White, particularly here as it is not played as a pawn sacrifice as is so often the case.

20...Bxe6 21.dxe6 Qe7 22.Bd5 f4 23.Qg2

23.Qd4! centralizing the queen looks even stronger.

23...Rf6?!

This is a critical moment. Black should have guarded b7 with 23...Rab8, but doesn't want to play passively and instead sacrifices the pawn.

24.Bxb7 Raf8 25.Bd5 Kh8?!

A better idea was 25...h5 26.Kh1 g4 but even after ...f3 Black will be far from equality as White can always open the queenside.

26.Kh1 Ne5 27.gxf4 gxf4

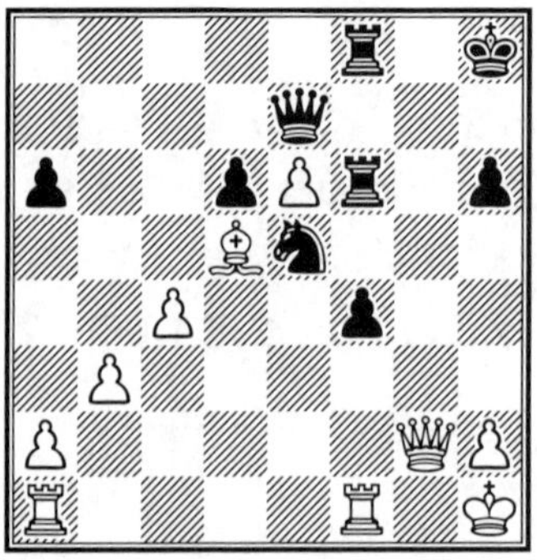

28.Qh3

The text is not bad, but 28.Rg1 was more direct. Black can continue 28...f3 (28...Rg6 29.Qb2 Rgf6 30.Raf1 with c4-c5 in the air.) 29.Qf2 Nd3

(29...Rf4 30.Rg3 Nd3 31.Qe3 f2 32.Rf1) 30.Qd4 f2 31.Rg2 Ne5 32.Rf1 Rf4 33.Qb2. These variations show that White's pieces are well-placed to cope with the advance of Black's f-pawn. This is not surprising as Doda effectively has an extra piece (Black's queen is tied down to watching the e-pawn).

28...f3 29.Rad1 Qh7 30.Rd4 f2 31.Rh4

White was winning after 31.Rd2! Qg7 32.Qc3 Rg6 33.Qa1 Rgf6 34.c5!

31...Rg8

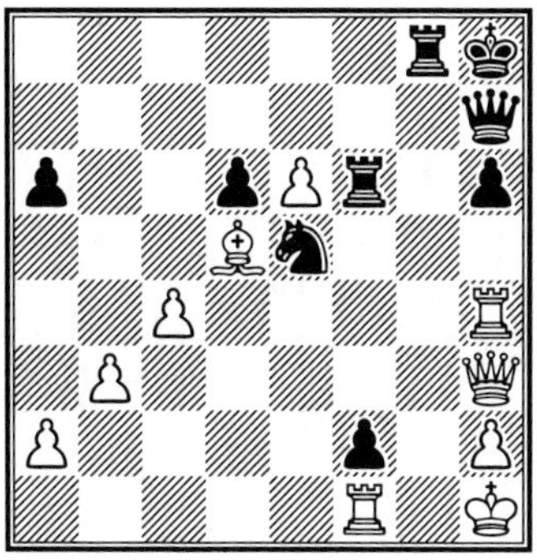

32.Be4⁇

32.Qe3 Qg6 33.h3 (Not 33.e7?! Qg1+ 34.Rxg1 Rxg1 mate) preserves White's advantage as 33...Qg1+⁇ would now be met by 34.Rxg1 Rxg1+ 35.Kh2 f1Q 36.Rxh6+ Kg7 37.Rxf6.

32...Qg7 33.Bg2 Nf3! 34.Rh5 Nd2 35.Rxf2 Rg6 36.Rhf5 Qa1+, 0–1.

How would Fischer have reacted if he had lost this game and suffered three consecutive defeats? This is a situation he had little experience with. During Bobby's entire career it appears he only twice "castled queenside"[1]—rounds twenty to twenty-two of the 1959 Candidates and rounds six through eight of the Second Piatigorsky Cup.

[1] To "castle queenside" is an expression in chess meaning three consecutive losses. It comes from the written notation for queenside castling of 0-0-0, read as zero-zero-zero.

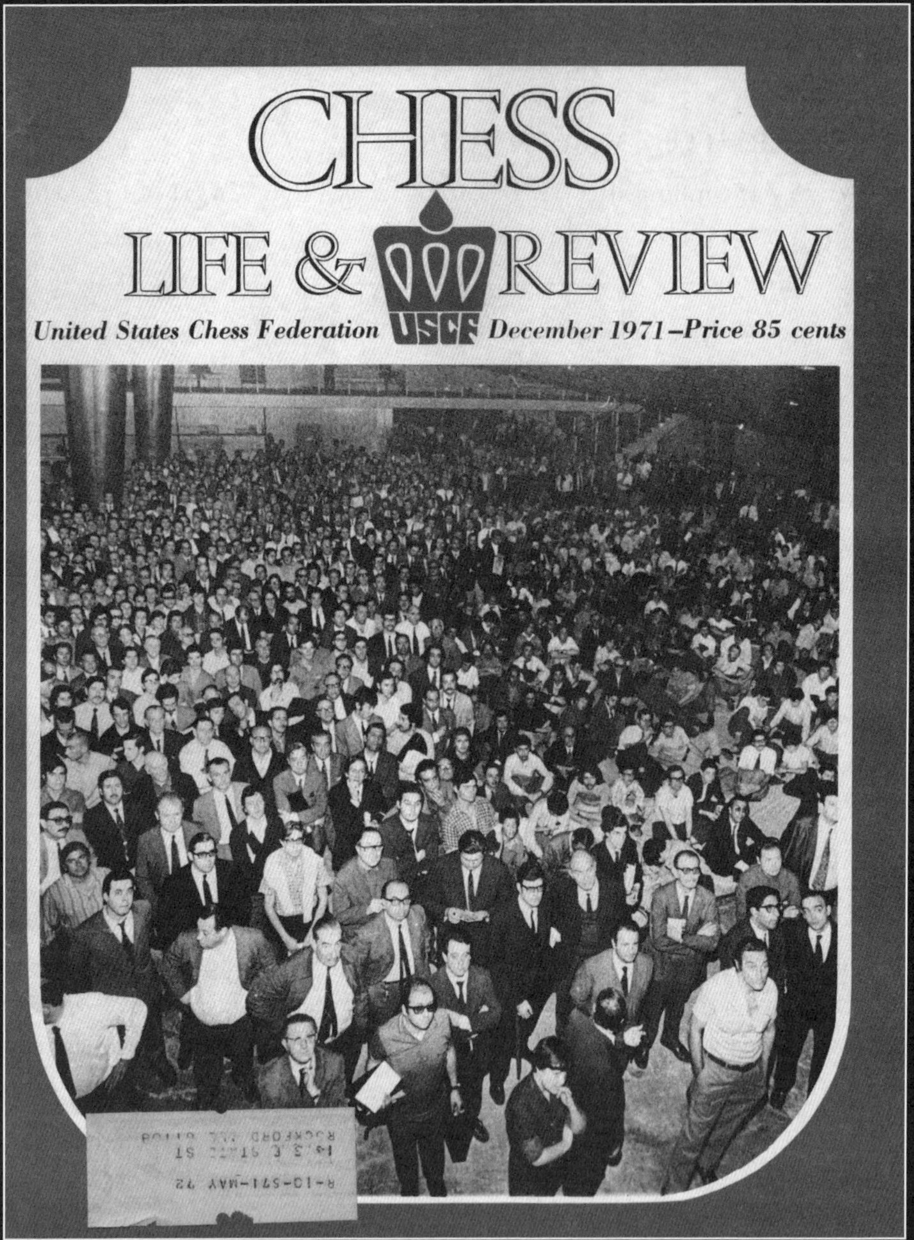

The lobby of the Teatro General San Martin in Buenos Aires. Crowds of enthusiasts who could not get in to see Fischer and Petrosian watch the game on giant demonstration boards (Photo: La Prensa).

PART SIX

the World Championship Cycle

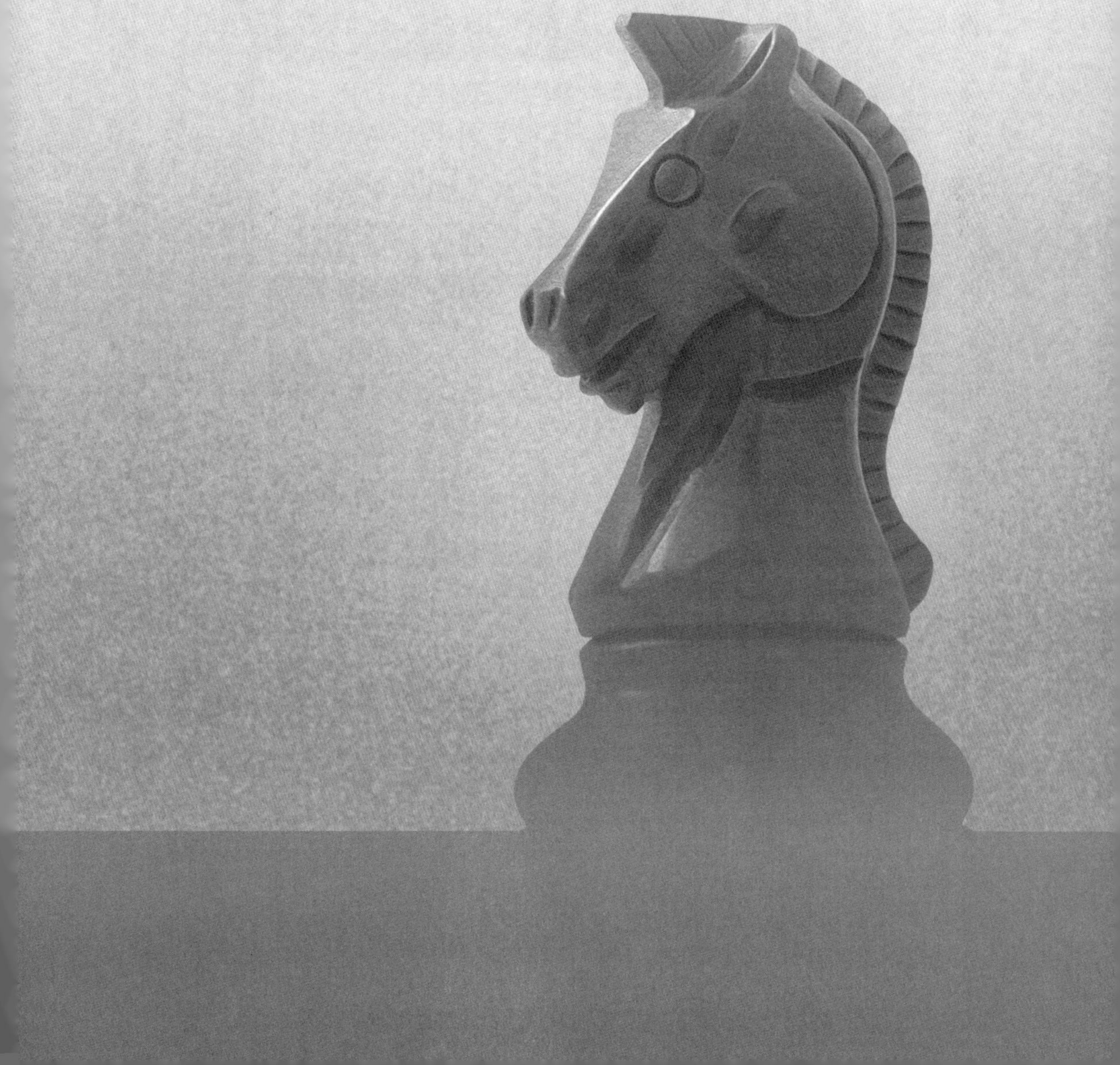

USCF

CHESS LIFE

UNITED STATES CHESS FEDERATION

EXTRA

SPECIAL ISSUE for You!

Announcing the

40th FIDE WORLD CHESS CONGRESS

SAN JUAN, PUERTO RICO

OCTOBER 9-24, 1969

BROUGHT TO YOU BY THE FEDERACION DE AJEDREZ DE PUERTO RICO (PUERTO RICO CHESS FEDERATION)

FOR THE FIRST TIME IN AMERICA

YOU

CAN PARTICIPATE IN A WORLDWIDE CHESS EVENT SPONSORED BY FIDE

Join the Masters at San Juan

SPASSKY • FISCHER • LARSEN • NAJDORF • GLIGORICH
SUETIN • PANNO • R. BYRNE • DONNER
YANOFSKY • POMAR • O'KELLY • KAPLAN

AND OTHER CHESS LUMINARIES ARE INVITED TO THE GRANDMASTER TOURNAMENT (FIDE Category 1A)

Be a spectator at this great International Chess Event

Play in the World Open

REGISTER NOW

AMONG THE STARS INVITED TO THE SAN JUAN GRANDMASTER TOURNAMENT

World Champion BORIS SPASSKY

U.S. Challenger BOBBY FISCHER

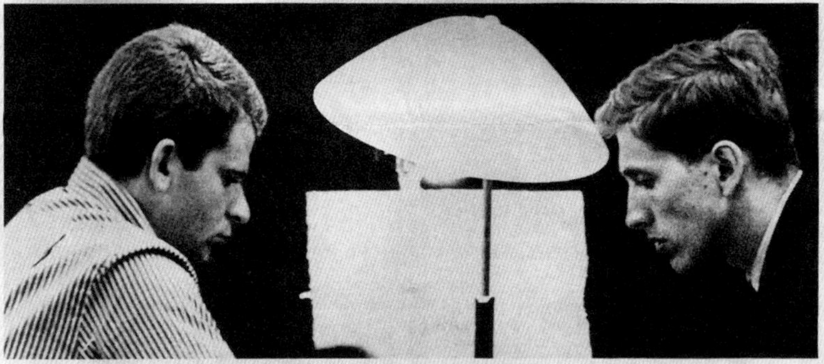

BORIS V. SPASSKY was born in Leningrad on January 30, 1937. In 1946, he joined a chess section of the Young Pioneers. His second place in the 1951 Russian Federal Republic Junior Championship earned him the title of Candidate Master. In 1953—just turned sixteen—he played in a strong international tournament in Bucharest. In the first round, he beat Smyslov and his overall score resulted in a FIDE title of International Master.

Spassky had a big year in 1955. In Moscow, he captured his first USSR Championship; he went on to win the World Junior Championship; and he became an International Grandmaster as a result of his score in the Interzonal Tournament (in which he tied for seventh). He again won the USSR Championship at Baku in 1961 and by 1964 he emerged as an outstanding possibility to succeed Petrosian as World Champion.

In 1964, Spassky scored 17-6 to tie for first with Larsen in the Interzonal Tournament. In the 1965 Candidates Matches, he beat Keres 6-4, Geller 5½-2½, and Tal 7-4. In 1966, he challenged Petrosian for the world title but was defeated 12½-11½.

Spassky's strength continued to grow during the next three years, and one of his most notable tournament victories was the Second Piatigorsky Cup at Santa Monica, 1966. He didn't lose a game and scored a clear first over Fischer, Larsen, Petrosian, and six more top Grandmasters.

In the 1968 Candidates Matches, he downed Geller 5½-2½, Larsen 5½-2½, and Korchnoi 6½-3½. Now at his peak, he defeated Tigran Petrosian by 12½-11½ in June of this year to become World Champion.

ROBERT J. FISCHER was born in Chicago on March 9, 1943. His sister Joan taught him to play chess in 1949 and his first contact with strong players was at an exhibition given by International Master Max Pavey in January 1951. Thereafter, he attended the Brooklyn Chess Club regularly and was taught much about the game by Carmine Nigro, President of that Club.

Bobby joined the Manhattan Chess Club in 1955 and, in the same year, played in his first national tournaments, the U.S. Amateur and the U.S. Junior Championships. In 1956, he began visiting the home of John W. Collins and in July of that year won his first national title; he became U.S. Junior Champion with an 8½-1½ score. In the same year, he tied for fourth place in his first U.S. Open and finished eighth in his first United States Championship.

In 1957, at the age of fourteen, Fischer came of age chesswise. He repeated as U.S. Junior Champion, this time with a score of 8½-½. He went on to win the U.S. Open Championship on tie-break after he and Bisguier finished with identical 10-2 scores. And he climaxed a great year by winning the United States Championship for the first time, finishing a point ahead of the veteran Reshevsky.

Fischer has now won the U.S. Championship an unprecedented eight times. He made chess history in the 1963-64 tournament by taking it with a perfect 11-0 score. But the nagging question still remains—how good is he? Only by proving himself internationally against the likes of Spassky can Bobby join the ranks of the few really great players, and we hope that he will seize this opportunity to do so.

Photo by Art Zeller

1
NEGOTIATIONS

Bobby Fischer won a fourteen-player round robin in Vinkovci, Yugoslavia, with a score of 11–2, two points ahead of Vlastimil Hort and Milan Matulović. The event, held in September 1968, was the only action Bobby would see the rest of the year except for a famous game against Anthony Saidy in the annual Manhattan versus Marshall match. Fischer didn't play again until the USSR vs. Rest of the World matches at the end of March 1970.

Now long-forgotten, an eight-page promotional insert received by *Chess Life* subscribers suggests Bobby was going to play in the 1969 San Juan Tournament. Arthur Bisguier wrote:[1]

> Before the tournament began there was considerable apprehension that some of the invited players would not show up. Actually, it was originally hoped that Bobby Fischer, Viktor Korchnoi, and Alexey Suetin might appear and that the tournament might actually consist of eighteen players rather than sixteen.

But in the end he was missing, as were Korchnoi and Suetin, Najdorf, Gligorić, Suetin, Panno, Yanofsky, and Pomar. Able replacements were found in Parma, Kavalek, Damjanović, and twenty-year-old Walter Browne, who as a last-minute addition to the sixteen-player event made his final grandmaster norm.

Fischer didn't play in the 1968/69 or 1969/70 U.S. Championships. His absence is explained in a letter to USCF Executive Director Ed Edmondson.

> October 29, 1969
>
> Dear Ed,
>
> Thank you for your inquiry as to my availability to participate in the 1969 USA Chess Championship. I am not available. Also, I would like to take this opportunity to make a correction of fact. It was stated in last year's *Chess Life* magazine that I never answered my 1968 invitation to the 1968 USA Chess Championship. This, as you know Ed, is a lie. I answered and declined in writing to you well over a month before the championship began. The reason I did not play last year and will not play again this year is the same—the

[1] *Chess Life*, December 1969, (p. 482).

tournament is too short. I feel the tournament should be twenty-two rounds as it is in the Soviet Union, Hungary, Romania, and other East European countries where chess is taken seriously, rather than eleven rounds that the present U.S. Championship is. As you know, Ed, this year's Championship is also the Zonal tournament for the U.S., which is the first step leading to the coveted World Championship. By my not participating in this U.S. Championship, I am not only giving up my chance to regain the U.S. Chess Championship which I have won eight times (every year I participated) but far more importantly I will lose my possibility of becoming official World Chess Champion in 1972, the next time a World Championship match will be held. So, the next opportunity for me to become World Chess Champion won't be until 1975. I want very much to play in the U.S. Championship this year—but not in a tournament where if a player has a bad start and loses a game or two at the beginning, he is practically eliminated from first place. I consider this to be too chancy an affair and it puts an undue burden on the favorite, who does not have enough time to make up for a bad start because the tournament is so short. Our U.S. Championship is the shortest of any major chess country. It is an affront to any professional chess player—such as I am.

In all probability the U.S. will lose its chance to have an American World Chess Champion for many years as a result of my not playing. You at the Chess Federation have an opportunity to see that this does not happen. You are supposedly dedicated to developing American chess—here is your chance to prove it, by lengthening the 1969 U.S. Championship scheduled to begin November 30 from eleven to twenty-two rounds.

Sincerely,

Bobby Fischer

Fischer engaged in an on going feud with the U.S. Chess Federation over the issue of expanding the national championship. It's true that the shorter the event the greater the potential for random results. However, there were other factors to take into consideration: Most of the players in the U.S. Championship were not chess professionals (in the financial sense) and would have been hard-pressed to take a month off. Expanding the event and adding eleven more players would have diluted the field at a time when the U.S. had six to eight high-level grandmasters but not much depth.

It's doubtful a bigger tournament would have changed anything beyond making the event last longer. The only close calls Bobby had in the eight U.S. Championships he played in were the first, 1962 and 1965/66. He lost consecutive games to Reshevsky and Robert Byrne in 1965/66, but even then finished a point ahead. If the field were expanded there is no reason to think other American grandmasters wouldn't have been just as efficient at beating the cellar dwellers as Fischer.

Tony Saidy commented:

> Fischer had a habit of making demands on the USCF that he knew would be impossible for them to agree to. He was an absolutist and had a powerful will, tempered by his desire to dominate, "...either you give me what I want, or I won't play."

Fischer's decision not to compete in the 1969/70 U.S. Championship had significant consequences. Because the U.S. Championship doubled as a Zonal, by not competing Fischer removed himself from the World Championship cycle and a chance to dethrone Boris Spassky. Tragedy was averted when two-time Candidate Pal Benko stepped aside. Reports he was paid by the U.S. Chess Federation to give his spot to Fischer were false.

Benko explained:[1]

> Incidentally, I must point out here that a misconception exists as to how Fischer came to play in the Palma Interzonal in 1970 even though he had not qualified in the previous Zonal. It has been widely and erroneously reported in the foreign press that I was paid a certain sum to give up my place in his favor (I had qualified in the 1969 U.S. Championship, which was the Zonal and in which Fischer did not play). The idea for me to step down and give Fischer my place was my own; it was made voluntarily and without pressure from anyone. I felt that as one of the world's strongest players he should have the right to participate in that critical Interzonal. The U.S. Chess Federation had always treated me well; by my action I hoped to show my gratitude. (The USCF had given me the opportunity to qualify for the Interzonal in Amsterdam in 1964 by arranging a match between Bisguier, who had qualified, and me, who had not. And there have been many other things for which I am grateful to the USCF.)
>
> The figure $2,000 is sometimes mentioned as the price I was paid for stepping down. Actually, that fee was paid, but it was for my services as second to Reshevsky and Addison at that tournament—and it is the same amount I would have received as an appearance fee had I actually played. The only condition I asked for stepping down was for Fischer to agree not to withdraw from the Interzonal or the ensuing matches should he qualify for them—and he fulfilled this.

Most of his career Fischer was disappointed by the lack of financial backing he received from the U.S. Chess Federation and the American Chess Foundation. Prior to his World Championship run the only monies Bobby received from these organizations, outside of prizes won in U.S. Championships, consisted of honorariums received for participating in Olympiads and travel reimbursements for playing in Interzonals and Candidates tournaments. This situation changed dramatically with his participation in the 1970–72 World Championship cycle.

---

[1] *Chess Life & Review*, July 1975, (p. 439).

This new support is spelled out in a letter from USCF Executive Director Ed Edmondson sent to Fischer shortly before the Palma de Mallorca Interzonal. A copy of this letter was also sent to key members of the three groups that were equal partners in funding Bobby's run—the U.S. Chess Federation, the American Chess Foundation and the Piatigorsky Foundation (Jacqueline Piatigorsky). Fischer, who was still negotiating for conditions at the very last minute (ten days before the start of the Interzonal), easily could have missed out completely on playing in the cycle.[1]

October 29,1970

Mr. Robert Fischer
Room 1525
HOTEL McALPIN
Broadway at 34th Street
New York, New York 10001

Dear Bobby,

As I told you on the phone last night, your letter which arrived October 27 can only be described as heartbreaking.

When you were here last week, we discussed how truly important your participation in the World Championship cycle is to you, to USCF and to chess in the United States. We discussed all conditions relating to the entire Cycle, including realistic honorariums—not only for the Interzonal but also for the Candidates and World Championship matches. I gave you a straightforward appraisal of the situation and promised to do everything that I possibly could on your behalf throughout the entire cycle.

After two days of what must have been careful consideration, apparently climaxing weeks of formative thought on your part, you told me on Thursday night that you had decided to play. We shook hands on it, all that is really necessary for a valid agreement between two sincere and honorable men—a category in which I place both of us.

I emphasized during our discussions last week that FIDE regulations require all contestants in the Interzonal be named to the host federation and to FIDE a minimum of fourteen days before the tournament commences. This includes any substitutions, such as Fischer for Benko and the requirement was particularly noted by the General Assembly last month when they voted to permit your entry. On the basis of our mutual agreement, and having heard nothing to the contrary by Saturday night, October 24, I wired both Spain and Dr. Euwe that you would be replacing Benko. They undoubtedly received these wires on Sunday, the deadline for naming Interzonal entrants.

Despite my dismay—almost disbelief—upon receiving your letter with its conditions quite beyond what we had agreed upon, I immediately contacted

[1] Edmondson letter in the DeLucia Collection.

USCF President Dubeck and Messrs. Kasper, Fried, and Reeves of the American Chess Foundation. I explained your letter to them and attempted to obtain financial support beyond that which I had promised last week. Each of these people—and several others contacted—feels very strongly that additional financial support will be forthcoming as you progress up the five steps leading to the World Championship. Certainly, by the time of the final Candidates match and the World Championship match there will be great excitement and enthusiasm over the prospect of your bringing the title to the USA. As this excitement mounts, we can no doubt gain financial backing (probably even from non-chess sources) to host at least two of the matches and to insure unprecedented prize funds for them. In my opinion, the honorariums and the prize money would amount to well over $30,000.

These are my honest expectations, concurred in by other reliable chess organizers and patrons. However, it is not easy to raise or guarantee tens of thousands of dollars when even the first step has not been taken. More than anything else, I want to help you to become World Champion—I can only do so if there is a high degree of cooperation and faith between us. I strongly urge you to play in the Interzonal and in the Candidates matches, trusting me as you progress to fight every step of the way for the best possible playing and financial conditions on your behalf. I ask this of you with the understanding that, if conditions for the final Candidates match and World Championship match are not satisfactory, then of course you need not play. But I think this is an extremely unlikely possibility; we will be able to secure exceedingly favorable conditions once you are that close to our mutual goal.

With the foregoing in mind, here are the conditions which we can guarantee at this time. I repeat that improvements will more than likely be possible and that the prize fund which come on top of these honorariums will be unprecedented. These, as I told you before we shook hands in agreement last week, are realistic conditions. I could say yes to anything you ask, knowing that my acquiescence was based upon a hope or even an outright lie. But I have never worked that way and don't intend to start now. I will only promise that which I am certain can be attained. I believe you appreciate this fact and ask that we again confirm agreement on the following:

1. Honorariums

Interzonal	$4,000
Candidates march, quarter-final	3,000
Candidates match, semi-final	3,000
Final Candidates match	4,000
World Championship match	5,000
Total guaranteed honorariums	$19,000

2. The honorariums are separate from prize money, which will be provided by the organizers and augmented to the maximum extent obtainable through the efforts of myself and your friends in American chess.

3. Reimbursement at first-class rates for all travel actually performed in connection with the Interzonal and the matches. For example, round-trip from New York to Palma de Mallorca for the Interzonal. (USCF already reimbursed you in Germany for a return to Los Angeles. I cannot justify paying you twice for the Los Angeles portion of a journey which will be performed only once.)

4. Incidental expenses (excess baggage, taxis, hotels en route,etc.) as you request, to a maximum of $300 for each event.

5.. Acting in your behalf, I will explain to the organizers of the various events in the Cycle that you must stay at the best hotels and eat at the best restaurants; depending upon the site of each event, we can agree in advance what the food expenses should amount to. If the organizer's reimbursement to you falls short of that figure, USCF will make up the difference. I will also guarantee that your "pocket money" will be twice that given to the other contestants in each event.

6. As I have already told you, your standards of lighting, spectator control, and control of photography and television will be met in every match. Mr. Puig has already assured us that absolutely no cameras or TV will be allowed at Palma once the games have begun and that spectators will be kept at a respectable distance and under control. The eagerness of the Spanish Chess Federation to have you play and to meet your requirements is shown by a cable just received. It reads "We guarantee installation for required lighting."

7. As I told you last night, there is a limit as to how much cash can be raised immediately—we must act now for the Interzonal—and as to how much we can predictably guarantee for a second of your choice throughout the match series. The only second practical at Palma is Benko. We are already committed to paying him $2,000 for stepping aside and making room for you; he is willing to act as your second in return. Evans wants $3,000 plus all expenses. Believe me, we can afford no second for the Interzonal other than Benko. During the matches, we can guarantee a second's expenses plus a $1,000 honorarium to him for each of the first two Candidates matches; a $1,500 honorarium for the final Candidates match; a $2,000 honorarium for the World Championship. Frankly, such guarantees mean a greater difficulty in raising the total amount needed and, therefore, could conceivably hold down the increase in amounts which eventually come to you. Please weigh this carefully against your need for a second to aid in winning each match.

8. You can depend upon me to see that your rights are protected during the events. USCF will do everything within its power to obtain satisfactory—

even a favorable—political balance of Tournament Directors and Arbiters, plus a western or neutral playing site in each instance.

As I explained last night, there is a very real danger in hesitating over a final decision on participation in the Cycle. On behalf of USCF, last Saturday I had to notify Spain and FIDE that our entrants in the Interzonal are Reshevsky, Addison, and Fischer. In an attempt to protect USCF's right to have three players in the Interzonal, today I wired Spain that your participation is after all uncertain and that Benko might yet play. In view of the strict fourteen days advance requirement of FIDE—specifically reconfirmed during the General Assembly Meeting at Siegen—I don't really know what to expect from the Spanish and FIDE. At this point, if you decide not to play, they could tell us that Benko had not been named and could not participate. Spain is very eager to put in one of its own players, but I have asked them to hold off until this Saturday for a final decision on your participation and to permit us to enter Benko if you do not play. I hope they will hold still for these few additional days while you consider the conditions given above.

This letter should reach you on Friday. You have been considering your course of action for a long time, and I urge you to contact me before your Sabbath commences Friday evening. Every hour's delay in reaching a final decision heightens the probability that FIDE will rule for only two USA players and tell Spain to name a participant to fill the vacancy. Let's not gamble needlessly on something as important as the World Championship. Trust me to do the best I can for you, and let's go!

Your friend,

E.B. Edmondson
Executive Director

After the Palma de Mallorca Interzonal (November 9–December 12), the guarantee of $19,000 for playing in the cycle was increased to $22,000 ($146,500 in 2020 dollars). This offer was made in a March 18, 1971, letter from Edmondson sent to the Hotel Fenix in Palma de Mallorca. Fischer's mailing address suggests that Bobby returned to Palma after giving simuls in Madrid during the Christmas holidays. An additional letter to Bobby from Edmondson, sent to another hotel on Palma dated February 21, 1971, provides further confirmation of this possibility. It appears Fischer spent three months in Spain after the Interzonal, much of it studying in seclusion, before returning to North America at the last minute for his Candidates match with Taimanov.

During his sojourn in Spain, Bobby took the opportunity to answer some of his critics. In a letter published in Ken Smith's magazine *Chess Digest*[1] he expressed his frustration with U.S. Chess Federation officials who failed to appreciate his reasons for wanting to double the length of the U.S. Championship—strange

1 *Chess Digest*, February 1971.

that he brought this up considering his Candidates match with Taimanov was right around the corner, but then again Bobby was adamant on the subject. Fischer also responded strongly to charges from his Olympiad team captain Isaac Kashdan that he was high maintenance. It's apparent from this letter that, aside from Fischer's "slanted articles" comment, relations between Bobby and Ed Edmondson were still quite good in early 1971. Sadly, that would not remain so.

January 21, 1971
From: Bobby Fischer
Madrid, Spain

Dear Ken,

I've been rather busy as you may know these last few months.

I have not had the time to answer some of the very slanted articles written by Mr. Ed Edmondson in several recent issues of *Chess Life* about our controversy over the length of the last U.S. Championship. In the meantime, Ed and I have gotten along pretty well at the team championship and at the Interzonal. I would like to say that I consider Mr. Edmondson to be the only person in American chess officialdom or among the chess patrons, etc. who have ever tried to do anything for me in my chess career and getting me on the road to the world chess title. A lot of people have tried to "help me" by publishing explanations of what they consider to be my mental disturbance, etc. I can do without their "help". Ed has consistently been raising money for me to play in many tournaments and especially in the FIDE cycle. He is working hard in FIDE to make some needed changes over the apoplectic rage of the Russians.

Having said all this I want to get back to this other thing (U.S. Championship). This is not a personal attack on Ed, just as his articles in his own words were not an attack on me etc.

It seems the real crux of Ed's argument is that the players are against expanding the championship to twenty-two rounds. Well in the first place why shouldn't they be? The way it stands now some of them feel they have a real chance of taking the title if I slip up in a game or two—have a slow start or bad finish, etc. It's just human nature not to want something that may be best if it goes against one's own personal interest. There is also a lot of garbage about the players not having time—until this last year where many, if not most, of them played much more than me. But, let's go back to the players meeting where the players supposedly voted 10–1 against expanding the tournament to twenty-two rounds.

There is a little bit of history to this player's meeting and how it came about that should be explained first.

In the 1962 U.S. Championship I lost a game to Edmar Mednis in an early round. After losing this one game I had to make a tremendous effort and win game after game to finally draw even with Arthur Bisguier in the last round. I won the last game against Bisguier and the title.

After this tournament the idea began in my mind that something was really wrong if a fellow couldn't lose a game in a U.S. Championship without practically being eliminated.

This attitude was reinforced after the 1964–65 Championship where I lost two in a row after having won almost all of my earlier games and I found myself in a very close finish taking the title.

At this stage I informed Mr. Kasper and the other organizers that I would not participate in anymore U.S. Championships unless they were considerably lengthened and I told them that I considered twenty-two rounds to be a good length. My feeling was that since I was obviously so much better than these guys that it was a farce to have a photo finish every year or two. I felt if it were longer it would give my percentage a chance to take hold.

Anyway, they hemmed and hawed and I guess they figured they would get me to play at the last minute. But I was determined to not play unless the championship was changed.

After the 1966 team championship in Havana, Cuba, I was called long distance by Mr. Kasper when I was in Mexico City. Mr. Kasper asked me to play as a special favor to him. He said he had made some kind of bet with some of the people at the "Chess Foundation" that I would play and it was very important to him to get me to play. He also offered $500 extra as a participation fee plus my usual hotel and living expenses during the tournament. I told him the tournament had to be lengthened like I said. He said there wasn't time to change it—it was up to the players at the yearly players' meeting. [Mr. Kasper is of the American Chess Foundation]

Suddenly Kasper was becoming very "democratic." Since when had we, the players, actually decided anything? I suspected this was just a play because he figured most of the players would be against it. But then Mr. Kasper made a promise which he completely broke. He said he would back my proposal at the players' meeting after the U.S. Championship and get it changed for next year. So, I said O.K.—flew back in a few days and played in the 1966–67 Championship which I won. Now to get to the players' meeting:

All the players were present except Reshevsky. Mr. Kasper opened discussion of my proposal to lengthen the tournament by saying "I'm for it" but that was precisely all the support he gave it. He then did his best to convince the players that the foundation couldn't possibly put up any more money for the prizes—in other words we play twice the length for the same money just to satisfy Fischer. What chance did the proposal have? Many of the players, to my surprise, actually seemed interested in making it longer. Benko, for example, said "he is right (Fischer). Of course, I'm so afraid of losing just one game and being eliminated. But we have to discuss the money and to play twice the length for the same money is ridiculous."

Kasper countered; well we have to develop these things. All of you who know financially well-off people should try to get them interested in supporting chess. You should get your contacts interested in supporting the foundation.

Donald Byrne countered "you are my contact, Mr. Kasper" and we all laughed.

Larry Evans who to my great surprise apparently smelling more money to be had by all was clearly coming around to a longer championship said "Mr. Kasper you're talking about pies in the sky—how much will you increase the prizes by?"

Kasper absolutely refused to discuss increasing the prize money in the proposed lengthened championship by one penny.

Anyway, after a very long discussion of the subject—at least one hour, maybe two—Mr. Kasper said we have to take a vote. Benko, Evans, Bisguier, Donald Byrne and others didn't even want to vote on it without discussing the money together with the length. This was Kasper's trick—this was the way he had planned it from the beginning. Obviously, no one, with the exception of me, would vote for it. This would put me in a very bad situation for getting it changed in the future.

Anyway, the vote was taken, but several players didn't even want to vote on it. For example, Zuckerman abstained—but Mr. Kasper seeing the way the vote was going said "you can't abstain—you have to vote yes or no." Zuckerman of course voted no. At least one other player and maybe more wanted to abstain but Kasper wouldn't allow them to. I think Addison also wanted to abstain. Naturally it's a little vague now. My big mistake was to vote for it. I should have voted against it because it was so ridiculous. But even after the vote was taken Benko and several other players begged Mr. Kasper to take another vote to see if the players were in favor of changing it with increased prizes. Mr. Kasper steadfastly refused to take this vote. Finally after another half hour or so of wrangling about this Mr. Kasper said "well you can't decide whether you want to change it or not" and finally the meeting broke up.

So that is the story of the ten to one vote against lengthening the U.S. Championship.

Now to move on to another point or two:

Ed says he tried to get me to play in the 1969 U.S. Championship [and World Championship Zonal qualifier] at the last minute—a day or two before the tournament began on the phone—after that conversation, nothing. There were absolutely no last-minute attempts to get my participation—there was absolutely no last-minute offer to make it a thirteen round [instead of eleven round] tournament. Ed told me I was "afraid" and "this" and "that". I finally hung up on him after saying a very loud "goodbye."

Oh, yes, Ed also said that "lying" wasn't going to do me any good in an apparent reference to my accusation that Burt Hochberg (writing in *Chess Life*) had published a lie stating that I had never answered my invitation to the 1967 U.S. Championship. This brings me to the next point—my accusation about this was never answered by Ed in *Chess Life* and I wonder why?

Also, Ed published an imbecilic letter by Mr. Kashdan. Mr. Kashdan makes some veiled accusations about my troublesome behavior at the Piatigorsky tournament. I guess he is referring to the fact that I kept asking him every day for a different chess set to play with—because the set we played with was exceptionally large. He would promise a new one eventually, but he never brought it. Naturally, I kept complaining to him for the new set. Finally, I asked Mrs. Piatigorsky herself and she got on it pretty fast. Kashdan also makes an oblique reference to my supposedly troublesome behavior in Leipzig, E. Germany. Apparently, he means the incident with Najdorf. To this day, I still don't know what that was all about. All I know is that the game was a draw and we signed the score sheets and analyzed for a couple of minutes then Najdorf made a remark I didn't care for—I pushed the pieces to the center of the board and left the hall. The next thing I knew they were talking about forfeiting. Apparently Najdorf's vanity was stung and he said I had pushed the pieces into the middle of the board while the game was still in progress. Anyway, nothing came of it and the draw stood. Mr. Kashdan overlooks the fact that I had the best score on first board in the finals and helped us to take second place behind the Russians. That's all forgotten—all he remembers is the "incident" which I in no way created with Najdorf.

On other points Ed makes it at the present time the USCF and the American Chess Foundation can't afford the increased expenses of a longer U.S. Championship. Well, quite frankly that is the only logical argument he has come up with. Unfortunately, I can't really say too much about this because I don't know the financial workings of either the USCF or the American Chess Foundation. Neither of which ever publishes any financial statements explaining how much money comes in and how much goes out to go to certain things like this. I am not saying they should—I have not thought about it that much. I do know the Foundation has taken in a tremendous amount more than they have spent; apparently, they are working on some plan to save a million dollars and then support chess with the interest. Well, I think it is better to invest the money in players than the bank—that's my opinion. So many countries can afford longer championships—why can't we?

Bobby Fischer[1]

---

1 Fischer's letter was originally published in *Chess Digest*, February 1971, (p. 25–27).

[top] CD Cover of a Mark Taimanov recording with his then wife Lyubov Bruk;

[middle] Fischer is studying the position after 13…Nxf5 in game six. Both players have played the opening quickly as reflected in the time elapsed on their clocks on opposite sides of the demonstration board. We have been unable to identify the wall-boy. (Photo: Northwest Chess, June 1971);

[bottom] Bobby Fischer and Mark Taimanov with match arbiter Božidar Kažić. (Photo: Chuck Jones).

2

FISCHER VS. MARK TAIMANOV

OFF TO MEET FISCHER

> With suitcase loaded with research material on Taimanov my plane left Dallas for New York April 20th. After a pleasant visit, and a side trip to Newburgh [then home to the United States Chess Federation], here it is Sunday, April 25th, as I jot down this short report on the plane home.
>
> "What about Fischer?" is of course the question that is important to you and the rest of the chess world. The answer can be put into two statements:
>
> (1) Fischer is in excellent physical shape–his mental attitude, at the present time, is one of determination toward winning the World Championship.
>
> (2) Fischer works at chess—takes nothing for granted in this short (too short) match coming up with Taimanov.
>
> I will end this short report with a few odds and ends:
>
> (a) Evans his second, at the present time, arrived one day after I did.
>
> (b) Of all the famous restaurants in New York to pick from, they outvoted me—and we went to a Japanese Steak House (but it turned out to be an excellent choice).
>
> (c) My legs were walked off by Fischer and Evans—they never heard of a taxi.
>
> Summary:
>
> If Fischer was easy to get along with, he would not be Fischer. I doubt (but hope so) that Evans will make it all the way as second. There will be problems before Fischer finishes this cycle of World Championship Candidates matches—but there is one thing I am certain of: Fischer has the genius and the great work (study) capacity that could make him Chess Champion of the World, if he so desires it enough.

Prophetic words from Ken Smith![1]

Mark Taimanov (1926–2016) was a man of many talents. Rated in the top twenty players in the world for a quarter of a century, he was also a respected theoretician and writer not to mention an accomplished concert pianist.

---

[1] *Chess Newsletter*, May 1, 1971.

A few years before the 1971 Candidates quarterfinals, Botvinnik had planned to play a match with Fischer. The match never took place but Botvinnik had drawn up a dossier on Fischer which he shared with fellow countryman Mark Taimanov:[1]

FISCHER DOSSIER

IN THE OPENING:

- Prior to each tournament Fischer prepares a new variation (sometimes several). He has variations (for example in the Sicilian Defense) that he has analyzed through and through, and plays with ease and confidence.
- Playing White in the Sicilian, he frequently uses the Nc3, Nb3, Bd3, Be3 and Qf3 setup.
- In several openings his preference is for Bg7, d6 and Ne5.
- In unexpected situations in the opening (especially in theoretical positions) his choices are almost always unhappy.
- Fischer does not like pawn chains. He needs room for his pieces.

IN THE MIDDLEGAME:

- Against opponents known to be weak he likes to advance forcefully with his K-side pawns.
- He likes clear-cut positions. When he enjoys a positional advantage, he welcomes any simplification
- In the face of sudden changes in the character of play (e.g. from attack to defense) his responses lack confidence.
- When he loses he does so mainly in sharp positions. Technical defeats are few in his case.
- He protects his pawn formations.
- He likes to spoil his opponent's pawns.
- He likes to sacrifice the exchange for central pawns.
- He likes to transfer his rooks via the third rank (Rf1-e1-e3).
- He likes long moves with his queen.
- He likes to advance the a-pawn against the knight on b3 or b6.
- He parts with bishops easily (frequently both Bf8-b4xc3 and Bc8-g4xf3).

IN THE ENDGAME:

- He likes to send his king on long raids.
- He likes bishops of different colors when there are rooks on the board.

[1] Dimitry Plisetsky and Sergey Voronkov, *Russians versus Fischer*. Moscow: Moscow Chess World, 1994, (p. 202–203).

GENERAL OBSERVATIONS:

- In the past he's willingly sacrificed pawns in exchange for mobility and action. Over the years he has become greedier toward material.
- He likes to gobble up pawns. In doing so he sometimes sells himself short.
- He has a keen positional sense, enabling him to evaluate the negative and positive features of piece interaction.
- He does not like his opponents to have strong pieces and seeks to exchange them as soon as possible.
- He is an excellent tactician and sees a lot.
- When a piece of his is attacked, he often replies by attacking a piece of his opponent's (zwischenzug).

SOME ADDITIONAL OBSERVATIONS:

- No material should be sacrificed to Fischer on general grounds alone. If there exists a specific refutation he'll find it.
- Aggressive action by Fischer must be countered!

Botvinnik's observations are a mixture of the obvious (Fischer's frequent use of the third rank attack against the Sicilian; i.e. Nc3, Nb3, Bd3, Be3 and Qf3) and the profound (Fischer's fondness for long queen moves, transferring his rooks to the third rank, and emphasis on exchanging off his opponent's strong pieces).

The last group of observations might seem self-evident, but they bring to mind the anecdote of Tal calculating deeply at a key moment in a game against Botvinnik. After the game Tal wanted to show his opponent what he had seen, but the "Patriarch" quickly cut him off, explaining that if he traded one pair of rooks and kept the others on, he knew he would be doing fine. Tal initially thought this assessment superficial, but the longer he analyzed the position the more he began to appreciate that Botvinnik had penetrated to the essence of the position. Some of the observations here are in a similar vein—simple but deep.

Botvinnik was one of the few to hold any hope for Taimanov in his match against Fischer. This assessment and a close reading of the dossier makes one wonder if the bad blood between him and Fischer might have affected his legendary objectivity. Taimanov barely made it into the Candidates matches and to expect the match would be close was optimistic.

The drawing of lots for the quarterfinals of the 1971 Candidates matches paired Mark Taimanov against Bobby Fischer. FIDE initially had trouble finding neutral ground for the East vs. West match, as Bobby wanted to play in the United States or Western Europe and Taimanov the Soviet Union or Eastern

Europe. Offers to stage the match in the U.S., USSR, Netherlands, Spain, and Italy were all rejected. Finally, a compromise was found in the Canadian city of Vancouver. The match was held there due to the generosity of long-time Canadian FIDE Zonal president and patron John Prentice (born Hans Pick in Vienna in 1907), who did so much to further chess in his adopted homeland.

The match was scheduled for ten games, with the winner the first to score five-and-a-half points. The experienced arbiter Božidar Kažić of Yugoslavia was the referee (as he had been for Bobby's two training matches with Matulović and Janosević in 1958) and for the most part he had an easy job. The Fischer mania that was to strike the United States in 1972 did not exist a year earlier. There was a respectable number of spectators in Vancouver, but never more than 200 and normally half that.

The games were played on the University of British Columbia campus in what was then called the Student Union Auditorium. This venue was selected by FIDE President Max Euwe and provided excellent conditions for the players and ample room for spectators. Luckily, Euwe was on-site to iron out details. The two players initially had trouble finding common ground on the playing site which led to the match starting three days later than originally scheduled.

This delay was to Taimanov's benefit. According to Robert Wade's report in the June 24 issue of *Chess*, the Soviet delegation only arrived in Vancouver on May 9th, which would not have allowed for proper time to acclimate if the match had begun on the original starting date of May 13.

UBC would host another important event later that summer, the 1971 Canadian Open. Boris Spassky and Hans Ree tied for first in the eleven round event ahead of Suttles, Browne, Kavalek, and Benko. This was truly a golden time for British Columbia chess. Future Grandmasters Duncan Suttles and Peter Biyiasas were students at the university taking math classes from the likes of UBC professors, *Canadian Chess Chat* editors and former Canadian Olympiad team members Dr. Elod Macskasy (winner of the 1958 Canadian Open and many times British Columbia champion) and Dr. Nathan Divinsky (author of several books devoted to chess history). There was plenty of upcoming talent including Bob Zuk, and two who went on to greatly contribute to Canadian chess, Jonathan Berry and Bruce Harper.

The modest attendance for the match could partly be attributed to some out-of-towners delaying their visit to Vancouver until what they thought would be the critical games seven to ten. They had no way of knowing Bobby was going to make chess history with his sweep.

Harder to explain is the lack of media coverage. Although the match ended June 1, readers of *Chess Life & Review* had to wait until the August issue for Robert Byrne's annotations (the July issue only included the game scores). Only

I.A. Horowitz, writing for *The New York Times*, offered a daily report on the beginning of Fischer's historic march to the title.

The games of the match between Fischer and Taimanov have been heavily analyzed in many places, but the best coverage of the match is to be found in Northwest Chess, edited at the time by Rob Hankinson of British Columbia. It reprinted several articles published in Vancouver newspapers, including several excellent pieces by Bill Rayner. From these accounts we know Taimanov had a strong team behind him in Yury Balashov and Evgeny Vasiukov with Alexander Kotov as head of the delegation. Fischer, meanwhile, had only Ed Edmondson who ran interference for him.

Larry Evans was to be Bobby's second, but as he explained in *Chess Digest:*[1]

> [I] had to decline because, among other reasons, one of Fischer's conditions was a ban on all journalistic activities.

This was not good news for Evans, who wanted to help Bobby. He had been earning good money writing for *Chess Life*, *Chess Digest*, and *Sports Illustrated*. Fischer also had two other conditions that were deal breakers for the Reno-based grandmaster: his wife had to stay home and he needed to arrive in Vancouver when Bobby did. Evans' absence left Fischer to play the most important competition of his life without a second. Evans wrote that Edmondson had his hands full as Fischer changed hotel rooms four times due to noise and ultimately, changed hotels. There is no question Edmondson's presence for this match, and the next two with Larsen and Petrosian, was critical. Without him it's doubtful Bobby would have stayed in the World Championship cycle.

The match started May 16 and the games were scheduled to be played every Thursday, Sunday, and Tuesday from 5:30PM to 10:30PM. Adjournments were Monday and Wednesday from 5:30PM to 9:30PM and Friday 2:30PM to 6:30PM. This program accommodated Fischer's religious beliefs, allowing him to observe the Worldwide Church of God's Sabbath from Friday evening to Saturday evening. The time control was forty moves in two-and-a-half hours and after five hours play games were adjourned.

Canadian Chess Chat had the games being played May 16, 18, 20, 25, 27, and June 1. The winner received $2,000 and the loser $1,000.

Ken Morton of Vancouver was the official games recorder for the match and, thanks to him, we know how many minutes the players used on specific moves (for example in game three Taimanov used thirty-five minutes to play his first nineteen moves but then went into a deep huddle, spending seventy-four minutes (!) on his next move (Taimanov says seventy-two minutes in *Russians versus Fischer*).

---

[1] *Chess Digest*, July 1971, (p. 146).

Several Vancouver players served as wall-boys during the match including future Grandmaster Peter Biyiasas who served for game one:[1]

> Question: When did you first meet Bobby Fischer?
>
> Biyiasas: It was at the match in Vancouver in 1971. I was the wall-boy for game one and believe Ken Morton and David Shapiro had the job the other five games. I remember being surprised by how Fischer talked. To me, he sounded like a motorcycle greaser. I had never heard a Brooklyn accent before.
>
> Question: Do you have any memories of being the wall-boy?
>
> Biyiasas: Yes, I remember Taimanov shook my hand before the game. Also, that he ate sugar cubes during the game for energy. Dr. Macskasy made fresh-squeezed orange juice for Bobby. After the first game was adjourned Taimanov spoke to Bobby in Russian and Fischer responded in English "Yes, it was a tough game."
>
> Question: Any other recollections?
>
> Biyiasas: Yes, I recall playing blitz with Duncan [Suttles]. At some point Bobby walked by and we asked if he wanted to join in, but he said he preferred to watch. After one game Duncan, asked me why I didn't play 1...g6 against 1.d4, which he thought was a better way to reach King's Indian middlegames. I said I didn't see what was wrong with the regular KID and Fischer immediately chimed in backing me up.

One of the few people to hold the grandmaster title for both over the board and correspondence chess, Duncan Suttles was born in San Francisco on December 21, 1945. He moved with his family to British Columbia a few years later, which explains how he was able to play in both the U.S. and Canadian Championships in 1965. Suttles played Fischer twice, losing both games.

One story Biyiasas didn't mention, but which has circulated around the Northwest for over four decades, concerns his relaying of the moves. The normal practice for wall-boys is to make the move on the demonstration board as soon as it is played in the game. Biyiasas, who was already a strong player and would become Canadian Champion the following year, allegedly played an automatic recapture before it was made in the game, earning a stern stare from Fischer. Conceivably this could have been 11...exf5, though it is not compulsory, 11...Nxf5 and 11...Bxf5 being legal if not good moves. A more likely candidate is the recapture 14.dxe6 (after 13...Bxe6), which is obligatory.

[1] From a 2014 interview with Peter Biyiasas.

Canadian Master Bruce Harper has a different take on this story. He recalled:

> Peter assumed that a move (I think a recapture) would be made and made it on the wall-board, but in fact one of the players made a different move. So, he was replaced as the wall-boy.

If this was the case, the incident might have occurred after 31...Kf7 with Biyiasas playing 32.Bxf8 instead of the game continuation 32.Be2.

Russians versus Fischer and *Northwest Chess* both confirm Taimanov was not feeling well after he lost two complicated games on the White side of the King's Indian and an easily drawn adjournment.

---

(68) Sicilian
Fischer – Taimanov
Vancouver (2) 1971

1.e4 c5 2.Nf3 Nc6 3.d4 cxd4 4.Nxd4 e6 5.Nb5 d6 6.Bf4 e5 7.Be3 Nf6 8.Bg5 Qa5+ 9.Qd2 Nxe4 10.Qxa5 Nxa5 11.Be3 Kd7 12.N1c3 Nxc3 13.Nxc3 Kd8 14.Nb5 Be6 15.0-0-0 b6 16.f4 exf4 17.Bxf4 Nb7 18.Be2 Bd7 19.Rd2 Be7 20.Rhd1 Bxb5 21.Bxb5 Kc7 22.Re2 Bf6 23.Rde1 Rac8 24.Bc4 Rhf8 25.b4 a5 26.Bd5 Kb8 27.a3 Rfd8 28.Bxf7 Bc3 29.Bd2 d5 30.Rd1 d4 31.Bxc3 Rxc3 32.Kb2 d3 33.Kxc3 dxe2 34.Re1 Nd6 35.Bh5 Nb5+ 36.Kb2 axb4 37.axb4 Rd4 38.c3 Rh4 39.Bxe2 Nd6 40.Rd1 Kc7 41.h3 Rf4 42.Rf1 Re4 43.Bd3 Re5 44.Rf2 h5 45.c4 Rg5 46.Kc3 Kd7 47.Ra2 Kc8 48.Kd4 Kc7 49.Ra7+ Kd8 50.c5 bxc5+ 51.bxc5 Ne8 52.Ra2 Nc7 53.Bc4 Kd7 54.Rb2 Kc6 55.Bb3 Nb5+ 56.Ke3 Kxc5 57.Kf4 Rg6 58.Bd1 h4 59.Kf5 Rh6 60.Kg5 Nd6 61.Bc2 Nf7+ 62.Kg4 Ne5+ 63.Kf4 Kd4 64.Rb4+ Kc3 65.Rb5 Nf7 66.Rc5+ Kd4 67.Rf5 g5+ 68.Kg4 Ne5+ 69.Kxg5 Rg6+ 70.Kxh4 Rxg2 71.Bd1 Rg8 72.Bg4 Ke4 73.Kg3 Rg7 74.Rf4+ Kd5 75.Ra4 Ng6 76.Ra6 Ne5 77.Kf4 Rf7+ 78.Kg5 Rg7+ 79.Kf5 Rf7+ 80.Rf6 Rxf6+ 81.Kxf6

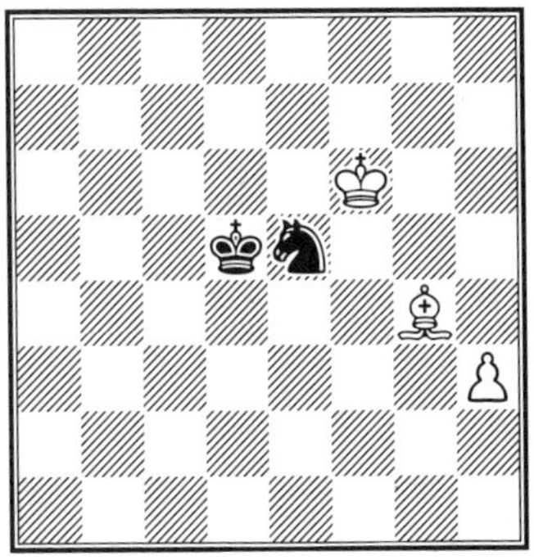

81...Ke4??

81...Nd3 82.h4 Nf4 83.Kf5 Kd6! 84.Kxf4 Ke7 draws or 81...Kd4 82.Bc8 Nf3 83.Bb7 Nh4 84.Kg5 Ke5 85.Kxh4 Kf6 drawing.

82.Bc8 Kf4 83.h4 Nf3 84.h5 Ng5 85.Bf5 Nf3 86.h6 Ng5 87.Kg6 Nf3 88.h7 Ne5+ 89.Kf6, 1–0.

Black's horrible blunder in the ending can partly be explained by Taimanov's state of mind after losing game three. It's also possible that his subconscious recalled an earlier game he played with Fischer. There, the young Bobby drew in textbook fashion, a similar, but different ending, where bringing the king behind the pawn was the correct plan.

(69) Nimzo–Indian
Mark Taimanov – Fischer
Buenos Aires 1960

1.c4 Nf6 2.Nc3 e6 3.d4 Bb4 4.e3 0-0 5.Bd3 d5 6.Nf3 Nc6 7.0-0 dxc4 8.Bxc4 Bd6 9.Nb5 Be7 10.h3 a6 11.Nc3 Bd6 12.e4 e5 13.Be3 exd4 14.Nxd4 Bd7 15.Re1 Qe7 16.Bg5 Nxd4 17.Nd5 Qe5 18.f4 Nf3+ 19.Qxf3 Qd4+ 20.Kh1 Ng4 21.hxg4 Qxc4 22.b3 Qb5 23.a4 Qa5 24.Red1 Bc6 25.e5 Bb4 26.Qe4 Bxd5 27.Rxd5 Qb6 28.f5 Bc3 29.Rc1 Bb2 30.Rb1 Bc3 31.Rc1 Bb2 32.Rc4 Rae8 33.f6 c6 34.fxg7 cxd5 35.gxf8Q+ Kxf8 36.Qxh7 Bxe5 37.Rf4 Qe6 38.Rf1 b5 39.axb5 axb5 40.Bd2 Ke7 41.Bb4+ Kd8 42.Rxf7 Rh8 43.Rf8+ Rxf8 44.Bxf8 Qf6 45.Bc5 d4 46.Kg1 Qf4 47.Qe7+ Kc8 48.Qf8+ Qxf8 49.Bxf8 Bg3 50.Kf1 d3 51.Bb4 Kd7 52.Be1 Bf4 53.Bc3 Bg3 54.g5 Ke6 55.g6 Ke7 56.Be1 Bf4 57.Bh4+ Kf8 58.g3 Bd6 59.Kf2 Bc5+ 60.Kf3 Kg7 61.Bg5 Kxg6 62.Bf4 Kh5 63.Ke4 Kg4 64.Kxd3 Kf3 65.Bc7 Bf2 66.Bd6 Be1 67.Kd4 Kg4 68.Kc5 b4 69.Kb5 Kf5 70.Kc4 Ke6 71.Bc7 Kf5 72.Kd3 Kg4 73.Bd6 Bc3 74.Kc4 Be1 75.Bxb4 Bxg3 76.Bc3 Bd6 77.Kd5 Be7 78.Bd4 Bb4 79.Kc4 Ba5 80.Bc3 Bd8 81.b4 Kf4 82.b5 Ke4 83.Bd4 Bc7 84.Kc5

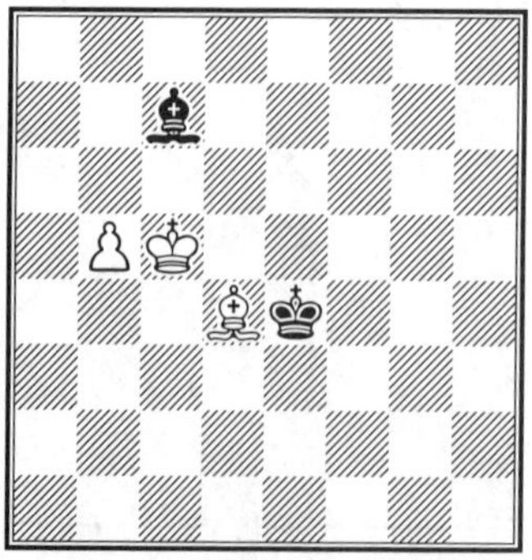

84...Kd3! 85.Kc6 Kc4 86.Bb6 Bf4 87.Ba7 Bc7, ½–½.

The match was suspended for three days with the score 3–0 as Taimanov was hospitalized for high blood pressure. When play resumed Fischer won the fourth game, arguably the best of the match, with a classic demonstration of the superiority of a bishop over a knight in the endgame. Then came the following tragedy.

(70) Grünfeld
Mark Taimanov – Fischer
Vancouver (5) 1971

1.d4 Nf6 2.c4 g6 3.Nc3 d5 4.Bg5 Ne4 5.Bh4 Nxc3 6.bxc3 dxc4 7.e3 Be6 8.Rb1 b6 9.Be2 Bh6 10.Nf3 c6 11.Ne5 Bg7 12.f4 Bd5 13.0-0 Nd7 14.Nxc4 0-0 15.a4 c5 16.Ne5 Nxe5 17.dxe5 f6 18.Rb2 Be6 19.Rd2 Qc7 20.Bg4 Qc8 21.Bf3 Rb8 22.Qe2 Rd8 23.Rfd1 Rxd2 24.Qxd2 Qe8 25.exf6 exf6 26.Qd6 Rc8 27.a5 Bf8 28.Qd2 Be7 29.Bd5 Qf7 30.Bxe6 Qxe6 31.Qd7 Kf7 32.Qxa7 bxa5 33.e4 Qc6 34.Rd7 Qxe4 35.h3 a4 36.Bf2 Kf8 37.c4 a3 38.Qxa3 Ra8 39.Qb2 Ke8 40.Qb5 Kf8 41.Rd1 Qxf4 42.Bxc5 Bxc5+ 43.Qxc5+ Kg7 44.Rf1 Qe4 45.Qc7+ Kh6

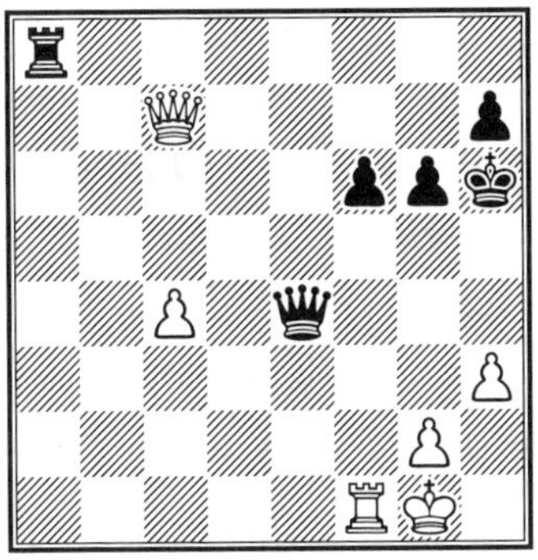

46.Rxf6?? Qd4+, 0–1.

According to *Russians versus Fischer* as Bobby played 46...Qd4+ he said, "I'm sorry."

Though Taimanov lost 6–0, all the games were tough fights except perhaps game six. Under normal circumstances he would likely have scored a couple of points (games two and five were easy draws).

Evgeny Vasiukov, in a 2012 interview with the Russian website Chesspro, blamed Taimanov's subpar result on poor nutrition. He stated:

> Fischer was much stronger, but as even he has admitted, the final result of the match didn't illustrate the real correlation of forces. Taimanov had to lose, but not in such a crushing manner.

> A significant role in this fiasco was played by Taimanov's malnutrition during the match, owing to which he just physically couldn't stand the workload.
>
> He was malnourished because he wanted to save money in order to buy some things he couldn't buy in the USSR. As long as I knew him Mark had a hearty appetite. I noticed that he was malnourished, so I told him he shouldn't be economizing on food, that it's very important for being able to stand five hours of tension during the game. Fortunately, we, the members of the delegation, received from the Sports committee of the USSR the normal daily subsistence for those times—eleven American dollars each, while Taimanov was getting even more from the organizer of the match, millionaire Prentice. He could eat properly, not denying himself anything. However, he didn't pay attention to me and continued saving. He never visited the restaurant of our five-star hotel, which was one story lower, during the match. Balashov and I, having a kitchen in our room, were buying all kinds of products in the supermarket and fed the excessively economical Mark. Does it sound like nonsense? Yes, unfortunately, but it happened.

Taimanov in his 1993 Russian language book on his games with Fischer (translated *I was Fischer's Victim* or alternatively *I was Fischer's Sacrifice*) concentrates primarily on the eight games they played (+7, =1) and doesn't mention food being an issue during the match.

Both Mikhail Botvinnik and Igor Bondarevsky point to the age difference of seventeen years (Taimanov forty-five to Fischer's twenty-eight) as a reason for the difference in energy between the two players. Bondarevsky mentions another important factor: Yes, Fischer had only played one previous high-level match (Reshevsky in 1961), but Taimanov had even less experience. His only previous one on one competition was a loss to Botvinnik for the 1952 Soviet Championship.

There was not much Taimanov could do about the age difference, nor the fact that in critical positions Fischer could calculate more deeply. Botvinnik suggested Taimanov consider playing the French Winawer, as Fischer had difficulties playing against it in the past.[1] He also acknowledged Taimanov had habitually used the Sicilian as his sole weapon against 1.e4 the past decade. Changing his stripes in a few months would have been difficult, if not impossible. In the final analysis Taimanov was simply overmatched. Yes, it could have been a little more even fight, but it was never going to be a close match.

International arbiter Božidar Kažić said Fischer was much more restrained than before, and on good speaking terms with Taimanov, and especially considerate towards Taimanov's young second, grandmaster Balashov.

---

[1] Recently unearthed records show Taimanov experimented with the French in training games against his seconds but without great success.

One of the spectators supporting Bobby in Vancouver was twenty-year-old Daniel Bailey, a future editor of *Northwest Chess* and proofreader for *Inside Chess*:

> In the summer of 1971, I went up to Vancouver to see one of the Fischer–Taimanov games. I sat near the front. All I can say is I have never been in the force field of more powerful human concentration. That includes master politicians, superb actors and consummate concert musicians. Fischer would come on stage from the wings and in three long strides reach the table, sit and start analyzing in one swift seamless motion. Then he'd freeze, his body motionless but his mind no more motionless than a big cat's riveted on prey. The intensity of his focus bumped up my pulse and blood pressure and made my breath come shallow minute after minute, hour after hour in the dark silence of the hall. I can only imagine what Taimanov must have been feeling from merely across the board.

To conclude coverage of Fischer–Taimanov, the man who was closest to the action in Vancouver, arbiter Božidar Kažić, had these observations.[1]

> Evans, Fischer's second, arrived in Vancouver only after the fourth game. The two did not meet even then. Ed Edmondson, U.S. Chess Federation Director, on the other hand, was Fischer's constant companion, chauffeur, bodyguard...
>
> Fischer got straight up from every game, not discussing one move of the match until it was finished when he did discuss the games with Taimanov for an afternoon.
>
> When the match had been decided 6–0, a proposal was put forward that the remaining four games be played as "friendlies." Taimanov had no objection. Fischer was willing, but only for the same fee as, proportionally, for the match. Nobody would put up the money.

No other report seems to have brought up the idea to play the last four games of the match. Considering the punishment Taimanov had received it seems unlikely he would have wanted to sit across the board from Bobby four more times. On the other hand, additional prize money in hard currency might have been an inducement.

Normally once a match has been decided, the action stops, but there have been a few exceptions, one being the 1993 title match between Kasparov and Short. When Garry reached 12½ points and retained his title there were still four days left on the schedule and the players filled them with seven exhibition games.

---

[1] *Chess*, August 1971.

One of Bent Larsen's many great tournament victories was his triumph at Le Havre 1966 where he took first with 9 from 11, two points ahead of the Soviet representatives Lev Polugaevsky and Nikolai Krogius, both of whom he defeated. Here he is in the opening stage of his game from round seven against Polugaevsky.

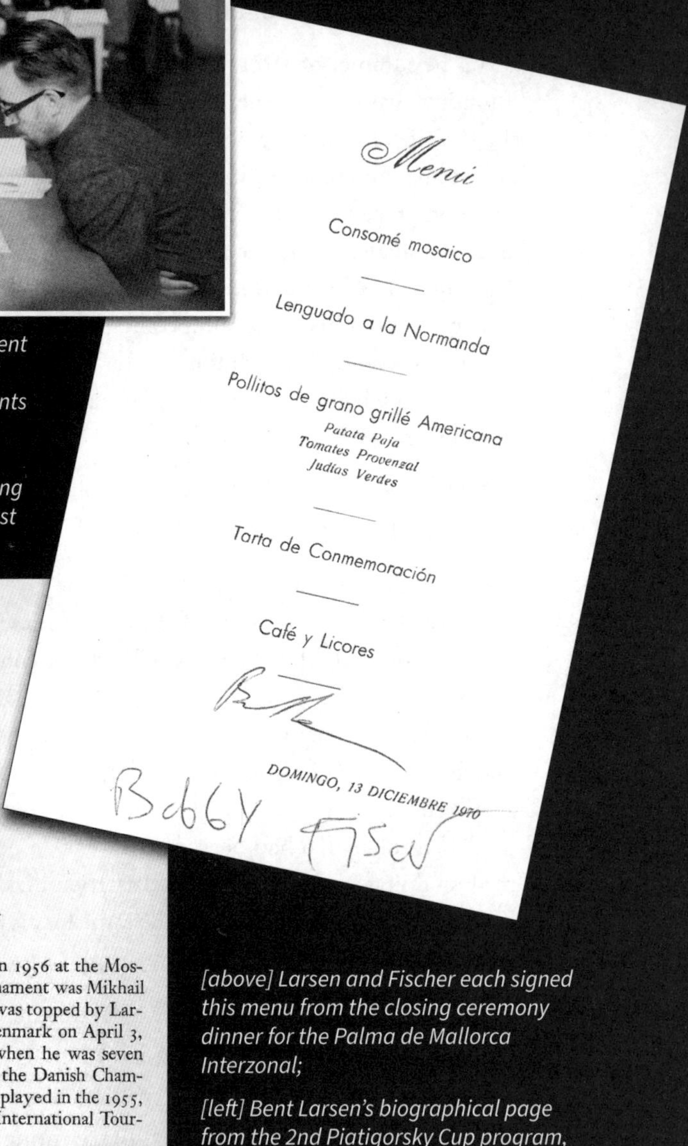

Menú

Consomé mosaico

Lenguado a la Normanda

Pollitos de grano grillé Americana
Patata Paja
Tomates Provenzal
Judías Verdes

Tarta de Conmemoración

Café y Licores

DOMINGO, 13 DICIEMBRE 1970

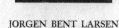

JORGEN BENT LARSEN

Jorgen Bent Larsen won his grandmaster title in 1956 at the Moscow Olympiade. Also participating in this tournament was Mikhail Botvinnik, who had achieved a 75% score, but was topped by Larsen with a 77.8% score. Larsen was born in Denmark on April 3, 1935. A young schoolmate taught him chess when he was seven years old. Twelve years later, in 1954, he won the Danish Championship, a crown he has captured whenever he played in the 1955, 1956, 1959, 1963 and 1964 championships. His International Tournament victories are impressive. As follows:

Scandinavian Championship, Oslo 1955. Tied with Olafsson and won the play-off with 4½-3½.

Hastings, 1956-1957. Tied with Gligoric for 1st and 2nd place.

Mar del Plata, 1958. Winner. Lombardy, 2nd. Panno, Eliskases and Sanguinetti in 3rd, 4th and 5th place.

Beverwijk, 1961. Tied with Ivkov, Uhlmann, 3rd and Olafsson, 4th.

Interzonal, Amsterdam, 1964. Tied with Spassky, Tal and Smyslov.

IBM Tournament, Amsterdam, 1964. Winner, Donner, 2nd.

Le Havre, April 1966. Winner. Polugajevski and Krogius, 2nd and 3rd. Matanovic and Forintos, 4th and 5th.

In the 1965 World Candidates Matches he beat Ivkov. In the second round after 9 games he had an even score against Tal but lost the match in the 10th game. In a recent match he beat Geller 5-4.

[above] Larsen and Fischer each signed this menu from the closing ceremony dinner for the Palma de Mallorca Interzonal;

[left] Bent Larsen's biographical page from the 2nd Piatigorsky Cup program, which he has signed. Larsen's win over Petrosian on the White side of a Maróczy Bind featuring a queen sacrifice is well remembered, but so should his beautiful positional squeeze near the end of the tournament using the King's Indian—an opening the reigning World Champion rarely lost against.

3
FISCHER VS. BENT LARSEN

The semi-finals of the Candidates matches started just five weeks after the quarter-finals. The match between the two best players in the West was eagerly anticipated and, unlike the previous round, there was no argument about what country would host the match, as Larsen preferred the United States to the Netherlands, Spain, or Sweden.

This might seem strange in view of the travel and jet lag Larsen would have to endure, but the August 1971 issue of *Chess* provides the answer: Larsen is said to have remarked, in memory of unfortunate experiences in other lands: "In the States I shall get the money!" Evidently, he had not been paid his honorarium/prize money by some European organizers.

The Great Dane had played in the United States several times before—Dallas 1957, the Second Piatigorsky Cup in 1966, and Aspen 1968 to name a few—and was comfortable there. Jack Spence, in his article on the match for *Chess* notes, wrote that Fischer was not the overwhelming fan favorite one might have expected playing on home ground. He wrote from Denver in July of 1971:

> The atmosphere is neutral. While the audience respects Fischer and holds his play in awe, few have witnessed him in action before, knowing him only as a name, which has dominated international chess for a dozen years or more. On the other hand Larsen, with his friendly personality, is well known to Denver chess fans primarily due to his popular victory in the 1968 U.S. Open at Aspen, a few hundred miles to the west.

Chess players in Colorado who attended Fischer's April 1964 exhibitions in Denver and Colorado Springs already had the opportunity of seeing Bobby in person, but Spence makes a good point. Larsen was a friendly person and great conversationalist who was a popular figure in the chess world.

Just as in Vancouver, Fischer came to Denver accompanied only by Ed Edmondson. Larsen merely brought his wife. This is likely the only time in the past fifty years that two world class players have met in a match connected with a World Championship cycle and not used seconds.

Larsen entered the match known for his fighting spirit and willingness to take risks. This aggressiveness had enabled him to win many important tournaments, but caused skeptics to question his ability to adjust to match play against strong opposition. The final score against Fischer reinforced this faulty perception—Larsen was in fact an excellent match player in the late 1960s and early 1970s. In the six years prior to Denver 1971 he had defeated Ivkov, Geller, Portisch, Kavalek, and Uhlmann in matches, split two with Tal, and lost to Spassky.

The lifetime score between the two players going into the match was close, 3½–2½ in Bobby's favor. Count only the four games played between them in the previous five years and they were even. Curiously, the player who had Black won every game.

His 1968 victory in Aspen (first place with 11–1) may have brought back good memories of Colorado for Larsen, but he would be in for a surprise as the Mile High City experienced a major heat wave in July 1971 with temperatures in the nineties, occasionally reaching triple digits. Larsen had not anticipated the heat and that it would have such a heavy impact on him. The age difference between the players was not significant as it was in the Taimanov match (Larsen age thirty-six to Fischer's twenty-eight), but Fischer, growing up in New York summers, was used to warmer weather. All this said, the playing hall was air conditioned (Fischer played in a suit) and major hotels of the time would have been as well.

Years later, in an interview he gave to *New in Chess*, Larsen blamed his defeat on the heat:

> They had the hottest summer in that place in thirty-five years. And very, very dry. This is not for me. I cannot sleep. It is absolutely impossible. After Round two I asked to see the doctor. The bad thing is that the doctor is part of the organization. He just thought I am someone who always runs around with high blood pressure and doesn't believe that I am not...I have to just put down my foot and leave or I have to play on. I didn't put down my foot.

In another article he stated:

> Yes, it was an insufferable match. The organizers chose the wrong time for this match. I was languid with the heat and Fischer was better prepared for such exceptional circumstances... I saw chess pieces through a mist and, thus, my level of playing was not good. It was a nightmare that I will never forget! Fortune didn't give me a single chance to win over him

The one-sided result did not cause Larsen any long-term problems as he quickly bounced back. Following the sound advice that the cure for a bad result is to have a good one, he got back in the saddle and had a successful year in 1972, winning two strong tournaments in England—Teesside, in which he won all six games with 1.b3 (an opening that now bears his name), and Hastings.

The playing schedule in Denver was the same as Vancouver. The match started July 6th with games scheduled to be played Tuesdays, Thursdays, and Sundays starting at 4:00PM. As in Vancouver, this schedule allowed Fischer to observe the Worldwide Church of God's Sabbath. The time control was forty moves in two-and-a-half hours and after five hours play the game would be adjourned.

The games were played July 6, 8, 11, 13, 18, and 20. Larsen took a postponement on grounds of health after game four, so no game was played July 15.

The playing hall was the Houston Fine Arts Center at Temple Buell College located in eastern Denver. Foote Music Hall in the same building hosted live commentary by Isaac Kashdan and Anthony Saidy.

The equipment used in Denver was not as grand as Vancouver where a beautiful table from the 1966 Havana Olympiad and a nice wooden set were provided. Fischer and Larsen played with a Drueke Players Choice set and a generic board placed on a table. No other important match is known to have used non-wood pieces, but Fischer was fond of the hard-plastic simulation wood Players Choice set and had played with it before in important competitions, one example being his game with Spassky from the 1966 Piatigorsky Cup when he was Black. Fischer's favorite set appears to have been the one made for the 1950 Dubrovnik Olympiad, which was used in the 1992 Fischer–Spassky match. Fischer praised this set on several occasions for the artistry of the design and the feel of the pieces. He appreciated that the Dubrovnik set had no hard edges, which is something it had in common with the more modest Player's Choice model. Larsen, who played in several American Swiss system tournaments between 1968 and 1970, would likely have been familiar with the Players Choice set, which debuted at the 1965 National Open.

John Howell and John Harris were key players in Colorado chess in the late 1960s and early 1970s and were responsible for Denver getting the match, beating out alternative bids from New York and Los Angeles. Paul Klein of Ecuador was the chief arbiter and he must have done a good job, as he was on Bobby's short list of officials to referee the never played 1975 World Championship.

There was much more press in Denver compared to Vancouver, where it was only local journalists and Al Horowitz writing for *The New York Times*. Horowitz was back but so were *Los Angeles Times* chess columnist Isaac Kashdan and International Master David Levy who would write the nice little book *How Fischer Plays Chess* a few years later. Judging from the photos of Fischer talking to journalists after the match and the interviews he gave at the time, Bobby appears to have been quite relaxed with the media, much different than a year later.

National Master Curtis Carlson and long-time Colorado chess player Mike Archer both attended the match. Carlson wrote:

> I also saw all six games, what great memories! The first was awesome. After Larsen tipped over his king the audience gave Bobby a well-deserved standing ovation. After winning the 1974 World Open Larsen gave a simul in Denver. After he crushed me (and thirty-five others) I asked him who would win a Fischer–Karpov match; he said no one could beat Bobby!
>
> It cost $3 a game to watch or $20 for a pass for the whole match. I made the mistake of buying a pass when it would have been cheaper to pay by the game!
>
> After the Larsen match Lubos Kavalek gave a simul in Denver before Bobby left town, and he came by to watch. He glanced briefly at my game vs. K (which was ultimately drawn), and his face contorted like he was looking at a dead animal or something. So much for my fifteen seconds of fame with the god of chess.

Carlson kept the time the players spent on each move for the first two games, the only record for this we know of.

Archer remembered:

> The entire match Fischer looked trim, fit, relaxed and perhaps even a bit dapper. He had a somewhat gangly but confident walk. I met him very briefly when he borrowed three books from my collection a few days before the match. He seemed like a regular guy to me with whom you'd be happy to go to a bar, push down a couple of brewskis. He was lanky, seemed a little awkward, really almost shy/self-conscious. Larsen on the other hand looked rumpled and tired from the get-go—I recall people mentioning this at the time. His hair was always a mess and his suit looked poorly fitted to me, but perhaps that was the style in Europe for all I know.
>
> Game One was the most exciting to watch. I remember everyone with their pocket chess sets analyzing it real-time. On one or two occasions I recall Fischer turning to the audience and giving us a quite stern look because of noise he apparently detected.
>
> In Game Three Larsen played a novelty in the Sicilian (as Black) which Fischer basically refuted over-the-board. At that point I don't think there was anyone following the match locally who would have bet any outcome other than 6–0. The remainder of the games definitely had an anti-climactic air about them.
>
> Larsen played the last games looking for wins only, so the 6–0 is a bit overblown in my eyes. Larsen eschewed drawing moves, always striving for "only" a win, and got clobbered because of it. Especially combined with his normal looseness, this created a disaster, but one that looks worse on paper than it really was.
>
> I would be curious to know when Larsen hit town vis-a-vis Fischer. I know for fact the latter was here several days early as my five-minutes-of-fame was at least a couple of days before the match.

Nebraskan Jack Spence, famous for the many tournament bulletins he produced, described the board mannerisms of the two players in the report he wrote for *Chess*:[1]

> When matters are going well Fischer has a tendency to sprawl back in his chair with his legs crossed at the ankles full length outside the table leg with his hands resting on his lap but a moment later he will be seated erect at the table with elbows resting close to the board with one hand on his chin or ear, stroking his hair back. He does not move around too often and seldom leaves the table while Larsen is studying. On the other hand Larsen leaves the stage at almost every opportunity. Generally he hunches forward in his seat with his elbows on his knees and his face close to the pieces. Occasionally he sits immobile for minutes at a time with his chin cradled in his hand and, when matters begin to worsen, runs his fingers nervously through his hair.

The following observation adds to Spence's account:[2]

> Several time Colorado state champion (1955, 1967, and 1970) E. Victor Traibush was the official scorekeeper for games one and two and he observed that whenever Fischer moved, he very carefully and politely slid the piece to the center of the square he was moving it to. However, there was an exception to this behavior in game one. When Fischer played 19.f5!, Traibush noticed that Fischer actually picked up the pawn and tilted it slightly toward Larsen as he moved it forward.

(71) French
Fischer – Bent Larsen
Denver (1) July 6, 1971

1.e4 e6 2.d4 d5 3.Nc3 Bb4 4.e5 Ne7 5.a3 Bxc3+ 6.bxc3 c5 7.a4 Nbc6 8.Nf3 Bd7 9.Bd3 Qc7 10.0-0 c4 11.Be2 f6 12.Re1 Ng6 13.Ba3 fxe5 14.dxe5 Ncxe5 15.Nxe5 Nxe5 16.Qd4 Ng6 17.Bh5 Kf7 18.f4 Rhe8 19.f5

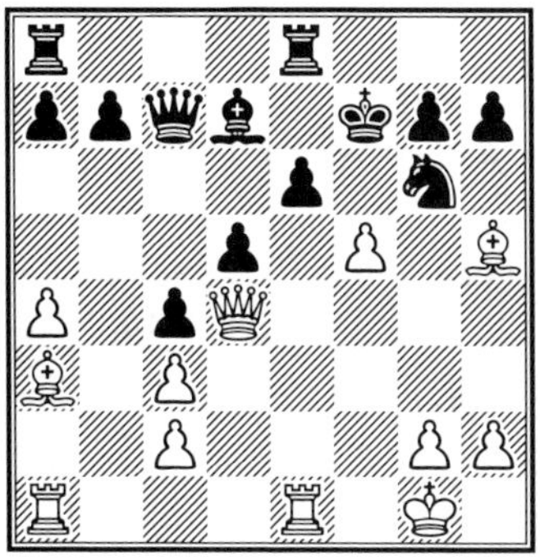

[1] *Chess*, August 1971.

[2] First reported in the *Rocky Mountain News* and later in the obituary for E. Victor Traibush in the *Colorado Chess Informant*, April 2011.

19...exf5 20.Qxd5+ Kf6 21.Bf3 Ne5 22.Qd4 Kg6 23.Rxe5 Qxe5 24.Qxd7 Rad8 25.Qxb7 Qe3+ 26.Kf1 Rd2 27.Qc6+ Re6 28.Bc5 Rf2+ 29.Kg1 Rxg2+ 30.Kxg2 Qd2+ 31.Kh1 Rxc6 32.Bxc6 Qxc3 33.Rg1+ Kf6 34.Bxa7 g5 35.Bb6 Qxc2 36.a5 Qb2 37.Bd8+ Ke6 38.a6 Qa3 39.Bb7 Qc5 40.Rb1 c3 41.Bb6, 1–0.

After the first game, Traibush drove Bobby to his home for dinner, and during the ride asked Fischer if he was aware of how he moved the f-pawn at move nineteen. The mortified Fischer had no idea what he had done and said, "That was very unprofessional."

Contrast that with the behavior of another World Champion as described by Yasser Seirawan.[1]

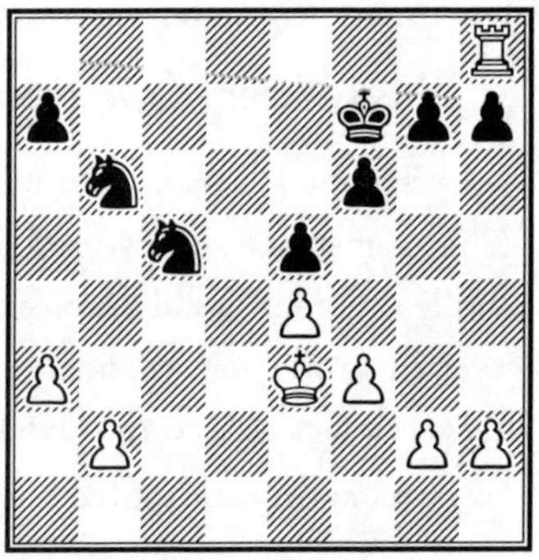

The position in the diagram, from Kasparov–Seirawan, Thessaloniki Olympiad 1988, is right before White played 29.Rb8!.

With this move Garry lashed out and smashed the clock with a closed fist. Unfortunately, the table happened to have little give to it and the end result was that all the pieces jumped off their squares. I was furious. Indeed, Garry had been so violent that on the adjacent board the game between Karpov and Gulko was also disturbed by Garry's outburst as their pieces jumped as well. So here I was, pieces spewed about, my clock running and now this. For the last few moves, Garry had been doing his "piece screwing" business, and I had had enough.

I decided right there and then that a solid right punch to the jaw was the required response and I clenched my fist. Garry's sense of self-preservation kicked into high gear faster than I could "make my move." Garry put his hands in the air and kept saying, "Sorry. Sorry. Sorry!" repeatedly. All the while readjusting the pieces and putting them on their proper squares. Garry's sudden change to a fawning apology disarmed me. The rush of adrenalin that wanted me to put Kasparov in a different time zone had nowhere to go, and I found that it took me many minutes to restore my concentration.

1 Yasser Seirawan, *Chess Duels: My Games with the World Champions*. London: Everyman, 2010, (p. 272–73).

> While not in time-trouble, I was beginning to drift in that direction, and the whole incident had a completely unnerving effect upon me. In my whole career I had never been in such a situation, although some opponents had been well and truly rude. But this? Talk about enfant terrible behavior. What had caused Garry to behave so badly? I have no idea of the pressures that he was under (or those expectations he placed on himself), but there was simply no excuse. It was a really unpleasant business and put me off from the tremendous respect I had, and have, for him as a player. A great player, but in this instance a terrible sportsman.

Fortunately, such behavior by world-class players is rare. Early in his book Seirawan writes of watching Paul Keres in his last tournament (Vancouver 1975) and what great manners he had.

Fischer was still very approachable in Denver, as evidenced by his going to Boulder to Traibush's house for dinner during the match and playing tennis with John Harris and several other local chess players. Things were much different a year later.

While both players got along well at the board, noise issues periodically caused problems throughout the match. This was always a problem for Fischer who was hypersensitive to even small sounds. Spence wrote:

> Until now Chief Arbiter Klein found matters running relatively smoothly but it was only a lull before the storm. At the start of the fifth game a cameraman from a national magazine was given permission to photograph the match in progress high above the stage in the projection booth. However he overstayed his time limit and the rustle of sounds from above forced a brief cessation of play while he packed his gear and departed. But as the ending approached Klein again had problems with the audience. After the last piece was exchanged Fischer had an outside passed pawn while Larsen had three pawns to two on the other wing. The ending became one of mathematics in a race to queen. Whispers became noticeably audible forcing Klein to descend into the auditorium where he gestured frantically to various spectators in an effort to eject them. They refused to move. Play halted as Fischer arose from the table in despair. Finally the worst offenders were removed and as play resumed Larsen was forced to journey over to stop the pawn while Fischer's king advanced to the other wing and victory.

Isaac Kashdan, in an unpublished article on the Fischer–Larsen match (originally planned for *Sports Illustrated*), explained how exacting Bobby was when it came to proper lighting:

> The lights were a problem, based on demands from Fischer. Most chess players are satisfied if they have a reasonably clear view of the board and men. Fischer had made a special study of the subject.

> His specifications called for twenty fluorescent fixtures, each with four daylight tubes, to be twenty feet above the playing surface. There must be no glare or shadow on the board or men. This was the ideal he had established after considerable experimentation in other matches and tournaments.
>
> The committee ordered the work done, and all was set when Fischer arrived. It turned out to be too bright. The electricians explained the fluorescent tubes are brighter than rated when newly installed.
>
> Fischer asked for changes, and changes were made, on the average of once each playing day. A typical request was: add four blue tubes, to replace the whites, and lower the fixtures three feet.
>
> Yellows were tried as well, but, were not successful. Soft-whites did better. All told, the committee owned close to 200 tubes, with only eighty needed during any one game, and none when the match was over.

Six-time U.S. Champion Walter Browne is one top player who shared Bobby's exacting standards concerning proper illumination, going so far as to withdraw from the 1978 U.S. Championship in a dispute over proper lighting.

4
FISCHER VS TIGRAN PETROSIAN

In 1960 Bobby confided to Spanish International Master and journalist Roman Toran that he thought Petrosian[1] was the top player in the world:[2]

> It's difficult to say. Botvinnik and Tal are among the best; I also like Spassky, but I think Petrosian is better than all of them. His weakness is too many draws, even against players he could beat easily. Maybe he lacks self-confidence.

Personal relations between Fischer and Soviet players cooled in 1962 after he accused them of cheating at Curaçao. While Bobby still respected Petrosian as a player, he didn't include Petrosian on his 1964 list of top ten players of all time (although when he revisited the topic in 1970, he did).

A month after taking the crown from Tigran Petrosian (late 1969), Boris Spassky stated[3] he believed Fischer would be the next World Champion—this at a time when it was not at all certain the American would be competing in the next cycle to determine the Challenger.

Spassky's comments about the weaknesses of Larsen ("plays feebly when his king is under attack") and Petrosian ("not ready to engage Fischer in a full-scale struggle for their entire match") are perceptive and support his reputation as one of the most astute chess psychologists of the twentieth century,

Spassky wrote[4]

> Even before the Candidates matches began I predicted that Fischer and Petrosian would meet in the final. Tigran Petrosian doesn't cede a thing to his rival in his understanding of chess, but I still saw Fischer as the favorite.

The relationship between Fischer and Petrosian on the eve of their 1971 match was one of mutual respect but with no love lost. Their previous encounters (eighteen games) left them dead even, but recent history favored Bobby due to

1 Petrosian became World Champion in 1963 when he beat three-time champion Botvinnik.

2 *Ajedrez Español*, July 1961, (p. 648).

3 In a letter written to the Canadian master Nathan Divinsky.

4 Spassky's article "Bobby Fischer in the 1971 Candidates Matches," written in Russian, was originally published in the English language magazine *Soviet Life* in a slightly different form.

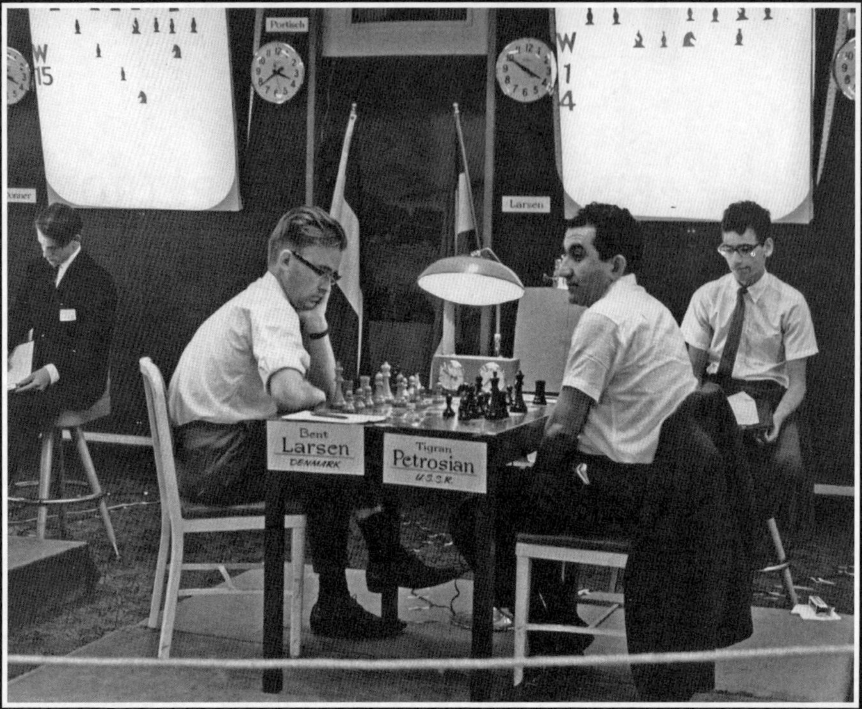

Bent Larsen and Tigran Petrosian at the start of their round seven game in the Second Piatigorsky Cup. Although Larsen won this, and their other match-up in Santa Monica, in brilliant style it was Petrosian who had usually dominated with a lifetime score of 13½–8½.

Fischer, Petrosian, I.S. Turover (the well-known brilliancy prize donor), Dražen Marović, and Risto Nicevski at Rovinj/Zagreb 1970.

his victory over Petrosian (3-1) the year before in the USSR vs. the Rest of the World. Another reason Fischer was favored was his performances in the first two rounds of the Candidates. While Fischer had defeated Taimanov and Larsen by a combined 12-0, Petrosian had only pasted Hübner and Korchnoi by the narrowest of margins, winning just two games out of seventeen played.

Spassky continued:

> The start of the match was in Petrosian's favor. After the third game the initiative was unquestionably on his side. The whole chess world was impressed by the second game of the match, which Petrosian won with a spectacular offensive. As Fischer's first defeat in the Candidates matches, it could have had unpleasant choices for him. I'm still convinced that after the second game Petrosian did not make the most of his favorable situation.
>
> I believe the former World Champion made the mistake of tempering his aggressive approach. Overcautious in the fourth and fifth games, he let Fischer recover his composure. At the same time, he preserved the equilibrium in the score.
>
> The sixth game showed the situation was changing. Winning this important game, Fischer completely mastered the lack of confidence he had shown after a difficult start. Another dangerous symptom was Petrosian's time trouble. No wonder the second half of the match was in sharp contrast to the first. Petrosian suffered a major setback in the sixth game, and after that he couldn't control his opponent's fiery attack.
>
> Fischer played the second half of the match brilliantly. The last four games left an indelible impression—all the strongest aspects of the American grandmaster's talents revealed themselves in the homestretch.
>
> In the first half of the Buenos Aires match Petrosian was in the picture while Fischer was not, but in the final part the opponent's changed roles. After the sixth game Fischer was obviously ahead. Of course, time trouble affected Petrosian's play, but I see the main reason for his failure somewhere else—he was not tuned up for a tough battle. I have played six matches in the Candidates matches during my chess career, and experience tells me that you only win when you put up a struggle to the very end. I think my upcoming match with Robert Fischer will be interesting. The thought of meeting a player as superb as Fischer puts one in a fighting mood.
>
> For the general chess public, I think the most interesting game Fischer played in 1971 was his first game against Larsen. It had everything—a sharp opening, attack and counterattack and mutual sacrifices. However, Fischer's seventh game against Petrosian is more to my taste. I consider it more characteristic of the American grandmaster's style.

(72) Sicilian
Fischer – Tigran Petrosian
Buenos Aires (7) 1971

Annotations by Boris Spassky.

1.e4

A traditional move for Robert Fischer—he starts all his games with the e-pawn.

1...c5

Petrosian's choice in the opening clearly shows that he intends to fight a real battle.

2.Nf3 e6 3.d4 cxd4 4.Nxd4 a6

In the first game of the match Petrosian also picked the Sicilian Defense, but instead of 4...a6 he played 4...Nc6. Chess fans know that after 5.Nb5 d6 6.Bf4 e5 7.Be3 Nf6 8.Bg5 Be6 9.N1c3 a6 10.Bxf6 gxf6 11.Na3, Black struck with the sudden counterblow 11...d5 which gave him excellent chances. Nevertheless, Black lost the game. Probably this fact played a part in Petrosian's decision not to continue the opening argument. Possibly he feared a surprise reply.

5.Bd3

This is exactly the way I played in the first and seventeenth games of the 1969 match with Petrosian.

5...Nc6 6.Nxc6 bxc6 7.0-0 d5 8.c4

I preferred 8.Nd2 in my games with Petrosian, with the intention of continuing b3 and Bb2. Fischer has worked out a different plan that is met with only rarely in tournament practice. Usually 8.c4 is not seen as posing any serious problems to Black. Fischer, however, has discovered an interesting method of strengthening White's play that sharply changes the assessment of this variation.

8...Nf6 9.cxd5 cxd5 10.exd5 exd5

I do not agree with the commentators who criticized Petrosian for this move. I think it was the wisest choice. Of course, the knight could have taken the pawn, but after 11.Be4 White has a rich choice of active continuations. The capture of the pawn with the queen also holds no special prospects for Black in view of the simple but strong reply 11.Nc3.

11.Nc3!

I have been told that White pondered over this move twenty minutes. Nonetheless, it seems to me that he charted the further plan of play not over the board but at home. Many people are inclined to consider the spectacular maneuver 11.Nc3 and 12.Qa4+ as a novelty especially prepared by the American grandmaster for his encounter with Petrosian.

This was Fischer's first opening surprise in the match. Formerly, the usual line of play was 11.Be3 Be7 12.Bd4 0-0, which permitted Black to preserve the equilibrium.

11...Be7 12.Qa4+!

Petrosian could have interposed the bishop, but evidently he was apprehensive about the variation 12...Bd7 13.Qc2 0-0 14.Bg5. The other continuation 13.Qd4 is also unpleasant for Black. It is clear that all this requires considerable analysis, but there is no doubt that White's position is preferable.

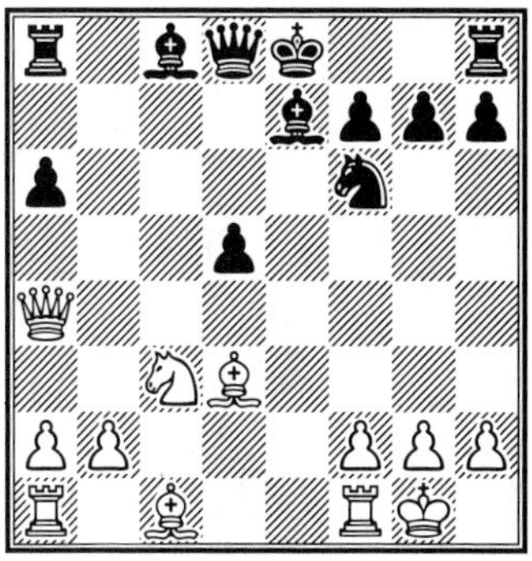

12...Qd7

Petrosian offers his opponent the sacrifice of the exchange, but Fischer rejects this Greek gift. It is easy to see that 13.Bb5 axb5 14.Qxa8 0-0 would give Black the chance for formidable counterplay.

13.Re1!

This calm continuation packs sufficient wallop that Black is now compelled to exchange queens and go over to a difficult defense.

13...Qxa4 14.Nxa4 Be6 15.Be3

White's positional superiority is becoming steadily more evident. He has an edge in pawns on the queenside, exercises control over the d4 and c5 squares, and is capable of getting hold of the c-file. I would even say that from the strategic aspect the outcome of the game is settled. The more so since Black's a-pawn is hopelessly feeble, while the king is still in the center.

15...0-0

Black is forced to postpone his plans while castling, since it would be too risky to leave the king in the middle of the game.

16.Bc5

The American grandmaster is consistently implementing his idea, planning the exchange of Black's most important piece—the bishop on e7.

16...Rfe8 17.Bxe7 Rxe7 18.b4!

Fixing Black's a-pawn in place and preparing for Nc5, Black has no active plan and is compelled to wait meekly for the situation to develop.

18...Kf8 19.Nc5 Bc8 20.f3

White, is in no hurry to rush things, preferring to strengthen his position gradually. Now he is opening the road to d4 for his king.

20...Rea7

Were Petrosian to exchange rooks, his pieces would be pinned down by the defense of the a-pawn.

21.Re5 Bd7

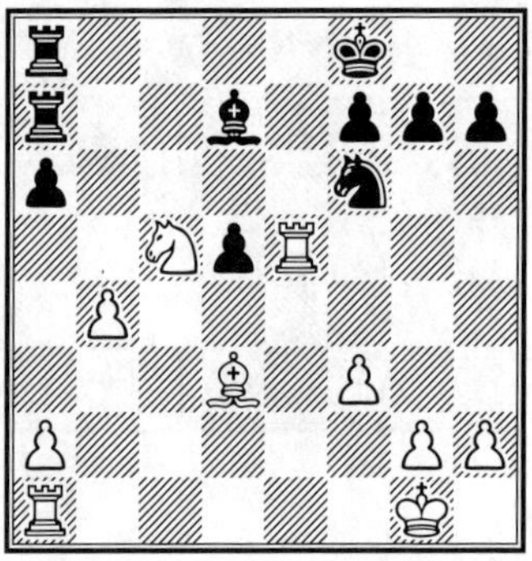

22.Nxd7+

Quite characteristic of Fischer. In exchanging his powerful knight for the bishop, the American grandmaster unerringly calculated that this was the clearest and most economical road to victory. Now all the files are at White's disposal, while no satisfactory defense against the threat of Kf2-e3-d4 can be seen.

22...Rxd7 23.Rc1

Threatening 24.Rc6 Raa7 25. g4 h6 26.h4.

23...Rd6 24.Rc7 Nd7 25.Re2 g6

Black does not start this pawn demonstration on the kingside for the pleasure of it. If for instance 25...a5, then 26.b5, while 25...Nb6 permits White to get another rook on the seventh rank.

26.Kf2 h5 27.f4 h4 28.Kf3 f5 29.Ke3 d4+

Otherwise White's king will occupy the important d4 square.

30.Kd2 Nb6 31.Ree7 Nd5 32.Rf7+ Ke8 33.Rb7 Nxb4

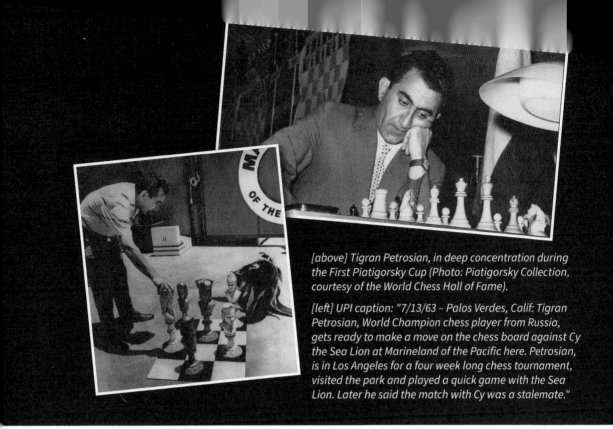

[above] Tigran Petrosian, in deep concentration during the First Piatigorsky Cup (Photo: Piatigorsky Collection, courtesy of the World Chess Hall of Fame).

[left] UPI caption: "7/13/63 – Palos Verdes, Calif: Tigran Petrosian, World Champion chess player from Russia, gets ready to make a move on the chess board against Cy the Sea Lion at Marineland of the Pacific here. Petrosian, is in Los Angeles for a four week long chess tournament, visited the park and played a quick game with the Sea Lion. Later he said the match with Cy was a stalemate."

Note that some sources, two being *Chess Life & Review* (February 1972) and Reuben Fine's *The Final Candidate's Match* (page 27), have Black playing 33...Nxf4 here.

34.Bc4, 1–0.

Because on 34...Nc6 there follows 35.Rg7 Rf6 36.Rg8+ Rf8 37.Bf7+ with mate to follow.

Tigran Petrosian speaks:[1]

The match, as is well known, ended very badly for me. Studying the course of the match carefully, it becomes clear that it divides into two halves, both completely unlike the other. Up to the fifth game, despite the scores being equal, the initiative was on my side. Starting from the sixth game, there seems to be another man playing...

I mentioned earlier in the article that the loser seems to have no moral right to seek the reasons for his failure in side-issues. I myself have never liked to look for excuses for defeat, and always consider that the decisive factor in a contest will be the relative strengths of the players.

The Argentinian government, highly valuing the role which our match had played in popularizing chess in their country, presented Fischer and myself with commemorative medallions. In a word, the hospitality of the Argentinians were unequaled, and I would hold treasured memories of Buenos Aires if only...I had not lost.

[1] Vik L. Vasiliev, *Tigran Petrosian: His Life and Games*, London: Batsford, 1974.

PROGRAM
THE WORLD CHESS
CHAMPIONSHIP MATCH
ICELAND
MÓTSKRÁ GEFIN ÚT AF SKÁKSAMBANDI ÍSLANDS · PUBLISHED BY ICELANDIC CHESS FEDERATION

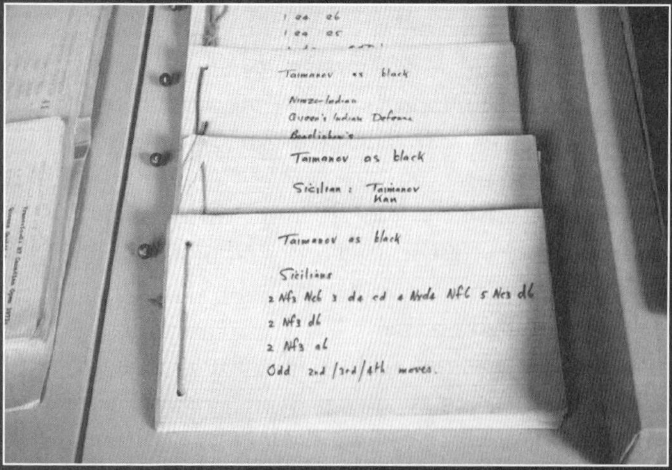

Ed Edmondson made an arrangement with Robert Wade at the conclusion of the Palma de Mallorca Interzonal to prepare reference materials for Fischer during his World Championship run. Approved by Bobby, this relationship extended up to the match in Reykjavík (Courtesy of the Rex and Jeanne Sinquefield Collection).

6
THE FIGHT FOR THE CROWN

GAME 1 AND THE PIVOTAL GAME 13

The match between Fischer and Spassky captured the world's attention in a way no other World Championship has before or since, with the action in Reykjavík the leadoff story in newspapers and television stations around the world for the better part of two months. Fischer's personality had a lot to do with this, as did the drama of an American and Soviet fighting it out during the Cold War.

The effect of the match in the United States was dramatic, with the U.S. Chess Federation's membership climbing from 10,000 to 60,000 in just a couple of years, and tournament attendance skyrocketing. The 1973 U.S. Open set a record with 725 players[1], a figure that is still the third highest ever. The same year the World Open, a mega-tournament that continues to this day, was held for the first time.

This was a great time for professional players in the United States, and not only because of the record prize money in tournaments. Publishers gave generous advances as they churned out chess books, trying to capitalize on the "Fischer Boom." For a period it was possible to earn a good living as a chess teacher as large numbers of beginners flocked to the game. Unfortunately, this golden time was short-lived.

Although the dozens of books published on the 1972 World Championship have extensively examined every aspect of the match, here is a fresh look at the first and pivotal thirteenth games, Games (73) and (74).

When thinking about Bobby Fischer's career, certain moves come readily to mind. In the opening, it might be his trademark 6.Bc4 against the Sicilian, his resurrection of 9.Nh3 in the Two Knights Defense, or his 11...Nh5 in the Modern Benoni. In the middlegame, it would be the start of famous combinations such as 11...Na4! versus Donald Byrne in the Game of the Century, or 19.Rf6! against Pal Benko in the 1963/64 U.S. Championship. But arguably Bobby's most famous move was in the endgame, his ill-fated capture of Spassky's h-pawn in the first game of their World Championship match.

[1] *Chess Life & Review* 1973, (p. 574).

(73) Nimzo-Indian
Boris Spassky – Fischer
Reykjavík (1), 1972

1.d4 Nf6 2.c4 e6 3.Nf3 d5 4.Nc3 Bb4 5.e3 0-0 6.Bd3 c5 7.0-0 Nc6 8.a3 Ba5 9.Ne2 dxc4 10.Bxc4 Bb6 11.dxc5 Qxd1 12.Rxd1 Bxc5 13.b4 Be7 14.Bb2 Bd7 15.Rac1 Rfd8 16.Ned4 Nxd4 17.Nxd4 Ba4 18.Bb3 Bxb3 19.Nxb3 Rxd1+ 20.Rxd1 Rc8 21.Kf1 Kf8 22.Ke2 Ne4 23.Rc1 Rxc1 24.Bxc1 f6 25.Na5 Nd6 26.Kd3 Bd8 27.Nc4 Bc7 28.Nxd6 Bxd6 29.b5

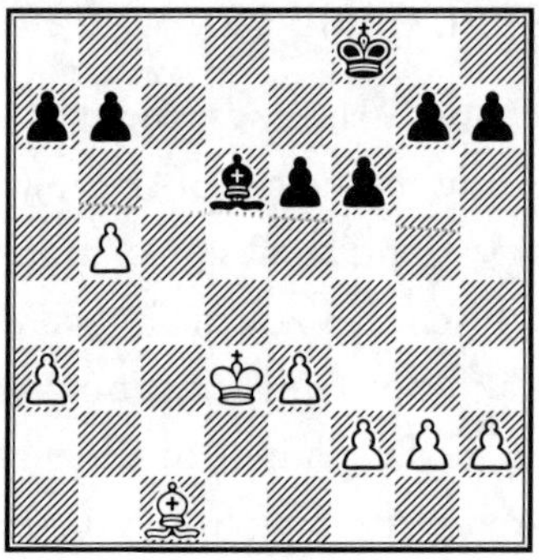

The game has been dull up to this point, but here Fischer uncorks a move that is still talked about close to half a century later.

29...Bxh2?!

Even club players know better than to take a poison pawn, but is it actually poisoned? Has Bobby seen something that Boris overlooked or did he miscalculate?

William Lombardy, in a talk at the Mechanics' Institute Chess Club on September 19, 2017, was asked to explain 29...Bxh2?! He answered it was a typical Fischer move, played to preserve possible winning chances. Rather than acquiesce to a draw in a few more moves, Fischer wanted to present some practical problems for Spassky.

A similar explanation is offered by Ivan Sokolov when annotating the game Korchnoi–Fischer, Sousse (Interzonal) 1967, in his book *Chess Middlegame Strategies*. He writes after White's twenty-first move:

[Sokolov] "A critical moment. Following the 'logic path,' Fischer is worried the game will peter out to a draw, so he sacrifices an exchange in order to keep the tension! Is it necessary? 'NO!' Is it Black's best move? Probably also 'NO.' Does it keep the tension, making the decision making process difficult (and hence mistakes possible)? 'YES!' Does it involve mutual risk ...with Fischer confident in himself and believing he will NOT be the one to err? 'YES' In some ways this resembles the famous Spassky–Fischer game one from the Reykjavík 1972 match with Fischer taking 29...Bxh2?! His decision here, however, is much sounder and White's task far from easy.

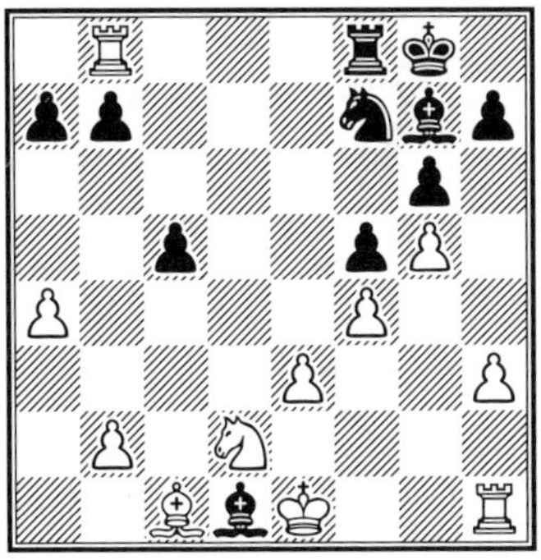

Korchnoi–Fischer, Sousse (Interzonal) 1967. Here Fischer sacrificed the exchange with 21...Bxa4 instead of playing 21...Rxb8.

The problem with 29...Bxh2?!, is that while Black may still draw with best play, it doesn't offer any realistic winning opportunities. It's not a practical decision. After the text Bobby is playing for two results–a draw or loss."

30.g3 h5 31.Ke2 h4 32.Kf3 Ke7

More than one annotator has speculated that Bobby probably planned 32...h3 33.Kg4! Bg1 34.Kxh3 Bxf2, but overlooked 35.Bd2!, when the bishop is trapped. It seems hard to believe Fischer could have overlooked something as simple this, but this is as good an explanation as any.

33.Kg2 hxg3 34.fxg3 Bxg3 35.Kxg3 Kd6 36.a4?

Kasparov criticizes this move in the volume dedicated to Fischer in his *My Great Predecessors* series. He quotes analysis by Ólafsson starting with 36.Kg4! as the path to victory.

36... Kd5 37.Ba3 Ke4 38.Bc5 a6 39.b6

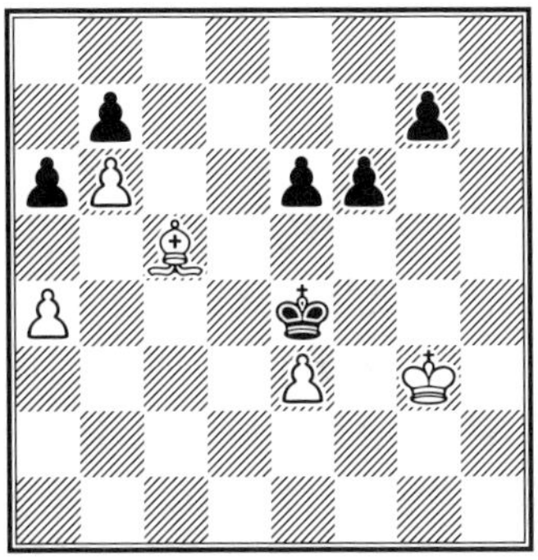

39...f5?

39...e5 40.Kg4 g6 41.a5 (41.Kg3 Kd3=) 41...Kd5 42.Be7 f5+ 43.Kg5 f4 44.exf4 exf4 45.Kxf4 Ke6 46.Bh4 Kd7 heading to c8 with a fortress was the last opportunity to draw. Sam Shankland overlooked this fortress resource, resigning in a similar position against Anish Giri at the Tata Steel Masters in 2019. The final position was a theoretical draw.

Lombardy saw this was drawing during the game, mentioning it to Fischer in the car ride back to the hotel after the game was adjourned. He remembers Bobby didn't say anything during the match, only acknowledging it after winning the title. Fischer had put it on the backburner, but his mind was always working on chess.

Many players do not respond well to the loss of a game, particularly when they have missed a chance to save it near the end. It's not uncommon to sleep poorly afterwards, replaying the painful experience over and over. This doesn't appear to have ever been a problem for Bobby.

40.Kh4 f4 41.exf4 Kxf4 42.Kh5 Kf5 43.Be3 Ke4 44.Bf2 Kf5 45.Bh4 e5 46.Bg5 e4 47.Be3 Kf6 48.Kg4 Ke5 49.Kg5 Kd5 50.Kf5 a5 51.Bf2 g5 52.Kxg5 Kc4 53.Kf5 Kb4 54.Kxe4 Kxa4 55.Kd5 Kb5 56.Kd6, 1–0.

The match had many memorable games, but perhaps none more than the thirteenth game, which Botvinnik claimed was Fischer's best achievement of the match.

William Lombardy, in his Mechanics' talk, pointed to this as the game that effectively ended the match. Spassky had started out with a gift point (29...Bh2?!) and a forfeit in game two, but after six games Fischer was already in the lead.

Wins in games eight and ten put Bobby three points ahead, but Boris fought back. He crushed Fischer's Poison Pawn Najdorf in game eleven and held comfortably in game twelve. Had he won game 13 Spassky would have only been a point behind with momentum on his side. Instead he lost and Fischer once again had a big lead.

---

(74) Alekhine
Boris Spassky – Fischer
Reykjavík (13) 1972

1.e4 Nf6 2.e5 Nd5 3.d4 d6 4.Nf3 g6 5.Bc4 Nb6 6.Bb3 Bg7 7.Nbd2 0-0 8.h3 a5 9.a4 dxe5 10.dxe5 Na6 11.0-0 Nc5 12.Qe2 Qe8 13.Ne4 Nbxa4 14.Bxa4 Nxa4 15.Re1 Nb6 16.Bd2 a4 17.Bg5 h6 18.Bh4 Bf5 19.g4 Be6 20.Nd4 Bc4 21.Qd2 Qd7 22.Rad1 Rfe8 23.f4 Bd5 24.Nc5 Qc8 25.Qc3 e6 26.Kh2 Nd7 27.Nd3 c5 28.Nb5 Qc6 29.Nd6 Qxd6 30.exd6 Bxc3 31.bxc3 f6 32.g5 hxg5 33.fxg5 f5 34.Bg3 Kf7 35.Ne5+ Nxe5 36.Bxe5 b5 37.Rf1 Rh8 38.Bf6 a3 39.Rf4 a2 40.c4 Bxc4 41.d7 Bd5 42.Kg3

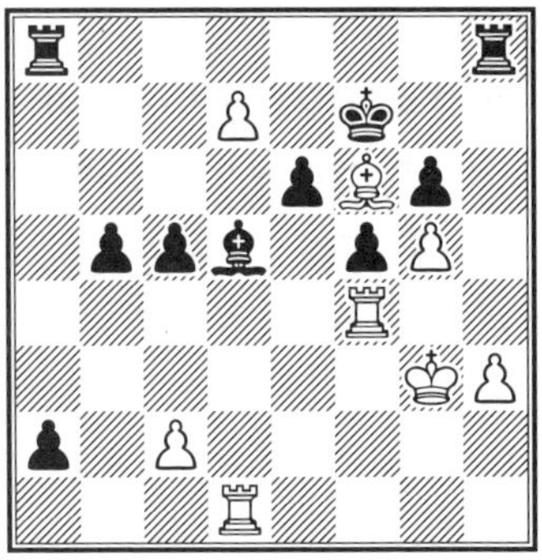

This was the sealed move. Lombardy in his Mechanics' talk mentioned Fischer had a significant time advantage (forty-two minutes) when the game was adjourned. He and Bobby were unable to find a win in their analysis of the adjournment—the main line was a draw. What to do? Lombardy counseled Bobby to use up some of his extra time in the hope of getting Spassky to drop his guard.

42...Ra3+

Fischer came to the adjournment twenty-five minutes late for the second session per Lombardy's strategy.

The time control for the match was forty moves in two and a half hours. Then sixteen moves an hour. The resumption of game 13 was a four-hour Friday adjournment session, which started at 2:30PM. The next two time controls were at move fifty-six (3:30) and move seventy-two (4:30).

43.c3 Rha8 44.Rh4 e5 45.Rh7+ Ke6 46.Re7+ Kd6 47.Rxe5 Rxc3+ 48.Kf2 Rc2+ 49.Ke1 Kxd7 50.Rexd5+ Kc6 51.Rd6+ Kb7 52.Rd7+ Ka6 53.R7d2 Rxd2 54.Kxd2 b4 55.h4 Kb5 56.h5 c4 57.Ra1 gxh5 58.g6 h4 59.g7 h3 60.Be7 Rg8 61.Bf8 h2 62.Kc2 Kc6 63.Rd1 b3+ 64.Kc3 h1Q 65.Rxh1 Kd5 66.Kb2 f4 67.Rd1+ Ke4 68.Rc1

At this point Spassky had seven minutes left to make the last four moves of the time control.

68...Kd3

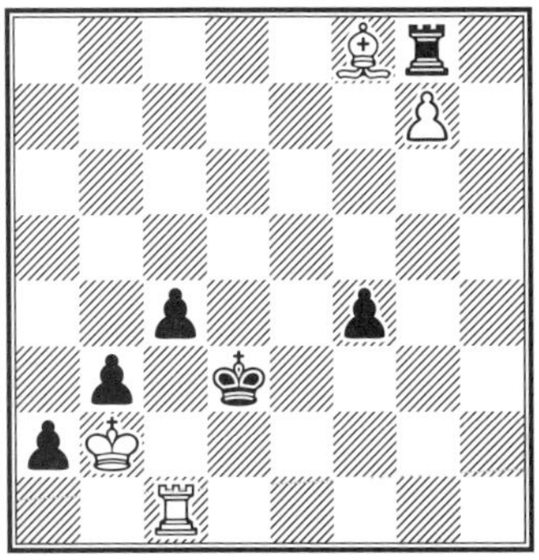

Spassky went to the rest room after move sixty-eight and then rushed back to the board where he instantly made his ill-fated sixty-ninth move. Seconds later he grabbed his hair realizing he had blundered.

69.Rd1+?

69.Rc3+ Kd4 70.Rf3 c3+ 71.Ka1 c2 72.Rxf4+ Kc3 73.Rf3+ Kd2 74.Ba3 was the drawing line.

69...Ke2 70.Rc1 f3 71.Bc5 Rxg7 72.Rxc4 Rd7 73.Re4+ Kf1 74.Bd4 f2, 0–1.

After the match Lombardy wrote an article for *Sports Illustrated* titled "A Mystery Wrapped in an Enigma," which caused Fischer to end their friendship." Lombardy wrote about game 13:[1]

> At 3AM Bobby turned suddenly and said: "Call Kavalek." The phone was at his left hand, but he seemed to fear the instrument. I protested, given the hour, but Bobby insisted, "Call him, call him."
>
> Kavalek picked up the receiver. "Lubos, sorry to awaken you," I said lamely. "Bobby would like you to come to look at the adjournment." Lubos arrived within minutes. The cycle of "Look," "No," "What do you think?" "Let me look at it alone" became a refrain. The playoff of game thirteen, as on every Friday, was set for 2:30PM. Bobby had not tired of analysis until 8AM. What's more, by noon he was up struggling with that beguiling position. There were chances, but the win, he knew, was just as far away as ever.
>
> Although Kavalek and I knew Bobby's plan of attack, Boris seemed uncomfortable when the game continued. The Russian nervously circled the table while Bobby considered this move, then that. A position was reached which many experts judged drawn. At this stage Bobby decided to go into a huddle. He stewed about ten minutes over move sixty-two, another ten over sixty-three, and then an hour over his sixty-fourth turn! Time spent in finding the best try in a drawn position. And suddenly Bobby had won.
>
> Watching the game's progress over the TV monitor in the lobby, the Soviet seconds were stunned by the result. Nikolai Krogius sadly admitted that Boris had erred on his sixty-ninth turn. "I didn't make enough of the fact that Fischer had consumed an entire hour over only one move," Spassky said later.
>
> Indeed he hadn't. Boris was jittery, waiting for Bobby to move. He seemed to prefer not to reason that Bobby might be weaving a trap. More often than not, he stayed away from the table instead of bolting himself to his swivel seat and studying the position while Bobby pondered. Boris popped in and out of the curtained entrance to the backstage. During Bobby's prolonged think, the champion, on occasion, sauntered over to the board and gazed down at the-position with a studied expression of boredom on his countenance.

---

[1] William Lombardy, *Sports Illustrated*, "A Mystery Wrapped in an Enigma," January 21, 1974.

GAME 13, AUGUST 10–11, 1972

(ar) indicates the player's arrival. (s) indicates a sealed move.

Spassky	Fischer
(White)	(Black)
(ar) (-0:02)	(ar) (0:06)

	White		Black	
1.	e4	(0:00)	Nf6	(0:07)

(Spassky left when he made his move and returned two minutes after Fischer made his move.)

	White		Black	
2.	e5	(0:02)	Nd5	(0:07)
3.	d4	(0:02)	d6	(0:07)
4.	Nf3	(0:03)	g6	(0:08)
5.	Bc4	(0:05)	Nb6	(0:08)
6.	Bb3	(0:06)	Bg7	(0:08)
7.	Nbd2	(0:23)	0-0	(0:14)
8.	h3	(0:25)	a5	(0:22)
9.	a4	(0:33)	dxe5	(0:25)
10.	dxe5	(0:33)	Na6	(0:26)
11.	0-0	(0:47)	Nc5	(0:35)
12.	Qe2	(0:50)	Qe8	(0:51)
13.	Ne4	(0:58)	Nbxa4	(0:54)
14.	Bxa4	(1:04)	Nxa4	(0:56)
15.	Re1	(1:08)	Nb6	(0:58)
16.	Bd2	(1:12)	a4	(0:59)
17.	Bg5	(1:14)	h6	(1:06)
18.	Bh4	(1:26)	Bf5	(1:16)
19.	g4	(1:29)	Be6	(1:16)
20.	Nd4	(1:31)	Bc4	(1:17)
21.	Qd2	(1:35)	Qd7	(1:19)
22.	Rad1	(1:37)	Rfe8	(1:23)
23.	f4	(1:38)	Bd5	(1:30)
24.	Nc5	(1:40)	Qc8	(1:31)
25.	Qc3	(1:51)	e6	(1:38)
26.	Kh2	(1:57)	Nd7	(1:40)
27.	Nd3	(2:00)	c5	(1:41)
28.	Nb5	(2:00)	Qc6	(1:42)
29.	Nd6	(2:04)	Qxd6	
30.	exd6		Bxc3	(1:42)
31.	bxc3	(2:04)	f6	(1:46)
32.	g5	(2:05)	hxg5	(1:47)
33.	fxg5	(2:05)	f5	(1:47)
34.	Bg3	(2:06)	Kf7	(1:50)
35.	Ne5+	(2:07)	Nxe5	(1:50)
36.	Bxe5	(2:07)	b5	(1:56)
37.	Rf1	(2:08)	Rh8	(2:02)
38.	Bf6	(2:12)	a3	(2:04)
39.	Rf4	(2:22)	a2	(2:08)
40.	c4	(2:27)	Bxc4	(2:09)
41.	d7	(2:36)	Bd5	(2:16)
42.	Kg3(s)	(3:08)		
		(ar)		(2:41)
42.	...		Ra3+	(2:42)
43.	c3	(3:08)	Rha8	(2:42)
44.	Rh4	(3:10)	e5	(2:42)
45.	Rh7+	(3:11)	Ke6	(2:42)
46.	Re7+		Kd6	
47.	Rxe5	(3:12)	Rxc3+	
48.	Kf2	(3:13)	Rc2+	
49.	Ke1	(3:13)	Kxd7	
50.	Rexd5+	(3:14)	Kc6	
51.	Rd6+	(3:16)	Kb7	(2:43)
52.	Rd7+	(3:20)	Ka6	(2:44)
53.	R7d2	(3:23)	Rxd2	
54.	Kxd2	(3:25)	b4	
55.	h4	(3:26)	Kb5	
56.	h5	(3:26)	c4	(2:45)
57.	Ra1	(3:37)	gxh5	(2:48)
58.	g6	(3:39)	h4	(2:49)
59.	g7	(3:50)	h3	(2:50)
60.	Be7	(4:08)	Rg8	(3:11)
61.	Bf8	(4:11)	h2	(3:49)
62.	Kc2	(4:11)	Kc6	(3:51)
63.	Rd1	(4:13)	b3+	(3:57)
64.	Kc3	(4:15)	h1Q	(4:02)
65.	Rxh1	(4:15)	Kd5	(4:02)
66.	Kb2	(4:18)	f4	(4:03)
67.	Rd1+	(4:19)	Ke4	(4:05)
68.	Rc1	(4:23)	Kd3	(4:06)
69.	Rd1+	(4:26)	Ke2	(4:07)
70.	Rc1	(4:27)	f3	(4:08)
71.	Bc5	(4:27)	Rxg7	(4:11)
72.	Rxc4	(4:28)	Rd7	(4:14)
73.	Re4+	(4:45)	Kf1	(4:15)
74.	Bd4	(4:49)	f2	
			0-1	

Note: The time used for both players during most of the games is posted at a website called The Crack Team! (http://www.crackteam.org/tag/chess/). Above is the time record for game 13 which doesn't always agree with Lombardy's recollections.

Although Fischer was twenty-five minutes late for the second session, he still had forty-five extra minutes for the second time control, which ended on move fifty-six. Bobby played the first eighteen moves of the next adjournment quite rapidly, until Spassky's 60. Be7 which caused him to consume thirty-eight minutes on his clock in finding a reply, his longest think of the match. Bobby spent an additional twenty-one minutes on the previous move that allowed his rook to be imprisoned, which makes it likely that the fifty-nine minutes he spent on moves fifty-nine and sixty was the longest for any two-move sequence in his career. All told the game ran nine hours and four minutes.

WHO WAS BOBBY'S SECOND?

Mark Wieder wrote:[1]

> When the musical *Chess* was playing on Broadway in New York in the mid-'80s, I attended with Bill. The show is (very) loosely based on the Fischer–Spassky match. The American player is abrasive and self-centered, the Russian polite and sympathetic. The American's second is also his girlfriend, who in the course of the play falls in love with the Russian (I did say *very* loosely). When the show ended, a man sitting right in front of us turned and asked, "Who was Bobby's second in Iceland?," to which Lombardy answered, "I was."

For William Lombardy the answer was simple, as he stated in his memoir:[2]

> I was the only person on the intimate inside during that Match of the Century, I choose to say very little because I do not delight in satisfying idle curiosity! As for my "uselessness" on the technical side of chess at Reykjavík, let me point out that there were fourteen adjourned games. Bobby and I worked together on those adjourned positions without making a technical error! Beyond that I bested the Soviet team psychology, even though the team had a so-called professional psychologist. For little renumeration, I dedicated my services in the Icelandic capital to guarantee that Bobby followed through and finished the match victoriously.

Frank Brady wrote in *Endgame* that Lombardy was not Bobby's only second, and that Argentinian Grandmaster Miguel Quinteros was also part of the team. Other say Quinteros was only present for part of the match and was in Iceland solely as Bobby's friend and supporter.

On another note, Tony Saidy quipped, "...Bobby never had seconds, he would consider the ideas of whomever [referring to grandmasters] walked into the room."

1 Mark Wieder, "In Memoriam, for Better and for Worse: Bill Lombardy (1937–2017)," *New In Chess*, 2017 #8, (p. 64–69).

2 William Lombardy, *Understanding Chess: My System, My Games, My Life*. In association with Russell Enterprises, 2011, (p. 218–219).

To complicate matters further in 2012, Lubos Kavalek stated in the pages of *New In Chess* that he was Fischer's second from the adjournment of game 13 until the end of the match:[1]

> In Reykjavík Bobby had two seconds: first it was Lombardy (the official one). I took over during the adjournment of game thirteen (Alekhine's Defense) and stayed with him till the end. I came to Reykjavík as a reporter for the Voice of America and reported on the games till the end. I came late to the match, game eight was the first I reported on from Iceland. Bobby listened to my broadcasts in Reykjavík and I got the first lengthy interview from him after he won (a small part is in the U.S. Chess Hall of Fame). Somehow it didn't bother him to ask me to analyze with him at the same time
>
> Brady is mistaken when he describes Miguel Quinteros as one of Bobby's seconds. The funny thing is Brady claims he was in our hotel all the time and yet Quinteros only came near the end of the match. He never took part in our analysis. He flew with Bobby to New York. I believed Quinteros was just Bobby's friend in 1971.
>
> We talk about Bill Lombardy. It was difficult for him to accept he was not what he was in 1960. It led to many unpleasant situations in the tournaments he played at the end of his playing career. I had no problem with him, although he probably didn't like being pushed away during the match.
>
> I thought the reason for the Bobby and Ed Edmondson split was the attention Ed was receiving and the implication that he was responsible for Bobby's success.

Throughout his career, in stark contrast to the Soviets, Bobby was known for not having seconds—preferring to do his own opening preparation and adjournment analysis. There were exceptions: Lombardy accompanied Bobby to the Portorož Interzonal in 1958; Bent Larsen seconded him a year later at the 1959 Candidates; and Arthur Bisguier helped Fischer and Pal Benko at the 1962 Candidates. In the first two instances the seconds doubled as chaperons as Bobby was still a minor.

Fischer did not have a second for his Candidates matches with Taimanov, Larsen, nor Petrosian, and for a long time there was a question of who would accompany him to Reykjavík. Correspondence between Fischer and Ed Edmondson (before he was removed from his duties) indicates that Fischer's first choice was Svetozar Gligorić with Larry Evans the backup, but they declined. Both had made previous commitments to do books on the match (and in Evans case, also television work for *ABC's Wide World of Sports*).

The U.S. Chess Federation had budgeted for the position and was paying the second directly, so it was not money out of Bobby's pocket, but up to the

[1] *New In Chess*, 2012 #6, (pp. 60–68).

beginning of the match the position was not filled, as Lombardy wrote in *Sports Illustrated*:[1]

> There were no long-range plans for me to serve as Bobby's second in Iceland. At the time the subject came up he had already missed the opening ceremonies in Reykjavík and nearly everyone was pessimistic about the chances of his appearing at the championship. I received a message to phone Dr. Anthony Saidy, a chess friend of Bobby's and son of the co-author of *Finian's Rainbow*. I guessed that Fischer might be holed up with the Saidys, and he was—he came to the telephone. I tried to convince him to go to Iceland, but he was noncommittal. "What about you? Can you come?" he asked. I told him I was committed to covering the event on cable TV. "You haven't signed anything, have you?" I had not.

Lombardy would prove to be a wise choice. While he was no longer the world-class talent he had been from 1958–1960, when he was one of the top fifteen players in the world, Lombardy was still a strong grandmaster with a deep understanding of the game.

The years in the priesthood had limited Lombardy's time to study chess and keep up on opening theory, and in that respect, Kavalek would have been more helpful—although in truth Bobby never needed help with openings. In 1972 Kavalek's rating of 2555 was only slightly higher, than Lombardy's 2520. However, Kavalek was a professional player who was improving quickly and by January 1974 he was number ten in the world with a FIDE rating of 2625.

Still, Lombardy had plenty to offer. The role of a second is not only to convey chess information. Often it's just as important to make sure the player is feeling confident and at ease. Lombardy, who had known Fischer for close to twenty years and watched him climb the mountain to the World Championship match, knew Bobby and his moods well. If he did nothing more than persuade Bobby to play game three Lombardy would have earned his keep and more.

In the end, what it comes down to is William Lombardy was paid by the USCF, put in long hours of work with Fischer, and should be considered Bobby's "official" second. It's clear that Lubos Kavalek helped Fischer in many critical adjournments in the second half of the match and therefore has claiming rights to be called one of Fischer's seconds. Miguel Quinteros has never spoken on the subject so it's a matter of hearsay as to how much input or influence he had.

---

[1] William Lombardy, *Sports Illustrated*, "A Mystery Wrapped in an Enigma," January 21, 1974.

PART SEVEN

the Dark Years

Bobby Fischer receiving his proclamation from Mayor Lindsay with Anthony Saidy on the lower left. Next to Saidy is his mother Marie, who took good care of Bobby when he stayed with the Saidy family before departing for Iceland.

1
A BRIEF PERIOD OF SUNLIGHT BEFORE THE DARKNESS

Fischer was in the limelight the first six months after he won the title. His first public appearance after being crowned World Champion was for "Bobby Fischer Day," September 22, 1972 at the New York City Hall. There had initially been talk of a parade, but Fischer declined the offer as he did the key to the city, remarking; "I live here, what do I need a key for?"[1]

Fischer agreed to a public ceremony where more than one thousand well-wishers turned up to watch Mayor Lindsay award Bobby a gold medal and proclaim him "the greatest master of them all." The World Champion then gave a short but witty speech (written by Anthony Saidy), which he delivered flawlessly.

> Mr. Mayor and Friends,
>
> First of all, I want to deny a vicious rumor that's been going around—I think it was started by Moscow. It is not true that Henry Kissinger phoned me during the match to tell me the moves.
>
> Chess is a great game, a game and sport for the mind.
>
> I never thought I'd see the day when chess would be all over the front pages here, but confined only to one paragraph in *Pravda*.[2] I guess that's my fault. It just depends who's winning.

The Associated Press' film clip shows Bobby accepting the award with Grandmasters William Lombardy and Miguel Quinteros standing next to him.[3]

The day after the event John Hess writing for *The New York Times*[4] reported:

> Fischer was unexpectedly accessible, circulating actively, shaking hands and signing autographs so busily that several times he snatched at a reporter's pen under the impression that it was being tendered.

Hess also stated that Bobby replied patiently to the standard questions about what he intended to do with his prize money, where and when he would play

1 Although Fischer moved to Los Angeles in 1968 he still considered himself a New Yorker.

2 *Pravda* ("Truth"), the Russian newspaper that was the official voice of the Soviet Communist Party from 1918 to 1991.

3 Available on YouTube: https://youtu.be/cMKwPKOCzNY.

4 John L. Hess, *The New York Times*, September 23, 1972.

next, and if he was still studying hard. But there was one exception to the usual exchange that foreshadowed Bobby's future lawsuit against Brad Darrach.

Hess continued:

> Fischer told a reporter that the story he had sold *Life* magazine an exclusive interview during the match with Spassky was "a dirty lie."
>
> "I was busy," he said. "If I'd given an interview to everybody that asked, I'd have lost the match."
>
> In addition to the city's Gold Medal, the champion received from Mayor Lindsay a parchment proclaiming yesterday Bobby Fischer Day in honor of "this unique, outstanding native of New York" and a leather-bound scrapbook of clippings about the Spassky–Fischer match.[1]
>
> Fischer gave the Mayor a pocket chess set, and commended the game as mental exercise.
>
> "It's full of discipline, isn't it?" asked Mr. Lindsay.
>
> "Not if you love the game," the champion replied.

A private person not known to seek the limelight, Bobby followed this event with several TV appearances. What motivated Fischer to step into the public eye? Did he enjoy the attention? Did the Worldwide Church encourage him? Whatever the reason, it's striking how quickly Bobby traded his status as a highly-visible celebrity for that of a recluse.

Early in his career, as a "boy wonder" he made two nationwide appearances on American television, both times on programs where the panelists had to guess his occupation—on the first occasion, *I've Got A Secret in 1958,* the panel was unsuccessful, but by 1961 on *Take a Good Look,* they succeeded.

Fischer's victory over Taimanov escaped the attention of the mainstream media, but after he defeated Larsen in July 1971, they started to take notice with Bobby appearing on *The Dick Cavett Show* and *The Mike Douglas Show* the following month. At the end of 1971, once he earned the right to play for the World Championship, attention on him increased dramatically. He appeared on *The David Frost Show* in early 1972 and that spring was a guest on *60 Minutes,* which introduced him to millions of non-chess playing Americans.

Dick Cavett, whom Bobby had gotten along with particularly well, invited him back for a second appearance, and then for a third time after Fischer won the crown. Watching the interviews Cavett did with Bobby it's clear the two had a special connection. Cavett's relaxed style put Fischer at ease and brought out his sense of humor. Fischer was funny, charming. and completely natural. Cavett who had no chess background, asked him intelligent questions and treated him with a respect not shown by other interviewers.

---

[1] The medal and scrapbook were among the items Fischer said were lost after his storage locker was auctioned off in early 1999. See page 609–619, The Day Bobby Lost his Treasures.

Cavett seemed to have understood, appreciated, and had great empathy for Bobby. This is apparent from the piece he wrote for *The New York Times,* after Fischer's death. Cavett was straightforward and wrote with great emotion. Following are some excerpts:[1]

> Among this year's worst news, for me, was the death of Bobby Fischer.
>
> Telling a friend this, I got, "Are you out of your bloody mind? He was a Nazi-praising raving lunatic and anti-Semite. Death is too good for him."
>
> He did, indeed, become all that. But none of it describes the man I knew.
>
> Towering genius, riches, international fame and a far from normal childhood might be too heady a mix for anyone to handle. For him they proved fatal.
>
> I'm still sad about his death. In our three encounters, I became quite fond of him. ...
>
> We ordinary mortals can only try to imagine what it might feel like to be both young and so greatly gifted at a complex art. And to be better at it than any other living being, past or present. There are plenty of geniuses and lots of famous people, but few are both. Is anyone really capable of surviving such a double burden? ...
>
> Until the advent of Bobby Fischer, my image of a young chess genius was not flattering. I pictured a sort of wizened and unpopular youth, small of frame, reclusive, short, with messy hair, untended acne, thick glasses and shirt sticking out in back...
>
> Getting Fischer on my show that first time, before the big match, was considered a major catch at the time. If anyone in the audience shared my image of what a chess genius probably looked like, Bobby's entrance erased it....
>
> There appeared, somewhat disconcerted, a tall and handsome lad with football-player shoulders, impeccably suited, a little awkward of carriage and unsure how to negotiate the unfamiliarity of the set, the bright lights, the wearing of make-up, the band music, the hand-shaking and the thundering ovation–all at the same time...
>
> And there were the eyes.
>
> Cameras fail to convey the effect of his eyes when they were looking at you. A bit of Svengali perhaps, but vulnerable. And only the slightest hint of a sort of theatrical menace, the menace that so disconcerted his opponents...
>
> I'm surprised in writing this how much emotion there still is in the subject for me. There's no story like it: genius kid, precocious, plunged into triumphant victory, money and world fame—no one under thirty should be subjected to fame—then gradual decline into raving lunatic. "Those whom the gods would destroy, they first make mad."

---

[1] Dick Cavett, *The New York Times,* "Was It Only a Game?", February 8, 2008. The complete article can be read at: https://opinionator.blogs.nytimes.com/2008/02/08/was-it-only-a-game/.

That fall, after winning the title, Fischer made the rounds of the talk shows. He traded jokes with Bob Hope like he was a natural comedian and, whether scripted or ad-libbed pulled off each appearance in fine style. Seeing Bobby then was to see him at his best—happy and on top of the world.

Fischer appeared on the following TV Shows (including two appearances prior the World Champion run):

I've Got A Secret (March 26, 1958)
Take A Good Look (February 9, 1961)
The Dick Cavett Show (August 5, 1971)
The Mike Douglas Show (August 31, 1971)
The Dick Cavett Show (January 4, 1972)
The David Frost Show (January 28, 1972)
60 Minutes with Mike Wallace (April 9, 1972)
The Bob Hope Special (October 5, 1972)
The Tonight Show with Johnny Carson (November 8, 1972)
The Dick Cavett Show (December 21, 1972)
Dinah's Place with Dinah Shore (February 1, 1973)

Fischer's television appearances made him a household name, but the disruption to what previously had been a normal part of his life—showing up at a chess tournament as a spectator—weighed on him. Fischer's visit to the 1972 American Open—then in its eighth year and attracting a record attendance of 428 players[1]—is an example of the commotion his celebrity now caused:

> One of those spectators was none other than the new World Champion, Bobby Fischer. He made his appearance without fanfare during the last round [November 26]. However, he no sooner entered the room than he was enveloped in a swarm of autograph seekers and camera buffs. I'm sure that Bobby would have enjoyed chatting with some of his friends who were present, and to have watched and studied some of the games. But this was not to be. His appearance at a chess tournament has the same effect as the arrival of a great movie star at a Hollywood premiere. Such is the burden that accompanies fame! Bobby endured the accolades of his admirers for about twenty minutes and then departed.

Seattle expert Mike Schemm, who was a participant in the 1972 American Open remembered Fischer's visit as if it were yesterday:

> I am sure you remember me saying I sat next to Joni Mitchell, but did not remember her. I do remember Bobby Fischer. He took a circle of the room. I was at the end of a row at the edge of the room. He stopped and spent

[1] According to Carl Budd, *Chess Life & Review*, February 1973, (p. 73).

> perhaps five or ten seconds looking at my game. A small thing, but I will never forget. I had a worse position in a gambit opening I had played, but I won the game. I remember the sound was like a beehive when Fischer walked in. He took a tour of the room and left. He was only there for a few minutes.

Bobby was no longer a private citizen who could come and go as he pleased. Unlike any other chess player before or since, he had lost his privacy. In retrospect, maybe it wasn't so surprising that soon after the American Open he disappeared from public life.

Fischer attended one other tournament in November of 1972, but after his experience at the American Open he understandably adopted a lower profile. David Levy, writing in *Chess Life & Review*[1] mentioned that one of the spectators for the last round of the great San Antonio event won by Anatoly Karpov, Tigran Petrosian, and Lajos Portisch, was Bobby Fischer. Fischer had flown in on the private jet of Garner Ted Armstrong who was in town for three days for Worldwide Church of God business. *Chess Life & Review* published a small photo of Bobby watching the games with binoculars. This would be his last public appearance for almost twenty years.

Stanley R. Rader, the number three person in the Worldwide Church of God hierarchy below Herbert and Garner Ted Armstrong, organized a well-attended press conference for Bobby at his home in Beverly Hills. The event, held on December 5, 1972, was reported on by *Los Angeles Times* staff writer Charles Maher. His angle for the story was how reserved Fischer was, in contrast to the match in Reykjavík a few months earlier.

Rader, who served as Bobby's business manager at the time, was quoted as saying. "Oh, Bobby's potential is much greater than that." This was a reference to a report that swimmer Mark Spitz, who had won seven gold medals earlier in the year, might make up to five million dollars in endorsements.

One of the less publicized events Fischer attended before going into seclusion was a banquet held in his honor at the Los Angeles Press Club on December 12, 1972 (it was announced in Isaac Kashdan's *Los Angeles Times* column two days before). The event was filmed, but regrettably, the footage no longer exists.

John Blackstone, who played for the U.S. Student team in 1968 and nearly beat Bobby in a clock simul in Davis, California, in 1964, recalled that evening:

> I and my wife (Julie), Don Steers, Rita Walker, and Earl Pruner all went to his banquet at the Los Angeles Press Club after he had won the world title. After the end of it, I and my party waited for him in the parking lot. When he came out with two women (one on each arm) I walked up to him and said you probably do not remember me. His reply was "Hello John. How

[1] *Chess Life & Review*, February 1973, (p. 66).

> have you been?" I then proceeded to ask if he would sign the books that he had written and he did so gladly. He then got into the limo with the two women and off he went. I never saw him again.

Two good friends of Fischer died in 1973, just a few months apart. Bobby's thoughtful responses show he was still engaging with his friends.

Alexander Liepnieks died in April. Liepnieks had directed the 1955 U.S. Junior Championship in Lincoln, Nebraska, and Bobby stayed with his family during the tournament. Alex and Bobby stayed in touch over the years and reunited in 1972 when Liepnieks served as Bobby's Russian translator in Reykjavík.

Liepnieks published the dual language (Latvian and English) magazine *Sacha Pasaule* for close to twenty years. Bobby was a subscriber to this journal, which published games that opened 1.e4 e5 2.Nf3 f5—has any other World Champions studied the Latvian Gambit as attentively as Bobby?

The following letter appeared in the May–June 1973 issue of *Sacha Pasaule*:

> AN INSPIRING EXAMPLE TO ME
>
> Thank you for your note informing me of your father's death. I was very sorry to hear this because I considered him to be a good friend. His enthusiasm, good will, dedication and love of chess was an inspiring example to me. And I am sure to many others.
>
> I have certainly enjoyed *Chess World* [*Sacha Pasaule*] very much over the years and especially the section on the Latvian Gambit, which was highly entertaining and instructive.
>
> It is my sincere hope that someone will follow in your father's footsteps and continue the monthly publication of this fine magazine. Again please accept my condolences.
>
> Sincerely,
> Bobby Fischer

Leonid Stein died on the 4th of July. Bobby sent the following telegram to the Soviet Chess Federation:

> I am stunned by the premature death of Leonid Stein—the remarkable international grandmaster and good friend. I express my condolences to his family and to all chess brotherhood.
>
> Sincerely,
>
> Bobby Fischer

Fischer and Stein met only a few times: the 1962 and 1967 Interzonals, the 1966 Havana Olympiad, and the USSR versus the World match in 1970, but that and the lack of a common language didn't stop them from being friends. They recognized in the other a total love of chess.

Mikhail Tal described how Stein and Fischer almost played a match:[1]

> During the Havana Olympiad in 1966, I met Leonid Stein and Robert Fischer at the seafront; they were talking and gesticulating lively. Both grandmasters were busy with an important problem: they remembered the position from their blitz games they played five years ago at Stockholm! And they argued, mixing Russian and English words, who was better.
>
> This argument continued until the next day, when the Cuban peoples' hero, Che Guevara[2], joined it. He offered them to play ten blitz games immediately. "And we'll invite Tal as the arbiter," he added. I agreed. I knew that Leonid was in great form then, and I was sure that he'd give Fischer a run for his money.
>
> But suddenly, everything became much more serious.
>
> "Why blitz?" Robert retorted. "I, as the current U.S. Champion, challenge Leonid Stein, the USSR Champion, for a match. Let's play seriously, until six wins."
>
> Stein agreed. Fischer found the president of the Cuban Chess Federation, Luís Barreras, and stated the idea. "Excellent", the president said, "a great idea! But I have no authority to make such decisions. Let's talk to the chairman of the organizing committee..."
>
> The chairman was Fidel Castro. He heard out both grandmasters and guaranteed that the match would be held in Havana. But when?
>
> "Right after the USSR Championship", Stein said, "the tournament begins in a month, and I can't miss it."
>
> "Well, no," Fischer said, disappointed. "You might lose your title, and our match won't be as interesting as it is now."
>
> Both champions were right in their own way. And so, the match Fischer–Stein that could have been very interesting never happened.

Initially, Fischer took an active role as World Champion, demonstrated by this telegram to FIDE delegates:[3]

> Greetings to all delegates on occasion of the Fiftieth FIDE Congress.
>
> I would like to address myself to some of the important matters that you will vote upon, and give you what I regard as the professional grandmaster's viewpoint. I hope you will give careful consideration to my opinions before you vote.
>
> I oppose decreased frequency of World Student Team Championship as hurting chess.
>
> I favor yearly FIDE Congress.
>
> Selection-by-committee of some players in Interzonal smacks of pure politics.
>
> I support re-election of Dr. Euwe as president because of background as World Champion and unique understanding of needs of professional and amateur players alike, because of his role in promoting chess worldwide.

---

[1] *The Ogonyok*, #9,1983.

[2] Tal most likely meant Fidel Castro. Guevara was not present at the Havana Olympiad.

[3] *Chess Newsletter*, September 15, 1974.

I oppose decreased frequency of Olympiad and Swiss System, which is imprecise and unscientific for Olympiad.

I oppose expulsion from FIDE of any country on political basis, on grounds that chess should be above politics.

Regarding World Championship, Cramer reflects my views, I would emphasize following points:

I oppose reducing cycle next World Championship from three years to two. For decades when title resided in Soviet Union, champion had to defend only once every three years. Now when Soviets have lost title there is proposal to increase mandatory frequency of match thus giving them more opportunity to regain title. I regard this as manipulation of rules to favor one country.

I have been interested in pre-1975 title or non-title match, not organized by FIDE directly, so as to avoid complex regulations and negotiations. However, I have not received a challenge from any player in the world, and my attempts to interest various backers regarding a return match with Spassky have failed because of adverse effects of negative statements in press by Soviet Chess Federation and former World Champion Spassky as to advisability, practicality, and availability of Mr. Spassky to face me before 1975.

During and after match, arbiters and appeal committee members must not engage in press activities, so as not to compromise their relations with the two players.

I oppose limitation of prize fund as limitation of rights of players and dignity of chess. Prize fund should be bid in gold because of worldwide inflation spiral.

I oppose splitting match site because it would double all problems. I oppose a possible fine for appealing arbiter's decisions as petty and decreasing players' rights.

When challenger is unavailable champion deserves to have up to one year at his discretion to prepare for substitute challenger.

World Championship is duel of individuals and not of federations, whose function should be to assist and not dictate to players. The two players are far more capable of reaching agreement without political intervention. Player should inform FIDE in writing whenever he delegates rights to his Federation.

I approve clause for flexibility in changing rules by mutual agreement.

Now I speak of a very important matter. Official World Championship occurs only once in three years. Temporary form, or team preparation, or luck should not be permitted to determine results. World Champion should be world's best player, and long match is necessary to reach a just result with nearly absolute certainty. For this reason I propose that match be won by first player to win ten games, with no limit on total number played.

Provision for drawn match with score nine wins to nine with champion retaining title and prize fund split equally is consistent with longstanding tradition of small advantage for champion. Yet those who have long enjoyed this advantage now wish to abolish it. Propaganda emanating from a certain

> country has falsely implied that I am seeking unprecedented advantage. These critics say that it is unfair to require a two-point margin of ten wins to eight in order for challenger to win the match, yet only in this way can champion's advantage be fairly preserved when there is no limit on total games. And critics deliberately overlook that champion also needs two-point margin of ten wins to eight in order to win match.
>
> Mr. Cramer can demonstrate the historical record, but for example, Alekhine needed at least a margin of six wins to four to become World Champion, whereas Capablanca needed only five wins to retain his title, draws not counting.
>
> Throughout my career I have always insisted on optimal conditions for my participation in chess competitions. I will not compromise on this principle for the 1975 World Championship match.
>
> Best wishes
> Bobby Fischer
> World Chess Champion

This telegram, as does the following letter,[1] provides clear evidence that among the reasons Fischer was respected by his colleagues were his attempts to obtain the best conditions for the players:

> Fischer Demands Professionalism!
>
> No one has done more in recent years to popularize the game of chess than current World Champion Robert Fischer. Now that he has fired the opening shot in the battle to upgrade the next title event by threatening to resign his championship unless his demands are met. It may be well to recall that Fischer has consistently worked for the improvement of playing conditions throughout his stormy career and has been instrumental in raising the cash prizes paid to professional chess masters. Here is part of an interview with Fischer that sharply illustrates his high standards excerpted from *Chess Express* and reprinted in *Chess in Australia*, December 1971.
>
> "My name is Robert James Fischer. Patzer and friends call me Bobby. I am a professional. I cannot do anything else but play chess, but what I can, I can do profoundly. I was born on March 9, 1943 in Chicago. I was born under the sign of the fish. I am a big fish. I swallow the grandmasters; the grandmasters from the Soviet Union I devour. It is my intention to beat Lasker's record, who was World Champion for twenty-seven years. I play anywhere, but the surrounding must be okay. What I need is quiet and good lighting. Foremost, I cannot stand noise, because I like not to be disturbed in my professional work in calculating and combining. I am not a computer but a human being, an extraordinary one for that. There are no wonders with me. I am just a professional. I play chess the whole day and try always to deepen my knowledge."

---

[1] Richard Shorman, *The Daily Review*, Hayward, California, July 7, 1974.

[top] The Ambassador Report;

[bottom] The Mokarow's home at 725 San Remo Road where Bobby often stayed.

2
THE WORLDWIDE CHURCH OF GOD

The least known part of Bobby Fischer's life is unquestionably the period between 1973 and 1991. During these wilderness years he made no public appearances, forfeited his World Championship title (attempts to arrange a match with Anatoly Karpov continuously failed), was arrested (as he described in *I Was Tortured in the Pasadena Jailhouse!*), entered into major lawsuits, lived at numerous locations ranging from comfortably middle class to one step from the gutter, and was heavily involved with the Worldwide Church of God.

Frank Brady's *Endgame* provides a through examination of Bobby's initial interest in Herbert W. Armstrong's Radio Church of God (later to become known as the Worldwide Church of God and today Grace Communion International). While never becoming a full-fledged convert—Bobby didn't subscribe to the church's prohibitions against premarital sex and listening to rock 'n' roll and rhythm and blues—Fischer's commitment can't be questioned. Bobby ended up tithing the church close to $100,000 ($700,000 in 2020 dollars). Not exactly chump change for someone who had often lived on less than $10,000 a year during the 1960s.

Fischer's faith in the Worldwide Church of God ended in the mid-1970s when the church experienced increasing turmoil. Garner Ted Armstrong was accused of sexual improprieties, Herbert of using the church for his own financial gain, and Stanley Rader and other church officials of high living in church owned "mansions" and jet planes.

In a rare 1977 interview Fischer expressed his disillusionment with Armstrong and the church. Published in the *Ambassador Report*[1] (an exposé of the Armstrong Empire), Fischer describes his relationship with Armstrongism and explains how even he, the "psych-out king," was able to be out psyched and manipulated by the Armstrongs through long-term exposure to subtle religious mind-control techniques.

This interview, stretched over the course of several weeks at various locations in the Pasadena area, was conducted by several staff members in a loose

---

1 *Ambassador Report*, "Bobby Fischer Speaks Out!," 1977, (pp. 54–55).

discussion style format. Only upon publication were these conversations turned into a formal question-and-answer format and organized under various topic headings.

WHY BOBBY CAME TO US

Len Zola: Bobby, how did you first come across our publication, and after several years of not making any statements to the media, why have you chosen to share your thoughts and perspectives regarding the Worldwide Church of God with us?

Bobby Fischer: I was walking by Bungalow News store in Pasadena, and a copy of *Ambassador Review* [the predecessor of *Ambassador Report*] was in the window. I'm really glad you guys put out that magazine. You really put a lot of work into it. I was coming around anyway, but that sped it up. It might have taken me another year or two to get where I am.

I didn't even want to give an interview in a sense, because my privacy is very important to me. But I feel that it is my duty to help out people, to help even one person. I just worry about the people in the Armstrong organization and those who may come into it. Why should they have to suffer because we rationalized that we didn't want to do anything?

I called you up about this. I hardly know you guys, but I want to help you. I think your publication is going to reach the people I want to reach. I really think that people should have information to make intelligent choices. I believe this.

Really my story is no different than that of any other jerk that was sucked into the organization. The only difference would be that I, Bobby Fischer, was saying it, and people would be more interested because of my name, my veracity, and the fact that I gave a lot of money.

However, I want to emphasize that I'm not trying to destroy the college or the Armstrong's. I know the Bible says, "Vengeance is God's." I'm not trying to "get" those guys. And I'm not interested in getting my money back. I'm trying to protect others. I just want to make sure that nobody gets ripped off mentally. That's the most important thing. I am not necessarily backing the whole magazine, but I'm using it because it is a good forum to get my views across.

INITIAL CONTACT WITH WORLDWIDE CHURCH

Zola: Was it in 1962 or around then that you said you first became involved with the Worldwide Church of God? Did you flip the radio to the Worldwide Church of God's radio broadcast by accident?

Fischer: I had some personal problems, and I started listening to a lot of radio ministers. I listened every Sunday all day, flipping the dial up and back. So, I heard just about every guy on Sunday. And then I heard Mr. Armstrong, and I said, "Ah, God has finally shown me the one, I guess. This guy really has power. Authority. He doesn't talk like the other guys. He really knows his stuff!"

When I started listening, it was to Herbert W. Armstrong mostly. Then Herbert and his son were alternating every day for a while. One day it was Herbert, and one day it was Ted. Then it was Herbert just on Sundays. And eventually, Herbert was just phased out.

Well, I kind of split my life into two pieces. One was where my chess career lies. There, I kept my sanity, so to speak, and my logic. And the other was my religious life. I tried to apply what I learned in the church to my chess career too. But I still was studying chess. I wasn't just "trusting in God" to give me the moves.

WHAT TITHING HAS DONE FOR ME

Zola: As you continued to listen to the WCG's "World Tomorrow" broadcast, did you begin sending donations?

Fischer: I never gave any money to a work or any church. I didn't believe in that stuff. But I got a whole bunch of literature from Armstrong. I felt guilty after awhile about getting so much. I was getting *The Plain Truth* for a couple of years. I had written for every last piece of literature I had ever heard him offering. Finally, I sent him five bucks or something. Then I got a co-worker letter. And then later on I sent them maybe $20. And then I remember in late 1963 I was in some tournament, and I said, "I'll send the whole tenth." It was a really big decision.

Bill Hughes: In 1972 when they got that money from you [$61,200], did they discuss what proportion they ought to receive?

Fischer: No, no. I wanted to do it. I was enthusiastic!

Hughes: What was it that you won in that chess tournament?

Fischer: I don't know exactly. It was about $160,000, plus I received a lot of royalties. I made about $200,000 that year.

Hughes: Well, didn't you donate more than 10% of your winnings?

Fischer: Yeah! Well, I told them that I wanted to give them a double tithe. Whatever it was, I wanted to do it the very right way, whatever that was. I did it on the gross amount. They cleaned my pockets out frankly. I have some money left, but not that much. I've got some assets. It's amazing they didn't get everything. Now my only income is a few royalty checks from my books. I was really very foolish, but I thought I was doing what I had to do. When I sent those checks off, I really didn't have the slightest qualms, no regrets, not the slightest. I don't really regret it that much, to tell you the truth, even now.

Now that I think about it, I never heard Armstrong once say, "Well, that's nice Bobby that you want to help us, but don't forget your family. Help them too." The Armstrongs never once said that.

> You know, I didn't improve my living standard one bit either. It wasn't like I just didn't help my mom. I didn't do anything for myself either. You know I don't even have a car. About the only luxury I got was quite a few $400 suits. I got ten maybe. But still what I'm saying is that it's still not a lot of money spent on me considering all the money I made. It wasn't like I was living high on the hog and neglecting my mom, but she's living real poor in a crummy apartment in England. She doesn't even have a bathroom. I just saw her a few months ago. I have to help my mom now. She's an old woman. She could soon be gone and here I was giving money so that Rader and these guys can have their parties in Beverly Hills. This whole thing is so sick.

The interviews were conducted in late 1976 and early 1977, and within a few months Bobby was having second thoughts. In the lawsuit he filed against Len and Margaret Zola, two of the editors of the *Ambassador Report*, he claimed that he had expressively forbidden the Zolas from using any of his private conversations. The Zolas countered this was not the case, asking for Fischer to show them the signed agreements to back up his claim. It's interesting that Fischer didn't dispute what the Zolas claimed he had said, only that he was taped without consent.

The Los Angeles County Hall of Records has documents from this case that reveal a pattern similar to Bobby's lawsuit against Brad Darrach, Time-Life International, and Stein & Day [see pages 491–500]. The legal merits of the respective positions were never resolved as Fischer repeatedly failed to respond to requests to be questioned by the Zola's attorney after the initial deposition. Due to this, the case ended up being dismissed.

Not only did Fischer fail to collect damages, he ended up losing money from his dealings with the Zolas. Not from legal fees, as Bobby received pro-bono legal work from Worldwide Church of God lawyers Ralph Helge and chief counsel Stanley Rader. Fischer's loss was the result of a separate, though related, lawsuit and an out-of-court settlement he had to pay Holly Ruiz.

Who was Holly Ruiz and why did Bobby have to give her money? Burt Hochberg provides the answers:[1]

> **BOBBY FISCHER UPDATE**
>
> The past several months have also seen a spate of rumors about Fischer's tangled relations with his church, the press, and the law.
>
> Fischer lives in Pasadena, California where the Worldwide Church of God has its headquarters. Fischer has been affiliated with the evangelical sect since the 1960s, and it is reported that over the years he has given it more than $95,000, including $62,000 from his winnings in the match with Spassky in

[1] Burt Hochberg, *Chess Life*, March 1978, (p. 119).

> 1972. He has been living on property owned by Ambassador College, which is funded by the church.
>
> Late in 1977, a ninety page magazine called the *Ambassador Report* was published by a small group of disaffected former church members. Nearly a year earlier, Fischer, evidently in sympathy with that group, had allowed himself to be interviewed for the magazine by Len Zola, one of its editors, by Mrs. Zola, and by Holly Ruiz, a reporter who recorded some of the conversations on tape.
>
> In April, Fischer apparently had second thoughts and broke contact with the magazine's staff. But in October, while the *Ambassador Report* was being prepared for the printer, Fischer was given an opportunity by Mr. Zola to inspect the dummy proofs. According to Mr. Zola, Fischer became infuriated when he read his own comments and demanded that they be removed from the magazine.
>
> In the days that followed, Fischer reportedly attempted to show that his participation in the *Ambassador Report* had been improperly obtained. He allegedly visited Holly Ruiz and demanded that she sign a statement to the effect that she had not been authorized by Fischer to record his conversations. She refused, and, according to a criminal complaint she filed later, Fischer struck her.
>
> A bench warrant calling for Fischer to answer the charges was issued on October 18. (This was not a warrant for his arrest, as has been reported.) At about that time Fischer was known to be in the New York City area. A few weeks later, however, he appeared at the offices of his Los Angeles lawyer, Oliver Moench. Mrs. Ruiz and her lawyer were present and accepted a financial settlement in exchange for withdrawing the criminal complaint.
>
> The nature of Fischer's present relationship with the church is not known.

A document in the John Collins Collection at Indiana University states that when the warrant was issued, Fischer flew to New York and went into hiding at John Collins' apartment in Stuyvesant Town. Bobby soon came to his senses and paid Ruiz the $5,000 she had requested.

Even though he had left the Worldwide Church of God by the mid-1970s, some of Bobby's closest friends for the next decade or more would be people he had met through it. This included personal trainer Harry Sneider, Bob Ellsworth and especially Arthur and Claudia Mokarow.

For much of the '70s Fischer lived at 300 Mockingbird Lane (a church owned property) next door to the Mokarows, and after that he lived on and off with Arthur and Claudia who had moved to a four-bedroom, four bath, 3100 square foot home at 725 San Remo Road in a fashionable neighborhood of Pasadena.

The relationship between Bobby and Arthur, who was a minster in the WCG and author of several books dealing with biblical prophecy and interpretation isn't clear, but Claudia was especially close to him and operated as his gate keeper.

Anthony Saidy, who had several interactions with Claudia and Fischer, believes that this started because Claudia was specifically tasked by the WCG to keep an eye on Bobby—he had already donated a lot of money to the church and offered the potential of giving more if he defended his title.

Claudia continued in this role even after Bobby left the church and moved away from Mockingbird Lane—first to a furnished room near Orange Avenue in Los Angeles (one block from Wilshire Boulevard), and later taking nightly or weekly rentals in a series of flophouses near MacArthur Park. The relationship with Claudia continued until the late '80s when the Mokarows relocated to Texas. Bob Ellsworth then became Bobby's trusted helper, until their falling out roughly a decade later.

3
ROBERT J. FISCHER, PLAINTIFF

The lawsuit with the Zolas was small potatoes compared to the one Bobby filed fours years earlier against Brad Darrach, Time-Life International, Stein & Day and several staff and officers of the U.S. Chess Federation. This case drove Bobby over the edge.

Written by Brad Darrach, and published in the summer of 1974, *Bobby Fischer vs. the Rest of the World* was seen by Bobby as a betrayal of the worst sort. Why? Because Darrach had offered repeated assurances, both orally and in writing, that he would not produce a book about the World Championship match or Fischer's preparations leading up to it, without Bobby's explicit consent. Fischer could not imagine that this promise would be broken. He was wrong.

Fischer had a distrust of journalists dating back to the thrashing he received in the early 1960s from the pen of Ralph Ginzburg that had left him angry and humiliated [see pages 254-260]. So why did Bobby talk with Brad Darrach and let him get so close, especially when William Lombardy and Frank Brady repeatedly warned him not to? This is not an easy question to answer. The only plausible explanation was Fischer's desire to see chess receive more favorable publicity in the United States.

Darrach was an accomplished writer, honored for the many articles he wrote that appeared in a variety of publications including: *Time, Life, People, Sports Illustrated,* and *Playboy*. As a seasoned interviewer he had a long track record of getting subjects to talk. He was the first writer to whom Marilyn Monroe revealed her traumatic childhood, and for another story, he courted Mel Brooks for five weeks until the comedian finally opened-up to him. Darrach was not only a fine writer but persistent, using his charm to gain Bobby's confidence. This made his betrayal all the crueler.

Why did Darrach act as he did? Why after gaining Bobby's friendship and trust, did he betray him? Unfortunately, Darrach can't be asked since he died in 1997. While he had a long career as a journalist and film critic, *Bobby Fischer vs. the Rest of the World* was the only book he ever wrote. Perhaps the desire to publish a novel motivated Darrach—he felt he had the story of a lifetime to tell.

The market for chess books in 1972 was seemingly insatiable (*Fischer vs Spassky: The Chess Match of the Century*[1] by Svetozar Gligorić, is routinely listed as one of the best-selling chess books of all times). *Bobby Fischer vs. the World,* aimed at the casual player, had great sales potential.

Darrach's duplicity is documented in a telegram sent during the match.

> Mr. Robert J. Fischer
> Hotel Loftleidir
> Reykjavík, Iceland
>
> Dear Bobby,
>
> I want to thank you for the series of exclusive interviews I have had with you, and through your good offices, with your team members, during the last several months.
>
> As we have discussed, I affirm my agreement that I will not use this material for a book or for any magazine article without first, obtaining your written approval. Of course, my present series of articles for *Life* magazine is exempted from the need for this approval.
>
> I look forward to a long and close relationship with you
>
> Sincerely,
> Brad Darrach

And, consider what photographer Harry Benson had to say:[2]

> Brad made a fatal error with it. This would be about the last week in Iceland, he gave Bobby a sign that he would not publish a book unless it was okayed by Bobby. I said: "Brad you're off your head, don't give it to him! You've got the story!" "Oh no, I must, Bobby wants it." A big mistake on Brad's part, he signed it.

It's clear Benson believes his fellow professional stepped over the line and was unaware of Darrach's numerous prior promises.

Benson had watched Darrach and Fischer together in close quarters since the fall of 1971 when *Life* magazine hired Darrach (as writer) and Benson (as photographer) to cover the Fischer–Petrosian match. This was at a time interest in Bobby was building outside the chess community following his victories over Taimanov and Larsen earlier in the year. With a potential World Championship match seemingly around the corner, *Life* was eager to tap into the chess fever starting to infect the American public.

When *Bobby Fischer vs. the Rest of the World* was published in June 1974, reaction was mixed, with many non-chess reviewers giving it the thumbs up while much of

---

1 Svetozar Gligorić, *Fischer vs Spassky: The Chess Match of the Century*. New York: Simon & Schuster, 1972.

2 *New In Chess*, issue 4, 2011, (p. 81).

the chess community was critical. How much of the book is fiction and how much is fact? Opinion varies.[1] Conceivably, Fischer might have accepted *Bobby Fischer vs. The Rest of the World* if it had portrayed him favorably, but it did nothing of the sort.

The only public response by Darrach after the book's publication, was a letter to the editor published in *The New York Review of Books* on February 23, 1975. Darrach shows no feelings of remorse in his lengthy defense to charges by Frank Brady and Burt Hochberg that he betrayed Bobby's confidence and put words in his mouth. Nor does he comment about breaking his agreement with Fischer.

Bobby had been aware of Darrach's book six months before its publication. Attorney Paul G. Marshall's letter to Bobby of January 21, 1974, addresses two brewing situations (Lombardy's article and Darrach's upcoming book). Marshall had served as his attorney in Reykjavík, but by the time of the letter he was no longer in Fischer's inner circle.[2]

> January 21, 1974
>
> Mr. Robert J. Fischer
> 300 Mockingbird Lane, Apt. #1
> South Pasadena, California 91030
>
> Dear Bob:
>
> I thought about our conversation, and I am quite distressed both from my point of view of law and morality about this entire matter.
>
> In the first place, as a matter of law, it is my view that any lawyer who tells you that you can succeed in litigation on the basis of the article in *Sports Illustrated* is patently incorrect; we would fail. Firstly, the article in *Sports Illustrated* is not only not damaging, but it is flattering to you. Secondly, it gives no "secrets" of any kind, which a court would understand as causing injury either economically or to reputation. Thirdly, it finally contravenes the basic constitutional right of a person to free speech and the implied right of the public to information. Finally, we have no written document we can show in court. Even if there was a written document, I think it would be unenforceable under the laws of the United States insofar as enabling us to prevent an article as was written in *Sports Illustrated*.
>
> Morally, I am even more distressed. Because of you, I have gotten to know and become good friends with Bill Lombardy. I haven't, however, spoken to Bill since our conversation in which you asked me to write this letter.
>
> In all the time I have known Bill, he has been the kind of friend to you that I would like to have. Where other people might say disparaging things about you, Bill never did. Where people might talk freely to Darrach, Bill, realizing

---

[1] Various arguments pro and con are discussed in Edward Winter's analysis "Brad Darrach and the Dark Side of Bobby Fischer" at www.chesshistory.com/winter/extra/fischerdarrach.html.

[2] Letter from the collection of David DeLucia.

that Darrach might hurt you, refused. Bill refused to talk to Darrach though he ran the risk of Darrach writing about Bill publicly in a most disparaging matter. It is my belief that Bill would do nothing to cause you any injury. Quite the contrary, he has gone a long way toward protecting you out of a feeling of friendship and affection.

You may remember Bill gave up the television program in New York to go with you to Iceland although the money for both was comparable. Therefore, I can't even tell Bill he made a lot of money out of you since he would have made the same had he done the show. Nevertheless, the decision, no matter how badly or uncharitable it is in my view, remains yours to make. I will not personally act against Bill Lombardy who I treasure as a friend. I know Bill a lot shorter time than you do and a lot less well, but I don't jeopardize my friendships.

When Bill was presented with the final document, the afternoon of the day that we went to Iceland he agreed, absolutely, to write nothing whatsoever which would be of a private nature in which he got from you by reason of his special friendship with you be it game analysis or otherwise. He made it clear that he would be free to write about his own experiences in Iceland provided that his own did not contravene the aforesaid clear rules. A writing evidencing this agreement was delivered by me to you and placed by me personally, at your instruction, in your safe deposit box in the Hotel Loftleider. I have never seen it since.

When I became aware of the article in *Playboy* and subsequently of the projected book, Bill assured me that neither dealt with your personal life during the Spassky match, or any personal matters, which he learned, from you during the match, or of any analysis of the games in the match.

I have read and reread the *Sports Illustrated* article, and while not flattering to me, it certainly is simply a recount of Bill's experiences, none of which, in any meaningful way whatsoever, dealt with non-public information which Bill learned from you.[1]

I have not seen any part of the manuscript of the book, but I am assured that the book deals with Bobby Fischer's growing up and his games during his formative period. This is by way of tribute to you.

I have always believed and I have told people that you are a person as big in spirit as you are in chess talent. While it makes no difference to my life one-way or the other, I would not like to be disappointed.

Now, so we can get the Darrach legal position correctly stated, I will set forth what I believe to be the facts and the law:

---

[1] Further to Marshall's opinion on Lombardy's *Sports Illustrated* article: Years later Lombardy wrote that the breakup between himself and Bobby was a misunderstanding due to faulty editing of the article after he submitted it for publication. The insinuation is that Fischer would have been fine with Lombardy's original unedited work. This seems highly optimistic as the article violated Fischer's cardinal rule that those who work for him should not profit financially.

(a) Brad Darrach's actions in writing anything which would hurt you are despicable. Brad Darrach promised, first in writing and then orally to me, and to others that he would never write anything that would hurt you. Based both on these writings and this clear oral agreement and under the pressure of events, he was allowed by you to have a special relationship. He used this special relationship to do a good job for *Time* and *Life* magazines. He is now misusing it I think, both illegally and immorally. In this case, I would certainly go out of my way to aid you to triumph, but only within the bounds of good sense and good law.

The law is difficult in this particular matter. Freedom of speech and the right of the public to information is one of the prime tenets of our Constitution and our legal system. The courts have shown increasingly stronger tendencies to allow people to write books and articles even in the face of agreements not to so do. The reason is that an agreement to keep secrets may not be in the public interest and thus is often not enforceable.

In this matter, I am worried about information. I don't want slanders and calumnies to appear which hurt you personally and hurt chess generally. It is important to the youth of our country that they look to you as a leader in morality, especially in times where our nation's morals are being so harshly questioned. A lawsuit will bring up all the offensive matters before the eyes of the public, and in fact, would increase these allegations believability. Witness Watergate; when one seeks to suppress information from the public, the public tends to believe the worst about the information suppressed.

Publication of the book would be equally bad in the terms of the public and you. Stein & Day, Inc. is a reputable publishing house. Their attorney, Maurice Nessen (Nickerson, Kramer, Lownstein, Nessen, Kamin & Soll) turns out to be an acquaintance of mine. I didn't know that he was their attorney until recently. I think he will be very sympathetic to your view point of view as he is both a patriot and a humanist.

Nevertheless, he is a very tough, able attorney and that such will protect his client's interest quite competently if challenged. There may be an attorney who will tell you you should sue before settlement negotiations, but in my view, such an attorney would be looking for fees and publicity.

Instead what should happen is the following:

Andrew Davis and I should sit down with Maurice Nessen and delete from the Manuscript any disgraceful references. While the public can get the truth, and you have never been afraid of letting the public know what happened in Iceland, references to your personal life should be taken out if they can bring you harm. I believe with all my heart that Nessen would cooperate to this end.

If this is done effectively, the following will be the result:

(a) A good book would come out by the best-informed writer covering the event; it might well be the most important book that you get on the match in terms of being well written.

(b) I believe you could get attorneys' fees paid and most important, you would be able to get an interest in the book and earn some substantial money in a valid work.

(c) Most important of all, the reputation of chess and your own reputation would be clean.

(d) Finally, in keeping with your moral principles, we would have stopped any book which did not conform to your agreement to the effect that Darrach could not write a separate book unless you approved. You would have approved the book subject to it being to the credit of chess and the credit of yourself, and Darrach would have been made to live up to his agreement.

When you go to a lawyer, you are not going to a servant. You are going to a professional man who tells you the treatment he will give you for the problem and then proceeds to treat your problem providing you are willing.

A lawyer, however, if he is true to his profession and honorable with his client, will not do what the client wants if the lawyer feels it will hurt the client. A doctor who feels his patient has pneumonia will not put a plaster cast on the patient's leg because the patient says his leg condition is caused by a broken ankle. In this case, to avoid litigation, and to get you to force Darrach to adhere to an American system of justice and to honor his promise to you is what should be accomplished. To risk the reputation of chess by an ugly lawsuit, which will only publicize the book and make it more successful is bad advice, and I will not give it, nor will I act upon it.

I wish you well.

Cordially,

Paul G. Marshall

Per his usual modus operandi Fischer followed none of Marshall's advice.

Fischer's understanding of the law was naive. He thought he understood the language and workings of the U.S. legal system but in reality, he didn't have a clue. His insistence that "he knew better" caused endless problems.

Why didn't Fischer receive satisfaction from the U.S. legal system?

Brady suggests that Bobby didn't have proper legal representation:

> And to solidify his reputation as a loner, Fischer prepared the legal brief himself, without the aid of an attorney.[1]

> Bobby ultimately did go to court but lost, the judge throwing the case out because it was so poorly presented and without sufficient evidence.[2]

Lack of proper legal representation wasn't an issue—throughout much of Bobby's life there were lawyers within the chess community and the Worldwide

[1] *Chess*, September 1977, Vol.42, (pp. 364–5).

[2] Frank Brady, *Endgame: Bobby Fischer's Remarkable Rise and Fall—from America's Brightest Prodigy to the Edge of Madness*. New York: Crown Publishers, 2011, (p. 216).

Church of God who offered him pro-bono council. However, no matter the circumstances, these lawyers' experiences were remarkably similar: They would begin the case on an optimistic note, soon come to realize Bobby was an exceptionally difficult client who didn't take instruction well or follow their legal advice, and invariably would decide Fischer wasn't worth the hassle.

Grandmaster Andy Soltis offered his view of Fischer's lawsuit against Darrach. He correctly points out Bobby was the poster child for the title "World's Most Impossible Client:"[1]

> **FISCHER'S TROUBLES WITH THE LAW**
>
> I have no great sympathy for Brad Darrach and considerable doubt about his style of journalism. But some dissent should be added to Frank Brady's version of the Bobby Fischer–Darrach legal hassle.
>
> Fischer may have a good case considering the key role that consent plays in invasion-of-privacy suits in American courts. But to obtain justice here as in any other country you have to act a bit more responsibly than the former World Champion has in his many legal affairs.
>
> Back in November of 1975 Fischer asked that his suit be moved from New York to Los Angeles to save on travel costs. The judge agreed but told Fischer that if he wanted the case heard he should see a lawyer. The original complaint Fischer filed was "almost unintelligible," the judge said.
>
> When the case was finally thrown out last April the judge noted that it had been the subject of "continuous hearings" during which Fischer had displayed "almost intentional disregard for the rules of discovery." The judge in question, by the way, was Matt Byrne, the man whose integrity was attested to by his handling of the Daniel Ellsberg burglary case a few years ago.
>
> Certainly, Fischer would have fared better had he been represented by Paul Marshall, his attorney during Bobby's rise to the championship. But Marshall eventually had to ask another court to be relieved of the responsibility of representing Fischer. He had found it impossible to contact his client, even by telephone, Marshall said. Fischer was so inaccessible during the long-running suit brought against him by filmmaker Chester Fox (remember him?) that Fox's lawyers eventually had to have a judge order Fischer to make depositions.
>
> If Fischer has been denied justice in this matter he has no one to blame but himself. And to suggest that these legal entanglements are what keeps Bobby from returning to the board is simply hard to swallow.
>
> Andrew Soltis
> New York, 18 October 1977

From the start, Bobby's lack of cooperation in his own lawsuit was apparent. Bobby was deposed on April 26, 1976.[2] The first day he was asked non-stop

---

[1] *Chess*, November 1977, Vol.43, (p. 55).

[2] This lengthy document is in Larry Finley's possession.

questions for the better part of eight hours. Bored with the process, he refused to continue with the depositions, failing to grasp they were integral to getting his complaint to trial.

What would have happened if Bobby had cooperated and Judge Byrne let the case go to trial. Could Bobby have won based on Darrich's promise that he wouldn't write a book? Anchorage attorney Robert Stoller offered an argument:

> Of particular interest to me (in my capacity as a lawyer) is the letter which Brad Darrach wrote to Bobby during Bobby's stay at the Loftleider Hotel stating that Darrach would not use materials gleaned from Bobby and his team members for a book without first obtaining Bobby's written permission. A question of law for the Court (had Bobby complied with the discovery orders and had his case then gone on to trial) would have been how long that negative undertaking could reasonably be deemed to be effective. There would also have been an implicit loophole to the effect that Darrach would not have been restricted from writing a book on Bobby using publicly available source information or Darrach's own personal observations obtained in public venues. And it might have been that Darrach tried to obtain Bobby's written permission, which Bobby then refused to give. Under that possibility, the legal question would have been whether Bobby had unreasonably refused to grant consent—in which event (i.e. a legally unreasonable refusal of consent), Darrach would have been at liberty to publish even without having obtained Bobby's consent.

Another question to consider is, had Bobby turned a "promising position" into an "unplayable one" by asking too much in damages and drawing in too many defendants. Robert Stoller comments:

> On top of all of these legal questions, the huge, over-riding economic question would have been how Bobby could have proven actual financial damage to him caused directly by the publication and sale of *Bobby Fischer vs. the Rest of The World*, much less the $20 million he was claiming against each and every one of the numerous defendants he had sued.
>
> Fischer's complaint named not only Darrach, but also twenty-seven other defendants including the author's wife (for typing the manuscript!). Leroy Dubeck (USCF president at the time[1]), Burt Hochberg (editor of *Chess Life & Review*), and Ed Edmondson (executive director) were included because the U.S. Chess Federation was advertising and selling the book.

Bobby would have had an impossible case proving $20 million in damages and most of those named had only peripheral involvement. He would not have won

1 Leroy Dubeck was USCF president from 1969 to 1972 and no longer in office at the time of Fischer's lawsuit. Bobby, who met with Dubeck many times in the early 1970s, probably didn't realize there was a new USCF president and as such went ahead and named him in the complaint.

what he was asking for. However, if he had asked for $100,000 or $200,000 (in the neighborhood of what he won in Reykjavík) and restricted the defendants to Darrach and his publisher Stein & Day, Bobby's chances would have increased greatly. It's likely that the defendants would have settled in such a case.

Was Stein & Day aware of Darrach's promise to Bobby? The angry response by the company's attorney when asked this question hints they might not have been. Stein & Day's papers ended up at the Columbia University Archives after the company closed in 1989, the answer may lie there. Stoller added:

> I have been giving a great deal of thought to the Fischer vs Darrach et al litigation recently, and it strikes me that one of the high-powered law firms representing the "deep-pocket" corporate defendants should have at least interviewed (if not formally deposed) Brad Darrach. I had heard stories about Darrach's written undertaking not to write a book on the Fischer/Spassky match without first obtaining Fischer's permission, and your research has now documented the existence of that letter. But before Stein & Day or Time/Warner (or any of the USCF officials who had also been named personally as defendants) could be held liable for any breach of that agreement, they at least would have had to have knowledge of it. Moreover, as I recall from our earlier review of the court's record log, Darrach allowed a default to have been entered against him. (I absolutely need to verify that my recollection is accurate on that point.) If my memory is accurate, then perhaps Darrach had some sympathy with Bobby's efforts to obtain some degree of compensation. In this regard, I think it is fair to say that Darrach had some degree of affection for Bobby. Approximately a year prior to the publication of *Bobby Fischer vs. the Rest of the World*, Darrach had published an article in *Playboy* magazine entitled "The Day Bobby Blew It", which recounted the machinations by which Bobby was—finally—seated on the flight to Reyjkavík. That article, by the way, was anthologized in a collection of best sports journalism of the 1970s. I read that article as revealing Darrach's respect and admiration for Bobby, notwithstanding many of Bobby's dubious antics during the World Championship.

This lawsuit shook Bobby to his core. He not only blamed Darrach, Stein & Day, and Time/Warner, but also the U.S. legal system and de facto the U.S. government. His feelings of mistreatment by the U.S. government (that bubbled to the surface in 1992, and again in 2001), appear to have their origins in this lawsuit. Starting in the mid-1970s Bobby retaliated by refusing to pay income taxes—though as his earnings dwindled, this gesture was largely symbolic. This incident is critical to understanding Fischer's thoughts from the mid-1970s—when he started to wander off to the dark side—until his death.[1]

---

[1] Bobby was successful in his legal fight against the newspaper *Plavi Vjesnik* and Dimitrije Bjelica. Dragoslav Andric, "Fischer Gets Money Through Court in Yugoslavia", *Chess Digest Magazine*, October 1973, (pp. 221–223).

This letter to Los Angeles District Attorney John Van de Kamp speaks to Bobby's mindset in 1977:*

May 31, 1977

Dear Mr. Van De Kamp

The original conspiracy to destroy my reputation and the criminal conspiracy to invade my privacy rolls on. Over a year ago I contacted you and showed your office overwhelming documentation of those charges. Deeply involved is your mentor Otis Chandlers' L.A. Times, Burt Prelutsky, Jim Murray, the L.A. Herald Examiner, Brad Darrach, Time, Inc., Stein and Day, New York Magazine and many others. I will not take indifference for an answer.

My good name, my reputation have been defamed, my privacy has been invaded. These are criminal offenses in the State of California. The laws are on the books and must be enforced.

I know you have a well deserved reputation of being in Otis Chandler's pocket. But now you are an elected official. Your duty is not just to Mr. Chandler but to the people of the state of California.

If you continue to turn a blind eye to these overwhelmingly documented charges, then I will be forced to strongly consider permanently not paying any income taxes to the state of California. I'm getting fed up with feeding the mouth that bites me.

Sincerely,

Robert J. Fischer

P.S. The Chandlers' are not Jesus, they can't save you, it time you became a moral decent man before God and mete out justice without fear or favor.

* The punctuation and emphasis are Fischer's.

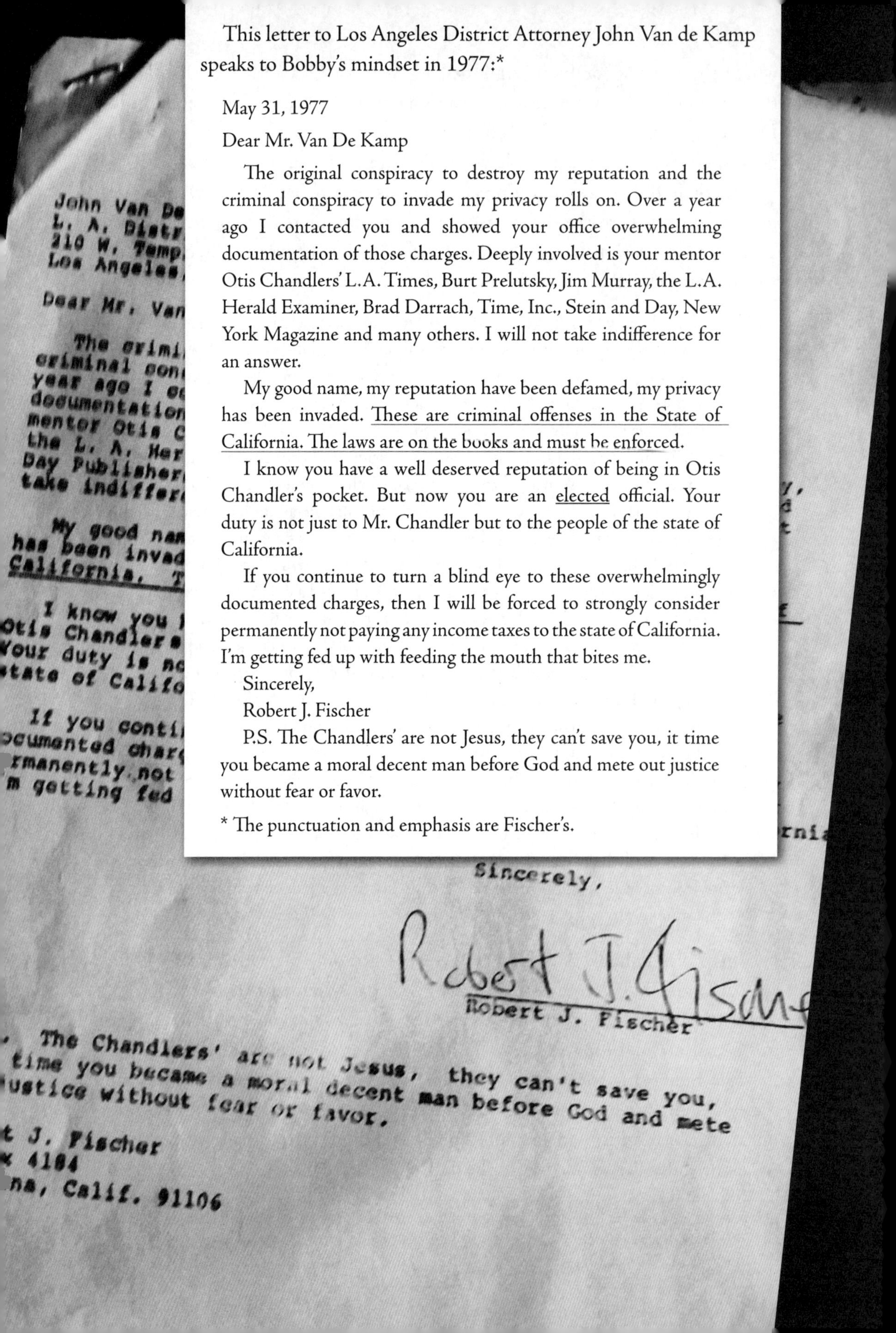

4
THE GREENBLATT PROGRAM

In the spring of 1977 Fischer played the Greenblatt Program and by the oddest of circumstances Games (75) to (77) are available to chess history. Odd, because it was the reclusive Fischer himself who brought this event to the world's attention by writing a letter to the *Computer Chess Newsletter*. Had he not done so the games might never have seen the light of day.

> © 1977 Bobby Fischer
> May 17, 1977
> Dear Mr. Penrod,
>
> I think your *Computer Chess Newsletter* is a very good idea. I recently played some games on a terminal with the Greenblatt program. Enclosed are three of them. I made the mistake of buying the "Chess Challenger." It's ridiculously weak—they really shouldn't have come out with it. They also made a botch of the keyboard so it's hard to follow the moves. Somehow they reversed the algebraic notation so that the files are numbered and the ranks are lettered, if you can believe that! I know I can give it a queen and a rook, because I gave them away in the opening and won. But I can probably give it much more. In the endgame it's almost impossible to lose to it. Provided you agree and acknowledge, that I have all the publication rights to the scores you can publish then in your newsletter.
> Regards
>
> Bobby Fischer

Fischer's letter confirmed the rumors circulating at the time that he was playing against computers.

Questions arise: Were the games Fischer played against the Greenblatt program a match? Support for that position comes from the fact that three games were given. Had Fischer clinched victory by winning game three as might be expected in a four game match? Reading Fischer's words literally it would seem this was not the case, "I recently played some games," which would suggest something more casual. Were there more than three games and Bobby only made public the more interesting ones? Where were the games/match played? Cambridge, Massachusetts, the home of MIT where the Greenblatt Program was housed, is commonly (and understandably) given as the location for the match, but does that mean that Bobby traveled across the country to play a computer? Or did he somehow play from southern California? What does Bobby mean that he played with the Greenblatt Program "on a terminal" in 1977? Finally, what enticed Bobby to play against the Greenblatt Program? Was it simple curiosity or was he paid to play? The answers to these questions remain unclear.

The Greenblatt Program, also known as MacHack, was started in mid-November 1966 by Richard Greenblatt at MIT. Almost from the start, unlike other computers, it competed in USCF rated tournament games against humans (as opposed to playing against other computers as was normal for the time). Greenblatt was fortunate in having three strong masters studying at MIT in the mid-1960s. Future Grandmaster Larry Kaufman, future Senior Master Carl Wagner, and Alan Baisley (who played in the U.S. Junior Closed) were all credited by Greenblatt with helping to improve the program.

Bobby responded to a question about man-versus-computer in his *Boys' Life* column in 1968:[1]

> Question: Have you ever played a computer? What do you think of the chance of a computer of grandmaster strength, and possibly becoming World Champion?
>
> Fischer: I've never played a computer. Eventually, though, I think a computer can become champion. After all, it can't be as hard as getting a man on the moon. But I hope it doesn't happen during my lifetime! Incidentally, here's an example of a computer game. Black's game was a disgrace to the human race. The computer (White) was called MacHack IV, and it took on Landey, the man.

Grandmaster Kaufman spoke of his involvement with the Greenblatt (MacHack) program in 2016:

> I worked on the MacHack chess program along with Greenblatt in 1967–1968. I wrote the opening book it used and proposed improvements based on playing it queen odds games. This seems odd as it got a rating in the 1500s from human tournaments and I can't give queen odds to a human so rated, but computers didn't know to simplify and avoid complications when ahead back then. Anyway, I graduated from MIT in mid-1968 and that ended my work on MacHack.
>
> I'm afraid that my knowledge of the Fischer match is as yours, from public sources. Although MacHack was improved by then, I doubt it was better than class A strength, as that was the level of the world's top engines then. Greenblatt was still in charge in 1977 as I saw him once after that and he was still in charge of it.

---

[1] *Boys' Life*, August 1968.

(75) King's Gambit
Fischer – Greenblatt Program
Cambridge 1977

1.e4 e5 2.f4 exf4 3.Bc4

Black was threatening ...Qh4+. This is normally met by 3.Nf3, but one school of thought, admittedly never the majority view, holds this move second best as it potentially exposes the knight to attack by ...g5-g4.

3...d5

The main line for many years has been this move and 3...Nf6, but Scottish Grandmaster John Shaw in his outstanding book *The King's Gambit* (Gambit Publishing 2013) makes a strong case for 3...Nc6!, claiming it refutes The Bishop's Gambit (3.Bc4). Bobby never faced this move which maintains all of Black's options ...g5,...d5 and ...Qh4+.

(A) 3...Qh4+ 4.Kf1 d6 5.Nc3 Be6 6.Qe2 c6 7.Nf3 Qe7 8.d4 Bxc4 9.Qxc4 g5= Fischer–Evans, U.S. ch. 1963/64.

(B) 3...Nf6 4.Nc3 c6 (4...Bb4 5.Nf3 Qe7 6.Qe2 0–0 7.e5 with a small edge, Fischer–Albert Sandrin, Chicago (simul) 1964.) 5.Bb3 d5 6.exd5 cxd5 7.d4 Bd6 8.Nge2 f3 9.gxf3 Nh5 10.Be3= Fischer–Zalys, Montreal (simul) 1964.

(C) 3...Ne7 4.Nc3 c6 5.Nf3 d5 6.Bb3 dxe4 7.Nxe4 Nd5 8.Qe2 Be7 9.c4 Nc7 10.d4= Fischer–Minić, Vinkovci 1968.

4.Bxd5 Nf6 5.Nc3 Bb4

5...Nc6 6.Nf3 Nxd5 7.Nxd5 g5 8.d4= Fischer–T. Cunningham, Houston (simul) 1964.

6.Nf3 0–0 7.0–0 Nxd5

7...Bxc3 8.dxc3 c6 9.Bc4 Qb6+ 10.Kh1 Nxe4 11.Qe1 Re8 12.Bxf4 and White soon won, Fischer–Nyman, Cicero (simul) 1964.

8.Nxd5 Bd6?

8...f5! 9.Nxb4 fxe4 recovers the piece with equal chances.

9.d4 g5?

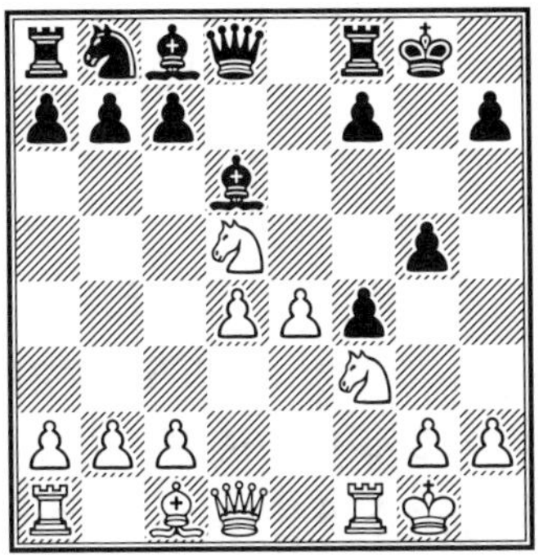

10.Nxg5!!

This shot wins on the spot.

10...Qxg5 11.e5 Bh3

11...Bxe5 12.dxe5 Qxe5 13.Bxf4 is crushing, but the text is no better.

12.Rf2 Bxe5 13.dxe5 c6 14.Bxf4 Qg7 15.Nf6+ Kh8 16.Qh5 Rd8 17.Qxh3 Na6 18.Rf3 Qg6 19.Rc1 Kg7 20.Rg3 Rh8 21.Qh6, 1–0.

---

(76) Sicilian
Greenblatt Program – Fischer
Cambridge 1977

1.e4 c5 2.Nf3 d6 3.d4 cxd4 4.Nxd4 Nf6 5.Nc3 a6 6.Be2 e5 7.Nb3 Be7 8.Be3 0–0 9.Qd3 Be6 10.0–0 Nbd7 11.Nd5 Rc8

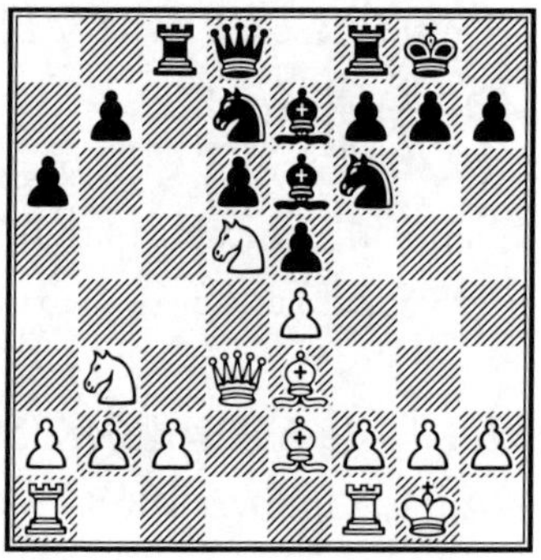

12.Nxe7+?

12.c4 would be more consistent supporting the good knight instead of trading it off for Black's bad bishop.

12...Qxe7 13.f3 d5!

Black is already better.

14.Nd2

14.exd5 Nxd5 15.c3 Rfd8 is clearly better for Black but preferable to what happens.

14...Qb4 15.Nb3 dxe4 16.Qd1

No better is 16.fxe4 Bc4 17.Qd1 Bxe2 18.Qxe2 Qxe4 with a large advantage for Black.

16...Nd5 17.Ba7

17.c3 Nxe3 18.cxb4 Nxd1 19.Bxd1 Bd5 and Black is again much better.

17...b6 18.c3 Qe7 19.fxe4 Ne3 20.Qd3 Nxf1 21.Qxa6 Ne3 22.Bxb6 Qg5 23.g3 Ra8 24.Ba7 h5 25.Qb7 h4 26.Kf2 hxg3+ 27.hxg3 f5 28.exf5 Rxf5+ 29.Ke1 Raf8 30.Kd2 Nc4+ 31.Kc2 Qg6 32.Qe4 Nd6 33.Qc6

Rf2+ 34.Kd1 Bg4 35.Bxf2 Qd3+ 36.Kc1 Bxe2 37.Nd2 Rxf2 38.Qxd7 Rf1+ 39.Nxf1 Qd1, 0–1.

(77) Sicilian
Greenblatt Program – Fischer
Cambridge 1977

1.e4 c5 2.Nf3 g6

Curiously when Fischer and Kasparov faced computers they both played the Accelerated Dragon variation of the Sicilian, something they never did before or after.

3.d4 Bg7 4.Nc3 cxd4 5.Nxd4 Nc6 6.Be3 Nf6

The fundamental idea behind the Accelerated Dragon is to try to play ...d5 in one move. White can stop that by playing 5.c4 (the Maróczy Bind), 7.Bc4 or the move played in the game.

7.Nxc6 bxc6 8.e5 Ng8

8...Nd5 is the alternative, but two of the greatest players of all time played the text.

9.f4 f6

9...Nh6 10.Qd2 0–0 11.0–0–0 d6 12.exd6 exd6 13.Qxd6 Qxd6 14.Rxd6 Nf5 15.Rd3 Ba6 16.Bc5 Bxd3 17.Bxf8 Bxf1 18.Bxg7 Bxg2 19.Rg1 Kxg7 20.Rxg2 Rb8 21.Re2 Rh8 22.b3 h5, intending ...h4-h3, was better for Black in Computer Fritz 2–Kasparov, Cologne 1992.

10.exf6?!

10.Bd4, as played in Kasparov–Ivanchuk, Prague 2002, is the main line and much more testing.

10...Nxf6 11.Bc4?!

11.Be2 would have saved a tempo.

11...d5 12.Be2 Rb8 13.b3?

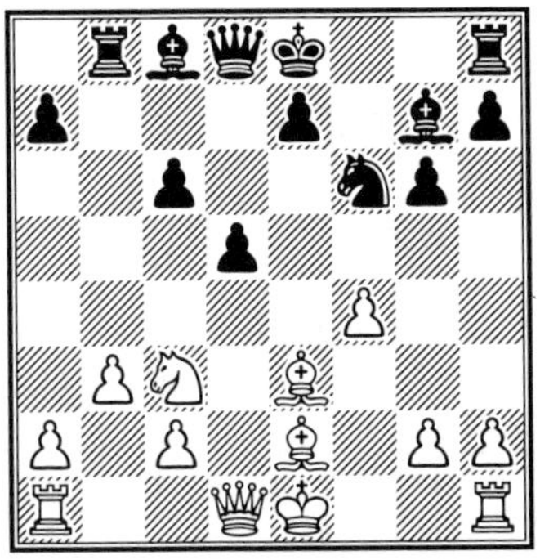

13.Bd4 would have kept White's disadvantage to a minimum.

13...Ng4! 14.Bd4 e5 15.fxe5 0–0

15...Qh4+ 16.g3 Qh3 17.Bf1 Qh5 18.Be2 Bxe5 was even stronger.

16.Bxg4 Qh4+ 17.g3 Qxg4 18.Qxg4 Bxg4

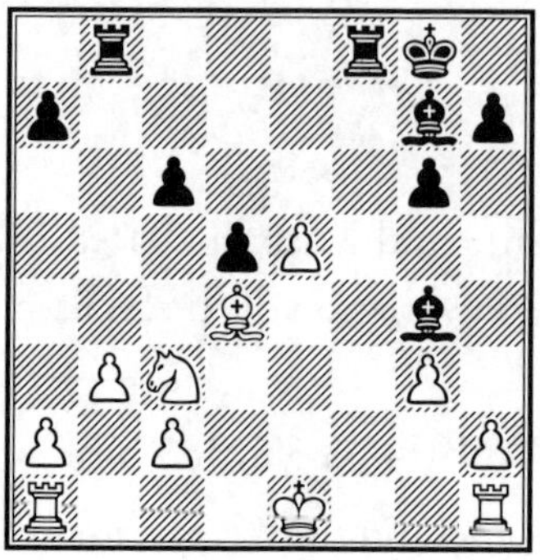

19.Rf1?

19.h3 Bd7 (19...Bf3? 20.0–0) 20.0–0–0=.

19...Rxf1+ 20.Kxf1 c5! 21.Bf2 Bxe5 22.Be1 Rf8+ 23.Kg2 Rf3 24.h3

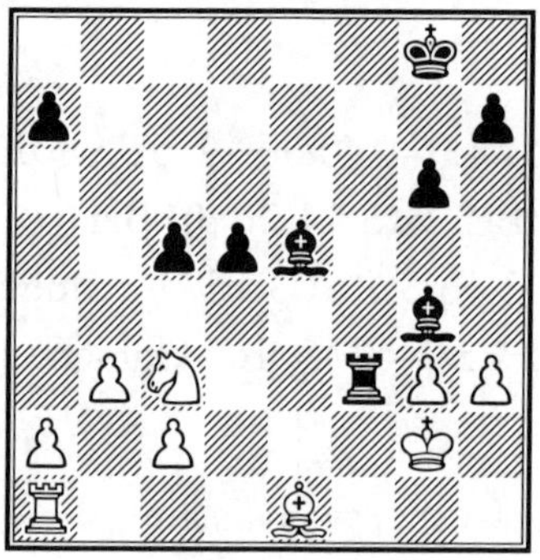

24...Rxc3 25.Bxc3 Bxc3 26.Rf1 Bf5 27.Rf2 h5 28.Re2 Kf7 29.Re3 Bd4 30.Rf3 Ke6 31.c3 Be5 32.Re3 d4 33.cxd4 cxd4 34.Re1 d3 35.h4 d2 36.Rd1 Bc3 37.Kf2 Bg4 38.Rh1 Bd4+ 39.Kg2 Kd5 40.a3 Ke4 41.Rf1 Kd3 42.Kh2 Ke2 43.Kg2 Bh3+ 44.Kxh3 Kxf1 45.b4 d1Q 46.Kh2 Qe2+ 47.Kh3 Qg2, 0–1.

National Master and computer developer Tom Crispin spoke of chess computers and his experience with Fischer:[1]

> At Lone Pine, 1976, I met a young woman chess player named Jennie Kiesling, and became friends not only with her and her family, but their friends—the family of Russ and Joan Targ who of course was Fischer's sister.

[1] From a correspondence in 2016.

I did eventually meet Fischer's mother during one of my later visits with the Targs. A few years later I did a little work for Russ with one of his psi experiments:

In May 1977 I received a phone call at work (in La Jolla) that opened with "Do you know Russ Targ?" I never understood how he got through the receptionist.

After allowing that I did in fact know Russ Targ personally, the caller identified himself as Bobby Fischer and wanted to know what I knew about computer chess. I did consider the possibility that it was a prank, for a short time. Why would Fischer call me?

After talking for some time he invited me to his place in L.A. for further discussion and a chance to experiment with his "Chess Challenger".

We met, his manager Claudia Mokarow delivered fast food, and I explained to him how computers play chess (more or less). Then we played some games on the machine. At the time I was still low expert and was reasonably pleased that I could follow the game blindfold (he didn't bother with pieces) and only took a few seconds to understand that when he said, "it's mate," he wasn't talking about the position on the board.

Even in that casual situation his intensity was evident. I did not even suggest the possibility of playing a few blitz games against him. Didn't ask for an autograph, either.

Don't remember why Fischer was with me as I retrieved some computer chess books from my car, but there he was. I left one volume behind, and he asked why. I said: "It's Samarian on the QGD. You could write it".

He actually cracked a smile.

About that time Doug Penrod was publishing the *Computer Chess Newsletter*.

On page two of *Computer Chess Newsletter* #2, Doug excerpts 7–8 paragraphs from me in which I admit to having played against Fischer's Chess Challenger. As he [Fischer] had admitted to buying one, I didn't think it remarkable that I should mention [Fischer] having played against it especially since I wrote earlier of having spoken with him.

TEXT OF CRISPIN'S LETTER:[1]

My experience with Bobby Fischer's Chess Challenger is that it should be considered weaker than 1,000, perhaps as low as 700. It falls for almost any two-mover. (ed. Note: Tom Crispin and Dennis Cooper have played against Russ McNiel's upgraded Chess Challenger and agree that it is much stronger).

...

My own preference is to sell listings of the program directly to micro-owners. It seems stupid to me to let large companies sell game packages to TV owners when for a little more $ the same owner could have a micro, with all the games: but also a computer. I want the micro industry to follow the

---

1 *Computer Chess Newsletter* #2 (1977).

> pattern of hi-fi. Software should be sold much like LP's—if it isn't simply placed in the public domain.
>
> I am hoping to collaborate with Bobby on the chess programming. I can provide the equipment and programming expertise; he could provide a somewhat better evaluation of the computer's play than I (though I am rated somewhere near 2100 I'm not too bad in that department)...
>
> After Doug died, his papers on computer chess were acquired by one of the popular microcomputer magazines of the time. They printed in full (?) my letter to Penrod in which I discussed in more detail my experience with the Chess Challenger. Every mention of the Chess Challenger—in their printed article—was prefaced with "Bobby Fischer's" in italics (and maybe even boldface), which implied endorsement. Even to me.
>
> This is pre-word processing so of course I didn't have an original copy of the letter, but I am pretty sure I would have identified the Chess Challenger as Bobby's only on the first reference to the machine.
>
> Fischer was livid. I became persona non grata to Fischer and Joan was careful to ask me to stay away anytime Bobby was visiting.
>
> Joan explained to me what had happened, and I wrote a scathing letter to the magazine in complaint, to which they wrote back saying that they would print my letter; but as I didn't read that particular journal I never learned whether or not they did. I continued to be friends with the Kieslings and Targs, but in 1983 we moved to Klamath Falls and pretty much lost contact.

When computer scientist and International Master Hans Berliner (1929–2017) died, his papers were donated to the World Chess Hall of Fame. Among the artifacts in Berliner's archive were two short letters from Fischer dated May 23, 1977, and July 12, 1977, which reinforce the view he was fascinated with computer chess at the time. Bobby's interest was serious enough that he wanted to meet face to face with Berliner to discuss the subject and asked for a copy of Berliner's thesis: "The Development of a Tactics Analyzer," which he wrote for his PhD from the Department of Computer Science at Carnegie Mellon in 1974.

The two letters also reveal a few more tidbits. Just as he did when writing to Penrod, Fischer affirmed his negative view of the Chess Challenger program, referring to it as a "piece of junk." More optimistically, Bobby noted the better programs were finally starting to avoid gross blunders.

Fischer wrote that not only was it fun and intellectually stimulating to play chess computers, but he saw commercial possibilities. A very prescient observation as dedicated playing machines, costing hundreds and sometimes thousands of dollars, were the bedrock of the U.S. Chess Federation's book and equipment sales department in the 1980s and 1990s. Rainer Rickford, publisher of the long defunct *Players Chess News*, also sold books and chess computers, and was another beneficiary of this lucrative but short-lived bonanza that ended with the emergence of stronger computers and low-cost chess playing software.

Bobby nearly endorsed the chess computer "Boris" in the late 1970s, according to its inventors Arleen and Steven Chafitz of New Midway, Maryland. They recalled traveling to Los Angeles to discuss an endorsement,[1] but like most of Fischer's business deals in the 1970s, it fell through.

1 Sonia Boin, *Frederick News-Post*, 2008.

Viktor Korchnoi and Fischer near the end of their round twelve game in Curaçao (Photo: Nathan Divinsky).

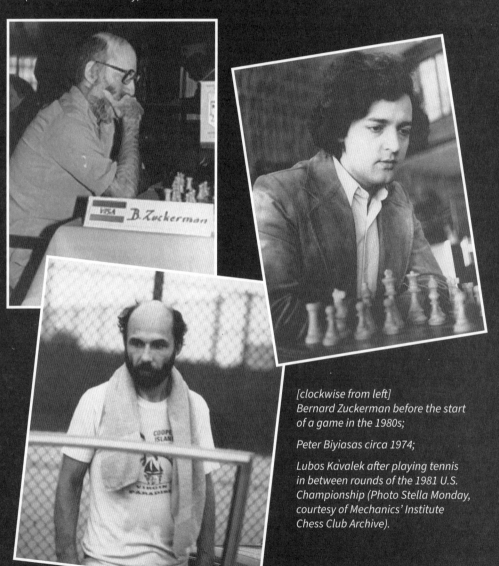

[clockwise from left]
Bernard Zuckerman before the start of a game in the 1980s;

Peter Biyiasas circa 1974;

Lubos Kavalek after playing tennis in between rounds of the 1981 U.S. Championship (Photo Stella Monday, courtesy of Mechanics' Institute Chess Club Archive).

5
ALIENATION

THE LAST MEETING WITH VIKTOR KORCHNOI

In his memoir *Chess is My Life*, Viktor Korchnoi wrote of his September 16, 1977 meeting with Fischer that took place in Pasadena, California:[1]

> The first thing I sensed was that he was terrible alone—that there was no single man or woman with whom he could be open...
>
> We talked about many things. I was staggered by his amazing chess memory. Whatever game I mentioned, he would answer instantly, as if he himself had been thinking about that game,
>
> ...[after the meeting with Fischer]I was due to start a talk and a simultaneous display. I was full of impressions of the day-time meeting, and of course, said something about this to the chess enthusiast. In the end as I understood it, Fischer's presence in Pasadena was hardly a secret for most residents of Los Angeles. But Fischer reasoned otherwise.
>
> The following day he sent me an angry letter, where he inferred that I was working for Soviet intelligence. That was enough for me. I never corresponded any more with Fischer, and had nothing more to do with him. And if I was asked if I wanted to play Fischer, I used to answer, and I still do, that apart from obligatory matches connected with the World Championship, I prefer to meet at the board with people who, I respect..."

In 2017 Genna Sosonko wrote an article about the meeting with Bobby which included the letter, discovered by Korchnoi's son Igor after his father's death:[2]

> September 25, 1977
>
> Dear Viktor,
>
> How are you? Hope you had a nice trip back.
>
> Just today I got a cassette tape copy of your speech at the Friday night September 16 exhibition (the day we met). I was very distressed. Hadn't I told you and hadn't you agreed just a few minutes earlier (before your speech) that you would keep our meeting and the substance of what we talked about

[1] Viktor Korchnoi, *Chess in My Life*. Zurich: Edition Olms, 2004.

[2] Genna Sosonko, "When Viktor met Bobby (for the last time)," *New In Chess*, #7, 2017.

completely confidential, except for the fact that we did indeed meet??? I don't understand this. Either your memory is very short or...

I told you about the severe persecution I'm undergoing by the conspirators. I thought you understood this well. I appreciate your open personality, humor, friendliness, goodwill and so forth. But I can't keep the line of communication open with someone who betrays my confidence. So the decision is yours. Incidentally some of the things you did say were quite garbled and distorted (not the tape—I mean you!). This may be due to the fact that our meeting was fairly brief or to your imperfect English or understanding of English. I know you still have your ties with the USCF and FIDE. I don't approve but that's up to you. I no longer have such ties and consider them vicious gangsters. Especially I don't want to give an "interview" with *Chess Life & Review.* It would be a great and malicious "coup" for them to gain such an "interview" directly or indirectly from you. Again I explained all this to you. You don't have to share my views but you must keep your word. You have not done this I'm sorry to say. I don't know how much damage has already been done. I guess you gave other speeches and perhaps interviews before leaving for Europe. I'll have to wait and see as these drift into print. I'd appreciate it if you you'd strictly adhere to our agreement from now on.

All the best,
Bobby

The words of both Korchnoi and Fischer speak for themselves. It's easy to empathize with both sides of the story—why Korchnoi would feel insulted by Bobby's letter, and why Bobby felt betrayed by Korchnoi. However, what can be drawn from these accounts is that while Bobby was still interacting with his peers, mistrust and paranoia were pulling him into alienation.

Sosonko remarked on Fischer's state of mind in 1977:[1]

> Bobby was thirty-four at the time, and although the ideas that would become an obsession had already taken root in his soul, he was still far from the paranoid man the world would see fifteen years later at the second match against Spassky in Sveti Stefan.

In his 1978 *Chess Life* column, Burt Hochberg commented on the likelihood of a Fischer–Korchnoi match:[2]

> It has been almost six years since Bobby played his last serious game of chess. Yet an unceasing flood of articles, rumors, speculation, and false reports have continued to circulate. Bobby no longer needs to play chess to capture the imagination of the public or to excite the curiosity of the press. He has transcended the game that gave meaning to his life, the game that one writer said seemed to have been created especially for him.

---

1 Genna Sosonko, *New In Chess,* "When Viktor met Bobby (for the last time)", #7, 2017.
2 Burt Hochberg, *Chess Life* "Bobby Fischer Update," March 1978.

During the last few years, Bobby's imminent return to the arena was announced several times in the press. As many then suspected, and as events have proved, those announcements were premature. Ex-Soviet Grandmaster Viktor Korchnoi told friends late in 1977 that in meetings with Fischer in California Bobby indicated a desire to play a match with him if a seven-figure purse could be arranged. There has been no further word on this possibility. However, the recent improvement in Korchnoi's status as a result of his victory over Boris Spassky may have increased the likelihood of a Fischer–Korchnoi match. The great publicity value of such a contest is more likely to attract the money, and Korchnoi's political independence avoids the obstacles which otherwise might have been imposed by the Soviet Chess Federation.

ZUCKERMAN, KAVALEK, AND LOMBARDY

The 1978 U.S. Championship held at the Worldwide Church of God's Ambassador College in Pasadena was the first time the event had been held in southern California.[1] By this time Bobby was clearly on the outs with the church. Unbeknown at the time, less than a year later the WCG would be in shambles, the State of California instituting criminal proceedings for a variety of charges including pilfering of church funds, liquidating assets, using church transactions for personal gain and living extravagantly.

The fifteen-player round robin (Walter Browne dropped out after a dispute over the lighting) was held during much of June and provided Bobby with a chance to meet up with several old friends who were playing or spectating, including childhood buddies William Lombardy, Bernard Zuckerman, and Anthony Saidy. As it turned out, he would never see any of them again.

Zuckerman's experience with Fischer is written about in a lengthy 1985 *Sports Illustrated* article on Bobby by William Nack (must reading for information about Fischer in the late 1970s to mid-1980):[2]

> In fact, he [Zuckerman] went to dinner with Fischer at a restaurant in Chinatown in Los Angeles—Fischer and Zuckerman are avid eaters of Chinese food—and they brought along young Larry Christiansen who was meeting Fischer for the first time.
>
> "We talked about chess," Christiansen says. "He didn't have much respect for Karpov's play... He launched into a tirade against the Jews, the world conspiracy. He seemed like a nice guy, then he launched into that tirade. I felt kind of sorry for him. I could see Zuckerman in the back seat, masking laughter."

---

1 Arnold Denker and Herman Steiner played a match for the U.S. Championship in Los Angeles in 1946.

2 William Nack, *Sports Illustrated*, "Bobby Fischer," July 28, 1985, (pp. 70–76, 78–84).

Zuckerman was close to Bobby for twenty years, but as with other old friends he found Bobby's involvement with the Worldwide Church of God troubling:[1]

> On a visit back to New York, while driving around Manhattan with his friend Bernard Zuckerman, Bobby made a reference to Satan. Zuckerman, ever sarcastic, said "Satan? Why don't you introduce me?" Bobby was appalled. "What? Don't you believe in Satan?"

Not long after, Zuckerman, who had become bored with Fischer's fascination with conspiracy theories and growing antisemitism, parted ways with Bobby.

Reminiscing in 2017, Lubos Kavalek, the top-rated American player of the 1970s after Bobby retired, wrote:[2]

> Bobby visited me in the fall of 1977 after I was helping to arrange his last meeting with Karpov in Washington, D.C. We were in touch by phone and mail.
>
> The last time I saw Bobby was in October 1978 when he visited us for two weeks before flying to Belgrade to see Gligo, who was running for FIDE presidency in Buenos Aires. I was still in touch with Bobby in 1979.
>
> After Browne left Pasadena (1978 U.S. Championship), Kashdan offered me his apartment. It was huge and belonged to some professor. It was far away from all the other players and Bobby was visiting me almost daily. We talked mainly about film and his movie role in a Milos Forman film. We also talked about making a chess video with another Czech-American director, but, did not discuss the championship at all. We cooked dinners there or went to some restaurants. Once in a grocery store, we bumped into Bill Lombardy and the conversation was quick.
>
> "Hi Bobby."
>
> "Hi. Do you still write for *Sport Illustrated?*" It took Bill aback. Bobby and I left, and I would not write what he said about Bill.

This story was corroborated by Lombardy—Fischer was still bitter over the article he wrote on Reykjavík for *Sports Illustrated*.[3]

The biography currently posted on Lombardy's website claims that many years after his article appeared Lombardy came to the conclusion that he had been maliciously edited:[4]

> Lombardy found that his text in the article had been conveniently and criminally edited (criminal tampering) by one Brad Darrack (a pen name!), who, by his editorship for and blithely allowed by *Time-Life*, "sweet ole Brad"

---

[1] Frank Brady, *Endgame: Bobby Fischer's Remarkable Rise and Fall—from America's Brightest Prodigy to the Edge of Madness*. New York: Crown Publishers, 2011, (p. 210).

[2] Lubos Kavalek in a 2017 email to John Donaldson.

[3] William Lombardy, *Sports Illustrated*, "A Mystery Wrapped in an Enigma," January 21, 1974,

[4] Williamlombardychess.com.

> sought to assure the undeserved success of his own planned fable *Bobby Fischer vs. the Rest of the World*.
>
> In short, Lombardy, only many years after the match discovered to what degree Darrach had tampered with the article Darrach conveniently named Lombardy's article "A Mystery Wrapped in Enigma"! Darrach had changed the tenor of the article by subtly inserting his own creative opinions and imperfect truths...

Were fabricated words responsible for the end of Lombardy's friendship with Bobby? Maybe, but there is no evidence to support Lombardy's allegations.

Bobby may have taken offense at what Lombardy actually wrote, but more likely it was a matter of principle, as Fischer had made it clear he did not want his second writing about the match. Bobby was always very sensitive to what he perceived as others benefiting from their relationship with him, be it for financial gain or publicity. Lombardy appears to have been found guilty of the former by Bobby and Ed Edmondson the latter. Becoming Bobby's spokesman seems to have made one vulnerable to getting the axe, as Lombardy mentions in his *Sport Illustrated* article, Edmondson's replacement Fred Cramer almost suffered a similar fate:[1]

> Fischer made no public statements himself, yet when his aides attempted to explain his actions he would object.
>
> After the objection he would retreat once again into seclusion. One time he opened some mail from Buenos Aires, dumping clippings on a table. A quick look at the newspaper stories raised his ire. "You're being quoted all over," he blurted out to Fred Cramer. "No more interviews. People think you are speaking for me."

Fischer and Kavalek remained close and were still corresponding in the late 1970s. Bobby wrote to Svetozar Gligorić on August 5, 1978:

> ...Anyway I'm mailing this letter to you c/o Brother Lubos (Kavalek). He told me he is leaving for Montilla on the 10th so I hope he gets it on time.

Kavalek received the letter from Bobby on schedule and was able to deliver it to Gligorić, one of several occasions he acted as a courier for Fischer during this period. Clearly, Kavalek had Bobby's trust, but after 1979 they would have no further contact.

Kavakek was not the only one of Bobby's close friends to stop hearing from him. As part of his gradual withdrawal from the world, sometime around the end of the 1970s, without warning, Fischer cut off correspondence with Svetozar Gligorić and Pal Benko. He had exchanged dozens of letters with these two long-

---

[1] William Lombardy, *Sports Illustrated*, A Mystery Wrapped in Enigma," January 21, 1974.

Steve Brandwein manning the wall-board for a game between Torre and Tal at the 1991 Pan Pacific International, San Francisco (Photo: Richard Shorman).

time friends in the mid to late 1970s, but around 1979 he stopped writing and would not make contact for over a decade.

Another old friend of Bobby's who suffered a similar fate to Lombardy was chess master and schoolteacher Ron Gross. They parted ways after Gross spoke about Bobby in an article which appeared in the *Orange County Register* in 1982. It didn't matter that what Gross said was complimentary—he had spoken to the press.

The break with Gross was permanent. Fortunately Lombardy and Fischer patched things up near the end of Bobby's life. Lombardy's letter in support of Bobby when he was imprisoned in Japan seemed to have broken the ice and the two spoke regularly—though never again face to face—after Fischer was released and settled in Iceland.

SAN FRANCISCO WITH BIYIASAS, BROWNE, BRANDWEIN, AND BUFF

In 1981 Fischer had two extended stays in San Francisco (these two visits appear to be the only occasions he left Los Angeles in the early '80s). William Nack described the circumstances of one of those visits:[1]

> In 1981 he had lived at the apartment of Greek-born Grandmaster Peter Biyiasas and his wife, Ruth Haring. Through Jim Buff, Biyiasas had invited Fischer to live with them.
>
> One day Buff called. "Peter, he's coming up. Bobby's coming up on the bus to stay with you!"
>
> Fischer arrived one early March morning with his suitcase of clothes and vitamins and a large orange-juice squeezer that he had bought in Mexico. He stayed for two months, returned to Los Angeles in the summer, then came back in the fall to stay two more months. They swam in the ocean, played pinball machines, bowled, went to movies, squeezed oranges, and played

[1] William Nack, *Sports Illustrated*, "Bobby Fischer," July 28, 1985, (pp. 70–76, 78–84).

[left] Steve Brandwein (Photo: Richard Shorman); [right] Jim Buff (Photo: Elliott Winslow).

baseball in Golden Gate Park. Fischer shagged Buff's fly balls and pegged them back to the plate as hard as he could.

"How was it coming in?" asked Bobby.

He was more overpowering at the chessboard with Biyiasas. During his four months in San Francisco, he beat Biyiasas seventeen straight speed games before Biyiasas finally surrendered.

"He was too good," Biyiasas says. "There was no use in playing him. It wasn't interesting. I was getting beaten, and it wasn't clear to me why. It wasn't like I made this mistake or that mistake. It was like I was being gradually outplayed, from the start. He wasn't taking any time to think. The most depressing thing about it is that I wasn't even getting out of the middle game to an endgame. I don't ever remember an endgame. He honestly believes there is no one for him to play, no one worthy of him. I played him, and I can attest to that. It's not interesting."

Walter Browne described another visit:[1]

When I returned home in August I was honored when Bobby Fischer visited my home for the first time [Walter lived in Berkeley]. I hadn't heard from him in almost nine years. I was in a rather unfavorable light in his eyes because of a *Sports Illustrated* article of January 12, 1976, where many comparisons were drawn between us by the creative writer Ray Kennedy, who had embellished part of my story. After Bobby was wined and dined and in excellent spirits, we gravitated to my game room as he inspected my book collection, plus we analyzed what I considered a nice batch of games from the recent U.S. Championship in Indiana. Overall, he was complimentary and for Bobby, who is naturally very critical this was extraordinary.

This was one of those magical moments in my life that could have been frozen in time. I hadn't felt so positive since 1975. I just won my fifth consecutive U.S. Championship and then an international event in Chile, and

[1] Walter Browne, *The Stress of Chess ...and its Infinite Finesse*. Netherlands: New In Chess, 2012, (pp. 219–220).

> my hero, the greatest natural talent in the history of chess, was imparting his knowledge and incomparable genius in my house!
>
> We played a game of pool but he never got to shoot as I ran from the break in 8 ball. Thanks to my son Marcelo's expertise in pool I had lots of practice at the time. We conversed during a roundabout walk in the hills, and he expressed many opinions on world affairs bordering on conspiracies, but also made sense with his complaints on the way he was treated by the World Chess organizers of FIDE, regarding the conditions for the match with Karpov and other issues.
>
> Bobby visited twice more, being accompanied as always by his long-time companion of many decades the affable Jim Buff, formally of New York, who has lived in San Francisco since the 1970s. On the third occasion he accepted my hospitality and stayed overnight. He enjoyed the book *666 Games* [*666 Kurzpartien* is a collection of 666 short games] by a German writer named Kurt Richter. The next day he was on the phone five to six hours straight! I told him there had to be a limit on phone use—after all, he was visiting us and I wanted to share more time with him. He must have taken offense and unfortunately the immature frustrated and naive child within him acted out. Bobby left soon after and never made contact with me again. We'd shared very good times and experiences of the early days and this is the way I've chosen to cherish him in my memory.

The event Walter won in Santiago, Chile was held August 2–14, so by Browne's timeline the visits with Fischer would have been in late August, September, or conceivably October.

Steve Brandwein remembered that Fischer visited San Francisco before and after the 1981 U.S. Open in Palo Alto (held August 2–14, 1981), while Fischer's arrest on May 26, 1981, in Pasadena, further tightens the timeline.

Nack got the dates right, but his account of Fischer's visit isn't quite accurate—Fischer had separate hosts during his stays in San Francisco. Peter Biyiasas and his wife, Women's International Master Ruth Haring (1955–2018), put him up, so did long-time friends Jim Buff (from childhood) and Steve Brandwein (since the mid-1960s). Jim and Steve lived at 521 3rd Avenue in the Richmond District of San Francisco. In the early '80s "Buff Manor" (as it was christened) was more often than not full to the brim with chess players. While a couch was good enough for International Master Jeremy Silman and FIDE Master Paul Whitehead, Bobby would have wanted some privacy and this would explain why he didn't stay with Buff and Brandwein on his second trip to the Bay Area.

Buff, Fischer, and Brandwein were known to strike terror in the heart of buffet owners. One of their favorite such establishments was Harry's Hofbrau in San Leandro, which was noted for its hearty German cuisine. The first time they visited the owner took one look at Fischer and Buff, both well over six feet tall and 220 pounds, and figured he was definitely not going to make any money off of them. Then he spotted Brandwein hidden between them and figured it would not be so bad after all, not realizing, that although of average height and weight, Steve was actually a formidable eating machine.

As expected, Fischer also played and studied chess during his stays in San Francisco. Biyiasas was not Fischer's only blitz opponent. Stephen Brandwein stopped playing in tournaments after reaching 2300 but continued to study several hours a day. He soon enjoyed a nationwide reputation as a blitz player par excellence, both incredibly fast and well versed in opening theory. He held his own against many strong blitz players in New York City in the '60s and '70s and not long before Fischer's visits had split a six-game match with Miquel Najdorf at the Mechanics' Institute Chess Club. Bobby and Steve played several sessions of three-minute chess with Fischer winning around 70% of them. Many years later Steve recalled most of the games he was White saw the Polugaevsky Najdorf (6.Bg5 e6 7.f4 b5) appearing on the board—interesting because this was a line Bobby only played once (Minić–Fischer, Skopje 1967).

Fischer was still sharp and up to date on current theory in 1981. Peter Biyiasas remembers showing Bobby his games from Wijk aan Zee 1980 where he had a great result. He was especially proud of his victory over Jan Timman, which opened **1.e4 c5 2.Nf3 d6 3.Nc3 a6 4.g3 Nc6 5.Bg2 Bg4 6.h3 Bxf3 7.Qxf3**

Now Timman played **7...g6**, which was strongly answered by **8.e5! dxe5? 9.Qxc6+!** with a much better endgame for White. Immediately after Biyiasas showed this, Bobby said he knew the idea from his game with Vlastimil Hort (Palma de Mallorca 1970). After he played 6...Bxf3 Hort spent a few seconds deciding on the best recapture (eventually taking with the bishop), time Fischer used to spot 7...g6 8.e5! dxe5? 9.Qxc6+!. Bobby kept this little nugget in his memory for over a decade.

Ruth Haring, whose USCF rating was around 2150, spoke of the time she came home from work, and to her horror, found Bobby playing through one of her games. He had unearthed a bunch of her game scores and spent the better part of the day going through them. She worried what he would think of her play, but to her surprise Bobby was kind and supportive and offered some helpful suggestions on how to improve.

His main advice? She was too self-critical of her play and should be more optimistic. Certainly, this was not a weakness Bobby suffered from! Interestingly, Fischer had offered similar counsel to Bernard Zuckerman twenty years before.

Ruth remembered playing tandem games, with Fischer and Jim Buff facing off against her and Peter with no consultation permitted. She also recalled visits to Chinatown with Bobby where he would stock up on various exotic tonics and medicines.

Bobby may have first developed a liking for hot springs and thermal baths during the 1972 match in Reykjavík. He was certainly a regular when he lived in Hungary and Japan, and such was the case during his stays in San Francisco where he faithfully visited the Kabuki Springs and Spa in Japantown.

One place Bobby did not visit during his 1981 stays in San Francisco was the Mechanics' Institute Chess Club, the nation's oldest (founded in 1854)—he had visited the club in earlier trips to the city in 1957 (U.S. Junior Open) and 1964 (simultaneous exhibition and lecture).

Not all was bright during Bobby's visits to the "Baghdad by the Bay." Fischer's certainty that Soviet players were fixing games was already set in cement and this obsession became more pronounced as time went on. He would accuse Kasparov and Karpov of prearranging the results of their matches—a view few grandmasters outside of ex-Soviets Josif Dorfman and Valery Salov shared. When Bobby started corresponding with Gligorić and Benko again in 1991, this idée fixe, that Kasparov and Karpov fixed their World Championship matches, was a constant theme. Later this delusion became public knowledge with Fischer's radio interviews in 1999.

More alarming to those who knew him was Fischer's growing fixation with antisemitism and various conspiracy theories. Even friends with well-reasoned arguments couldn't sway him as the following anecdote illustrates.

Bobby and Steve Brandwein visited a couple of Russian language bookshops in the Richmond section of San Francisco, home to many who left the Soviet Union. Their first stop was Znanie ("knowledge" in English) where Bobby bought a bunch of Russian language chess material. Then they ventured to another bookshop that Steve had never been to before—which says a lot as Brandwein was an insatiable reader who sometimes devoured three books in a day.

This bookstore was filled with so much anti-communist literature that Steve, with his far-left leanings, may have felt like a vampire immersed in holy water, but he hung around long enough to hear Bobby ask the sales clerk, "Where is the good stuff." This got Steve's attention. "The good stuff? What could Bobby mean? San Francisco being San Francisco it couldn't be adult material—that would be on the shelves." The sales clerk pretended to ignore the question, but Fischer pressed him until he finally relented and went to a back room. Several minutes later he returned with a stack of antisemitic literature of the vilest kind. *The Protocols of the Elders of Zion* was at the top of the heap and Bobby was beaming. A few minutes later, selections made and paid for, the two left the store.

Heading back to Jim Buff's place, Bobby proceeded to lecture Steve on *The Protocols of the Elders of Zion* and what a brilliant book it was. Big mistake. Steve casually mentioned to Bobby that the book was of course a well-known fraud and proceeded to systematically tear it apart. Initially Bobby tried to defend himself, but after ten minutes he gave up and changed the subject, especially after Steve suggested they dispense with the second-rate stuff and create their own conspiracy theory! Fischer had inadvertently found one of the few people on the planet who didn't suffer fools, no matter how famous, and who knew just about everything under the sun. This episode was typical Steve and evidence that once Bobby had made up his mind he couldn't be persuaded to listen to logic. Canadian International Master Camille Coudari had a similar experience with Bobby when he interviewed him for *The Great Chess Movie*, as did Svetozar Gligorić during their long correspondence.

Bobby kept a very low public profile throughout the 1980s with one notable exception: Bobby sent a letter to the *Encyclopedia Judaica* claiming he wasn't Jewish. This was a particularly nasty affair and brought up a topic that Fischer would mention on numerous occasions the next two decades—his belief that circumcision was mutilation performed on helpless babies.

QUEST FOR COMPANIONSHIP

Without tournament play to occupy him, Bobby was lonesome and spent a lot of time trying to find a partner—though with little success. He developed a close friendship (but nothing more) with Women's International Master Shernaz Kennedy who played for the United States in the 1986 Olympiad in Dubai. Kennedy, who moved from India to the United States in 1976, has taught chess to children in New York City for four decades. She is working on a book to be titled *King's Indian: Inside the Mind of Bobby Fischer* that will include a section on Fischer's marriage proposal to her.[1]

After Shernaz Kennedy, Petra Stadler (now Dautov) entered Bobby's life. Their experiences were similar. A fan letter from Petra (Boris Spassky was the matchmaker) was well received and followed by a phone call from Bobby, albeit at 4AM in her location, Germany (Fischer always lived on Fischer time). In April 1988, after surviving the interview—according to Petra she needed to be able to mate with bishop and knight versus king, and be of Aryan blood to pass—she flew to Los Angeles and spent several weeks there with Bobby.

Petra returned to Germany and there was no immediate follow-up because Fischer didn't have the money to relocate to Germany. That changed in the spring of 1990 when Dutch organizer Bessel Kok invited Fischer to Brussels where Kok was living and the now long defunct Grandmaster's Association was headquartered.

After his weeklong stay in Belgium, where he registered at the Sheraton Hotel under the alias Bobby Brown (Robert Dallas James and Robert James were other

---

[1] At this writing there is no information as to if, or when, this book will be published.

names he had used in the past to avoid detection), Fischer moved on to Germany. The fee Fischer received from Kok, his mother's Social Security income and his book royalties enabled Bobby to spend roughly a year in Germany.

Bobby Fischer—wie er wirklich ist. Ein Jahr mit dem Schachgenie[1] (*Bobby Fischer as He Really Is: A Year with a Chess Genius*) was published in 1995. According to Petra Dautov (she married Rustem Dautov, a German grandmaster of Tatar origin, in 1992), this book offers a look at the "real Bobby"

Petra described Fischer's first few months in Germany spent in her town of Seeheim, a forty-minute drive south of Frankfurt. He met with Boris Spassky and French-Lebanese Grandmaster Bachar Kouatly to discuss a possible Fischer–Spassky rematch in the Middle East, and spent time with German Grandmaster Lothar Schmid. It's nice to think that the reunion with the arbiter of the '72 World Championship (he also arbitrated the '92 rematch) might have taken place in Schmid's home—Bobby, with his great love for chess literature, would have been in heaven in Schmid's extensive world-famous chess library. A few personal details are revealed in the book, including Fischer's love of fresh juices and large salads. However, he was hardly a vegetarian. Petra, who was, wrote that Bobby ate large quantities of meat. There is also an amusing chapter on his search for a particular leather chess wallet that he had used for many years. Bobby was always very specific in the type of chessboards and pieces he used, and this extended to the chess wallet—he liked one that was real-leather. Such wallets were popular among top players in the 1950s and 1960s but were gradually replaced by synthetic ones.

Even though things didn't work out with Petra, Fischer stayed in Germany, only returning to the United States when journalists discovered his whereabouts.

Bobby spent three months in Waischenfeld at the Hotel Pulvermühle with the chess-playing Bezold family. This hotel, run by Kaspar Bezold, an enthusiastic German club player, had hosted Petrosian when he played in an international tournament in Bamberg in 1968, and other players over the years. Bobby was very much at home with the Bezolds enjoying privacy, the good food and beer, and the beautiful countryside. Maybe the Bezolds even had a dog that accompanied Bobby on his walks—he clearly loved animals but apparently had no pets as an adult.

Fischer played the role of chess mentor to young Michael Bezold, a master at the time (he later earned the grandmaster title), who enjoyed showing Bobby different endgame studies. Bezold joins a select group of young players who are known to have studied chess with Fischer post-Reykjavík. Some of the others

[1] Petra Dautov, *Bobby Fischer–wie er wirklich ist. Ein Jahr mit dem Schachgenie*. P. Dautov California-Verlag: Germany, 1995.

include the Polgar sisters, Péter Lékó, and American players Grandmaster Alex Sherzer and Master Lael Kaplan. Sherzer and Kaplan met Bobby several times at one of the famous baths in Budapest around 1994. Kaplan remembers that Bobby still had an excellent memory, recalling games he played from the early 1960s without a problem. One other youngster, who was not a famous player, that should be added to this list is Claudia and Arthur Mokarow's son Kevin. He played as a teenager and the World Chess Hall of Fame in St. Louis has a Chess Informant that Bobby dedicated to him.

Fischer might have continued living in Germany indefinitely if his cover had not been blown. Once he saw the journalists coming it was back to the United States. Petra wrote about Fischer's fear of journalists and his desire to maintain his privacy as some sort of paranoia—maybe, maybe not, but the press did find him in the end.

This was not the first time the press interfered with Bobby's tranquility in Germany. During a visit to West Berlin in 1978 to meet his mother he met up with an old acquaintance, Alfred Seppelt. The two had first met during the 1958 Interzonal and two years later Seppelt had arranged a match between the best players of West Berlin and the U.S. Olympiad team where Bobby defeated Klaus Darga. Bobby and Seppelt made a visit to the famous department store KaDeWe where they found the future Correspondence Grandmaster Arno Nickel demonstrating Mephisto, an early commercial chess program. Bobby couldn't resist playing the machine but beat a hasty retreat when Nickel recognized him. Unfortunately, what was once a good friendship became forever etched in Bobby's mind as treachery when Seppelt sold a photo of Bobby to the *Berliner Morgenpost*.

"MACKIE'S BACK IN TOWN..."

One day in 1986 Dodd Darin walked into the Los Angeles office of *Players Chess News* where International Master Jeremy Silman was editor. Dodd's father, singer Bobby Darin (Dodd's mother was actress Sandra Dee), was a well-known chess enthusiast and Dodd shared his father's passion. Bobby Darin died suddenly in December 1973 shortly before the scheduled first annual Bobby Darin Classic a sixteen-player grandmaster round robin that Darin was sponsoring. The tournament offered a prize fund of $25,000 (the largest for a tournament at that time) and a list of entrants that included most of the top players in the world including Boris Spassky, Tigran Petrosian, and Mikhail Tal. Sadly, the event was canceled upon Darin's death.

Dodd, a 1600 rated player—not bad at all for someone who started playing as an adult—was hoping he could resurrect the Bobby Darin Classic and was

Bobby Darin playing chess with actor José Ferrer.

trying to get contacts in the chess world. Silman, knowing Fischer would be interested in meeting the son of the Rock & Roll Hall of Fame singer, put Dodd in contact with Shernaz Kennedy who in turn put Dodd in contact with Fischer.

A love of chess and the Bobby Darin connection (Fischer was a big fan of his music) made Dodd and Bobby fast friends. The two met often to play racquetball, and Dodd, a strong varsity tennis player in college (and eighteen years younger) consistently crushed Bobby. Not being one who would took losses lightly, Fischer attributed his defeat to Dodd "getting lucky" and would vow revenge—though it rarely came.

Fischer "hung-out" at Dodd's home for long hours, playing on Dodd's chess computer—he was adamant about making sure his games were erased. Bobby loved to eat and would say to Dodd, "I'll bring the food;" oddly, what he usually brought was food from a Jewish Deli. While Dodd enjoyed this time with Bobby he eventually tired of the endless conspiracy talk—Dodd's father, an outspoken liberal, had been an active supporter of Robert Kennedy's presidential bid. Dodd drew the line when Fischer took him to a white supremacist bookstore and refused to accompany him to such stores after that.

Fischer would not give Dodd his phone number and never revealed where he lived. To meet, Fischer would phone Dodd and request to be picked him up at a particular bus stop. After Fischer's visit, Dodd would attempt to return him to the same bus stop. However, at what seemed a random location, Fischer would suddenly yell, "Stop the car! I'll get out here." On one occasion Dodd actually watched in his rear view mirror as Fischer jumped behind some bushes, lying in wait until he was sure Dodd was out of sight and couldn't follow him.

They lost touch when Fischer went to Europe in 1992. Dodd did receive one 3 AM (Los Angeles time) call from Europe, but nothing after that.

6

LIARS, CHEATERS, AND PREARRANGED GAMES (FISCHER'S ANALYSIS AND ANNOTATIONS)

On many occasions from the mid-1980s on, Fischer talked of writing a book about what he believed were prearranged matches between Karpov and Kasparov. It's unknown how far he got, but a March 30, 1991 letter to Svetozar Gligorić (the first in a dozen years), suggests Bobby had given the matter a great deal of thought:[1]

> Dear Gligo (or is it Gliga and I forgot) it was very nice to get back in touch after so many years—I think about twelve! The predominant factor in chess today is cheating, and as you added, lying. Of course the two go hand in hand. Even the allegedly anti-Soviet Ljubojević is making deals. In *Informator #49* in his game with Kasparov (White) he played the opening so incredibly badly, and Kasparov returned the compliment. I have to believe it was prearranged.

(78) Nimzo – Indian

Garry Kasparov – Ljubomir Ljubojević

Linares 1990

Annotated by Fischer.

1.d4 Nf6 2.c4 e6 3.Nc3 Bb4 4.f3 d5 5.a3 Be7 6.e4 dxc4⁇

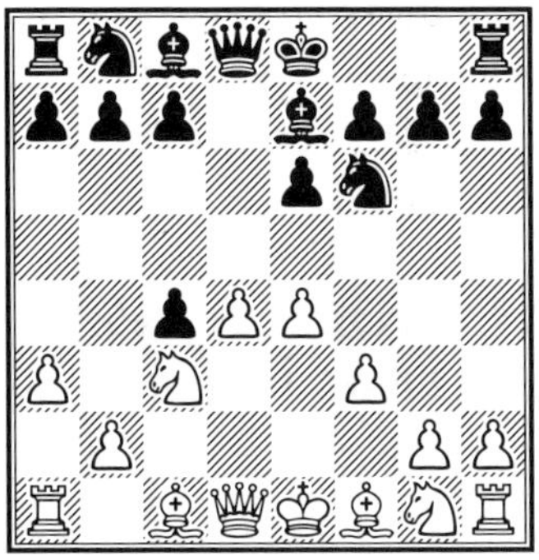

Is this a move?

7.Bxc4 c5 8.dxc5⁇

[1] Fischer's letter to Gligorić is in the DeLucia Collection.

And after suspicious sharp play the game was drawn. First of all, after the not terribly hard to find 8.Nge2, doesn't White have a clear positional advantage? Secondly, what about instead of capturing playing for even more with the restraining move 7.Be3!?.

When I showed this to some German players last year I was informed that Ljubojević was on the organizing committee in Linares. Could it be no one talks about prearrangements because no one is clean except yours truly?

Also it's interesting to note that Ljubojević sprung a novelty against a variation Kasparov never, or almost never plays.... very suspicious, very suspicious indeed. I have a nose for prearrangement and this game was prearranged—period. No questions about it.

Starting with Karpov we had a new breed of Soviet chessplayers. Before Karpov the Soviets were fairly good to mediocre players who heavily employed the device of cheating by prearrangement. That is to say, they were chessplayers who regularly cheated on orders from the Soviet government. But starting with Karpov we have the first Soviet "chess actor" rather than chess player. And of course the trend continued with Weinstein–Kasparov (even his name is phony).

What is the difference between a Soviet chess player and a Soviet "chess actor"? A top Soviet chessplayer is primarily a chess player who vastly enhances his results (on orders from his government) by prearranging games, whole matches, etc. A top Soviet "chess actor" is primarily an actor who on orders from his government plays the role of "world chess champion" or "world chess challenger" etc. Chess ability, incredible as this may sound, is a minor almost totally insignificant factor. Chess actors are chosen not for their chess ability but more for their acting ability. Their main requirement is they must be completely ruthless and immoral, and lack all self-respect and culture, and above all follow instructions to the "T."

The plain fact of the matter is most (not some) of Kasparov games are prearranged. Ditto for Karpov. All of the games from their last match were prearranged. This becomes clear when one studies the openings, the times per moves, etc. When you write a book about this match and fail to state that the match was prearranged you are doing a great disservice to chess and chess fans and players around the world...

8...Qxd1+ 9.Kxd1 Bxc5 10.Nb5 Bb6 11.e5 Nd5 12.Nd6+ Ke7 13.f4 Nc6 14.Nf3 Ne3+ 15.Bxe3 Bxe3 16.g3 Rd8 17.b4 f6 18.Ke2 Bd4 19.b5 Bxa1 20.bxc6 fxe5 21.Nxc8+ Raxc8 22.Rxa1 exf4 23.Rb1 Rxc6 24.Rxb7+ Kf6 25.Rb4 fxg3 26.hxg3 h5 27.Ke3 e5, ½–½.

What can be said about Fischer's comments to the game Kasparov–Ljubojević, Linares 1990, confining ourselves to matters of fact and not speculation? First, Fischer is correct: 6...dxc4 is a rare move—the game between Kasparov and Ljubojević might be the first time it was tried, but it was played subsequently by several strong players.

Objectively speaking Ljubojević's novelty is not terribly impressive. 8.Nge2 may or may not be better than 8.dxc5, but Bobby's 7.Be3!, as played in Milov–Ricardi, Buenos Aires 1996, is the reason this line is seldom seen in grandmaster practice.

It's true that Kasparov had not played 4.f3 prior to this game, his two main anti-Nimzo lines being 4.Nf3 and 4.Qc2. However he did play the Saemisch (4.a3) against Beliavsky in 1983, and 4.f3 d5 5.a3 Bxc3+ 6.bxc3 is a common way to reach Saemisch positions while avoiding set-ups in which Black has not committed to ...d5.

How to explain the opening choices of both players? Ljubomir Ljubojević (b. 1950) was one of the most talented players of the 1970s and 1980s. A gifted tactician with a strong intuition, he reached as high as number three on the FIDE rating list (in 1983), but never qualified for the Candidates. He was never known for being an opening specialist, something that proved to be a serious handicap in his games against Kasparov who owned him (12½–3½) despite being Black in 12 of the 16 games they played at a classical time control.

Whether Kasparov played 4.Qc2, 4.Nf3 or 4.f3 against the Nimzo-Indian he was going to be better versed in opening theory. It's almost certain that 6...dxc4 was improvised at the board by Ljubojević who was constantly trying to avoid Kasparov's opening preparation. Although this didn't offer him any success as White (he lost a miserable series of anti-Sicilian games after ditching 3.d4), Ljubo did manage a few half-points as Black with sidelines (1.d4 d5 2.c4 c6 3.Nc3 Nf6 4.e3 g6 with a quick ...a5 led to a draw at Brussels 1987) where he caught Garry off-guard early on. Their game from Linares 1990 belongs in this category.

Fischer loved the endgame studies Jan Timman showed him during their meeting in 1990 and reciprocated by showing the Dutch grandmaster discoveries he had made in the games of Garry Kasparov and Anatoly Karpov. According to Timman, Fischer was still using *Chess Informant* as his main source of information at that time.

(79) Sicilian
Vassily Ivanchuk – Garry Kasparov
Tilburg 1989

1.e4 c5 2.Nf3 d6 3.d4 cxd4 4.Nxd4 Nf6 5.Nc3 a6 6.Bg5 e6 7.f4 Qc7 8.Qe2 Nc6 9.0–0–0 Nxd4 10.Rxd4 Be7 11.e5 dxe5 12.fxe5 Nd5 13.Bxe7

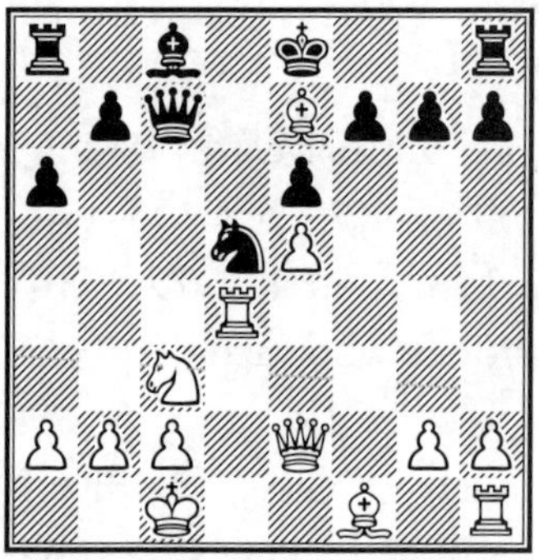

13...Nxe7

The main alternative was 13...Nxc3 when Kasparov in *Chess Informant* gave the following analysis:

14.Qg4 Qxe5 15.Bh4 Qe3+ 16.Rd2 Nxa2+ 17.Kd1 0–0 18.Qa4 e5 and after a few more moves concludes White is better. His then second Alexander Nikitin gave the same analysis in *New in Chess* 1989/8.

Timman writes that Fischer had worked out that this analysis was wrong. Then instead of 18…e5?, the correct move for Black was 18...Qe5! with the point that 19.Qxa2? would be met by ...Qh5+. That after the superior 19.c3 b5 20.Qd4 Qxd4 21.Rxd4 e5 White is behind in material without any compensation. Twenty years later the silicon oracles are in complete agreement with Bobby.

Fischer had a nice variation worked out after the stronger 17.Kb1 in 17…Qxd2 18.Qxg7 Rf8 19.Qf6 Qd7 20.Kxa2 and the position is very unpleasant for Black. Timman points out the second player can improve with: 19...Nc3+! 20.bxc3 Qd6 21.Be2 Bd7 22.Rd1 Qc5 23.Bh5 Qb6+ 24.Kc1 Qe3+ and the White king is unable to escape the checks.

Timman concludes Fischer 17.Kb1 was indeed stronger than Kasparov and Nikitin's 17.Kd1.

14.Ne4 0–0 15.Qh5 Ng6 16.Ng5 h6 17.Nf3 b5 18.Bd3 Bb7 19.Bxg6 fxg6 20.Qxg6 Bd5 21.Kb1 Rac8 22.Rc1 Qe7 23.Rg4 Rc4 24.Rxc4 bxc4

25.c3 Qa7 26.Qc2 Bxf3 27.gxf3 Qe3 28.Qa4 Qd3+ 29.Ka1 Rxf3 30.a3 Qd5 31.Qxa6 Rh3 32.Rg1 Rxh2 33.Qc8+ Kh7 34.Qc7 Rg2 35.Rxg2 Qd1+, ½–½.

(80) Queen's Gambit
Anatoly Karpov – Lajos Portisch
Linares 1989

1.d4 d5 2.c4 e6 3.Nc3 Be7 4.cxd5 exd5 5.Bf4 c6 6.e3 Bf5 7.g4 Bg6 8.h4 h5 9.g5 Bd6 10.Nge2 Na6 11.Bxd6 Qxd6 12.Nf4 Nc7 13.Be2 Qb4 14.Qd2 Ne7 15.Bf3 Ne6 16.Nce2 Nxf4 17.Nxf4 Qxd2+ 18.Kxd2 Be4 19.Bxe4 dxe4 20.Rac1 0–0–0 21.Rc5 Nd5 22.Nxd5 Rxd5 23.Rhc1 Rhd8 24.b4 Kc7 25.Ke2 a6 26.f3 exf3+ 27.Kxf3 R5d6 28.Rf5 R8d7 29.Rcc5 Re7 30.Rce5 Kd8 31.a4 g6 32.Rxe7 Kxe7 33.Re5+ Kf8 34.Ke4 f6 35.gxf6 Rxf6 36.b5 axb5 37.axb5 Kf7 38.Rc5 Ke7 39.Rg5 Kf7 40.Rg2 Rf5 41.bxc6 bxc6 42.Rc2 Rf6 43.Ra2 Ke7 44.Ra7+ Kd6 45.Rg7 Ke6 46.Kd3

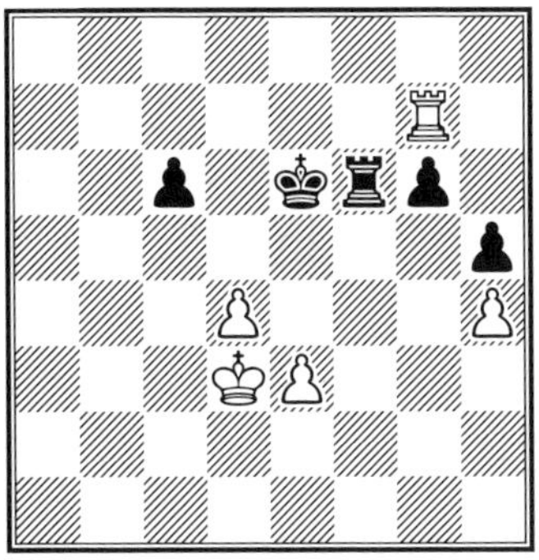

Here Portisch played 46...Kd6? and after 47.e4 he was hopelessly lost.

Fischer indicated Portisch could have drawn with 46...c5!, tearing down White's pawn structure. He supported this conclusion with the following nifty piece of analysis: 47.Ke4 (47.dxc5 Kd5 is the simple line) 47… cxd4 48.exd4 Kd6 49.d5 Kc5 50.Rc7+ Kd6 51.Rc6+ Ke7 52.Rxf6 Kxf6 53.Kf4 Kf7 54.Ke5 (54.Kg5 Kg7 55.d6 Kf7) 54...Ke7 55.d6+ Kd7 56.Kd5 g5!.

46...Kd6 47.e4 Rf4 48.e5+ Ke6 49.Rxg6+ Kd7 50.Kc4 Rf1 51.Rh6 Rc1+ 52.Kd3 c5 53.d5 c4+ 54.Kd2 Rh1 55.Rh7+ Ke8 56.Rxh5 Rh3 57.Kc2, 1–0.

Timman concludes: "There is no doubt that Fischer has analyzed more positions this deeply, but unfortunately all that work has been lost." Sadly this appears to be the case.

This analysis suggests that Fischer wasn't sitting on his hands in the 1980s. He was doing what he always did—studying chess. Bobby might not have been keeping up with opening theory the way he did in the past, and he certainly wasn't as physically fit, but his analytical skills and understanding of the game were still intact.

PART EIGHT

Comeback

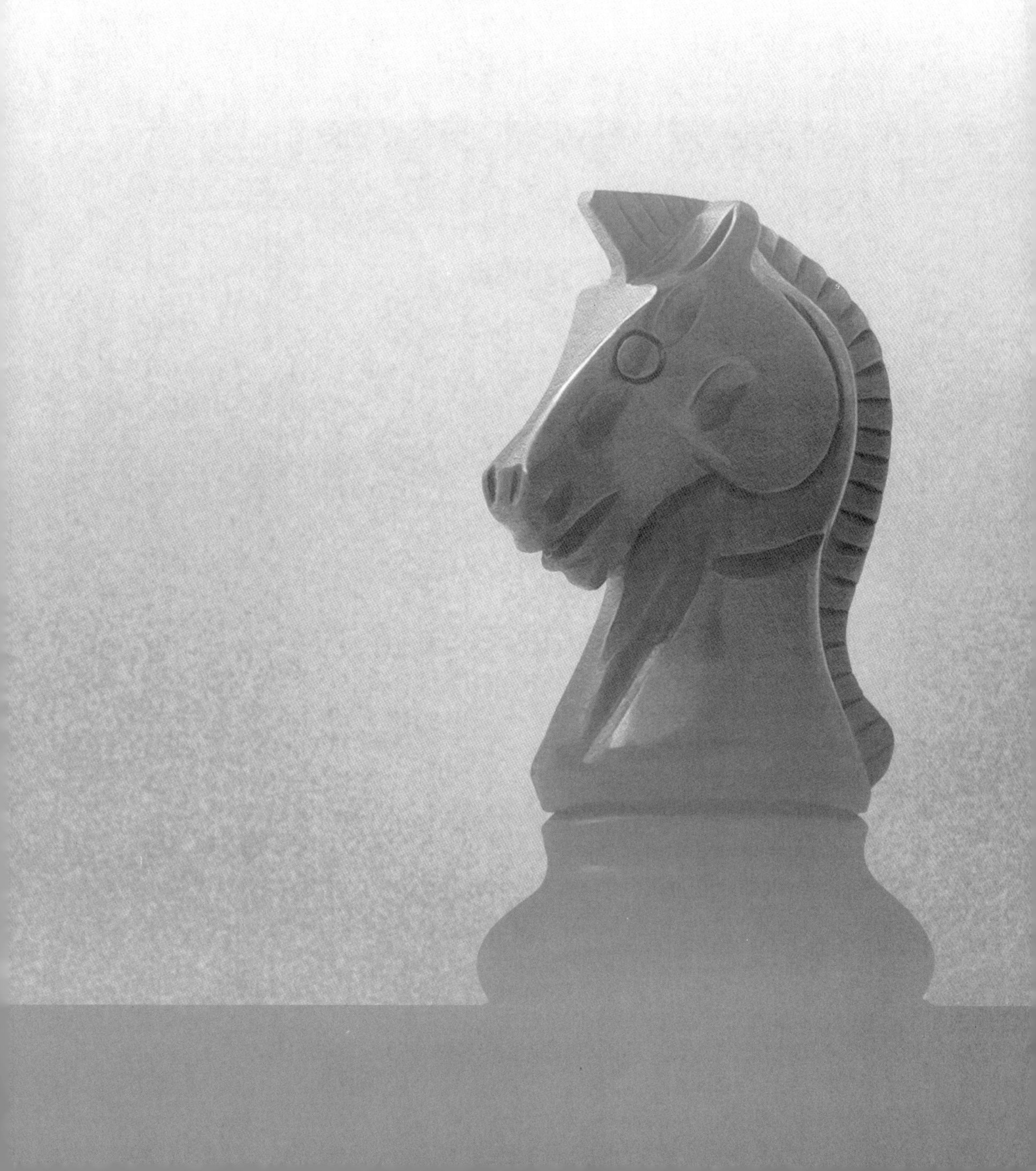

Sakkvilágbajnokok Budapesten
Reykjavík, 1972: Fischer–Szpasszkij 12,5:8,5
Világbajnok: Robert James Fischer!
SAKKVILÁGBAJNOKOK BUDAPESTEN
BUDAPEST 8, 1993. 10. 22.
Sveti Stefan, Belgrád, 1992:
Fischer–Szpasszkij 17,5:12,5
MAGYARORSZÁG 15 Ft

LES GRANDS MAITRES DES ECHECS
BOBBY FISCHER
REP. CENTRAFRICAINE 500F

LES GRANDS MAITRES DES ECHECS
SPASSKY
JEU VENITIEN
POSTE AERIENNE
REP. CENTRAFRICAINE 300F

1
WHY BOBBY FISCHER CAME BACK
by Lou Hays

After years of living in obscurity, the 1992 Fischer–Spassky rematch returned Fischer to the public eye. What brought Fischer out of retirement? Who was responsible for arranging and persuading Fischer to play after so many failed attempts over the previous twenty years? Lou Hays supplied a first-hand glimpse of one part of the story.[1]

> WHY BOBBY FISCHER CAME BACK
> My Extraordinary Adventure with the World Chess Champion
>
> [Ed. Tom Braunlich's Note]: Lou Hays was a regular tournament chess competitor from 1973 to 1995 and a longtime member of the Dallas Chess Club, where he served several terms as president. He and his wife, Susan, hosted many famous players including Boris Spassky, David Bronstein, Yasser Seirawan, John Donaldson, Ronald Henley, Larry Christiansen, Anatoly Lein, and Susan Polgar, who celebrated her eighteenth birthday at the Hays' home. He is the author/publisher of many books on the game of chess.
>
> INTRODUCTION
>
> Bobby Fischer. The name itself was magical from 1956 through 1972, evoking terror from chess opponents and marvel from the public. His fame reached every corner of the earth in 1972, when he singlehandedly wrested the World Chess Championship from Boris Spassky. Fischer broke over two decades of Soviet ownership of the title and Cold War propaganda of communist superiority. Shortly after winning the title, however, he mysteriously disappeared into obscurity and didn't play chess again for twenty years.
>
> In 1992 I was a witness to and participant in some of the key events that led to Fischer's decision to end his exile from chess.
>
> The standard narrative is that he needed the money and a banker in Yugoslavia put up a five million dollar prize with no strings attached. But

[1] Lou Hays, *Oklahoma Chess Monthly*, "Why Bobby Fischer Came Back," June 2017.

these are only the surface facts of a deeper story about Fischer's motivations, a story I want to set straight here.

The truth is, he was inspired by a teenager.

Fischer was living in dire poverty early in 1992, but this had been the case for many years. Since 1972 he had made a habit of torpedoing proposed chess matches and product endorsements ("I don't use them," he would say) that could have brought him many millions of dollars. He had a brief change of heart early in 1992 and became willing to play chess again. This article gives an account of his thinking and activities leading up to the 1992 rematch with Boris Spassky.

I met with Bobby Fischer on two occasions for a total of five days in Pasadena, California, both times in the month of April 1992. I never saw him after that, but now and then he would call me, usually to ask for help locating chess books.

A friend and I provided Bobby with the funds to entertain Zita Rajcsányi, a young Hungarian lady who, through letters and phone calls had earned his trust. Ultimately, Zita was responsible for inspiring his return to the board. Had she not come into his life when she did, he might well have died in poverty and oblivion in Los Angeles.

I made a record of these events on cassette tapes as they occurred. I subsequently put the tapes away and didn't listen to them for a quarter of a century. When you get into your seventies, it becomes more important to tell a meaningful story than to bother about who will or won't believe it.

Tangible proof of my meetings with Fischer is fleeting, as he shunned photographs and autographs. His psychological state was such that I never wanted to risk losing his trust by asking for such things. He did give me a leather pocket chess set from Germany, but there is no proof it was from Fischer. I do, however, have a voice recording of Fischer leaving a message on my answering machine in June of 1992, just a month before the announcement of the 1992 Fischer–Spassky rematch. Fischer, in his inimitable voice, called to ask me to locate copies of the *Chess* and *British Chess Magazine* annuals for 1984 and 1985. He was cordial, offered to pay for the materials, and thanked me at the end of the message. Anybody can listen to this message by going to youtube.com and searching for "Voicemail from Bobby Fischer." I also have included the image of a note Fischer wrote to a friend of mine who met with him in Pasadena on April 29, 1992 as part of this story. Bobby's handwriting and signature are distinctive.

In the fall of 1972, Bobby Fischer, newly crowned world chess champion, was the most famous person on earth. No American chess player before or since has achieved such a degree of international notoriety. Throughout the summer of 1972, Fischer's pre-match hysterics, antics, and demands made headlines all over the world. When he took the crown from the Soviet chess machine, the mass publicity that ensued prompted new chess players to sprout up all over the globe. Everywhere you looked, it was chess, chess, and more chess. New members flooded the United States Chess Federation. The Fischer era had begun.

Or had it? Shortly after the match, Bobby Fischer, to the shock and dismay of chess fans, disappeared from public view for almost twenty years.

I. THE BEGINNING 1989–1990

Like millions of others, I became fascinated with Bobby Fischer—and with chess—in 1972. My relationship with him happened much later, and entirely by accident. It started in 1989 when a client at my Dallas travel agency, Mark Robinson, walked in to pick up an airline ticket. Mark noticed the chess set I kept in the office, and told me he'd recently dined with Bobby Fischer.

The Bobby Fischer? Impossible. I didn't believe a word of it. Seventeen years had passed since Fischer's World Championship victory. Questions about him and his whereabouts ran thick and fast in the chess community. Rumors had him holed up somewhere in Pasadena, but nobody was able find out anything about him. The only sign he was still alive was a one dollar booklet he published in 1982 in which he described how the Pasadena police arrested and jailed him because he resembled a bank robbery suspect.

My client, Mark Robinson, was not a chess player, but he seemed honest and believable. He told me he had belonged to the Worldwide Church of God, the same church Fischer joined in the early 1970s and to which Fischer had donated a large portion of his prize winnings. Mark had a close friend, fellow church member Bob Ellsworth of Pasadena, who had been friendly with Fischer since the early 1970s.

Ellsworth was a non-chess playing businessman who helped take care of Fischer's business affairs and often lent him money. He and Fischer had dined together several times a month for many years. Robinson and Ellsworth both knew Fischer was a well-known chess celebrity, but at that time neither understood he was considered the strongest player in history.

I told Robinson I would love a chance to meet Fischer. Over the next couple of years, he mentioned this to Ellsworth several times. The answer always seemed to be "Perhaps, but don't count on it." I soon learned that Fischer always charged a fee for meetings with strangers.

It wasn't until later that I learned how Fischer rationalized his meeting fees. He knew that if he met a person, that person would be able to say they met with Bobby Fischer—a tangible benefit. He said also he believed most of these people would have nothing to offer him in return, so it would be a one-sided arrangement unless he received financial compensation. Fischer was destitute in those years, surviving on part of his mother's social security check plus a few book royalties and whatever he could borrow from friends. By the time I met him, in 1992, his meeting fee was $5,000.

II. GETTING CLOSER 1991

In January of 1991 I started a chess publishing house. To my knowledge, no complete compilation of Fischer's games existed at that time, so that became one of several book projects I began researching. Mark Robinson and I had become friends, and in the fall of 1990 we had taken a trip with our wives to southern California. I met Bob Ellsworth, but Fischer was nowhere to be found that weekend—probably no accident

I tried to keep the door open with Ellsworth over the following year, but by autumn 1991 any hope of contact with Fischer still seemed as remote as the day I first talked with Robinson. I was working hard on compiling Fischer's games for publication, and around Christmas of that year I completed a book called *My System–21st Century Edition*. This book was a re-edit of a seventy-five-year-old book by Aron Nimzowitsch, one of the world's top players in the early twentieth century. I sent a copy to Ellsworth and asked him to give it to Fischer. Bobby was delighted with the gift, as he had been searching in vain for the old edition in libraries and bookstores around Los Angeles.

III. EARLY 1992

I received a phone call from Bob Ellsworth one day early in 1992. He told me Fischer wanted to invite a young Hungarian lady, Zita Rajcsányi, to visit him in Pasadena. A strong chess player herself, Zita had written several fan letters to Fischer. He was her hero, she wrote to him, and she wanted to come to California to see him. Fischer called her several times and eventually invited her to come. Now he needed money for her plane ticket and expenses.

My opportunity had come. In March, Ellsworth contacted me and said if I could come to Pasadena soon, Fischer would reduce his fee to half, or $2,500, plus the cost of a few chess books he wanted me to pick up at Ken Smith's Chess Digest warehouse in Dallas. I was a few months away from finishing my book of Fischer's games, and I reasoned that a onetime royalty payment of that amount would be justifiable. Also, Fischer wouldn't be able to say I had used his games to earn money without compensating him.

The situation was perfect. At Ellsworth's suggestion, he and I split the $1,200 cost for Zita's air ticket. She was set to arrive in Los Angeles the first week of April.

"Chess, like love, like music, has the power to make men happy." This quote from famous chess grandmaster Siegbert Tarrasch was about to apply to Bobby Fischer. He already loved pop music and chess. But in 1992, with Zita Rajcsányi, he experienced true love for the first time in his life. His desire to become financially independent in order to forever make Zita part of his life gave him the final push to come out of retirement and play chess again.

Fischer lived in a tiny apartment, smaller than the size of the master closet of a modern home. He traveled everywhere by metro bus. He often had to borrow money from Ellsworth just to keep his bills paid.

Ellsworth and I were talking regularly on the phone by this time. I outlined to him a plan that could earn Fischer millions of dollars in a short time. The two of us composed a letter to Fischer explaining that we would like to help him promote himself and make enough money to live comfortably for the rest of his life. Fischer was receptive to the letter, but nineteen and a half years of inactivity had left him unmotivated. He was in no state of mind to get busy doing anything, much less negotiating the terms of a high-stakes chess match.

First, we told Fischer he needed to drop his senseless meeting fees. A fee for meeting with him was fine for autograph seekers and chess fans, but the idea of a meeting fee for wealthy and influential people who could help him make a fortune was preposterous. Ellsworth and I suggested simultaneous chess exhibitions, TV and magazine interviews, and book publications, but the three of us ultimately agreed a high-stakes match was the simplest way for Bobby to acquire a fortune quickly.

But who would he play? Bobby immediately said Boris Spassky. The two had already spoken about playing a rematch a year or so earlier, but like always with Bobby in those days, it had been just talk.

Just before my visit to Pasadena, I sent Ellsworth a copy of a recently published book, *Karpov on Karpov*, to give to Fischer. Karpov had been named world chess champion after his 1975 match with Fischer fell apart over disagreements on the rules of play. In his book, Karpov had some nice things to say about Fischer and how he had elevated financial rewards for all top players. Ellsworth said he handed the book to Fischer one evening as they sat down to eat dinner. Fischer took one look at it then threw it aside as though he wasn't interested. But he kept glancing over at it, Ellsworth told me, until he finally picked it up and said, "I guess I'd better see what those 'blankety-blanks' are up to."

Zita arrived in California on Friday, April 3. She stayed at Ellsworth's condo, and Fischer began riding the bus back and forth from his tiny apartment every day to see her. Everything was about to change.

IV. THE FIRST TRIP TO PASADENA

On April 10, Ellsworth called and said I needed to get there as soon as possible. I was certain Fischer needed money to entertain Zita. I canceled my plans to play in a chess tournament the following week and told Ellsworth I'd be there the following Friday. Two days later, Ellsworth faxed me a list of the books Fischer wanted from Chess Digest. Much of the material he wanted was about Karpov's and Kasparov's match games. I thought at the time that Fischer might be thinking of challenging one of them. Later I learned he wanted their games and analysis in order to prove to the world that all their games were prearranged.

I got what I could find of the books Fischer wanted from Chess Digest and I arrived in California on April 17. I checked in at the Ritz Carlton of Pasadena, just a few minutes from Ellsworth's condo. Ellsworth and Fischer agreed to meet me in the hotel bar at eight. I got there a few minutes early, ordered a Perrier, and nervously waited.

Ten minutes later, Ellsworth and Fischer arrived and made their way to my table. Fischer's appearance startled me. He didn't look anything like he had in 1972. He was balding, and he had a short beard and a middle-age spread. Both were wearing sports coats and Fischer had on a tie. After greeting me and shaking hands, Fischer ordered the bar's chicken teriyaki with pineapple appetizers and quesadillas. He drank a gin and tonic.

I took care of business first, reaching into my pocket and handing Bobby his fee. He thanked me and pulled out small leather chess set.

"This is for you," he said as he opened the set. "Lou, take a look at this."

He set up an opening position from the 1984 Karpov–Kasparov match and declared that the game had to have been prearranged, since by 1984 everybody already knew that in this position, such-and-such had been proven to be a bad move. It was difficult for me to see, particularly on such a small board in the bar's dim lighting. I nodded and tried to act interested, but I told him I was unfamiliar with that analysis.

We spent the next forty-five minutes on small talk and Fischer finally asked me my chess rating. I told him I was a longtime expert and that I had started playing tournament chess after his 1972 match against Spassky. I mentioned I had played in the New York Open more than once. We discussed some of the New York players he knew and I told him I had won a game against his old friend Ariel Mengarini in the 1986 New York Open.

"Ah, yes, he exclaimed. "Mengarini. I should never have given him a draw in that position." He spoke as though the game had been played that same afternoon, not thirty-five years earlier. [Author's note: The game was played in round three of the 1957 New Jersey Open and Bobby was better (32...Rb3) when they drew but not winning as he had been a few moves earlier (28..f6 was correct not allowing White to play e5.]

Ellsworth had made us a nine o'clock dinner reservation. We had just started out the door of the bar when Fischer suddenly dashed back to the table. As he walked back, I was struck by the fact no patrons in the crowded bar recognized him. In his coat and tie he fit right into the Ritz-Carlton crowd. Apparently he could travel anywhere in Los Angeles and never be recognized.

While Ellsworth went to pick up his car from the valet, Bobby and I headed to my room to get the chess books I had brought from Dallas. As we entered the room, he looked around and exclaimed, "Wow, these rooms are fantastic. I've never been in one before."

I got out the suitcase with his books and Bobby dug through them like a kid in a candy store. He had asked for some opening books, but much of the material he wanted was on the 1984–1985 Kasparov–Karpov match games and analysis of these games. He began telling me again how these match games had all been prearranged and that he was going to prove it. It was nonsense, and eventually it became tiresome.

Before my trip, Bob Ellsworth warned me that Fischer loved to discuss his "enemies," all of whom he called Jews, whether they were Jewish or not. I discovered Fischer used the word "Jews" to describe anybody or anything he disliked, feared, or harbored jealousy toward. It was a reflexive mental tape that played over and over in his head. Ellsworth told me to ignore Fischer and just change the subject whenever he brought it up. This was strange to me, as Fischer was himself Jewish.

In his book *Chess Duels*, Yasser Seirawan describes how in 1992 he put the Kasparov–Karpov "prearranged games" question to Fischer. He asked Bobby how it might have worked with the Soviet authorities managing thirteen moves and sending runners to each player's hotel room the night before with the prearranged moves and desired result. It's a hilarious exchange, and Seirawan, grandmaster and chess champion himself, used perfect logic to neatly put Fischer's absurd theory in its place.

As we rode to the restaurant, Fischer suddenly asked me what I thought about Grandmaster Patrick Wolff. I said I knew he was one of the strongest players in the country at the time. I remember reading an article where Wolff said he had patterned his play after Fischer's. Perhaps Fischer had read this article too.

Zita had arrived two weeks earlier, but she didn't join us that evening. The three of us went to a nice Italian restaurant. Ellsworth ordered wine, Fischer had another gin and tonic, and we had appetizers once again before enjoying a delicious meal.

As we ate, I mentioned Grandmaster Samuel Reshevsky, (many times U.S. Champion and one of Fischer's fiercest rivals), who had died two weeks earlier. Fischer became pensive, and he hesitated before he spoke.

"You know," he said, "in the old days Sammy was the greatest American chess player, better even than Reuben Fine. He should have been World Champion. He was that good." I could tell from the seriousness and hint of sorrow in his voice that, despite their intense battles, Fischer had tremendous respect for Reshevsky.

I found out during this meal Bobby still considered himself the undefeated World Champion who had been blacklisted by the chess authorities. In his mind, these "authorities" had been conspiring to prevent him from playing and making any money since 1972. Here was a man who, without much effort could have made fifteen to twenty million dollars in a year or two. But his intransigence, his meeting fees, and his childlike fear that someone else might make a little money of their own by helping him had left him frustrated, angry and penniless. He got by on his mother's social security check and by borrowing two or three hundred dollars at a time in hopes that a royalty check might someday show up and bail him out.

"I have to find some way to make some real money," Bobby said to me several times. This was the Zita Rajcsányi effect. Bobby Fischer was motivated.

After dinner, we went to Ellsworth's condo and I met Zita. She was a charming young lady. She spoke perfect English, and she was mature, polite, and proper in every way. She was also a strong chess player, perhaps 2200 USCF.

Zita had been there for only two weeks, but it was obvious that Bobby already had feelings for her. He was protective and in Bob Ellsworth's condo they would sit close to each other with Bobby's arm around her.

Zita and I were settling in at the chessboard for a blitz session when Bobby suddenly went pale and exclaimed that he'd left his briefcase at the restaurant. Ellsworth had already warned me about Fischer's chronic absentmindedness. He told us to sit tight and play chess while he went back and found Fischer's valise stashed under the table where we had eaten.

Bobby had a Toshiba 386SX laptop that had been given to him by the U.S. Chess Federation. I told him at dinner that I had bought some programs to run on it for his enjoyment. His computer already had ChessBase (which he had never opened), a program called MChess, and another unusual program, the Bobby Fischer Increment Chess Clock, a software program someone had written and placed on the laptop for him. As I remember, the shift keys served as timer buttons.

I loaded a text file of all of Fischer's chess games along with Chess Reader, a .pgn reader which he could use to play through all the games in any text file, including the file I had just given him. I also put on a chessplaying program called Zarkov.

Zita and I sat down to play using the new chess clock. Fischer first set it up for four minutes with one second added per move. After a few games, he changed it to three minutes with two seconds added per move. Although these time controls are common today, in 1992 I had never played chess with a time increment. Zita and I played sixteen blitz games for an hour or so.

"How do you like the clock?" Fischer kept asking me. "Do you like the idea of playing with increments?" I did like the new clock, but playing chess with Bobby Fischer looking on was an interesting experience, to say the least—something like practicing your new piano piece with Chopin sitting in the room. By then it was almost 3 AM Dallas time—and I was exhausted.

As Ellsworth's car idled at the curb outside my hotel, I shook hands with Fischer, thanked him for the chess set, and told him how much I had enjoyed the evening. I wasn't scheduled to fly back to Dallas until Monday and I hoped I hadn't already used up my royalty money.

Ellsworth called and invited me back over at about one pm the next day. This time I drove my rental car. Bobby hadn't arrived yet, so Zita and I got out the clock and began another blitz session. Ellsworth had a meeting to go to for a couple of hours. Before he left, he told us he wanted to take us to a Cuban restaurant, La Havana, that evening at eight.

Bobby showed up later that afternoon. He wanted to take a walk to a local supermarket and buy oranges for Zita. As I walked with him, we passed a small church along the way. I dared to ask him what he thought of religion.

He shrugged. "I'm not into religion anymore," he said. He still had a bitter taste in his mouth from the Worldwide Church of God, which he had left many years earlier.

I later asked the same question of Zita, and she also said she wasn't religious. I asked her what she believed in.

"I believe in myself," she replied. I was beginning to believe in her, too.

When we got back from the store, Bobby wanted to play chess against the Zarkov program. I operated the computer as Bobby watched the screen and told me his moves. I was surprised when he began dictating the moves in the old descriptive chess notation. By 1992, most chess players and publications had changed to algebraic notation.

Bobby had no problem defeating the Zarkov program, which played at perhaps an 1800 level on his 386 laptop. The last game of the half dozen he played against Zarkov was automatically saved on the disk. It appears here for the first time. The game has no theoretical importance; its only value is that it's a previously unpublished Bobby Fischer game. It is somewhat novel because Bobby gave up each of his bishops for a knight by the sixteenth move.

Zarkov played white with five minutes and Fischer had black with seven minutes, allowing two extra minutes for me to enter his moves. He moved quickly and time was never a factor in any of the games.

(81) Queen's Pawn
Zarkov – Bobby Fischer
Pasadena, April 18, 1992

[Lou Hays]: Previously unpublished game against computer program, on a Toshiba 386SX.]

1.d4 Nf6 2.Nc3 d5 3.Nf3 g6 4.Bf4 Bg7 5.e3 0-0 6.Bd3 Bg4 7.h3 Bxf3 8.Qxf3 c6 9.0-0 Nbd7 10.a4 a5 11.Rfe1 Re8 12.Bg3

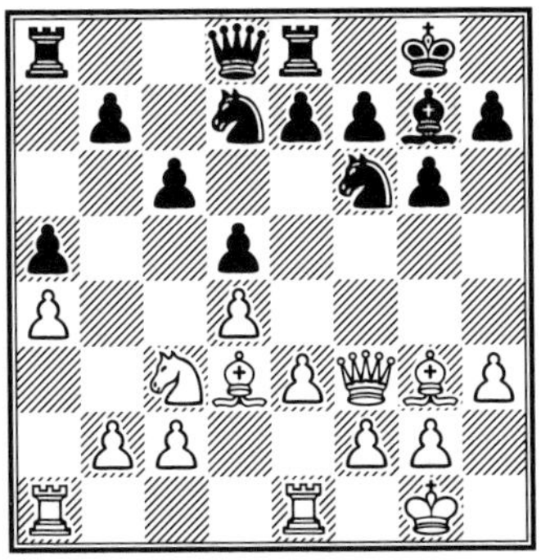

12...e5 18 13.Qd1

[Fischer]: "Lousy move."

13...exd4 14.exd4 Qb6 15.Ne2 Nh5 16.Bd6 Bxd4 17.Nxd4 Qxd4 18.Rxe8+ Rxe8 19.c3 Qf6 20.Bc7 Ne5 21.Be2 Nf4 22.Bxa5 Qg5 23.Bg4 h5 24.g3 hxg4 25.gxf4 Qxf4 26.Bc7 Nf3+, 0–1.

Bob Ellsworth had just returned from his meeting and was looking on as Bobby played. There were no flashy moves or startling tactical sacrifices, just Bobby Fischer chess, the simplest moves to win.

"This computer isn't showing me anything," Bobby said when it was clear his game was won. "Resign for it, Lou. I'm hungry. Let's go eat." The man loved good food.

Ellsworth, Bobby, Zita and I went to La Havana for dinner. Bobby had his usual appetizers, along with a gin and tonic. We discussed a high-stakes match and looking for a sponsor. Bobby seemed all in on the idea, as did Zita.

During the meal, I made the mistake of casually saying I believed Bobby's mom would be happy to see him playing chess again. Bobby seemed irritated that I had brought her into the conversation.

He turned red and looked at me. "What kind of comment is that?" he said. "Of course she wants somebody to play me." Fortunately, his anger dissipated quickly and we were back discussing a match.

After a hearty meal, we got back to Ellsworth's condo around ten. Ellsworth said he felt a cold coming on and went to bed. Zita and I played a few more blitz games using Fischer's clock, and then she said she wanted to retire.

Fischer and I stayed up and discussed the match. He said he would like to play in Los Angeles or Dallas. I mentioned Yasser Seirawan as a possible opponent. Yasser had been U.S. chess champion several times by 1992, and he was a popular and very well known grandmaster. Fischer claimed that Seirawan was Jewish. I told Fischer that Seirawan's father was Syrian and his mother was British. Fischer wasn't convinced. He claimed Seirawan was definitely Jewish, and just like Anatoly Karpov, had had facial surgery to hide it. It was more nonsense, but Bobby seemed to believe it.

Through my publishing business, I had become acquainted with Grandmaster Seirawan and International Master John Donaldson, associate editor with Seirawan at *Inside Chess* magazine. The two had been upcoming junior players at the peak of the Fischer era. When I told them that Bobby was talking about playing again they were ecstatic at the prospect.

Fischer gave me two reasons for rejecting the idea of playing Seirawan. First, he said he was unhappy that Seirawan had referred to him as The Great Ghost of Pasadena in an *Inside Chess* article. Second, he told me he'd had some California politician (I don't remember the name) fax a story on his new chess clock to *Inside Chess*. The magazine had only mentioned the clock in passing instead of running the full article.

I wondered if these were the genuine reasons Fischer wasn't interested in playing Seirawan, who at thirty-two years old was a world-class player in his prime. I can't predict who would have won the match, but Fischer was forty-nine, obviously out of shape, and hadn't played a tournament game in almost twenty years. Boris Spassky was fifty-five, and Fischer was certain he could beat him again. Besides, they were friends; Fischer trusted Spassky not to cross him.

So Fischer and Seirawan would not play one another, but the two would meet during Fischer's upcoming 1992 match with Spassky. Seirawan later wrote of the meeting:

"After September 23 [1992], I threw most of what I'd read about Fischer out of my head. Sheer garbage. Fischer is the most misunderstood, misquoted celebrity walking the face of the earth." He added that Fischer was not camera shy, smiled and laughed easily, was "a fine wit" and a "wholly enjoyable conversationalist."

Yasser was right. That's the same Bobby Fischer I had come to know when I met him. Bobby and I had found some common ground in that we both loved the Spanish language. That weekend we had several conversations in Spanish. He was quite proficient and had a good working vocabulary. He was also very funny, loved jokes, and liked to laugh in either Spanish or English. This was the Bobby Fischer I liked.

But Fischer also had his dark side that Yasser didn't see.

> Paranoia (noun) – A mental condition characterized by delusions of persecution, unwarranted jealousy, or exaggerated self-importance, typically elaborated into an organized system. It may be an aspect of chronic personality disorder, of drug abuse, or of a serious condition such as schizophrenia in which the person loses touch with reality.

The above description from Webster's Dictionary, minus the drug abuse, fits the other Bobby Fischer of 1992, except Fischer symptoms would come and go without warning.

After the Seirawan discussion, Fischer wanted to look at some chess material. He picked up one of the books I had brought from Dallas. I sat at the board across from him as he set up a position and played through a few moves. Then, staring intently at the board, he made another move or two and said, "Look at this position. Black can exchange here and this is forced, allowing this and this to force a queen ending. Black can easily win from there."

I don't remember what game it was and I didn't care. I just remember that watching Bobby Fischer analyze at the chessboard was a remarkable and unforgettable experience. We looked at another position for a few minutes and then he said he was ready for me to take him home. It was 1:30AM on Easter Sunday.

We got into my rental car and Fischer immediately noticed the car phone under the console. I hadn't asked for the phone when I made the reservation, and I had no intention of using it. That was before the age of cell phones, back when car phones were rare and mystical products.

"Look," said Fischer, who loved electronic gadgets of all kinds, "There is even a slot where you can slide your credit card."

There was no traffic at that hour and I drove about 50 mph toward L.A. Bobby liked that. He said I'd live a long time if I kept driving so safely. In truth, I was trying to maximize the time I could spend visiting with him. He

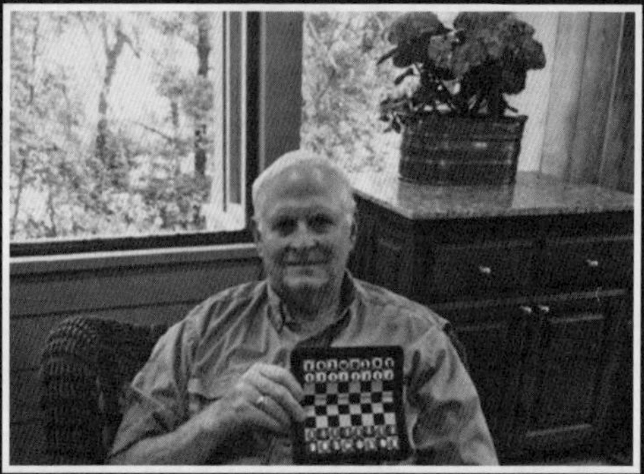

[above] Lou Hays at home in Oklahoma showing the travel set Fischer had given him.

[left] Bob Ellsworth, a pivotal figure in Bobby Fischer's later life, with Mark Robinson in 1992 (Photo: Dianne Robinson);

eventually directed me off the 110 freeway to the west, and we rambled back and forth through some dark streets until he finally pointed out his bus stop. It was around 2AM and this was definitely not Beverly Hills.

Fischer instructed me to drive to a nearby alley where we could talk while we waited for his bus to arrive. We spoke about Spassky and about the rules of the match. Fischer insisted that the winner should be the first player to win ten games, draws not counting. This, he asserted, was the only way to prove who really was the better player. I told him I fully agreed with the format.

When I realized I had no idea how to get back to the 110, I asked Fischer and got a blank stare. He didn't know. I don't believe he ever had a driver's license or drove a car.

Eventually the outline of his bus appeared a couple of blocks away. He started looking all over the car, patting his pockets, and grabbing the chess books and his briefcase. In fifteen seconds he loaded up, exited the car, and loped over to the bus stop. He looked back and nodded to me as he boarded the bus. It was surreal.

As his bus disappeared into the darkness, I wondered how this could be the same Bobby Fischer who had been the world's most famous person twenty years earlier, riding a city bus on his way to a small apartment that he didn't want me to see. Other than his chess memorabilia, he had no worldly possessions. I could barely get my mind around this sad spectacle. Mental illness, I thought, is no respecter of persons.

Late in the afternoon of Sunday, April 19, Fischer arrived at Ellsworth's condo and said he wanted to go back to La Havana for dinner.

"That place is dynamite!" he said. This was a word he used often. When we arrived, Bobby grabbed the one-page menu and started ordering everything in sight. Drinks, appetizers, fried bananas, main meal, and more.

After dinner, I excused myself to the men's room, while Zita, Bobby, and Ellsworth exited to the street. Ellsworth told me later that once they were outside, Fischer kept asking him how much he thought I would charge him for my help in setting up a match. Bobby never comprehended that my purpose wasn't to make money for myself. All I wanted was to work with him and try to bring him back to the chess world.

The magical weekend came to a close late that night. As I left Ellsworth's condo and said goodbye to Zita and Bobby, I asked him one last time to relent on his meeting fees, but he refused. This would make finding a sponsor for his match more difficult, but I told him I'd try.

V. BETWEEN VISITS TO PASADENA

The following week I contacted chess promoter John Carlson of the Intermark Group in Los Angeles. Carlson was reported to be a difficult man to reach, but the mention of Bobby Fischer's name got me through to him immediately. He had to call me back, however, as he suddenly had to hang up and talk to World Chess Champion Garry Kasparov, who was calling him from Europe on another line. We discussed setting up a match, but when I said Fischer insisted on a fee even to talk to Carlson, he told me to forget it. Through Yasser Seirawan, I also spoke to Min Yee, a wealthy Microsoft executive. Yee didn't know me, but again the mention of Bobby Fischer immediately got me a meeting with him. All went fine until we got to the meeting fee. That ended Min Yee's interest.

Either of these men would have been able and willing to arrange a multi-million dollar match, but neither would acquiesce to Fischer's $5,000 fee to meet and discuss it. I didn't blame them. It was bad business, and one reason Bobby stayed broke for most of twenty years.

Fischer's paranoia manifested itself in other ways. For example, every time I spoke by phone with him, he first warned me to be careful what I said, since Israeli intelligence listened in on all his conversations. He needed therapy and medicine, but, being Bobby Fischer, he would never admit it or see a doctor.

VI. SECOND TRIP, APRIL 29–30, 1992

As the month wore on, Fischer needed more money to entertain Zita for the remainder of her stay. I told Ellsworth I had a chess friend I believed would be happy to pay a fee to meet with him. Fischer, of course, was extremely suspicious of any stranger and had Ellsworth call me back with numerous questions about him. I will call my friend by the pseudonym "Milos" here because he has reasons now to not have his name associated with Fischer—a reminder of Bobby's unkind legacy. He was a chess expert and a huge Fischer fan at the time.

I made it clear to Bobby that Milos didn't belong to any conspiracy against him and would have no trouble coming up with the $5,000 meeting fee. He finally agreed, and I accompanied Milos to Pasadena on April 29.

I was certain Bobby would like Milos. As I expected, the two of them hit it off. Ellsworth picked us up at the Ritz-Carlton and we had dinner at the British Raj Indian restaurant in Santa Monica.

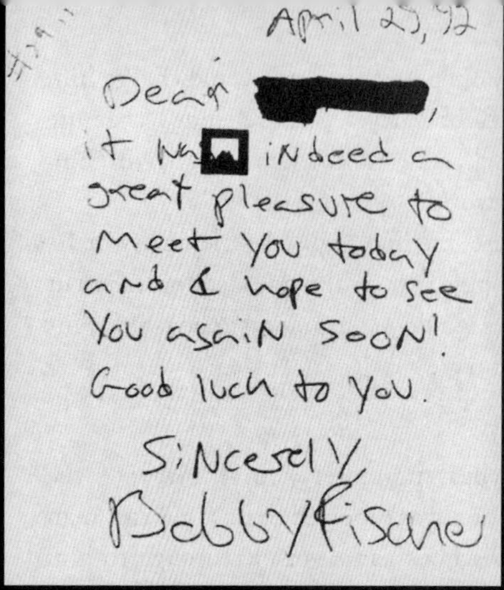
April 23, 92

Dear [redacted],
it wa[redacted] indeed a
great pleasure to
meet you today
and I hope to see
you again soon!
Good luck to you.

Sincerely,
Bobby Fischer

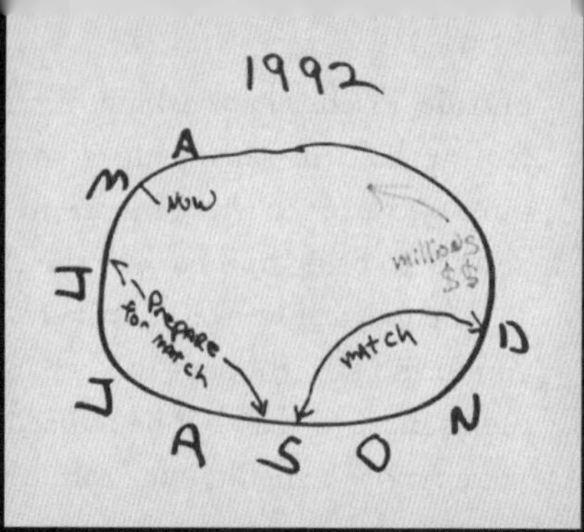

[left] The autograph for "Milos";

[right] Crude visual-cue circular calendar Lou Hays gave to Fischer to help him visualize the match potential.

After dinner, Milos, Zita and I played more blitz chess on the increment clock with Bobby occasionally grimacing and asking, "Why did you play *that* move?"

Between my visits to Pasadena, I handmade a 1992 calendar for Bobby. My hope was that a spatial thinker like Fischer would be able to see on a simple, circular calendar what he couldn't seem to grasp just talking about future events. The calendar was as crudely made as the one you see above, running from April through December. I marked four important points: 1) Now 2) Preparing for the match 3) Playing the match itself, and 4) Being wealthy by December. I handed him the calendar and told him if he stayed focused on it, he had everything he needed to duplicate the year as shown.

Bobby may have thrown my calendar in the trash that very night, or he might have used it to keep his mind fixated on what he was about to accomplish. I'll never know, but I hoped it would create a clear and positive picture in his mind.

VII. JUNE–JULY 1992

After the quick trip to Pasadena with my friend Milos, I never saw Bobby in the flesh again. I spoke with him a couple of times on the telephone, and in June he left the message on my answering machine that can be heard on youtube.com.

Although I didn't know it, by June he was already in negotiations for a five million dollar match with Spassky, thanks to another fortuitous feat by the remarkable Zita Rajcsányi (detailed below). On July 25, I got a call from my friend, national chess master Mike Richards. He told me to buy a copy of *The New York Times* ASAP. He read the headline to me: "Fischer and Spassky Said to Sign for Chess Rematch in Yugoslavia."

I was surprised, but only mildly so. Despite the demons in his head, Bobby Fischer was going to play chess again and make his millions.

EPILOG

At the end of the 1992 Fischer–Spassky rematch, I received an urgent call from Joan Targ, Bobby's sister in California. Bobby knew I was publishing a book on the match and that I had hired Grandmaster Leonid Shamkovich as game analyst. Bobby wanted to see a draft immediately. I told Joan the book wasn't yet fully proofread, but she insisted that I print a copy of whatever I had and overnight it to her. A couple of days later a spiral bound copy was in her hands and on its way to Bobby.

Mark Robinson, my travel agency client and later dear friend, who first mentioned having dinner with Bobby Fischer, tragically died of heart failure in 2009 while still in his fifties.

Bob Ellsworth, Bobby's close friend and confidant for twenty years, accidentally failed to pay the rent on Bobby's storage locker a few years after the rematch, causing Bobby to lose a large portion of his memorabilia. Bekins Storage put the contents of the locker up for auction to recoup the lost rent. Ellsworth was shocked when he realized what had happened. He told me he had paid the bill in advance once every few months for many years. The storage locker company changed hands and somehow his billing address was lost or the billing changed to monthly. By the time Ellsworth realized the mistake, it was too late, and the auction had already taken place. Ellsworth spent about $8,000 of his own money to buy back many of the items, but much of it was lost.

Fischer was furious over the loss for the rest of his life, and sadly, Ellsworth became persona non-grata, part of the conspiracy against Bobby Fischer.

The last time I spoke with Ellsworth was right after Bobby's death in 2008. As I wrote this story, I tried unsuccessfully for several months to locate him in hopes of rehashing details. The last I heard, he was living overseas.

Zita Rajcsányi should be credited more than any other person for the chess revival of Bobby Fischer and the match of 1992. She inspired him and added a new dimension to his life at just the right moment.

When Zita returned to Hungary in May of 1992, Bobby trusted her with a letter of intent to seek a sponsor for a high-stakes chess match. Through her chess connections she located organizer Janos Kubat, who in turn found Jezdimir Vasiljević, a banker who provided five million dollars to sponsor the match. It was announced barely two months after she left Pasadena. Quite an accomplishment for a teenager.

Zita didn't reciprocate Fischer's romantic feelings. Reportedly she eventually gave up chess, got married, had kids, and moved to New Zealand.

Bobby Fischer earned $3.65 million for winning the 1992 match against Spassky. By playing in Yugoslavia he violated a U.N. embargo on commercial activity in that country. He paid no taxes to the U.S. government from his winnings and never returned to this country. Before the match started, the U.S. government sent Fischer a letter threatening a $250,000 fine and ten years' imprisonment for playing chess in a country under sanctions (Boris

Fischer at the home of Andor and Olga Lilienthal in Budapest in the 1990s.

Spassky received no such treatment). At a press conference a day before the match started, Fischer publicly spat on the letter in defiance, saying, "That is my reply."

Fischer spent the next dozen years living in Yugoslavia, Hungary, Japan, and the Philippines. His anti-U.S. and anti-Jewish rants became more vicious as the years went by. His already-damaged legacy was wholly destroyed when on 9/11 he openly rejoiced, saying on the Bombo Radyo station in Baguio City, Philippines, that the U.S. had gotten what it deserved. As always, he blamed the Jews. This and subsequent radio broadcasts from this station were posted online and Fischer's odious rants were heard all over the world.

In July of 2004 Fischer was arrested and jailed at the Narita airport in Tokyo for trying to board an airplane with a revoked U.S. passport. He remained incarcerated in Japan for approximately nine months. After much legal wrangling, Iceland granted him full citizenship rights. He was released from jail and flown directly to Reykjavík in March of 2005, where he lived until his death from kidney failure on January 17, 2008. He was sixty-four.

On September 6, 2004, while imprisoned in Japan, Fischer married his longtime friend, Miyoko Watai, chess player and official in the Japanese Chess Association. He had known Watai since the 1970s. He left no will or trust. Watai, after a court fight, was awarded the remainder of his estate, reportedly around two million dollars (before U.S. taxes). A middle-of-the-night exhumation to extract Fischer's DNA was required to verify that he was not the father of a Filipino child whose family had made a claim to his estate.

Many years ago, I discussed Bobby's mental condition with Dr. Kay Hale, a psychologist and chess friend from Dallas. After listening to my anecdotes, Hale told me he believed Bobby would never seek treatment and that his paranoia would continue to worsen with time. This, in turn, would lead to a stressful existence, and he predicted Bobby would die at a relatively young age. How prophetic Dr. Hale was.

Over the past twenty-five years, I have often wondered how Bobby Fischer's life would have unfolded if Mark Robinson had never entered my travel office, if Bob Ellsworth and I hadn't provided the funds for Zita's ticket to California, and if Milos and I hadn't financed Fischer during Zita's California visit.

Perhaps he would have found other patrons, but I cannot imagine how. Zita was writing to him, I was in contact with Bob Ellsworth, I was publishing a book on his games, and I knew Boris Spassky. The stars were aligned.

The grim probability is that Bobby Fischer would have died alone and impoverished in his tiny apartment in west Los Angeles. But is that better or worse than what eventually happened?

He would not have fallen in love. He would not have played another chess match, and he would not have acquired his millions. The amazing story of his winning the world chess championship at the height of the Cold War in 1972 would have been his enduring legacy. To the general public, he was a former World Champion and curiosity. To those of us in the dedicated chess community, Bobby Fischer would have been remembered as the greatest player ever, but also a flawed and fallen superhero.

Nowadays, I look back at 1992 with some degree of remorse, seeing the devastation Fischer ultimately brought to his reputation and to himself as a human being. It was a grand and exciting adventure, but in view of how Bobby Fischer's life and legacy turned out, if I had the opportunity to do it all over again, I wouldn't.

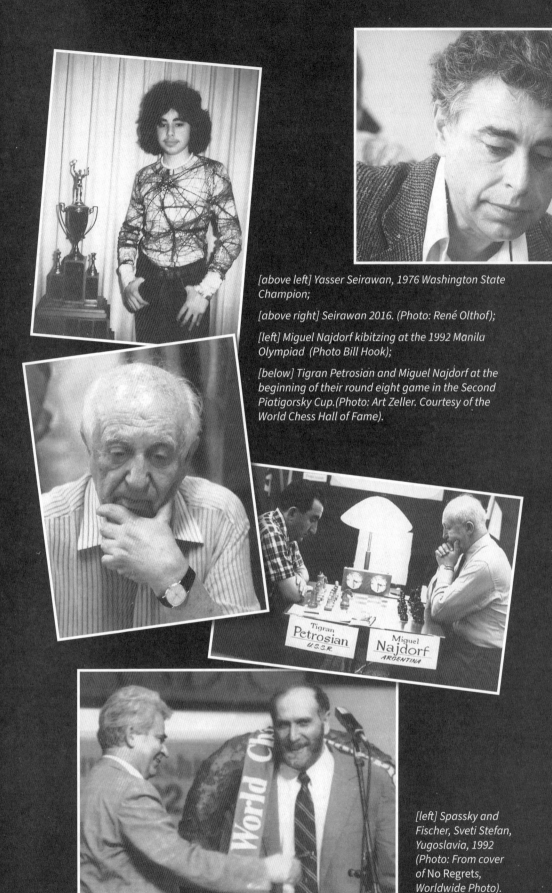

[above left] Yasser Seirawan, 1976 Washington State Champion;

[above right] Seirawan 2016. (Photo: René Olthof);

[left] Miguel Najdorf kibitzing at the 1992 Manila Olympiad (Photo Bill Hook);

[below] Tigran Petrosian and Miguel Najdorf at the beginning of their round eight game in the Second Piatigorsky Cup.(Photo: Art Zeller. Courtesy of the World Chess Hall of Fame).

[left] Spassky and Fischer, Sveti Stefan, Yugoslavia, 1992 (Photo: From cover of No Regrets, Worldwide Photo).

2
"PERFECTION HAS NO STYLE"

Yasser Seirawan was in Yugoslavia to cover the Fischer–Spassky confrontation for his magazine *Inside Chess*, and shortly after published a book about it, *No Regrets*. The only American Grandmaster to attend the match and the sole representative of his generation to spend significant time with Bobby, he offered a unique perspective:[1]

> It is often written, and correctly, that Bobby has an aversion to the media and this is often extended to mean *all* journalists. At no time during our period together did Bobby forbid me to write or talk about our meetings. He never spoke "off the record." He knew I was the publisher of *Inside Chess* and fully expected I would in fact be writing about our time together.

However, Bobby eventually turned on Seirawan as he did so many others. Seirawan wrote:[2]

> I had met eight of the thirteen World Champions—I missed Steinitz, Lasker, Capablance, and Alekhine as they had all died long before I was born. That left one I was yet to meet, my compatriot Bobby Fischer.
>
> I finally met Bobby Thursday, September 17, 1992 in Sveti Stefan, Yugoslavia during his match with Boris Spassky. It was a free day and we were at the beach. My wife Yvette roused me, "Bobby and Eugene [Grandmaster Eugene Torre] are going for a swim." I turned to watch them for a few minutes and went back to sun bathing. After a while Yvette shook me awake again to say, "Bobby's coming over!" and indeed he was. We scrambled to our feet and shook hands all around. For me it was a magic moment.
>
> Bobby was a big guy. Around six foot two, with big hands and a warm, friendly face. He smiled and laughed easily
>
> Eugene made the introductions and we spoke easily together for about fifteen minutes. I had mentally prepared myself to meet Bobby for twenty years. Suddenly we were just two guys talking about a common love—chess.

[1] Yasser Seirawan and George Stefanović, *No Regrets: Fischer–Spassky 1992*, Seattle: International Chess Enterprises, 1993, (p. 307).

[2] This material is covered in *No Regrets* in a slightly different format.

For what seemed like an endless time Bobby complimented me on my book on the Kasparov–Karpov match, *Five Crowns.*[1] He praised the book to the skies—he *really* liked it! I remember thinking to myself while receiving his praises, "thank goodness for my editor and proof-reader!" Bobby said that he would like some extra copies and I told him I had copies at the hotel and I would give him ten. He was very pleased and then said, "But you know... The book has two mistakes." I was stunned.

The book is 250 pages covering twenty-four games all deeply annotated with hundreds of variations and very strong opinions. Yes, I knew of two mistakes. One I found at random when I literally first opened a new copy hot off the press. Seeing the mistake had terrified me—if it was so simple to find one I was fearful there would be many. So I asked Bobby what were the mistakes that he had found? He carefully told me what they were and why and I nodded my head, indeed these two mistakes were the very same ones I discovered as well. It occurred to me that Bobby must have spent hundreds of hours carefully considering every move to find them. It gave me great pleasure to think that Bobby had read my book so closely.

[The next day Yasser traveled to Cetinje to play for the chess club from Niš in the Yugoslav Team Championship and it was not until September 21 that he and Bobby met again. Yasser describes what happened.]

Bobby invited my wife Yvette and myself to his suite and we had a most enjoyable time together analyzing his brilliancy from the day before with Eugene Torre and Svetozar Gligorić. What I remember best is how much we all laughed together. Bobby was extremely warm, friendly and quite humorous. Spontaneous things happened all around him and he was very comfortable.

That evening Bobby asked us to dinner and we went to a Chinese restaurant where we gorged ourselves on excellent food. After we were all completely stuffed the chef brought out a marvelous whole Peking duck. The whole table groaned in disappointment. It seems extraordinary to me now but Bobby and I ate the whole thing together. I do not know how we managed to do this. We convinced ourselves that it would be an insult to the cook so we plowed right through it. The chef, the restaurant owner, was very proud and asked Bobby if he would be so kind to autograph his guest book? Bobby more than happily complied and wrote a fine inscription indeed. The chef beamed in delight and his little boy hid behind his father's legs fascinated by the celebrity sitting in his father's restaurant signing the guest book. The chef generously offered Bobby a gift, a ceramic bottle filled with his own home-made Slivovitz (plum brandy). Bobby thanked him for the gift and we began our walk home, as soon as we were out of sight, Bobby gave the bottle to Grandmaster Svetozar Gligorić and said, "Here you take this. But save me a drop okay?"

[1] Yasser Seirawan and Jonathan Tisdall, *Five Crowns: Kasparov–Kaspov World Chess Championship 1990 New York–Lyon*. Seattle: International Chess Enterprises, 1997.

This immediate act of generosity spoke volumes for me. Bobby was very generous to his friends.

The last time I saw and spoke with Bobby was at the closing ceremony in Sveti Stefan. I didn't attend the second half of the match in Belgrade as I had a tournament to play in Tilburg.

Thinking back, I can appreciate how the time Yvette and I spent with Bobby differed markedly from the experiences of *New In Chess* editor Dirk Jan ten Geuzendam who interviewed Bobby in Sveti Stefan.[1] Dirk's experiences seem to have been "dark" in great contrast to our own. Likely the conversations he had drifted into areas that triggered Bobby.

After Fischer's death in 2008, Seirawan was interviewed by the French periodical *Europe Echecs* and was asked the question, Are youngsters in the United States today motivated to play in "Fischer's style?" Seirawan responded:[2]

I'm not sure what, "Fischer's style," is or if it even exists. A very dear friend, Grandmaster Miguel Najdorf, who had very strong, opinions on just about every topic, delighted in baiting me and drawing me into animated, emotional discussions. He was a passionate man who loved chess very much. He postulated a theory which I've thought about often and think he was right. His theory went like this:

"Jasser (Miguel would always mispronounce my name in this Spanish way) you know, Bobby had no style."

Such an opening gambit to start a conversation was perfect bait.

"You see, when you show me a game of Capablanca, I think, 'Aha. Very nice. Very smooth. Logical. Beautiful play. Must be a game of Capa!' Then you show me another game, I think, 'My God! Who is this bandit playing the White pieces? Look at these reckless, daring sacrifices. And this quiet move as well! Incredible! Down two pieces and he stops to make such a move. And he won! Of course, I realize, this is Tal.' And another game. 'I can't understand what the player is doing. He is taking extraordinary precautions and his opponent isn't even attacking. Now he has maneuvered his pieces backwards and then to nice squares. He improves his position but has done nothing concrete. My God! The opponent is suffocated and is dead. Of course, that is Petrosian.' You see Jasser! I recognize style. But you see when I play a game of Bobby, there is no style. Bobby played perfectly. And perfection has no style." We argued for hours, but in the end, I found Miguel's theory quite convincing.

---

[1] Dirk Jan ten Geuzendam, *Finding Bobby Fischer: Chess Interviews*. Alkmaar, The Netherlands: New In Chess, 1994.

[2] *Europe Echecs*, 2008 #575. This article was translated into English and appeared on the ChessBase website.

Svetozar Gligorić.

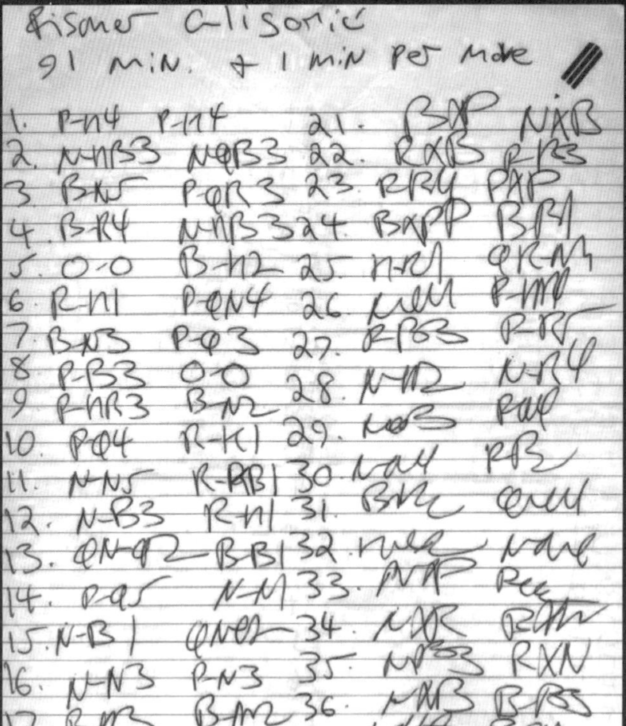

Deciphering Fischer's score sheets was not an easy task. Belgian Grandmaster Luc Winants did a particularly good job on this one, Game (87).

3
TRAINING MATCH WITH GLIGORIĆ

Bobby Fischer and Svetozar Gligorić first met in 1958 and soon became fast friends—"Gliga", was twenty years older than Bobby, and became something of a father figure to him. Bobby always had a high opinion of his elder's chess understanding and during his 1971–72 World Championship run hoped to have the Yugoslav Grandmaster as his second, particularly in Reykjavík. This didn't come to pass as Gligorić had other commitments, but the two stayed close corresponding regularly until the late 1970s when Bobby cut off contact with the chess world. When Fischer returned in 1990 "Gliga" was one of the first people he reached out to and his support was critical for the 1992 rematch with Spassky, which might never have taken place without him.

Gligorić didn't act as Bobby's second, nor hold an official position, but Bobby leaned heavily on his old friend. "Gliga", wrote about his time spent time with Bobby in Belgrade:[1]

> My friendship with Bobby started when he was fifteen years old, and I was thirty-five. It lasted about forty years. During the two decades of his self-isolation I was one of the very few people who was in regular contact with him.
>
> In 1992 Bobby arrived in Belgrade, several weeks before the beginning of his second match with Spassky. In advance of the match he asked for my help in delivering to him all games played during the twenty years of his absence from chess. I had a little-known computer, and Bobby was unpleasantly surprised by the enormous increase in the number of games with each opening variation which he had in his repertoire. That is when he began to think of reforming the rules of chess at all costs, removing the very tiring task of preparing openings in advance for each game. He spent a year or two trying to persuade me to write a book about Fischerandom chess. I eventually did so. My book, *Shall We Play Fischerandom Chess?*,[2] was published in London in 2002, while he was still alive.
>
> During Bobby's stay in my country he asked me to be in his company all the time and we went to Sveti Stefan together. He had plenty of time at his

[1] From Gligorić correspondence to Edward Winter, Chess Notes March 2012.

[2] Svetozar Gligorić, *Shall We Play Fischerandom Chess?* London: B.T. Batsford, 2002.

disposal and since he had not played chess for twenty years he probably felt uncertain about whether he had maintained his previous form. He therefore asked me to do him a favor: to play ten secret training games against him, with his new chess clock (now valid in the whole chess world), which was due to be used in the Spassky match. The games were played in Sveti Stefan, while we were waiting for Spassky's arrival. Bobby and I had two bungalows close to each other, and he was in the best one, where Sophia Loren had stayed during an earlier visit. As far as I recall, we played our ten games there, one per day. It was agreed that there would be no spectators at all. Bobby did his best, after twenty years away from the board. He made no particular comments about his play but expressed satisfaction with several of the early games. Afterwards he had time to play a few games against Eugene Torre, following his arrival.

Unfortunately, I cannot be of much help now in deciphering Bobby's handwriting or in providing other details about the game-scores. At that time my wife was seriously ill (she died in 1994), and I was rather absent-minded about chess matters. I remember very little about the ten games which Bobby and I played, except that I won as White in the final game. I think that Bobby had at least three wins. If I had kept my easily readable score sheets, we would have no problems today, but after the match I gave them all to Bobby, without his asking, to show him that the material would never be used for any publicity purposes.

When Bobby departed from my country in 1993, moving to Budapest, he asked if he could leave many of his possessions in my house for safekeeping. I do not recall the exact date, but subsequently, before his departure to Tokyo, I hired a driver and a car, filled with Bobby's belongings for delivery to him, but the Hungarian customs officials would not allow the car to continue its journey to Budapest without Bobby's personal presence at the frontier. He was too lazy to come, and all the material was returned to me in Belgrade. I still have everything. There are many packages but, in accordance with Bobby's wishes, I have never looked inside them.

My assumption was always that he had probably destroyed most of the game-scores, except the ones where he was particularly interested in the opening variation. I was surprised to learn from you that one score sheet in my handwriting has been found.

FISCHER (2780) 7½ – GLIGORIĆ (2450) 2½

The games from this training match are arranged by opening, as no definitive information exists as to the order in which they were played. The choice of variations, which did not overlap with known Spassky preferences, indicates the purpose of this match was to get the rust off and not test novelties for the upcoming battle with Boris. Despite the age and rating difference Gligorić held his own for the most part, only fading in the later stages in many games.

(82) King's Indian
Svetozar Gligorić – Fischer
Sveti Stefan 1992

1.d4 Nf6 2.c4 g6 3.Nc3 Bg7

The King's Indian was Fischer's main defense against 1.d4 throughout his career but he only played it against Spassky in their 1992 match, using the Grünfeld in their 1960s tournament games and 1...Nf6 2...e6 in 1972.

4.e4 d6 5.Nf3 0-0 6.Be2 e5 7.0-0 Nc6 8.d5 Ne7 9.Nd2

The text was always one of Gligorić's favorite ways to combat the KID as White. He also had a lot experience with this variation with Black as the King's Indian was his main weapon against 1.d4 for much of his career.

Besides the flexible text, which prepares b4, c5 and Nc4—while stopping ...Nh5, White can also try 9.Ne1, 9.b4, 9.Bd2, 9.a4 and 9.Kh1.

9...a5

This was something new for Bobby. Previous to this training match he had played the main alternative 9...c5. For example: 9...c5 10.Rb1 (10.a3 Ne8 11.b4 b6 12.Rb1 f5 13.f3 f4 14.a4 g5 15.a5 Rf6 16.bxc5 bxc5 17.Nb3 Rg6 18.Bd2 Nf6 19.Kh1 g4 20.fxg4 Nxg4 21.Rf3 Rh6 22.h3 Ng6 23.Kg1 Nf6 24.Be1 Nh8 25.Rd3 Nf7 with equal chances in Korchnoi–Fischer, Herceg Novi 1970 (blitz) though Bobby later outplayed his opponent.) 10...Ne8 11.b4 b6 12.a4 f5 13.a5 Nf6 14.Qa4 Bd7 15.Qa3 Bh6 16.Bd3 Qc7 17.bxc5 bxc5 18.exf5 gxf5 19.Bc2 a6 20.Nde4! was slightly better for Larsen in the fourth game of his match with Bobby in Denver in the summer of 1971. Fischer later outplayed him with a direct attack on the king.

Bobby never played the King's Indian in the style of Hikaru Nakamura who has successfully met both 9.Nd2 and 9.b4 with 9...Ne8 followed by an all out kingside versus queenside attack. Fischer more typically preferred to defer his attack, taking steps to slow down White's operations with 9...a5 or 9...c5 and often took time to swap his bad bishop with ...Bh6.

10.a3 Bd7

The most commonly played move here is 10...Nd7 which would have been familiar to Gligorić as his game with Vukić from the 1989 Yugoslav Team Championship was drawn after 11.Rb1 f5 12.b4 Kh8 13.Qc2 b6 14.Bb2 Nf6 15.f4 exf4 16.Rxf4 axb4 17.axb4 Bd7 18.Rbf1 g5 19.R4f2 f4 20.h4 gxh4 21.Rxf4 Ng6 22.R4f2 Qe7 23.Nd1 Ba4 24.Qd3 Bxd1 25.Bxd1 Nd7 26.Rxf8+ Rxf8. The plan with f4 instead of the usual f3 (playing for c4-c5) is interesting, but likely not as effective.

10...Ne8

This was played in another game of the training match.

11.b3

This quiet move prepares a gradual b2-b4 as 11.Rb1 would be met by 11...a4 (one of the points of 10...Bd7).

11...c5 12.Bb2

Much more commonly seen is 12.Rb1 Ne8 13.b4 axb4 14.axb4 b6 15.bxc5 bxc5 16.Nb3 f5 17.f3 Nf6 18.Bd2 f4 and White has a choice between 19.Nb5 and 19.Ra1 with a typical King's Indian queenside versus kingside battle brewing. Towards the end of his career Gligorić experimented with placing his bishop on b2—the aforementioned game with Vukić and another with Pikula from 1996 being two examples.

12...Bh6

12...Ne8 intending ...f5 was the other way to handle the position. With the text Fischer activates his"bad" bishop with the possible idea of trading it off so as to not be left with an inferior minor piece.

13.Qc2 b6 14.Nd1!?

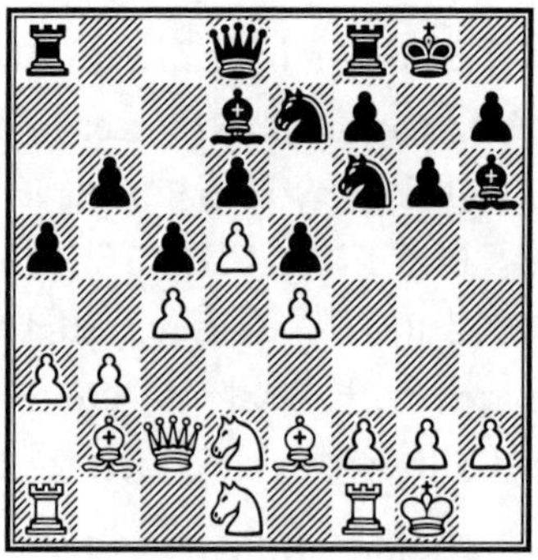

With the text Gligorić aims to blast open the position with f2-f4 (note the unprotected knight on f6) and forces Bobby to take up the challenge.

14...Bxd2

This wins a pawn, but White's two bishops provide good compensation. The alternative was 14...Ne8 15.Qc3 f5 16.f4 with sharp complications.

15.Qxd2 Nxe4 16.Qd3 f5

16...Nf6 17.f4 allows Gligorić to realize his idea of bringing the bishop on b2 into the game in a big way.

17.f4 exf4

17...g5 18.fxe5 dxe5 19.Bxe5 Ng6 20.Bb2 Nf4 21.Rxf4 leads to murky play, but 19.g4!, undermining the knight on e4, is good for White.

18.Rxf4

18.Nf2 Nf6 (18...Nxf2?? 19.Qc3 winning) 19.Nh3 leads to play that is similar to the game continuation.

18...Nf6 19.h4 Rf7 20.Nf2 Qf8 21.Nh3 h6

The text not only stops Ng5 but also allows ...Kh7 to neutralize pressure on the a1-h8 diagonal by allowing the h8 square to be covered.

22.Raf1 Re8

Queenside play with 22...a4 or 22...b5 was possible, but Fischer prefers more center-oriented action.

23.Bd1 Nc8 24.Qg3 Rg7 25.Qc3 Re5

25...Ne4 26.Qxg7+ Qxg7 27.Bxg7 Kxg7 28.Re1 b5 29.Bc2 Nf6 30.Rxe8 Bxe8 intending ....bxc4 and ...Ng4-e5. With an extra pawn in the pocket, this probably offers Black enough compensation for the exchange, but no more.

26.Qc1 Qe7 27.R4f2

27.Bxe5 dxe5 28.R4f2 Nd6 would give Black one pawn and considerable positional compensation for the exchange—a strong pawn center and an excellent blockading knight on d6 for starters.

27...Kh7 28.Nf4 Ne4 29.h5 gxh5

29...Nxf2 30.hxg6+ Kg8 31.Rxf2 and sooner or later White will recover the exchange with balanced play.

30.Rf3 Qg5 31.Qc2 Ne7?

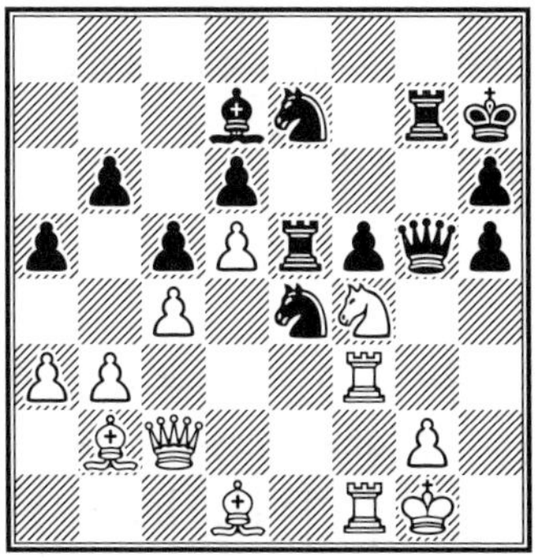

This leaves the queen precariously placed. Essential was 31...h4 (to anchor the knight on g3) 32.Bc1 Ng3 33.Nh5 Ne2+ 34.Qxe2 Qxc1 35.Qf2 Rg6 36.Qxh4 Qg5 with equal chances in the ending.

32.Bc1! h4

As 32...Ng3 fails to 33.Rxg3 Qxg3 34.Nxh5.

33.Ne6

Thematic and stronger was 33.Nd3! Qg6 34.Bb2 Ng5 35.Nxe5 dxe5 36.Re3 and the critical pawn on e5 falls.

33...Qf6 34.Nxg7 Kxg7 35.Bb2 Ng3 36.Qf2 Qg5?

36...Nxf1 37.Qxf1 Qg5 38.Bc2 Kf6 and ...Ng6 to follow leaves White in a position to recover the exchange but no more. Since Black cannot save the rook on e5 he had to grab the material while he could.

37.Re1 Ng6 38.Bc2?

38.Bxe5+ dxe5 (38...Nxe5 39.Rfe3 f4 40.Rxe5 dxe5 41.Qb2 Kf6 42.b4!) 39.Kh2! anticipates ...h3 and meets 39...e4 with 40.Rxg3 hxg3+ 41.Qxg3, leaving White with good winning chances.

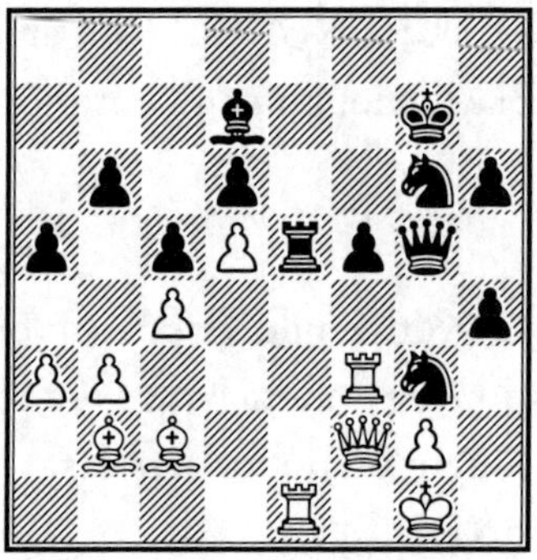

38...f4?

It was necessary to immediately break the pin with 38...Kg8 39.Bxe5 Nxe5 40.Rfe3 f4 41.Rxe5 dxe5. With the bishop on c2, the queen does not have access to the critical square b2 where it is perfectly placed for attack and defense. The text mistakenly activates the bishop on c2, justifying Gligorić's last move.

39.Bxg6 Kxg6 40.Bc1??

40.Bxe5 dxe5 41.d6!

(41.b4 looks quite promising with the idea of meeting 41...h3 with 42.Rxg3 fxg3 43.Qf8. Now the king looks very exposed but after 43...Qf4! 44.Qxf4 exf4 45.bxc5 bxc5 46.Re4 h2+ White has to force a draw right away and can easily lose if he presses. 47.Kh1 Kg5 48.Re5+ [48.d6?? Bc6 49.a4 (49.d7 Bxd7 50.Re5+ Kg4 51.Rxc5 f3) 49...f3 50.gxf3 Bxe4 51.fxe4 Kf6 52.e5+ Ke6 53.Kg2 h5 54.Kh1 h4 55.Kg2 h3+ 56.Kh1 Kd7 57.e6+ Kxe6 58.d7 g2+ 59.Kxh2 Kxd7] 48...Kg6 49.Re4 Kg5 draws.)

41...h3 42.Rxg3 fxg3 43.Qc2+ Bf5 (43...Qf5 44.Qxf5+ Kxf5 45.gxh3; 43...Kf6 44.Qd3 with Rf1+ and Qf3 to follow.) 44.Rxe5 winning.

40...Qe7

Black could have forced a pawn up rook ending where he would have been playing for two results (win or draw) with 40...h3!? 41.gxh3 Bxh3 42.Bxf4 Ne2+ 43.Kh1 Nxf4 44.Rg1 Bg2+ 45.Rxg2 Qxg2+ 46.Qxg2+ Nxg2.

41.Rxe5 dxe5 42.Qe1

42.b4!?, opening lines for the rook, better meets the needs of the position.

42...Qg5 43.Kh2

43.Bb2 e4 44.Rxg3 falls short after 44...hxg3 45.Qxe4+ Qf5.

43...Bg4 44.Bxf4?

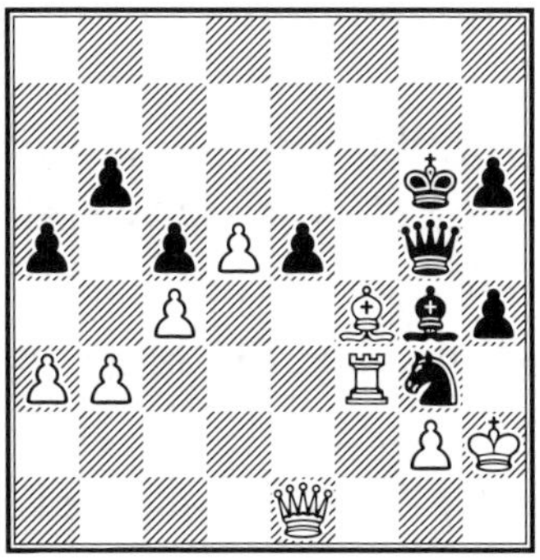

At first glance this looks like it might draw based on the exposed position of the enemy king, but it shouldn't work. Necessary was 44.Rf2 preserving the rook.

44...exf4 45.Qe8+ Kg7 46.d6 Bxf3?

Bobby decides to split the point, but 46...Bh5 47.Qe6 Bf7 48.Qe1 Qf5 49.d7 Qxd7 50.Qe5+ Kg6 51.Rxf4 Nf5 looks convincing as Black's pieces coordinate perfectly.

47.Qd7+ Kf8 48.Qc8+ Kf7 49.Qd7+ Kg6 50.Qe8+ Kf5 51.gxf3 Nf1+ 52.Kh1 Ng3+ 53.Kh2,Draw.

---

(83) King's Indian
Svetozar Gligorić – Fischer
Sveti Stefan 1992

1.d4 Nf6 2.Nf3 g6 3.c4 Bg7 4.Nc3 0-0 5.e4 d6 6.Be2 e5 7.0-0 Nc6 8.d5 Ne7 9.Nd2

The text is similar to 9.Ne1 in that White prevents 9...Nh5 (planning to come to f4 as well as play ...f5) and aims to bring the knight to the queenside to support play on that wing. The difference is that from d3 the knight not only supports c4-c5, but can also go to f2 to defend the king. With the knight on d2, White envisions attacking Black's pawn chain with b4, c5 and Nc4 pressuring d6.

9...a5 10.a3 Ne8

Bobby deviates from 10...Bd7 which was played in two of the other training games.

11.Rb1 f5 12.b4 Nf6 13.f3 Bh6

Fischer's favorite way of handling this position, first seen in game four of his match with Larsen, has rarely been played. With the text he seeks to get rid of his "bad bishop", but much more common are 13...f4, 13...axb4 and 13...Kh8.

14.Nb3

The sharpest test of 13...Bh6 is the pawn sacrifice 14.c5. After 14...Be3+ 15.Kh1 dxc5 16.bxc5 Bxc5 17.Nc4 Bd4 White has sufficient compensation for the pawn, but no more.

14...Bxc1 15.Qxc1 axb4 16.axb4 f4 17.c5 g5 18.Nb5 g4 19.cxd6 cxd6 20.Qc7

Thematic, but Black's play down the a-file holds the balance.

20...Qxc7 21.Nxc7 Ra2 22.Nc1 Rc2 23.Nb5 gxf3 24.gxf3 Bh3 25.Rf2 Rfc8 26.Nd3 Ne8 27.Bf1 Bd7 28.Rxc2 Rxc2 29.Rc1 Rc8

If 29...Rd2, then 30.Na3 followed by Nc4.

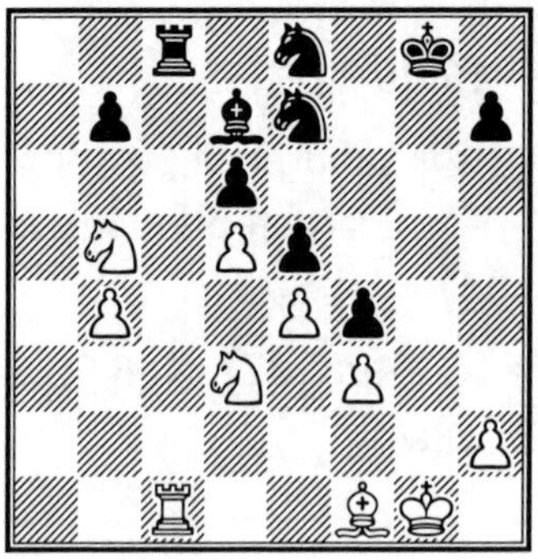

30.Rxc8 Nxc8 31.Nxd6!?

Gligorić sacrifices a knight for two connected central passed pawns with a third soon to come after Nxf4, but Fischer is equal to the challenge. 31.Na3 Kf7 was equal.

31...Nexd6 32.Nxe5 Bb5 33.Bxb5 Nxb5 34.Nd3 Nd4 35.Kf2 Nc2 36.e5 Kf7 37.d6 Nxd6 38.exd6 Ke6, Draw.

(84) King's Indian
Svetozar Gligorić – Fischer
Sveti Stefan 1992

1.d4 Nf6 2.c4 g6 3.Nc3 Bg7 4.e4 d6 5.Nf3 0-0 6.Be2 e5 7.0-0 Nc6 8.d5 Ne7 9.Nd2 a5 10.a3 Bd7 11.b3 c5 12.Rb1 b6 13.b4 axb4 14.axb4 Bh6

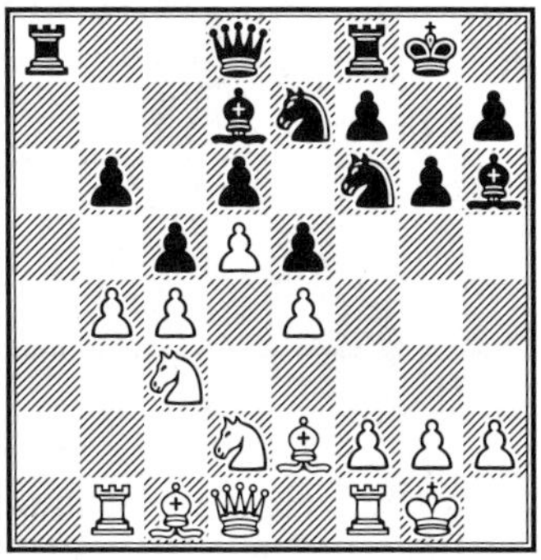

Fischer played this move in all three training games with 9.Nd2. On the plus side Black trades off his potentially bad bishop, but at a cost. The loss of several tempi could have been better spent developing kingside play, meaning Black's attack comes more slowly or maybe not at all.

Bobby's treatment is in some ways less dynamic than the standard King's Indian strategy, but also means Black is not necessarily reliant on an "all or nothing" kingside attack.

More commonly seen is 14...Ne8 15.bxc5 bxc5 16.Nb3 f5 17.f3 Nf6 18.Bd2 f4 19.Nb5 Nc8 20.Ra1 Rxa1 21.Qxa1 when White holds a small advantage, having made more progress on the queenside than Black on the other wing.

15.bxc5 bxc5 16.Nb3 Bxc1 17.Qxc1 Nc8 18.Ra1 Rb8 19.Ra3

19.Na5, eyeing c6 and with f4 in the cards, looks a little better for White.

19...Rb4 20.Qe3

20.f4 is also quite playable as Black has trouble making use of the e5 square.

20...Nb6 21.Nd2 Ng4 22.Bxg4 Bxg4 23.f4 exf4 24.Qxf4 Rb2 25.Ra7 Bd7 26.Nf3

Another option was 26.Nd1 when 26...Rc2 leads to a drawish endgame after 27.Rb7 Nxc4 28.Nxc4 Rxc4 29.Qxd6 Bc8 30.Qxd8 Rxd8 31.Rbxf7 Rxe4. Fischer might also have considered the exchange sacrifice 26...Rxd2 27.Qxd2 Nxc4 28.Qc3 Ne5 with decent compensation.

26...f6

Bobby prefers to keep the tension and prevents Gligorić from simplifying the position by a timely e5. For example: 26...Nxc4 27.e5 Nxe5 28.Nxe5 dxe5 29.Qxe5 Re8 30.Qc7 Qg5 31.Qg3 leads to an equal endgame as White will soon recover his pawn; e.g. 31...Qxg3 32.hxg3 Rd8 33.Rc7.

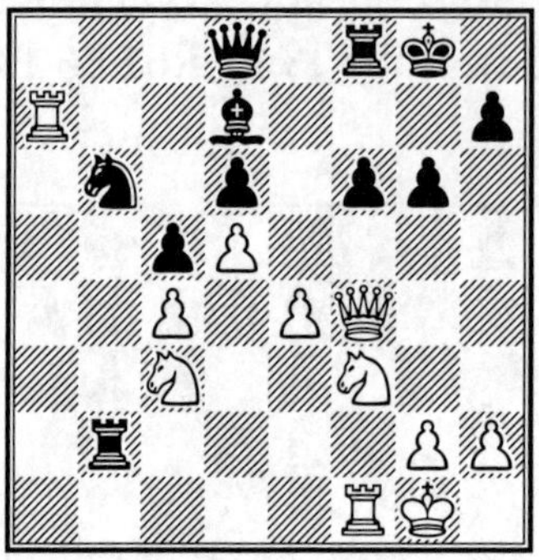

27.Qxd6?

This is the right idea, but the wrong execution. Correct was interpolating 27.Nd1, saving an important tempo which should lead to a drawn ending. Houdini gives the following sample line: 27...Re2 28.Qxd6 Rxg2+ 29.Kh1 Re2 30.Rb7 Bh3 31.Qxd8 Rxd8 32.Rf2 Rxe4 33.Rxb6 Rde8 34.Ng1 Re1 35.Rd2 Bg4 36.Kg2 Rxd1 37.Rxd1 Bxd1 38.Rc6 Bb3 39.Rxc5 Kf8 40.Rc6 Re4 41.Rxf6+ Ke7 42.Rb6 Bxc4 43.d6+ Kd7 44.Rb7+ Kxd6 45.Rxh7.

27...Rxg2+ 28.Kh1 Rc2!

This is the difference picking up a critical tempo against the unprotected knight.

29.Nd1?

Better chances for survival were offered by 29.Nb5 Bh3 30.Rg1 Qxd6 31.Nxd6 Nxc4 32.Nxc4 Rxc4 33.Rg3.

29...Bh3 30.Qxd8 Rxd8 31.Ne3

31.Rg1 Nxc4 leaves the knight completely out of play on d1.

31...Bxf1 32.Nxc2 Nxc4 33.Na3 Nd6 34.e5 Be2

The immediate capture of the e-pawn might have been even stronger as 34...fxe5 35.Nxe5 is met by the bone crusher 35...Bh3! with ...Rf8 looming.

35.Ng1?

35.Kg2 leads to a two pawn deficit in the ending, but with some practical chances due to Black's loose pawns and poor king position. The text loses on the spot.

35...Bd3!

Black's bishop dominates both of White's knights. Fischer finishes in convincing fashion.

36.Nh3 fxe5 37.Ng5 h6 38.Ne6 Rc8 39.Rg7+ Kh8 40.Rd7 Nf5 41.d6 c4 42.Nd8 Be4+ 43.Kg1 Bd5, 0–1.

Game (85) and (86) were most likely games eight and ten in the training match. We base this on Gligorić's recollection that he won the last game, that the match games appeared to be have been played as in a thematic tournament (first the KID games, then the Queen's Indian etc.), and the score sheets for these two games had the logo for the Fischer–Spassky match, while some of the earlier games were recorded on notebook paper.

(85) Queen's Indian
Svetozar Gligorić – Fischer
Sveti Stefan (8) 1992

1.d4 Nf6 2.c4 e6 3.Nf3 b6 4.Nc3 Bb7 5.e3 Ne4

This is not a commonly played move. It's seen more often after 5.a3, but the idea behind the knight advance is different in this position—Black wants to double White's c-pawns without having to exchange his dark-squared bishop for a knight. By playing 5...Ne4 Fischer is hoping to gain a tempo over the variation: 5...Bb4 6.Bd3 Ne4 7.0-0 Nxc3 8.bxc3 Be7 which has been tried (admittedly with modest success) by Grandmasters Romanishin, Miles and Chiburdanidze.

6.Bd3 Nxc3 7.bxc3 Be7 8.0-0 0-0 9.e4 d6

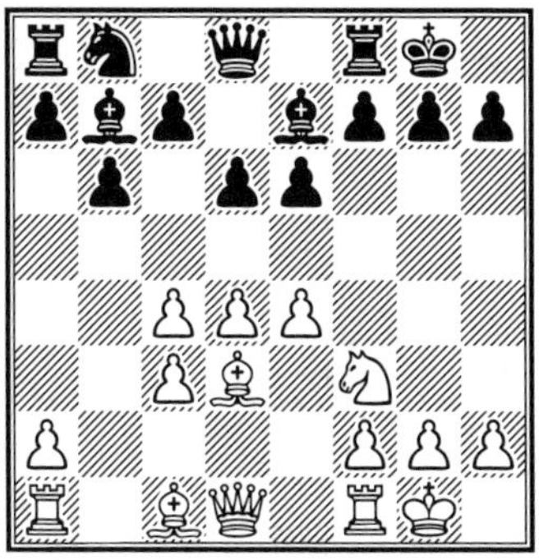

This is the position Bobby has been aiming for. He has inflicted double pawns on White without having to surrender the bishop pair, but in return Gligorić has an advantage in space. These two games convinced Bobby that the passive positions Black obtained were not something he wanted to repeat in his match with Spassky.

10.Ne1 Nd7 11.Nc2 e5 12.f4

This move is necessary in such positions. White needs to play actively to compensate for the doubled c-pawns.

12...Bf6 13.Rb1

This removes the rook from the diagonal and can sometimes help to get in c4-c5.

13...Re8 14.Qf3 Nf8 15.fxe5 dxe5 16.d5 Nd7 17.Ba3

This stops ...Nc5 and works well as Black cannot challenge the bishop with ...Be7 due to the unprotected pawn on f7.

17...Bc8 18.Qf2 Kh8 19.c5 Nxc5 20.Bxc5 bxc5 21.Bb5 Bd7 22.Qxc5 Be7 23.Qc4 Rb8

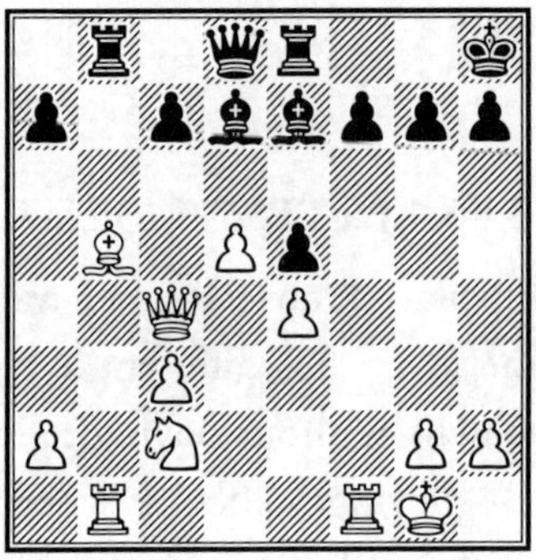

24.Bc6?!

White has played very well the past few moves and with 24.Bxd7 Qxd7 25.Nb4 he would maintain a small, but clear, positional advantage.

24...Bxc6 25.Qxc6 Rf8 26.Ne3

26.Nb4 still makes sense.

26...Rb6

Chances are now even.

27.Rxb6 axb6 28.Nf5?

28.Nc4 was preferable.

28...Bc5+ 29.Kh1 g6 30.Nh6?

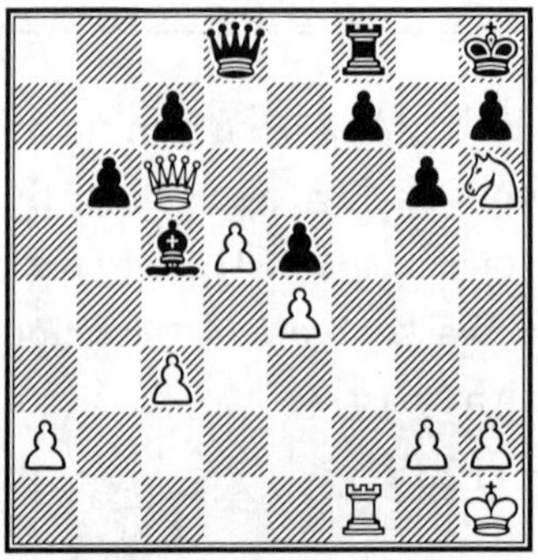

30.Ng3 was necessary.

30...Qg5

30...Bd6! and 30...Qh4! 31.Nxf7+ Kg7 (similar to the game) were both winning for Black. The text allows White a chance to save himself.

31.Nxf7+?

31.d6! (to open the c4-f7 diagonal) 31...Qxh6?? (31...cxd6 32.Nxf7+ Kg8 33.Qd7 =) 32.dxc7 Rc8 33.Qd7 and White wins.

31...Kg7 32.Qxc7 Qe7 33.Qxe7 Bxe7 34.g3 Rxf7 35.Kg2 Ba3 36.Rxf7+ Kxf7 37.Kf3 Ke7 38.h4 h5 39.g4 Kd6 40.gxh5 gxh5 41.Ke2 Kc5 42.Kd3 b5, 0–1.

---

(86) Queen's Indian
Svetozar Gligorić – Fischer
Sveti Stefan (10) 1992

1.d4 Nf6 2.c4 e6 3.Nf3 b6 4.Nc3 Bb7 5.e3 Ne4 6.Bd3

6.Nxe4 Bxe4 7.Bd2 Be7 8.Be2 0-0 9.0-0 d5 didn't offer White much in Kaidanov–Seirawan, U.S. Championship 2003.

6...Nxc3 7.bxc3 Be7 8.e4 d6 9.0-0 0-0 10.Be3

10.Ne1 was seen in Game (85)

10...Nd7 11.Nd2 e5 12.f4 Bf6 13.Rb1 Re8 14.Qf3 exf4 15.Qxf4 Nf8 16.Qg3 Ng6 17.Rf5 Bc8 18.Rh5 Nf8 19.Rf1 g6

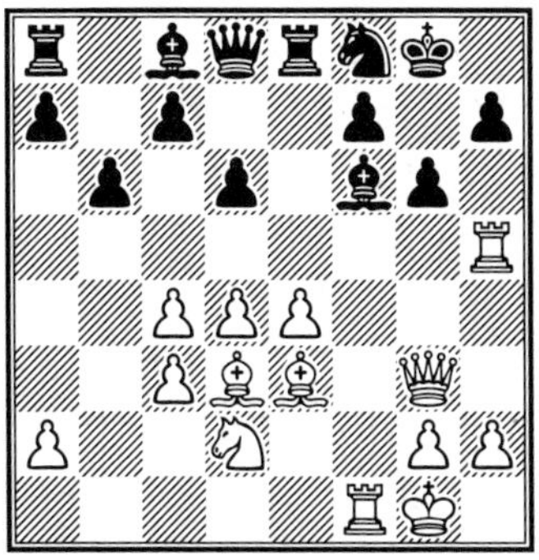

20.Rd5!?

White dominates after 20.Bh6 Bh8 21.Nf3 Qd7 22.h3 Ne6 23.Nh2 c5 24.Rhf5 winning.

20...Bg7

On 20...Be6, either 21.Rb5 or 21.Qf2 leave White with a strong initiative.

21.e5! Be6 22.Be4

Just as in the King's Indian games, Gligorić is quite happy to part with the exchange if needed, provided he obtains enough positional compensation.

22...Nd7 23.exd6

23.Rb5! was even stronger.

23...c6 24.Rg5 Bxc4

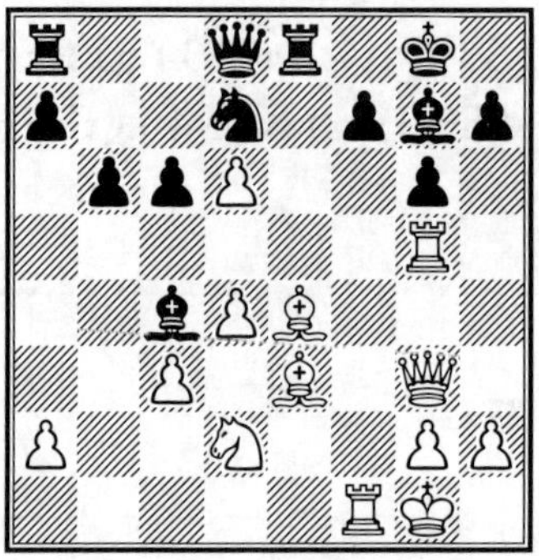

On 24...f6, White breaks through with 25.Rxg6 hxg6 26.Qxg6 Nf8 27.Qg3 Qd7 (27...Rc8 28.Bh6 Qd7 29.Rxf6 Kh8 30.Bxg7+ Qxg7 31.Qh4+ Kg8 32.Rf3) 28.Rxf6.

25.Bxg6 hxg6 26.Nxc4 Re6 27.Ne5 Nxe5 28.dxe5 Qd7 29.Bf4 Rae8 30.h4 Rf8 31.h5 Qe8

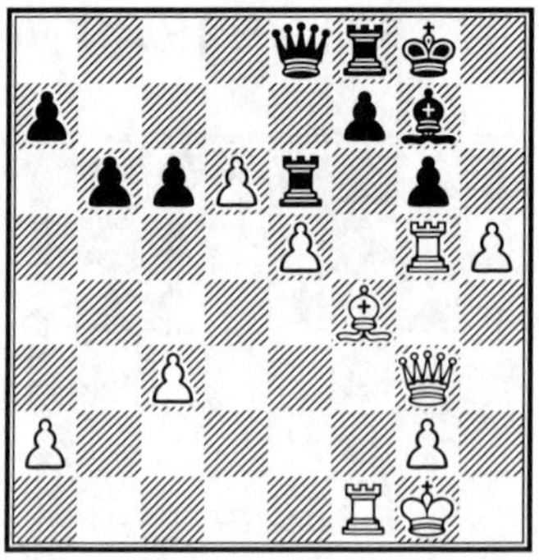

32.Rg4 c5

32...Bxe5 33.Bxe5 Rxe5 34.hxg6 f6 35.Qh4 Qd7 36.g7 winning.

33.Qd3 c4 34.Qd5 gxh5 35.Rxg7+ Kxg7 36.Bg5 Qd7 37.Bf6+ Rxf6 38.exf6+ Kg6 39.Qe4+ Kg5 40.Qe5+ Kg6 41.Qe4+ Kg5 42.Qf4+ Kg6 43.Rf3, 1–0.

(87) Ruy Lopez
Fischer – Svetozar Gligorić
Sveti Stefan 1992

1.e4 e5 2.Nf3 Nc6 3.Bb5 a6 4.Ba4 Nf6 5.0-0 Be7 6.Re1 b5 7.Bb3 d6 8.c3 0-0 9.h3 Bb7 10.d4 Re8 11.Ng5 Rf8 12.Nf3 Re8 13.Nbd2 Bf8 14.d5 Nb8 15.Nf1 Nbd7 16.Ng3 g6 17.Be3 Bg7 18.Qd2 Qe7 19.Rf1

Grandmaster Luc Winants had this to say about the position:[1]

The 19th move was one moment of doubt because what I read on the score sheet was KR-e1 instead of KR-B1. However, Rf1 is a very common move in such variations of the Ruy López. Among the many examples are:

- 22 Rf1 in Tal–Portisch, Interzonal play-off, Biel
- 1976 21 Rf1 in Spassky–Portisch, ninth game, Candidates' match
- 1977 22 Rf1 in Tal–Spassky, Tilburg, 1980
- 22 Rf1 in Anand–van der Sterren, Wijk aan Zee
- 1998 19 Rf1 in Bacrot–Postny, French team championship, 2009.

I took 19 Rf1 because it is a common move, but 19 Red1, to stop c7-c6, seems very logical as well and perhaps even more appropriate to the situation. Even 19 Rec1 (to support c3-c4) has its points. I had other doubts later on, but after I reached the position following 34...Bxa4, when 35 Rxa4 is refuted by 35...Nf1+ and 35 Nc6 by 35...Bb5, I thought that this was most probably the correct version.

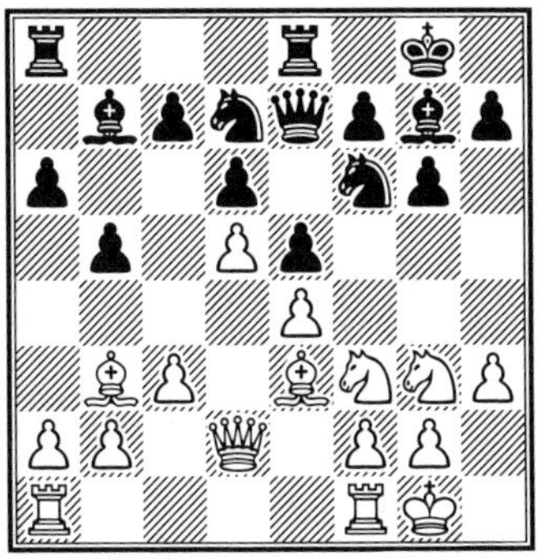

19...Nb6 20.a4 bxa4 21.Bxa4 Nxa4 22.Rxa4 c6 23.c4 cxd5 24.cxd5 Bc8 25.Rfa1 Rb8 26.Ne1 h5 27.f3 h4 28.Ne2 Nh5 29.Nd3 f5 30.Nb4 f4 31.Bf2 Qg5 32.Kh2 Ng3 33.Nxa6 Bd7

White can meet 33...Rb7 with either 34.Rb4 or 34.Nb4 Bd7 35.Nc6

34.Nxb8 Bxa4 35.Nc3 Rxb8 36.Nxa4 Bf6 37.Nb6 Bd8 38.Nc4 Qe7 39.Qc2, 1–0.

[1] Edward Winter's Chess Notes.

(88) Ruy Lopez
Fischer – Svetozar Gligorić
Sveti Stefan 1992

1.e4 e5 2.Nf3 Nc6 3.Bb5 a6 4.Ba4 Nf6 5.0-0 Be7 6.Re1 b5 7.Bb3 d6 8.c3 0-0 9.h3 Bb7

9...Nb8 10.d4 Nbd7 11.Bc2 Bb7 12.Nbd2 Re8 13.Nf1 Bf8 14.Ng3 was seen in games one, three and five of the 1992 match between Fischer and Spassky.

10.d4 Re8 11.Ng5

Fischer has no intention of repeating the position three times, but is eager to grab some extra clock time by repeating the position.

11...Rf8 12.Nf3 Re8 13.Nbd2 Bf8 14.d5

The text was played in three games of the training match and 14.Bc2 in another (where White played d5 the very next move).

14...Nb8 15.Nf1 Nbd7 16.Ng3 h6

16...g6 was tried in another game, but the main line is 16...Nc5 17.Bc2 c6.

17.Nf5 Nc5 18.Bc2 c6 19.b4 Na4!

Black's two bishops will provide adequate compensation for the doubled a-pawns.

20.Bxa4 bxa4 21.c4 cxd5 22.exd5 Bc8 23.Ne3 Bd7 24.Nd2 Qb6 25.Ba3 Qd4 26.Rc1 Qd3 27.Bb2 Rac8 28.Rc3 Qg6 29.Qc2 Qxc2 30.Nxc2 Nh5 31.h4?!

31.Ba3 Nf4 32.Ne3, trying to play c4-c5, seems more consistent.

31...f5 32.g3 Nf6

32...f4! 33.Ne4 Bf5 leaves Black on top.

33.Ne3 g5?!

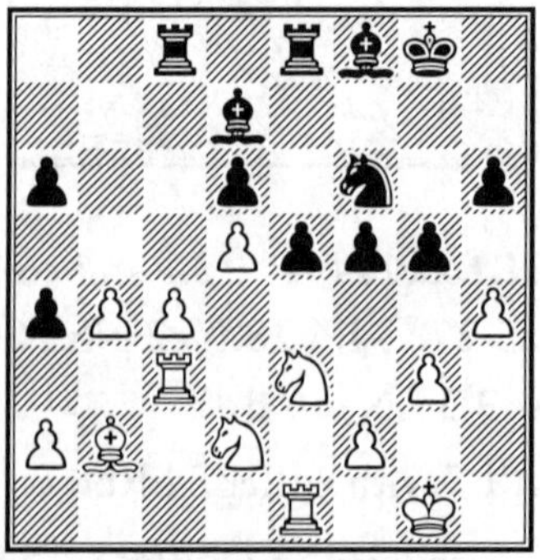

33...f4!

34.Nxf5!

White uses tactics to keep the position under control.

34...Bxf5 35.Rf3 Nxd5 36.Rxf5 Nxb4 37.hxg5 Nd3 38.Rb1 Rb8 39.Ba3 Rxb1+ 40.Nxb1 hxg5 41.Rxg5+ Kf7 42.Nc3 Be7 43.Rg4 Rc8 44.Kf1 Nc5 45.Ke2 Nd7 46.Kd3 Nf6 47.Rh4 Rg8 48.c5 dxc5 49.Rxa4 Ra8 50.Bc1 Rd8+ 51.Ke2 Rd6 52.Be3 Rc6 53.Kd3 Ke6 54.Rh4 Rb6 55.Rh6 Kf7 56.Rh8 Rb2 57.Ra8 e4+ 58.Nxe4 Rxa2 59.Nxc5

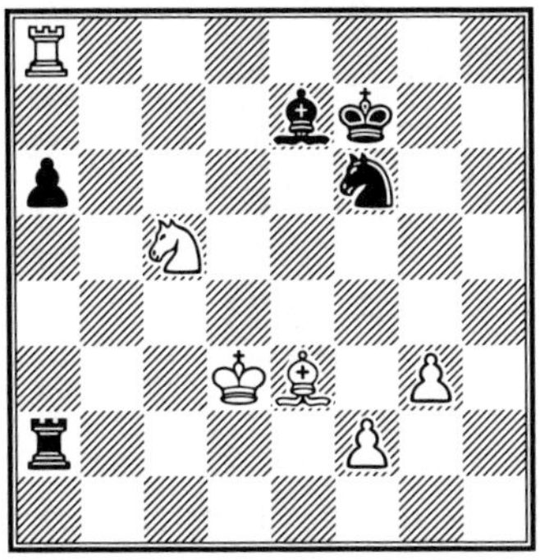

59...Ng4 60.Ne4 Ra3+ 61.Ke2 Nxe3 62.fxe3 Ra1 63.Ra7 Ke6 64.g4 Bb4 65.Rb7 a5 66.Rb5 Be7 67.Ng3 a4 68.Nf5 Bf6 69.Rb6+ Kf7 70.Nh6+ Kg7 71.Nf5+ Kf7 72.Nd6+ Ke7 73.Ne4

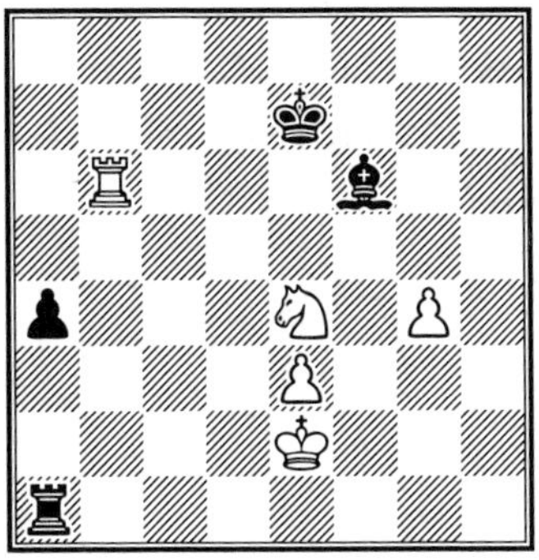

73...Be5 74.Rb5 Bh8 75.Rb7+ Ke6 76.Ra7 Kd5 77.Nd2 Bc3 78.Kd3 Bxd2 79.Kxd2 Ke4, ½–½.

---

(89) Ruy Lopez
Fischer – Svetozar Gligorić
Sveti Stefan 1992

1.e4 e5 2.Nf3 Nc6 3.Bb5 a6 4.Ba4 Nf6 5.0-0 Be7 6.Re1 b5 7.Bb3 d6 8.c3 0-0 9.h3 Bb7 10.d4 Re8 11.Ng5 Rf8 12.Nf3 Re8 13.Nbd2 Bf8 14.Bc2 g6

14...Nb8

15.d5 Nb8 16.b4

16.b3 is the main line.

16...c6 17.dxc6 Nxc6 18.a4 Qc7 19.axb5 axb5 20.Rxa8 Rxa8 21.Bd3

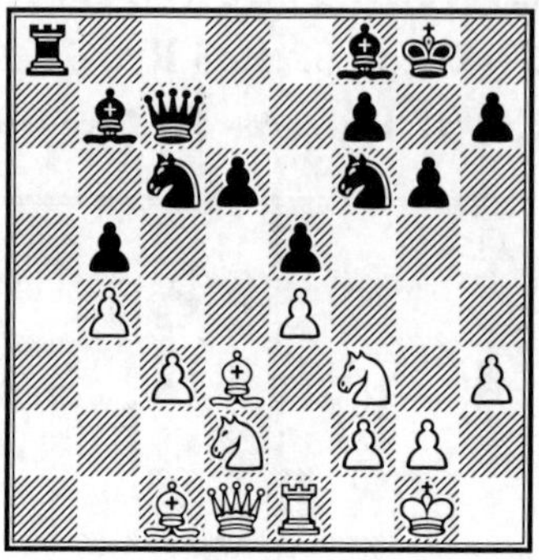

21...Nd8!

Gligorić's huge experience on the Black side of the Ruy Lopez shows here. Instead of defending his b-pawn, Black launches a counterattack against White's c-pawn while preparing ...Bc6 and the ...d5 break. The knight will come into play on e6.

22.Bb2 Bc6 23.Qe2 Qb6

23...Ra2 was a good alternative.

24.Nb3 Ne6 25.Bc1 Rc8 26.Na5 Be8 27.Qb2 Qb8 28.Qb3 Bg7 29.Be3 Rd8 30.Ng5 Nxg5 31.Bxg5 Rc8 32.c4 Nh5 33.Rd1 Nf4 34.Bxf4 exf4 35.cxb5 Bxb5 36.Bc4 Be8?!

36...Rc7 37.Rd5 Bxc4 38.Nxc4 Qa7, intending ...Bd4, looks fine for Black.

37.Bd5?

37.b5! and White is in control.

37...Rc3! 38.Qa2 f3! 39.gxf3

If 39.g3 Black has 39...Qc8.

39...Rxf3

39...Qd8! followed by ...Qh4.

40.e5 Rf4! 41.exd6

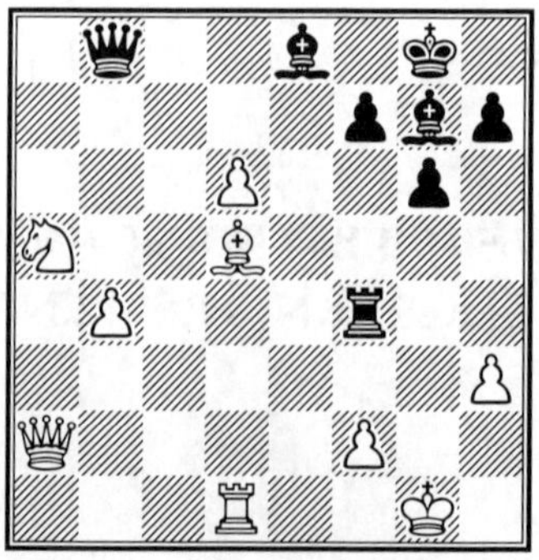

41...Qxd6?

41...Bd4! and Black is winning!

42.Qe2 Qf8 43.Bc6 Bxc6 44.Nxc6 Bf6 45.Rd7 Qc8

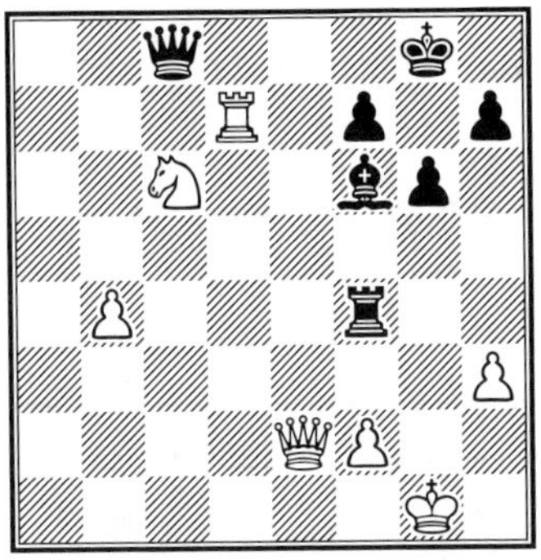

46.Qe7!? Bxe7??

Gligorić must have had a complete hallucination. 46...Qf8 was necessary and would have held.

47.Nxe7+ Kg7 48.Nxc8 Rxb4 49.Nd6 Rf4 50.Rc7 g5 51.Rc4 Rf3 52.Kg2 Rd3 53.Rd4 Ra3 54.Nf5+ Kg6 55.Ne3 Ra6 56.Nc4 f6 57.Rd6 Ra7 58.Ne5+, 1–0.

---

(90) Ruy Lopez
Fischer – Svetozar Gligorić
Sveti Stefan 1992

1.e4 e5 2.Nf3 Nc6 3.Bb5 a6 4.Ba4 Nf6 5.0-0 Be7 6.Re1 b5 7.Bb3 d6 8.c3 0-0 9.h3 Bb7 10.d4 Re8 11.Ng5 Rf8 12.Nf3 Re8 13.Nbd2 Bf8 14.d5 Nb8 15.Nf1 Nbd7 16.g4

16.Ng3 was played in two of the other training games.

16...Nc5 17.Bc2 c6 18.b4 Ncd7 19.dxc6 Bxc6 20.Ng3 Nb6 21.Bb3 Rc8 22.g5 Nfd7 23.Nh2 Bb7 24.Qf3 Nc4 25.Ng4

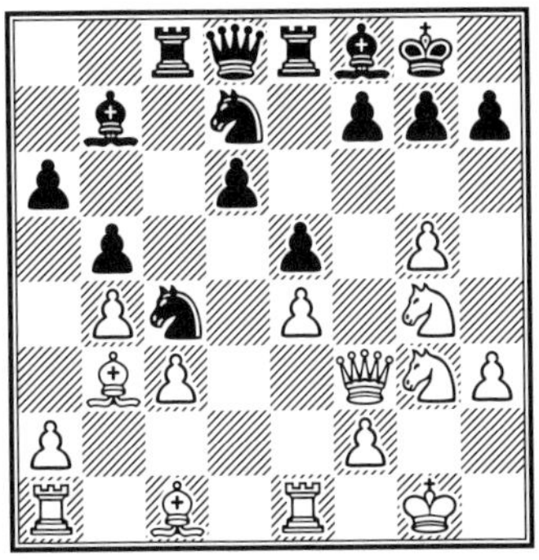

25...Re6

Black has a comfortable position and had good alternatives in 25...a5 and 25...Ndb6.

26.Be3 Be7

26...Ndb6 intending ...Na4 was also promising.

27.h4 Nf8?!

Starting to go passive. Why not 27...Qc7?

28.Nf5 Qe8

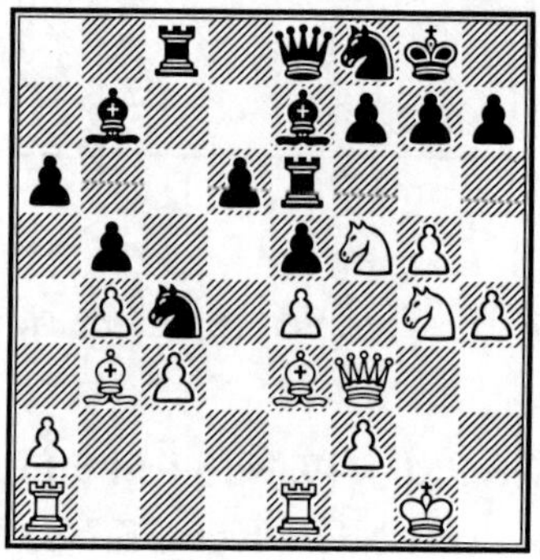

Continuing the trend of deactivating Black's pieces.

29.a4

29.h5! with the idea h5-h6.

29...Nxe3?

29...Qc6

30.Rxe3 Ng6 31.axb5 axb5 32.Ra7

Black's position has collapsed.

32...Rc7 33.Bd5! Bxd5 34.Rxc7 Bc4 35.h5 Bxg5 36.hxg6 Rxg6 37.Qh3! h6 38.Rg3 Kh7 39.Qh5 Qa8 40.Nge3 Qxe4 41.Nxc4 Qxf5 42.Ne3 Qe6 43.Qf3 Bf4 44.Rxg6 Qxg6+ 45.Qg4 Qb1+ 46.Nf1, 1–0.

Fischer played 1.e4 in four games. It seems probable they were number 1,3, 5 and 7 and Game (91) is number 9.

(91) English
Fischer – Svetozar Gligorić
Sveti Stefan (9) 1992

1.c4 c5 2.b3 Nc6 3.g3 Nf6 4.Bg2 d5 5.cxd5 Nxd5 6.f4

Only six moves have been played and already a position has been reached which is brand new! Fischer's sixth move seeks to stop Black from setting up a Maróczy Bind with ...e5.

6...e6

Solid, but Black has many choices here, including the more active 6...Nd4 or 6...Bg4.

7.Bb2 h5

Both players are in an adventurous mood.

8.Nh3

8.Nf3 h4 9.Nxh4? Rxh4 10.gxh4 Qxh4+ 11.Kf1 Nxf4 would lead to a quick win for Black.

8...Nf6 9.Nf2 h4 10.Nc3 hxg3 11.hxg3 Rxh1+ 12.Bxh1 Bd7

12...Qd7, planning, ...b6 and ...Bb7, was a sensible alternative.

13.e3 Qa5 14.g4!

Nowadays advancing the g-pawn to gain space is all the rage. Once again Fischer was ahead of his time.

14...0-0-0 15.g5 Ne8 16.Qh5 f5

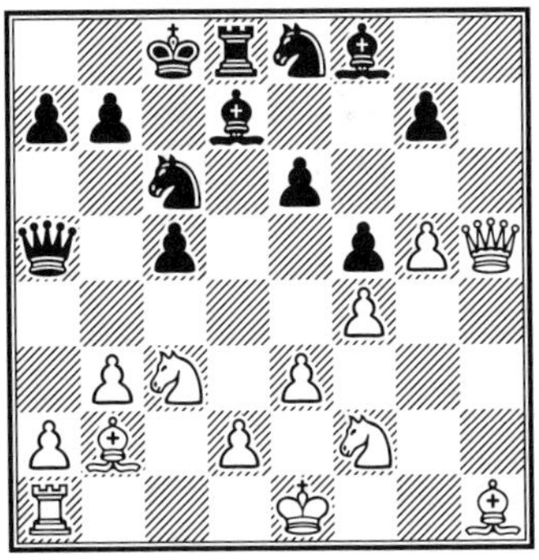

16...Nd6 was less committal.

17.Bxc6!?

Concrete play by Fischer. 17.gxf6 Nxf6 18.Qf7 was the alternative.

17...Bxc6 18.Qf7 Nc7 19.Nd3! Rxd3 20.Qxf8+ Ne8 21.Qe7

Fischer takes care to restrict the activity of Black's pieces.

21...Rd6

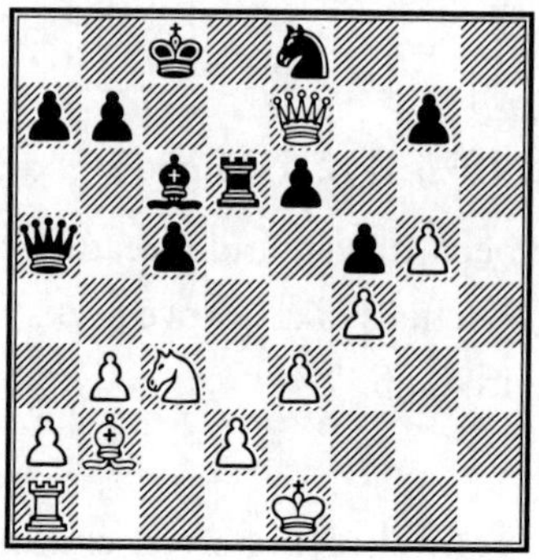

22.0-0-0

The computer move 22.Nb1, with the powerful threat of Be5, forces Black to either offer a queen trade with 22...Qd8 or head for obscure complications with 22...Qb4 which favor White: 23.Be5 Qe4 24.Kd1! (24. Bxd6 Qh1+ 25.Kf2 Qg2+ 26.Ke1 Qg1+ 27.Ke2 Bf3+ 28.Kxf3 Qf1+=) 24...Rd5 25.Nc3 Qh1+ 26.Kc2 Qxa1 27.Qxe6+ Kd8 28.Nxd5.

22...Qd8 23.Qxd8+ Rxd8 24.Na4 b6

As 24...Bxa4 25.bxa4 leaves White with much the better minor piece which more than compensates for the doubled a-pawns.

25.Be5 g6 26.Nb2 Rd7 27.Nc4 Bf3 28.Rf1 Bd5 29.Rd1 Rh7

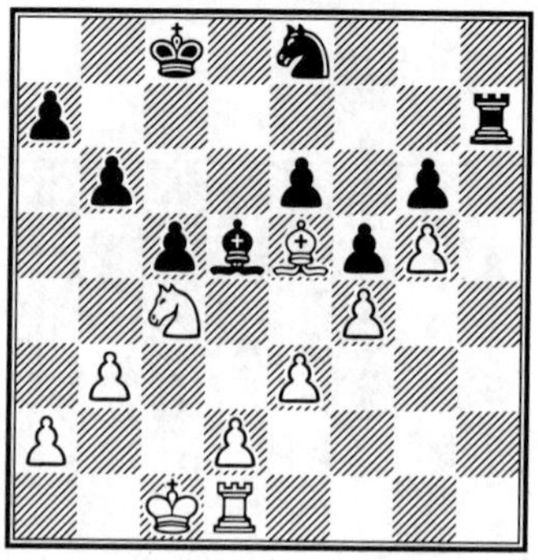

Black has the h-file, but no targets to attack.

30.a4 Rh3 31.Kc2 Kb7 32.Kc3 a6 33.b4 cxb4+ 34.Kxb4 Rh2

34...a5+ was necessary.

35.a5! Bf3?

35...b5 36.Nb6 Bc6 37.d3 with e4 to follow, also favors White.

36.Rc1 b5 37.Nb6!

The start of a far-sighted maneuver to attack the base of Black's pawn chain.

37...Bc6

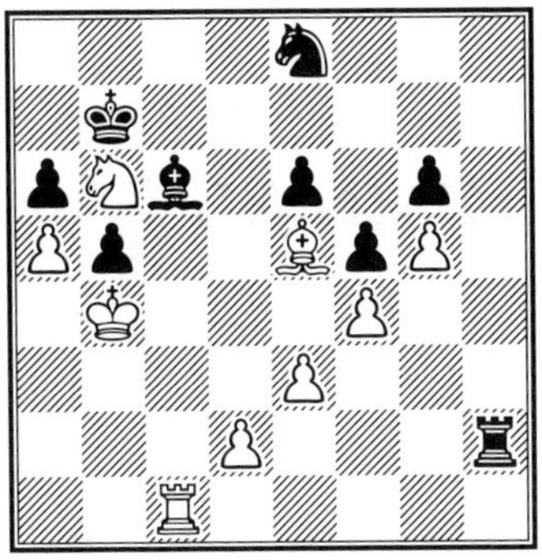

38.Nc8! Rxd2 39.Ne7 Bd7 40.Nxg6 Ra2 41.Ne7 Ra4+ 42.Kb3 Re4 43.Rd1 Rxe3+ 44.Kb2 Re2+ 45.Kc1, 1–0.

4

TRAINING GAME WITH TORRE

After his match with Gligorić, Bobby played a few games with his second Eugenio Torre. Game (92) is the only one that has surfaced as of this writing.

(92) Sicilian
Eugenio Torre – Fischer
Sveti Stefan (Training Game) 1992

1.e4 c5 2.c3 Nf6 3.e5 Nd5 4.d4 cxd4 5.Nf3 Nc6 6.Bc4 e6 7.cxd4 d6 8.0-0 Be7 9.Qe2 0-0 10.Qe4 a6

While this looks like a time waster compared to the regular moves 10...Bd7, 10...Qc7 and 10...Ndb4, it might not be that bad. By getting in ...b5 Black has the potential to obtain more activity than is usually the case in this line.

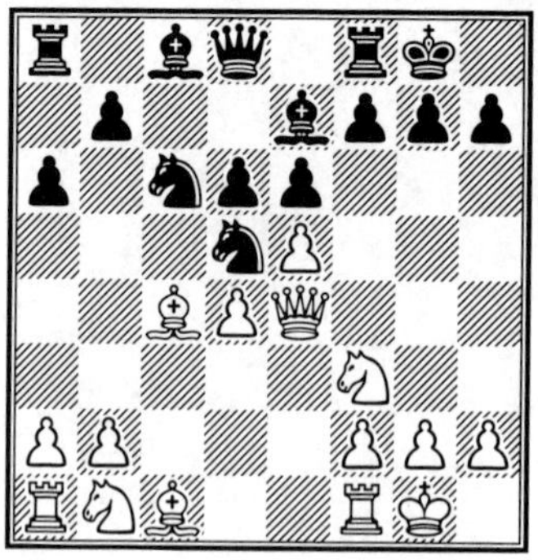

11.a3 b5 12.Bd3

12.Bxd5? exd5 13.Qxd5 Bb7 offers Black excellent compensation for the pawn.

12...g6 13.Bh6 Re8 14.Nbd2 Bb7 15.Rfe1 Nb6

This looks to be a novelty. 15...dxe5 16.dxe5 Nb6 17.Bb1 Qc7 18.Qg4 Rad8 19.h4 Rd5 20.h5 Nxe5 21.Nxe5 Rxe5 22.Rxe5 Qxe5 23.hxg6 f5

24.Qh5 Rd8 25.Ba2 Nd5 26.Nf3 Qf6 27.gxh7+ Kh8 28.Ng5, 1–0 was Jurković–Janković, Rijeka 2005 and serves as a cautionary example of the difficulties Black faces if he does not generate enough counterplay—White has an easy attacking plan in h2-h4-h5.

16.Bf1

Black's last move introduced the threat of trading on e5 and moving the knight on c6, leaving the bishop on d3 in an awkward position. This begs the question where it should relocate. The normal response would be 16.Bb1 keeping the bishop on the b1-h7 attacking diagonal, but locking in the queen rook. 16...dxe5 17.dxe5 Na5 18.Qf4 and now 18...Nd5 19.Qg3 Nc4 20.Nxc4 (20.Ne4 Nxb2 21.h4 Nc4 22.h5 Qc7 23.hxg6 fxg6 offers White compensation for the pawn, but nothing concrete.) 20...bxc4 offers chances for both sides.

16...Rc8 17.Qf4

The immediate 17.Qg4 was also possible, but Torre prefers the Black knight on d5 where it stands well, but blocks the d-file.

17...Nd5 18.Qg4 dxe5 19.dxe5 Nb8

This is an interesting redeployment by Fischer who prepares to bring the knight to d7 where it can go to f8 or c5 as needed.

20.Rac1 Nd7 21.h4 Rxc1 22.Rxc1 Qb8 23.Re1 Qc7 24.Bd3 Nc5?!

This takes the knight away from the kingside. 24...Rd8!? is interesting meeting 25.h5? with 25...N7f6! 26.exf6 Nxf6. White should instead play 25.Bb1, when 25...Nf8 is a solid reply.

25.Bb1 f5

This creates a weakness on e6, but Black needs the breathing space for his pieces.

26.exf6 Nxf6 27.Qd4 Qd6

27...Rd8 28.Qc3 Rc8 29.b4 Ncd7 30.Qxc7 Rxc7 31.Ba2 picks up an important pawn.

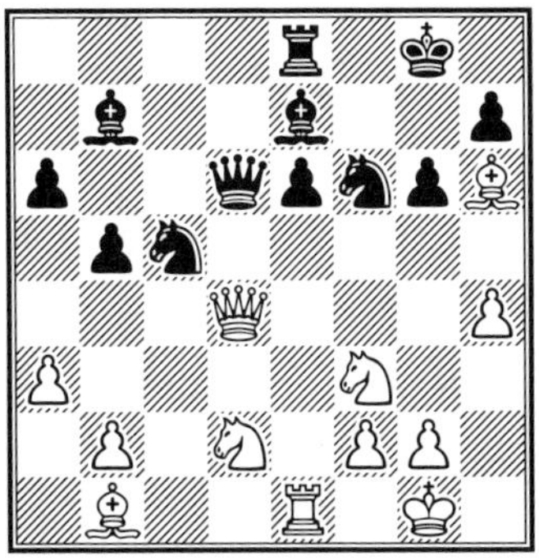

28.Bg5

28.b4! Na4 29.Ba2 Qxd4 30.Bxe6+ Kh8 31.Nxd4 would have left White a clean pawn up.

28...Qxd4 29.Nxd4 Bd5 30.Rc1 Na4 31.Nc6 Kf7 32.Ne5+ Kg8 33.Nc6 Kf7 34.Nxe7 Rxe7 35.b3 Nb6 36.f3 Rb7 37.Bd3 Nbd7 38.Kf2 Ne5 39.Be2 Nc6 40.Ke3 Ne7 41.g4 Rd7 42.Bxf6 Kxf6 43.Ne4+ Kg7 44.Nc5 Ra7?!

44...Rd6 was more solid.

45.Bd3 Kf7 46.Be4 a5?!

46...Rc7 was better. Now Black gets into trouble.

47.Bxd5 Nxd5+ 48.Kd4 Nb6

Black wants to play ...a4, but overlooks White's threat.

49.Nd3?

49.Nxe6! Rd7+ 50.Kc5 Kxe6 51.Kxb6 Rd3 52.Rc6+ Ke7 53.Rc7+ Ke6 54.b4 a4 55.Kxb5 Rxa3 56.Rxh7 winning.

49...a4 50.Ne5+ Kf6 51.b4 Nd7 52.g5+ Kf5 53.Nc6

53.Nd3! is better.

53...Ra6 54.Ke3 e5 55.Ne7+ Ke6 56.Nc8 Nb8 57.Rc7 Rc6 58.Re7+ Kd5 59.Na7 Rc3+ 60.Kf2 Rxa3 61.Rxh7 e4?!

61...Ra2+ 62.Ke3 (62.Kg3 Ra1 63.Nxb5 Kc4=) 62...Ra3+ holds.

62.fxe4+ Kxe4 63.Nxb5 Rb3

63...Ra2+ 64.Kg3 Ra1 also held.

64.h5! Rb2+

64...Rxb4 is inferior: 65.Nd6+ Ke5 66.hxg6 Rf4+ 67.Ke3 with good chances to win.

64...gxh5 looks like it just holds: 65.g6 Rf3+ 66.Ke2 Rg3 67.g7 Na6 (67...Nc6 68.Nc3+ Ke5 69.b5 winning) 68.Nd6+ Ke5 69.Ne8 Nxb4 70.Rxh5+ (70.Rh8 a3 71.g8Q Rxg8 72.Rxg8 a2 73.Rg1 Nc2=) 70...Ke6 71.Kf2 Rg4 72.Rh4 Nd3+ 73.Ke2 Rg3 74.Rh8 a3 75.g8Q+ Rxg8 76.Rxg8 Nc1+ 77.Kd2 a2 78.Ng7+ Kf7 79.Ra8 a1Q drawing.

65.Kg3 Kf5?

Black holds with 65...gxh5 66.g6 Rb3+ 67.Kh4 Kf5 68.g7 Rxb4+ 69.Kh3 Rb3+, draw.

66.Nd4+ Kxg5 67.Nf3+ Kf6 68.h6 Rxb4

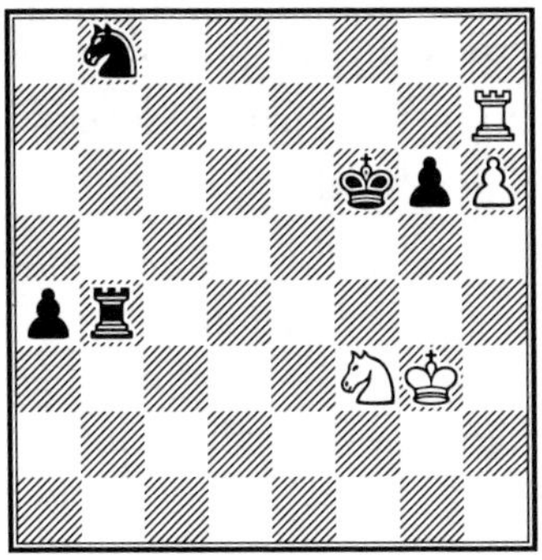

69.Ra7⁈

69.Rh8 Rb7 (69...Nd7 70.Rd8 Ke7 71.h7) 70.Rf8+ Ke6 (70...Rf7 71.Rxb8 Rh7 72.Nh2; 70...Ke7 71.h7) 71.h7 winning.

69...Rb5 70.Nh2

70.h7 Rh5 71.Rb7 Nc6 72.Rb6 Rxh7 73.Rxc6+ with a draw is just what Black is hoping for. White has to hang onto his h-pawn.

70...Rh5

70...Rb3+ 71.Kh4 g5+ 72.Kg4 Rb4+ 73.Kg3 was one way to draw.

71.Ng4+ Ke6 72.Rxa4 Nd7

72...Nc6 (intending ...Ne7-f5) 73.Ra6 Kd6 74.Kf4 Rf5+ 75.Ke4 Rh5 is simpler.

73.Ra6+ Kf7 74.Ra7 Rd5

74...Ke6 draws.

75.h7 Kg7 76.Nf6!

A beautiful move, but not one to change the result from a draw to win if Black keeps his head.

76...Rd1, ½–½.

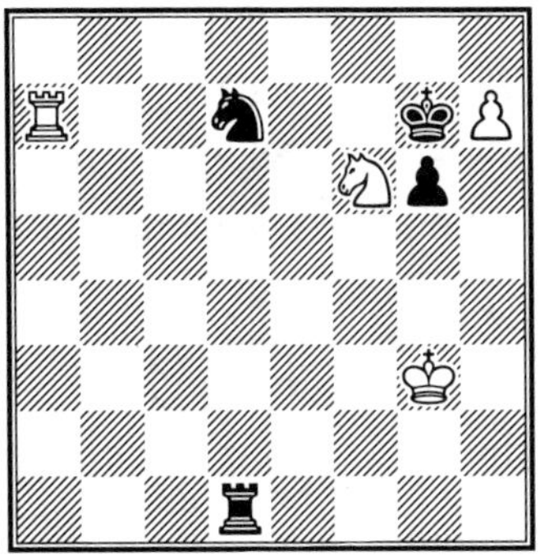

The players agreed to a draw here which is the correct result. The key for Black's defense is that rook and knight versus rook is a draw in all but a few special positions. It's important that Black play ...g5 when given the chance to give breathing space for his king.

Play might have continued:

(A) 77.Kg4

Black has to watch out for one beautiful trick made possible by passive play:

77...Rg1+

77...Rh1 78.h8Q+ Kxh8?? (78...Rxh8 79.Kg5 Kf7 draws) 79.Rxd7

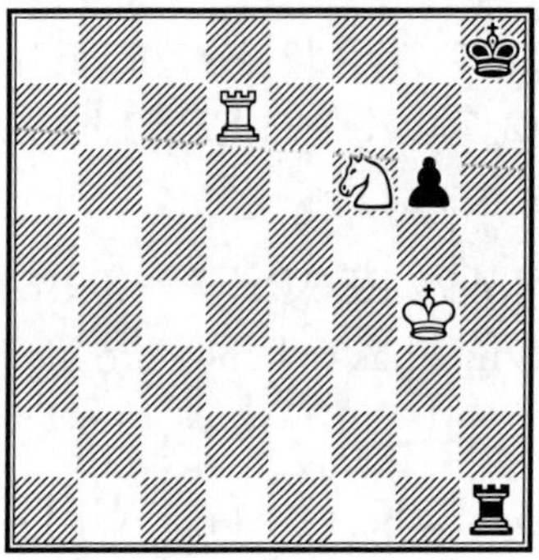

This position could have been a study. It's Black's move but he is totally paralyzed and unable to prevent White's king from coming to f8. 79...Rh2 80.Rf7 Rh1 81.Kf4 Rh2 82.Ke5 Re2+ 83.Kd6 Rh2 84.Ke7 Rh1 85.Kf8 with Rg7 followed by Rg8 mate!

78.Kh3 Rh1+ 79.Kg2 Rd1 80.Ra8 Rd2+ 81.Kg3 Rd3+ 82.Kf4 Rh3 83.Nxd7 Rxh7 draws

(B) 77.Kh3

Threatening Ra8 which if played immediately is met by 77...Rh1.

77...g5!

The easiest way to draw. Black can still get into trouble: 77...Rh1+ 78.Kg2 Rh4 (78...Rd1 79.Ra8) 79.Kg3 Rh1? (79...g5) 80.Nxd7 Kxh7 81.Nf6+ Kh8 82.Rf7 Rh6 83.Kf4 Rh1 84.Ke5 Rh3 85.Ke6 Rh4 86.Ke7 Rh2 87.Kf8 with the same theme we saw before.

78.Ra8

78.Kg2 Rd4 79.Kg3 Rh4 80.Nxd7 Kxh7 81.Nf8+ Kg8 (81...Kh6 82.Rh7 mate!) 82.Ne6 is a draw.

78...Rh1+ 79.Kg2 Nxf6, Draw!

5

FISCHER VS. SPASSKY TWO (THE REMATCH)

After a twenty year layoff—one without precedent among top players—Fischer returned to the tournament arena for a much anticipated rematch with Boris Spassky. Fischer–Spassky Two is superbly covered by Seirawan and Stefanović in *No Regrets*,[1] hence this chapter is limited to an evaluation of the quality of play.

The first game, played on September 2, 1992 twenty years and a day after the first match ended, was universally hailed as a masterpiece, combining brilliant positional (29.Nb1!) and attacking play (36.g4!). Everyone was stunned Fischer could play so well after such a long layoff. In retrospect, this turned out to be the highlight of the match.

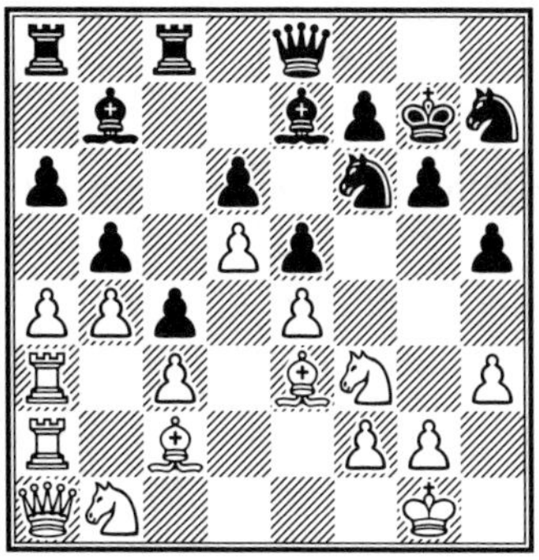

Position after 29.Nb1! in game 1.

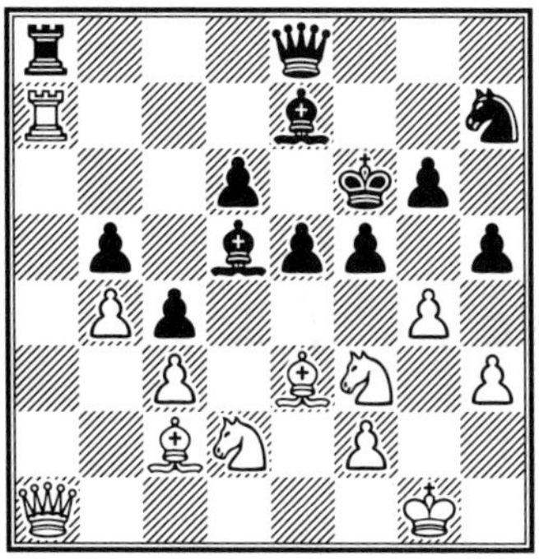

Position after 36.g4! in game 1.

[1] Yasser Seirawan and George Stefanović , *No Regrets: Fischer–Spassky 1992*, Seattle: International Chess Enterprises, 1993.

The young Fischer playing Spassky at the Havana Olympiad in 1966.

This was a long battle. The rules required a player to win ten games (draws not counting), with no adjournments, the conditions used in the first World Championship match between Wilhelm Steinitz and Johannes Zukertort in 1886. It took Fischer thirty games to get the ten victories and win by a score of 17½–12½.

Spassky might have made it closer if he had not lost two games right out of the opening.

(93) Ruy Lopez
Fischer – Boris Spassky
Sveti Stefan/Belgrade (9) 1992

1.e4 e5 2.Nf3 Nc6 3.Bb5 a6 4.Bxc6 dxc6 5.0-0 f6 6.d4 exd4 7.Nxd4 c5 8.Nb3 Qxd1 9.Rxd1 Bg4 10.f3 Be6 11.Nc3 Bd6 12.Be3 b6 13.a4

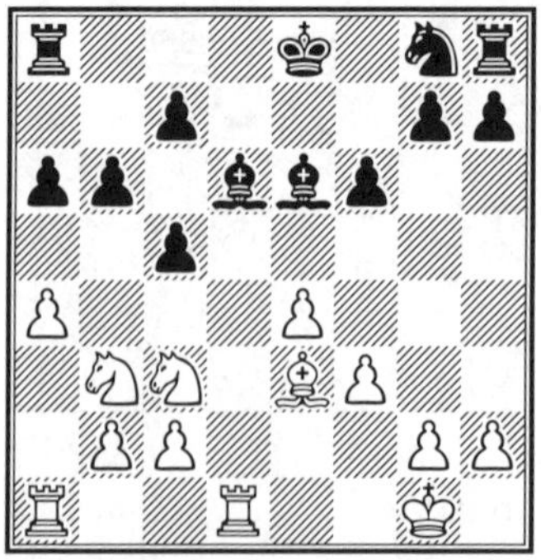

13...0-0-0?!

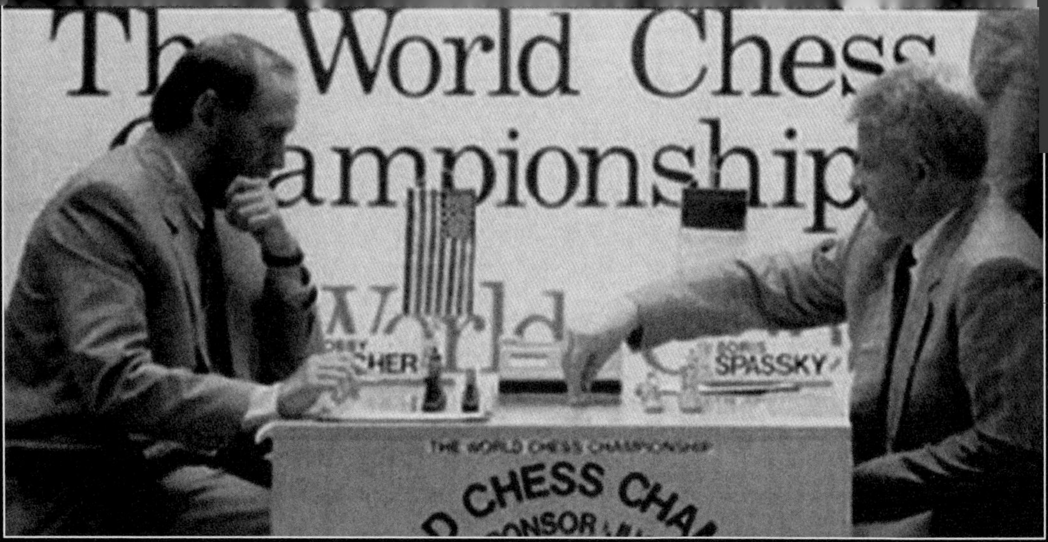

Fischer and Spassky in 1992.

This line isn't seen much anymore in part because 13...Kf7 14.a5 c4 15.Nd4 b5 is considered to be fine for Black.

14.a5 Kb7?! 15.e5! Be7

15...fxe5 16.axb6 cxb6 17.Ne4 Bxb3 18.Nxd6+ Kc7 19.Nb5+ axb5 20.Ra7+ Kb8 21.Rxd8+ Kxa7 22.cxb3 with an easy win for White.

16.Rxd8 Bxd8 17.Ne4

This was a novelty, 17.axb6 having been played in Adorjan–Ivkov, Skope 1976.

17...Kc6?? 18.axb6 cxb6

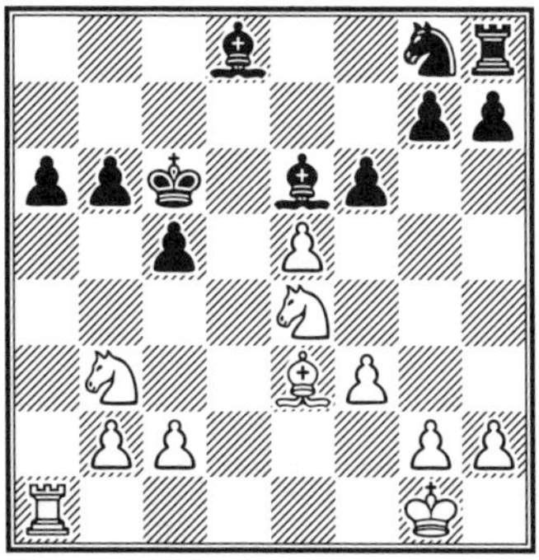

19.Nbxc5!

With the pretty variation 19...bxc5 20.Rxa6+ Kd5 21.Bf4 fxe5 22.Nc3+ Kd4 23.Nb5+ Kc4 24.Na3+ Kd4 25.Rd6+ Bd5 26.c3+ Kd3 27.Rd5+ Ke2 28.Rxe5+ Kd3 29.Rd5+ Ke2 30.Rd2+ Ke1 31.Nc2 Mate!

19...Bc8 20.Nxa6 fxe5 21.Nb4+, 1–0.

(94) Benoni
Boris Spassky – Fischer
Sveti Stefan/Belgrade (16) 1992

1.d4 Nf6 2.c4 c5 3.d5 d6

Fischer had a couple of surprises prepared for 1.d4. One was his adoption of the Queen's Gambit Accepted four times, an opening he had never previously played. Another was the use of the Gheorghiu Benoni where Black delays ...e6 and in so doing side steps some of White's sharper tries in the Modern Benoni.

There is no free lunch in chess and Black has to give up something to get something—in the Gheorghiu Benoni that means offering White the option of answering ...exd5 with exd5. The resulting positions with a symmetrical pawn structure—as opposed to the usual Modern Benoni theme of central pawns versus queenside pawn majority—give White a small, but clear, advantage due to his greater space. Spassky adopted this approach in game 26 of the match and won a fine game.

4.Nc3 g6 5.e4 Bg7 6.Bg5 h6 7.Bh4 g5 8.Bg3 Qa5 9.Bd3?

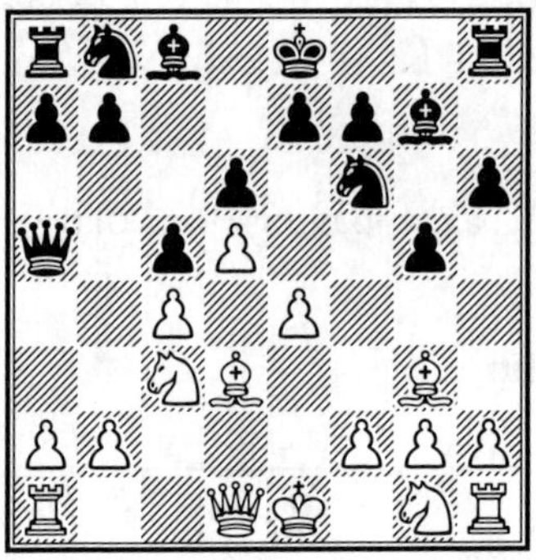

This move makes sense from a positional standpoint—White avoids the exchange of his dark-squared bishop after 9.Qd2 Nh5—but has a tactical drawback.

9...Nxe4! 10.Bxe4 Bxc3+ 11.bxc3 Qxc3+ 12.Kf1 f5 13.Rc1 Qf6 14.h4

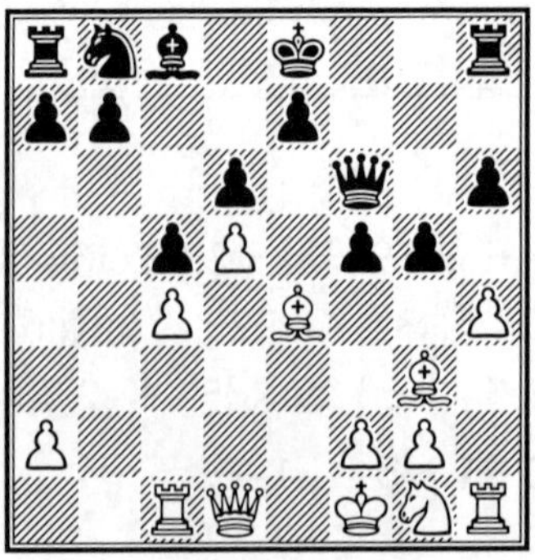

14...g4!

Thematic and strong. Fischer was quoted at the postgame press conference as saying that 9.Bd3?? was "an old trap." It seems pretty clear that Fischer was aware of 14...g4! for a long time. The more difficult question to answer is whether Spassky intentionally went into this line counting on the recommended 14.h4 or if he was forced to improvise earlier.

15.Bd3

15.Bxf5 Bxf5 16.Ne2 is only modestly in Black's favor.

15...f4 16.Ne2 fxg3 17.Nxg3 Rf8 18.Rc2 Nd7 19.Qxg4 Ne5 20.Qe4 Bd7 21.Kg1 0-0-0 22.Bf1 Rg8 23.f4 Nxc4 24.Nh5 Qf7 25.Qxc4 Qxh5 26.Rb2

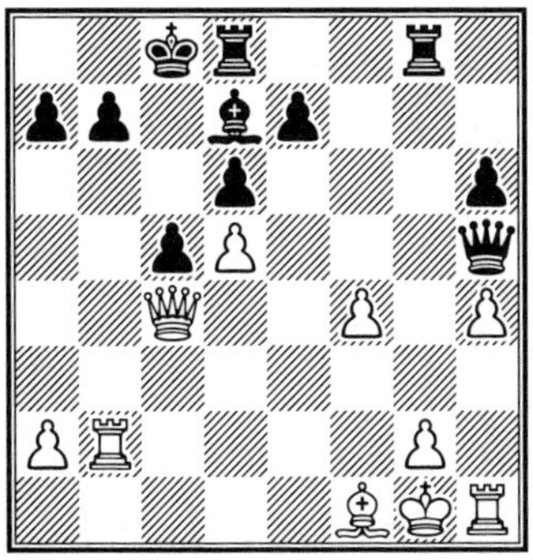

26...Rg3! 27.Be2 Qf7 28.Bf3 Rdg8 29.Qb3 b6 30.Qe3 Qf6 31.Re2 Bb5 32.Rd2 e5 33.dxe6 Bc6 34.Kf1 Bxf3, 0–1.

Those who refer to this as a match between two players past their prime often cite their nineteenth game as evidence. It's true that in 1992 Spassky was no longer the giant that had played three World Championship matches between 1966 and 1972. He maintained his position in the top ten in the world for over a decade after Reykjavík, but by 1987 was no longer a World Championship contender. Spassky's rating of 2560 at the time of the second match with Fischer ranked him number 106 in the world.

Part of the reason for Spassky's rating decline was his increasingly peaceful nature, which often resulted in him offering short draws to his opponents irrespective of rating. However, Spassky was still strong enough to finish in the middle of the field in the 1988–89 World Cup against top class opposition. A year after facing Bobby, Spassky played Judit Polgar and lost by the narrowest of margins, 4½–5½. These results indicate Spassky could still play at a high level when motivated.

When he stopped playing in 1972 Bobby was rated 2780, over 100 points above the next player, and had just won the 1972 World Championship in convincing fashion.

Fast-forward twenty years. Fischer is now forty-nine having lost his prime playing years. Could he possibly be as strong as he was in 1972? Not likely, but possible. Viktor Korchnoi played World Championship matches against Anatoly Karpov at roughly the same age. As of this writing, Viswanathan Anand (age fifty) is still rated in the top fifteen in the world, while Michael Adams (forty-eight), Vassily Ivanchuk (fifty-one) and Boris Gelfand (fifty-two), are still world class players, albeit no longer at the very top. Of course Fischer had an additional handicap—he was not only close to fifty, but hadn't played for two decades. There is no comparable absence by a top chess player, but also no one with his work ethic.

Now let's look at the nineteenth game, Game (95), where Fischer fails to win a queen ending two pawns up.

(95) Sicilian
Fischer – Boris Spassky
Sveti Stefan/Belgrade (19) 1992

1.e4 c5 2.Nc3 Nc6 3.Nge2 e5 4.Nd5 Nge7 5.Nec3 Nxd5 6.Nxd5 Be7 7.g3 d6 8.Bg2 h5 9.h4 Be6 10.d3 Bxd5 11.exd5 Nb8 12.f4 Nd7 13.0-0 g6 14.Rb1 f5 15.b4 b6 16.bxc5 bxc5 17.c4 0-0 18.Qa4 Bf6 19.Rb7 Nb6 20.Qb5 Rf7 21.Rxf7 Kxf7 22.Bd2 Rb8 23.Qc6 Nc8 24.Re1 Ne7 25.Qa4 Qc7 26.Kh2 exf4 27.Bxf4 Be5 28.Re2 Rb6 29.Kh3 Ng8?

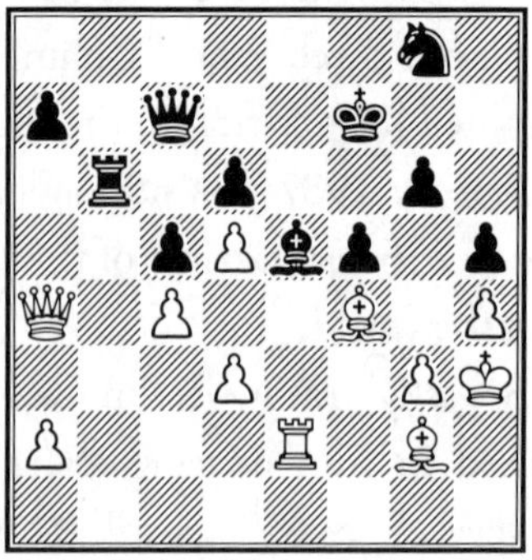

30.Rxe5! dxe5 31.Bxe5 Qe7 32.d6 Rxd6 33.Bxd6 Qxd6 34.Bd5+ Kf8 35.Qxa7 Ne7 36.Qa8+ Kg7 37.Qb7 Kf8 38.a4 f4 39.a5 fxg3 40.a6 Qf4 41.Bf3 Nf5 42.Qe4 g2 43.Qxf4 g1Q 44.Be4 Qa1

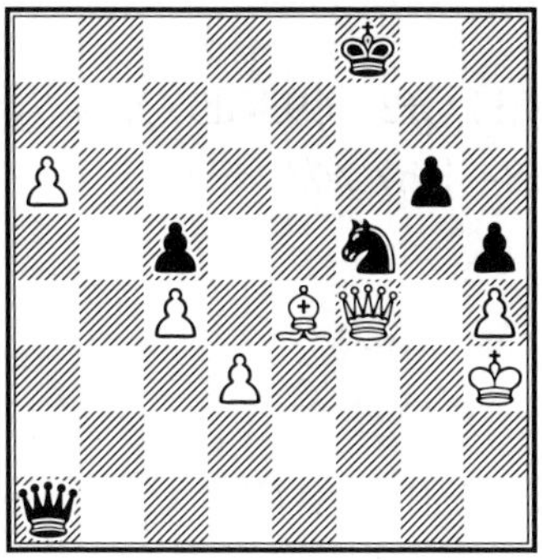

45.a7?

45.Bxf5 and 45.Qb8+ Kg7 46.a7 both won on the spot.

45...Qxa7 46.Bxf5 gxf5 47.Qxf5+ Kg7 48.Qg5+ Kf8 49.Qh6+ Kg8 50.Qxh5

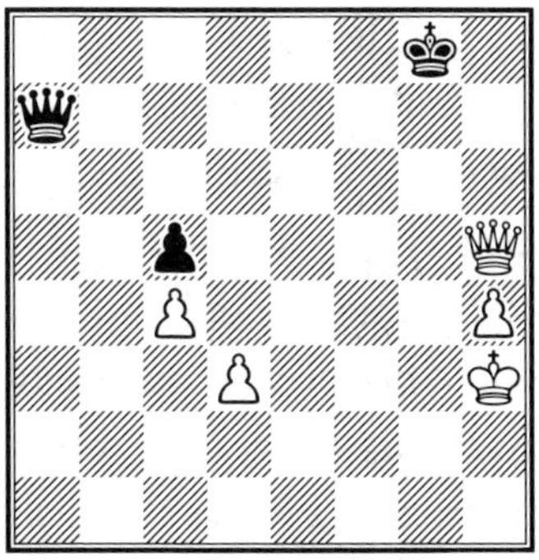

White is two pawns up and yet unable to win. Fischer critics had a field day with this game. Despite some technical difficulties (i.e. one Black pawn is holding two of White's and there are some stalemate possibilities for the second player) Bobby should have won this game. So what happened?

50...Qc7 51.Qg6+ Kh8 52.Qf6+

52.h5?? Qh2+ 53.Kg4 Qf4+.

52...Kg8 53.Qe6+ Kh8 54.Qd5 Qf7 55.Kg2 Qg6+ 56.Kh3 Qf7 57.Qe5+ Kh7 58.Kg4 Qg6+ 59.Kf4 Qh6+ 60.Kf3 Qg6 61.Qe4 Kh8 62.Ke2 Qd6 63.Qe3 Qh2+ 64.Ke1 Qh1+ 65.Kd2 Qh2+ 66.Kc3 Qxh4

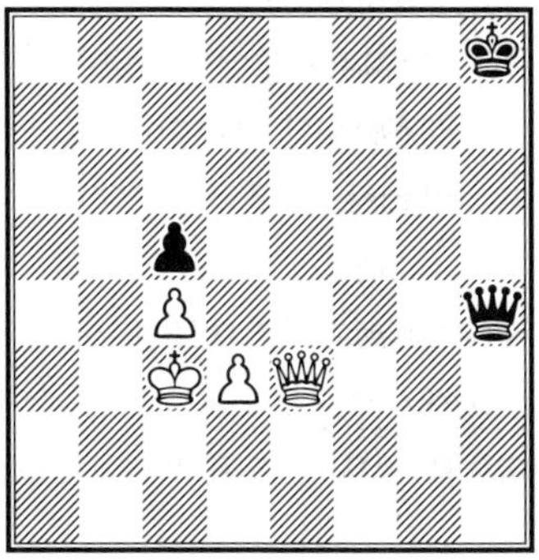

67.d4

67.Qxc5! Qe1+ 68.Kd4 Qf2+ 69.Kd5 Qf5+ 70.Kc6 Qxd3 71.Qf8+ Kh7 72.Qe7+ Kh8 73.Qe8+ Kh7 74.Qd7+.

67...Kh7 68.d5?

68.dxc5 was the last easy win.

68...Qf6+ 69.Kc2 Qd6 70.Qg5

70.Qe8 Kg7 71.Qc6 Qh2+ 72.Kb3 Qb8+ and White is not making progress.

70...Kh8 71.Kd2 Qb6 72.Qe5+ Kg8 73.Qe8+ Kg7 74.Qb5 Qc7 75.Kc2 Kf8 76.Qa6 Qh2+ 77.Kb3 Qb8+ 78.Qb5 Qc7 79.Ka3 Qa7+ 80.Kb3 Ke7 81.Kc2 Kd8 82.Kd2 Qc7 83.Qa6 Qf4+ 84.Kc2 Qe4+, ½–½.

What is the explanation for this total collapse? In a word—fatigue! The Fischer–Spassky rematch not only witnessed Bobby's return to the tournament arena but the birth of a new era in chess time controls. The match was the first time Fischer's new increment chess clock was publicly tested and the correct settings for the clock were still being worked out.

Today clocks with increment or delay are the standard and have been around for almost three decades so it's easy to forget Bobby and Boris were guinea pigs back in 1992. In retrospect it's clear Fischer seriously underestimated just how long the games were going to last.

The terms of the match were that:

- each player starts with 110 minutes on the clock
- after each move, 1 minute is added
- after move 40, 40 minutes are added
- after move 60, 30 minutes are added
- after move 80, 20 minutes are added

This meant that each player had 150 minutes, or two-and-a-half hours, for the first 40 moves. A 60-move game would give each player three-and-a-half hours each; an 80 move game four hours and twenty minutes apiece.

Fischer and Spassky played games that were 84, 80, 68, 67, 61, 59, 58, 58, 54, 50, and 50 moves long. The 84-move game went almost nine hours! Fischer's time control made a 60 move game last around six hours, much longer than the 40 moves in two-and-a-half hours followed by adjournment that was the norm for many years.

By comparison Garry Kasparov, who retired at forty-one, never came close to playing a game as long as the ones Boris and Bobby did. The most Garry and previous World Champions might have played was seven hours during an Olympiad, but note this would have been in two sessions - a two hour adjournment in the morning and a regular five hour session in the afternoon and evening. Taking this into account is it any wonder that Bobby and Boris were feeling a little punch drunk at the end of some of the longer games?

GRANDMASTERS CRITIQUE FISCHER–SPASSKY TWO

Andy Soltis:[1]

> Fischer's play in that game (the first one) evoked memories of 1972. In fact, the match games were of a fairly high quality particularly when compared with Kasparov's championship matches of 1993, 1995, and 2000, for example. Yet the games also reminded many fans how out of place Fischer was in 1992. He was still playing openings of the previous generation. He was, moreover, the only strong player in the world who didn't trust computers and wasn't surrounded by seconds and supplicants. He was a player from the past.

Yasser Seirawan wrote the match proved Fischer's playing strength was:[2]

> ...somewhere in the top ten in the world.

Kasparov was dismissive of Fischer and stated:[3]

> Bobby is playing OK, nothing more. Maybe his strength is 2600 or 2650. It wouldn't be close between us.
>
> ...Yes, Fischer played well, but Black's play was too helpless: "gifts" such as 19...Nh7?, 30...f5? and 33...Kf6? are no longer made by the leading grandmasters of today.[4]

Grandmaster Duncan Suttles, who played Bobby twice (1965/66 U.S. Championship and 1970 Interzonal) and spent a lot of time with him during the Taimanov match, made a careful study of the 1992 match and shared his thoughts in two interviews that are unlike anything else written on the contest. Suttles points out Fischer's calculating ability had slipped in the twenty years since the Reykjavík match, but puts more emphasis on Bobby's increased strategical understanding, which he attributes to two decades of diligent study. Suttles also notices a stylistic change in Fischer's play which caused him to seek out more semi-closed/closed positions whereas twenty years before he had preferred more

---

1 Andy Soltis, *Bobby Fischer Rediscovered*, London: B.T. Batsford, 2003, (p. 278).

2 Yasser Seirawan and George Stefanović, *No Regrets: Fischer–Spassky 1992*. Seattle: International Chess Enterprises, 1993, (p. 283).

3 Fred Waitzkin, *Mortal Games: The Turbulent Genius of Garry Kasparov*. New York: Putnam 1993, (p. 298).

4 Garry Kasparov referring to game one of the Fischer–Spassky rematch. *Garry Kasparov on Fischer: My Great Predecessors Part IV*. London: Everyman Chess, 2004.

open games. To the Canadian grandmaster these changes translate to Fischer having a deeper and more mature understanding of the game. Suttles noted some slips in technique by Bobby, but attributes this to rustiness, something that would disappear with more practice..

Interview with GM Duncan Suttles by Bruce Harper:[1]

Question: What is your assessment of the level of play in the match?

Suttles: I would say Spassky is, maybe, 2650. I don't know how you determine Fischer's performance from that number. It depends on how you count the draws. Not counting draws, maybe 2800…

Question: Really?

Suttles: Why not? He beat him two to one, didn't he? What does that mean? I would say somewhere between 2750 and 2800. What's Kasparov's rating? About 2780? Let's just say Fischer's within about 25 points of Kasparov—plus or minus.

Question: How do you think Fischer would fare in a match against one of the top players in the world, such as Anand, Ivanchuk, Short or Timman?

Suttles: I think he would be favored against any one of them. Mind you, someone who plays as fast as Anand might pose a little bit of a problem.

Question: How would Fischer do against Kasparov?

Suttles: Well, I think right now it would be pretty close, but if Fischer plays himself back in form, I think he would beat him.

Question: Kasparov has said that Fischer isn't playing "modern chess." Do you think chess has changed since Fischer last played?

Suttles: I didn't see what wasn't "modern" about his chess in the match.

Question: Is there such a thing as "modern chess?" I think Kasparov was referring to a better understanding of the dynamic possibilities inherent in the game.

Suttles: I think Fischer tries to seek the truth in the position. Seeking the truth in the position and playing what might practically be the best line are not necessarily the same thing. If they mean by modern chess trying practically to beat the opponent over the board by not playing the best move but by posing a problem for him, then maybe Fischer doesn't exactly go for that. I would say, on the other hand, whether or not what's referred to as "modern chess" has uncovered some new truth behind the game, I sort of doubt it. To figure this out would probably require computers to figure out whether Fischer's strategies in fact work.

---

[1] Yasser Seirawan and George Stefanović, *No Regrets: Fischer–Spassky 1992*. Seattle: International Chess Enterprises, 1993, (pp. 277–279).

I saw some games in which Fischer plays what might be considered from the "modern chess" point of view to be risky positions, in that they were cramped and his opponent had a space advantage or might have had a temporary plus in mobility. However, it's difficult to say whether, objectively, those were bad positions for him. They might have been good.

Question: So Kasparov tries to win and Fischer seeks the truth?

Suttles: Well, they both try to win, but Fischer tries to win by playing the best move, while Kasparov tries to win by finding the weakness in his opponent's psychology. I think that's the difference between the so-called "modern chess" and Fischer's style of chess. Fischer's style is more related to the truth in the position—or what he perceives to be truth. Fischer seeks a deeper understanding of the actual position on the board, not just the dynamics of the particular opponent.

Question: Are we approaching the "death of chess?"

Suttles: In what sense? Computers will be unbeatable in a few years, but I don't know if that will matter. It depends on human chess players. One of the problems will be that computers will add more and more to opening theory, which will make the problem of people being booked up greater and greater.

Question: Is it becoming increasingly difficult for a good player to show that he's good?

Suttles: Well, a player who can memorize key lines from an extended computer analysis will be difficult to beat in the opening and will always achieve a decent position going into the middlegame. So in that sense the game might be played out. I can see some problems developing similar to what happened to checkers, where openings have to be drawn by lot. In chess wins could become less and less frequent. I think computer analysis will significantly increase the margin of draw in chess. As in the match, as opposed to playing with bishop against knight only twice. Does this mean anything? In the 1972 match Fischer traded knights for bishops just about as often as he traded bishops for knights.

In this match a significant number of positions were relatively closed. In blocked or semi-blocked positions knights are usually better than bishops.

Question: So Fischer seemed to be playing for closed positions?

Suttles: (Laughs) Maybe they both were. There were clearly quite a few closed positions. I think Fischer may have been doing it to create a larger number of long-range strategic possibilities, as opposed to violent tactics which would clarify things. Presumably to give himself a chance to outplay his opponent.

So the knights against bishops is only the result of the type of position Fischer was playing. I think the games also show that Fischer was playing for structural advantages, generally speaking. Again, I think this might signify a shift in style. Perhaps Fischer has come to the conclusion that defense offers more possibilities than had been previously thought.

Question: Does this make a Fischer–Kasparov match even more interesting?

Suttles: I think so, because you would have a clash between a style which attempts to strive for activity and dynamic chances, so to speak, versus an attempt to exploit structural advantages through long-term strategy. Especially if Fischer goes for long-term advantages and goes on the edge to do it—for that to work against Kasparov, he has to play himself into the best possible technical form too, obviously, because you can't afford any slips when you're using that strategy.

Question: That's for sure. I guess I don't have to ask which side you'd be cheering for, stylistically?

Suttles: (Laughs) Of course, I'm more inclined towards the structural.

Question: Any other comments?

Suttles: I think generally...the problem coming back after twenty years is one of getting your technique to be even, but I have the feeling he has evolved in his understanding of the game. In other words, he showed a lot of finesse in this match—there was a lot under the surface. Some of the criticisms of his play have looked too much at the result of the games. You have to be careful—there's a tendency to push forwards the moves of the winner and push back the moves of the loser...I don't think Fischer panicked with his king walk [game 8]—I think he was just trying to win the game.

PART NINE

Adrift

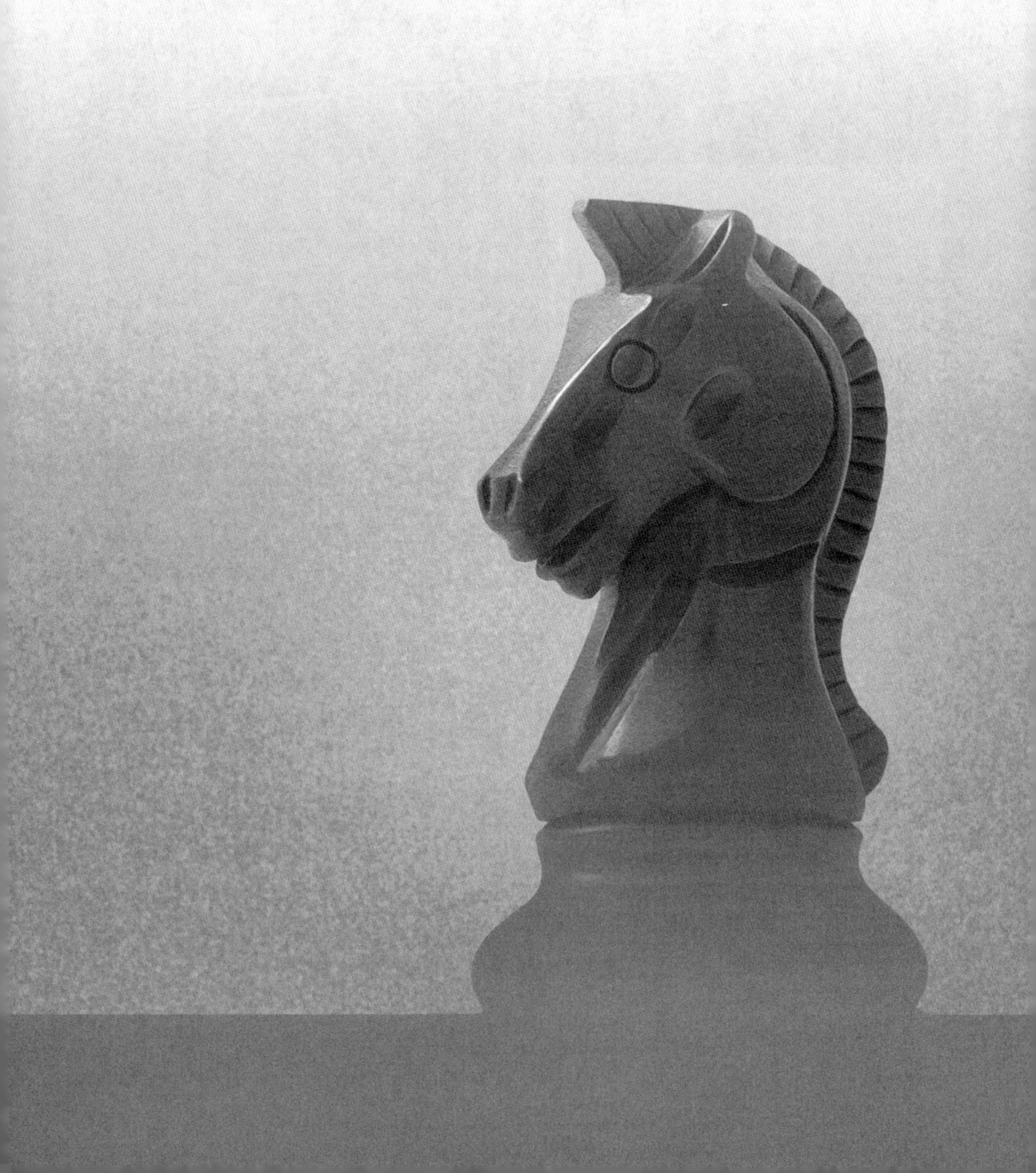

William Lombardy and FIDE Master Paul Whitehead at the Mechanics' Institute Chess Club of San Francisco, September 14, 2017 (Photo: Ralph Palmeri).

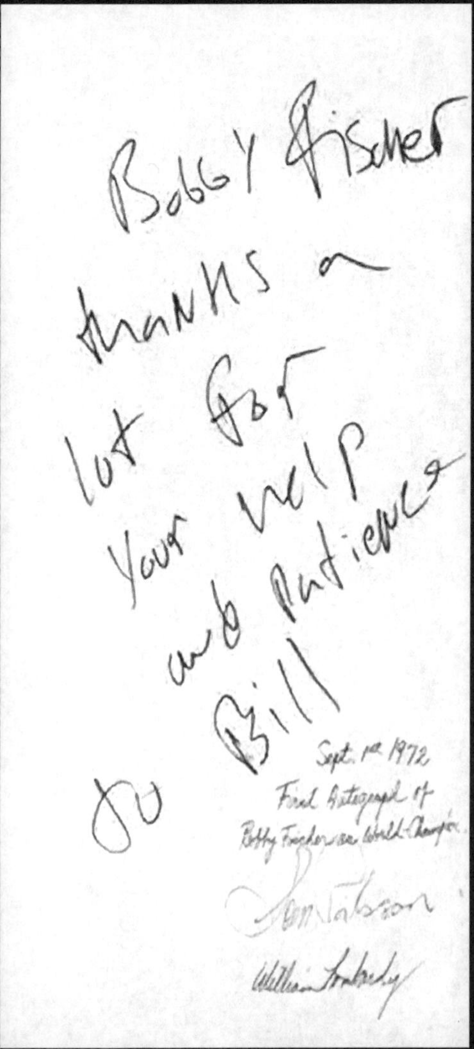

Fischer's autograph in My 60 Memorable Games *inscribed to "Bill" [Lombardy]. The book was annotated and signed by Lombardy, and also signed by Saemundur "Saemi" Pálsson, Fischer's bodyguard/driver in Reykjavík [Described by Bonhams on page 623, item 1].*

In his 1974 article in Sports Illustrated *("A Mystery Wrapped in an Enigma"). Lombardy describes the last day of the 1972 World Championship:*

On the way to the hall Bobby sat analyzing in the front seat. I thrust a copy of My 60 Memorable Games *into his hands.*
"What's this?" Bobby asked.
"Sign it," I urged "I want your first autograph as World Champion!"
"No, no. It's not official. Later," he replied, returning the book. ...
On the way back to the hotel, I thrust My 60 Memorable Games *once more on Bobby.*
"Sign."
"I mean Bill, what's in it for me?" he teased.
"You want to know what's in it for you?"
"Yeah, what's in it for me." Repeated Bobby.
"A big congratulations."
At the top of the first leaf of the book, Bobby put his signature, his first autograph as champion. "Should I write anything?" he asked.
"If you want, write what you feel,"
Bobby wrote: "To Bill: Thanks for your help and patience."

1
A BOOKSTORE IN ARGENTINA

Originally published in the Spanish magazine *Jaque*, this article by FIDE Master Pedro F. Hegoburu (translated by FIDE Master Jonathan Berry[1]) was written after Bobby's 1996 visit to Argentina to promote Fischer Random Chess. Fischer's love for chess literature shines through.

I came to know Bobby Fischer through the hand of Destiny. The afternoon of Wednesday, June 26th, I dropped over to Juan Morgado's bookstore at about 6:30. As usual, I had nothing in particular in mind. Upon arrival, I saw a very tall man leaning over some books; he supported himself with his left arm to inspect the books closest to the floor. I did not see his face. Nearby was another person, with Asiatic features, much shorter, and also leafing through chess literature. Before I can take a step, Morgado tells me:

"Have you seen who is looking at books? It's Bobby Fischer!"

I could not believe it. The American genius had arrived just a few moments before, accompanied by Filipino Eugene Torre (that would explain his Asiatic features) and Armando de Hiebra, well known in this part of the world as director of Argentine chess.

Bobby went on looking at books. He was scanning the Yugoslav Informant opening monographs. At some point, he said to Torre:

"You know, chess players are all hungry for this kind of material, for opening theory. Larry Evans told me that years ago, people want these books." Torre grunted in assent.

After this verbal rapture, Bobby continued looking at books. He noted that he felt at ease among chess players (I do not feign to call us peers). It is an atmosphere that agrees with him, as opposed to press conferences, where he is sure to waste time with people who know nothing of chess. On a higher bookshelf he found *Bled 1931* and *Moscow 1936*. He enjoys the books for a moment, then remarks that he knows them and that they are two of his favorites. He finished with those and took the two volumes of *Fifteen Pretenders to the World Crown*, by Najdorf.

"These are two good books." He showed them to Torre and after leafing through them, returned them to their place.

---

[1] *Inside Chess*, Volume 9, issue 25–26, (pp. 4–9).

Fischer: "Morgado, don't you have the tournament book of Curaçao 1962? And the one with the two matches between Reshevsky and Najdorf?"

It is now late. Bobby looked at the books he had chosen and took out an envelope full of dollars. He put on his short chestnut-colored leather coat, and a black leather cap to protect his grey matter from the cold Buenos Aires winter.

My attention was drawn to the fact that he did not much resemble the Fischer whose image sells periodicals. He is not so old, nor so bald, and he is very accessible. To see Fischer is to behold a most human image: he is no unapproachable deity. Bobby Fischer is a child who scatters books, who will argue any strange point, who is convinced of what he says. His love for chess remains, although he promotes Fischerandom. Beneath his arm were three volumes of games by Tal, an endgame book by Kasparian, the book *Chess Kaleidoscope* by Karpov and Gik; *Karpov/Korchnoi* by Román Torán; a recent *New In Chess*; and the two most recent bulletins of the *Argentine Postal Chess Circle* (CAPA).

Bobby promised to return another day; he would like to examine more books. For me, there was still much to learn. One doesn't often meet an idol face to face, even rarer might that idol be so generous with his time. As he left, we asked him to autograph a copy of the CAPA bulletin. Before signing, he honored us by leafing through it.

Fischer: "This is a postal chess magazine?"

Hegoburu: "Yes, we publish it four times a year for the members of our circle."

Fischer: "This is serious material: all the games are annotated . . ."

Fischer went over to the chess board and showed us from memory the games that Spassky played with Tal and with Karpov from the Montreal 1979 tournament. His fingers dance with agility around the board. He grasps each piece with confidence and moves it at once to the correct square. From time to time he pauses for a few seconds, remembering the precise move order. Nonetheless, he did not make a single mistake.

Fischer: "Remember that Karpov, for many years starting in 1975, never lost to Russian or ex-Russian players outside the Soviet Union. Inside the Soviet Union he lost games, but when he played international tournaments abroad he was never defeated by Russians or by former Russians. Really, it's very strange."

[Translator's note: Divinsky shows no Karpov losses against the top Soviet (or ex-) players abroad between 1975 and 1986, aside from Korchnoi. Then he lost to Andrei Sokolov at Bugojno 1986 and Belfort 1988, to Beliavsky at Tilburg 1986 and Brussels 1988, to Salov at Rotterdam 1989, to Ivanchuk at Linares 1991, to Kamsky at Tilburg 1991, and many times to Kasparov. A database search turned up a loss to Spassky in Hamburg 1982, but that was a TV game.]

Bobby selected a pile of books to buy. In Buenos Aires he didn't have a lot to do. He probably spent the free time reading all he could about chess. From a top shelf he took *The Even More Complete Chess Addict* and asked if it was the same book as *The Chess Addict*. Even though it is different, he refused it, saying that it was full of foolishness, it wasn't a serious chess book.

Hegoburu: "But Bobby, you can't spend twenty-four hours a day studying serious chess! I think that would be a good book to read in the bathroom. You don't know how much I read in the bathroom!"

Fischer laughed and put the book in the buy pile. It was another interesting stack: *Kasparov* by Angel Martín; *Capablanca/Alekhine* from Editorial Sopena; *Grossmeisterskie Kompozitsii* by Archakov, in Russian; *The Inner Game* by Dominic Lawson; *The Even More Complete Chess Addict; Timman's Selected Games* by Timman; *Chess Scandals; Kasparov New World Champion* by Kasparov; *Steinitz Complete Games*.

Bobby put on his coat and hat, and got ready to leave. Morgado found a camera, but Bobby firmly refused to be photographed. Torre, one foot on the street, called back to tell us that there would be no problem with photographs at the next press conference, at La Plata city.

2
FISCHER REVIEWS KASPAROV

Throughout the 1980s and 1990s Bobby told friends he was working on a book that would prove Garry Kasparov and Anatoly Karpov prearranged the results of games during their World Championship matches.

A hundred page manuscript dated November 18, 1997 with the title *What Can You Expect From Baby Mutilators*, exists in a private collection and might be a draft of the book Fischer was referring to. The portions of the manuscript that deal directly with chess make for interesting reading—although the question arises: If Fischer was correct and the matches were fixed, why was only Kasparov allowed to win?

Unfortunately, the title of the manuscript, which references Fischer's negative view of circumcision, correctly suggests the bulk of the content is related to Bobby's fringe theories. Much of the excerpted material is painful to read, an antisemitic screed railing at what Fischer sees as the Jewish conspiracy.[1]

The manuscript expands on Bobby's often voiced assertions that Batsford "butchered" his classic book *My 60 Memorable Games* when they reprinted it. There is little new here.

Bobby's unpublished reviews of two books by Garry Kasparov are considerably more interesting.[2]

> In 1986 The Macmillan Chess Library published a book entitled *Garry Kasparov Teaches Chess* by Garry Kasparov. Significantly, the book was printed in Great Britain. The book, with a few cosmetic touches, is virtually identical in every way to the Batsford edition of *Garry Kasparov Teaches Chess* by Garry Kasparov, which I once possessed. I could tear this pitiful book apart, but this is not the time and place to do it. But I'll give you a little taste of what a joke of a book this is. On page 2 of *Garry Kasparov Teaches Chess* by Garry Kasparov (published by Macmillan) we read: "I want to win, I want to beat everyone, but I want to do it in style, in an honest sporting battle." This from a crook who has played hundreds and hundreds of tournament

[1] David DeLucia's *Bobby Fischer Uncensored* contains a sixteen-page excerpt from the manuscript. While Hungarian International Master Janos Rigo is listed as the contact person for distribution, it seems pretty certain DeLucia has the only copy.

[2] Material in the DeLucia Collection.

and match games that were prearranged move by move! And on pages 42 and 43 of the same book we read: [The review continues with Fischer's comments interspersed with Kasparov's published annotations]

(96) Philidor
Evgeny Vasiukov – Boris Lebedev
Moscow 1960

1.e4 e5 2.Nf3 d6 3.d4 Nd7

[Kasparov]: Black's unsophisticated deployment of his pieces is very frequent in the games of amateurs. The entirely sound idea of strengthening the advance post in the center (e5) is brought about in a somewhat fanciful manner whereby the bishop on c8 gets blocked.

4.Bc4 h6

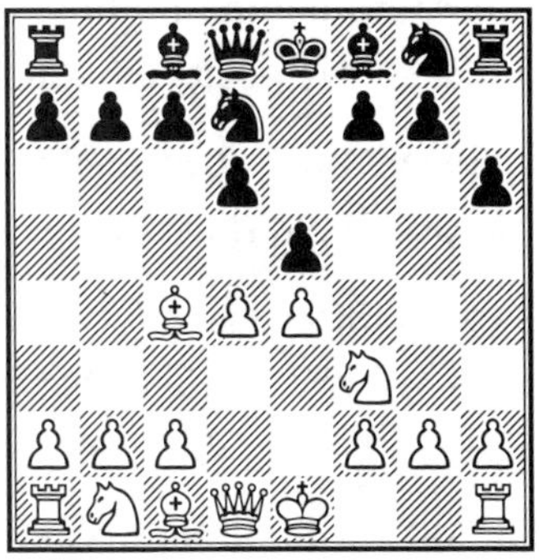

[Kasparov]: This is an altogether dubious decision—instead of developing his pieces (for instance, 4...Be7) Black, planning to move his knight to f6, loses time trying to prevent the intervention of the White knight on g5. However, to prove the unsoundness of Black's strategy in the opening White had to play very resourcefully and vigorously.

[Fischer]: Of course, Kasparov's 4...Be7?? is a well-known blunder since after 5.dxe5! White has won a healthy pawn for nothing. For example after 5...Nxe5 6.Nxe5 dxe5 7.Qh5! g6 8.Qxe5 White has a technically won game. Let's follow the great Kasparov's analysis a little further.

5.dxe5 dxe5

[Kasparov]: After 5...Nxe5 6.Nxe5 dxe5 7.Bxf7+! Black's position would have been hopeless.

6.Bxf7+ Kxf7 7.Nxe5+ Kf6

[Kasparov]: Anything else would bring the end even faster.

8.Nc3!

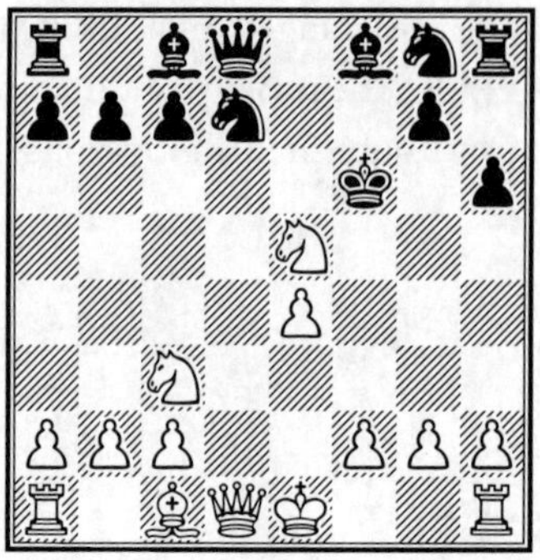

[Kasparov]: In order to bring the Black king into the open White sacrifices his knight.

8...Kxe5

[Kasparov]: The threats of 9.Nd5+ and 9.Qd4 may be countered in only one way, as all other variations fail to save him, for example: 8...c6 9.Qf3+ Kxe5 10.Qf5+ Kd6 11.Bf4+ Ne5 12.Qxe5+ Kd7 13. Rd1+.

[Fischer]: This is all horrendously bad analysis! Instead of the blunder 9.Qf3+?? White should play 9.Qd4! with an easy win, i.e.

(A) 9...c5 10.Nxd7+ (or 10.Nd5+ Ke6 11.Nf4+ Ke7 12.Qd5!) 10...Ke7 11.Qe5+ Kxd7 12.Bf4 Qe7 (12...Kc6 13.Rd1—it's all over) 13.0-0-0+ Ke8 14.Qh5+ Qf7 15.Rd8+! etc.

(B) 9...Ke6 10.Ng6! Rh7 11.Qc4+ Kf6 12.Nf4—again bad news for Black.

Returning to Kaspy's analysis after 9.Qf3+?? Kxe5 10.Qf5+ (10.Qf7!? g5! White hasn't got enough for the two pieces.) 10...Kd6 11.Bf4+

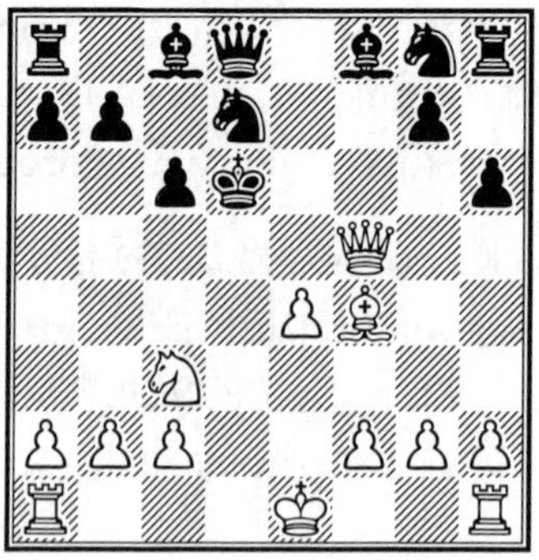

[Fischer]: Now instead of Kaspy's absolutely unbelievable 11...Ne5????????, Black should play the sane 11...Ke7! Of course after 12.0-0-0!, White in spite of his two-piece deficit can still struggle on (he's threatening mate in two), but with accurate play by Black it's a lost cause. Now I like 12...Qe8!, forcing White to simplify by 13.Bd6+ Kd8 14.Bxf8 Ne7 15.Bxe7+ Qxe7 and Black little by little will extricate himself and grind out the win.

The rest of Kasparov's notes to this game are not much better. For example, after 8.Nc3 Lebedev played 8...Kxe5 and now Kasparov fails to point out that instead of the fishy 9.Qh5+ Vasiukov should have played 9.Qd5+!. Kasparov's book, *Kasparov's Teaches Chess*, replete with faulty diagrams, is a disgrace. Obviously, it was ghostwritten for him. [End of Fischer and Kasparov notes.]

Since Vasiukov–Lebedev, Moscow 1960, is not given in Mega Database, the full game score follows with light notes for the record.

9.Qh5+

9.Qd5+! (Fischer) 9...Kf6 10.Qf5+ Ke7 11.Nd5+ Kd6 12.Bf4+ Kc6 13.Qe6+ Bd6 14.Nb4+ Kb6 (14...Kb5 15.a4+ Ka5 16.Qc4 c6 17.Nd5) 15.Bxd6 Ndf6 16.Bc5+ Kxc5 17.Nd3+ wins.

9...g5 10.Bxg5 hxg5 11.f4+ Ke6

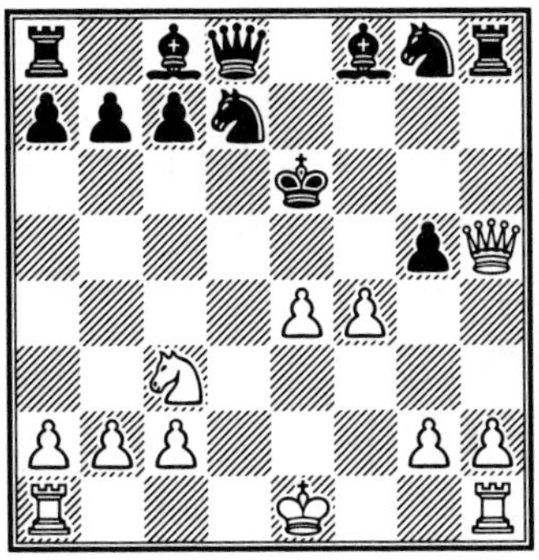

12.f5+

Delaying capturing the rook is necessary as 12.Qxh8 Nh6 is fine for Black.

12...Ke7 13.Nd5+ Kd6 14.Qxh8 Ngf6 15.0-0-0 Kc6 16.Rhe1 b6 17.Nb4+ Bxb4?

17...Kb7 18.e5 Qe7 19.Nd3 Ng4 with chances for both sides.

18.Qxd8 Bb7 19.Rxd7

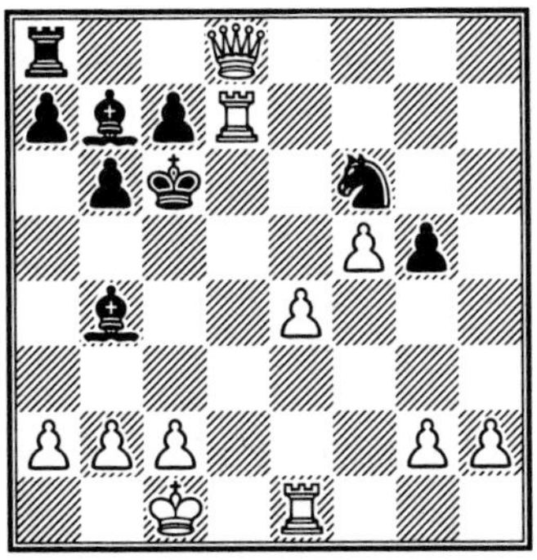

19...Nxd7⁈

Here 19...Rxd8 20.Rxd8 Bxe1 21.e5 Ng4 22.e6 Bf2 (22...Bb4? 23.Rd4) 23.e7 Nf6 24.e8Q+ (24.Rf8 Kd7) 24...Nxe8 25.Rxe8 Kd7 had to be played. Now Black is lost.

20.Qxg5 Bxe1 21.Qe3 Bh4 22.Qh6+ Bf6 23.e5 Rf8 24.exf6 Rxf6 25.Qf4 Bc8 26.g4 Nc5 27.b4 Nb7 28.Qe4+ Kd7 29.Qd4+ Rd6 30.Qg7+ Kc6 31.f6 Nd8 32.f7 Nxf7 33.Qxf7 Be6 34.Qe8+ Kd5 35.Qa8+ Ke5 36.Qxa7 Rc6 37.Qa4 Rc4 38.Qb5+ Kf4 39.g5 c6 40.Qxb6, 1–0.

Bobby then shifted his attention to *Kasparov on the King's Indian*, offering his views on a game Garry annotated, here Game (97).

---

(97) King's Indian
Anatoly Karpov – Garry Kasparov
New York (11) 1990

[Fischer]: In 1990 Karpov and Kasparov played a so-called "World Championship" chess match in New York City. The match, as all the previous Karpov–Kasparov matches, was prearranged. The opening moves of game 11 were as follows:

1.d4 Nf6 2.c4 g6 3.Nc3 Bg7 4.e4 d6 5.Nf3 0-0 6.Be2 e5 7.Be3 exd4 8.Nxd4 Re8 9.f3 c6 10.Qd2 d5 11.exd5 cxd5 12.0-0 Nc6 13.c5

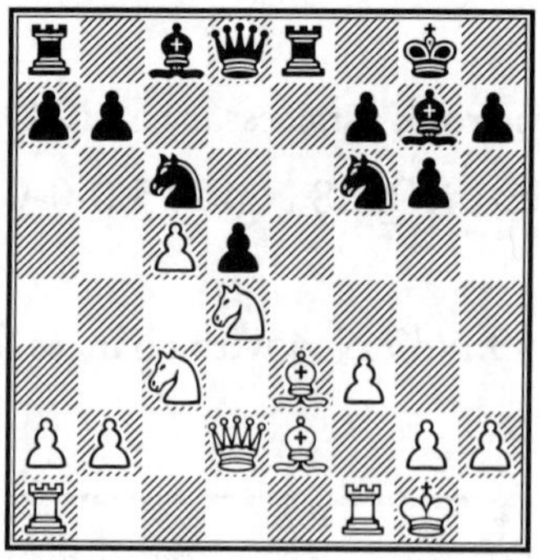

[Fischer]: In the book *Kasparov on the King's Indian* by Garry Kasparov with Raymond Keene published by B.T. Batsford Ltd. (London 1993) on pages 45 and 46 Kasparov analyses this position. Here is what he writes; try not to laugh out loud.

[Kasparov]: And now 13...Qe7!? 14.Bf2 Qxc5 15.Ne6 Qxf2+! 16.Rxf2 Bxe6

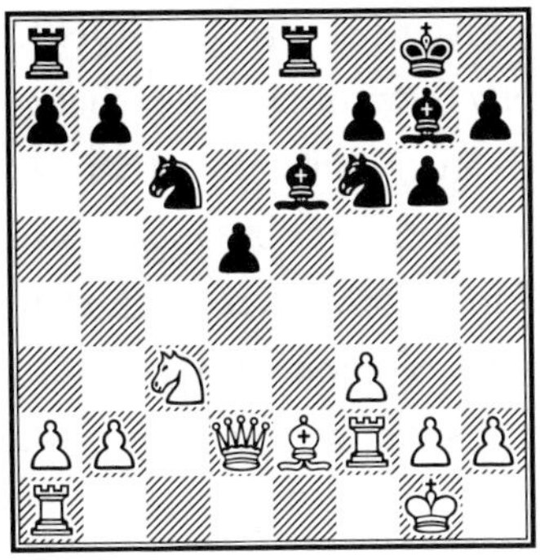

[Kasparov]: When I first showed this to my helpers in New York, practically all of them reacted ironically to this idea, to put it mildly, and regarded it as some sort of manifestation of the "third game complex". To a certain extent they were right. [Kasparov is referring to game three of the match where with the same colors and opening variation he sacrificed his queen for two minor pieces and a pawn.]

But when we embarked (under considerable pressure from me!) on a serious analysis, it transpired that Black gains quite good counterplay! Thanks to what? To do justice to traditionalism, I will endeavor to list the positional components of Black's unexpected great positional compensation. They are: his strong dark-square bishop, with the e3 and d4 squares in White's position being extremely weak: Black's overwhelming superiority in the center—the most important sector, in which White does not have a single strong point: and the inability of White in the immediate future to undertake anything active.

All this smacks of a superficial establishment of obvious truths, but a more respectful attitude to "general considerations" helps White to find the correct plan, by which he retains (although without any guarantee of a win!) an enduring advantage. For this he must foresee that as soon as possible he has to exchange a pair of minor pieces, and at least one pair of rooks.

After weighing up everything "for" and "against," and taking account of the features of my constant opponent's style, I considered the practical risk of an adverse development of events to be excessive, but the idea of a positional sacrifice for the achievement of the same strategic aims was by no means buried. In fact, after "all that has been experienced", its correct implementation did not look so unusual. Indeed, why sacrifice a "whole queen," when one can make due with a "modest" exchange sacrifice? And so

13...Rxe3.

> [Fischer]: All this is nonsense. After 13...Qe7!? 14.Bf2 Qxc5?? Instead of 15.Ne6?? simply 15.Nxc6! winning the exchange gives White a clearly won game. 15.Nxc6! is such an obvious move that even Yasser Seirawan couldn't fail to find it although for some strange reason he gives this obviously decisive move an !?. Furthermore Seirawan claims that 14...Qxc5 15.Ne6 Qxf2+ 16.Rxf2 Bxe6 was a game Tolush–Geller, Moscow 1950.[1] I believe this to be absolutely false. So far as I know no such game between Tolush and Geller exists!
>
> However there was a game Tolush–Geller, XX Russian Championship, USSR 1952, which went as follows 1.d4 Nf6 2.c4 g6 3.Nc3 Bg7 4.e4 d6 5.f3 0-0 6.Be3 e7 7.Nge2 Nbd7 8.Qd2 Nb6 9.b3 exd4 10.Nxd4 Re8 11.Be2 c6 12.0-0 d5 13.exd5 Qe7 14.Bf2 cxd5 15.c5 Qxc5 16.Nf5 Qxf2+ 17.Rxf2 Bxf5 and Black, although he is probably quite lost, went on to win the game in fifty-one moves. Trust anything Seirawan says at your own risk! The book *Kasparov on the King's Indian* is more ghosted garbage. It's chock-full of beautiful and prearranged draws!
>
> In May of 1997 in New York City when for once in his life Kasparov was called upon to play an honest match against a reasonably strong opponent (the IBM "Deep Blue" computer) he not only lost the match, but almost everyone says his play was completely "unrecognizable". I wonder why. Immediately after losing the last game of the match Kasparov made some imbecilic statements to the press to the effect that the "Deep Blue" computer now needed to play in some strong tournaments "to prove itself." Garry, you just lost. You're the one who needs to "prove himself". Clearly Kasparov, whose entire career is based on cheating, has never developed any sportsmanship....

What to make of Fischer's critique? First, Bobby's analysis of Vasiukov–Lebedev is correct and likely Batsford published the two books with little, if any, involvement by Kasparov beyond lending his name to the titles. He certainly would not have made the mistakes in analysis that are present in the notes to Vasiukov–Lebedev.

The Tolush–Geller game is more complicated. They did play in 1950 in the Soviet Championship and Geller won, but it was a Sicilian not a King's Indian. When they played in 1952, it was again in a Soviet Championship.

As Fischer points out the position in the 1952 game, although very similar to the one given in Kasparov on the King's Indian, is not identical. In Tolush–Geller Black's knight is on b6: in the analysis based on Karpov–Kasparov, game

---

[1] Yasser Seirawan and Jonathan Tisdall, *Five Crowns*. Seattle: International Chess Enterprises, 1991, (p. 109).

11 of their 1990 World Championship match, it is on c6. Also White has played b3 in Tolush–Geller. Black's missing move in that game is accounted for by taking two moves for his knight to reach b6 instead of reaching c6 in one jump. Different positions!

Fischer is correct that with the knight on c6, 14...Qxc5 loses to 15.Nxc6. This was not an option in Tolush–Geller, but the move played there, 16.Nf5, left Geller with a difficult position. The queen sacrifice is not as strong as Black's knight is poorly placed (b6 instead of c6), but allowing the trade of Black's dark-squared bishop with White's remaining on the board doesn't look appealing: for example 16...Qb4 17.Nxg7 Kxg7 18.Bd4.

Geller's decision to sacrifice his queen was the best practical choice, even though Fischer is correct in calling it not quite sound. One wonders if Kasparov, grounded in the classics (games from Soviet Championships being part of the curriculum), didn't have Geller's queen sacrifice idea in his subconscious. What's pretty certain is Kasparov would not have overlooked 15.Nxc6!. This is likely Keene's doing. Seirawan having the wrong position/game reference was not uncommon before computer databases became the norm in the late 1990s.

Harder to explain is the poor analysis in *Garry Kasparov Teaches Chess*. Kasparov is definitely not responsible for it beyond signing on as the author, but according to the advertisement for the book this series of twenty-four chess lessons was first published in *Sport in the USSR*. One would have thought the errors would have been spotted not long after the material was first published.

Bobby was correct in his analysis to the two games (he probably played over Tolush–Geller, 1952 USSR Championship, when he was a kid) and his remarks about Kasparov's comments after the Deep Blue match were accurate. Clearly Garry was frustrated at the end, but, blaming his well-known opening blunder in game six on Deep Blue's coaches Grandmasters Miguel Illescas and Joel Benjamin made no sense. Today Kasparov accepts that he was wrong.

Fischer claims Kasparov prearranged hundreds of games which is a gross exaggeration. If he said Garry had agreed to a few last round draws it would be another matter; aside from Bobby it would be hard to find a top player who hasn't. Many World Championship matches have witnessed short draws. They occur, not because they were prearranged, but because they suited the contestants. Sometimes both players are tired after a tough fight, or a player who lost and now has White wants to regain their equilibrium with a short draw (Petrosian subscribed to this rule). There are many other reasons. Here Bobby was mistaken.

[top] Flier from the Collection of David DeLucia;

[middle] The 1966 Havana Olympiad table. Pictured is Irish first board Wolfgang Heidenfeld's table now in the possession of his son Mark. Along with the table and chairs, came a set of beautiful wooden chess pieces complete with its own storage case. The table came with built in flag holders and cushioned areas for resting ones arms—this was something unique in the 1960s and later incorporated into the design of the 1972 and 1978 World Championship tables (Photo: Alexander Baburin);

[bottom] Various drafts of what would become My 60 Memorable Games.

ANNOUNCING A GROUP OF SINGULAR CHESS BOOKS AND PERIODICALS FROM THE LIBRARY OF THE ENIGMATIC AND NOW EXILED WORLD CHAMPION, BOBBY FISCHER
PRESENTED AT THE 32ND CALIFORNIA INTERNATIONAL ANTIQUARIAN BOOKFAIR
CONCOURSE EXHIBITION CENTER, SAN FRANCISCO
FRIDAY, SATURDAY, AND SUNDAY, FEBRUARY 12-14, 1999
BOOTH #125
THE BOOK SHOP
"first-class second-hand books"™
134 N. Citrus Ave.
Covina, CA 91723
1-(800)-507-READ
BookShop@compuserve.com
http://www.the-book-shop.com
Roger Gozdecki, Proprietor

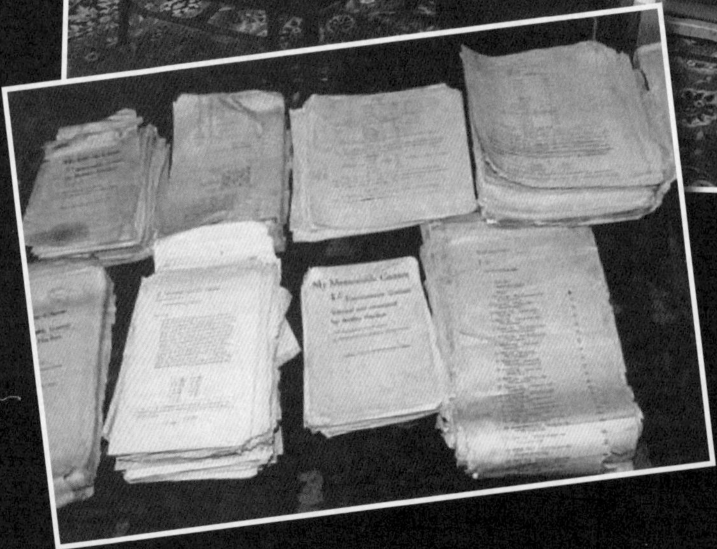

3
THE DAY BOBBY LOST HIS TREASURES

CHESS CHAMP LIVID AT REPORTED PROPERTY SALE[1]

PASADENA — It seemed like a simple procedure. The renter at A-American Self Storage hadn't paid his bill in six months so the contents were sold in a lien sale to cover back rent.

It didn't seem the makings of international intrigue. But then it wasn't common knowledge that the man was an apparent friend of former world chess champion Bobby Fischer, and that the unit, which rents for $80 a month, allegedly contained some of Fischer's prized possessions. [Continued on page 611]

The pain, anger, and stress caused by the loss of the treasures he had accumulated over a lifetime put Bobby over the edge. His good friend Pal Benko summed it up well when he said, "Bobby went wild when they sold his things."

The '90s had already dealt Bobby a failed relationship (with Zita Rajcsányi whom he saw as the love of his life) and the botched reworking of *My 60 Memorable Games* (which made him furious). He was reeling after the U.S. Government indictment which made it clear he would face prosecution if he returned to the United States—resulting in the inability to attend the funerals of either his sister (in 1997) or mother (in 1998). And now his possessions were stolen!

What were these treasures, how were they lost, and what became of them?

The story starts in 1968 when Bobby moved from New York to Los Angeles. By the early 1970s more of his personal treasures had traveled to the West Coast—although many of his books appear to have stayed in storage with friends in New York.

Not long after the World Championship match in Reykjavík, the Worldwide Church of God provided Fischer with an apartment near Ambassador College in Pasadena. After that, it's difficult to construct a precise timeline of where Bobby lived and when, as he came and went, moved to different apartments, and stayed off and on with various WCG church members and other friends.

[1] Jim Walters, *Los Angeles Times* (San Gabriel Valley edition), February 19, 1999.

Some time around 1986 Bobby put most of his treasures into storage at a Bekins facility located at 511 South Fair Oaks Drive in Pasadena. Claudia Mokarow's name and address went on the lease along with that of fellow renter Robert D. James. Using an alias to protect Bobby's privacy might have seemed a good idea at the time, but it would later cause serious trouble.

When Fischer traveled to Europe to face Boris Spassky in the summer of 1992 he had no inkling there would be no returning to the United States. The indictment issued against Bobby for breaking sanctions (playing the match with Spassky in Yugoslavia) gave him a major problem and a minor headache. The problem, of course, was that he was now subject to arrest if he returned to the United States. The headache was that all his worldly treasures were in Pasadena. Rather than having them brought to him in Europe, Bobby chose to continue paying the storage fees, entrusting Bob Ellsworth to handle the payments.

What was Bobby thinking? Did he believe the warrant for his arrest would eventually be lifted? Did he have plans for his possessions to be brought to him? Most likely he wasn't sure what to do and continuing to pay to have them stored was the default option.

Fischer was not the most trusting of individuals. Not knowing he would be unable to return to the United States, Bobby had no reason to give Ellsworth access to the storage locker containing his treasures. Consequently, Ellsworth probably had no idea of its contents. One person who knew, besides Claudia Mokarow and Bobby, was Fischer's old trainer, champion weight lifter Harry Sneider. It wouldn't be a surprise if he were the person who helped Fischer move the heavier items (the safes and cabinets) into the storage unit.

Why was Ellsworth given this job, and not the Mokarows, or his attorney Joseph Choate Jr.? Arthur and Claudia might have seemed obvious choices but they moved to Texas in the late 1980s and Bobby was no longer close to them. As to the choice of Ellsworth over Choate: It was Ellsworth (along with Lou Hays) who helped Bobby meet and court Zita, and in so doing made the 1992 match possible. In the fall of 1992 Ellsworth, living in Pasadena, was the logical person for Bobby—a friend who had done him many favors, asking little in return.

The next six years Ellsworth performed his duties perfectly. Bobby sent a check each year for $5,000 that covered the cost of storage unit number 120020 ($80 per month) and Ellsworth's management fee. The majority of the money was for taxes on two undeveloped Florida properties (in Clearwater and Tarpon Springs)—land originally owned by his grandfather and bought from his mother in 1992.

Things went sour in late 1998 when Ellsworth failed to make a payment. The ownership had changed from Bekins to A-American Self Storage in early 1998, and what appears to have happened is Ellsworth made the January payment to

Bekins for the first half of 1998 but for some reason neglected to make a payment in July. Noticing that the account was overdue the new owners sent out a bill for the remaining six months of the year. The bill would have been sent to the parties on the lease, but the addresses and other contact information were out-of-date—Fischer was in Europe, and Claudia Mokarow in Texas. A-American Self-Storage would not have known about Ellsworth, and with unpaid bills piling up they were well within their legal rights to auction off the contents of the storage locker to recover lost rent and any associated costs (including the expense of transporting the items from Pasadena to the auction house in Irvine). Once the back rent, associated costs, and auction house's percentage were deducted, any remaining proceeds should have gone to Fischer, but this was complicated by the fake name he used when the lease was signed. Since ownership of the storage unit could not be determined, it's very likely the State of California ended up receiving the balance.

The auction took place on January 10, 1999. The *Los Angeles Times* reported:[1]

> [Continued from page 609] While the friend [Ellsworth] could not be reached for comment at his home or office, another longtime Fischer acquaintance—Olympic coach Harry Sneider—said he was very familiar with the items that Fischer had held in storage since his recluse days in Pasadena, following his 1972 world title win over Russian Boris Spassky.
>
> Sneider, a former physical education teacher and weightlifting coach at Ambassador College in Pasadena and now an Arcadia resident, said he met Fischer in 1972 when the chess champion came looking for conditioning help. The two forged a friendship that has lasted twenty-seven years.
>
> "There was a chess set from that World Championship, two file cabinets full of game notes and personal diaries, a letter from Richard Nixon, two 3,000-pound safes," said Sneider describing the items he recalled being stored in the rental unit.
>
> "He (Fischer) said all of the stuff lost is worth $100 million. I think several million is more like it. We've been able to recover some of the things."
>
> Some of the items were consigned for sale to Dreyer's Auction Inc. of Irvine, which publicized the availability of Bobby Fischer memorabilia on the Internet for its Jan. 10 auction.
>
> "There wasn't much. The entire gross was about $8,500," said Dreyer's co-owner, Chuck Dreyer. "There were no chess sets. Just miscellaneous letters, books, correspondence, a bronze bust of Fischer."
>
> It was unclear what might have happened to the other items that Fischer and Sneider claimed were stowed away in the storage unit.
>
> During the past five weeks, Fischer, from his home in Budapest, Hungary, has railed over the sales during broadcasts on Bomba Radyo in the Philippines and over the Internet.

[1] Jim Walters, *Los Angeles Times* (San Gabriel Valley edition), February 19, 1999.

In interviews posted on the Internet, the fifty-six-year-old Fischer said the "confiscated items"—as he described them—included a famous statue of three horses that he won in a 1970 tournament in Yugoslavia, a bronze bust he sat for in 1961, a bag of fifty to a hundred rare silver dollars, hundreds of chess books, thousands of racy Mexican comic books, and Japanese posters from a Los Angeles movie theater that gave them to him when it closed down. Other items were 600 to 1,000 unpublished games—from simultaneous games played in exhibitions, following his win over Tigran Petrosian for the right to play Spassky in '72.

A spokesperson for A–American, which bought the storage building from Bekins Storage in January 1998, said no one was aware of the contents when the lien sale took place.

"We called someone down from the corporate office, they took pictures of the contents we could see from outside the door," [the spokesperson] said. "There was no inventory. We had no knowledge of what was in there."

The Atlantic gave another account of the auction:[1]

As for the Bekins theft,[2] it, too, is a fiction. He did maintain a Bekins storage room in Pasadena for twelve years, and the memorabilia inside it were confiscated, but not in some nefarious plot. The contents of the storage room were sold at a public auction, because Fischer's account—maintained by a Pasadena businessman named Bob Ellsworth, whom Fischer had met through the Worldwide Church of God—was in arrears. The Pasadena storage facility had been sold in the late 1990s, and the new owners noticed that the account was overdue. "It was my responsibility to pay the bill, and I didn't pay it because I didn't know there were new owners," Ellsworth says. "So they put Bobby's stuff up for auction. I felt really bad and spent about eight thousand dollars of my own money buying back all the significant memorabilia."

The storage room was not a treasure trove worth "hundreds of millions of dollars," as Fischer has claimed. "A lot of it," Ellsworth says, "was old magazines and things that were of personal interest to Bobby: books on conspiracy theories, racy Mexican comics, lots of John Gunther books. Things you could go down to Olvera Street and replace for a dime a copy. That stuff I passed on. But anything of intrinsic value I snagged." At the auction Ellsworth acquired "about 80%" of the various lots.

Harry Sneider corroborates Ellsworth's story, and says that his son personally delivered the reclaimed memorabilia to Fischer in Budapest. When a list of the numbered lots was read off to him, Sneider confirmed that each one is again in Fischer's possession. Lot 151: Box Lot of Telegrams to Bobby Fischer during World Chess Championship. "Delivered." Lot 152: Box Lot of Books Inscribed to Bobby Fischer (not by authors). "Delivered." Lot 153:

---

1 *The Atlantic*, "Bobby Fischer's Pathetic Endgame" by Rene Chun, December 2002.

2 Bobby continually referred to "the Bekins theft," apparently unaware that the storage facility had changed ownership before the time of the auction.

> From the People of New York given to Bobby Fischer—Leather Scrapbook with Letter and Telegram from Mayor John V. Lindsay of New York City. "Delivered."[1]

According to Ellsworth, the auction was held on short notice, not well publicized, and was one of many Dreyer's held that day. In his account he states the auction was lightly attended and Harry Sneider came along to lend moral support in the quest to recover Bobby's belongings. Roger Gozdecki, at the time owner of The Book Shop in Covina, California, was another probable attendee. Gozdecki made the statement:[2]

> ...recently, we sold a genuinely historic group of chess books that once belonged to Bobby Fischer, which had been presented to him by the authors with some marvelous inscriptions, around the time that he became the World Chess Champion in 1972.

While this isn't irrefutable evidence that Gozdecki was in Irvine on January 10, 1999, the timing and his shop being located in Covina, only thirty-seven miles from the Irvine auction site, strongly suggests that he was—how else would he have come by this material and advertise it for a February 1999 sale?

FISCHER'S CLAIM

The sale of his possessions became an obsession with Fischer and inevitably came up whenever he was given a forum. On January 14, 1999, a few days after the auction, Bobby, understandably angry, aired his outrage in a radio interview:

> I have spent on this...just in storage fees alone over $10,000. I have spent in buying the custom-made safes, custom-made file cabinets, with secret built-in safes in the file cabinets, another file cabinet, a safe with special drill-proof doors, with a second door inside, combination locks, both timers, in case somebody tries to force you to open it. The works! To preserve my memorabilia. My stuff from Marcos, my letters from President Nixon, books dedicated to me by President Nixon, former President Nixon when he dedicated the books, but he was President Nixon when he wrote to me. All kinds of stuff, photo albums, statues, the works!
>
> What the hell, am I gonna give away all of the stuff which I have taken years to accumulate and to preserve over $400. I've got $300 million in

1 According to Sarah Sneider (Harry's widow) who was contacted in 2019, Harry's son brought only two suitcases of material reclaimed from the auction to Bobby in Budapest. They did not receive a favorable reception from Bobby. When the younger Sneider gave the boxes to Bobby the response was, "Where's the rest?" Sarah Sneider felt Bobby may have viewed these two suitcases as tainted. She remembers Bobby calling her several months after the luggage was given to him, asking for the combinations to the bags—he apparently had not opened them as yet. Sarah Sneider also states that Harry was not at the auction with Bob Ellsworth.

2 Alibris online profile of Gozdecki.

> Switzerland. I got dough here in Hungary. They did it all behind my back. Nobody contacted me. Nothing. They didn't contact my lawyers. Nothing.

This was the first in a series of similar interviews where Fischer bitterly attacked Ellsworth, suggesting, but providing no evidence, that he was part of a conspiracy to steal his possessions. While Ellsworth did miss at least one payment, there's nothing to suggest it was anything more than an unintentional error—once he discovered his mistake, he did everything in his power to get Bobby's possessions back. But now in Fischer's view, Ellsworth was a criminal and a twenty-year friendship was over. The interview then digressed into vicious antisemitic tirades that were part and parcel of the radio interviews Fischer gave from 1999 to October of 2006.

Some fact checking: The $10,000 figure for storage fees Fischer claimed he spent sounds about right for the dozen or so years he paid for the space. However, Fischer's statement that he had assets of $300 million in Switzerland, was off by two zeros (!)

A–American never took an inventory, so the contents of the storage locker has to be reconstructed from Fischer's interviews and firsthand witnesses.

Besides the statue of three horses, the bronze bust Fischer sat for, the bag of silver dollars (one can only speculate what happened to these coins which alone might have covered the amount owed on the storage unit), chess books, comics, and posters, of greatest interest are the still unaccounted for "600 to 1,000" unpublished games from simultaneous exhibitions Fischer gave in Argentina after his victory over Tigran Petrosian:

> After I played [Petrosian in 1971] I gave...twenty-five, thirty simul exhibitions [in Argentina]... all the players had to give me their copy of the score... maybe between six hundred and a thousand scores...What the hell are they worth? Thousands, millions of dollars.

The number of games Fischer mentioned was a bit of an exaggeration. Fischer spent a month on that simul tour and ended up playing around 400 games (roughly twenty exhibitions with a fixed limit of twenty boards). These score sheets were in Fischer's opponents' handwriting and as such their monetary value would be significantly affected by whether or not he signed them. However, the real value of these games is their contribution to Fischer's legacy and therefore it becomes difficult to put a dollar value on them.

On more than one occasion Bobby remarked that he had played a number of instructive miniatures on his 1971 simul tour. Fischer realized early on that sthe Argentine amateurs he faced (rated 1800–2200), though out of touch with modern opening theory, were strong practical players in other phases of the game. Hence, Bobby tried to beat them as quickly as possible—or, at least get a big advantage from the opening. Unfortunately, the roughly dozen games preserved from the tour don't emphasize this, as they are mostly the rare games Fischer lost or drew. Players typically don't like to publish their losses.

These score sheets were probably the most important items housed in the storage locker that are still missing—hopefully these games are in the possession of some collector and not thrown out by someone who didn't recognize their worth. It is a real pity Fischer never wrote about these games as he sometimes talked of doing.

Los Angeles Times reporter Jim Walters raised an important question in his 1999 article about the storage locker fiasco. Did all of Fischer's treasures make it to the auction in Irvine? Was there a pre-auction or lien sale to unload some of the items to make transportation to the auction site, about an hour away, easier? Fischer, in his radio interviews said that his ten-foot by ten-foot storage locker was completely filled and contained close to 100 boxes, two 3,000-pound safes, and filing cabinets. This doesn't seem physically possible, but there can be no doubt he had a lot of stuff stored there.

It seems likely that something happened before the auction, as there is no indication the massive safes were auctioned off nor the numerous collectible coins Bobby spoke of. The auctioneer in Irvine, Chuck Dreyer, says Bobby's effects only grossed about $8,500. Compare this to the $8,000 Ellsworth claims to have spent at the auction buying back all important items, which strongly suggests he got pretty much everything of Bobby's—but he didn't. Among the missing items were the Argentina simul games, and several early drafts of *My 60 Memorable Games*—these drafts were later found elsewhere. Therefore it stands to reason some of the items in the storage locker were sold before the auction, or they were held back when their value was realized.

COLLECTING FISCHER

The person who ended up with the bulk of this treasure trove of Fischer memorabilia was none other than Larry Finley, the boy who had befriended Bobby in the summer of 1958 at the Brussels World's Fair. Finley never again came face to face with Bobby, but in a fashion, their paths did cross. Visiting a flea market in Long Beach, California, in the spring of 1999, Finley was stunned to find boxes and boxes of chess material, that on closer inspection he recognized to have belonged to Bobby Fischer. Like chess players everywhere, Finley was familiar with the storage locker story and the anguish the episode had caused Bobby. Finley immediately bought everything and envisioned the day when he would visit Fischer and return the rescued items.

For close to six years Finley tried, with no success, to contact Bobby. In the late spring of 2005 Finley thought he would be successful—Fischer had arrived in Iceland and his exact whereabouts was known. Six months and many repeated attempts later, Finley gave up. He came to the realization (rightly as it turns out) that Bobby wanted nothing to do with the treasures he once held so dear.

A tournament player since his high school days, Finley had been rated as high as 1800. However he was not a serious chess collector, certainly not to the extent of his Fischer purchase, so, he decided to sell some of the material. He carefully sorted through the treasures, retaining about ten boxes of personal items, and listed the rest on eBay. He reasoned that if Bobby ever changed his mind it would be the more personal items he'd want back.

The initial listing elicited a torrent of hate mail from chess fans around the world who felt selling Bobby's treasures, even if legally acquired, was in poor taste. Finley quickly removed the items from eBay, but a little while later had second thoughts and relisted them. The second offering on eBay attracted widespread media attention with major articles appearing on the ChessBase website and in *The New York Times*.

Finley's eBay offer, item number 8736084948, was described as follows:

> **BOBBY FISCHER'S CHESS BOOK COLLECTION AND OTHER ITEMS PURCHASED AT A CA FLEA MARKET, BF'S STORAGE LOCKERS**
>
> Purchased at a southern California Flea market about six years ago, here are some of Bobby Fischer's personal items presumably from the infamous storage locker, which was said to have been sold for lack of rent payment. It is a unique opportunity for someone in the International Chess community to preserve the legacy of whom many feel is the most talented chess player of all time. I have tried many times in the last few years to reach Mr. Fischer about these items, but have had no response. What is being offered is:
>
> 1. The original manuscript and galley prints of Bobby's bestselling book, *My 60 Most Memorable Games* (originally titled, *My Life in Chess*). This covers an entire table top and contains numerous notes and corrections which should make fascinating study for years to come. (Note, this is said to have been written on a typewriter, which he won at one of his early tournaments).
> 2. A ceramic plaque given to Bobby, Bahia Blanca, on November 3, 1971.
> 3. About twenty meticulously crafted "crib" notes for tournament preparation: [long list of subjects given]. Note, each book contains at least fifty games all written by hand and categorized by opening moves.[1]
> 4. *Chess Informants* #2 to #38.

[1] These were specially prepared for Bobby's World Championship run by Robert Wade with Les Blackstock and Kevin O'Connell assisting.

5. About 300 foreign chess books (Bobby has been heard to say that he felt he had one of the best collections anywhere). These are roughly divided between modern as well as many older issues. Some are signed "Bobby Fischer."
6. About 200 English language chess books, many inscribed to Bobby with a personal message. One is signed by his mother on his birthday.
7. About thirty-five mint copies of Bobby's book about being incarcerated in the Pasadena Jail overnight.
8. An original manuscript of a chess story "End Game" by Walsashek
9. Legal papers about Bobby's attempt to copyright a chess move
10. Two boxes of non-chess reading material containing a variety of spiritual, political, religious, and other material of an extremely personal nature.
11. For an example of the chess books, one box contains the following: [long list of books and magazines given].

    The entire collection is boxed in seventeen cardboard boxes, with a total weight of approximately 500 lbs.

The starting bid of $15,000 failed to generate any takers and the listing was taken down. Not long after, an East Coast dealer purchased the items from Finley, and subsequently, they resurfaced in a 2009 auction at Bonhams in New York City that brought a winning bid (including auction fees) reputed to be $61,000.

The Bonham sale was a record for Fischer related memorabilia, but subsequent auctions, including two in New York around the time of the 2015 World Championship match, did not generate the same level of excitement.

In addition to the Finley material, the Bonham lot contained other interesting items. One prize was the Spassky red book from the *Weltgeschichte des Schachs* series, which was Fischer's constant companion during the run-up to the 1972 match—the book contained Fischer's personal handwritten annotations.

Where is everything now? Private individuals and public institutions have preserved many of Fischer's treasured possessions with the following the most important:

- The Marshall Chess Club. This material, the Russell Targ Collection, is pre-1961;
- The World Chess Hall of Fame in St. Louis;
- In the possession of Larry Finley;
- In Budapest with Pal Benko's family (Benko had stored many of the items that were transported to Hungary after the auction of the Pasadena storage locker). A few of the items in Hungary may still be in the possession of Hungarian International Master Janos Rigo who Fischer accused of misappropriating some of his belongings;

- In the private collection of David DeLucia.

[Note: the collections of the World Chess Hall of Fame, DeLucia, and Finley all contain a number of Fischer's non-chess books that do not reflect well on him. Many of these books are extremely unpleasant and antisemitic in nature. Vile as they are, these books express some of what Fischer believed for several decades, and like it or not are part of his legacy.]

The World Chess Hall of Fame has one of the famous chess tables created for the 1966 Havana Olympiad which were subsequently given to all first boards and a few high ranking FIDE officials. Theirs previously belonged to Fred Cramer, a U.S. Chess Federation official who was a key helper during the 1972 World Championship match. Bobby sold his table to Burt Hochberg, whose widow Carol still has it [see photo page 608].

While Bobby liked the Havana Olympiad table, he was also very pleased with the Swiss made chess table he played on at the Zurich 1959 tournament and later had shipped home. He sold this table, which he used heavily throughout the 1960s, to Bernard Zuckerman when he moved to Los Angeles in 1968.

One item that may have come from Fischer's storage locker was sold for $16,800 by Bonhams (Los Angeles branch) on October 15, 2008 (at this writing its location is unknown):

FISCHER, BOBBY. 1943–2008.
BOBBY FISCHER'S CHESS NOTEBOOK.

Autograph Manuscript Signed integrally ("Fischer"), 31 pp recto and verso, 12mo, n.p., 1959–1963, being a chess notebook used by Fischer during the time period and including a record of thirteen games played against Samuel Reshevsky plus manuscript notes on the games in progress, on printed "Litokarton" notebook published in Yugoslavia, in leatherette boards with "Fischer Robert" stamped to lower right corner of upper cover, some wear and soiling to leaves.

A fascinating piece of Fischer memorabilia from the early part of his career, featuring Fischer's own notes on USA Championship matches and other important games, many played against leading Grandmaster of chess Samuel Reshevsky, plus his notes on at least one of the matches: "This is just what I had hoped for! Reshevsky plays for the KB square too soon and thereby ruins his game...."

SNEIDER AND ELLSWORTH

Paul Heaton, a noted Fischer expert from London, spoke with Harry Sneider and Bob Ellsworth in 2013 about Bobby's treasures, here is his take-away:[1]

> Harry Sneider was one of the nicest people you could ever meet—a BIG, warm personality (I think his interviews in *Bobby Fischer vs the World* are a good reflection of how his personality could fill a room)...
>
> Sneider said that Bobby's reliance on Claudia Mokarow became so encompassing it almost ended her marriage to Art and this was one of the reasons they moved to Texas. ...the Mokarows won't speak about Bobby. Sneider confirmed the belongings did go back to Bobby in Budapest...not only did his son go, but Bobby paid for him and his wife to visit in Budapest as well. ...He remembered going to Las Vegas with Bobby in Ted Armstrong's jet to discuss a match, but nothing happened... and said Bobby struggled in the real world, e.g. not paying electricity bills, as he thought he was above mundane stuff like that.
>
> It's difficult to know what to make of Bob Ellsworth—Harry introduced us. Ellsworth confirmed some of the details about the auction, but then he started asking me how much various items of Bobby's would fetch (though said he didn't have anything). I specifically remember when I said that *I was Tortured in the Pasadena Jailhouse!* would fetch around $150–200 he remarked that Art Mokarow had a box of them in his garage, and he wondered how he could get hold of them. I found this exchange a bit strange in response to asking him about Bekins, but perhaps he had warmed to me as he was asking me for investment advice beforehand. I seem to recall he had just sold a house.
>
> Ellsworth complained Rene Chun never published "that book," after he spent the best part of two days driving him around Los Angeles, and he confirmed Chun was correct that Bobby lived in a small flat on Orange Street near the Fairfax district in Los Angeles. He said he mainly came into Bobby's life when the Mokarows moved to Texas in late '80s, and Claudia asked him to look after Bobby. His first memory was Claudia calling him one night and saying, "Bobby is feeling cold, can you take him some blankets".
>
> Ellsworth offered that Bobby had been preparing to leave the U.S. for some time as part of playing a match and would walk around Los Angeles putting stuff he did not want in public bins—but he would only put a little bit in each bin in case someone came along and reconstructed everything he was throwing away. ...Bobby would come to parties in his flat for the Pasadena Tournament of Roses Parade, and speak to people there (none of who recognized him), introducing himself as Dallas James and generally being friendly. He recalled one episode where Bobby started speaking to a Jewish guest, and he got very nervous—but nothing happened.
>
> Ellsworth gave me one of the chess sets Bobby left behind, which is exactly the same as Lou Hays received from Fischer.

1 Excerpted from correspondence between Paul Heaton and John Donaldson.

WILLIAM LOMBARDY

William James Joseph Lombardy and Robert James Fischer had plenty in common besides sharing the same middle name.

Both grew up in economically challenged circumstances and had questions about who their fathers were. Fischer's story is well-known, with Hans-Gerhardt Fischer listed on Bobby's birth certificate, but Paul Nemenyi was almost certainly his real father.

Lombardy's situation is more confusing. By his account, shortly before his twelfth birthday he discovered papers indicating he was born in the New York Foundling Hospital. This suggested that he had been adopted:[1]

> Later I raised the subject of adoption, which he calmly ignored. Raymond [Lombardy] was a soft spoken and loving father, so "adoption" wouldn't have changed my love for my parents, even though from that day on, I have always wondered. ... Parenthetically, in December of 2007 [when trying to obtain a baptismal certtificate] I learned that I could not get the certificate at the church where supposedly I was baptized, but only at the Foundling [where infants were often abandoned and/or given up for adoption]! At age seventy, I believed that I finally had evidence of my adoption. But I was really no longer interested in pursuing the matter! Such thoughts at my age have become no more than mere curiosity.

Their mutual distaste of the U.S. Chess Federation has already been referred to although it should be pointed out the organization provided strong support for Fischer during his World Championship run and that Lombardy was given $10,000 by the USCF's Professional Players Health and Benefits Program late in his life to help him get back on his feet (he had fallen behind on rent and was eventually evicted).

Fischer and Lombardy shared a distrust of conventional medicine, something that may have hastened their deaths. This aversion to Western medicine was curious in Fischer's case, with his mother being a doctor and his sister a nurse. Dr. Anthony Saidy remembers a discussion the two had around 1977 in which Bobby shared his distrust of blood transfusions. When Saidy mentioned he had personally known at least a dozen people whose lives had been saved by a blood transfusion, Bobby said he "would rather take his chances" than undergo the procedure (the World Wide Church of God never had prohibitions against blood transfusions so that wasn't the root of his belief.)

Both were tough negotiators, sticking to their principles even to financial detriment—Fischer turned down many endorsement deals after winning the

---

1 William Lombardy, *Understanding Chess: My System, My Games, My Life*. In association with Russell Enterprises, 2011, (p. 10).

World Championship. Lombardy subscribed to Fischer's "nobody makes money on my name" thesis as expressed in his memoir:

> For the latest HBO mythological film *Bobby Fischer Against the World* that company wanted to interview me gratis. "How nice," I mused, "a corporation only in it for profit and with a million dollar budget thinks to do without spending a dime to interview me who knows the subject." Perhaps HBO feared the unforeseen that I might reveal and which views HBO would rather decline to publish. Without access to appropriate knowledge HBO created new myths based on its own preconceptions...

They also had their differences. Unlike Fischer, whose behavior at the board was beyond reproach, Lombardy could behave in ways that did not endear him to his colleagues. A case in point is Game (98).

(98) Sicilian
Edmar Mednis – William Lombardy
Pasadena (5) 1978

1.e4 c5 2.Nf3 e6 3.d4 cxd4 4.Nxd4 Nf6 5.Nc3 Nc6 6.Ndb5 d6 7.Bf4 e5 8.Bg5 a6 9.Bxf6 gxf6 10.Na3 Be6 11.Nc4 Rc8 12.Ne3 Ne7 13.Bd3 Qb6 14.0-0 Qxb2 15.Ncd5 Bxd5 16.Nxd5 Nxd5 17.exd5 Qd4 18.Qf3 Ke7 19.a4 Rc7 20.Rfd1 Qc3 21.Rab1 Qa5 22.Qe4 Bh6 23.Rb3 Bd2 24.Rdb1 Rb8 25.Rb6 Bc3 26.Rxa6 bxa6 27.Rxb8 Bd4 28.g3 h6 29.Kg2 Ba7 30.Rh8 Rb7 31.Qf3 Qd2 32.Bxa6 Rb8 33.Rxb8 Bxb8 34.Qb3 Bc7 35.Bd3 Qa5 36.Qb7 Qb6 37.Qxb6 Bxb6 38.f3 Kd8 39.Kh3 Ke7 40.Kg4 Kf8 41.Kf5 Ke7 42.Bb5 Bg1 43.h3 Bf2 44.g4 Be1 45.Bc6 Bf2 46.Bb7 Be1 47.Ke4 Bf2 48.Bc8 Kd8 49.Bf5 Be1 50.Bh7 Kd7 51.Kd3 Kd8 52.Kc4 Kc7 53.Kb5 Bg3 54.a5 Be1 55.Bd3 Bh4 56.Be4 Be1 57.Ka6 Bh4 58.Bh7 Bg5 59.Bg8 Bd2 60.Bxf7 Bc3 61.Bg6 Be1 62.Bf5 Bc3 63.Kb5 Be1 64.a6 Bf2 65.Kc4 Kb6 66.Bc8 Kc7 67.Bb7 Kd8 68.Kd3 Ke7 69.Ke4 Bb6 70.Bc8 Bc5 71.Be6 Kf8 72.Kf5 Kg7 73.c3 Bf2

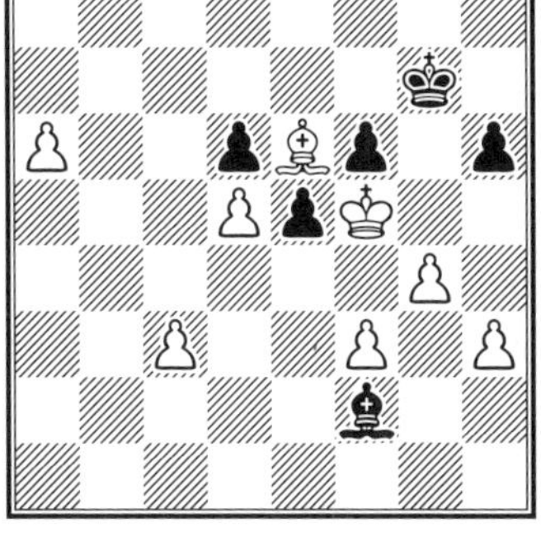

White wants to play a7 or bring his king to e6. How does he force zugzwang?

74.Bg8! Bc5 75.Ke6 Kxg8 76.Kxf6 Kh7 77.Kf7 Bf2 78.h4

Black could resign, but he plays on. The game was adjourned at move ninety with White two queens up. The next morning, while Lombardy slept in, Mednis had to wait in the tournament hall for his flag to fall.

Larry Christiansen provided a somewhat different account of the game's conclusion while doing online commentary for the Internet Chess Club. He said the adjourned position was actually the final position in the game. When play resumed the following day, the adjournment envelope was opened and instead of a sealed move, Lombardy had written "@#$% YOU!".

It isn't certain which version transpired, but in either case Black's conduct was not very sportsmanlike.

78...Bc5 79.g5 hxg5 80.hxg5 Bb6 81.g6+ Kh6 82.g7 Kg5 83.g8Q+ Kf4 84.Qg4+ Ke3 85.Qg1+ Kxf3 86.Qxb6 e4 87.a7 e3 88.a8Q e2 89.Qe8 e1Q 90.Qxe1, 1–0 (Black's flag fell).

Lombardy and Fischer had something else in common, the loss of their "treasures." Throughout his life Lombardy endured financial difficulties. After his death, Mark Wieder (the same fellow who called Bobby Fischer during the Palma de Mallorca Interzonal) wrote a piece on Lombardy for *New In Chess* and addressed what lead up to the loss of his belongings. [1]

> [In the late 1980's Bill was introduced to Ted Field an heir to the Marshall Field department store fortune and a good friend to chess who for many years was a silent backer of the American Open. Field became interested in taking chess lessons and extended his generosity to Lombardy.]
>
> Bill began working with Field...
>
> Ted asked what Bill's rate was after the first session of about four hours. I think Bill asked for $125 an hour. Ted wrote a check for $25,000 and told Bill to take this on account for future sessions, and that he wanted Bill to be available and not have to worry about money.
>
> ...
>
> Field sponsored the New York half of the 1990 World Championship match between Karpov and Kasparov and promised Lombardy an important, although unspecified, role in the proceedings. At the end of the twelve New York games, Bill went over the games with Kasparov (while Ted Field watched) and commented later as to Garry's incredible objectivity in assessing the positions. But Bill felt that Field had reneged on his promise of a role in

[1] Mark Wieder, "In Memoriam, for Better and for Worse: Bill Lombardy (1937–2017)," *New In Chess*, #8, 2017, (pp. 64–69).

> the match, and became disillusioned with the relationship. The two severed their ties shortly thereafter and Field's interest in chess eventually went completely by the wayside...
>
> Bill thought he had found an annuity in Field and that he would never have to worry about money again. Outside of some funds generated by sporadic lessons, lectures, and writing, Bill lived out his life over the next 25+ years by gradually exhausting the savings accumulated from the billionaire's largesse, and by late 2016 he was, tragically, homeless on the streets of New York.

The loss of Field's support affected Lombardy's equilibrium. He had always felt unappreciated, especially by the U.S. Chess Federation. Lombardy had represented the United States with distinction in seven Chess Olympiads and seven Student Team Championships, played in numerous U.S. Championships, written for *Chess Life* for over three decades and had served in various USCF governance positions. He believed this lifetime of work merited some sort of pension that would offer him financial security.

Field's generosity might well have felt like karmic justice to Lombardy. When this support ended he became increasingly embittered towards chess powers from the American Chess Foundation to the USCF.

Lombardy possessed one valuable resource that could have rescued him from homelessness, his extensive collection of chess memorabilia, but he chose not to sell any of it. When he was evicted in 2016 Lombardy placed a higher priority on his treasures than keeping a roof over his head, sleeping rough in Union Square Park and the subway to save money to house them.

Most of Lombardy's belongings were stashed in two different storage facilities, and in a replay of Bobby's tragedy, one was auctioned off sometime before his death due to non-payment. These items were purchased by Gotham Thrift Store of New York, located in Queens, which is offering them for sale on eBay, often for optimistic prices.

The fate of the items in the other storage locker is less clear, but it appears at least some of them were auctioned off by Bonhams in early December of 2017. One lot, which sold for $1,875, included the following items as described by the auction house:

1. *My 60 Memorable Games*. New York: Simon and Schuster, (1969). 8vo. Some wear to jacket. First edition, inscribed to his coach Bill [Lombardy] on the occasion of his first World Championship, "thanks a lot for your help and patience." Annotated and signed by Lombardy, "Sept 1st, 1972/First autograph of Bobby Fischer as World Champion" [see photo page 596].
2. *Bobby Fischer Teaches Chess*. New York: Basic Systems, (1966). Illustrated boards, without d.j. as issued. Cracking to joints, some soiling. *First edition, signed by Fischer, Bill Lombardy's copy*, with his signature to paste-down.

3. Signed traveler's check ("Bobby Fischer"), accomplished in Fischer's hand to Bill Lombardy, and endorsed by Lombardy to the verso.

4. Five Icelandic postal covers, each signed by both Fischer and Lombardy, dated 2.VII.1972 to 1.IX.1972 and numbered, with various representations of Fischer–Spassky, and including one dated the day of Fischer's momentous victory.

5. Original watercolor by Halldór Pétursson, depicting Fischer and Spassky, along with Lombardy, lettered in English, pen and ink with watercolor, 367 x 478 mm, inscribed by the artist to "Grandmaster William Lombardy," Reykjavík, July 1972, lower right, small tear to left hand margin, not affecting image.

Less than $2,000 for the entire lot was well below what might have been expected in this little publicized auction. Not surprisingly, since the winning bid was offered by a professional book dealer Matt Raptis (Raptis Rare Books), they were quickly on the market again and this time the premier item, Lombardy's copy of *My Sixty Memorable Games,* the first book signed by Bobby Fischer after becoming World Champion, sold for $15,000! This appears to be the most paid for a Fischer related item since 2009. Bill Lombardy probably had no idea what his "treasures" might fetch. He certainly could have used the money.

4
"I WILL NOT MENTION CHESS."

Once hailed as a U.S. national hero, the millennium found Fischer a man without a country roaming from Budapest to Asia, and back and fourth between Manila and Tokyo. His public popularity had waned and many old friends had turned their backs on him (his ranting and hate speech made him impossible to be around).

Fischer first visited Iceland in 1960 before the Leipzig Olympiad. His next visit was a dozen years later to check out Reykjavík as a possible venue for the upcoming World Championship. While in town he paid a visit to the 5th Reykjavík International that was in progress only to be disappointed when Raymond Keene agreed to a draw against Leonid Stein in a position Fischer believed to be winning. In the words of Icelandic Master Bragi Kristjánsson:[1]

> When Fischer came to Iceland in February 1972 it was during the bi-annual International Reykjavík tournament. I took him to the playing hall. He rushed in and walked so fast that I had difficulty keeping up with him, and took a short look at one of the in play boards. I recall that it was the Soviet Grandmaster Stein playing the British International Master Keene. He immediately declared:
>
> "Stein is completely lost." At the same moment there came up a sign. The players had agreed on a draw. Fischer shook his head, lost his interest in the tournament, and walked out.
>
> The next day on our way to the airport I asked him whether he was sure that Stein had a lost game. He took from his pocket a chess set, and with quick movements put up the position which he had in his mind, although he had only glimpsed it for a second the day before and showed me several possible variations and said:
>
> "Completely lost. There is nothing he can do."

---

1 Eduard Gufeld, Carlos Almarza-Mato, Mike Morris, Wolfgang Unzicker, Gudmundur Thorarinsson, Bragi Kristjánsson, and Bob Long, *Bobby Fischer: From Chess Genius to Legend.* Davenpart, Iowa: Thinkers Press, 2002, (pp. 147–149).

(99) Grünfeld
Raymond Keene – Leonid Stein
Reykjavík 1972

1.d4 Nf6 2.c4 g6 3.Nc3 d5 4.Bg5 Ne4 5.Bh4 Nxc3 6.bxc3 Bg7 7.e3 c5 8.cxd5 Qxd5 9.Nf3 Nc6 10.Be2 cxd4 11.exd4 Qa5 12.0-0 Qxc3 13.Rc1 Qb4 14.Rb1 Qd6 15.Bg3 e5 16.Nxe5 Qxd4 17.Nxc6, ½–½.

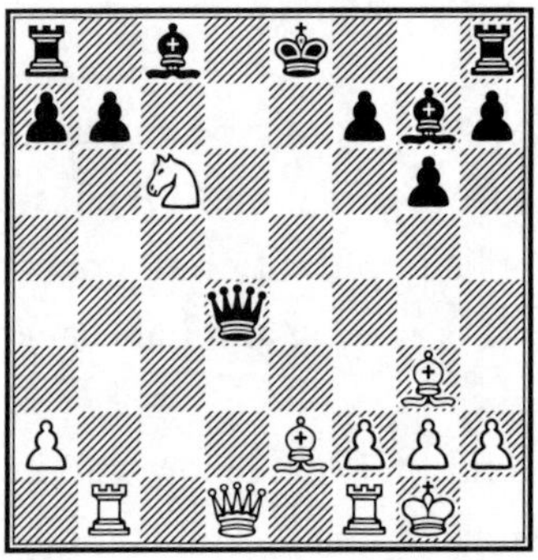

Fischer's evaluation of the position is correct:

17...bxc6 (17...Qxd1 18.Rfxd1 bxc6 19.Bd6 is equally bad for Black) 18.Bd6 Be6 19.Qxd4 Bxd4 20.Rb7 Bd5 (or 20...0-0-0 21.Rfb1) 21.Bf3 Bxf3 22.Re1+ Kd8 23.gxf3 Re8 24.Rd1 wins.

Helgi Ólafsson, was the oldest of a group of Icelandic players (Margeir Pétursson, Jón Árnason, and Jóhann Hjartarson), who inspired by Bobby, turned the small nation into a chess powerhouse in the late 1980s and early 1990s (three top ten finishes in Olympiads and Hjartarson becoming a Candidate in 1988).

Ólafsson was also one of the group that was instrumental in getting Bobby released from Japan's custody by arranging for Iceland to grant him citizenship. During the three years Bobby lived in Iceland Ólafsson spent many hours with him—going to movies, restaurants, and even a fishing trip in the wilds of Iceland. Ólafsson clearly viewed Fischer with an objective eye:[1]

> Bobby's coming "home" to Iceland stirred up a lot of emotions. Generally our effort was appreciated, but some were unable to forget or forgive his radio interviews...
>
> There were many good reasons not to lend Bobby Fischer a helping hand whilst in jail in Japan, but given the strong possibility that the man was/is seriously ill was reason enough to try to help him. I will never regret that. Personally I make no distinction between, say, a schizo-paranoid, a person

[1] Ólafsson, Helgi. *Bobby Fischer Comes Home: The Final Years in Iceland, a Saga of Friendship and Lost Illusions*. The Netherlands: New In Chess, 2014, (p. 69).

with cancer, a brain tumor or any other disease. Everyone should have some basic human rights. Jail was certainly not the correct place for Fischer.

...

Friðrik Ólafsson, [no relation to Helgi] decided to invite Bobby, Boris [Spassky] and his wife Marina, and me for a lunch...

Hendrik [a chef and restaurant owner] understood the situation and generously offered to open the restaurant only for us. We were supposed to be there at 1 pm and I was going to pick up Bobby. When I came to his flat I told him where we were going.

"Out of the question. The press is going to be there. We will go to a place of my choice" he said. I explained to him that it was Friðrik who was inviting us for lunch and orders had to be made well in advance. "It's my way or no way," he continued in his stubborn manner. I suggested various ways to smuggle him into the restaurant, but he did not give in. "Tell them to come over and from here we will decide" he said. There was no point arguing, so I told him I would drive to the restaurant. When I got there Friðrik, Boris and their wives had already ordered some drinks. "I am sorry, but Bobby refuses to come with me," I said. Neither Friðrik nor Boris seemed too surprised. Friðrik suggested that Boris would telephone Bobby and so he did. "Bobby, what shall be our next move?" was Spassky's first sentence. I could not hear his answer but it was decided that I, together with Boris, would go to Bobby's flat and try to persuade him to come over to the restaurant. Spassky had not been to Bobby's place before. "Bobby, this is a very good flat," Spassky said. He started to walk around, casting an appreciative look at what he saw. Without any real reason he turned to me and in passing said, "So you are the ambassador of Bobby Fischer in Iceland?"

Now we had to solve the issue about the restaurant. Bobby had already "won" by getting Boris to come over, so I suggested an alternative route to the restaurant. We would drive around downtown Reykjavík, and as the street facing the Skolabru was an open area, any journalist would be spotted immediately. Hesitantly Bobby agreed on this...

A few days later I received the following email from Spassky:

Dear Helgi, ...It was funny for me to see how you deal with Bobby. He can torture everybody....

Everybody, included Bobby, who was often his own worst enemy.

Throughout his life, music was Bobby's constant companion while he studied chess—rock 'n' roll, rhythm and blues, a radio station playing Motown classics.

Hans Ree, who spent a lot of time with Fischer during the Netanya tournament in 1968, observed:[1]

He knew a lot about American popular music and knew nearly all Aretha Franklin's songs by heart. On one occasion he did an amusing imitation of the

---

1 Hans Ree, *My Chess*, Milford, CT: Russell Enterprises, Inc., 2013, (p. 102).

Four Tops, a popular Motown group in those days to the delight of the few people still out and about.

Jackie ("Mr. Excitement") Wilson was one of Bobby's all-time favorites. The Detroit born member of the Rock & Roll Hall of Fame was frequently referenced by Bobby from his singing "No Pity (In The Naked City)" on one of his Philippine interviews to an email to Pal Benko[1] in which he wrote "[I'm] alone here in the apartment listening to soul singer Jackie Wilson's golden oldies."

There are many other clues to Bobby's favorite music. A cover of the March 1968 issue of *Chess Life* that Bobby owned has written on it, in his hand, some of the lyrics to Percy Sledge's "Take Time to Know her." Songs by Edwin Starr of "War" fame, are also to be found.

Bobby's musical taste seem to stop with the late '60's although it would be nice to think he heard Tom Petty's song "I Won't Back Down" at least once. The lyrics "You can stand me up at the gates of hell, but I won't back down," capture Fischer perfectly.

The Godmother of Punk, Patti Smith, shared Bobby's love of early rock and roll. Ólafsson described the meeting of two legends:[2]

> Bobby Fischer was from the baby boomer generation, but it seemed his path never crossed with any of the radical members of his generation, be they beatniks, the rock 'n' roll generation, hippies or anyone involved in the happenings of the sixties. In that respect he was somewhat out of touch. The music of the Beatles came up one evening when we were dining at a restaurant called Jarlinn in downtown Reykjavík. Bobby liked their music, but preferred their earlier efforts from 1961 to 1965.
>
> He had never heard of rock singer Patti Smith when in August of 2005 I was asked to arrange a meeting between the two of them. A concert promoter called me and said that at the top of her wish list during her stay in Iceland, which was part of a European tour, was a meeting with Bobby Fischer. Just weeks before she came to Reykjavík she had been in Paris, where she was made *Commander of the Ordre des Arts et des Lettres* by the French Minister of Culture.
>
> They met in the restaurant at the Hotel Borg, the hotel Bobby had stayed in during his first visit to Iceland in 1960. Bobby didn't have the faintest idea that he was meeting the grandmother of punk. I was not quite sure what was expected of me. Hotel Borg was within walking distance of Bobby's home on Klapparstigur. I told Bobby that I intended to leave and either he could walk home or he could also give me a call later and I would drive him home. "Oh, please stay," Patti said to me and I did. I would have liked to discuss two of her

[1] A 2006 correspondence in the collection of David DeLucia.

[2] Ólafsson, Helgi. *Bobby Fischer Comes Home: The Final Years in Iceland, a Saga of Friendship and Lost Illusions*. The Netherlands: New In Chess, 2014, (p. 138).

> "favorite lads'" with her, Arthur Rimbaud and Jim Morrison, but she took me for a bodyguard and that was all right.

This was not their first meeting. They had first crossed paths in 1966 during a promotional event for the newly released *Bobby Fischer Teaches Chess,* held in a Manhattan bookstore where she worked.

What could these two possibly have had in common? Smith said she didn't even know the moves to the game. The fact is they shared several things: A love of early rock 'n' roll; the birthplace of Chicago; and coming-of-age in the early 1960s (Bobby was three years older). But where these two legendary figures most connected was the burden of being famous. Patti and Bobby both knew the alienation and loneliness brought on by the loss of their privacy. Perhaps they recognized each other as kindred souls, artists who didn't compromise their integrity.

Smith wrote in *M Train:*[1]

> I received a call from a man identifying himself as Bobby Fischer's bodyguard. He had been charged with arranging a midnight meeting between Mr. Fischer and myself in the closed dining room of the Hotel Borg. I was to bring my bodyguard, and would not be permitted to bring up the subject of chess...
>
> Bobby Fischer arrived at midnight in a dark hooded parka. ...Bobby chose a corner table and we sat face-to-face. He began testing me immediately by issuing a string of obscene and racially repellent references that morphed into paranoiac conspiracy rants.
>
> "Look, you're wasting your time, I said. I can be just as repellent as you, only about different subjects."
>
> He sat staring at me in silence, when finally he dropped his hood.
>
> "Do you know any Buddy Holly songs?" he asked.
>
> For the next few hours we sat there singing songs. Sometimes separately, often together, remembering about half the lyrics. At one point he attempted a chorus of "Big Girls Don't Cry" in falsetto and his bodyguard burst in excitedly.
>
> "Is everything all right, sir?"
>
> "Yes," Bobby said.
>
> "I thought I heard something strange."
>
> "I was singing."
>
> "Singing?"
>
> "Yes, singing."
>
> And that was my meeting with Bobby Fischer, one of the greatest chess players of the twentieth century. He drew up his hood and left just before first light. I remained until the servers arrived to prepare the breakfast buffet.

---

[1] Patti Smith, *M Train*. New York; Alfred A. Knopf, 2015.

In a 2015 interview to promote her memoir, Patti elaborated on how the two bonded over their love of rock 'n' roll and books:[1]

> Bobby loved rock 'n' roll, just loved it, since a boy....We spent till Dawn singing songs.—everything, the Chi-Lites, the Four Tops, Chuck Berry, Darlene Love, all these old songs. Some he didn't know and I'd sing them. And, he was a terrible singer, god bless him, just the tinniest ear.
>
> I had told him the story about how we had met when I was quite young at Scribners bookstore—I was a clerk there. He didn't remember, and then said to me, "Can you still get books?"

I said "I can get you any book you want because I'm a real book sleuth."

Till the end of his life, he sent me emails asking me for very obscure history books. They were really hard to find, but, I found them for him. And that's how we continued our sort of abstract friendship. Books and rock 'n' roll.

Fischer clearly had an effect on her:

> ROBERT JAMES FISCHER
> "Bobby"
> (March 9, 1943–January 17, 2008)
>
> I met with him in Iceland at midnight in a dark corner of an empty dining hall. Our designated body guards were appointed to stand vigil outside. We were not to speak of chess. What we did speak of, until dawn, was rock 'n'roll. It was his boyhood passion.
>
> Through the night we must have sung a hundred songs. He knew every lyric to every fifties rock song, to every Motown song. He had all the dance moves.
>
> He still possessed the heart of the kid who dressed in sharkskin. The kid who beat the old fellows at chess in Washington Square for money to buy tickets to the Brooklyn Fox and Paramount.
>
> We had a good time. I watched him pull on his parka as we said goodbye. He was somewhat shattered and paranoiac yet within those dark eyes the intelligence, rage and humor that he possessed as a young Grandmaster still burned.
>
> No one owned him. He was a force that could not be contained. Genius is dangerous. Those that think it can be packaged are fools.
>
> Farewell, Bobby. I mourn you gone. If we meet again I will not mention chess. I will sing your favorite Buddy Holly song. You know the words.

[1] *PBS News Hour,* October 20 2015.

EPILOGUE

Bobby Fischer gave thirty-five radio interviews between 1999 and 2006. These interviews can be painful (or impossible) to listen to when Fischer gets on a roll and expands upon his conspiracy theories with a vengeance. However, there were eyes in these storms, and when Bobby stuck to chess he was as insightful as ever. In conclusion, a few observations from his last interview, given in 2006, where he pays tribute to some of the great players of the past:

> In chess so much depends on opening theory, so the champions before the last century did not know as much as I do and other players do about opening theory. So if you just brought them back from the dead they wouldn't do well. They'd get bad openings. You cannot compare the playing strength, you can only talk about natural ability. Memorization is enormously powerful. Some kid of fourteen today, or even younger, could get an opening advantage against Capablanca, and especially against the players of the previous century, like Morphy and Steinitz. Maybe they would still be able to outplay the young kid of today. Or maybe not, because nowadays when you get the opening advantage not only do you get the opening advantage, you know how to play, they have so many examples of what to do from this position. It is really deadly, and that is why I don't like chess any more.
>
> [Capablanca] wanted to change the rules already, back in the twenties, because he said chess was getting played out. He was right. Now chess is completely dead. It is all just memorization and prearrangement. It's a terrible game now. Very uncreative.
>
> Morphy and Capablanca had enormous talent, they are two of my favorites. Steinitz was very great too. Alekhine was great, but I am not a big fan of his. Maybe it's just my taste. I've studied his games a lot, but I much prefer Capablanca and Morphy. Alekhine had a rather heavy style, Capablanca was much more brilliant and talented, he had a real light touch. Everyone I've spoken to who saw Capablanca play still speak of him with awe. If you showed him any position he would instantly tell you the right move. When I used to go to the Manhattan Chess Club back in the fifties, I met a lot of old-timers there who knew Capablanca, because he used to come around to the Manhattan club in the forties—before he died in the early forties. They spoke about Capablanca with awe. I have never seen people speak about any chess player like that, before or since. Capablanca really was fantastic. But even he

had his weaknesses, especially when you play over his games with his notes he would make idiotic statements like 'I played the rest of the game perfectly.' But then you play through the moves and it is not true at all. But the thing that was great about Capablanca was that he really spoke his mind, he said what he believed was true, he said what he felt.

INDEX OF NAMES

WC = World Champion
WWC = Women's World Champion
GM = Grandmaster
IM = International Master
* = World class player who died before 1950 when the GM title was created.
Illustrations are indicated in ***bold-italic***.